CHINA STEPS OUT

What are Beijing's objectives towards the developing world and how they have evolved and been pursued over time? Featuring contributions by recognized experts, *China Steps Out* analyzes and explains China's strategies in Southeast Asia, Central Asia, South Asia, Africa, Middle East, and Latin America, and evaluates their effectiveness. This book explains how other countries perceive and respond to China's growing engagement and influence. Each chapter is informed by the functionally organized academic literature and addresses a uniform set of questions about Beijing's strategy. Using a regional approach, the authors are able to make comparisons among regions based on their economic, political, military, and social characteristics, and consider the unique features of Chinese engagement in each region and the developing world as a whole. *China Steps Out* will be of great interest to students and scholars of Chinese foreign policy, comparative political economy, and international relations.

Joshua Eisenman, PhD, is Assistant Professor at the LBJ School of Public Affairs at University of Texas at Austin, and Senior Fellow for China Studies at the American Foreign Policy Council.

Eric Heginbotham, PhD, is Principal Research Scientist at the Center for International Studies at the Massachusetts Institute of Technology.

China Steps Out is a brilliant guide for both policy-makers and academics alike. The authors masterfully detail China's strategic goals and expansive relations with the developing world through comparative regional analyses and unique insights.

Ambassador Paula Dobriansky, *former Under Secretary of State for Global Affairs*

China Steps Out is the most up-to-date and comprehensive assessment of China's broad footprint across the developing world—examining relations with numerous regions of the "Global South" and the complex toolbox of instruments Beijing uses to advance its interests. This is the best textbook available on the subject, which should be read widely by students, scholars, journalists, the business community, and government officials.

David Shambaugh, *Gaston Sigur Professor of Asian Studies, Political Science and International Affairs, George Washington University*

China's economic clout in the developing world is transforming geopolitics as nations from Latin America to Africa bandwagon, balance, and bend under the weight of Beijing's newfound influence. Eisenman and Heginbotham have brought together a first-rate team of scholars to assess China's strategic intentions and the consequences and contradictions of Xi Jinping's ambitious bid to lead the developing world. This new volume is a must-read for anyone trying to make sense of China's sudden and important impact around the globe.

Michael Green, *Associate Professor, Edmund A. Walsh School of Foreign Service, Georgetown University and former senior director for Asian affairs at the National Security Council*

China Steps Out captures the most important shift in the Xi Jinping era of Chinese foreign policy: China's relations with the developing world. China's relations with great powers are discussed in many books; this book, by contrast, is a rare study of the geographic areas where strategic competition between the U.S. and China will most likely play out. Its well designed and executed chapters survey China's "comprehensive engagement" strategies around the world, including Beijing's increasingly important military relationships.

Christopher P. Twomey, *Associate Professor of National Security Affairs, Naval Postgraduate School*

CHINA STEPS OUT

Beijing's Major Power Engagement with the Developing World

*Edited by Joshua Eisenman
and Eric Heginbotham*

Routledge
Taylor & Francis Group

NEW YORK AND LONDON

First published 2018
by Routledge
711 Third Avenue, New York, NY 10017

and by Routledge
2 Park Square, Milton Park, Abingdon, Oxon OX14 4RN

Routledge is an imprint of the Taylor & Francis Group, an informa business

British Library Cataloguing-in-Publication Data
A catalogue record for this book is available from the British Library

Library of Congress Cataloging-in-Publication Data
A catalog record for this book has been requested

ISBN: 978-1-138-69232-9 (hbk)
ISBN: 978-1-138-20293-1 (pbk)
ISBN: 978-1-315-47265-2 (ebk)

Typeset in Bembo
by Apex CoVantage, LLC

Printed in the United Kingdom
by Henry Ling Limited

Dedicated to the memory of
Ambassador James R. Lilley

CONTENTS

FOREWORD

Our last book, *China and the Developing World: Beijing's Strategy for the Twenty-first Century* (2007), was published a decade ago. At that time, China had already become a major presence in what Mao Zedong had dubbed the Third World, and was shaping political, economic, and social outcomes in dozens of countries. Beijing's presence in the developing world has since grown and evolved, and for many regions China is now a top investor and trading partner. Meanwhile, Beijing's influence has expanded apace, and a variety of new, China-initiated international organizations now provide a robust institutional framework for its activities.

For much of the Cold War, the United States and the Soviet Union struggled for dubious advantages in forgotten ramparts in East Asia, Latin America, the Middle East, and Africa. Places like the Ogaden in Ethiopia, Jambo in southern Angola, and the mountainous jungles of Nicaragua all saw conflict and competition as part of a seemingly inexorable global game of dominos. China participated in this early era of strategic competition—during a particularly vigilant period of ideological intensity in the late 1960s and Sino-Soviet rivalry in the 1970s—building railroads and providing military support and ideological sustenance to radical regimes across the globe, but withdrew to focus on domestic imperatives after 1978.

When the Cold War ended it was widely hoped that the major powers would shift their attention from military confrontations in the developing world toward a multifaceted agenda to advance prosperity, including poverty alleviation and trade promotion. Alas, it did not turn out that way. After decades of neglect, particularly for Africa, many parts of the underdeveloped or slowly developing world continue to receive little resources and attention from the United States and other industrialized democracies. Since the turn of the millennium, however, China has stepped into this generally bleak picture and the strategic and economic consequences have been profound.

This book could not come at a more opportune moment. China has returned to the developing world with a powerful economy and a message of non-intervention that resonates in autocratic states, kleptocracies, Islamic republics, and with anyone suspicious of the West. Beijing is building extensive economic, political, and military relationships with developing countries' governments and political parties in an effort to obtain resources to power its economy, markets for its products, and diplomatic partners to support its international positions. This rapid expansion of Chinese power and ambition means that for the first time in history its leaders are now making decisions that determine the course of events far beyond the Asia–Pacific region.

Over the last decade, China has become engaged in the developing world more deeply and across a wider range of issues than ever before. While in 2007 Beijing was primarily focused on economic objectives, today ideological and military ambitions have resurfaced. China must still secure energy and other raw materials from its partners, yet its multibillion-dollar investments in military modernization and deployments, foreign cadre training, Confucius Institutes, and state-run media platforms mean that politics and security have again become essential areas of concern for Beijing. Rather than a single-minded approach toward the developing world, China's policies are now highly diversified. It has economic policies, energy policies, Taiwan policies, and policies designed to promote multipolarity. To introduce and coordinate these initiatives, Beijing has created institutions, such as the Shanghai Cooperation Organization, the Forum for China–Africa Cooperation, and the Asian Infrastructure Investment Bank (AIIB).

Meanwhile, domestic changes since President Xi Jinping took power in 2011 are also reflected in China's foreign relations. The country's economic growth has leveled off and its new leadership remains as intent as ever on cracking down on corruption and ensuring the Communist Party's continued dominance over all aspects of Chinese society. For the first time in over three decades, there are real questions about Beijing's commitment to free market principles and foreign access to Chinese markets. Whereas a decade ago it seemed that China had determined that its needs were best met by seeking to shape the current global framework from inside the tent, it has since proved willing to establish alternative institutions and structures when it regards its own voice as insufficiently represented in existing ones. China's international behavior in its immediate vicinity raises questions about the "peaceful rise" mantra it proclaimed during the 1990s and 2000s and its intentions vis-à-vis its neighbors, while in Washington the longstanding consensus that China's rise is good for the U.S. has begun to erode.

Thankfully neither China nor the U.S. has returned to the zero-sum logic of Cold War competition. It is often China's support for the status quo, rather than regime change, that works at cross-purposes with the U.S. and its partners' efforts to improve governance and human rights in more autocratic developing countries. Moreover, Chinese investment and trade have contributed to economic growth and poverty alleviation in many countries. Critics ought not forget that Western firms have been guilty of many of the same deleterious corporate practices, from corruption to environmental degradation, as their Chinese counterparts. Still, Chinese firms' lack of transparency and weak government oversight and accountability in many developing countries remain serious concerns, especially in those countries where human rights abuses preclude Western firms from investing.

Despite Beijing's evolving aspirations, significant continuity with twentieth century objectives endures. Since the Bandung Conference of 1954, China has consistently identified with the developing world, referring to itself as the "world's largest developing country" and making constant reference to shared historical solidarity and "friendship" with the states of Asia, Africa, and Latin America. The acceptance of China's sovereignty over Taiwan remains a condition for any country to establish official diplomatic ties with Beijing. China also continues to view the support of developing states as critical to its efforts in the international arena, particularly at the United Nations.

Although China considers its relations with the developing world a "cornerstone" of its foreign policy strategy, until recently the topic had received surprisingly little attention in either academic or policy circles. Most books and articles on Chinese foreign policy dealt with the topic only peripherally, as part of works on China's relations with its neighbors in the region and the West. To fill that void, in 2007, this book's editors, Joshua Eisenman and Eric Heginbotham, joined with Derek J. Mitchell and a group of scholars focused on China's relations with individual regions to publish the first full-length treatment of the subject since 1986. That book, which one senior observer hailed as "the first comprehensive assessment of China's rapidly growing relationship with the developing world," did much to aid policymakers in their understanding of a topic that has since grown rapidly in prominence and importance for U.S. foreign policy.

Much has changed, both within and beyond China's borders, between the appearance of *China and the Developing World* and this volume. China's relations with developing countries have received more attention in academic circles; a half-dozen books have been published on the topic and countless others on China's relations in specific geographic regions. What continues to set *China and the Developing World* apart from those that followed, however, was its authors' attention to a common set of policy relevant research questions that traversed the chapters and allowed the reader to make cross-regional comparisons that elucidated continuities in China's global strategy. That approach is employed to even greater effect in this new book, producing a product that, although written by many experts, boasts a high degree of consistency that is rare among edited volumes.

Perhaps the most important observation to come out of this book is that China's strategy toward the developing world—largely a work in progress in 2007—has now reached a new stage. China has gone from a capital-scarce destination for foreign investment, to a capital-abundant country seeking higher returns from investments in less developed countries. In this way, China's development pattern is similar to that of earlier developing-cum-middle income countries: falling returns to capital at home have driven investors to seek high returns abroad. Still, questions abound. Can China's state-owned enterprises consistently succeed in identifying profitable opportunities in developing countries? How will Beijing react if the current downturn in extractive industries results in major losses? Can China ensure the security of its growing community of overseas compatriots, who have gone abroad in search of small-scale, private investment and trade opportunities? Tensions between different priorities and among domestic and foreign actors are already apparent, and are likely to grow more discordant over time as government resources become increasingly scarce.

Another important set of questions addressed in this volume, which has come more sharply into focus, is the response of developing countries to China's expanded presence. Beijing continues to skillfully interact with governments and elites across the political spectrum. In many countries, however, its relations with civil society, including universities, the media, non-governmental organizations, and labor unions, remain strained. Beijing's ability to improve its interactions with nongovernmental and social actors in developing countries—even as it limits their freedoms at home—is essential to the success of ambitious initiatives like the AIIB and "One Belt, One Road." If local concerns are not taken into account, particularly in places like Central Asia, Africa, and Latin America, then China's massive infrastructure investments may face an increasingly hostile political and security environment. In the best case, such ambitious endeavors promise to create infrastructure networks connecting China to the world, much like the empires of old, while in the worst, they threaten to overcommit Beijing and draw resources away from an already weakened Chinese economy to finance white elephant projects in far-flung foreign lands. More likely than not, reality will fall somewhere in the middle.

This book comes at a critical moment in U.S. relations with China. It will serve as a guide for government, private sector, and nongovernmental organization practitioners, a researcher's desk reference, a university textbook, and an engaging read for non-specialists and long-time watchers alike. By combining a detailed examination of Chinese strategic thinking with region-specific policy analysis and easy-to-use trade and energy datasets, this volume explains China's objectives and methods as well as their implications for developing countries and the United States. It is an important contribution to the literature, that, like its predecessor, will not soon be superseded.

Kurt M. Campbell
Chairman of the Center for a New American Security
Former Assistant Secretary of State for East Asia and Pacific Affairs
Washington, D.C.

BIOS

Joshua Eisenman is Assistant Professor at the LBJ School of Public Affairs at the University of Texas at Austin and Senior Fellow for China Studies at the American Foreign Policy Council in Washington, D.C. He has served as a policy analyst for the U.S.–China Economic and Security Review Commission. Dr. Eisenman is coauthor of *China and Africa: A Century of Engagement* (2012) and coeditor of *China and the Developing World: Beijing's Strategy for the Twenty-first Century* (2007). His forthcoming book is *Red China's Green Revolution: Technological Innovation, Institutional Change, and Economic Development Under the Commune* (2018). He holds a Ph.D. in political science from the University of California, Los Angeles.

Eric Heginbotham is Principal Research Scientist at Massachusetts Institute of Technology (MIT) Center for International Studies. Before joining MIT, he was a senior political scientist at the RAND Corporation and was a senior fellow of Asian studies at the Council on Foreign Relations. Dr. Heginbotham is the lead author of RAND's *U.S.–China Military Scorecard* (2015), coauthor of *Chinese and Indian Strategic Behavior: Growing Power and Alarm* (2012), and was coeditor of *China and the Developing World: Beijing's Strategy for the Twenty-first Century* (2007). He holds a Ph.D. in political science from MIT.

R. Evan Ellis is Research Professor of Latin American Studies at the U.S. Army War College Strategic Studies Institute. His research focuses on the region's relationships with China and other non-Western Hemisphere actors. He has authored three books: *China in Latin America: The Whats and Wherefores* (2009); *The Strategic Dimension of Chinese Engagement with Latin America* (2013); and *China on the Ground in Latin America* (2014). Dr. Ellis holds a Ph.D. in political science from Purdue University.

Sarah Kaiser-Cross works for a private financial institution based in Dubai, focusing on the nexus of contemporary security threats and finance in the Middle East.

She holds an M.A. in global policy studies and Middle Eastern studies from the University of Texas at Austin, where her thesis on Chinese influence on U.S. interests in the Arabian Gulf received the Emmette S. Redford Award for Outstanding Research.

Derek J. Mitchell is a senior advisor at the Albright Stonebridge Group and U.S. Institute of Peace. He has held senior positions on Asia policy at both the State and Defense Departments, and served as U.S. ambassador to Myanmar (Burma) between 2012 and 2016. Ambassador Mitchell was coeditor of *China and the Developing World: Beijing's Strategy for the Twenty-first Century* (2007).

Mao Yufeng is Assistant Professor at Widner University, specializing in modern Chinese history, race and ethnicity, and transnational history. Her article, "A Muslim Vision for the Chinese Nation: Chinese Pilgrimage Missions to Mecca during World War II," appeared in *The Journal of Asian Studies*. She holds a Ph.D. in East Asian history from George Washington University.

Matthew Oresman is a counsel in Pillsbury's Public Policy and International Trade Practice, located in the law firm's Washington, D.C. and London offices. He founded the China Eurasia Forum, a think tank focused on China's engagement with its periphery, and has published and spoken extensively on China–Central Asia relations.

Raffaello Pantucci is Director of International Security Studies at the Royal United Services Institute (RUSI) in London. From 2009–2013 he was Visiting Scholar at the Shanghai Academy of Social Sciences. He coauthored "China's Eurasian Pivot: The Silk Road Economic Belt" (RUSI Whitehall Paper series, Number 88, 2017).

David H. Shinn served for 37 years in the United States Foreign Service with assignments at embassies in Kenya, Tanzania, Mauritania, Cameroon, and Sudan, and as ambassador to Burkina Faso and Ethiopia. He has taught African politics at The George Washington University's Elliott School of International Affairs since 2001. Ambassador Shinn is the coauthor of *China and Africa: A Century of Engagement* (2012) and *Historical Dictionary of Ethiopia* (2013). He holds a Ph.D. in political science from The George Washington University.

Jeff M. Smith is Research Fellow for South Asia at The Heritage Foundation and author of *Cold Peace: China-India Rivalry in the 21st Century* (2015). He was previously Director for Asian Security Programs at the American Foreign Policy Council.

PART I
Background and History

1

CHINA AND THE DEVELOPING WORLD

A New Global Dynamic

Joshua Eisenman and Eric Heginbotham

Introduction

On May 14, 2017, over 1,500 people, including twenty-nine national leaders and delegates from 130 countries, gathered at the China National Convention Center in the Olympic Center in Beijing to hear President Xi Jinping's remarks opening the One Belt, One Road (OBOR) Conference. "What we hope to create is a big family of harmonious co-existence," Xi said, then announced another 100 billion yuan ($14.49 billion) for the Silk Road Fund, bring the total to nearly $55 billion. Moreover, he added: "The China Development Bank and the Export–Import Bank of China will set up special lending plans respectively worth 250 billion yuan and 130 billion yuan to support Belt and Road cooperation." During the group photo, Xi was flanked by Russian President Vladimir Putin and Turkey's President Recep Tayyip Erdogan, who both spoke at the ceremony. Ethiopian Prime Minister Haile-mariam Desalegn summed up the mood among the attendees: "China has taken the leadership in laying the foundations for the realization of our shared vision for an open, fair and prosperous world. Achievement of this vision will require our political commitment and a huge sum of resources."[1]

For centuries, Western observers have predicted that China would someday emerge as a major political and economic force in regional and world affairs and—as the 2017 OBOR Conference and dozens of similar events demonstrate—that that day has arrived: *China has stepped out.* Since 2000, by nearly every measure—trade, investment, aid, diplomacy, media, culture, education, party-to-party, person-to-person, military-to-military, and many more categories—China's engagement with developing countries has witnessed an historic expansion. On a nearly weekly basis, China's state-owned firms and banks conclude multibillion-dollar investment or financing agreements throughout Asia, Africa, Latin America, and the Middle East.

Indeed, the pace and scope of China's emergence has been breathtaking. Between 2000 and 2016, China's real GDP increased more than fourfold to roughly

$11.4 trillion at the 2016 exchange rate;[2] its foreign trade climbed from $642 billion to $3.7 trillion (in 2016 dollars);[3] and its share of the global economy grew from 3.6 percent to 14.9 percent.[4] Chinese FDI, which was about $70 billion in 2013, exceeded $170 billion in 2016.[5] When Beijing abandoned isolation and began its economic "opening" to the world in the mid- to late 1970s, even the most optimistic Chinese policymaker could not have predicted such a precipitous expansion of economic scale or global engagement.

To cope with excess industrial and construction capacity and gain higher returns, Beijing's "going out" policy has been expanded into the ambitious OBOR initiative. To help Chinese state-owned and private firms take advantage of new economic opportunities in lesser-developed regions, China has created policy banks and other funding mechanisms (e.g., the China Ex–Im Bank, China Development Bank, the China–Africa Development Fund, and the Silk Road Fund) to lend money to foreign governments to execute infrastructure projects employing Chinese firms. The Beijing-based Asian Infrastructure Investment Bank, unlike the others, is a multilateral institution, but it is also part of China's larger international development and trade promotion strategy. According to an official media outlet: "With the 'Belt and Road' initiative and other strategies serving as a powerful engine . . . China's overseas investment will continue to maintain a double-digit growth rate."[6]

Politically, Beijing continues to expand the depth and breadth of its "strategic partnerships" with developing countries. China has also created a multilateral institutional framework for its interactions with every region of the developing world except South Asia, where rivalry between India and Pakistan precludes such an effort.[7] China's influence in developing countries has expanded under President Xi, who in 2014 exhorted his comrades: "We should increase China's soft power, give a good Chinese narrative and better communicate China's messages to the world."[8] Indeed, Beijing is spending more time and resources hosting and visiting counterparts from developing countries' political parties than ever before, the People's Liberation Army (PLA) is building military-to-military ties, Chinese arms suppliers are doing a brisk business, and in 2017 Beijing christened its first overseas military base in Djibouti. Chinese language schools, media training, cultural exchanges, educational and training programs, and other forms of aid and assistance have increased China's soft power in many countries.[9]

Yet, China's push into the developing world has not been without setbacks and problems. China's economic slowdown, especially the sharp downturn after 2015, precipitated a drop in global commodity prices and raised new questions about the profitability of many government-driven commodity investments. Similarly, after making tens of billions in politically driven loans at favorable rates to high-risk developing countries including Venezuela, Zimbabwe, and Sri Lanka, China now faces problems recouping its capital. One hotly debated question as this book goes to press is whether OBOR will reverse these trends or, more likely, exacerbate them.

Growing trade deficits and asymmetric investment have engendered concern among leaders in numerous developing countries, and, in some cases, drawn protests from local populations. China's growing hard power, combined with its more assertive approach to territorial and boundary issues in the South China Sea, has also caused some states around China's periphery to seek closer military or strategic ties with the United States and Japan. Farther afield, in the Middle East and to a lesser extent Africa, Beijing's commitment to neutrality and non-interference in regional disputes are increasingly being tested as its economic interests expand in ways that require it to behave like a more traditional major world power.

This book has four goals: to assess China's primary objectives in different parts of the developing world and how they have evolved over time; to unpack and summarize the primary means Beijing uses to pursue those objectives; to evaluate how effective Chinese efforts have been; and to understand how other countries perceive and respond to China's growing engagement and influence.

China's Emergence and Evolution as a Major Power

Domestic context is essential to understanding any country's foreign relations, and this is nowhere truer than when examining China's relations in the developing world. Prior to the Sino–Soviet split in 1958–59, China viewed developing countries largely through the political prism of Afro-Asian solidarity initiated at the 1954 Bandung Conference. The leaders of the newly founded People's Republic of China (PRC) sought to establish bilateral relationships with as many countries and revolutionary groups as possible, primarily to gain external validation of Communist Party legitimacy and demonstrate the correctness its own domestic communist ideology. Throughout the 1960s and 1970s, as the rivalry between Beijing and Moscow heated up, China provided military largesse, weapons, guerilla training, and rhetorical support to both anti-colonial and anti-Soviet groups in Asia, Africa, and, to a lesser extent, Latin America. Throughout the Mao era, Beijing cultivated support among the newly independent developing nations of Africa and (less successfully) Asia, and juxtaposed its policies with those of the "imperialist powers," namely, the Soviet Union and the Unites States.

Under Deng Xiaoping's leadership, China jettisoned Maoism and adopted a distinctly non-ideological, domestic development-first approach to foreign policy, following the maxims of "keeping a low profile" and "biding time and hiding capabilities" (韬光养晦).[10] Chinese leaders began referring to a period of "strategic opportunity," during which China, free from external threats, could focus on internal development. To ensure a peaceful international environment suitable for growth, China worked with its neighbors to resolve longstanding border disputes, expand trade, and attract foreign investment. Meanwhile, country by country, Beijing built positive international relationships—particularly with the United States, Japan, and other Asian neighbors—and quietly isolated Taipei as an international political entity. Throughout the 1980s, China's trade with the developing world increased rapidly, both in real terms and as a percentage of its total trade (see Appendix I). Under the mantra of "peace and development," China's non-ideological and conciliatory approach to international relations, which Joshua Kurlantzick dubbed China's Charm Offensive, proved highly successful.[11]

By the 1990s, Beijing's growing need for raw materials and markets motivated expanded political engagement with developing states and the establishment of policy banks to support an export-oriented growth strategy. In 1999, China formally initiated its "go out policy," which aimed to expand export markets and gradually increase foreign direct investment (FDI) to countries around the world. Then, in 2002, Foreign Minister Tang Jiaxuan outlined China's "new security concept," emphasizing cooperative security and confidence building with both developed and developing countries.[12] Zheng Bijian, an influential Chinese think tank leader, suggested that Beijing should promote its foreign policy under the slogan "'peaceful rise' to great power status," though the leadership ultimately adopted the less forward-leaning formulation, "peace and development."[13] These concepts, enabled China to enhance its "comprehensive national power" while minimizing the insecurity of neighbors. They prioritized flexibility, dispute resolution, and involvement in regional institutions. China joined the World Trade Organization, ratified the United Nations Convention on the Law of the Sea, and expanded its participation in UN peacekeeping operations. For three decades China's well-considered diplomacy succeeded in improving its global image and cultivating international partners.

Since the end of the 2000s, and especially since Xi Jinping's accession in 2012, China has pursued a more self-confident and assertive approach to foreign affairs. Under the banner of "Chinese Dream" of national rejuvenation, Xi has advanced its concept of "major power diplomacy with Chinese characteristics."[14] China's rapidly expanding overseas economic interests and growing military capabilities have combined to produce a more muscular foreign policy toward the developing world. Beijing has been more willing to show leadership on the one hand, and has been more assertive in pursuing its narrower "core national interests" (including territorial ones) on the other. Its coast guard and naval ships have confronted foreign vessels in the East and South China Seas, it has established an air defense identification zone in the East China Sea, and it has employed land reclamation to transform tiny features in the South China Sea into military outposts.

Xi Jinping has also sought to buttress "major power diplomacy" with a variety of bold initiatives designed to win hearts and minds and expand Chinese influence in the developing world. The PLA has continued to expand military diplomacy, and the Chinese navy now holds regular port calls throughout the developing world, anti-piracy patrols off the Somali coast, and is actively engaged in a broad range of peacekeeping efforts. Most dramatically, Beijing has also doubled down on economic diplomacy with the 2013 launch of OBOR, which seeks to create a new Sino-centric era of globalization using both traditional tools of Chinese statecraft as well as new types of economic incentives and debt financing arrangements. In spite of these activities, many countries on China's periphery continue to harbor serious concerns about Beijing's long-term ambitions and others are ambivalent about excessive dependence on trade with and investment from China. Addressing these concerns while pursuing Beijing's material goals will challenge Chinese foreign policy leaders for the foreseeable future.

The Developing World in Chinese Strategic Thinking

Chinese foreign policy practice has long parsed political relations according to the characteristics of partner states: specifically, relations with major power (大国); relations with states around China's periphery (周边国家); relations with developing states (发展中国家); and, since the 18th Party Congress in 2012, relations with multilateral (多边) forums.[15] The definition and boundaries among these different types of partnerships are somewhat ambiguous, and many states fall into more than one group.

Major powers are economically developed states of a certain size, including the United States, Russia, Japan, Germany, Britain, or the EU as a whole. States on the periphery include a wide array of both developing states and major powers in East Asia, Central Asia, South Asia, Russia, and Southeast Asia. Former President Hu Jintao is credited with the formulation: "Major powers are the key, surrounding (peripheral) areas are the first priority, developing countries are the foundation, and multilateral forums are the important stage."[16] Under the Xi administration, the sequence of discussions and their content, suggests relations with major powers, especially with the United States, remain Beijing's top priority.

Developing states, however, have gradually assumed a larger role in China's thinking on both political and economic affairs. Over the last two decades, Chinese foreign policy strategists have adopted an increasingly nuanced view of the developing world that differentiates "major developing states" (发展中大国) or "newly emerging powers" (新兴大国) from "other" developing states.[17] While there is no set definitive list of major developing states, they appear to include a handful of large, rapidly developing and politically influential states such as the developing members of the G-20—Argentina, Brazil, Mexico, South Africa, India, Indonesia, Saudi Arabia, Turkey, Iran, and Thailand.[18] Some analysts also suggest Russia should be included in this category.[19] As this volume's chapters make clear, in each region Beijing has identified one or two states of strategic importance as "gateway" countries, on which it lavishes particular attention.

China sees itself as both a major power and first among a group of large developing states. Its policies are intended to accentuate common interests and promote the emergence of a more "democratic" international order, consistent with what Chinese analysts see as the emergence of a "multipolar world." To advance common political interests, Beijing has concluded bilateral "strategic partnership" agreements with major developing states and has collectively engaged subsets of them, most famously the BRICS grouping—Brazil, Russia, India, China, and South Africa—to help balance Western dominance.[20]

Established in 2009, the BRICS organization has held annual summit meetings to coordinate political–economic positions and public statements. The BRICS have sought reform of international financial institutions, including voting shares within the IMF, to increase their collective influence. Impatient with the pace of IMF reform, the BRICS established a $100 billion currency reserve to lessen dependence on that institution, and authorized another $100 billion to establish the New Development Bank (NDB).[21] For the most part, BRICS' leaders and Western analysts see the NDB as complementing existing institutions and adding to overall capacity.[22] Yet they also see it is as an important statement; major developing states will be represented or they will establish parallel institutions that balance Western dominance. Nevertheless, the BRICS countries have as many divergent interests and perspectives as common ones, thus limiting the extent and degree of cooperation on many important issues such as UN Security Council reform.

A portion of the developing world falls within China's "periphery" (周边), sometimes also translated less literally, but closer to the actual meaning, as "strategic periphery"—that is, a geographic belt around China that is of particular importance for China's strategic interests. Some Chinese strategists now argue that China's strategic periphery has expanded apace with Chinese power and influence and that Beijing's strategy should adjust accordingly. Previously, the periphery was limited to Northeast Asia, Southeast Asia, South Asia, and Central Asia, but over the last five years the "greater periphery" (大周边) has been expanded to include West Asia, the South Pacific, and, by some definitions, East Africa.[23]

In part, this new interpretation reflects China's growing reach and interests—a waypoint between China's recent past as a regional power and its future as a global one. But the complexity of the political and security environment in these regions also makes the greater periphery increasingly important. The U.S. pivot to Asia, the troubled aftermath of Washington's democracy promotion in the Middle East, the now defunct Trans-Pacific Partnership (TPP), and Japan's reemergence as a political–military actor have all been cited by Chinese analysts as challenges in the greater periphery. In response, they argue, China must maintain the political initiative in these areas by establishing unifying narratives, maintaining leadership in regional organizations, and knitting regional structures.[24]

In sum, the aforementioned evolution in Beijing's grand strategy has taken place amid a simultaneous evolution China's own identity and sense of its place in the world such that China continues to perceive and portray itself as both a developing state, and, increasingly, also as a major power. Maintaining that China is the largest developing country serves to identify the country with other developing states, insulate China from the strictest demands on, for example, climate change, and dampen fears that China may aggressively challenge the United States. As Foreign Minister Wang Yi said in 2016:

> Although China is the world's second-biggest economy, in per capita terms we are behind over 80 other countries. This is why we say we remain . . . a developing country, and we still must focus our efforts on development, not just at present, but for a very long time to come. We will not vie against others, nor do we have the intention to replace others.[25]

This same logic—that China cannot afford to become bogged down in conflict while seeking to catch up—led Deng Xiaoping to offer the admonition that China should "keep a low profile" in international affairs. While that strategy has never officially been repudiated, it has been supplemented by other concepts that provide China with a more proactive vision. At the 17th Party Congress in 2007, for instance, Hu Jintao said China would seek to create a "harmonious world," asserted that the world cannot "enjoy prosperity and stability without China," and strongly implied China would become a counterweight to the United States.[26] Since 2009, Beijing has aggressively sought to consolidate maritime territorial claims, and since 2012, Xi Jinping has further accelerated the trends towards a bolder and more proactive approach to international relations.[27] According to Yan Xuetong, an outspoken advocate of nationalist positions, "From 2012 to 2014, Chinese diplomacy transformed from 'keeping a low profile' to 'striving for achievements.'"[28]

In 2012, Xi proposed a "new type of great of major power relations" with the United States, thus acknowledging China's status as a major power. Others have since expanded on Beijing's broader global "major power diplomacy."[29] He Yafei, former Deputy Minister of Foreign Affairs, observed in 2016 that China's approach involves a dense network of global partnerships, oriented towards win–win cooperation and full participation in global governance. China, He writes, is "an important participant in, constructor of and contributor to global governance, as well as a central motive force in the reform of global governance." He emphasized the importance of reassuring Washington that China supports the existing international order but also advocated building partnerships with other nations that seek a "multi-polar world and democratic international relations."[30] To that end, He argues developing countries should remain "the bedrock and strategic focus of China's major-country diplomacy." Not only does Chinese history and identity provide a special bond with these countries, but the narrowing of capabilities between the developed and developing world also increases Chinese interests in the latter.[31]

China's leadership in the developing world serves multiple national goals. It advances Beijing's vision of a more democratic and multipolar international order. It serves Chinese economic interests by promoting its trade and investment in those parts of the world with the fastest growth potential. Chinese engagement with the developing world also provides external legitimacy for China's autocratic political system. Chinese elites have long believed that liberal democracy causes political instability and exacerbates social divisions, particularly in developing countries. As one senior Chinese diplomat explained: "Western democracy cannot work in poor countries. It does not make much sense to promote good governance without development."[32] When violence swept Kenya in 2008 following a disputed election, an editorial in the *People's Daily* echoed this view: "Western-style democratic theory simply isn't suited to African conditions, but rather carries with it the roots of disaster."[33] Over the last decade, Beijing has substantially stepped up its activities in cadre training for political parties in partner states.

Literature on China and the Developing World

The literature on China and the developing world has gone through a number of evolutions since the establishment of the PRC. Scholarly debates in the fields of development studies, China studies, and international relations have substantially influenced publications on the subject. During the 1960s and 1970s, the United States and the Soviet Union were engaged in a strategic and ideological struggle for influence in what Mao Zedong called the Third World. At that time, China's policy towards the developing world was well covered in western surveys of Chinese foreign policy.[34] Numerous publications addressed Beijing's role in Latin America, the Middle East, and Southeast Asia.[35] In 1963–66 alone, at least four books were written on China's foreign policy towards Africa, touting what one author titled *Red China's African Offensive*.[36] Between 1974 and 1976, no fewer than five books, as well as countless articles, focused on China's relations with the African continent.[37]

During the 1980s and 1990s, as China looked inward and abandoned Maoism, the scholarly literature and expertise on China's relations with the developing world diminished. While China's relations with major powers such as the United States, Russia, and Japan received due attention, Beijing's engagement with nations in the developing "South" receded from view.[38]

During the 2000s, China's reinvigorated economic relations with developing countries generated a flood of media reports and policy studies, yet there was little effort to place these developments in the broader context of China's overall foreign policy toward those regions. Indeed, our previous volume, published in 2007, represented the first book-length treatment of China's role in the developing world in almost two decades.[39] Since 2010, many researchers, including a number of leading Sinologists and development experts, have acknowledged the importance of Chinese relations with developing countries, precipitating a resurgence of publications on the topic.[40]

The contemporary literature is distinguished from earlier generations in that it is generally organized around functional themes, as well as in its sheer quantity. Some researchers have stressed that Chinese trade, investment, and lending have increased economic growth and improved infrastructure in developing states.[41] Others have questioned the political consequences of China's rapidly expanding economic engagement and political training, particularly with autocratic regimes.[42] Still other scholars note the paucity of oversight within China and examine the implications of Chinese overseas corporate activity on corruption and environmental protection in host nations.[43]

Generally speaking, although there is a large literature on China's broader foreign policy and intentions, the contemporary literature on China and the developing world is less explicitly about geopolitical goals and competition than it was during the Cold War.[44] The most notable exception is scholarly work on China's relations in Southeast Asia, where Beijing's assertiveness in the South China Sea has drawn ample attention. There are also vigorous debates about the extent to which China's expanding economic presence may enhance its political influence on its partners or even adversaries.[45] Yet, these debates often turn on which metrics or standards are applied. How, for example, should "influence" be understood or operationalized?[46] Should the behavior of Chinese firms with regard to, for example, environmental impact be evaluated against that of Western companies, in which case they often fall short, or against that of firms from other developing states, in which case their behavior is more typical.[47]

Another feature of the contemporary scholarship on China and the developing world is that many publications focus on a single region or country. Perhaps because China's activities in Africa epitomize its dramatic quest for resources and consumer markets, studies on Africa are overrepresented in the literature.[48] Southeast Asia has also received significant attention, since that is where Chinese economic interests, military power, and trade and investment links are the most extensive.[49] Latin American scholars, many steeped in the "dependency" school of political economics, have produced a sizable literature on economic relations with China, the latest major power to expand its involvement in that region.[50] These national and regional studies often offer depth, but their coverage and treatment of different regions remains uneven and limited by an inherent inability to place Chinese policies in a comparative perspective. Central Asia, the Middle East, and South Asia are largely overlooked, while the literature on Africa, Southeast Asia, and Latin America tends to vary widely in quality, perspective, and research methodology.

Research Design

This book is *not* a compilation of scholarly conference papers. It a calculated intervention by a select and diverse group of researchers intended to elucidate China's strategy toward the developing world. Because the regional chapters examine Chinese engagement with states in a single area, the authors are able to make comparisons between countries within that region based on their economic, political, military, and social characteristics, and consider the unique features of Chinese engagement in the region as a whole. Each chapter is informed by the functionally organized academic literature and addresses a uniform set of questions about Beijing's strategy. To do this work, we recruited coauthors that had recently produced scholarship on their topic that is both high quality *and* policy relevant.

To maintain the book's logical coherence and guide our research, we adopted a research design derived from the comparative politics tradition: the "structured, focused comparison" case study methodology.[51] The work is "structured" in the sense that each author considered an identical set of general questions that reflect the research objectives, and it is "focused" in that it examines specific aspects of all five regional "cases." Yet, as Alexander George and Andrew Bennett warned, the "structured, focused comparison is more difficult to carry out in collaborative research when each case study is undertaken by a different scholar."[52] To help mitigate this problem, we edited all chapters with an eye towards standardizing their structure and highlighting common themes.

To simplify cross-regional comparisons we used three strategies prescribed by George and Bennett. First, we identified specific objectives and questions and created a research strategy to achieve them. Second, rather than relying on *ad hoc* press reports, we insisted all chapters use standardized data sets from authoritative sources.

Data on trade from the IMF's Direction of Trade Statistics; data on energy imports from UN Comtrade; and arms imports from SIPRI's database on arms transfers are provided.

Third, to avoid bias, we used China's own conceptions of the Third World to identify a defined and finite universe of cases.[53] We included only those regions China itself considers part of the developing world, while other regions that might from other perspectives be consider "developing" (e.g., Eastern Europe, Micronesia, and Antarctica) were omitted. Then, applying the notions of "strategic periphery" and "outer periphery" identified above, we ranked regions in accordance with their strategic importance to Beijing and sequenced the book's chapters accordingly— Southeast Asia, Central Asia, South Asia, Africa, Middle East, and Latin America.[54] This prioritization also mirrors China's Ministry of Foreign Affairs (MFA) website, which lists its regional departments in nearly the same order.[55] The only exception is South Asia, which the MFA lists as part of the Department of Asian Affairs. We examine South Asia separately, because of its great strategic importance and the separate international and internal dynamics at play. It is also noteworthy that China has established international institutions and published official White Papers to coordinate its interactions with each region of the developing world—except South Asia: ASEAN+1, Forum on China–Africa Cooperation, Forum of China and the Community of Latin American and Caribbean States, Shanghai Cooperation Organization, and China–Arab States Cooperation Forum. The relevant official White Papers issued by the 18th National Congress of the Communist Party of China between November 2012 and October 2017 are available in Appendix II.

Like government agencies, we had to make hard choices about boundaries, which sometimes raised difficult questions. For instance, should Myanmar be included as part of South or Southeast Asia? Since Myanmar is a member of ASEAN we chose to include it in Southeast Asia, at the cost of reduced attention to Myanmar's relations with South Asian countries. Should Afghanistan be included as part of South or Central Asia? We chose to include it as part of Central Asia because we wanted the South Asia chapter to examine in detail the China–India–Pakistan trilateral relationship.

Each regional chapter addresses four sets of questions, which we return to in the concluding chapter when we assess the common patterns and themes in China's strategy toward the developing world:

1. How has China defined its interests in the region, and how has that changed over time? What policies does China pursue to support its declared interests and its larger foreign policy goals?
2. What methods or tactics does Beijing employ with nations in the region to achieve its objectives? What assets does it bring to bear, and what weaknesses continue to hamper its efforts?
3. How successful has Chinese diplomacy been in the region? Has Chinese influence grown and, if so, upon what does its influence rest? If not, what are the obstacles to Chinese influence?
4. What are the implications of China's policies for other actors? What impact does Beijing's new outreach have on regional affairs, including governance and

the overall welfare of the region's citizens? What impact does Beijing's recent engagement have on U.S. interests? And what impact does it have on the preservation or evolution of international norms and institutions?

Each chapter is organized in seven parts. An introduction summarizes key findings and distinctive features of the region. A "historical overview" section briefly summarizes the history of Chinese interactions with the region, focusing largely on the period since China's reform and opening but also commenting on more distant events or features that shape or inform contemporary relations. The "objectives" section distills the major interests and goals that appear to inform Chinese strategy in the region, with judgments based on both Chinese rhetoric and action. The "methods" section unpacks the political, economic, cultural, and military means employed by Beijing and how those means have evolved over time. The "regional perspectives" section evaluates how Chinese activity is viewed by regional states and the extent to which Beijing has succeeded or failed in attaining regional objectives. The "implications" section examines the impact of Chinese activities on the U.S. regional position and objectives and how Washington and other actors might respond. Finally, the "conclusions" section summarizes findings and assesses how China's regional engagement is likely to evolve in the coming decade. Taken together, the goal is to allow the reader to compare and contrast China's approach across regions and to identify broad patterns of similarity and difference between regions and over time.

Book Outline

After this chapter, Derek J. Mitchell opens the volume with an historical overview of China's relations with the outside world from the imperial era to the present day. He traces continuities and change in China's approach over the centuries, from its tributary relationships with "barbarians" beyond its cultural and territorial boundaries during its imperial days, to Beijing's support for national liberation movements in the Third World during the Cold War, to the reawakening of economic and political interest in the developing world in recent years. Mitchell explains that echoes of China's traditional principles and approaches to dealing with lesser-developed areas along its border and beyond continue to inform its contemporary international outlook and policies.

In Chapter 3, Eric Heginbotham highlights China's deep and complex interests in Southeast Asia and the tensions between them. Over time Beijing has increased attention to the region to prevent the emergence of an anti-China coalition, maximize trade and investment, build strategic relationships with regional states, and secure territorial claims. Since roughly 2009, Beijing has more actively sought to advance its control of contested territory in the South China Sea, while using political, economic, and military engagement to mitigate regional reactions. While many regional states remain wary of China's growing power, Heginbotham notes that Beijing's diplomatic efforts and large side-payments to several weaker states have effectively prevented a unified ASEAN opposition from coalescing against Beijing's position in the consensus-driven regional grouping.

In Chapter 4, Raffaello Pantucci and Matthew Oresman describe China's growing economic and security relations in Central Asia. They explain that China's engagement with Central Asia is informed by a desire to develop and stabilize China's western provinces, especially Xinjiang. Central Asia arguably provides the most important nodes in China's broader OBOR vision. Central Asia, they argue, is a "testing ground" or predictor for how China's broader global strategy of building mutual prosperity through loan financing will fare in other regions of the developing world. Pantucci and Oresman also examine the importance and limitations of the Shanghai Cooperation Organization (SCO) in helping regional states build confidence and address terrorism. They suggest that the recent expansion of the SCO to include India and Pakistan may blur its focus.

In Chapter 5, Jeff M. Smith addresses the evolving balance that Beijing has struck in its relations with its traditional partner, Pakistan, and a rising India. He highlights the historical distrust that has long kept India and China at arm's length and the quickly expanding commercial linkages and political engagement that have added new dimensions to bilateral relationship. Beijing's interest in preventing the emergence of a U.S.–Indian coalition provides powerful motivation for rapprochement. But China's growing power projection capabilities, its increasingly deep relations with other South Asian states, and its interests in developing the capability to protect its SLOCs into the Indian Ocean have prompted increased concerns in Indian strategic circles. Smith concludes by acknowledging the progress India and China have made in bilateral relations while cautioning that there are still many unresolved tensions and uncertainties.

In Chapter 6, Joshua Eisenman and David H. Shinn examine China's extensive network of economic, political, and military relationships in Africa. They note that China's once strongly ideological foreign policy in Africa has become largely a quest for resources, markets, and strategic influence. The establishment of the China–Africa Cooperation Forum has ushered in a new era in China's relations with African nations and allowed Beijing to institutionalize a growing array of technical training, debt relief, financial aid, political cadre training, and infrastructure development projects. Eisenman and Shinn note that while China's economic assistance, investment, and debt financing generally contribute to GDP growth in Africa, trade deficits may have pernicious long-term consequences. Of more immediate concern, Chinese norms of "non-interference" and its lack of discrimination in arms sales have helped sustain a number of oppressive autocratic regimes.

In Chapter 7, Sarah Kaiser-Cross and Mao Yufeng explain China's increasing activism and influence in the Middle East and the Arab world. China's increasing dependency on oil imports from the Middle East and concerns about its own large Muslim minority have led Beijing to mobilize both substantial hard and soft power resources to promote economic, political, and cultural relations with countries in the region. Kaiser-Cross and Mao write that Beijing has prioritized economic interests, worked to avoid confrontation with the United States in the region, and studiously avoided taking sides in intra-regional conflicts such as the Saudi–Iran rivalry and the Israeli–Palestinian conflict. Still, as in other regions, as China's presence expands it has become increasingly difficult to maintain a strictly neutral position.

In Chapter 8, R. Evan Ellis examines China's fast expanding relations with the Latin American nations. Ellis highlights China's primarily economic objectives in the region, but also notes Beijing's regional efforts to foster multipolarity together with like-minded regional states. China's economic involvement has grown rapidly, but the impact has been mixed. Chinese investment and financing have boosted growth and precipitated an impressive improvement in Latin American port, rail, and road transportation, especially along the Pacific coast. Yet, they have also weakened the domestic manufacturing sector, thus making Latin America more susceptible to boom and bust cycles in primary goods, and produced a large and growing number of "white elephant" projects that are either not completed or quickly go bankrupt.

Finally, in Chapter 9, we weave together the findings of the individual chapters into a concluding analysis. To enhance their accessibility we have summarized the five key themes in the section immediately below.

Five Themes in China's Relations with the Developing World

Generalizing about China's activities in the developing world and their impact is a hazardous enterprise, and for every generalization there are likely to be important exceptions. Nevertheless, five key themes in China's relations with developing countries emerge from the regional-case study chapters in this volume.

1. **China pursues a "comprehensive engagement" strategy**: Beijing employs a "comprehensive engagement" strategy that includes political, economic, cultural, and military elements. While all countries pursue diplomacy across multiple tracks, the components of China's comprehensive approach are mutually reinforcing and overlapping, with a single event or delegation often including multiple elements. As a senior Chinese foreign policy official observed, Beijing's approach involves "multi-centric, multi-layered and multi-pivotal sub-networks of regional and international cooperation that are interconnected and interwoven."[56] In addition to diplomatic exchanges and summit meetings, political engagement conducted by cadres in the International Department of the Central Committee of the Communist Party of China provide an essential conduit for outreach to political parties and training programs for party leaders and state administrators.

2. **Beijing looks to promote a more "democratic" international order**: While Beijing supports the international economic order and international institutions, it works with like-minded partners to gain a greater say in how those institutions are structured and administered. It seeks to work with the

United States and avoid conflict with it across a wide range of issues, but it also looks to foster a more "democratic" or multipolar world order to constrain the United States' space for unilateral action. To this end, China works to build strategic relations with major developing states and work with them in organizations like the BRICS and G-20 to pursue common interests. It has also built overlapping multilateral regional forums with a wider range of states that help to harmonize China's relations with developing countries. Given the political differences between the circumstances and interests of developing states around the world, these efforts often build on a relatively narrow range of economic issues, though there are some political issues (e.g., the defense of sovereignty norms) upon which Beijing and others cooperate.

3. **Money talks, but debt creates risk**: Despite its extensive political outreach and military engagement, China's checkbook remains the most important tool in its kit. China's large, sometimes dominant, economic presence in developing countries ensures its interests cannot be ignored. The rapid growth of China's FDI over the last decade, albeit from a low base, expands Beijing's options in economic diplomacy. Given the central role that policy banks play in the Chinese system, it is easier to provide debt financing to developing countries than FDI. OBOR represents a massive expansion of China's lending and places unprecedented emphasis on infrastructure-related financial investment in foreign countries, many with poor credit ratings. The drop in commodity prices in 2015 and political crises in partner states (e.g., Venezuela and South Sudan) highlight the risks of expanded investment—especially in the context of China's large and growing total debt and the decline in its foreign currency reserves.

4. **Military diplomacy is expanding, but remains underdeveloped**: Although relatively new, China's "military diplomacy," or military-to-military engagement, is fast becoming an important component of Beijing's larger diplomatic effort. In its immediate periphery, China has moved to deepen security ties by establishing defense and security consultation mechanisms with important neighbors. It is expanding the scope of combined military exercises with a growing number of partners, primarily in Southeast Asia, South Asia, and Central Asia (as well as Russia). Farther afield, the PLA Navy is now a regular visitor at ports from Mombasa and Lagos to Port Zayed and Rio de Janeiro. Chinese military-industrial firms have dramatically increased the value of their defense exports, which are poised to continue growing and are likely to facilitate China's pursuit of other political and economic interests throughout the developing world.

5. **China's political influence is growing, but remains uneven**: Although the limits of major power influence over smaller nations are well explored in numerous academic studies, the continuing limitations of Chinese influence appear to have disappointed expectations in Beijing. To be sure, as China's economic and political weight has grown, it has become increasingly important for developing nations to carefully consider how to manage relations with Beijing.

But Chinese influence is highly uneven. It depends, first and foremost, on the issue and whether the political costs of adjusting behavior to meet Chinese expectations are high (e.g., issues involving territorial sovereignty or alliance partners) or low (e.g., repudiating the Dalai Lama or Taiwan independence). Other factors, including the country's distance from China, relative size, level of economic development, regime type, and relationship with other major powers, are also important. Where asymmetry in size and power is extreme and where the state has few other partnership options, such as Cambodia and Zimbabwe, Beijing has been able to effectively turn some poor and isolated regimes into client states. But in most cases, China's ability to positively influence policy or action on issues where compliance entails significant political or economic costs remains modest.

Acknowledgements

We would like to thank our wives, Iris and Katsue, for their support and encouragement. We would also like to acknowledge the support of the University of Texas at Austin, LBJ School of Public Affairs, and the Massachusetts Institute of Technology's Center for International Studies. Special thanks go to Leanne Hinnes who approached us to write this volume and Stephanie Rogers who saw the project to the end; Mi Siyi who compiled the data, did essential research, and standardized the citations; and Adam Jankowski, Luo Siyu, and Benjamin van der Horst who provided research support. Michael Glosny provided an invaluable sounding board on broad directions in Chinese foreign policy thinking.

Notes

1 "Quotes From Leaders at China's New Silk Road Meeting," *ABC News*, May 14, 2017.
2 International Monetary Fund (hereinafter referred to as IMF), World Economic Outlook Database, gross domestic product, constant prices (national currency) and gross domestic product, current prices (U.S. dollars). GDP growth is most meaningfully measured in local currency, but note that growth in GDP U.S. dollar value is higher—growing in real terms almost sevenfold between 2000 and 2016.
3 IMF, Direction of Trade Statistics, 2016. Figure from 2000 adjusted using IMF estimated U.S. GDP deflator, since original current figures are provided in U.S. dollars.
4 IMF figures, using exchange rates; purchasing power parity figures will yield different results.
5 Guo Xiaohong, "EY: China's 2016 Outbound FDI to Exceed US$170 bln," *China.org. cn*, September 29, 2016; "Mixed Messages," *Economist*, October 1, 2016; "MOFCOM Department Official of Outward Investment and Economic Cooperation Comments on China's Outward Investment and Cooperation in 2016," Website of the Ministry of Commerce of the People's Republic of China, January 18, 2017.
6 Guo, "EY: China's 2016 Outbound FDI to Exceed US$170 bln."
7 For more on this issue, see Jeff M. Smith's chapter on South Asia.
8 "Xi Eyes More Enabling Int'l Environment for China's Peaceful Development," *Xinhua*, November 30, 2014. Also see: David Shambaugh, "China's Soft-Power Push," *Foreign Affairs*, July/August 2015.

9 Professor Joseph Nye coined the phrase "soft power" in the early 1990s to describe, as he put it, "the ability to get what you want through attraction, rather than coercion or payments." Alternatively, Nye defined the term as "shap[ing] the preferences of others" to do things in your interest through the attractiveness of one's culture, political ideals, and policies, and leading by example. See Joseph S. Nye, Jr., *Soft Power: The Means to Success in World Politics* (New York: Public Affairs, 2004), X, 5.

10 The four Chinese characters *tao guang yang hui* are part of a longer 24-character statement by Deng Xiaoping. The full 24-character statement has been translated in a variety of ways, including, "Observe calmly; secure our position; hide our capacities and bide our time; be good at maintaining a low profile; and never claim leadership." See "Deng Xiaoping's Lasting Legacy," *The Japan Times*, August 27, 2014. For a discussion of the origins and evolution of Deng's 24-character formulation, see Shin Kawashima, "The Development of the Debate Over 'Hiding One's Talents and Biding One's Time (tao-guang yanghui)'," *Asia-Pacific Review* 18, no. 2 (2011): 14–36.

11 Joshua Kurlantzick, *China's Charm Offensive: How China's Soft Power Is Transforming the World* (New Haven, CT: Yale University Press, 2007).

12 For a comprehensive overview of China's outlook on the international security environment, and on Chinese foreign and security strategy as outlined by then-Foreign Minister Tang Jiaxuan, see "Chinese FM: China's Int'l Status Grown in Last 13 Years," Statement at 16th National Congress of the Communist Party of China, *Xinhua*, October 9, 2002.

13 Zheng Bijian coined the phrase "peaceful rise." The senior leadership ultimately adopted "peace and development" as a less provocative formulation of the same idea. Zheng Bijian, "China's 'Peaceful Rise' to Great-Power Status," *Foreign Affairs*, September/October 2005; Robert Suettinger, "The Rise and Descent of 'Peaceful Rise'," *China Leadership Monitor* no. 12 (Fall 2004): 1–10; Zheng Bijian, *China's Peaceful Rise: Speeches of Zheng Bijian 1997–2005* (Washington, DC: Brookings Institution Press, 2005).

14 This concept was first advanced in Li Junru, *The China Dream: China in Peaceful Development* (Beijing: Foreign Languages Press, 2006). Also see Liu Mingfu, *China Dream: Great Power Thinking and Strategic Power Posture in the Post-American Era* (New York: CN Times Books, 2015).

15 "Shibada zhihou de Zhongguo waijiao xin jumian" 十八大之后的中国外交新局面 [China's New Foreign Policy after the 18th Party Congress], *Sina News*, January 9, 2014.

16 The phrase appears to be a summary of Hu's comments during an August 29, 2004 meeting of Chinese diplomatic envoys. "Zhongguo zouxiang 'dawaijiao'" 中国走向"大外交" [China Moves Towards 'Big Power Diplomacy'], *People's Daily*, February 8, 2011. See also "The 10th Conference of Chinese Diplomatic Envoys Stationed Abroad Held in Beijing," *People's Daily*, August 30, 2004.

17 "Xi Jinping chuxi zhongyang waishi gongzuo huiyi bing fabiao zhongyao jianghua" 习近平出席中央外事工作会议并发表重要讲话 [Xi Jinping Chairs Central Conference on Work Relating to Foreign Affairs and Delivers an Important Speech], *Xinhua*, November 29, 2014. Although it has only recently begun to generalize about this distinction, Chinese diplomacy has long implicitly differentiated the importance of different states, in part by concluding different levels of "strategic partnership" with them. But the category of "major developing state" appears reserved for a smaller subset of states.

18 In July 2008, Hu Jintao met with four other leaders of "major developing states," including India, Brazil, South Africa, and Mexico. "China's Hu Proposes Priorities for Further Cooperation Among Five Major Developing Countries" [Meeting held July 8, 2008 during an outreach session of the G-8 Summit in Sapporo], *People's Daily*, July 8, 2008.

19 Peng Gang and Guan Xueling, "Eluosi shi yige fazhanzhong guojia ma?" 俄罗斯是一个发展中国家吗? [Is Russia a Developing Country?], *Eluosi zhongya dongou yanjiu* 俄罗斯中亚东欧研究 [Russian, Central Asian and East European Studies] 1 (2004): 31–35.

20 Feng Zhongping and Huang Jing, "China's Strategic Partnership Diplomacy: Engaging With a Changing World," European Strategic Partnership Observatory (ESPO), Working Paper 8, 2014. Note that the definition of strategic partnership is elastic enough that

it also pertains to China's relations with several states with which competition is as salient as cooperation (including the United States, Vietnam, and Japan).

21 Jordan Totten, "BRICS New Development Bank Threatens Hegemony of U.S. Dollar," *Forbes*, December 22, 2014; "BRICS Cooperation Helps Build New International Framework," *Global Times*, July 13, 2015.

22 Michael A. Glosny, "China and the BRICs: A Real (But Limited) Partnership in a Unipolar World," *Polity* 42, no. 1 (January 2010): 100–129; Mayamiko Biziwick, Nicolette Cattaneo, and David Fryer, "The Rationale for and Potential Role of the BRICS Contingent Reserve Arrangement," *South African Journal of International Affairs* 22, no. 3 (August 2015): 307–324; and "BRICS Bank Is a Fine Idea Whose Time Has Come," *Financial Times*, April 5, 2012.

23 On these points, see Chen Xiangyang, "Zhongguo tuijin 'dazhoubian zhanlue' zhengdangshi" 中国推进"大周边战略"正当时 [The Right Time for China to Advance a "Greater Periphery" Strategy], China Foundation for International Studies website, January 1, 2015.

24 Chen Xiangyang, "Zhongguo tuijin 'dazhoubian zhanlue' zhengdangshi."

25 "A Changing China and Its Diplomacy—Speech by Foreign Minister Wang Yi at Center for Strategic and International Studies," Ministry of Foreign Affairs of the People's Republic of China website, February 26, 2016.

26 "Full Text of Hu Jintao's Report at 17th Party Congress," *Xinhua*, November 24, 2007; Friso M.S. Stevens, "What Happened to Deng's Maxim 'Tao Guang Yang Hui'," *Atlantisch Perspectief*, April 2014.

27 Elizabeth C. Economy, "China's Imperial President: Xi Jinping Tightens His Grip," *Foreign Affairs*, November/December 2014.

28 Yan Xuetong, "China must not overplay its strategic hand," *Global Times*, September 8, 2017.

29 David M. Lampton, "A New Type of Major-Power Relationship: Seeking a Durable Foundation for U.S.–China Ties," *Asia Policy*, July 16, 2013.

30 He Yafei, "China's Major-Country Diplomacy Progresses on All Fronts," *China.org.cn*, March 23, 2016.

31 He, "China's Major-Country Diplomacy."

32 Interview by Jonathan Holslag with an official from the Ministry of Foreign Affairs, Beijing, June 2, 2010. See Jonathan Holslag, "China and the Coups: Coping with Political Instability in Africa," *African Affairs* 110, no. 440 (2011): 382. For additional work on this topic as it related to Africa see He Wenping, "Minzhu yu Feizhou de zhengzhi fazhan" 民主与非洲的政治发展 [Democracy and Political Development in Africa], *Xiya Feizhou* 西亚非洲 [West Asia and Africa], no. 1 (January 2004): 59–63; Wang Yingying, "Dui Feizhou minzhuhua de zhai sikao" 对非洲民主化的再思考 [Rethinking Democratization in Africa], *Guoji Wenti Yanjiu* 国际问题研究 [International Studies], no. 6 (June 2002): 28–33; Li Anshan, "Feizhou minzhuhua yu guojia minzu jiangguo de beilun" 非洲民主化与国家民族建构的悖论 [The Paradox of Nation Building and Democracy in Africa], *Shijie Minzu* 世界民族 [World Ethno-nationalistic Studies], no. 5 (2003): 10–18.

33 "The Sound of Silence," *Economist*, February 7, 2008.

34 Before 1978 Chinese foreign policy was almost synonymous with its role in the Third World, the topic receives substantial coverage in most treatments of the former. See, for example, G.W. Choudhury, *China in World Affairs: The Foreign Policy of the PRC Since 1970* (Boulder, CO: Westview Press, 1982); King C. Chen, *The Foreign Policy of China* (Roseland, NJ: East West WHO, 1972); Michael B. Yahuda, *China's Role in World Affairs* (London: Croom Helm, 1978). For works specific to China's relations with the Third World, see W.A.C. Adie, "China, Russia, and the Third World," *China Quarterly* no. 11 (July–September 1962): 200–213; Wolfgang Bartke, *China's Economic Aid* (London: C. Hurst, 1975); Janos Horvath, *Chinese Technology Transfer to the Third World: A Grants Economy Analysis* (New York: Praeger, 1976); Alvin Z. Rubinstein, *Soviet and Chinese Influence in the Third World* (New York: Praeger, 1975); Charles Neuhauser, *Third World Politics:*

China and the Afro-Asian People's Solidarity Organization 1957–1967, Harvard East Asian Monographs no. 26 (Cambridge, MA: Harvard University Press, 1970); Shen-Yu Dai, *China, the Superpowers and the Third World* (Hong Kong: Chinese University of Hong Kong, 1974); Jerome Alan Cohen, *The Dynamics of China's Foreign Relations* (Cambridge, MA: Harvard University Press, 1970); James C. Hsiung and Samuel S. Kim, *China in the Global Community* (New York: Praeger, 1980); Udo Weiss, "China's Aid to and Trade With the Developing Countries of the Third World," in *China and the Current Era of Détente*, edited by *Centre d'Etude du Sud-Est Asiatique et de l'Extrême-Orient* (Brussels: Université Libre de Bruxelles, 1974); George T. Yu, "China and the Third World," *Asian Survey* 17, no. 11 (1977): 1036–1048.

35 Cecil Johnson, *Communist China and Latin America 1959–1967* (New York: Columbia University Press, 1970); Yitzhak Shichor, *The Middle East in China's Foreign Policy* (Cambridge: Cambridge University Press, 1979); Leo Suryadinata, *"Overseas Chinese" in Southeast Asia and China's Foreign Policy: An Interpretative Essay* (Singapore: Institute of Southeast Asian Studies, 1978); Robert G. Sutter, *Chinese Foreign Policy After the Cultural Revolution, 1966–1977* (Boulder, CO: Westview Press, 1978); Melvin Gurtov, *China and Southeast Asia, the Politics of Survival: A Study of Foreign Policy Interaction* (Baltimore: Johns Hopkins University Press, 1975); Joseph Camilleri, *Southeast Asia in China's Foreign Policy* (Singapore: Institute of Southeast Asian Studies, 1975); James C. Hsiung, *Beyond China's Independent Foreign Policy: Challenge for the U.S. and Its Asian Allies* (New York: Praeger, 1985).

36 These include Sven Hamrell and Carl Gosta Widstrand, *The Soviet Bloc, China and Africa* (London: Published for the Scandinavian Institute of African Studies, Uppsala [by] Pall Mall Press, 1964); John C. Cooley, *East Wind Over Africa: Red China's African Offensive* (New York: Walker and Company, 1965); Emmanuel John Hevi, *An African Student in China* (New York: Praeger, 1963); Emmanuel John Hevi, *The Dragon's Embrace: The Chinese Communists in Africa* (New York: Praeger, 1966).

37 Books on Africa published between 1974 and 1976 include Alan Hutchison, *China's African Revolution* (London: Hutchison, 1975); George T. Yu, *China's Africa Policy: A Study of Tanzania* (New York: Praeger, 1975); Alaba Ogunsanwo, *China's Policy in Africa 1958–1971* (Cambridge: Cambridge University Press, 1974); Martin Bailey, *Freedom Railway: China and the Tanzania-Zambia Link* (London: Rex Collings, 1976); Richard Hall and Hugh Peyman, *The Great Uhuru Railway: China's Showpiece in Africa* (London: Victor Gollancz, 1976). At least three additional books were written on the subject during the 1970s: Bruce D. Larkin, *China and Africa 1949–1970: The Foreign Policy of the People's Republic of China* (Berkeley: University of California Press, 1971); Richard Lowenthal, *Model or Ally? The Communist Powers and the Developing Countries* (New York: Oxford University Press, 1977); Warren Weinstein, *Soviet and Chinese Aid to Africa* (New York: Praeger, 1980).

38 The exceptions were Samuel S. Kim, *The Third World in Chinese World Policy* (Princeton, NJ: Princeton University, 1989); Lillian Craig Harris, ed., *China's Foreign Policy Toward the Third World* (New York: Praeger, 1985); and Lillian Craig Harris and Robert L. Worden, eds., *China and the Third World: Champion or Challenger?* (Dover: Auburn House, 1986).

39 Joshua Eisenman, Eric Heginbotham, and Derek Mitchell, *China and the Developing World: Beijing's Strategy for the Twenty-first Century* (Armonk, NY: M.E. Sharpe, 2007).

40 Manochehr Dorraj and Carrie Liu Currier, *China's Energy Relations With the Developing World* (New York: Continuum, 2011); Lowell Dittmer and George T. Yu, eds., *China, the Developing World, and the New Global Dynamic* (Boulder, CO: Lynne Rienner Publishers, 2010); David Shambaugh, *China Goes Global: The Partial Power* (New York: Oxford University Press, 2014); Dennis Hickey and Baogang Guo, eds., *Dancing With the Dragon: China's Emergence in the Developing World* (Lanham, MD: Lexington Books, 2010); Yang Yao and Ho-Mou Wu, eds., *Reform and Development in China: What Can China Offer the Developing World* (New York: Routledge, 2010); Elizabeth Economy and Michael Levi, *By All Means Necessary: How China's Resource Quest is Changing the World* (Oxford: Oxford University Press, 2014); Jan Wouters, Jean-Christophe Defraigne, and Matthieu Burnay,

China, the European Union and the Developing World: A Triangular Relationship (Cheltenham, Gloucestershire: Edward Elgar Publishers, 2015); Carla Freeman, *Handbook on China and Developing Countries* (Cheltenham, Gloucestershire: Edward Elgar Publishers, 2015); Evelyn Goh, *Rising China's Influence in Developing Asia* (New York: Oxford University Press, 2016). For an official account see Xu Shuai, Guo Xinning, and Wang Fangfang, *China's Relationship With the Developing Countries* 论中国与发展中国家关系 (Beijing: National Defense University Press, 2012).

41 See, for example, Sumedh Deorukhkar and Le Xia, "Gauging the Impact of China's Growth Slowdown on Emerging Asia," *BBVA Research, Asia Economic Watch*, March 2, 2016; Deborah Brautigam, *The Dragon's Gift: The Real Story of China in Africa* (New York: Oxford University Press, 2009); Kevin P. Gallagher and Roberto Porzecanski, *The Dragon in the Room: China and the Future of Latin American Industrialization* (Stanford: Stanford University Press, 2010); Mattias Busse, Ceren Erdogan, and Henning Muhlen, "China's Impact on Africa—The Role of Trade, FDI, and Aid," *Kyklos International Review for Social Sciences* 69, no. 2 (May 2016): 228–262; and Angus Deaton, "Why Poor Countries Need Strong Government More than Anything Else," *Market Watch*, October 12, 2015.

42 Part of this literature revolves around whether there is a "Beijing consensus" that stands in opposition to a "Washington consensus." Stefan Halper, *The Beijing Consensus: Legitimizing Authoritarianism in Our Time* (New York: Basic Books, 2010); Scott Kennedy, "The Myth of the Beijing Consensus," *Journal of Contemporary China* 19, no. 65 (April 2010): 461–477; John Williamson, "Is the 'Beijing Consensus' Now Dominant," *Asia Policy* 13, no. 1 (January 2012): 1–16. Other work on China's political impact includes Holslag, "China and Coups: Coping With Political Instability in Africa," 367–386; David Dollar, "China's Investment in Latin America," Brookings Institute Geoeconomics and Global Issues Paper 4, January 2017; Julia Bader, "China, Autocratic Patron? An Empirical Investigation of China as a Factor in Autocratic Survival," *International Studies Quarterly* 59, no. 1 (March 2015): 23–33; and David H. Shinn and Joshua Eisenman, *China and Africa: A Century of Engagement* (Philadelphia, PA: University of Pennsylvania Press, 2012).

43 On the issue of corruption, see, for example, Frank Stroker, "Perceptions of Chinese Firms in Africa Tainted by Corruption and Other Abuses," *Corporate Compliance Trends*, February 27, 2015; and Daniel C. O'Neill, "Risky Business: The Political Economy of Chinese Investment in Kazakhstan," *Journal of Eurasian Studies* 5, no. 2 (May 2014): 145–156. On the environment, see David H. Shinn, "The Environmental Impact of China's Investment in Africa," *Cornell International Law Review* 49, no. 1 (Winter 2016): 25–67; Carla P. Freeman and Yiqian Yu, "China as an Environmental Actor in the Developing World—China's Role in Deforestation and the Timber Trade in Developing Countries," in *Handbook on China and Developing Countries*, ed., Carla P. Freeman (Cheltenham, UK: Edward Elgar Publishing, 2015); Rebecca Ray, Kevin Gallagher, Andres Lopez, and Cynthia Sanborn, *China and Sustainable Development in Latin America: The Social and Environmental Dimensions* (New York: Anthem Press, 2017).

44 On China's general foreign policy, objectives, and strategy, see Alastair Iain Johnston, "Is China a Status Quo Power?" *International Security* 27, no. 4 (Spring 2003): 5–56; Evan S. Medeiros, *China's International Behavior: Activism, Opportunism, and Diversification* (Santa Monica: RAND Corporation, 2009); Elizabeth Economy, "The Impact of International Regimes on Chinese Foreign Policy-Making: Broadening Perspectives and Policies . . . But Only to a Point," in *The Making of Chinese Foreign and Security Policy in the Reform Era*, ed. David M. Lampton (Stanford: Stanford University Press, 2001); Robert D. Blackwill and Ashley J. Tellis, *Revising U.S. Grand Strategy Toward China* (New York: Council on Foreign Relations, 2015); David Shambaugh, "China Engages Asia: Reshaping the Regional Order," *International Security* 29, no. 3 (Winter 2004/2005): 64–99.

45 See, for example Goh, *Rising China's Influence in Developing Asia*; Shambaugh, *China Goes Global*; and Scott L. Krastner, "Buying Influence? Assessing the Political Effects of China's International Trade," *Journal of Conflict Resolution*, 60: 6 (2016), 980–1007.

46 Goh, *Rising China's Influence in Developing Asia*.

47 This point is made by, among others, Economy and Levi, *By All Means Necessary*; and John Ghazvlnian, *Untapped: The Scramble for Africa's Oil* (New York: Mariner Books, 2008). A similar point is made about some aspects of state-level behavior in George J. Gilboy and Eric Heginbotham, *Chinese and Indian Strategic Behavior: Growing Power and Alarm* (Cambridge: Cambridge University Press, 2012).

48 Examples include Shinn and Eisenman; Howard W. French, *China's Second Continent: How a Million Migrants Are Building a New Empire in Africa* (New York: Vintage, 2015); David N. Abdulai, *Chinese Investment in Africa: How African Countries Can Position Themselves to Benefit From China's Foray Into Africa* (New York: Routledge, 2016); Harry Verhoeven, "Is Beijing's Non-Interference Policy History? How Africa is Changing China," *Washington Quarterly* 37, no. 2 (2014): 55–70; Matthias Busse, Caren Erdogan, and Henning Muhlen, "China's Impact on Africa—The Role of Trade, FDI, and Aid," Ruhr University Institute of Development Research and Development Policy Working Paper 206, 2014.

49 Goh, *Rising China's Influence in Developing Asia*; David B.H. Denoon, ed., *China, The United States, and the Future of Southeast Asia: U.S.-China Relations, Volume II* (New York: New York University Press, 2017); Zhang Biwu, "Chinese Perceptions of US Return to Southeast Asia and the Prospects of China's Peaceful Rise," *Journal of Contemporary China* 24, no. 91 (2015): 176–195. Michael Green, Kathleen Hicks, Zack Cooper, John Schaus, Jake Douglas, *Countering Coercion in Maritime Asia: The Theory and Practice of Gray Zone Deterrence* (Washington, DC: Center for Strategic and International Studies, 2017); Michael D. Swaine and M. Taylor Fravel, "China's Assertive Behavior, Part Two: The Maritime Periphery," *China Leadership Monitor*, no. 35 (Summer 2011), 1–29; Evan S. Medeiros, Keith Crane, Eric Heginbotham, Normal D. Levin, and Julia Lowell, *Pacific Currents: The Responses of U.S. Allies and Security Partners in East Asia to China's Rise* (Pittsburgh, PA: RAND Corporation, 2008).

50 Margaret Myers and Carol Wise, eds., *The Political Economy of China-Latin America Relations in the New Millennium* (New York: Routledge, 2017); Kevin P. Gallagher, *The China Triangle: Latin America's China Boom and the Fate of the Washington Consensus* (New York: Oxford University Press, 2016); Robert Evan Ellis, *China on the Ground in Latin America: Challenges for the Chinese and Impacts on the Region* (New York: Palgrave Macmillan, 2014).

51 Elucidated by Alexander L. George and Andrew Bennett in their seminal text *Case Studies and Theory Development in the Social Sciences* (Cambridge, MA: MIT Press, 2005).

52 George and Bennett, *Case Studies and Theory Development in the Social Sciences*, 71.

53 George and Bennett, *Case Studies and Theory Development in the Social Sciences*, Chapter 3.

54 Andrew J. Nathan and Andrew Scobell, *China's Search for Security* (New York: Columbia University Press), 3–7.

55 "Homepage," Ministry of Foreign Affairs of the People's Republic of China, accessed October 2016.

56 He, "China's Major-Country Diplomacy Progresses on All Fronts."

2

EXPANDING THE "STRATEGIC PERIPHERY"

A History of China's Interaction with the Developing World

Derek J. Mitchell

Introduction

On his most famous voyage in 1492, Christopher Columbus led a fleet of ninety sailors aboard three ships, the longest of which was 85 feet. This historic journey was heralded as a breakthrough in maritime exploration. Yet a half century earlier, Zheng He, the Chinese Muslim eunuch, commanded 28,000 sailors on 300 ships of up to 400 feet, equipped with the most advanced maritime technology of the day, to conduct maritime exploits far from the shores of China. Zheng's sophisticated fleet dwarfed anything sailing out of Europe at the time, and during his seven historic voyages he spread Chinese goods and culture from Southeast Asia to India and on to the shores of Africa. China was at the height of its global power during the early years of the Ming Dynasty (1368–1644 CE), and Zheng He's voyages were a landmark in China's interest and outreach to the world.[1]

Zheng He's expeditions emerged out of an intermittent Chinese maritime tradition and rich interaction with its neighbors reaching back to the first millennium. It was China, after all, that invented the compass during the Han Dynasty (206 BCE–220 CE) and first applied the invention to seafaring during the Song Dynasty (960–1279) when China established its first national navy as the most powerful and sophisticated of its day.[2] During the Han Dynasty, Buddhism was introduced to China via overland trade routes that extended to Central Asia and Persia. During the Tang Dynasty (618–907), pilgrims from India and scholars and traders from China and Central Asia traveled along the Silk Road, over which trade in silks, spices, and tea reaching as far as Rome introduced commercial and cultural exchange to the seat of the emperor in Chang' an (Xi'an). The Tang period led to growing Chinese influence in Japan and Korea, whose people adopted the Chinese writing system and other cultural, artistic, and philosophical concepts. Even today, the Chinese look to the Han and Tang dynasties as a hallowed historic era during which China assumed its rightful place as the acknowledged regional, if not global, leader.

Indeed, had it not been for a power struggle in which suspicious, xenophobic Confucian scholars prevailed in the late fifteenth century, it might have been Zheng He, rather than Columbus, who "discovered" America and officially established America's patrimony as Chinese rather than European. Instead, China's official engagement with the world beyond its immediate periphery ended soon after Zheng returned home. As China turned inward, it dismantled its maritime forces, and inaugurated several centuries of self-imposed semi-isolation in which all foreign interaction was highly regulated and ritualized in a manner that fueled China's sense of self-importance, but led to complacency in science, commerce, and military affairs that would eventually lead to the tumultuous end of China's Imperial era.

Decades of humiliation, division, and war in the nineteenth and twentieth centuries led China to reevaluate the traditional attitudes that allowed the Middle Kingdom to become weak and vulnerable to external challenges. Although sometimes considered the latest Chinese dynasty, the Chinese communists under Mao Zedong took a much different approach to China's security and to its relationship with the world. During the early years of the Cold War, which pitted two competing ideologies and power blocs against one another, China chose to focus on the so-called Third World of post-colonial developing nations to promote its own ideological and political agenda. By the 1980s and 1990s, with the decline of ideology and rise of economic reform and pragmatism, China's relationships with the developing world were subordinated to its need to develop constructive political and economic relationships with the developed world. This was done to promote domestic development and stability, and to return China to the ranks of the world's great powers.

Today, China continues to call itself the world's largest developing nation, even as it reaches out and connects itself to the international community to a degree unprecedented in China's long history. Nonetheless, the basis for China's approach to international affairs generally—and the developing world specifically—has been built upon the foundation of China's centuries of experience in dealing with the outside world. Examining the themes of China's external relations throughout its history can provide the necessary context for understanding China's current approach, and where its foreign policy may be headed in the twenty-first century. This chapter seeks to provide this context, and to assess what elements remain relevant today as China emerges as a major global player.

Imperial Dynasties and Governments of China

- Xia Dynasty: 2206–1766 BCE
- Shang Dynasty: 1766–1122 BCE
- Zhou Dynasty: 1122–770 BCE
- Spring and Autumn Period: 770–476 BCE
- Warring States Period: 476–221 BCE

- Qin Dynasty: 221–206 BCE
- Han Dynasty: 206 BCE–220 CE
- Three Kingdoms Period: 220–265
- Jin Dynasty: 265–420
- Northern and Southern Dynasties: 420–581
- Sui Dynasty: 581–618
- Tang Dynasty: 618–907
- Five Dynasties and Ten Kingdoms: 907–960
- Song Dynasty: 960–1279
- Northern Song: 960–1127
- Southern Song: 1127–1279
- Liao (Khitan) Dynasty: 916–1125
- Jin (Jurchen) Dynasty: 1115–1234
- Yuan (Mongol) Dynasty: 1279–1368
- Ming Dynasty: 1368–1644
- Qing (Manchu) Dynasty: 1644–1911
- Republic of China: 1912–present (relocated to Taiwan in 1949)
- People's Republic of China: 1949–present

Note: For excellent comprehensive discussions of Imperial China's external relations, see *The Chinese World Order: Traditional China's Foreign Relations*, ed. John King Fairbank (Cambridge, MA: Harvard University Press, 1968); John King Fairbank and Edwin O. Reischauer, *China: Tradition and Transformation* (Boston: Houghton Mifflin Company, 1973); and Mark Mancall, *China at the Center: 300 Years of Foreign Policy* (New York: The Free Press, 1984). For an outstanding analysis that traces Chinese strategy from the Imperial period to the present, see Michael Swaine and Ashley Tellis, *Interpreting China's Grand Strategy: Past, Present, and Future* (Santa Monica, CA: RAND, 2000).

The Imperial Era

While China has historically maintained substantial and productive interactions with peoples and cultures beyond its borders, Imperial China's external relations through the centuries were infused more by alienation than embrace. Imperial China's policy and perspective toward the outside world drew greatly on its cultural heritage, unique geopolitical situation, and consistent requirement to attend to its endemic internal challenges. Specifically, China's adherence to Confucian philosophy, its proud self-image, its constant concern over the vulnerability of its periphery to external challenges, and its consistent fear of domestic turmoil if not dissolution due to internal corruption, civic unrest, or palace intrigue drove what was often an essentially defensive approach to external relations. During periods of strength, however, Chinese emperors often displayed more aggressive, expansionist tendencies. Each of these themes, and the interplay among them, will be examined in the following pages.

Self-Image, Cultural Values, and Statecraft

During the Imperial period, China's view of the world and its place in it was reflected in the name the Chinese gave their country—Zhongguo, or "Middle Kingdom"—and in the term used to describe the scope of their imperial suzerainty—*tianxia*, or "all under heaven." By early in the first millennium, China's advanced culture and material and philosophical achievements had produced a self-reverence that informed every aspect of the nation's behavior, from imperial rites and rituals to how the Chinese viewed themselves in relation to the outside world.

Those outside Chinese civilization were officially termed "barbarians," and thus unworthy of study or emulation. During the Ming Dynasty, for instance, Chinese descriptions of foreign lands portrayed foreigners in mystical and fantastical terms—akin to exotic animals—and described them in deliberately condescending or belittling language.[3] It may be said that during the Imperial era Chinese leaders viewed the world outside their borders as the developing world, with which the Chinese emperor, as the "Son of Heaven," might engage only with great condescension and charity.

The Chinese emperor and Confucian scholar–official viewed the world as they viewed the organization of their own society, through a Confucian notion of hierarchy and reciprocal responsibility akin to that between ruler and subject, father and son, or older brother and younger brother. China put itself at the pinnacle of this world order, with its leader holding the self-proclaimed "mandate of heaven" as the basis of his legitimacy to rule.

The emperor's mandate was based on a moral authority conveyed by adherence to the Confucian value system. According to Confucianism, the international system—like the social system—should be led by a civilized force that exercises rule by virtue rather than by naked power.[4] Confucian bureaucrats tended to disdain the professional military as a matter of principle, viewing military power as beneath the dignity of an advanced civilization. They even declined to include warriors in their social and occupational hierarchy of scholar–bureaucrat, farmer, artisan, and merchant, in descending order of status.[5] An exception to Confucians' antipathy toward military force was when an external power failed to acknowledge Chinese superiority, thus requiring the Middle Kingdom to firmly restore the violator to its appropriate place in the Sino-centric order.[6]

China's lack of interaction with societies of equal cultural achievement, at least from China's perspective, facilitated its presumed superiority over outsiders. During the Imperial era, interaction between Chinese traders and foreign counterparts[7] was either with relatively undeveloped militant nomadic and seminomadic cultures on northern and western borders, or with neighbors in southeast and northeast Asia whose cultures often were influenced by China. China's ritualized interaction with these border nations and tribes over the centuries only served to reaffirm its sense of superiority and exceptionalism. And even when unsuccessful in preventing occupation by non-Han peoples, as during the Mongol (Yuan Dynasty: 1279–1368) and

Manchu (Qing Dynasty: 1644–1911) dynasties, the eventual preservation of the Confucian order and cultural assimilation of their occupiers only further reaffirmed the superiority of the Chinese culture.

Imperial China was generally self-sufficient in terms of natural resources, which also enabled its rulers to feel little need to compete with other nations to sustain its power or legitimacy. What China might have received from the outside world tended to be viewed as luxuries or objects of curiosity rather than materials critical for the stability and sustainability of the national economy and polity.[8] Generally, Chinese leaders focused their energies and strategies internally to secure their rule from rivals, rather than externally to dominate foreign powers.

Superiority and Weakness: Imperial Chinese Relations With the Strategic Periphery

Despite China's confident sense of its own cultural superiority relative to the world around it, its leaders were quite aware of the country's vulnerability to challenges from its immediate inland periphery—particularly to the north and west (China tended to ignore its maritime borders as they were largely safe from foreign challenges until the middle of the Qing dynasty). The purpose was to safeguard the Chinese heartland, which was generally defined as encompassing the maritime eastern shore, north through the Yellow River plains and tributaries to today's Beijing, south through the Yangtze River region to the shores of the South China Sea, and as far west as the mountains and high plains of modern Sichuan and eastern Qinghai.[9]

Attention to challenges from the west began at least as far back as the first millennium CE, during the Han Dynasty, which suffered from attacks primarily from the Turkic Xiongnu (Hun) tribes. Safeguarding trade along the Silk Road required securing the areas along China's border with Central and South Asia. Invasions from the north led to the establishment of two major dynasties not run by the ethnic Han people during the second millennium—the Mongol (Yuan Dynasty) and Manchu (Qing Dynasty)—as well as several small dynasties that ruled over parts of China—the Qidan (Liao Dynasty: 916–1125) and the Jin Dynasty (1115–1234). The security of China's periphery was an immediate, strategic concern to Chinese leaders. Pacification of Inner Asia became consistent elements of Chinese Imperial strategy.

Chinese leaders handled the challenge from its periphery in several ways, depending on China's internal situation. When China was beset by internal troubles, usually during a period of dynastic consolidation at the start of a new era, or during the late, turbulent years of a dynasty, Chinese leaders took an essentially defensive position to hold off border threats and challenges. When stronger, it took the fight to the "barbarians" and expanded its strategic periphery accordingly.

During the Han Dynasty, for instance, leaders sought to fight off, buy out, or pit barbarian against barbarian.[10] At a military disadvantage fighting far from the

Chinese heartland, Han Dynasty emperors often resorted to a policy of "peace and kinship" toward nomad leaders in the west, appeasing them with lavish gifts, entertainment, and even betrothal to Han princesses.[11]

Imperial Chinese Statecraft

A wildcard in any examination of themes in Imperial China's relations with the outside world, particularly one that seeks to detect themes relevant to the present day, is the issue of classical Chinese strategic concepts and statecraft.

Despite official Confucian disdain for the military arts, a well-developed strategic culture nonetheless emerged during the earliest days of the Chinese nation that arguably remains embedded within the Chinese popular—and perhaps elite—imagination today. Ancient Chinese statecraft reaching back nearly three thousand years, to the Spring and Autumn (722–481 BCE) and Warring States (403–221 BCE) periods through the dynasties of the first millennium CE have been immortalized in Chinese classic literature and oral histories that told of the exploits of kings, generals, political strategists, and philosophers as they jockeyed for power and defended the realm during periods of political turmoil in China.[12] This strategic culture included military tactics, but accentuated diplomatic cunning and political maneuver to achieve consolidation of one's power and triumph over one's competitors. As Michael Hunt has written,

> (T)his tradition shows Chinese functioning in an amoral interstate system characterized by constant maneuver and ruthless competition. Its leading figures are not burdened in their decision by hoary tradition; rather, they repeatedly resort to the classic realist calculus, trying to achieve the desired end by the most economical means. Temporary accommodation, alliances made and abandoned, ambush and treachery, the careful cultivation of domestic resources and morale, psychological warfare, and of course raw military power all occupied an important place in the arsenal of the statesmen of these periods of disunity.[13]

The essence of this strategic approach was captured in the so-called 36 Stratagems, which used stories from Chinese history—apocryphal or otherwise—to compile a series of pithy sayings instructing the practitioner on how to achieve one's strategic objectives. The sayings are divided into six sections to address situations of advantage and disadvantage, offense and defense. The theme that runs through each stratagem, however, is the utility of deception to achieve an objective.[14]

Although developed to address power struggles among warring fiefdoms on the battlefield and in the halls of power, and not necessarily for China's interactions with the wider world, these political and military methods—embedded in popular literature—remain part of China's cultural memory.

Mao Zedong, for example, was a notable student and practitioner of classical Chinese statecraft. The classical tradition remains a potential guide for any modern Chinese (or indeed Western) strategist who seeks to gain strategic advantage over others in a complicated security environment.

Over time such interactions became ritualized as a method of economic (trade) and diplomatic intercourse between China and non-(ethnic) Han peoples. To preserve the nation's self-image, the Confucian bureaucracy came to frame these ritualized interactions as demonstrations of Chinese superiority and benevolence, as barbarian "tribute" to the superior (virtuous) Chinese empire.[15] The visiting state was required to use highly specific and formalized language of subservience, present the Chinese court with gifts (sometimes including a prominent hostage), and perform the ritual kowtow—or "three kneelings and nine prostrations"—in a minutely choreographed display of fealty that, in the Chinese mind, provided the Middle Kingdom with a formal acknowledgment of its cultural and political superiority. In return, the Chinese provided lavish gifts and allowed limited trade between the two sides.[16]

China usually gave far more than it received from foreign missions, reflecting the court's attitude that its smaller neighbors had little to offer their great nation, and demonstrating Chinese generosity and benevolence. In return for receiving Chinese political recognition and protection, China required reciprocal obligations from tributary states to assist in keeping the peace, including serving alongside Chinese armies whenever called upon.[17]

In the end, the system primarily served the practical purpose of facilitating trade for the tributary states rather than incurring loyalty and obedience. Issues of relative status, superiority and inferiority, and reciprocal responsibility were generally of lesser importance to them. While flawed, the tributary system offered mutual benefit from both economic and security standpoints to the tributary states and China alike. Tributary states received trade benefits and, in some cases, security guarantees, while China got strategic peace of mind, reaffirmation of its self-regard, and an effective means of saving the cost of maintaining a large standing army to patrol all its borders.

Periods of Strength and Confidence: Imperial China Reaches Out

Once an Imperial dynasty consolidated its control within China and felt relatively strong and confident, however, a different China often emerged from the one that assumed a defensive posture during periods of vulnerability. This China sought to exert more direct control over its periphery, and even expanded through military means its territorial and tributary boundaries.[18]

Vietnam and Korea were favorite targets. The Han Dynasty overran northern Vietnam, leading to Chinese rule down to modern Hanoi.[19] The Sui sought to extend Chinese dominion to southern Vietnam.[20] The Song failed in its campaign against its southern neighbor. The Ming initially succeeded but found the cost of trying to formally absorb Vietnam into the Chinese empire too high, resorting ultimately to a traditional tributary relationship.[21] Similarly, Korea experienced repeated Chinese efforts at direct control or subjugation. The Han, Sui, and Tang each launched military campaigns to absorb the peninsula (or parts thereof) into the Chinese imperium, until the Ming and Qing settled for a dominant tributary relationship that made Korea a virtual protectorate.[22]

The Ming Dynasty's founding emperors, still worried about the Mongol threat even after successfully casting off the Yuan Dynasty, took the offensive against nomadic threats from the north and northwest to extend their Confucian suzerainty even farther. Beginning in 1405, and for the next two decades, Ming Emperor Zhu Di sent Zheng He on at least seven maritime expeditions to forcefully secure new tributary relationships and economic benefits for China in the South Pacific, Indian Ocean, Persian Gulf, and the eastern coast of Africa[23]—including helping to overthrow the leaders of Sri Lanka and Sumatra and replace them with more tributary-friendly rulers.[24]

Although private maritime and overland merchant trade to Southeast, Central, and South Asia had occurred for centuries, these official voyages to nearly fifty new countries constituted the most extensive official contact with the non-Confucian world in Chinese history to that point. While Chinese officials retreated into relative diplomatic isolation in the ensuing centuries, Zheng's voyages nonetheless set the stage for the dominant presence of Chinese traders in Southeast Asia.

Through both military conquest and political cooptation, Ming and Qing Dynasty leaders continued territorial expansion into regions previously considered outside the Chinese heartland. The founding Ming emperor, for instance, referred in an early proclamation to the "countries of Yun-nan and Japan,"[25] suggesting that both were independent entities outside China's frontiers. Officials from the Ming Bureaucracy gradually coopted local authorities until the formerly autonomous (or semiautonomous) entity became formally incorporated into the Chinese empire.[26] This process of absorption was not unique to Yunnan or the Ming, but it provides a window into one way that China was able to expand its territory steadily over the centuries.

Early Qing emperors also expended much effort to influence and control China's periphery beyond that achieved by earlier dynasties, including invasions, often labeled "pacification," against Burma, Nepal, and Mongolia. In the process, Qing leaders aggressively incorporated Chinese Turkestan (Xinjiang today), Taiwan, and Tibet into its Imperial order as protectorates, which set the stage for later claims of explicit sovereign rights to these relatively autonomous regions.[27]

The expansion of the Chinese Imperial Empire through military action and gradual assimilation of surrounding peoples thus offers an alternative way to view China's posture toward the developing world along its border during this period, one that belies China's preferred narrative about itself. In fact, the Chinese imperium tended to expand and contract throughout history, making historic "China" a geographically difficult concept to define, and cross-border aggression difficult to identify. The Great Wall, meant to protect China from outside (non-Han) aggressors, exists far inside the borders assumed by today's People's Republic of China, for instance. Today's Tibet, Xinjiang, Manchuria (Heilongjiang), Inner Mongolia, and Taiwan, among other areas, were historically considered by ancient China as dangerous sources of barbarian threats, and thus were hardly part of the imperium.

In the end, as China forcefully absorbed many of the peoples on its northern and western borders into its imperial orbit, the definition of China's strategic periphery necessarily expanded as well. As the Chinese imperium expanded, so did the territory required to serve as a buffer to protect it. A neighbor's inherent sovereign legitimacy was not often the determining factor in whether a border nation, people, or area maintained its sovereign independence. In the end, what was most important was military strength, which either successfully repulsed Chinese aggression or withstood the charge long enough to tire the empire into accepting the limited suzerainty of a tributary relationship. The traditional notion that Chinese identity is based on culture rather than ethnicity rationalized and facilitated this process of territorial expansion in the Chinese mind. As countries and ethnic groups on China's periphery were invaded and gradually assimilated Chinese culture and customs, it was natural that over time they became incorporated into a new, ever-expanding "Chinese" polity.[28]

End of the Imperial Era: China Confronts the West

As mentioned, during the Ming period China began to isolate itself from interaction with the wider world outside its immediate periphery. Following Zheng He's expeditions, increasingly powerful neo-Confucian scholar–bureaucrats advocated a more traditional focus inward on agriculture and cultural purity. Emperor Zhu Di's successors renounced Zheng He's voyages as wasteful and embraced Confucian introspection, leading to a decline in interest in the outside world and in science and technology. Maritime exploration was forbidden, and large ships were destroyed.[29] China ceded its maritime strength to Europe, and by 1503, the Chinese navy was one-tenth the size of a century earlier.[30]

For centuries, China remained inward-looking and xenophobic, uninterested in fully engaging in a world it viewed as inferior. The outside world, the resurgent Confucian bureaucratic elite believed, would taint the superior Chinese culture. Eventually the outside world, whether inferior or not, would come to China.

Western traders and missionaries had begun to flow into China in the late Ming period of the sixteenth century, despite China's desire for isolation. For the first time China was confronted by nations with aggressive political, economic, and military cultures that had little patience for or reasons to cater to Chinese pretensions of centrality or superiority. As a result, in the seventeenth century, faced with a military threat from Russia, Imperial China displayed a more flexible and pragmatic side to its Confucian orthodoxy with respect to international affairs. The Qing entered its first international treaty, the Treaty of Nerchinsk, suggesting a relationship between equals. A Qing mission even accepted to perform a small kowtow in Moscow, requiring reciprocity of course, in an attempt to prevent Russia from aiding the Mongols who were (as always) challenging the Chinese heartland.[31]

Over time, trade restrictions were eased. In the late eighteenth and nineteenth centuries, European powers reached the Middle Kingdom's shores. After 1760, the "Canton system" was established whereby all foreign trade was restricted to Canton (Guangzhou) to allow the Qing regime to manage the growing European trade.[32] Europe's lust for the China trade, however, led eventually to war to open the China market. Centuries of isolation and complacent assumption of its own superiority had left the empire militarily weak and unable to meet the new threat from across the sea when it came. China was defeated in the Opium Wars (1839–1842) and compelled to sign the Treaty of Nanjing, the first in a series of "unequal treaties" that thoroughly altered China's relationship with the outside world.

The steady loss of domestic sovereignty and territorial integrity at the hands of foreign powers launched China's so-called century of humiliation. The Qing Empire fell, ending China's Imperial era. Warlords appeared in its place, as well as a Republican era that focused China's energies inward as the country struggled with both a devastating civil war and foreign invasion. Only with the end of World War II in 1945 was China able to regain its sovereignty.

Post-1949: The Communist Era

China and the Third World

With the founding of the People's Republic of China (PRC) in 1949, China entered a new phase in its external relations that focused specifically on building relations with developing countries. Distinct from its Imperial relationships, these interactions were based on a self-conscious ideology that promoted equality among nations (albeit with some more equal than others) and that involved China deeply in global affairs.

In a June 1949 speech commemorating the founding of the Chinese Communist Party (CCP), Mao Zedong stated that

> in order to win victory and consolidate it, we must lean to one side. . . . [A]ll
> Chinese without exception must lean either to the side of imperialism

or to the side of socialism. Sitting on the fence will not do, nor is there a third road.

In this same speech, he asserted that China would work to

> unite in a common struggle with those nations of the world which treat us as equals and unite with the peoples of all countries. That is, ally ourselves with the Soviet Union, with the People's Democracies and with the proletariat and the broad masses of the people in all other countries, and form an international united front.[33]

Despite Mao's statement of fealty to communist solidarity and internationalism, however, China's actual policy began to adhere to a "third road" of engagement and identity with the developing world, particularly as its relations with both superpowers faltered. The PRC began to accentuate its relationships with developing countries in a series of stages. In the first stage, China sought to consolidate its position domestically and counter isolation imposed by the United States, which included the establishment of the anti-communist Southeast Asian Treaty Organization (SEATO) on its doorstep immediately following the Korean War. Premier Zhou Enlai—consistent with classical Chinese strategy—worked first to stabilize China's relations with nations along its periphery, signing agreements with the Mongolian People's Republic (Outer Mongolia) and the Democratic People's Republic of Korea (North Korea), and promoting ties with post-colonial nations India and Burma (now Myanmar), as well as Vietnamese revolutionaries fighting French colonialism.

Crystallizing China's new diplomatic approach, at a meeting with an Indian delegation on December 31, 1953, Premier Zhou Enlai outlined the "Five Principles of Peaceful Coexistence" as the framework under which its foreign policy would be conducted.[34] The Five Principles—mutual respect for territorial integrity and sovereignty, non-aggression, non-interference in internal affairs, equality and mutual benefit, and peaceful coexistence—all appealed to a developing world that, like China, had felt the brunt of colonialism by Western capitalist powers.

The Five Principles were enshrined the following year at the Bandung Conference in Indonesia. The Bandung Conference, which involved delegates from twenty-nine Asian and African nations, promoted Asia–Africa solidarity and inaugurated China's new role in international diplomacy among the nations of the Third World.[35] Bandung was the precursor to the "Non-Aligned Movement," in which Third World nations ostensibly refused to side with either the United States or the Soviet Union in what was rapidly becoming a bipolar international environment. China's involvement at Bandung opened the door to greater cooperation with a host of countries around the world that had previously refused to recognize the PRC in favor of the Republic of China on Taiwan, and offered China an opportunity to assert international leadership.

Maoist Radicalism and the Decline of Third World Solidarity

Bandung and the Five Principles of Peaceful Coexistence were just the first of many theories that defined (and redefined) China's relationship with the developing and developed world during the second half of the twentieth century. These theories evolved as China's foreign policy priorities and national interests evolved.

In 1963, Mao elaborated on his "Dual Intermediate Zones" theory, which he had first discussed more than a decade earlier.[36] This theory argued that a spacious intermediate zone existed between the United States and the USSR. Countries in the intermediate zone, like China, were independent and should band together to form a united front against imperialist America. The intermediate zone itself was broken down into sections. One part consisted of the developing countries and colonies in Asia, Africa, and Latin America, which formed the core of the anti-United States coalition. The other part consisted of Japan, Canada, Oceania, and the capitalist countries of Western Europe, countries that, in the PRC's opinion, were being controlled or negatively influenced by the United States.[37] According to this view, the developing countries of Asia, Latin America, and Africa were placed at the forefront of a righteous struggle against imperialism.

The 1960s eventually became the "high point of China's sponsorship of Third World radicalism."[38] China's anti-colonial rhetoric gave way increasingly to an ideological campaign. From 1963 to 1964, Zhou Enlai toured thirteen Asian and African nations to gain support for the Chinese model of socialism. Later, he declared, "The revolutionary movements of the people of the world, particularly in Asia, Africa and Latin America, are surging vigorously forward."[39]

China began to provide material assistance—arms, money, military instructors, and economic aid—to help guerrilla movements in Angola, Indonesia, Malaysia, Mozambique, the Philippines, Rhodesia (Zaire), Thailand, and Uganda, and actively fought on behalf of communist insurgents in Vietnam, who received nearly $20 billion in Chinese aid. During the radical height of the Cultural Revolution in the late 1960s, China's leadership limited its engagement with Third World governments in favor of Maoist insurgents inside their countries. Beijing also used its well-honed propaganda machine to spread the communist message in Southeast Asia, for example, through radio broadcasts. These activities predictably soured its relations with many Third World nations, which must have questioned the PRC's commitment to the Five Principles of Peaceful Coexistence. Although SEATO had disintegrated by the mid-1960s, Southeast Asian nations formed the Association of Southeast Asian Nations (ASEAN) to counter China's support for communist insurgencies in the region.

As before, spreading communism in the Third World was as much a political aim as an ideological one, as China began to compete not only with the United States but also with the Soviet Union over leadership in promoting global communism following the Sino–Soviet split that became ever wider as the 1960s progressed. In his famous 1965 essay, "Long Live the Victory of People's War," China's Defense Minister Lin Biao predicted that the developing world would usurp power from the superpowers and establish a Chinese-led new world order.[40]

In the end, however, despite being the largest non-OPEC donor to developing countries between 1953 and 1985, the PRC's ability to influence Third World developments decisively during the Cold War was limited.[41] Chinese aid to insurgent movements in reality was modest. With the exception of Vietnam, the largest single recipient of Chinese aid was the Pakistani government (ironically in a balance of power struggle against its erstwhile Third World/Bandung ally, India), not African or Latin American rebel groups. The overall Chinese effort in the Third World was disorganized, reflecting the chaos of China's leadership during the period leading up to and during the Cultural Revolution. Rebel groups eventually became disillusioned with their militant Chinese benefactors.

Meanwhile, border wars with India in 1962 and Vietnam in 1979 also revealed many rifts in Third World solidarity and challenged China's presumption of leadership. China's performance reflected a nation as concerned with traditional balance of power considerations and periphery security as extraordinary ideological affiliation with the developing world. China's framing of these two short wars as "teaching a lesson" to these border countries also echoed the attitude of superiority and tributary-style approach to periphery relations that China assumed during its Imperial era—a fact that was not lost on border states.[42]

As conflict and competition with the Soviet Union deepened, China also began to rethink its strategic orientation. By the early 1970s, Beijing began to reestablish diplomatic ties that had withered or been cut off during the more violent days of the Cultural Revolution. China gradually reentered the community of nations, replacing the Republic of China in the United Nations in 1971 and opening a new era in relations with the United States in 1972.

Nonetheless, even late-Maoist China continued to promote "anti-imperialist" solidarity and a new international economic order based around the developing world. In a 1974 speech at the United Nations, Deng Xiaoping introduced Mao's "Theory of the Three Worlds" that divided the world into three zones. The first zone included the United States and the Soviet Union, whose competition threatened world war. The second zone included the rest of the industrialized world, including Europe, Japan, Canada, Australia, and New Zealand. The third zone included the non-aligned Third World, led by China. The theory called for the second and third zones to unite against imperialism and an unjust world economic order. While on the surface this statement appeared to be little more than a recapitulation of past theories, Mao's Three World Theory was in fact a significant departure from earlier delineations of the world into socialist and capitalist camps. It abjured ideology and pitted the superpowers against the rest of the world. China made clear, however, that the Soviet Union posed a greater threat to the world than the United States, enabling it to pursue closer ties with Washington.[43]

Post-1979: The Decline of Ideology

Beginning in the late 1970s, however, China steadily downplayed the ideological components of both its domestic and foreign policy as it pursued economic liberalization and began to open itself up to foreign trade and investment. China shifted from giving aid to seeking and receiving foreign assistance (although its foreign aid picked up again in the 1980s, particularly to Africa).[44] In 1980, China joined the World Bank and the International Monetary Fund—two of the instruments of the "imperialist" financial order China once sought to disband. That same year, Japan began its Overseas Development Assistance program in China, both to aid China's reform process and as a tacit form of penance for the damage Tokyo wrought in the 1930s and 1940s. In the 1980s, China became one of the largest recipients of World Bank loans ($5.5 billion for fifty-two projects).[45]

China continued to affirm that its international relations were based on the Five Principles of Peaceful Coexistence, although China's foreign policy was now conducted without regard to a nation's political system or ideology. In 1982, Deng Xiaoping established China's commitment to an "independent foreign policy of peace" to reassure the international community of Beijing's new non-aligned and pragmatic orientation.

While China accentuated economic development and its relationship with the United States became a top priority, Beijing continued to seek constructive relationships with Third World countries based on affirmed principles of "equality and mutual respect," and in the economic arena based on "mutual benefit" (what China termed "win–win" results). Because the developing world had little to offer China economically, Beijing's financial aid declined during this period. However, the rhetoric of South–South cooperation continued. Deng did not abandon the notion of people's war, but did change its definition to anything that strengthened the hand of Third World nations against pressure from the United States and other First or Second World powers.[46] China began to provide military aid to Third World nations such as Algeria, Iran, Iraq, Pakistan, Saudi Arabia, and Syria to gain capital, buy influence, and demonstrate its continued fealty and leadership in the developing world. China turned to the developing world in a more concentrated and strategic way following the violent suppression of the Tiananmen Square demonstrations in 1989, when the regime felt the brunt of Western-led condemnation, sanction, and political isolation for its behavior.

During the 1990s, China's pragmatism and economic openness paid dividends politically, as it normalized relations and developed closer economic ties with countries throughout the developing and developed world. Beijing continued to pressure developing nations for diplomatic recognition and to adhere to a "One China policy" that meant de-recognition of the "Republic of China" on Taiwan. Beijing used its growing strength and pragmatic international orientation to isolate Taiwan in the international community, particularly as the PRC began to perceive the island as drifting toward a posture of permanent separation in the late 1990s and 2000s.

During the same period, China continued to suspect that the United States sought to divide China and contain China's rise. Observing that the end of the Cold War did not lead to a division of power in the world but to heightened American predominance, Beijing began to promote the concept of a multipolar world to dilute U.S. global power and influence, a posture that resonated well in most of the developing world and led to common cause in international organizations such as the United Nations and the World Trade Organization. With the expansion of its economic interests in Africa, Latin America, the Middle East, Central Asia, South Asia, and Southeast Asia, China's strategic attention to the developing world witnessed a renaissance as the twenty-first century dawned.[47]

China and the Developing World in the Early Twenty-First Century

Although Chinese leaders no longer took an ideological approach to its relations with the developing world as during the Cold War, the spirit of Bandung still lived on during the first decade of the twenty-first century. China continued to identify itself as the world's largest developing country, speak of relations with the developing world as the foundation of its foreign policy, and tout the Five Principles of Peaceful Coexistence as the foundation of its international diplomacy, whether in the guise of its "New Security Concept" or in its accession to Southeast Asia's Treaty of Amity and Cooperation.[48]

Beijing self-consciously sought to promote its "soft power" through educational and cultural initiatives around the world, including in developing countries. China continued to attend G-77 (developing world) meetings, and held numerous bilateral and multilateral summit meetings with developing world leaders at which substantial economic aid and investment deals were announced, reflecting China's growing economic muscle and use of such for strategic purposes.[49] Its businesses in turn responded to the government's announcement of its "go out" (*zou chuqu*) policy in 1999 by indeed going out around the world, supported by Chinese diplomats and foreign aid money, in search of new export markets, investment opportunities, and natural resource deals to fuel China's rapid growth.[50]

In the process, China leveraged its relationship with the developing world to achieve other national objectives, including ensuring votes in the United Nations on issues in China's interest, isolating Taiwan diplomatically, and balancing the power and influence of the developed world, particularly the United States, to ensure China's global and domestic interests were protected against Western pressure.

Over time, China's self-identification as a developing nation as its national wealth and power grew rapidly in the first two decades of the twenty-first century came under question, with some viewing it as a way for China to absolve itself of responsibility for addressing global challenges. As China entered the Xi Jinping era, however, several new initiatives spotlighted growing Chinese power and assertiveness in dealing with both the developed and developing world. Announcement of an Asian Infrastructure Investment Bank (AIIB) to be headquartered in Beijing, resourced to rival the World Bank and Asian Development Bank, demonstrated China's desire to leverage its massive dollar reserves to put money where its mouth had been in supporting development needs in developing countries. Announcement of the "One Belt, One Road" initiative—including both a land-based Silk

Road Economic Belt and twenty-first-century Maritime Silk Road—promised to solidify infrastructure links between China and Eurasia on land and at sea.

China's vision of a Regional Comprehensive Economic Partnership (RCEP) among Asian nations, excluding the United States, and negotiation of several bilateral and multilateral free trade agreements with neighbors further reflected China's intention to develop its "strategic economy." Indeed, even as China rapidly modernized and resourced its military in the early years of the twenty-first century and engaged more assertively in regional and global affairs, China's economic attractiveness and ability to dole out economic favors to selected nations (and perhaps leaders) appeared to be the preferred method of gaining political advantage and asserting strategic leverage. The Trump Administration's formal withdrawal from the twelve-nation Trans-Pacific Partnership trade agreement in January 2017 only enhanced China's prospect as a leader in the establishment of new trade standards going forward.

Nonetheless, while China is now the largest trading partner of most countries in Asia, Chinese companies and diplomats have faced a backlash in many countries in the region and beyond based on the way China has done business. Many countries bordering China in Asia, for instance, appear unwilling to accept the implicit deal that economic relations with China means they must respect China's conception of its national interests, even if at the expense of one's own political independence, or security requirements.[51]

Conclusion

China's historical sense of superiority over, and responsibility toward, lesser developed neighbors dating back to the tributary period and its experience of victimization and subjugation in the nineteenth and first half of the twentieth centuries led China over much of the last half-century to assert itself as a natural leader of less fortunate nations around the world. It is clear, however, that China's ideological goals today are different than they were during the Cold War, when Beijing promoted an insurgent revolutionary agenda of ideological hostility to the capitalist world. Today, China seeks to attain First World economic and political status with a prominent seat at the table.

China's view of the world and its place in it has evolved greatly over the centuries. While China historically measured itself as a highly developed power largely according to its cultural achievements, today economic development, technological advancement, and military prowess have assumed priority as measurements of China's sense of itself in relation to the world's major powers. This change has had substantial impact on China's current foreign and domestic policy, and places the PRC on a more traditional track in international affairs. For instance, contrary to its Confucian tradition, Beijing has sought in recent years to embrace global trade as an essential priority in achieving comprehensive national development and international prestige, and to develop a military commensurate with its growing economic and political strength. Only too late did Imperial China begin to realize the danger of relying on its sense of cultural superiority and virtue alone to protect itself from the will and depredations of stronger outside powers.

China's traditional perception of its "strategic periphery" has also grown due to modern realities. While once this periphery encompassed Tibet and the nomadic areas of the northern and northwestern steppe, today such areas are considered proper Chinese territory, requiring a new and expanded definition of China's overland strategic requirements. Today China must also look south and east toward the security of its maritime coastline. This includes the island of Taiwan, whose deep emotional resonance to China transcends security, as well as the East China Sea and South China Sea—each of which involves elements of both military and economic security.[52]

One might argue that in today's globalized world, China's urgent domestic needs extend its strategic periphery even farther to those areas that may offer the markets, investment destinations, and natural resources that are required to keep China developing economically so Beijing may maintain domestic stability, global influence, and the Communist Party in power. Contrary to its Imperial days, China's days of proud self-sufficiency are past.

As described in this chapter, China has had many different historical experiences with the outside world that may inform its future approach to the developing world. How might China's past inform its future? Xi Jinping's reverential commentary about "the great resurgence of the Chinese nation," and "great rejuvenation of the Chinese nation," and China as a "re-awakening lion," are part of a campaign to realize an incompletely defined "Chinese Dream." This nationalistic approach has given pause to neighbors and distant powers alike about the trajectory of a modernizing China.[53] Questions raised a decade ago about whether China's self-image and history may lead over time to assertive challenges to the international system, international norms, and therefore the interests of other states are less and less under debate, particularlly given China's actions in recent years in the South China Sea.

That China's assertiveness and nationalism appear to be rising commensurate with its per capita income is perhaps to be expected. Some contend that East Asia is simply returning to its natural order from centuries past, when China was preeminent in its neighborhood. That "natural order," however, involves other independent nations with their own sense of sovereign pride. History may not be as appealing in hindsight to neighboring countries as it is to China. And their dreams may not match.

Indeed, there is little in the tradition of Chinese history that suggests it is China's natural state to forge international partnerships of equality and mutual respect, particularly with lesser powers. While in the first decade of this century it was common for Chinese leaders to tout that "big powers and small powers are equal" in sovereignty and rights, that adherence to international law must remain paramount, and that "hegemony and power politics" have no place in international affairs, one can argue China has reversed itself on each of these counts in both words and practice in recent years.[54] China's credibility not only with developed nations but also developing nations, particularly in Asia, is coming into question as a result.

In the end, Beijing faces constraints on its ability to dominate its neighbors or assert its cultural superiority in the same way it did when China's emperors believed they ruled "All Under Heaven." Perhaps the most compelling constraint is the presence today of another proud, rather self-reverential, and sometimes arrogant nation with its own sense of exceptionalism that considers itself the world's Middle Kingdom in all but name. Managing its relationship with, and the influence of, the United States around the world, particularly along China's border, will remain Beijing's most critical challenge. Likewise, how the United States and the world handle the emergence of history's Middle Kingdom will go far to determine the continued peace and stability of Asia and beyond in the twenty-first century.

Notes

1 For an extensive account of the seven expeditions by Zheng He, see Roderich Ptak, *China and the Asian Seas: Trade, Travel, and Visions of the Other (1400–1750)* (Aldershot; Brookfield: Ashgate, 1998), 97–107.

2 Bruce Swanson, *Eighth Voyage of the Dragon: A History of China's Quest for Seapower* (Annapolis, MD: Naval Institute Press, 1982); John R. Dewenter, "China Afloat," *Foreign Affairs* 50 (1972): 738–751; Bernard Cole, "Waterways and Strategy: China's Priorities," *China Brief* 5 (2005): 1–3.

3 Jonathan Spence, *The Search for Modern China* (New York: W.W. Norton & Company, 1990), 119.

4 Mark Mancall, *China at the Center: 300 Years of Foreign Policy* (New York: Free Press, 1984), 7.

5 John King Fairbank and Merle Goldman, *China: A New History* (Cambridge, MA: The Belknap Press of Harvard University Press, 1998), 108–9.

6 Examples include the Xiongnu during the Han Dynasty, the Tibetan kingdom during the Tang, and the Ly Dynasty of Vietnam during the late Tang/early Song period. Michael D. Swaine and Ashley J. Tellis, *Interpreting China's Grand Strategy: Past, Present, and Future* (Santa Monica, CA: Rand, 2000), 54.

7 It is revealing about the Confucian mindset toward the outside world to note that merchants were placed on the lowest rung of the Confucian social hierarchy. Traders were considered too parasitic and nonintellectual for the Confucian scholar. Qing-era Chinese who traveled to or traded with the outside world, in fact, were viewed as having abandoned their country. Nonetheless, Chinese merchants were leaders in China's historical outreach to the world, in the Asian region and beyond. See Spence, *The Search for Modern China*, 119.

8 The Qing emperor Qian Long's famous letter to King George III in 1792, responding to British emissary Lord George Macartney's mission to establish closer trade relations between the two countries, encapsulated with rare efficiency the historical attitude of Chinese emperors toward such entreaties: "We have never valued ingenious articles, nor do we have the slightest need of your country's manufactures. Therefore, O king, as regards your request to send someone to remain at the capital, while it is not in harmony with regulations of the Celestial Empire we also feel very much that it is of no advantage to your country." Needless to say, Macartney left without achieving trade concessions. Spence, *The Search for Modern China*, 122–23; Mark Mancall, "The Ch'ing Tribute System; An Interpretive Essay," in *The Chinese World Order: Traditional China's Foreign Relations*, ed. John King Fairbank (Cambridge, MA: Harvard University Press, 1968), 89.

9 Swaine and Tellis, *Interpreting China's Grand Strategy*, 22–3.

10 This "pitting barbarian against barbarian" strategy was common throughout Chinese history and is a key element of classical Chinese statecraft, as discussed below. During the Han period, the strategy was manifested in its unsuccessful attempts to enlist peoples in Central Asia as allies to combat the Xiongnu threat along its border, while the Ming's similar "divide and rule" strategies sought to pit potential enemies against one another to make them less threatening, and perhaps more susceptible, to absorption by the Chinese state. Indeed, many will note echoes of this strategy in communist China's relations with the United States and Soviet Union during the later years of the Cold War. John King Fairbank and Edwin O. Reischauer, *China: Tradition and Transformation* (Boston: Houghton Mifflin, 1973), 63; Geoff Wade, "Ming China and Southeast Asia in the 15th Century: A Reappraisal," *National University of Singapore Asia Research Institute Working Papers Series* 28 (2004): 39, 24.

11 Fairbank and Goldman, *China: A New History*, 61.

12 These volumes include Luo Guanzhong's "The Romance of the Three Kingdoms," Sima Qian's "Records of the Grand Historian of China," and other Chinese dynastic histories. Sun Zi's classic "The Art of War" remains a standard exposition of classic Chinese battlefield tactics and military strategy. For an excellent and entertaining exposition of the various competing political philosophies and military strategies developed during this period of ancient China, see in particular Dennis Bloodworth and Ching Ping Bloodworth, *The Chinese Machiavelli: 3000 Years of Chinese Statecraft* (Somerset, NJ: Transaction Publishers, 2004). For an authoritative and landmark study of China's strategic culture, see Alastair Iain Johnston, *Cultural Realism: Strategic Culture and Grand Strategy in Chinese History* (Princeton, NJ: Princeton University Press, 1998).

13 Michael H. Hunt, "Chinese Foreign Relations in Historical Perspective," in *China's Foreign Relations in the 1980s*, ed. Hany Harding (New Haven, CT: Yale University Press, 1984), 7–8.

14 Examples of the stratagems include: "Befriend a distant state while attacking a neighbor"; "Wait at ease for the fatigued enemy"; "Sacrifice the plum for the peach"; "Make a feint to the east while attacking in the west"; and "Inflict injury on oneself to win the enemy's trust." See Koh Kok Kiang and Liu Yi, trans., *The Thirty-Six Stratagems: Secret Art of War* (Singapore: AsiaPac Books, 1992).

15 The Chinese themselves actually used the terms "tribute" or "tributary system" to describe their interactions with outside powers. In fact, there is no such Chinese word or phrase. The two terms are Western appellations. To the Chinese, such interactions were characterized as that between "civilization" and "barbarism" with a corresponding lexicon that reflected this state of relations. Gungwu Wang, "Early Ming Relations With Southeast Asia," in *The Chinese World Order: Traditional China's Foreign Relations*, ed. John King Fairbank (Cambridge, MA: Harvard University Press, 1968), 41–43; Mancall, "The Ch'ing Tribute System," 63.

16 By the nineteenth century, under the tribute system, Korea paid tribute once a year; the Ryukyu Kingdom (today's Okinawan islands) once every two years; Annam (Vietnam) once every three years; Siam (Thailand) once every four years; the Philippines once every five years; and Burma and Laos once every ten years. John K. Fairbank, "A Preliminary Framework," in *The Chinese World Order: Traditional China's Foreign Relations*, ed. John K. Fairbank (Cambridge, MA: Harvard University Press, 1968), 11. It is noteworthy that feudal Japan alone rejected tributary status, although by the early Qing Dynasty its leaders had chosen to withdraw into seclusion and trade with China only indirectly. Nonetheless, Japan did model its culture after China, again offering the Middle Kingdom reaffirmation of its superiority over those in its orbit. John Miller, "The Roots and Implications of East Asian Regionalism," *Asia-Pacific Center for Security Studies Occasional Paper Series* (2004): 11.

17 China periodically demonstrated its seriousness in upholding the reciprocal nature of tributary responsibility. For instance, Chinese forces helped Korea expel invading Japanese forces in 1592, fulfilling its side of the bargain in protecting a close tributary state (although one might argue that more practical calculations concerning the security of China's northeast frontier were more decisive, as they were in 1950). In 1788, the

Chinese went to the aid of the ruling Le Dynasty in Vietnam, citing their right and obligation to do so under the tributary system, but later switched sides to the Nguyen family when the latter proved more committed to its tributary obligations. Spence, *The Search for Modern China*, 119.

18 It should be noted that this examination excludes consideration of the Yuan (Mongol) Dynasty, whose alien incorporation of China into an intercontinental empire, and singular culture of aggression, is considered an anomaly in Chinese history.

19 Fairbank and Reischauer, *China*, 63.

20 Fairbank and Reischauer, *China*, 96.

21 Swaine and Tellis, *Interpreting China's Grand Strategy*, 52.

22 Swaine and Tellis, *Interpreting China's Grand Strategy*, 52.

23 Among the far-flung places Admiral Zheng reached were Java and Sumatra (modern Indonesia), Ceylon (Sri Lanka), Siam (Thailand), Vietnam, Cambodia, India, Bangladesh, Yemen, Arabia, Somalia, and Madagascar.

24 Fairbank and Reischauer, *China*, 198; Philip Bowring, "China's Growing Might and the Spirit of Zheng He," *The New York Times*, August 2, 2005.

25 *Tai-zu shi-lu, juan*, as cited in Wade, "Ming China and Southeast Asia in the 15th Century: A Reappraisal," 39 (lb).

26 Wade, "Ming China and Southeast Asia in the 15th Century: A Reappraisal," 22.

27 Evelyn S. Rawski, "Re-Envisioning the Qing: The Significance of the Qing Period in Chinese History," *Journal of Asian Studies* 55 (1996): 829–50; Swaine and Tellis, *Interpreting China's Grand Strategy*, 60–61.

28 Today's Outer Mongolia makes an interesting exception to this rule, although one might argue that Mongolia's independence was an accident of history due more to the legacy of Soviet communism and Cold War dynamics than to any inherent difference in Mongolia's historical status with China. The leaders of Mongolia today surely recognize this situation as they deal delicately with growing Chinese influence in their economy and society.

29 Ptak, *China and the Asian Seas*, 105.

30 Spence, *The Search for Modern China*, 119.

31 Fairbank and Reischauer, *China*, 253.

32 For a comprehensive summary of the process of institutionalizing the Canton system, see Earl H. Pritchard, *The Crucial Years of Early Anglo-Chinese Relations, 1750–1800* (New York: Octagon Books, 1936), 128–141.

33 Mao Zedong, "On the People's Democratic Dictatorship, June 30, 1949," in *Mao Zedong Xuanji* [Selected Works of Mao Zedong] (Beijing: People's Press, 1991), vol. IV, 1477.

34 Zhou Enlai, *Zhou Enlai Waijiao Wenxuan* [Selected Works of Zhou Enlai on Diplomacy] (Beijing: Central Documents Press, 1990), 63.

35 Coined by economist Alfred Sauvy in a 1952 article in the French magazine *L'Observateur* as a deliberate reference to the Third Estate of the French Revolution, the term "Third World" was originally used to describe those nations that were nonaligned in the Cold War, "those less-industrialized countries opposed to political and economic domination by the superpowers and the developed world," *L'Observateur* 118 (1952). See also Anthony I. Akubue, "Gender Disparity in Third World Technological, Social and Economic Development," *Journal of Technology Studies* 27 (2001): 64. The term came to prominence following the Bandung Conference when developing nations explored ways to counter a world dominated by "American imperialism" and, to a lesser extent, the Soviet Union.

36 The theory was first presented during a talk between Mao and American journalist Anna Louise Strong in 1946. See Mao Zedong, *Mao Zedong Xuanji*, vol. IV, 1194.

37 Mao Zedong, "There Are Two Intermediate Zones," in *Mao Zedong Waijiao Wenxuan* [Selected Works of Mao Zedong on Diplomacy] (Beijing: Central Documents Press, 1994), 506–509.

38 Donald W. Klein, "China and the Second World," in *China and the World: New Directions in Chinese Foreign Relations*, ed. Samuel S. Kim (Boulder, CO: Westview Press, 1989), 130.

39 Premier Zhou Enlai's Speech at the National Day Reception, September 30, 1966.

40 Lin Biao, "Long Live the Victory of People's War!" *Peking Review* 8, no. 36 (September 3, 1965): 9–30. During this period, China also supported Indonesia's call for a new United

Nations for developing nations. Harry Harding, "China's Changing Roles in the Contemporary World," in *China's Foreign Relations in the 1980s*, ed. Harry Harding (New Haven, CT: Yale University Press, 1984), 187.

41 Organisation of Economic Co-operation and Development, *The Aid Programme of China* (Paris: OECD, March 1987), 5.

42 China's intervention in the Korean War in 1950 might also be viewed as an echo of China's long-time concern about the vulnerability of its periphery, albeit without the formal tributary or "virtue-based" components. For an excellent discussion of how Chinese communists have framed their military campaigns in terms of "teaching a lesson," see Allen S. Whiting, "China's Use of Force, 1950–96, and Taiwan," *International Security* 26 (2001): 103–131.

43 For instance, "Speech by Deng Xiao-Ping, Chairman of Delegation of People's Republic of China at Special Session of United Nations General Assembly," *Peking Review* (1974), I–II.

44 Organisation of Economic Co-operation and Development, *The Aid Programme of China*, 5.

45 Klein, "China and the Second World," 163.

46 Thomas W. Robinson, "Chinese Foreign Policy From the 1940s to the 1990s," in *Chinese Foreign Policy: Theory and Practice*, ed. Thomas W. Robinson and David Shambaugh (Oxford: Clarendon Press, 1994), 575.

47 Council on Foreign Relations, *More Than Humanitarianism: A Strategic U.S. Approach Toward Africa*, Report of an Independent Task Force (2006): 42.

48 Beijing developed its "New Security Concept" in the mid-1990s to challenge the notion that international security, particularly in East Asia, requires the underlying guarantee of U.S.-based alliances. The concept stresses development of informal strategic partnerships between nations, adherence to the Five Principles of Peaceful Coexistence, and multilateralism, which itself promotes a more equal role for the developing nations in setting the rules of international affairs. See *Zhongguo Guanyu Xin Anquanguan de Lichang Wenjian* [Document on China's Position on the New Security Concept], submitted by the Chinese delegation to the ASEAN Regional Forum on July 31, 2002, *People's Daily*, August 2, 2002, 3.

49 Trefor Moss, "Soft Power? China Has Plenty," *The Diplomat*, June 4, 2013; Carola McGiffert et al., "Chinese Soft Power and Its Implications for the United States: Competition and Cooperation in the Developing World," *Center for Strategic & International Studies*, March 2009; David Shambaugh, "China's Soft-Power Push: The Search for Respect" *Foreign Affairs*, July/August 2015.

50 Jeffrey Reeves, "China's Unraveling Engagement Strategy," *The Washington Quarterly*, (Fall 2013), 139–149.

51 China's aggressive response to the Republic of Korea's decision to deploy the Theater High Altitude Area Defense (THAAD) system against a rapidly modernizing North Korean missile threat, a response that included popular boycotts and official restrictions on Korean companies and goods, was only the most dramatic demonstration in early 2017 of China's use of economic means to punish neighbors for taking action it considered against its interests. Popular sentiment toward China in Korea plummeted as a result. Javier C. Hernandez, Owen Guo, and Ryan McMorrow, "South Korean Stores Feel China's Wrath as U.S. Missile System Is Deployed," *New York Times*, March 9, 2017; Park Jae-Hyuk, "Anti-China Sentiment Rising Over THAAD Row," March 2017, *The Korean Times*.

52 "China's Worries At Sea," *Global Times* (reprinted in the *People's Liberation Daily*), January 2, 2004.

53 Owen Guo, "'Sleeping Lion' China Awakened, Says President Xi Jinping, *Global Voice*, March 29, 2014; "Chasing the Chinese Dream," *Economist*, May 4, 2013; Carrie Gracie, "The Credo: Great Rejuvenation of the Chinese Nation," *BBC News*, November 7, 2014.

54 John Pomfret, "U.S. Takes a Tougher Tone With China," *The Washington Post*, July 30, 2010; Tim Daiss, "China Has Defied International Law, Now What? Experts Speak Out," *Forbes*, July 16, 2016.

PART II
Regional Profiles

3

CHINA'S STRATEGY IN SOUTHEAST ASIA

Eric Heginbotham[1]

Introduction

In August 2015, Chinese Minister of Foreign Affairs Wang Yi said,

> China views ASEAN as the priority in its diplomacy with neighboring states,
> as a critical area for establishing the 21st century maritime silk road, and for
> establishing a new form of international partnership with cooperation and
> mutual benefit at its core.[2]

Beijing's recent record in Southeast Asia is mixed, and it is doubtful whether China
can succeed in achieving all of Wang Yi's stated goals without moderating its political behavior, but there is little question that China has become a central actor—if
not the central actor—in Southeast Asia.

Leading trends in Chinese foreign policy are often observed first in Southeast
Asia. During the early to mid-2000s, China's "charm offensive" and the soft power
associated with it was said to be "transforming the world."[3] Nowhere was this more
on display than in Southeast Asia, where there was some concern that Chinese
charm—and money—might undermine the appeal of the United States as partner.
During the 2010s, on the other hand, Southeast Asia became the primary venue
for "China's new assertiveness," and a range of activities there have alarmed many
in the region and beyond about Beijing's provocative behavior.[4] China's interests in
the region have remained broadly consistent. But its emphasis in the means used to
pursue those interests has evolved with circumstances, and they will likely continue
to evolve in the future.

The combination of proximity, politics, and economics gives China greater and
more immediate interests in Southeast Asia than it has in any other developing
region. Beijing employs the full array of diplomatic, economic, and military tools in

Southeast Asia. China's coercive behavior in the South China Sea captures the most prominent headlines in the West. And indeed, China's coast guard, military, and other elements of coercive power are more on display in Southeast Asia than in any other region. But Beijing has also sought to offset regional suspicion through intensive bilateral and multilateral diplomacy, as well as through the continuous pursuit of deeper economic ties. And although it may not accomplish all its goals, it has already been remarkably successful in expanding and consolidating its economic position, in securing its territorial claims, and in finding enough willing political partners to blunt opposition.

Historical Overview

Chinese interactions with Southeast Asia have a deeper and richer history than those with any other developing region. Early Chinese relations with Southeast Asia were governed by the tributary system, first established under the Han Dynasty (206 BCE–220 CE).[5] The number of regional kingdoms providing obeisance and tribute varied over time, depending on the health and capacity of successive Chinese rulers and dynasties. The tributary system depended heavily on soft power, especially trade, diplomacy, and cultural exports, though in nearby kingdoms it also involved the occasional dispatch of armed forces to resolve disputes and cement Chinese influence. Chinese merchants settled in pockets throughout Southeast Asia and established a network of trading ties across the region.

Although the tributary system survived more than three hundred years after first contact with the West, both tribute missions to and trade with China gradually collapsed as European states strengthened their position in South and Southeast Asia. That trend accelerated during the nineteenth century with the sharp decline in Qing power, symbolized most strikingly with its abject defeat at the hands of Britain in the Opium Wars (1839–1842 and 1856–1860). As Chinese imperial majesty declined, however, the number of Chinese in Southeast Asia ballooned, with the coolie trade bringing large numbers of Chinese laborers to join the established Chinese merchants in Southeast Asia.

By the time the Qing fell, much of Southeast Asia was divided into European colonies or dependencies (the important exception being Siam), and state-to-state relations between the new Republic of China and Southeast Asia were therefore virtually non-existent. Nevertheless, the new Chinese government arguably did more than past imperial governments to reach out to overseas Chinese populations, foster a sense of ethnic identity among them, and work diplomatically to secure their rights—though at the cost of having those populations seen by other regional actors as more "separate and apart" than might have otherwise been the case.

Shortly after sweeping into Beijing in 1949, the new Chinese Communist government demonstrated its willingness to support insurgency, providing material assistance to the Viet Minh within months of taking power.[6] More broadly, the CCP's foreign policy was mixed, supporting revolutionary movements selectively during the 1950s, and with greater energy during the 1960s. Insurgency, and China's support for it, enjoyed indifferent success everywhere in Southeast Asia except Indochina (where initial success quickly soured) and helped push many regional governments towards the United States. Chinese support for insurgency prompted the 1955 formation of the short-lived Southeast Asian Treaty organization (SEATO) and influenced the 1967 creation of the Association of Southeast Asian States (ASEAN) by founding members Indonesia, Malaysia, the Philippines, Singapore, and Thailand.

By the early 1970s, however, growing Chinese trepidation about Soviet military power and its deployments along the Sino–Soviet border motivated China to rethink and moderate its foreign policy. U.S. President Richard Nixon's visit to Beijing in 1972 provided the opening for Beijing to reach out to Southeast Asian governments. As part of that outreach, Beijing greatly reduced and, after 1978, severed ties to insurgent groups. At the same time, it moved to restore informal political and trade relations with most Southeast Asian states, establishing formal diplomatic relations with Malaysia (1974), the Philippines (1975), and Thailand (1975).

Chinese efforts in Southeast Asia were further energized by the launch of reform and opening and the Vietnamese invasion of Cambodia in December 1978. In 1979, the PLA launched an offensive to "punish"Vietnam, setting in motion more than a decade of involvement in Indochinese conflict. Beijing sought to strengthen relations with other Southeast Asian states to isolate Vietnam, and the 1980s saw a number of positive developments for Chinese diplomacy in the region. Trade between China and regional states blossomed. In 1990, China normalized relations with Indonesia and Singapore, the last of the ASEAN states with which it had not yet done so, clearing the way for China to begin dialogue with ASEAN as an organization the following year.

The 1990s saw continued growth in trade and cultural ties, but also increased tensions between China and several ASEAN members over South China Sea issues. After having bested Vietnam in a battle for the Paracel Islands in 1974, China took possession of six features in the Spratly Islands in 1988, built structures on a number of those features during the 1990s, and was engaged in mutual tussles over oil exploration and drilling rights in disputed areas. In 1994, it occupied a seventh feature, Mischief Reef. Although rival claimants, most prominently Vietnam, engaged in similar behaviors, China's growing military power cast Chinese actions in a more ominous light and heightened regional insecurities.

Towards the end of the 1990s, China moderated its behavior in response to proto-balancing by several regional states. Beijing launched the so-called charm offensive mentioned on page 000. During the 1997 Asian Financial Crisis, China extended limited aid to hard-hit countries and, more importantly, agreed not to devalue its own currency. It signed a Declaration on the Conduct of Parties in the South China Sea with ASEAN in 2002, and concluded the ASEAN–China Free Trade Area (ACFTA) agreement in the same year. At the same time, it deepened bilateral political relations with most regional states, intensifying military-to-military contacts and confidence building in the process.

We have, however, seen yet another shift in China's regional behavior since roughly 2009, with more assertive behavior by China in the South China Sea and, since Xi Jinping's accession to Party leadership in 2012, a more decisive style of leadership.[7] While much of this chapter concerns events during this period, it is important to remember that, even as Beijing's interests have remained relatively stable, its behavior has changed periodically in response to new domestic and international circumstances.

China's Interests in Southeast Asia

China arguably has greater interests in Southeast Asia than it does in any other region treated in this volume. But its pursuit of them is complicated by the tensions between different types of national interests.

Broadly framed, China has four types of interests in the region. The first is maintaining amicable relations with neighbors and preventing any outside power, especially the United States, from dominating the region. During the later stages of the Cold War, the apparent success of the Soviet Union and its Vietnamese proxy in expanding their military presence in Southeast Asia prompted Chinese fears of encirclement. More recently, U.S. regional diplomacy in South Asia and Southeast Asia, together with bases in Northeast Asia, has prompted fears that the United States might now be aiming at containment or encirclement of China.[8] Put more positively, China has an interest in maintaining positive ties throughout the region and establishing strategic relations with key states, not only to limit regional influence and leverage of external powers but also to further its economic and domestic political agendas. Although Beijing likes to demonstrate leadership in all developing regions, only in East Asia, where the imprint of Chinese philosophy and exchange is profound, can it make a case for organic and comprehensive leadership.

The second set of interests is economic—cultivating trade with and investment in Southeast Asia to support sustainable growth at home. Economic interests are central to China's position in every developing region, but as we detail further on page 000, China does more trade with the countries of Southeast Asia than it does with those of any other region. Perhaps more importantly, Chinese trade with Southeast Asia is highly diversified and includes large quantities of electronic and other manufactured or processed goods. This diversity is largely a function of the region's integrated supply chains.[9] Increasingly, Chinese firms are also going "off shore" in Southeast Asia, as wage inflation and environmental concerns push manufacturers in some low value-added industries to relocate.[10]

A third set of interests involves what Chinese leaders would describe as defending or maintaining national sovereignty and unity—or strengthening and consolidating territorial and maritime claims and preventing rival claimants from doing the same. Although such formulations sound straightforward, Chinese claims in Southeast Asia have been ambiguously framed. Many Chinese documents (including some legal documents, such as those submitted to the United Nations in 2009) contain maps with a "nine-dash line" that encompasses virtually all of the South China Sea and within which Beijing claims "historic rights."[11] Other documents, including China's 1992 Law on the Territorial Sea and Contiguous Zone, refer only to sovereignty over and rights accruing to named islands and features within the South China Sea.[12] It is also unclear what status China will claim for the rocks and "low tide elevation" (LTE) features it has converted into artificial islands.[13]

Also related to Chinese external security is Beijing's interest in protecting its sea lines of communications (SLOCS). Hu Jintao's "new historic missions" called on the military to prepare for a diversified mission set, and the requirement to defend sea lines has become sharper and more explicit in subsequent Chinese defense white papers. Chinese academics and strategists have long discussed the so-called Malacca dilemma, or the vulnerability of sea-lanes from the east coast of Africa through the South China Sea.[14] Although an objective assessment might conclude that SLOC protection will remain well beyond the Chinese navy's capacity even 10 or 15 years from now, the PLA Navy has been directed to prepare for just this task.[15]

There is, of course, interplay between the interests described above. In some cases, there may be synergy; initiatives designed to improve political relations can be sweetened to include trade or investment provisions, and closer trade and investment relations may shape regional states' perceptions of their own national interests. Yet some interests are in tension with one another. Efforts to strengthen legal or moral claims to contested territory by, for example, patrolling around contested features, can and often does sour political relations and may drive regional states into Washington's arms.

Given the range of Chinese interests at play in the region and the tensions between them, it should come as no surprise that Chinese priorities in the pursuit of its regional interests have shifted over time, depending on leadership and circumstances. More changes in the future are not just possible, but likely. Circumstances will continue to evolve and China will continue to struggle with the question of what kind of major power it wants to be. Arguments can be made for the primacy of each of the interests outlined above, and all are consistent with China's definition of its "core national interests" (核心利益).[16] But emphasis on one or another can profoundly affect the nature of Beijing's diplomacy, and its impact on regional states.

China's Methods

Parsing Chinese diplomatic, economic, and military means in Southeast Asia is complicated by the obvious interconnections between component elements of Chinese strategy. In one sense, China's economic outreach takes pride of place, given the obvious appeal of China's growing market to Southeast Asian partners and the ability of China and its firms to finance projects overseas. Chinese military power, in contrast, generates regional concern, and Beijing's cultural and political outreach works only slowly, when it works at all. Despite this, we begin with a discussion of China's diplomatic means, given the centrality of political motives—but we do so on the understanding that readers will bear in mind the importance of economic tools and the growing scope afforded military power and military engagement.

Diplomatic Means

Beijing's exercise of hard power—specifically its coercive activity in the South China Sea—works, on balance, against China's ability to achieve other objectives and makes the task of its regional diplomats more challenging. Perhaps for that reason, Beijing has redoubled and energized its diplomatic efforts, seeking to prevent regional states' suspicions from turning to coordinated opposition and looking to cement relations with those states least affected by the maritime disputes. Beijing pursues its diplomatic efforts at the bilateral level and, since the 1990s, through multilateral mechanisms, primarily through ASEAN-related groups and activities.

Bilateral Diplomacy

Beijing's bilateral strategy looks, primarily, to deepen partnerships wherever the grounds for positive relations exist and, secondarily, to isolate opponents while still leaving the door open to future improvement with these states. While China engages all states economically, it offers more inducements to political partners or pliant states. Where circumstances permit, partnership includes military and strategic cooperation.

China has increasingly come to differentiate its approach to developing states based on the political weight and importance of the partner in question. Distinctions have increasingly found their way into China's official diplomatic lexicon, with more important states now labeled "major developing states" (发展中大国) to differentiate them from "other," less important developing states.[17] Perhaps nowhere in the developing world do states differ more in terms of size, wealth, and governance standards than in Southeast Asia. Singapore's GDP per capita, $52,000, stands in sharp contrast to that of Cambodia or Myanmar, both below $1,500. Similar divergence is seen in the overall size of regional economies. Laos' economy is just 1.5 percent as large as Indonesia's.

TABLE 3.1 Southeast Asian Economies by GDP and GDP Per Capita, 2017 (Projected)

	Nominal GDP (in U.S. millions of dollars)	Population (in millions)	GDP (nominal) Per capita
Indonesia	$1,020,515	263.5	$3,873
Thailand	$432,898	68.3	$6,338
Philippines	$329,716	103.9	$3,173
Malaysia	$309,860	32.0	$9,683
Singapore	$291,860	5.6	$52,118
Vietnam	$215,829	92.7	$2,328
Myanmar	$72,368	54.8	$1,321
Cambodia	$20,953	15.6	$1,343
Laos	$14,971	6.5	$2,303
Brunei Darussalam	$12,326	0.4	$30,815

Sources: GDP figures are from the International Monetary Fund. Population figures are from the United Nations Department of Economic and Social Affairs.

Although Beijing's engagement with each state is unique, some generalizations can be made based on the size and capabilities of the regional state, the intensity of disputes with that country, and idiosyncratic political developments that pose particular challenges and opportunities. Specifically, Beijing prioritizes the building of broad and robust partnerships with ASEAN's strongest states; fosters patron–client relations with poor, weak neighbors; and seeks to isolate states with which it has the most significant disputes—while still holding the door open to improvements in those relationships. These are, of course, fluid categories; some states fall into more than one category, while others may shift from one to another.

Prioritizing Strategic Relations with ASEAN's Strongest States

China has prioritized relations with the region's heavyweights—Indonesia, Malaysia, and Thailand, which together account for 65 percent of ASEAN's GDP. During Xi Jinping's maiden trip to Southeast Asia as president, conducted in October 2013, he traveled to Indonesia and Malaysia. Following the trip, Foreign Minister Wang Yi declared, "China's relationships with the two countries always ranked at the top of China's relationship with other ASEAN countries." "Further improving the bilateral relations," he said, "will play a leading and exemplary role in stepping up China's relations with ASEAN."[18]

Indonesia has the largest population in Southeast Asia, including a large number of ethnic Chinese, and has by far the largest economy in ASEAN. Jakarta, which does not claim islands within China's nine-dash line, has nevertheless grown warier of Chinese intentions in the South China Sea. It issued a formal protest about Chinese Coast Guard activities in Indonesian waters in March 2016, and Indonesian President Joko Widodo visited the Natuna Islands aboard an Indonesian naval warship following two more incidents near the islands in May and June of that year.[19] In June 2016, Indonesia announced that it would reinforce bases on the islands with additional aircraft, warships, and marines.[20] Yet, from a larger strategic perspective, Indonesia continues to seek a middle path between the United States and China under the banner of a "free and active" foreign policy.[21]

For all these reasons, Indonesia has been a natural priority for China, and it has received more visits by high ranking Chinese officials than any other ASEAN state (see Table 3.2). China's Maritime Silk Road dovetails nicely with President Joko "Jokowi" Widodo's appeal to make Indonesia a Global Maritime Fulcrum.[22] At the 2014 APEC summit, Jokowi invited China to invest in the development of 24 seaports, and he has continued to press for funding through the Chinese-led AIIB.[23] Indonesia is one of a handful of countries anywhere that has engaged in defense-industrial cooperation with China, with Indonesia license producing Chinese C-705 anti-ship cruise missiles.[24] And in April 2017, an Indonesia–China consortium signed a $4.7 billion contract to build a high-speed rail line between Jakarta and Bandung.[25]

China's increasingly complicated relationship with Malaysia also demonstrates how Beijing has pursued its territorial claims and how it has sought, with some

TABLE 3.2 Visits to Southeast Asia by Top Chinese Foreign Policy Officials, March 2013–April 2017

Destination	Visits by President Xi Jinping	Visits by Premier, State Councilor, FM	Total High-Level Total Visits
Brunei Darussalam		3	3
Cambodia	1	5	6
Indonesia	2	5	7
Lao		3	3
Malaysia	1	5	6
Myanmar		4	4
Philippines	1	1	2
Singapore	1	4	5
Thailand		2	2
Vietnam	1	6	6

Source: Data on visits was assembled through a systematic search of English- and Chinese-language media sources.

success, to mitigate the impact on overall relations. Malaysia shares many of the same characteristics that make Indonesia an appealing partner to China, and Malaysian officials have long described their ties as a "special relationship." Malaysia was the first ASEAN state to normalize diplomatic relations with China (1974). Disputes concerning overlapping claims in the South China Sea remained largely dormant until 2015, when it was revealed that Chinese Coast Guard vessels had been anchored at the contested Luconia Shoals for two years.[26] Malaysia lodged an official protest and dispatched Defense Minister Hishammuddin Hussein to a meeting with U.S. Defense Secretary Ash Carter on board a U.S. aircraft carrier in the South China Sea in November 2015.[27]

But despite intensified territorial disputation, China has managed to score several striking successes with Malaysia—partly by manipulating Malaysian domestic politics. In mid-2016, evidence emerged that some $700 million from a troubled state development fund may have been funneled into Prime Minister Najib Razak's personal accounts.[28] China rode to the rescue with a $2.3 billion purchase agreement for the fund's assets, easing its debt burden.[29] Shortly thereafter, Najib visited Beijing and agreed to Malaysia's first major defense deal with China, purchasing four Littoral Mission Ships.[30] He also brought back $34 billion in MOUs, though it remains to be seen how many will be fulfilled.[31]

Beijing's relations with Thailand are perhaps the most robust and multi-faceted. In 1975, Thailand became the second ASEAN state to normalize relations with China, and after the Vietnamese invasion of Cambodia in 1979, Beijing and Bangkok forged a strategic partnership, including an arms sales component, to balance against the expansion of Vietnamese and Soviet power. Economic relations also developed quickly and relatively smoothly. Several of Thailand's business groups were among the biggest investors in China during the 1980s, and China signed an FTA with Thailand in 2003.[32]

Thailand has long prided itself on playing a middle power role in regional politics—aligning itself with Japan during World War II before joining the allies as the tide of war shifted. Today, Thailand's primary military partnership is clearly with the United States. In 2003, the United States designated Thailand a major non-NATO U.S. ally. But Bangkok is also China's closest military partner in the region, and unlike several other Southeast Asian states, Thailand has no overlapping territorial claims or disputes with China. Thai *coups d'état* in 2006 and 2014 resulted in a partial cutoff of U.S. assistance and cooperation, and opened the door to overtures by China. Since 2014, Thailand's military government has increased the pace of weapons purchases from China, including modern tanks, armored personnel carriers, and submarines.[33]

Fostering Patron–Client Relations with Weak Neighbors

Along China's immediate periphery are several relatively weak, poor states that are particularly susceptible to Chinese influence. These include Myanmar, Laos, and Cambodia. Geographic proximity would likely make them naturally large trade and investment partners to China; their small size and poverty ensures that economic dependence is asymmetrical. Politics—and the fact that none of these states is democratic—has limited both political and economic engagement with the West and provided further scope for Chinese diplomacy. Although China has not actively undermined democratic rule in Southeast Asia, it has exploited economic and political circumstances in weak non-democratic states to build effective patron–client relations.

In Cambodia, Beijing has made itself an indispensable ally of Prime Minister Hun Sen's Cambodia People's Party (CPP) government, which has effectively suppressed opposition since 1997.[34] China has provided the largest share of foreign direct investment (FDI) in the country—more than 30 percent of Cambodia's total in 2015.[35] Beijing's political and economic support to the CPP has paid political dividends. In 2009, Cambodia expelled Uyghur refugees seeking asylum; in July 2012, it blocked ASEAN's adoption of joint statement on the South China Sea; and in June 2016, Prime Minister Hun Sen offered moral support to China in rejecting the Permanent Court of Arbitration's jurisdiction in South China Sea issues.[36] In July 2016, China announced a $600 million aid package for Cambodian election infrastructure, education, and health projects."[37]

A similar pattern holds with regard to China's strategy towards Laos, where China supports the isolated People's Revolutionary Party (LPRP), is the largest source of FDI, and has committed to building a $6.28 billion high-speed rail line between China's Kunming and Vientiane.[38] Much like Cambodia in 2012, Laos, which held ASEAN's rotating chair during a special ASEAN–China Foreign Minister's meeting in June 2016, blocked a resolution that would have raised the issue of tensions in the South China Sea and cited China by name after reportedly being lobbied by Beijing.[39]

Even (or perhaps especially) small states are loath to become overly dependent on a single patron. Laos maintains close political and economic ties to Vietnam, and even before recent leadership transition, Myanmar had sought to cultivate closer relations with India and Thailand.[40] Developments in Myanmar are evidence that some of Beijing's closest relationships may become less special as political reform takes hold and new diplomatic possibilities open. The November 2015 victory of the National League for Democracy in Burma's fairest elections in decades has brought an easing of U.S. sanctions and an opening to the West, though Burma's leaders will have to balance new relationships with existing ties to Beijing.[41]

Isolating Front-Line Opponents

Maritime territorial and boundary disputes have most severely affected China's relations with Vietnam and the Philippines. In 2009, the territorial and maritime disputes between China and the Philippines and Vietnam escalated. The latter two submitted a joint application for recognition of extended continental shelves to the United Nations, and China responded by submitting its nine-dash line and an assertion of "indisputable sovereignty over the islands in the South China Sea and adjacent waters."[42] While China has undertaken direct coercive action to demonstrate administrative control over areas disputed with the Philippines and Vietnam (discussed in the section on "military means" from page 000), it also launched a public relation offensive against its rivals.

It sought to "isolate" the Philippines (in the words of one *Huanqiu Shibao* headline).[43] In July 2013, the Philippines foreign minister complained that he had visited Beijing three times since assuming his post in 2011, without a single reciprocal visit by the Chinese foreign minister.[44] No high-level visit occurred until January 2015, when State Councilor Yang Jiechi arrived in Manila. Troubled political relations also appeared to affect investment. According to UNCTAD statistics, Chinese FDI stocks in the Philippines showed less than a 1 percent increase from 2009 to 2012 (the latest for which the organization has compiled statistics), while Chinese investment stocks in ASEAN as a whole rose some 92 percent.[45]

But although China is more than willing to isolate or throttle back ties with adversary nations, the goal is inevitably to bring them back to positions more advantageous to Beijing. The political and economic picture with the Philippines changed dramatically after the election of Rodrigo Duterte in May 2016. During the election campaign, Duterte vowed to rebalance relations with Beijing and Washington, and after being elected, returned from his first state visit to Beijing with $24 billion in "funding deals."[46] It is unlikely that anywhere near that amount will be invested even if the rapprochement lasts, a proposition that appears increasingly unlikely. Nevertheless, Beijing had sent a clear message—cooperation with China pays not just political dividends, but financial ones as well.

Bilateral Political Means

Regardless of the category or bin within which any given relationship is placed, Beijing employs a relatively standardized toolkit in its engagement, including summit meetings, party meetings, economic incentives, cultural outreach, and military diplomacy. A breakdown of the 44 visits by China's top four political and foreign policy leaders[47] between March 2013 and April 2017 demonstrates both the breadth of Chinese leadership engagement, and the priority accorded diplomacy with different states (see Table 3.2). Indonesia, Malaysia, Vietnam, and Cambodia received more high-level Chinese visits than anywhere else in the region, reflecting the role that these states play in Beijing's calculations.

In addition to meetings between individual state leaders, the Chinese Communist Party pursues party-to-party outreach, which can be particularly important in relations between China and other one-party states, but which is also important in some other cases. The CCP International Liaison Department may change its favorite interlocutor, as it did when it shifted from Cambodia's royalist FUNCINPEC to the People's Party (CPP) after the mid-1990s, or maintain positive ties with multiple parties in a given state, as it does today with Indonesia.[48]

Multilateral Diplomacy

Beijing understands that its regional efforts are more likely to succeed when partner states feel that China is engaging with ASEAN institutions and accepts the consensus-based decision-making upon which the organization is founded. In some cases, ASEAN provides a force multiplier for China, enabling it to gain efficiencies in efforts that would otherwise have to be replicated with individual states. And Chinese leaders are happy to exploit ASEAN's consensus-based style to smother and blunt opposition to China's hard-power activities, especially in the South China Sea. Beijing's multilateral engagement therefore not only serves to further its bilateral agenda, but also works to bind potential opponents in a framework that impedes unilateral action by them.

China became a full dialogue partner of ASEAN in 1996. In 2003, it became the first extra-regional state to sign the Treaty of Amity and Cooperation in Southeast Asia, seen as a symbol of willingness to abide by the organization's commitment to multilateral processes. The China–ASEAN Free Trade Area (CAFTA) agreement was signed in 2002 and took effect in 2010. Beijing appointed its first ambassador to ASEAN in 2008, and has maintained a permanent mission to ASEAN since 2012. As of 2013, China was a participant in some 12 ministerial-level mechanisms within ASEAN.[49] In 2015, the ASEAN–China Defense Ministers' Informal Meeting (ACDMIM) held its inaugural meeting—one year after ASEAN established similar mechanisms with the United States and Japan.[50]

At the 16th ASEAN–China Summit meeting in October 2013, Premier Li Keqiang advanced what he called a "2+7 cooperation framework," with provisions that strongly suggest Beijing's strategy for mitigating the backlash from its *fait accompli* in the South China Sea while advancing other objectives. It contains two political consensuses (the "2" in "2+7"). The first is that deeper strategic trust is central to closer cooperation. Disputes in the South China Sea should be addressed through "consultation and negotiation" and joint development pursued in the interim. The second is that focusing on economic development is crucial by Chinese analysts to deeper cooperation. Both of these "consensus" points underpin the seven specific proposals:

- Conclude a treaty on good-neighborliness, friendship and cooperation;
- Upgrade the China–ASEAN Free Trade Area (CAFTA);
- Expedite the development of infrastructure and connectivity;
- Improve regional financial cooperation and risk prevention;
- Advance maritime cooperation;
- Strengthen exchange and cooperation in the security field;
- And intensify cultural, scientific, technological, environmental and people-to-people exchanges.[51]

In August 2015, State Councilor Wang Yi advanced a similar "ten-point proposal on China–ASEAN cooperation" that referenced Li Keqiang's 2+7 formulation and modified or added points to the list, including a proposed protocol to the Treaty on the Southeast Asia Nuclear Weapon-Free Zone.[52]

In China's overall engagement with ASEAN and in the case of the "2+7 cooperation framework," Beijing seeks to exploit ASEAN's consensus style of decision-making. It embraces ASEAN's peaceful resolution of disputes to mitigate the threat that adversaries might employ unilateral means against China, while offering economic incentives for cooperation. At the same time, it places the blame for disputes squarely on the United States and miscreants within ASEAN. As Xu Bu, China's ambassador to ASEAN, wrote in early 2016, "U.S. wanton incitement has led a small number of regional states to set their gaze on individual advantage, and as a result, East Asian cooperation, based around economic development, has been significantly obstructed."[53]

Economic Means

Economic measures are central to China's engagement in Southeast Asia and remain the most potent and attractive tool in Beijing's foreign policy arsenal. For Southeast Asian leaders, economic considerations do not necessarily trump military security. Indeed, some states may react negatively to economic entreaties, looking to limit over-reliance or dependence on the Chinese economy as those ties deepen. But given the large and growing economic importance of China to all regional economies, the economic implications of political decisions are a consideration for every regional state. In several countries where China's economic presence is overwhelming, leaders appear more willing to do China's bidding on even sensitive issues.

Beijing clearly believes that Chinese economic scale and growth make regional states more likely to respect China's international interests.[54] In 2011, the vice president of one of China's leading foreign policy think tanks wrote, "In terms of foreign exchange reserves, export capability, increases in foreign investment, domestic demand drive and other areas, China has accumulated massive international economic influence, and to a certain extent raised China's political and military influence."[55] Asymmetric dependence on trade is often taken by Chinese analysts as a surrogate for influence. Below, we discuss the growth of Chinese trade and investment in Southeast Asia over the last decade and outline the ambitious set of political–economic initiatives it has rolled out to stimulate deeper integration and, in its view, build influence.

Growth in Trade and Investment

China's trade with Southeast Asia is greater than that with any other develop-ing region, and it is growing rapidly. Between 2001 and 2016, China's trade with Southeast Asia increased, in real terms, by 726 percent, or a compound annual growth rate (CAGR) of 15.1 percent per year.[56] In 2001, trade with Southeast Asia represented 8.2 percent of China's total trade, a figure that grew to 12.4 percent in 2016. As important as trade with Southeast Asia is to China, it is even more central to Southeast Asian states. In 2001, ASEAN states did almost three times as much trade with the United States as they did with China. By 2016, China was the dominant trade partner. In that year, 20 percent of Southeast Asia's trade was with China, and only 10 percent with the United States (see Figure 3.1). The remarkable growth of Chinese trade in Southeast Asia has profoundly affected the interests and calculations of Southeast Asian states.

Through the 1990s, foreign direct investment (FDI) flowing *into* China played a major role in underpinning China's economic growth, but Chinese companies had virtually no investment position overseas. That began to change in 1999, when the Fourth Plenum of the 15th National Party Congress launched the so-called going out strategy (走出去战略), encouraging firms to "establish branches overseas" and "explore international markets." China's external FDI position built only slowly

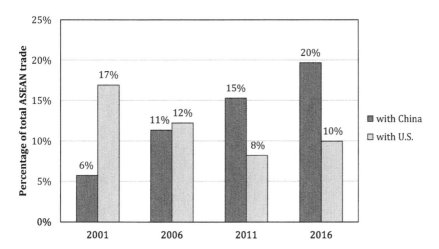

FIGURE 3.1   Percentage of ASEAN Total Trade with China and the United States

Source: International Monetary Fund, Direction of Trade Statistics.

until the banking and oversight mechanisms to support overseas efforts were established by the mid- to late 2000s.

In 2001, China's outward FDI flow to the ASEAN states was only a fraction of 1 percent of ASEAN's total incoming FDI.[57] In 2011, China accounted for 6.7 percent of ASEAN's incoming FDI flow, and by 2016, it was 9.5 percent. Even in 2016, China's FDI flow to Southeast Asia was significantly less than that of either the United States or Japan (see Figure 3.2), and its total stock of FDI in each of those years represented a smaller percentage of total FDI stock, given that Japanese and Western firms have invested significant money in Southeast Asia for decades. Nevertheless, Chinese firms have moved from having virtually no equity stakes in Southeast Asia (or elsewhere) to being significant investors.

China's economic relationships with the ASEAN states varies as widely as the ASEAN states themselves differ from one another in terms of their developmental levels and distance from China. In 2016, trade with China (including Hong Kong) constituted fully 37 percent of Myanmar's trade with the world, whereas trade with China accounted for only 17 percent of total Indonesian trade and 16 percent of Thailand's total. Even larger differences in FDI are apparent. In 2016, Chinese investment counted for 10 percent or less of total investment in most ASEAN states, but fully 22 percent of total investment in Cambodia and 66 percent of investment in Laos. Investment figures fluctuate more dramatically from year to year than trade values, and, for example, Chinese investment comprised 67.6 percent of Myanmar's total in 2010, but only 6.9 percent in 2016.

In all cases, the economic relationship is highly asymmetrical, a point not lost on Chinese political and economic analysts. For the smaller states of Southeast Asia, the

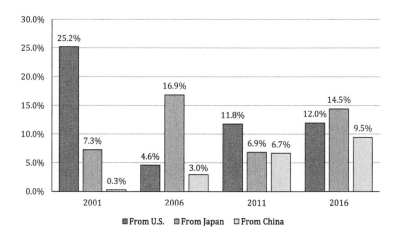

FIGURE 3.2 Percentage of Total FDI Flow into ASEAN from U.S., Japan, and China, 2015

Source: ASEAN Statistical Yearbook, various years.

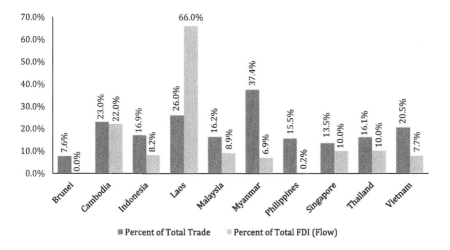

FIGURE 3.3   Trade (in Goods) with and FDI Inflow from China as a Percentage of National Totals, 2015

Sources: "ASEAN Foreign Direct Investment (FDI) Dashboard," ASEAN Stats, 2015 data; and "ASEAN Trade in Goods (IMTS) Dashboard," ASEAN Stats, 2015 data.

asymmetry is extreme. In 2015, China accounted for 27.2 percent of Cambodia's trade in goods, but Cambodia accounted for only 0.1 percent of China's (see Figure 3.3). But the asymmetry is large even for the major trading states of Southeast Asia. In 2015, China accounted for 20.0 percent of Singapore's trade, but Singapore accounted for only 2.3 percent of China's total.

"One Belt, One Road" (OBOR)

The centerpiece of China's recent political–economic efforts is its "one belt, one road" (OBOR) initiative, rolled out in September and October 2013. OBOR, Xi Jinping's signature foreign policy project, consists of infrastructure projects designed to promote Chinese trade with and investment in more than 60 countries.[58] The Silk Road Economic Belt (SREB) is primarily continental and runs through Central Asia, West Asia, the Middle East, and Europe. The Maritime Silk Road (MSR) connects China to countries in Southeast Asia, Oceania, and parts of North and East Africa—the South China Sea, South Pacific, and Indian Ocean regions. Southeast Asia will have projects associated with both the belt and road portions of OBOR. According to Wang Huiyao, Counselor for China State Council, several features of Southeast Asia make it a central starting point for OBOR, including geographic proximity, the large number of ethnic Chinese in Southeast Asia, and the historical and cultural similarities shared by China and the region.[59]

One of the core elements of the "belt" portions of OBOR is a transportation corridor (primarily consisting of high-speed rail links) running between Kunming in southwestern China and Singapore—which will transit Laos, Thailand, and Malaysia. The 3,000-kilometer line would link a number of major cities: Kunming–Bangkok, Bangkok–Kuala Lumpur, and Kuala Lumpur–Singapore. As in other high-profile OBOR projects, several points related to history and context are important. First, the plan builds on several longstanding proposals, including some of the elements most likely to be profitable. For example, Malaysia and Singapore have been considering the Kuala Lumpur–Singapore line for many years. Second, China cannot dictate terms, and the failure to secure agreement with any one partner could imperil the profitability of the entire scheme.[60] And third, even if such agreement with all parties is reached, potentially unprofitable portions of the line could produce losses for the project as a whole. Maintenance costs on high-speed rail are high, and cheaper means exist for moving goods from Kunming to Southeast Asia.[61]

In Southeast Asia, Jakarta and Singapore are identified as key hubs in the maritime Silk Road, together with several Chinese ports that front the South China Sea. A Chinese report from July 2016 suggested that Chinese and Malaysian businesses were exploring plans for the expansion of port facilities at Port Klang near the Strait of Malacca.[62] The most enthusiastic reception, though, has been from Indonesia's President Joko Widodo, who, as noted earlier, invited Chinese companies to help develop 24 seaports.[63] In 2015, China and Indonesia reached agreement on a $5.5 billion joint venture, to be financed by the China Development Bank, to build a high-speed rail between Jakarta and Bandung. Despite Chinese gains, it is important to maintain perspective. Japan's investment in Indonesia was twice that of China in 2016.

Financing for OBOR projects, which different estimates suggest could reach between one trillion and four trillion dollars, may ultimately come primarily from the AIIB (discussed immediately below on page 000) and the Silk Road Fund (currently funded at $40 billion), but current financing comes largely from Chinese policy banks.[64] Chinese officials suggest that OBOR projects dovetail with ASEAN initiatives and priorities, such as the Master Plan on ASEAN Connectivity (MPAC). Launched in 2010, MPAC is meant to improve physical infrastructure, institutional connectivity, and people-to-people relations. The Asian Development Bank estimates that the Master Plan will require about $70 billion a year for the next five to ten years, and ASEAN leaders are concerned by shortfalls in funding.[65] Both Premier Li Keqiang and State Councilor Wang Yi have stipulated that they will look to harmonize funding agencies, OBOR, and MPAC.[66]

Asian Infrastructure Investment Bank (AIIB)

Xi Jinping announced China's intention to establish the AIIB in October 2013, and it began operations in December 2015.[67] Four interrelated motivations likely drove AIIB's creation. First was a perceived need to better and more rapidly utilize

China's vast foreign reserves. Second was the reluctance of established institutions, such as the IMF and Asian Development Bank, to grant China a larger governing role, despite a willingness on Beijing's part to bear a more significant share of the financial burden.[68] Third was the greater willingness of some regional states to accept investment from multilateral institutions than directly and bilaterally from China.[69] And fourth was the need for a finance vehicle or platform to facilitate and coordinate regional OBOR investments.[70]

At its launch, the bank had 57 founding member states—including 37 regional and 20 non-regional states. Washington was deeply ambivalent about the bank, with some seeing it as a challenge to existing institutions such as the IMF, and others viewing it as a natural—and non-threatening—development. In the context of the coordinated U.S. and Japanese decision to reject membership, the quick accession by several close European allies of the United States was both an apparent surprise and embarrassment.[71] Initial capital was $100 billion, about two-thirds of the capital of the Asian Development Bank and about half of the World Bank.[72] In 2016, the AIIB approved loans totaling $1.7 billion, including loans for projects in Azerbaijan, Oman, Pakistan, Indonesia, Bangladesh, Tajikistan, and Burma.[73]

Regional Comprehensive Economic Partnership (RCEP) and the Trans-Pacific Partnership (TPP)

During the November 2012 East Asian Summit, members announced their intention to create RCEP, an FTA that would include the ten ASEAN states plus six countries with which ASEAN has bilateral FTAs, including China, India, Japan, South Korea, Australia, and New Zealand. RCEP's ostensible goals are to harmonize the terms of trade, currently defined by a wide variety of bilateral agreements, and reduce tariff and nontariff barriers.[74] Exceptions are to be made for some of the poorer developing states. And China, in the interests of hastening approval, has advocated "early harvest" provisions that would enable those parts of the agreement with broadest appeal to come into force early—perhaps even before the rest of the agreement is finalized.[75]

The shape and membership that RCEP took in 2012 represents a compromise between China and Japan. Originally, Beijing sought an East Asian FTA with more limited membership, including only ASEAN, China, Japan, and South Korea. In contrast, Tokyo sought the inclusion of a larger group of states, as well as more flexible rules for future expansion.[76] Although many Japanese actors supported a relatively exclusive approach to East Asian integration during the 1990s and 2000s, by 2012, Japanese policymakers had come to believe that the narrowest groupings, especially those that excluded the Commonwealth states of Australia and New Zealand, would be dominated by Beijing.[77] Beijing's willingness to accede to many of Tokyo's preferences, for its part, was spurred by concerns that momentum for the Trans-Pacific Partnership (TPP) was building.

TPP grew out of the Trans-Pacific Strategic Economic Partnership Agreement (TPSEP), signed by Brunei, Chile, Singapore, and New Zealand in 2005. In 2008,

12 states began negotiations on TPP. The finalized proposal was signed in February 2016, and was awaiting ratification when President Donald Trump withdrew U.S. participation in January 2017. The membership of TPP was quite different from RCEP's—it included only four members of ASEAN and did not include China, but did include five countries in the Western Hemisphere, including the United States.[78] Many, but not all, specialists on both sides of the Pacific viewed TPP as being in direct competition with RCEP.[79] Beijing was skeptical of U.S. assurances that China could join TPP later and showed little interest in doing so. Zhuang Guotu, director of Southeast Asian Studies at Xiamen University, argued that if Southeast Asian states joined TPP, "China would then be isolated."[80] Many in Asia also feared that, with a membership that cuts across Asia and the Americas, TPP would undermine the larger project of Asian integration.[81]

Prior to January 2017, it appeared that TPP had the clear upper hand. Most TPP members had clear interests in tying Asia closer to the United States, while RCEP faced a number of challenges. Several of the non-ASEAN states in RCEP (e.g., China and India) did not have FTAs with each other, so those states needed to consider a higher level of potential impact.[82] India, which is largely interested in service sector provisions, firmly rejected an early harvest agreement, which is more likely to favor trade in goods.[83] Several NGOs, as well as some poorer members, were critical of draft language pushed by Japan and South Korea that calls for strict provisions on intellectual property rights.[84] But U.S. withdrawal from TPP has breathed new life in RCEP negotiations, and most have recommitted themselves to a relatively rapid conclusion of the treaty.[85]

Military and Coast Guard Means

China has employed its improved military and coast guard capabilities coercively to secure its territorial interests in the South China Sea, and the broad and sustained use of coercive means now distinguishes China's military behavior in Southeast Asia from the pattern of Chinese behavior in other developing regions. At the same time, Beijing has sought to mitigate the backlash in Southeast Asia through increased military engagement. Regional activities by the PLA and Coast Guard can be divided into three overlapping categories: presence missions; coercive measures; and military diplomacy.

Military Presence

Between 1996 and 2016, China's official defense budget grew by an inflation-adjusted 650 percent. China's military modernization has given it increased reach, and that, in turn, translates into a dramatically increased presence in the South China Sea and Southeast Asia more broadly.[86]

Over the last 20 years, the Chinese Navy has moved from a brown water force to a blue water, ocean-going one. In 1996, China had a single destroyer larger than 4,000 tons; today, it has 17 such ships (as well as several more awaiting commissioning), in addition to many smaller warships. Similarly, in 1996, China had just taken delivery of its first two modern (*Kilo*-class) submarines; it now operates 40 modern submarines, most manufactured in China. The PLA Navy is currently operating its first aircraft carrier, a test-bed platform with little operational value, and in March 2017 it announced the launch of its first domestically built, and much more capable, carrier. The PLA Navy has deployed 20,000-ton underway replenishment ships, and will soon take delivery of replenishment ships twice that size.

The PLA Navy has deployed flotillas to the Gulf of Aden for counter-piracy operations since 2009, and has been far more active than previously in waters in the East China Sea, South China Sea, Western Pacific, and Indian Oceans. In January and February 2014, the PLA dispatched a surface action group, consisting of a 25,000-ton *Yuzhao*-class amphibious transport dock (LPD) and two destroyers, through the South China Sea, the Sunda Strait, the Lombok Strait, the Makassar Strait, and the Philippine Sea, before returning home via the Bashi Channel. The fleet halted at several points along the way to conduct a variety of offensive and defensive training exercises.[87] In September 2016, Chinese and Russian naval flotillas conducted eight days of naval exercises (primarily island landing and defense) in the South China Sea—the first time their combined forces have exercised in that area.[88] And in February 2017, three warships, including the Chinese aircraft carrier *Liaoning*, conducted exercises in the South China Sea before cruising on to the Indian Ocean.[89]

Similar developments have occurred in the Chinese air forces, which now boast roughly 800 fourth generation fighter aircraft and a large force of medium bombers. In early 2017, the PLA began series production of its new large cargo aircraft, the Y-20, and it is likely that a variant of the Y-20 will serve as an aerial refueling tanker, giving Chinese aircraft greater range and loiter time over the South China Sea than their current small fleet of outdated tankers allows. At the same time, China has gained situation awareness in the South China Sea with the development of a robust space-based surveillance capability.[90]

With coast guards taking a leading role in many of the region's territorial disputes, several countries are engaged in what might be termed a coast guard arms race.[91] In 2013, the Chinese centralized most assets of their five disparate maritime law enforcement agencies under the Chinese Coast Guard (海警).[92] Between 2010 and 2016, the tonnage of ships associated with these agencies increased by an estimated 73 percent, making it, by tonnage, the largest in the world.[93] The Chinese Coast Guard has taken converted naval frigates into service, and has it has recently commissioned two 10,000-ton patrol ships—the largest coast guard vessels in the world. Chinese media reports celebrate the fact that these new ships will be capable of ramming and possibly sinking 9,000-ton ships without sustaining significant damage to themselves.[94]

Combined with the airfields and support facilities provided by China's land reclamation efforts in the South China Sea (discussed on page 000), China is now far more capable of maintaining a significant military presence in the region and pursuing its territorial and other goals there.

Coercive Employment of Hard Power

Beijing has employed its rapidly improving military capabilities to strengthen and con- solidate its territorial claims in the South China Sea (as well as in the East China Sea, an area not covered in this chapter). It has pursued those ends largely through coercive means—demonstrating administrative control of contested areas in the South China Sea and muscling out others trying to do the same. In a number of significant incidents, Beijing was ostensibly reacting to the actions of others, but its response exceeded the initial provocation in scale or intensity and ultimately changed the status quo in its own favor. Chinese goals and policy with respect to disputes has remained consistent over the last several decades, but its behavior with respect to pursuing its objectives has shifted with circumstances.

In 1974, as the Vietnam War was drawing to a close, Beijing wrested control of the Paracel Islands from South Vietnam after a brief naval skirmish. Starting in early 1988, with other claimants having moved to garrison features deeper in the South China Sea, China occupied seven features in the Spratly Islands. In March 1988, PLA Navy ships attacked Vietnamese troops on Johnson Reef, killing 74.[95] Later, as China consolidated its holdings and built small platforms or forts on occupied features, it took a more accommodating diplomatic position—partly in response to nascent balancing by regional states. In 2002, China and ASEAN signed the Declaration on the Conduct of Parties in the South Chinese Sea.[96] In 2005, China, the Philippines, and Vietnam signed an agreement to conduct joint oil exploration surveys over an area of 143,000 square kilometers.[97]

Starting in 2009, analysts observed increased Chinese "assertiveness" in the South China Sea, with the expulsion and, in some cases, arrest of foreign (especially Vietnam- ese) fishermen operating "illegally" in Chinese-claimed waters.[98] The intensification of conflict, which was not limited to China, coincided with the May 2009 deadline for states to make seabed hydrocarbon claims under UNCLOS. In addition to the mutual arrest of fishermen, China and Vietnam have confronted one another over oil exploration and drilling—as well as over China's continued building on the Paracel Islands. In May 2014, a Chinese oil platform moved to and operated from a position 120 miles east of Vietnam's Ly Son Island, sparking large-scale demonstrations and riots in Vietnam.[99] The same Chinese platform made repeat visits in 2015 and 2016.[100]

Elsewhere, Chinese Coast Guard vessels have challenged the Philippines for con- trol of two disputed features. At the Second Thomas Shoal (roughly 200 kilometers from the Philippine's Palawan Island), the Philippines has maintained a garrison onboard a grounded military ship since 1999. China has maintained a Coast Guard presence there since May 2013, and attempted to blockade resupply in March 2014. With U.S. support, the Philippines has continued to resupply, but Chinese ele- ments have remained in place, occasionally harassing resupply.[101] At Scarborough Shoal, Chinese maritime surveillance ships prevented the Philippines from arresting Chinese fishermen in April 2012 and have remained in place since. Chinese Coast Guard ships at Scarborough regularly turn away Philippine fishing boats, despite a purported agreement for both sides to withdraw government ships.[102]

Several incidents have also raised tensions with Indonesia and Malaysia. In June 2015, Malaysia detected Chinese Coast Guard vessels near the Luconia Shoals—100 kilometers off the Sarawak coast of Borneo and well within Malaysia's claimed EEZ. Indonesia is not a party to the dispute over the Spratly Islands, but Indonesia's EEZ, which extend from the Natuna Islands, overlaps with China's nine-dash line.[103] In 2016, Chinese Coast Guard ships obstructed Indonesian patrol vessels and were involved in other incidents with Indonesian Coast Guard ships within Indonesia's claimed EEZs.[104]

The most striking Chinese escalation has been its land reclamation and building program, which followed reclamations efforts by others but exceeded them massively in scale. In 2014–2015 China reclaimed more than 3,200 acres of land on seven features (including four features that had been "low tide elevations" and three "rocks").[105] It has established cement factories, barracks, and other facilities on the new land, as well as runways of approximately 10,000 feet each on three of the islands.[106] By February 2017, indications suggested that China might have deployed its most advanced surface-to-air missile systems to those islands and few doubt that it will deploy other military and coast guard assets there.[107]

In November 2013, China declared an air defense identification zone (ADIZ) across much of the East China Sea, raising the question of whether, and under what conditions, China might establish an ADIZ in the South China Sea. At the start of 2014, analysts believed that China might be many years from establishing a South China Sea ADIZ, since it did not have the intelligence and surveillance capabilities necessary to maintain situational awareness across the area. However, the land reclamation projects in the Spratly Islands alter that equation; Chinese radar and patrol aircraft operating from the new islands will significantly enhance the PLA's ability to monitor air activity in the southern portions of the South China Sea. Chinese operators are already challenging U.S. surveillance flights near the new artificial islands, and if Beijing establishes a South China Sea ADIZ, the scope and intensity of its activities may increase.

Military Diplomacy

China has capitalized on differing threat perceptions throughout the region to advance strategic relationships wherever possible and to mitigate the political fallout from its efforts to consolidate its territorial position. Indeed, China's "military diplomacy" (军事外交), or what the U.S. military calls "partnership building," has become an important element of China's larger diplomatic toolkit. Although military outreach goes back to the revolutionary period, and high-level military delegations often followed normalization with Southeast Asian states, the broader concept of military diplomacy is newer and received a major boost from Jiang Zemin's 1998 "new security concept." Key components include high-level defense meetings; combined exercises and other unit-level activities; individual exchanges for training; and arms sales.

High-Level Visits and Dialogue Mechanisms

The Chinese Central Military Commission sets Chinese military policy and has command authority, and the PLA's general departments exercise administrative responsibilities. The one important function remaining to the Ministry of Defense is external PLA liaison. Military contacts with Southeast Asian states followed normalization, though the speed and pace of developments varied significantly. Thailand normalized relations with China in 1975, and military relations became central to the relationship immediately following Vietnam's invasion of Cambodia in December 1978. Malaysia, on the other hand, normalized in 1975, but the first high-level military exchange did not occur until 1992, when Malaysia's then-Defense Minister Najib Tun Razak visited Beijing.

With its most important partners, especially those in China's immediate periphery, China has established Defense and Security Consultation (DSC) or Defense Policy Dialogue (DPD) mechanisms. In Southeast Asia, it has established such mechanisms with Thailand (2001), the Philippines (2005), Indonesia (2006), Singapore (2008), Vietnam (2010), and Malaysia (2012) (see Table 3.3). Significantly, the overall size and influence of the state appears to be more important in determining whether such mechanisms are established than how close the state's relations are to

TABLE 3.3 PLA Military-to-Military Engagement, Summary

	Defense and Security Consultation Mechanisms	Bilateral military exercises start (number to date in parentheses)	Military exercise partners (service, branch)	Arms sale value, 2007–2016 (in constant 2016 US$, millions)
Brunei	—	—		—
Cambodia	—	2016 (1)	Medical, Engineer, Rescue	189
Indonesia	2006	2011 (5)	Army (SOF), Airborne	476
Laos	—	—		61
Malaysia	2012	2014 (3)	Military Staff, Navy, HQ Staff	8
Myanmar	—	—		1,982
Philippines	2005	—		—
Singapore	2008	2009 (4)	NBC, Police, Army (infantry), Navy	—
Thailand	2001	2005 (9)	Navy, Army (SOF), Marines, Air Force	237
Vietnam	2010	2016 (1)	Border Police	—

Sources: Defense and Security Consultative mechanisms and information on combined exercises are derived from a systematic review of Chinese- and English-language sources. Arms sale values are from SIPRI, Arms Transfer Database, converted to constant 2016 US dollars.

China—China does not have such mechanisms with client states Cambodia, Laos, or Myanmar.

The DSC, in which China engages at the deputy defense ministry level, are intended to enable the exchange of views on regional security issues (including potential disputes) and to facilitate the discussion of educational exchanges, fleet visits, exercises, arms sales, and other means of cooperation. Ostensibly held annually, DSC meetings are sometimes episodic. Malaysia, for example, held its first DSC with China in 2012 and its second in 2015; meetings with Vietnam have been more regular. Whatever their parameters, the DSC are important for maintaining continuity and enabling other aspects of military diplomacy to be renewed in the event that political differences interrupt other forms of military-to-military engagement.

Unit-Level Activities

Unit-level engagement with foreign militaries is a recent phenomenon. The PLA Navy's first foreign port visit did not occur until 1985. Its first combined exercise with a foreign nation took place in 2002, when it held an exercise with Kyrgyzstan. In Southeast Asia, China's first combined exercises were with Thailand, starting in 2001, and it has held a total of 19 named exercises since that time. (It has also participated in a variety of multilateral exercises and fleet visits, including some that encompassed cross-deck visits and smaller drills.) The PLA has conducted nine named exercises with Thailand, five with Indonesia, four with Singapore, three with Malaysia, and one each with Cambodia and Vietnam. Similar to its pattern with DSC mechanisms, China has focused its bilateral exercise efforts on countries with relatively advanced military practices.

The nature of China's bilateral exercises has evolved over time. Its first two exercises in Southeast Asia were naval (beginning in 2005). Later exercises added, successively, Army SOF (2007), Marines (2010), Airborne (2013), and Air Force fighter units (2015). With the exception of the Airborne exercises (conducted twice with Indonesia), new service or branch elements were added to the mix first with Thailand. In July 2007, the PLA undertook its first "combined *training* exercise" (联合训练), which Chinese reports emphasized differed significantly from the other types of "combined exercises" (联合演习). Rather than displays of combat power, combined training exercises are generally smaller (typically companies or battalions) but involved the full integration of Chinese and foreign elements—often down to the squad level and often for a period of weeks.[108]

Combined exercises demonstrate goodwill, build confidence, and allow the sharing of military "best practices." In September 2016, China and ASEAN agreed to a code for unplanned encounters at sea (CUES) in the South China Sea. When two Singapore warships conducted drills with a Chinese frigate off Shanghai later in the same month, they rehearsed the CUES protocols.[109] China often pushes for exercises with elite foreign units, many of which are close partners with U.S. military counterparts. Chinese units participating in such exercises are sometimes packed with officers, indicating that learning military "best practices" is a key motivation.[110]

Arms Sales and Licensed Production

Of potentially even greater significance to political relations are nascent but grow-ing arms sales ties that could become more robust as the Chinese arms indus-try matures. China has periodically sold arms to a limited number of purchasers (including Pakistan and Thailand). The list of regional customers has widened, and arms relationships have evolved to include a broader range of goods and licensed production and limited joint development. Within the next decade or two, mili-tary-industrial cooperation is likely to become a larger factor in China's relations with regional states.

Cultural Means

The Chinese state also actively pursues cultural diplomacy, which is perhaps more important in parts of Southeast Asia, where several states have large ethnic Chinese populations, than it is elsewhere in the world (Table 3.4). China has established 30 Confucius Institutes in Southeast Asia, with the largest number in Thailand (14), Indonesia (6), the Philippines (4), and Malaysia (2).[111] The Chinese state also pro-motes student exchanges and tourism, as well as Chinese media outlets in Southeast Asia, and it has established a formal "people-to-people mechanism" with Indonesia to cultivate bilateral cultural ties.[112]

Although China has sought to highlight its cultural ties to Southeast Asia, it should be noted that a large ethnic Chinese population does not necessarily serve to facilitate the pursuit of the PRC's political ends. Indeed, the presence of large Chinese populations often works against Chinese efforts. Ethnic Chinese families are greatly overrepresented in elite business communities in several Southeast Asian states, including Thailand, Indonesia, and Malaysia, but their political position is often delicate. Any appearance of political fealty towards China would place these

TABLE 3.4   Ethnic Chinese Population in the World

	Estimated Chinese ethnic population	*Ethnic Chinese as percentage of total population*
Brunei Darussalam	44,972	10.3%
Cambodia	15,957	0.1%
Indonesia	3,099,793	1.2%
Lao	7,019	0.1%
Malaysia	6,994,691	22.6%
Myanmar	1,706,713	3.0%
Philippines	820,994	0.8%
Singapore	4,290,042	74.2%
Thailand	9,548,115	14.0%
Vietnam	952,610	1.0%

Source: CIA World Factbook.

populations in an untenable position. And even where that is not the case, as in the ethnic Chinese majority in Singapore, it may not be a population friendly to Beijing's politics or position. Nevertheless, an important Chinese business community can and often does facilitate economic integration, which can have spillover effects on political interests.[113]

Tensions Between Different Parts of China's Strategy

The goal of deepening political, economic, military, and cultural relations in Southeast Asia stands in tension with Beijing's unilateral efforts to expand or consolidate its claims of sovereignty over disputed territorial features in the South China Sea. To an extent, Beijing's diplomacy may mitigate some of the diplomatic and political fallout from territorial conflict, and China's recent largess may be motivated by the need to undo the damage done to its regional political position. The "2+7 framework" reads very much like a navigation chart for troubled political waters. But whether China succeeds in this balancing act will depend on a host of variables, not least Beijing's own self-control in its future disputes and the extent to which neighboring states place trade above securing their own claims to contested features.

It is unclear the extent to which Chinese officialdom as a whole understands and the tensions between the two tracks in China's Southeast Asian approach, but at least some have voiced concerns. In 2010, Shi Yinhong, professor at Renmin University and occasional advisor to the Chinese government, suggested that although China should defend its core interests, it "must have a constructive attitude toward all countries, no matter large or small, rich or poor" and it should "listen to, and coordinate and cooperate with other countries."[114] In 2015, a researcher associated with the Chinese Academy of Social Sciences warned, "The challenge to 'one belt, one road' posed by the South China problem is all encompassing, and it is the most important factor affecting China's entire perimeter security." "Over the last 10 or even 20 years," she observed, "ASEAN has been the most successful example of Chinese regional cooperation," but "ultimately the South China Sea problem erodes mutual trust between China and ASEAN, and will inevitably affect the prospects for OBOR."[115]

Nor are such views expressed only in the academic community. Wu Jianmin, one of China's most prominent diplomats, famously wrote in 2009 that Mao's admonition to "keep a low profile" should remain the governing principle of Chinese foreign policy for another hundred years, and he continued his outspoken advocacy of win–win approaches to Chinese foreign policy until his premature death in June 2016.[116] Others, however, appear to believe that China's dual-track strategy is working and securing China's historical claims without producing undue damage to its international position. PLA Navy Rear Admiral Zhang Zhaozhong, a theorist (and sometimes loose cannon) with the PLA National Defense Academy, observes that China's strategy of "seal and control" used at Scarborough Shoal has achieved Chinese ends without "resort to war" and should be employed more broadly.[117] Which Chinese view predominates may ultimately determine whether

Chinese strategy and policy returns to a course of moderation and compromise or continues to favor the divide, conquer, and mollify strategy it has recently pursued in the South China Sea.

Regional Reactions

Given the variation in economic and political conditions within the region and in China's approach to individual countries, it should come as no surprise that the region's reaction has varied. Not only have different states reacted differently to China, but also in a number of cases, individual states have changed course dramatically in terms of how they position themselves vis-à-vis China and the United States. Overall, China has been relatively successful in achieving territorial and other unilateral objectives without engendering a broad-based balancing reaction. But in considering political outcomes, care must also be taken not to exaggerate Chinese gains or the extent to which most regional states hedge their position and welcome an active U.S. partner.

At least three groups of variables appear to have shaped contrasting reactions. The first group includes geostrategic factors. States with the most significant and immediate territorial disputes with China have, naturally, had a more contentious relationship with Beijing. Thailand, lacking territorial disputes with China, has been more receptive to its entreaties over time than Vietnam or, until recently, the Philippines. As Duterte's election in the Philippines demonstrates, however, the intensity of such disputes is not always decisive. The second geostrategic variable is military. Military vulnerability is a function of both national power and geography. Small, weak states that are close to China have shown a far greater likelihood to appease China than stronger, more distant ones. This is most obvious in the cases of Cambodia and Laos, but is also a factor in the Philippine's about face.[118]

Economic and social variables also shape outcomes. Smaller states tend to trade more than larger ones, and the impact of trade liberalization will therefore affect smaller countries more than larger ones.[119] Laos has a population less than 3 percent the size of Indonesia's, and offers to expand aid or trade, especially on concessionary or positive terms, will be difficult for it to dismiss. Middle-income ASEAN countries, especially Vietnam, also stand to benefit from the Chinese movement of production offshore, a phenomenon that is already evident in apparel and footwear industries.[120] At the same time, higher income countries might see increased competition from China in, for example, the production of intermediate goods, such as electronic parts and components.[121] As noted earlier, large or powerful ethnic Chinese business communities tend to promote trade ties that are more robust than proximity and productive factors alone would predict.

Finally, a third set of variables relates to domestic politics issues. Where military coups or the forceful suppression of dissent by authoritarian government has led to even limited U.S. sanctions (e.g., Thailand, Laos, Cambodia, and Myanmar), governments have often found a more receptive audience in Beijing. Even in the absence of sanctions, U.S. government criticism of potential abuses during the Philippines drug war and a Justice Department probe into potential graft by Prime Minister Najib in Malaysia appear to have nudged the leadership in those countries to reevaluate their position vis-à-vis China, at least in the short term. However, this is not an argument for Washington to change its stance on these issues; the opportunities afforded to Beijing by such episodes are likely to be fleeting, and U.S. principles give it important advantages in the long-term competition for hearts and minds across a wider swath of territory.

Overall, China has been remarkably successful in achieving its regional objectives. China has been able to deepen its economic and political relationships with regional states, advance Beijing's narrow unilateral interests (especially territorial ones), gain significant policy influence in some weak neighboring states, and avoid a strong or unified balancing reaction by the region's larger powers. Nevertheless, China's assertive behavior in the South China Sea has kept the region's most important states looking to the United States and elsewhere for political and military support.

Implications for the United States

U.S. and Chinese interests in Southeast Asia are not entirely zero-sum, and they overlap on a number of issues. Nevertheless, with two treaty allies (the Philippines and Thailand), a number of other close strategic partners, and its own independent interests in Southeast Asia, Washington will want to ensure that Chinese presence and influence do not come at the expense of the United States. Below, I outline four implications for U.S. policy.

First, U.S. bilateral efforts should engage all regional states, but priority should be given to cultivating deeper relations with the major "anchor states" of ASEAN— especially Singapore, Malaysia, and Indonesia. To be sure, U.S. political and military relations with several other regional states, especially the Philippines and Thailand, are deeper than those with Malaysia and Indonesia, and U.S. ties with existing allies should be maintained and further developed. But America's skillful and patient diplomacy with Myanmar demonstrates what might be accomplished with even the most unlikely partner. Indonesia has by far the largest population and economy in ASEAN and is effectively its political center, while Singapore and Malaysia are also critical. In addition to their economic and political value, these states are also sufficiently distant from China to chart an independent course.

Second, most states in Southeast Asia are focused largely, if not overwhelmingly, on economic development and economic security, and U.S. economic engagement will be central to maintaining Washington's relevance. Clearly, China's regional appeal is, first and foremost, economic. The United States cannot and should not compete on the same terms as Beijing. It cannot, for example, offer the same level of subsidized infrastructure investment that Chinese state banks do. But the United States and U.S. firms are, in many ways, more attractive partners, and deepening economic integration will likely carry political dividends. Withdrawing from TPP will do immense damage to the U.S. political position in Asia without providing any compensating net economic benefit for the United States.[122] But having abandoned TPP, Washington should find other ways of advancing its economic relevance, and one way of doing so would be through bilateral trade agreements.

Third, the U.S. military should remain actively engaged with regional partners in Southeast Asia. Given growing concerns about the direction of Chinese military power and the uses to which it might be put, regional interest in deepening strategic relations is growing. Without active U.S. involvement, there is no coalition of Asian states willing to balance, or capable of balancing, Chinese power—the imbalance of power is simply too great for even a combination of regional states to maintain their position without support. With U.S. backing, however, a number of regional states are likely at least to improve their defensive capabilities and may be more inclined to present a united political front if and when Beijing overreaches. Given the emphasis that most Southeast Asian states place on technology development in military procurement arrangements, Washington should consider agreements that facilitate technology transfer (similar to the Defense Technology and Trade Initiative that it established with India in 2012).

Finally, the United States should directly address differences with China, while looking for opportunities to deepen political, economic, and military cooperation with Beijing in areas where interests overlap. Chinese are rightly proud of their country's legitimate international contributions, such as the large role its soldiers and police play in international peacekeeping. Publicly recognizing and embracing these Chinese contributions would help make it clearer to Beijing that when the United States criticizes Chinese actions, it does so on the basis of specific behavior, rather than on the identity of the actor. Within Southeast Asia, the U.S. military should look for opportunities to organize a wider range of multilateral exercises with China than it has to date.

Notes

1 Special thanks are due to Michael Glosny, who read an early draft of this chapter and offered a number of important suggestions and sources.
2 "Wang Yi: Open the new horizon for China-ASEAN relations based on the proposed 'one road, one belt' and the development strategies of ASEAN states," Ministry of Foreign Affairs of the People's Republic of China (hereinafter referred to as FMPRC website), August 5, 2015.
3 Joshua Kerlantzick, *Charm Offensive: How China's Soft Power Is Transforming the World* (New Haven, CT: Yale University Press, 2007).
4 There are different views of China's activities in the South China Sea since 2009. For those that view the behavior as new and more assertive, see Brantly Womack, "Beyond Win–Win: Rethinking China's International Relationships in an Era of Economic Uncertainty," *International Affairs* 89, no. 4 (July 2013): 911–928; Nian-Chung Chang Liao, "The Sources of China's Assertiveness: The System, Domestic Politics or Leadership Preferences," *International Affairs* 92, no. 4 (July 2016): 817–833; and Michael D. Swaine and M. Taylor Fravel, "China's Assertive Behavior, Part Two: The Maritime Periphery," *China Leadership Monitor*, no. 35 (summer 2011): 1–29. For those who argue there has been little change, see Alastair Iain Johnston, "How New and Assertive is China's New Assertiveness?" *International Security* 37, no. 4 (Spring 2013): 7–48; and Bjorn Jerden,

"The Assertive China Narrative: Why It Is Wrong and How So Many Still Bought Into It," *Chinese Journal of International Politics* 7, no. 1 (2014): 47–88.

5 For brief historical surveys of China in Southeast Asia, see Martin Stuart-Fox, *A Short History of China in Southeast Asia: Tribute, Trade and Influence* (Crows Nest, NSW: Allen & Unwin, 2013); John E. Wills Jr., ed., *China and Maritime Europe, 1500–1800: Trade, Settlement, Diplomacy, and Missions* (Cambridge: Cambridge University Press, 2011); and Victor Lieberman, *Strange Parallels: Southeast Asia in Globalized Context, c. 800–1830, vol. 2: Mainland Mirrors: Europe, Japan, China, South Asia, and the Islands* (Cambridge: Cambridge University Press, 2009).

6 Michael S. Goodman, *The Official History of the Joint Intelligence Committee, Volume I: From the Approach of the Second World War to the Suez Crisis* (New York: Routledge, 2014), 336.

7 Cheng Li, *Chinese Politics in the Xi Jinping Era: Reassessing Collective Leadership* (Washington, DC: Brookings Institution, 2016); Elizabeth C. Economy, "Xi Jinping Tightens His Grip," *Foreign Affairs*, October 2014.

8 This fear is evident in official and popular discussions of the U.S. "pivot" to Asia and U.S. Asia policy more generally. See, for example, 寿晓松 [Shou Xiaosong], *Zhanlue xue* 战略学 [Science of Military Strategy 2013] (Beijing: Academy of Military Science Press, 2013), 79, 96–97; Dai Xu, "U.S. Building 'Asian NATO' to Encircle China," *China.org.cn*, August 11, 2010; and Hu Qingyun, "US to Increase Troops Stationed in Australia: Deal Seen as Move to 'Encircle' China," *Global Times*, August 13, 2014.

9 Willem Thorbecke, "Understanding the Flow of Electronic Parts and Components in East Asia," RIETI Discussion Paper Series, June 2016.

10 "How China Is Changing Its Manufacturing Strategy," *The Wall Street Journal*, June 7, 2016; and "China to Move Production Capacity Offshore," Parliament of Australia website, July 8, 2015.

11 Variants of the map date back to an "eleven-dash line" on maps generated by the Nationalist government of China in 1947. Subsequent maps published by Communist China have dropped dashes along the Gulf of Tonkin and include either nine or ten dashes.

12 United Nations, "Law on the Territorial Sea and Contiguous Zone," 25 February 1992, www.un.org/depts/los/LEGISLATIONANDTREATIES/PDFFILES/CHN_1992_Law.pdf.

13 The distinctions between islands, rocks, and low tide elevations have important implications for the extent of control or sovereignty of water surrounding them. See Paul Gerwirtz, "Limits of Law in the South China Sea," East Asia Policy Paper 8, Brookings, May 2016; and Christopher Mirasola, "What Makes an Island? Land Reclamation and the South China Sea Arbitration," CSIS Asia Maritime Transparency Initiative, July 15, 2015.

14 Tong Xiaoguang and Zhao Lin, "Dui 'Maliujia' kunju yu Zhongguo youqi anquan de zaisikao" 对"马六甲困局"与中国油气安全的再思考 [Rethinking China's Oil and Gas Seurity and the 'Malacca Strait Dilemma'], *Policy Research* 政策研究, no. 7 (November 2010): 17–22; Zhongguo shiyou yunshuzhong de Maliujia kunju 中国石油运输中的马六甲困局 [The Malacca Dilemma in Chinese Oil Transport], January 8, 2014; "Shi Qiping: Maliujia kunju shi Zhongguo zuida diyuan zhanlue tiaozhan" 石齐平: 马六甲困局是中国最大地缘战略挑战 [Shi Qiping: The Malacca Dilemma is China's Greatest Geo-Strategic Challenge], *Phoenix Television* [Hong Kong], November 27, 2015.

15 China's 2015 "Military Strategy" white paper stipulates, "It is necessary for China to . . . safeguard its national sovereignty and maritime rights and interests, and protect the security of strategic SLOCs and overseas interests." Chinese Ministry of National Defense, "China's Military Strategy," May 2015.

16 The islands in the South China Sea are not mentioned explicitly as part of China's core national interests in official formulations. On the core national interests, see Michael D. Swaine, "China's Assertive Behavior, Part One: On 'Core Interests'," *China Leadership Monitor*, no. 34 (2011), 1–25.

17 On these categories, see Zhang Qiaosu, ed., "Xi Jinping chuxi zhongyang waishi gongzuo huiyi bing fabiao zhongyao jianghua" 习近平出席中央外事工作会议并发表重要

讲话 [Xi Jinping Chairs Central Conference on Work Relating to Foreign Affairs and Delivers an Important Speech], *Xinhua*, November 29, 2014.

18 Wang Yi, "Creating a New Landscape for the Diplomacy with Neighboring Countries and Boosting the Asia–Pacific Regional Cooperation," FMPRC website, October 9, 2013.

19 Yenni Kwok, "Indonesian President Jokowi Visits the Natuna Islands to Send a Strong Signal to China," *Time*, June 23, 2016.

20 "Indonesia Set to Upgrade Military Base in Islands Perched on Edge of South China Sea," *The Japan Times*, June 29, 2016.

21 Natasha Hamilton-Hart and Dave McRae, "Indonesia: Balancing the United States and China, Aiming for Independence," The United States Studies Center at the University of Sydney, November 2015.

22 "President Jokowi at IMO Forum: I'm Committed to Making Indonesia a Global Maritime Fulcrum," Indonesian Cabinet Secretariat website, April 20, 2016.

23 C.P.F. Luhulima, "Superimposing China's 'Maritime Silk Road' on Indonesia," *The Jakarta Post*, June 10, 2016; Chris Brummitt and Haslinda Amin, "Jokowi Leans on China, Central Bank to Revive Indonesia GDP," *Bloomberg*, February 11, 2016.

24 "Indonesia to License Produce Chinese C-705 Missiles," *Defense Update*, January 31, 2013.

25 Dylan Amirio, "Indonesia Might See High-Speed Rail Costs Swell Amid Changes," *The Jakarta Post*, April 15, 2017.

26 "Beijing Keeps Close Check on Latest 'Colony' Malaysia: Chinese Navy Constantly Patrolling Luconai Shoals While Najib Regime Sent Only One Vessel—Report," *Malaysia Chronicle*, April 2017.

27 Yeganeh Torbati, "Pentagon Chief Visits U.S. Carrier in Disputed South China Sea, Blames Beijing for Tension," *Reuters*, November 5, 2015.

28 "1MDB: The Case That Has Riveted Malaysia," *BBC News*, July 22, 2016.

29 Praveen Menon, "Malaysia's Najib Aims to Take China Ties to 'New Highs' on Visit," *Reuters*, October 27, 2016.

30 Prashanth Parameswaran, "Malaysia's New China Warship Deal: Promises and Prospects," *The Diplomat*, February 4, 2017.

31 Joseph Sipalan, "Malaysia's Najib Risks Backlash at Home After Deals With China," *Reuters*, November 7, 2016.

32 On the development of Thailand's economic ties with China, see Evan S. Medeiros, Keith Crane, Eric Heginbotham, Norman D. Levin, Julia F. Lowell, Angel Rabasa, and Somi Seong, *Pacific Currents: The Responses of U.S. Allies and Security Partners in East Asia to China's Rise* (Santa Monica: RAND Corporation, 2008), 132–141.

33 Mike Yeo, "Thailand to Buy More Chinese Tanks, Reportedly for $58M," *Defense News*, April 4, 2017; Patpicha Tanakasempipat, "Thailand Approves $393-mln Purchase of Chinese Submarines," *Reuters*, April 24, 2017.

34 John D. Ciorciari, "China and Cambodia: Patron and Client?" International Policy Center Working Paper, no. 121, Gerald R. Ford School of Public Policy, University of Michigan, June 14, 2013.

35 "Investment Trend," Council for the Development of Cambodia (CDC), accessed October 20, 2016, www.cambodiainvestment.gov.kh/why-invest-in-cambodia/investment-enviroment/investment-trend.html. Altogether, China provided more than $8 billion in investment between 2005 and 2015. "China Global Investment Tracker," American Enterprise Institute, accessed October 20, 2016, www.aei.org/china-global-investment-tracker/.

36 Carlyle A. Thayer, "New Commitment to a Code of Conduct in the South China Sea," *National Bureau of Asian Research*, October 9, 2013; "Hun Sen and the South China Sea," *Khmer Times*, June 22, 2016.

37 Sok Khemara, "China Gives $600m to Cambodia in Exchange for International Support," *VOA*, July 16, 2016.

38 China is responsible for 70 percent of the cost, though repaying loans for the remaining 30 percent may strain Cambodia's finances. Prashanth Parameswaran, "China, Laos to Build $6 Billion Railway by 2020," *The Diplomat*, November 16, 2015.

39 David Tweed and David Roman, "South China Sea Talks End in Disarray as China Lobbies Laos," *Bloomberg*, June 14, 2016.

40 Fanny Potkin, "Is Laos Moving Away From China With Its Leadership Transition," *The Diplomat*, February 3, 2016.

41 "U.S. Ambassador Derek Mitchell: 'I Feel Gratitude for What I've Been Able to Witness'," *The Irrawaddy*, March 15, 2016; Thant Myint-U, "Why Burma Must Reset Its Relationship With China," *Foreign Policy*, January 12, 2016.

42 United Nations, "Note Verbale," CML/17/2009, May 7, 2009, www.un.org/depts/los/clcs_new/submissions_files/mysvnm33_09/chn_2009re_mys_vnm_e.pdf.

43 Han Shuo, "Feifang shou Zhongguo lengluo buganxin rang Yuenan daihuai yaoqing Wang Yi fangfei" 菲方受中国冷落不甘心 让越南带话邀请王毅访菲 [Philippines Dissatisfied with Being Subject to Isolation by China, Has Vietnam Deliver an Invitation for Wang Yi to Visit Philippines], *Global Times*, August 6, 2013.

44 Han Shuo, "Feifang shou Zhongguo lengluo buganxin rang Yuenan daihuai yaoqing Wang Yi fangfei."

45 UNCTAD Statistics, accessed October 2016, http://unctad.org/Sections/dite_fdistat/docs/webdiaeia2014d3_PHL.pdf.

46 Andreo Calonzo and Cecilia Yap, "China Visit Helps Duterte Reap Funding Deals Worth $24 Billion," *Bloomberg*, October 21, 2016.

47 In order of rank and importance, those leaders include President Xi Jinping, Premier Li Keqiang, State Councilor Yang Jiechi, and Foreign Minister Wang Yi.

48 Carlyle A. Thayer, "China's Relations With Laos and Cambodia," in *China's Internal and External Relations and Lessons for Korea and Asia*, eds. Jung-Ho Bae and Jae H. Ku (Seoul: Korea Institute for National Unification, 2013).

49 Prashanth Parameswaran, "Beijing Unveils New Strategy for ASEAN-China Relations," *Jamestown Foundation China Brief* 13, no. 21 (October 2013): 9–12. By a different 2015 count, it was a member of 20 major multilateral mechanisms with ASEAN. See Gerald Chan, "China Eyes ASEAN: Evolving Multilateralism," *Journal of Asian Security and International Affairs* 2, no. 1 (April 2015): 75–91.

50 Prashanth Parameswaran, "China Reveals New Proposal to Boost Defense Ties With ASEAN," *The Diplomat*, October 17, 2015; Zhu Ningzhu, "Shanghai Summit to Explore New Asia Security Outlook," *Xinhua*, April 16, 2014; and Ankit Panda, "China Creates New 'Asia for Asians' Security Forum," *The Diplomat*, September 15, 2014.

51 "Remarks by H.E. Li Keqiang Premier of the State Council of the People's Republic of China at the 16th ASEAN-China Summit," FMPRC website, October 10, 2013.

52 "Wang Yi Brought Forth a Ten-Point Proposal on China-ASEAN Cooperation," FMPRC website, August 6, 2015.

53 Xu Bu and Yang Fan, "Zhongguo-Dongmeng guanxi: xinde qihang" 中国—东盟关系：新的启航 [China–ASEAN Relations: Setting a New Course], *Guoji wenti yanjiu* 国际问题研究 [China International Studies], no. 1 (January 2016): 35–48.

54 Michael A. Glosny, "Chinese Assessments of China's Influence in Developing Asia," in *Rising China's Influence in Developing Asia*, ed. Evelyn Goh (Oxford: Oxford University Press, 2016).

55 Fu Mengzi, "Guanyu Zhongguo guoji yingxiangli wenti de ruogan sikao" 关于中国国际影响力问题的若干思考 [Some Reflections on the Issue of China's International Influence], *Xiandai guoji guanxi* 现代国际关系 [Contemporary International Relations], no. 1 (2011): 4, as cited in Glosny, "Chinese Assessments of China's Influence in Developing Asia," 34.

56 Data from this paragraph is from IMF, Direction of Trade Statistics.

57 All statistics in this paragraph are from *ASEAN Statistical Year Book*, various years.

58 "Tuidong gongjian sichou zhilu jingjidai he 21 shiji haishang sichou zhilu de yuanjing yu xingdong" 推动共建丝绸之路经济带和21世纪海上丝绸之路的愿景与行动

[Vision and Actions on Jointly Building Silk Road Economic Belt and 21st-Century Maritime Silk Road], National Development and Reform Commission of the PRC, March 28, 2015.

59 Qi Wei, ed., "Dongnanya zai 'yidaiyilu' jianshe zhong jiang fahui zhongyao zuoyong" 东南亚在"一带一路"建设中将发挥重要作用 [Southeast Asia Will Play an Important Role in Building 'One Belt, One Road'], *Jingji cankao* 经济参考 [Economic Information Daily], July 6, 2015.

60 As of early 2017, work has begun on China and Laos segments, but negotiations are ongoing with all other partners.

61 Shang-su Wu, "Singapore–Kunming Rail Link: A 'Belt and Road' Case Study," *The Diplomat*, June 17, 2016.

62 "Port Investment Shows Belt and Road Vigor," *China Daily*, July 6, 2016.

63 Antoine Duquennoy and Robert Zielonka, "Bridging Asia and Europe Through Maritime Connectivity: China's Maritime Silk Road and Indonesia's Maritime Axis," *European Institute for Asian Studies*, March 2015; C.P.F. Luhulima, "Superimposing China."

64 "Our Bulldozers, Our Rules," *Economist*, July 2, 2016.

65 "AIIB, Silk Road Fund Crucial for Developing Countries in Asia: Cambodian Transport Minister," *Xinhua*, August 29, 2016.

66 "Remarks by H.E. Li Keqiang Premier of the State Council of the People's Republic of China at the 18th ASEAN Plus China, Japan and ROK Summit," FMPRC website, November 23, 2015; Zhang Chunxiao, "Yearender: China-Proposed Initiatives Synergize with ASEAN's Development Strategies," *Xinhua*, December 22, 2015.

67 Jane Perlez, "China Creates a World Bank of Its Own, and the U.S. Balks," *New York Times*, December 4, 2015.

68 "A Tale of Two Rail Lines: China and Japan's Soft Power Competition in Indonesia," *The Diplomat*, May 12, 2017.

69 Mike Callaghan, "The $100 Billion AIIB Opens for Business: Will China's Multilateral Ambitions Soar or Sour?" *Lowey Institute*, January 19, 2016.

70 Callaghan, "The $100 Billion AIIB Opens for Business."

71 "Is China-Led Bank a Lost Opportunity?" *The Japan Times*, April 15, 2015.

72 "Why China Is Creating a New 'World Bank' for Asia," *Economist*, November 11, 2014.

73 AIIB, "Approved Projects," viewed November 2, 2017.

74 Murray Hiebert, "ASEAN and Partners Launch Regional Comprehensive Economic Partnership," Center for Strategic and International Studies, December 7, 2012.

75 Ouyang wei and Xia Fan, "RCEP Talks Should Focus on Early Harvest," *China Daily*, May 13, 2014.

76 Hiebert, "ASEAN and Partners Launch Regional Comprehensive Economic Partnership."

77 Much of Japan's economic bureaucracy was sympathetic to the East Asian Economic Caucus (EAEC), proposed by Malaysian Prime Minister Mohamad Mahathir in 1990. The grouping would have included the ASEAN states, plus Japan, South Korea, and China. Although Japanese political leaders decided to remain aloof from the EAEC, Tokyo later led the drive for various ASEAN+3 initiatives and structures that included the same group of nations. See Hitoshi Tanaka and Adam P. Liff, *Japan's Foreign Policy and East Asian Regionalism* (New York: Council on Foreign Relations, 2009); and Tadahiro Yoshida, "East Asian Regionalism and Japan," IDE APEC Study Center Working Paper Series, no. 9, March 2004.

78 Current signatories include Brunei, Malaysia, Singapore, Vietnam, Australia, Japan, New Zealand, the United States, Canada, Chile, Peru, and Mexico.

79 See, for example, Peter A. Petri and Michael G. Plummer, "The Trans-Pacific Partnership and Asia-Pacific Integration: Policy Integration," Peterson Institute for International Economics, Policy Brief 12–16.

80 Teddy Ng, "Xi Jinping, Li Keqiang Mount Diplomatic Offensive in Southeast Asia," *South China Morning Post*, October 17, 2013.

81 Jingyang Chen, "TPP and RCEP: Boon or Bane for ASEAN," Asia Foundation, September 9, 2015.

82 "RCEP Leaders to Skip 2016 Completion Target," *Kyodo News*, September 7, 2016.
83 Banikinkar Pattanayak, "RCEP Meet: India Says 'No Early Harvest,' Differences Widen Split," *Financial Express*, July 28, 2016.
84 Ariane Kupferman-Sutthavong, "Activists Fret About RCEP Impact," *Bangkok Post*, October 20, 2016.
85 Shefali Rekhi, "Will RCEP Be a Reality by the End of 2017?" *The Straits Times*, April 23, 2017; "RCEP Put on Fast Track to Fend Off US: Japan and ASEAN Aim to Conclude Talks Soon," *Bangkok Post*, April 12, 2017.
86 On Chinese military modernization and the impact on the broader balance of power, see Eric Heginbotham, Michael Nixon, Forrest E. Morgan, Jacob L. Heim, Jeff Hagen, Sheng Li, Jeffrey Engstrom, Martin C. Libicki, Paul DeLuca, David A. Shlapak, David R. Frelinger, Burgess Laird, Kyle Brady, and Lyle J. Morris, *The U.S.–China Military Scorecard: Forces, Geography, and the Evolving Balance of Power, 1996–2017* (Santa Monica: RAND Corporation, 2015); and Roger Cliff, *China's Military Power* (Cambridge: Cambridge University Press, 2015).
87 "China's Navy Extends Its Combat Reach to the Indian Ocean," U.S.–China Economic and Security Review Commission Staff Report, March 14, 2014.
88 Shuhei Yamada, "China, Russia Begin Naval Exercises in South China Sea," *Nikkei Asian Review*, September 13, 2016.
89 Michael Martina and J. R. Wu, "China Says Aircraft Carrier Testing Weapons in South China Sea Drills," *Reuters*, January 4, 2017.
90 Eric Heginbotham et al., *The U.S.–China Military Scorecard*, 154–157.
91 Ryan D. Martinson, "China's Second Navy," *Proceedings Magazine* 141 (April 2015): 346; Lyle J. Morris, "Blunt Defenders of Sovereignty," *Naval War College Review* 70, no. 2 (Spring 2017): 72–112.
92 Lyle Morris, "Taming the Five Dragons? China Consolidates its Maritime Law Enforcement Agencies," *Jamestown Foundation China Brief* 13, no. 7 (March 2013): 8–10.
93 Morris, "Blunt Defenders of Sovereignty." See also Jeremy Page, "The Rapid Expansion of China's Navy in Five Charts," *Wall Street Journal*, April 10, 2015; and Todd Crowell, "A Coast Guard Arms Race," *Real Clear Defense*, May 23, 2016.
94 Zhang Hui, ed., "Jiemi Zhongguo haijing budui: 'Zhongguo haijing 2901' cheng shijie zuidai haijingchuan" 揭秘中国海警部队: "中国海警2901"成世界最大海警船 [Unveil Chinese Coast Guard: 'China Maritime Police 2901' Becomes the World's Largest Coast Guard Cutter], *Phoenix Television*, April 19, 2016.
95 M. Taylor Fravel, "China's Strategy in the South China Sea," *Contemporary Southeast Asia* 33, no. 3 (2011): 298.
96 Leszek Buszynski, "ASEAN, The Declaration on Conduct, and the South China Sea," *Contemporary Southeast Asia*, 25, no. 3 (2003), 343–362; and Brantly Womack, "Beyond Win–Win: Rethinking China's International Relationships in an Era of Economic Uncertainty," *International Affairs*, 89, no. 4 (July 2013), 911–928.
97 "China, Philippines, Vietnam Sign Joint South China Sea Oil Search Accord," *Radio Free Asia*, March 14, 2005.
98 M. Taylor Fravel, "Maritime Security in the South China Sea and the Competition Over Maritime Rights," in *Cooperation from Strength: The United States, China and the South China Sea*, ed. Patrick M. Cronin (Washington, DC: Center for a New American Security, January 2012), 39.
99 "Vietnam Boat Sinks After Collision With Chinese Vessel," *BBC News*, May 27, 2014.
100 Shannon Tiezzi, "Vietnam to China: Move Your Oil Rig Out of the South China Sea," *The Diplomat*, April 9, 2016.
101 Michael Green, Kathleen Hicks, Zack Cooper, John Schaus and Jake Douglas, *Countering Coercion in Maritime Asia: The Theory and Practice of Gray Zone Deterrence* (Washington, DC: CSIS, May 2017), 169–201; "China–Philippines navy spat captured on camera," *BBC News*, March 30, 2014.
102 Green, Hicks, Cooper, Schaus, and Douglas, *Countering Coercion in Maritime Asia*, 95–123.

103 Ina Parlina and Haeril Halim, "Govt to Fortify Flashpoint Island," *The Jakarta Post*, June 30, 2015.

104 Steve Mollman, "Indonesia Confirms It Shot at 'Criminal' Chinese Fishing Boats Near Its Natuna Islands," *Quartz*, June 20, 2016.

105 Office of the Secretary of Defense, "Annual Report to Congress: Military and Security Developments Involving the People's Republic of China 2016," April 26, 2016, 13.

106 Office of the Secretary of Defense, "Annual Report to Congress: Military and Security Developments Involving the People's Republic of China 2016," 31.

107 Thomas Gibbons-Neff, "New Satellite Images Show Reinforced Chinese Surface-to-Air Missile Sites Near Disputed Islands," *Washington Post*, February 23, 2017.

108 "Zhongguo jundui shouci yu waijun lianxun: Zhongtai 'tuji-2007'," 中国军队首次与外军联训: 中泰"突击－2007 [The Chinese Military Conducts First Combined Training with a Foreign Military: China-Thai 'Strike 2007'], *Xinhua*, July 16, 2007; "Special Forces Train in China," *The Nation* (Thailand), July 18, 2007. See also "Chinese Army Troops Spring Surprise, Sing Jana Gana," *The Economic Times*, December 6, 2008.

109 "ASEAN, China Agree on Code for Unplanned Encounters in South China Sea," *Xinhua*, September 7, 2016; Prashanth Parameswaran, "China, Singapore to Hold Naval Exercise," *The Diplomat*, September 9, 2016.

110 In an exercise with India, 40 of the 130 PLA participants were officers—whereas the expected number might be five or six. See "India, China Begin Second Leg of Historic Military Exercise," *The Indian* (online), December 6, 2008.

111 Hanban, "Confucius Institute Headquarters," accessed October 14, 2016, http://english.hanban.org/node_10971.htm.

112 "China, Indonesia People-to-People Exchange Mechanism Enhances Mutual Trust, Friendship," *Xinhua*, May 29, 2015.

113 See, for example, James E. Rauch and Vitor Trindade, "Ethnic Chinese Networks in International Trade," *The Review of Economics and Statistics* 84, no. 1 (February 2002): 116–130; Sarah Y. Tong, "Ethnic Chinese Networking in Cross-Border Investment: The Impact of Economic and Institutional Development," University of Hong Kong paper, April 2003.

114 Shi Yinhong, "How to Boost China's Peaceful Rise," *China Daily*, May 18, 2010.

115 Qi Wei, ed., "Dongnanya zai 'yidaiyilu' jianshe zhong jiang fahui zhongyao zuoyong" 东南亚在"一带一路"建设中将发挥重要作用 [Southeast Asia Will Play an Important Role in Building 'One Belt, One Road'], *Jingji cankao* 经济参考 [Economic Information Daily], July 6, 2015. The passages quoted in the text are Zhang Jie's.

116 Zhang Zailin, ed., "Wu Jianmin shu Zhongguo waijiao 60 nian bianhua: taoguang yanghui rengyao guan 100 nian" 吴建民述中国外交60年变化：韬光养晦仍要管100年 [Wu Jianmin Speaks on the Evolution of China's 60 Years of Diplomacy: China Should Continue to "Keep a Low Profile" for Another 100 Years], *China News* 中国新闻网, June 1, 2009.

117 "A Game of Shark and Minnow," *New York Times*, October 27, 2013.

118 During the 2015 election, Duterte stipulated, "We cannot go to war, we cannot fight China." See Allan Nawal, "Buying F-16 Fighter Jets a Mistake, Says Duterte," *Inquirer*, August 14, 2015.

119 Alberto Alesina and Romain Wacziarg, "Openness, Country Size and Government," *Journal of Public Economics* 69 (1998): 305–321.

120 "How China Is Changing Its Manufacturing Strategy."

121 Ronald U. Mendoza, Keven C. Chua and Monica M. Melchor, "Revealed Comparative Advantage, International Production Chain and the Evolving ASEAN–China Trade Linkages," *Journal of Asian Development Studies* 4, no. 1 (March 2015): 23–36.

122 An assessment by the United States International Trade Commission found that TPP would have had different effects on different sectors of the U.S. economy, but the net impact would have been marginal. See U.S. International Trade Commission, *Trans-Pacific Partnership Agreement: Likely Impact on the U.S. Economy and on Specific Industry Sectors* (Washington, DC: U.S. International Trade Commission, 2016).

4

CHINA'S STRATEGY IN CENTRAL ASIA

Raffaello Pantucci and Matthew Oresman

Introduction

In September 2013, new Chinese President Xi Jinping gave a speech at Nazarbayev University, Astana, in which he put forward his vision for a "Silk Road Economic Belt" (SREB). Xi's Astana, Kazakhstan speech presaged his keynote foreign policy concept known as "One Belt, One Road" or OBOR (also known as the Belt and Road Initiative, BRI).[1] The speech came over a decade after China held its first joint military exercise in a generation with Kazakhstan's Central Asian neighbor Kyrgyzstan. Aimed at preparing border forces on both sides to respond to a terrorist insurgency, this event highlighted Central Asia's growing importance to China.[2]

"One Belt, One Road" is an omnidirectional vision of a world interconnected to China through a series of trade and economic corridors emanating out from the Middle Kingdom, with SREB the first route. The subsequent twenty-first-century Maritime Silk Road (paradoxically the "Road" of the "Belt and Road" vision) was an attempt to replicate this model to the seas, while other routes subsumed under this banner—the China–Pakistan Economic Corridor (CPEC), the Bangladesh–China–Myanmar–India (BCIM) corridor, or the China–Mongolia–Russia route—are all strategic trade and economic corridors that had previously been considered in one form or another.[3] The "Belt and Road" vision has provided a broader theme to Xi's foreign policy agenda, and at its core sits the Central Asian "Silk Road Economic Belt." Central Asia has once again become China's foreign policy testing ground.

Historical Overview

China's engagement in Central Asia has been one of the more under-explored and yet intriguing developments since the end of the Cold War. China's interest in building relations with Central Asia dates back to the foundations of the Silk Road. This history includes such revolutionary events as the Battle of Talas in 751, which stopped the greatest expansion of China's borders in its history, and the Chinese conquest of Xinjiang beginning in 1757.[4] During the period of the Great Game between Russia and the United Kingdom, Kashgar, in the far west of the region, became the center of the two powers' regional competition with both capitals directing their intrigue from consulates in the city.[5] Today, both consulates are hotels, a historical curiosity reflecting China's economic re-shaping of the region. The start of Xinjiang's modern history is also the launching point for China's engagement with Central Asia. Beginning in 1949 when the People's Liberation Army (PLA) conquered the region and defined the outline of a modern PRC's borders, it also established the boundaries between China and Central Asia.[6]

During the Cold War, except for efforts to secure the area from Soviet invasion, this border was largely ignored. Beijing sought to assert authority over Xinjiang from afar with the creation of the Xinjiang Production and Construction Corps (XPCC or *Bingtuan*), a paramilitary construction force made up of demobilized soldiers.[7] This militarization of the area was matched on the Soviet side with Moscow fearful of the region becoming the soft underbelly into Russia. During the period of deterioration in relations between China and Russia, the two powers faced off against each other in Central Asia. In Afghanistan, China supported American and Saudi efforts to arm the mujahedeen fighting the Soviet forces, and allowed the U.S. to use listening posts in Xinjiang to eavesdrop on Soviet communications.[8]

After the Cold War, relations improved and China moved quickly to engage the newly created Central Asian powers. The Shanghai Five grouping was established to delineate borders between China and the region—bringing together China, Russia, Kazakhstan, Kyrgyzstan, and Tajikistan.[9] Although largely ignored in the west, this grouping generated a positive "Shanghai Spirit" that was mentioned in news reports at the time. This sentiment, or harmonious interaction and cooperation, as it was characterized, remains the primary sentimental underpinning for China's relations with Central Asia and has had a profound geopolitical effect on a part of the world that Western policymakers have traditionally relegated into the second tier of concerns.

The agility and creativity China has exercised in orchestrating its re-emergence in Central Asia has surprised many observers, but has received little attention in the West. In the wake of the September 11, 2001 attacks, attention towards Central Asia increased sharply. For the United States in particular, Central Asia suddenly became a key point of entry and support for its forces in Afghanistan.[10] Meanwhile, China's relationship with the region evolved with the establishment of the Shanghai Cooperation Organization (SCO), coincidentally the same year.

The SCO's creation was overshadowed by the conflict in Afghanistan, but it marked an important shift in regional relations—for both China and Central Asian nations. For the first time China had created a multilateral security organization; a dramatic new approach for the country. Uzbekistan, traditionally a hesitant participant in any multilateral organizations, joined the SCO, underscoring the new dynamics at play in the region with China's entry.

Since the end of the Cold War, Western attention in Central Asia was largely focused on large energy projects and local security threats. China, for its part, used the Shanghai Five as a venue to delineate and disarm its borders with Russia, Kazakhstan, Kyrgyzstan, and Tajikistan. Then it formed the SCO to deepen multilateral and bilateral economic and security ties, and alleviate Central Asian states' long-standing suspicions about its intentions. By contrast, the United States' attention has come and gone, largely reflecting the degree to which policymakers in Washington prioritize the conflict in Afghanistan. The west's history more generally with the region is one of occasional opportunistic engagement, compared to China's steady rise and Russia's persistent presence.

China's Central Asia Strategy

Objectives

China has four principal sets of strategic and diplomatic objectives that define its actions in Central Asia. First is Xinjiang's domestic development and stability. China wants to help improve the region's economic prospects to help Xinjiang prosper, and prevent Central Asian states from becoming a staging point for Uighur "splittists." Second, China wants to open economic and trade corridors through the region as part of the "Belt and Road" foreign policy vision that Xi Jinping has enunciated. Third is exploiting the abundant regional natural resources to help fuel China's growth. Fourth is to manage other regional powers' presence in the region (e.g., Russia and the United States) and ensure they do not harm China's interests.

These objectives reflect China's historical approach to the region, as well as the increasingly important role Central Asian states play in stabilizing Xinjiang. In July 2009, Xinjiang was wracked with a wave of violence that included a major riot in the capital Urumqi.[11] At least 200 were killed in the most vicious recorded inter-ethnic violence in the region for some time—with the situation escalating to the point that President Hu Jintao had to leave the G8 Summit in L'Aquila, Italy to help manage the situation. This humiliating turn of events re-focused Zhongnanhai's attention towards the region and led to a raft of measures to try to stabilize it. These measures ranged from firing the former provincial leadership and strengthening the security apparatus to a renewed emphasis on economic development and prosperity. The heavy focus on economic development was fundamentally linked to Central Asia. Xinjiang, like the Central Asian states it borders, is landlocked and its development requires access to markets and greater connectivity to the region. For Xinjiang's economy to thrive it not only requires improved internal infrastructure, but also needs accessible markets and a more prosperous and stable neighborhood.

This logic is not new, but it does help explain a fundamental driver of Chinese engagement with Central Asia, one that has intensified apace with separatism in

Xinjiang. In the wake of the violence in 2009, there was a wholesale change of the province's leadership, as well as a push towards greater international engagement by Xinjiang into Central Asia and beyond. The previously moribund Urumqi "Trade Fair" was upgraded to the "China–Eurasia Expo" and promoted by the most senior leadership in China as an opportunity to highlight Urumqi's role as the "gateway to Eurasia."[12] Representatives from most Central Asian countries attended the Expo as they sought to develop trade and economic links into the region. Chinese companies in Xinjiang were actively encouraged to look across the border into Central Asia, and the Xinjiang leadership made regular visits to strengthen ties.

While the fundamental underlying logic of China's economic push into the region is that it will help bring stability, this soft security approach is matched by an equally uncompromising hard security approach. Continually concerned about Uighur or other dissident networks that might organize in unstable spaces across the border to plot attacks in China, Beijing's security leadership has built up a network of contacts regionally to ensure this cannot happen. The primacy of domestic stability and security as a concern when looking towards Xinjiang and its links to Central Asia cannot be underestimated, as a failure in this regard would cut to the very *raison d'être* of the Communist Party leadership and undermine its political legitimacy.

This underlying driver of policy—whereby enhanced trade is used to create economic prosperity and political stability—has become a central part of China's national strategic vision. Captured under the rubric of "One Belt One Road," the first public announcement of this strategic vision was in a speech by Xi Jinping's during a visit to Nazarbayev University, Astana, in September 2013. Xi spoke of the creation of a "Silk Road Economic Belt" through Central Asia that would open up the region and re-create the ancient Silk Road trading routes.[13] The next month, during a speech at the Indonesian Parliament, the president spoke of the twenty-first-century Maritime Silk Road.[14] Subsequently, the two have been merged into the "One Belt and One Road" initiative, which over time was abbreviated into the "Belt and Road," "OBOR," or "BRI." This has since become one of the signature foreign policy concepts advanced by Xi Jinping, and has gradually emerged as the umbrella under which almost every foreign policy relationship is conceived, especially those in China's near abroad.

In May 2013, during a visit to Islamabad, Li Keqiang inked the Memorandum of Understanding that announced the China–Pakistan Economic Corridor (CPEC). Although that announcement came three months prior to Xi's proclamation of the "Silk Road Economic Belt" in Astana, the model that underlies both (and the broader "Belt and Road" vision) is one that builds on the approach that China has been undertaking in Central Asia for the past decade.[15]

The approach was developed and implemented in Central Asia first, but now China pursues a consistent global strategy whereby China uses national policy banks to fund the construction of infrastructure and open markets (also using Chinese firms), and seek to improve stability through prosperity. Consequently, Central Asia can be read as a testing ground or predictor for China's broader global strategy, as well as some of the problems which China is likely to encounter as it continues to expand its approach into other regions of the developing world.

The vision as laid out by Xi Jinping and followed up through various speeches, strategy papers, and statements has a larger significance beyond Central Asia. The "Belt and Road" that runs through Central Asia ultimately leads to Europe. In this way, Central Asia becomes tied into China's broader Eurasian strategy, helping provide the connective tissue that ties China across the continent to European markets.

There is also a larger geopolitical context. Belt and Road projects are being offered in some cases by China as an alternative to the U.S.–led Trans-Pacific Partnership (TPP). China is attempting to construct an integrated regional trading platform that removes barriers, but does not require the national policy sacrifices that are required by TPP. However, it may require certain strategic political commitments to support Chinese interests or help advance Chinese policy goals. Accordingly, many Asian maritime nations had been hedging between TPP and the Maritime Silk Road in an effort to obtain the best of both without fully committing to one world view. Following the Trump administration's withdrawal from TPP, however, it seems increasingly unlikely it will be enacted in the near future. Cash-strapped Central Asian nations, which are not eligible to join TPP, have even fewer alternatives to the Belt and Road.

Ultimately, the size and potential of Central Asian markets are limited. Thus it seems China's larger goal, in addition to the development of Xinjiang, is to improve access to European markets. China seeks to diversify its trade routes and lines of communication to Europe, to avoid relying solely on traditional sea routes. In this way, China's approach to Central Asia is tied to its interests in the Caucasus, Iran, Russia, Turkey, the broader Middle East, and across Europe.

This objective is visible not only in the public declarations by various leaders, but also in the companies, institutions, and approaches on the ground. At a strategic level, Chinese leaders speak of connecting the "Belt and Road" vision with the Kazakh "Nurly Zhol," the Russian Eurasian Economic Union (EEU), and the British "Northern Powerhouse" ideas.[16] And all the partner countries are happy to reciprocate. While these are all distinctive concepts—a Russian-led supranational common customs space, a Kazakh vision for national rejuvenation, and a British strategy for development in the nation's under-developed north—linking them to the "Belt and Road" is useful to Beijing.

Chinese companies that are building projects and connecting infrastructure along OBOR can expand their presence beyond Xinjiang, to Central Asia and Europe. Xinjiang Hualing, for example, a primarily construction and real estate development firm with roots in Xinjiang, has become one of the largest foreign investors in Georgia and has signed contracts worth at least £60 million in the north of the United Kingdom.[17] In 2016, CEFC China Energy Company, a firm with purported links to the People's Liberation Army (PLA) bought half of the Kazakh state-owned energy firm KazMunaiGas (KMG), which has subsidiaries in countries across Eurasia.[18] The same Chinese company has also explored building a hydropower plant in Albania and other deals in the Czech Republic.[19] In 2016,

CEFC's CEO joined President Xi during a visit to Prague to promote the "Belt and Road."[20] A key component of the "Belt and Road" strategy is to help deploy excess Chinese production and construction capacity despite a slowing domestic economy, an objective that is visible through Beijing's corporate diplomacy.

Chinese infrastructure firms generally follow a furrow that has already been ploughed in Central Asia by Chinese energy and mineral companies. Even in the face of a slowing economy, Chinese demand for raw materials from Central Asia continues to grow. From Turkmen gas, to Kazakh oil or copper, to Tajik gold, China continues to see Central Asia's natural resources as important to future economic expansion. As PLA General Liu Yazhou has said, "Central Asia is the thickest piece of cake given to China by the heavens."[21] Indeed, the region remains a largely untapped source of potential future natural resource supplies. With proper infrastructure, resources from Iran, the Caucasus, or Russia could also traverse the region into Xinjiang and help feed China's growth.

China was actually a late participant in the battle for regional energy supplies. Russia has long-standing ties in the region, and in the immediate wake of the Soviet Union's collapse, Western companies gained a foothold, securing access to many of the largest and most accessible fields. Chinese energy firms' access was long relegated to older Soviet fields. While China was able to rapidly build basic infrastructure—like the China–Central Asia pipeline which was constructed in 18 months—it lacked the technical ability to mine new fields.[22] More recently, however, there has been a dramatic shift, with Chinese firms not only winning contracts where others were unable (like Turkmenistan), but also moving into larger consortia led by western energy giants—like Kazakhstan's supergiant "Kashagan."[23] China is building a regional energy infrastructure network that touches on every aspect of regional energy flows. Politically, the objective is to manage other powers' influence in a region, and limit foreign influence in Xinjiang, one of China's most sensitive regions.

China's main tool in regional geopolitical influence is its unrelenting economic drive. Landlocked and surrounded by instability, the Central Asian countries are constantly seeking outside investment and support. Historically, Russia has dominated the region, yet China's expansion into the area has had a transformative economic effect. The Central Asian states are wary of a single power gaining overwhelming presence, and have sought greater external investment from further afield. Unfortunately, interest from outside powers has oscillated wildly, from intense and narrow attention to utter disinterest—a pattern that has taught Central Asian powers to not expect much, and left them with an overbearing Russia and China's ever tightening economic embrace.

From China's perspective, Russia continues to be the main potential geopolitical rival in the region. Concerns that the region could become home to American or western bases that could be used to launch strikes against China or undermine China's stability have largely receded as U.S. interest in the region—as well as its deployment in Afghanistan—has faded. China has increasingly sought to engage with the U.S. in Afghanistan and both the Americans and Europeans have explored cooperation with China in Central Asia.[24] China has also used its influence with the Central Asian states to ensure they do not grant the U.S. privileges that might threaten China's perceived territorial security.

Russia has the potential to de-stabilize the region and undermine Chinese interests; however, the overwhelming force of the global geopolitical alignment between the two powers means that it is unlikely that Moscow will undermine Beijing in Central Asia. Moscow may fear a loss of regional influence to China, but the Russian need for Chinese investment and support in the UN Security Council mean it will prioritize the bilateral relationship over Central Asia. Chinese officials regularly deny that their country's policies undermine Russian influence in Central Asia, and are often in fact keen to illustrate how they always consult with Russian partners when undertaking activity in Central Asia.

Methods

China's objectives in Central Asia are interlinked. The ultimate goal of making its western regions stable and prosperous is tied into a broader vision for reconnecting the Eurasian landmass to China and using Chinese power and influence to implement it. China's efforts to perfect the use of its power and influence in Central Asia provides the underlying logic for the broader "Belt and Road" strategy. Because the "Belt and Road" projects are focused on investment in infrastructure and opening trade corridors and markets, it is easy to gain the support of potential partners. From Beijing's perspective, these projects also use tools that are comprehensible and controllable: liquid capital and state-owned infrastructure and extractive companies. Consequently, the narrative of the "Silk Road Economic Belt" is one of re-building infrastructure, Chinese companies going out to implement large-scale projects and gradually moving into new markets. Chinese companies and nationals are also increasingly finding themselves drawn into regional security questions—in some cases, hard security ones, and in others, local political quagmires. China's methodology in implementing its approach through this space can be broken down into three broad baskets: economic, security, and political.

Economic

The dominant narrative of China in Eurasia is one of economic investment. From a third world power, China has in the past few decades transformed itself into a global economic powerhouse. For Chinese leaders, this prosperity, bringing stability and security at home and abroad, justifies the ruling Communist Party's continuing dominance over the country. As outlined above, one of China's key strategic imperatives in Central Asia is to stabilize Xinjiang and improve its economic situation by developing its foreign markets and regional connectivity. Many of the approaches that are undertaken are similar (or in some cases extensions of) strategies or visions that have already been implemented at home.

Chinese success in these Eurasian investments rests on the use of Chinese development banks to lend large amounts of money to countries to implement projects using Chinese firms. The approach is not new—the approach is one that Korean and Japanese policy banks have long undertaken in Asia and beyond.[25] Chinese policy banks have long been at the forefront of providing linked loans to Central Asian powers to build infrastructure.[26] One difference between older investments and those associated with the "Belt and Road" is the increase in size and scale. A second is that China has added new funding vehicles with the creation of new international financial institutions and new policy banks.

At the core of this new constellation of financial institutions are the Silk Road Fund (SRF) and the Asian Infrastructure Investment Bank (AIIB)—two institutions characterized as "sisters" by Chinese officials but with different interests and approaches. Created in December 2014 (and drawing on funds from the China Development Bank, the Export–Import Bank of China, and other state-owned financial institutions), the Silk Road Fund will be capitalized at $40 billion. The National Development and Reform Commission (NDRC) will oversee its operations.[27] The goal of the fund is to create profitable investments along the "Silk Road" routes. So far, the projects that the SRF has undertaken have been fairly broad in their approach—from investments into Russian energy fields, Italian tire company Pirelli, and a Pakistani hydropower plant. The key determinant of SRF approval appears to be that they are commercially viable.

In contrast, the AIIB has been created in the model of an international financial institution aimed at developing regional infrastructure projects. The AIIB was conceived partly as a response to the slow reform of existing financial institutions like the World Bank or International Monetary Fund, and partly as a response to the perceived dominance in Asia of the Japanese-led Asian Development Bank (ADB). Launched using Chinese seed capital, and drawing on international staff expertise, the AIIB has a very different mandate to the SRF and is focused on building infrastructure across the region.[28] Constrained by a mandate that requires it to place all project calls out to open tender and a still nascent staff capability, the AIIB has so far funded few projects. Thus far, it has bought into pieces of infrastructure projects in Kazakhstan, Tajikistan, Myanmar, Indonesia, and Pakistan, for the most part paying into existing projects rather than creating new ones. Analysts at the bank say that this is to allow the institution to learn how to do projects. It has also undertaken smaller projects by itself in Bangladesh and Indonesia. Its creation was a masterful display of Chinese economic diplomacy and included the recruitment of experts from around the world and the persuasion of numerous Western countries to join—often over the objection of the United States.

These SRF and AIIB join the constellation of pre-existing Chinese policy banks that have been injecting capital into Central Asia for many years. They reflect a Chinese view that financial institutions are important keys to its influence and power in its near neighborhood. Given the shortage of liquid capital in Central Asia, China offers these nations large amounts of financing—often with the stipulation that Chinese firms implement the projects, that goods are sent to China, or that the money is spent in China. When project money is spent in China, it is generally denominated in Renminbi, encouraging the internationalization of the Chinese currency.

An example of Chinese practice is provided by the Kazakh mining firm, Kazakhmys (which changed its name to KAZ Minerals and Kazakhmys Corporation in 2014). The company initially obtained a loan through an inter-governmental agreement from the China Development Bank (CDB) to purchase and develop copper mines in Kazakhstan.[29] After the success of the first deal, the company went back direct to CDB to request a second loan, this time direct from the Bank rather than through an inter-governmental agreement. The deal was focused on purchasing and developing a copper mine near the Kazakh border with China and came in two parts, with $1.34 billion in US dollars and an additional 1 billion in Renminbi (approx. $158 million at contemporary rates). The company guaranteed that at least 50 percent of the material extracted would be sent to China, a promise with limited meaning given 60 percent of the entire firm's output already goes to China.[30] Finally, the firm used Chinese contractors during production, further ensuring China benefitted substantially from the project.

In other contexts, even more specific Chinese contracts have been issued. For example, in Tajikistan, the government received a loan from the China Export–Import Bank to build a system of traffic cameras in the capital. This was finalized with the stipulation that a Chinese company implement the project. Huawei won the contract and Dushanbe now has a sophisticated system of cameras monitoring its traffic. Tajikistan is using the money from fines generated to pay back the loan. This project also demonstrates how China is able to invest in sensitive national infrastructure, something that has raised concerns around the world.

China is also a member of other more aspirational regional policy banks that may ultimately play substantial roles in the region. The BRICS New Development Bank (NDB) emerged from the BRICS international grouping—with China joined by Brazil, Russia, India, and South Africa. All five have purportedly committed funds towards its establishment, aimed at capitalization of $100 billion though so far discussions appear only underway for the first half. A headquarters has been established in Shanghai with an Indian executive in charge. Beyond this, though, it is unclear what additional progress has been made. The Shanghai Cooperation Organization (SCO) Bank, an institution that China has long mooted under the auspices of the SCO, is at an even earlier stage of development and has been held back by others' fears of Chinese dominance.

In addition to funding, Chinese companies are building and implementing a new network of infrastructure and connectivity across the Eurasian landmass. Roads, rail, and port (land and sea) infrastructure is being developed across the region. Chinese companies are not only building roads to link China to the region, but also slowly becoming the most dominant players in Central Asian business more generally.

To focus on a specific sector: energy. Chinese companies are not only active in extracting oil, gas, and uranium, but also in building refineries, helping refurbish aging gas metering systems, re-developing old solar furnaces, building hydropower plants, and exporting wind and solar energy equipment and expertise. At the other end of the Silk Road, China is also pushing a similar strategy of slow expansion in Europe. In less-developed Central and Eastern European countries, China has already been investing on the massive scale familiar to Central Asia. For example, in 2015, the Belarusian government announced a "One Belt, One Road initiative" project to build an entirely new city. If completed, the city would become a hub for connectivity with China.[31] A similar, but more limited project is being undertaken by Xinjiang Hualing Group in Georgia.[32] In Serbia and Albania, Chinese investments are increasingly displacing Russian or European ones as the cheapest and quickest offerings on the table.[33] In the United Kingdom, China is seeking to build new nuclear power plants and invest in the redevelopment of Manchester and Liverpool.[34] In Germany, it is purchasing expertise, and in Scandinavia, Chinese telecom companies are establishing research and development hubs.

Many of China's investments in Central Asia are state-driven and implemented by state-owned enterprises—but private investment is steadily increasing. In some cases those Chinese businessmen and women who began in market stalls of Kara Suu or Barekholka have slowly built local empires.

China's regional trade and investment is driven more by entities in China's western provinces, which have not benefitted as much from China's earlier export boom as those on the coast. For example, in October 2015, the Georgian government co-hosted the first Tbilisi Silk Road Forum, an event that brought together top policymakers from across the Eurasian continent and was ostensibly hosted by both the Georgian and Chinese governments.[35] In reality the Chinese side was represented by the Xinjiang and Shaanxi governments, which both sent senior figures to speak at plenary events. This pattern holds more generally. It is often important to look at the provincial or local level to understand the direction of Chinese planning. While senior central government leadership visits often result in large deals being signed, the practical provisions are hammered out and implemented at a regional level.

Security

Still a hesitant actor in international security affairs, Chinese policy thinking clings rhetorically to the concept of non-interference in the affairs of other countries. In reality, most in Beijing would acknowledge that China shed this approach in practice, though no alternative formulation has yet been fully developed or articulated. Instead, there has been a gradual but noticeable increase in China's security presence and concerns around the world. From needing to evacuate nationals from conflict zones in response to state collapse, to finding nationals kidnapped by groups like ISIS, Boko Haram, or Al Qaeda, to launching increasingly international policing operations, China's security apparatus is slowly being drawn outwards. This comes atop growing assertiveness in its maritime periphery. It is clear that the old logic of avoiding foreign security entanglement no longer holds.

In Central Asia, China's security problems are less pronounced, though as the attack in August 2016 on the Chinese Embassy in Bishkek illustrated, there is a potential for terrorism against Chinese interests in the region. While neighboring Afghanistan continues to be a source of concern and potential instability, the situation in the rest of Central Asia is more stable, though Chinese companies and workers have often found themselves as the targets of local anger. As a result, Chinese security efforts in the region remain fairly limited and focused on a few narrow interests—protecting China from threats that might spill over from Afghanistan, and the protection of nationals and investments from local anger or criminality.

A final concern is that Uighur groups might use safe havens in the region to plot attacks back in China. Beijing seems to have confidently resolved that concern through bilateral engagements and pressure on local authorities to address specific issues. Security Minister Meng Jianzhu makes regular trips through the region to meet with his counterparts, and security officials in all Central Asian countries (including Afghanistan) highlight instances of direct support for China's anti-separatist efforts. This support sometimes runs against the sentiments and interests of native Uighur populations in Central Asia. In Kazakhstan and possibly elsewhere, Chinese authorities have reportedly pressured Uighur diaspora communities to report on anti-Chinese activity. Through intensive regional diplomacy, China has successfully choked off Central Asia as a route for dissatisfied Uighurs fleeing China to Turkey. The largest ex-flow of Uighurs recently appears to flow through Southeast Asia rather than Central Asia, notwithstanding the ethnic proximity Uighurs enjoy to other regional Turkic peoples of Central Asia.[36]

In terms of external threats, the focus for China (as well as most in the region) is the potential for threats from unstable Afghanistan to spill over into Central Asia. China has played a variety of roles in trying to mitigate this threat. It has played an increasingly influential role within Afghanistan, contributing to the establishment of the Quadrilateral Contact Group (QCG) with the United States, Pakistan, and Afghanistan to try to bring peace to the country.[37] China has also sought to bolster the border capabilities of the countries it has identified as weakest—Kyrgyzstan and Tajikistan—providing them with uniforms, barracks, communications equipment, and other support, as well as undertaking bilateral training exercises focused mostly on counter-terrorism and border security questions.[38] Beijing's military relations with Kazakhstan, Uzbekistan, and Turkmenistan consist largely of military sales, with China making inroads into a market that Russia previously dominated.

Within Central Asia, China's security concerns (outside of Uighur groups plotting attacks within China) are that general instability, criminal and narcotics trafficking groups, Islamic extremists, or separatists might adversely affect Chinese projects in the region or might somehow migrate to China. Beijing's main approach to these complex problems beyond bilateral and multilateral regional security cooperation is to invest heavily in the region on the understanding that economic development may indirectly mitigate instability and criminality. However, the large-scale investments undertaken through policy banks and state-owned firms are government-to-government projects from which locals will see little benefit (aside from the resulting infrastructure). Chinese workers are often brought in to build the projects, reducing local content. Not unaware of these problems, China has explored ways in which local benefit can be enhanced—for example, through the development of special economic zones or local industrial parks that might host Chinese companies that have been priced out of China. While the effectiveness of these projects is questionable, China is attempting to address some of the local pushback through softer approaches of offering scholarships to help train locals to manage such sites, encouraging Chinese firms to move operations, and encouraging direct twinning between regions and SEZs in Central Asia.

Political

The Shanghai Cooperation Organization (SCO), a multilateral organization founded in 2001 with all the Central Asian powers except Turkmenistan, is a key fixture in China's political approach to the region.[39] Indeed, despite its original mandate as a security organization, it has so far proven to be more of a political player than security or economic actor. While the SCO provides the auspices under which the Central Asian powers hold regular security training missions with their Chinese counterparts, there has been little evidence so far that these large multilateral "peace missions" have provided any direct security support or helped mitigate the security threats that the Central Asian states see from Afghanistan or elsewhere in the region. Similarly, efforts to use the SCO to facilitate regional economic integration and investment have stumbled, with most Chinese investment in the region being handled bilaterally. SCO channels have been limited to technical exchanges and coordination.

China's "win–win" rhetoric on the SCO reflects the approach that it continues to take with the region and the world. Whilst the SCO first provided China with multilateral cover to engage with Central Asia without arousing suspicion, China did not exclusively keep its relations within this context. It has continued to push its regional relations equally strongly at the bilateral level (a topic discussed further in the next section). The SCO became whatever its members needed it to be—with China continuing to pursue the idea of a Free Trade Area or Development Bank through the organization, while Russia has instead floated an SCO University and pushed for an expansion of SCO membership in an effort to dilute China's influence.

China has also at various moments sought to engage other Central Asian multilateral entities. For example, China has championed the long-standing but largely overlooked Conference on Interaction and Confidence-Building Measures in Asia (CICA). Similarly, China has supported the "Heart of Asia" or "Istanbul Process" around Afghanistan. However, none of this has become a substitute for bilateral engagement with each country in Central Asia.

China's political engagement captures the basic essence of Chinese larger approach to foreign policy, pushing forwards on every level and in every direction. Until it encounters pushback, China will continue to bulldoze forwards, and when it does find resistance, it will deploy wide-ranging tools of engagement that will, more often than not, deliver what China wants.

TABLE 4.1 Country Profile of Central Asian Nations, 2017

	Population (million)	GDP (billion)	Size (Km²)
Kazakhstan	18.6	$451.2	2,724,900
Uzbekistan	29.8	$205.6	447,400
Kyrgyzstan	5.8	$21.5	199,951
Tajikistan	8.5	$26	144,100
Turkmenistan	5.4	$95.5	488,100

Source: Central Intelligence Agency, The World Factbook.

Regional Perspectives

It is important to note that the Central Asian states each have a different relationship with China, though the broad thrust from Beijing's perspective is often similar. Each pursues its own interests through independent foreign policies that often include engagement with Russia, the United States, India, Turkey, and others to prevent dominance by one state. This section will briefly touch upon each country in turn to highlight the key pressure points with each one that China faces and the nature of their perspective on China.

Kazakhstan

Kazakhstan is central to China's relationship with Central Asia. The largest and wealthiest regional power, it shares the longest border with China. China has found it relatively easy to achieve its goals in the country, and the Kazakh leadership has also benefitted from the relationship. Kazakhstan has attracted the largest share of regional Chinese investment. The Kazak story is a microcosm of China's larger regional diplomacy—from large-scale investment in infrastructure and energy, to shuttle trade (i.e., small scale import/export), to sensitive political negotiations over Kazakhstan's relationship with and treatment of dissident Uighur communities. For example, China's state-owned Sinopec energy company was given approval by the Kazakh government to purchase Lukoil's stake in a major Kazakh energy producer for nearly $1.1 billion, reflecting China's deep investment in Kazakhstan and Kazakhstan's constant rebalancing between China and Russia.

At the same time, Kazakhstan has also been a forerunner of problems that China is encountering elsewhere. Anti-Chinese sentiment has affected investment in some cases. The efforts of Chinese agricultural firms to secure long-term land leases have sparked large-scale protests.[40] In 2009, protests against a land deal with China forced the government to back away from the proposal.[41] Protests also erupted after legislation was passed allowing foreign ownership of land. And Chinese businessmen and companies often encounter difficulties in securing visas.

In part, these protests are a reflection on other local tensions. Chinese deals provide a pretext and cover for locals to express dissatisfaction with Kazakh authorities without directly attacking the state. But in some cases, the anger seems focused on the overwhelming and overbearing nature of Chinese investment, as well as the treatment of workers employed by Chinese firms. The net result is occasional dissonance between the government's eagerness to do business with China and the local population's unwillingness to accept the Chinese presence. This complicated balance plays against an increasingly close Kazakh economic relationship with Russia, as well as fears of Russian meddling in domestic politics.

From a Kazakh perspective, the economic future of the country is inevitably tied to China, but it is unclear how it will balance its relationship with Beijing and that with other powers.

Uzbekistan

Uzbekistan is Central Asia's most populous and industrialized country, and China sees potential economic opportunities in deepening ties with it. But as with all other players in Uzbekistan, Chinese companies have encountered difficulties in moving into the market. With tight currency controls and an investment climate that favors players with senior official connections, Uzbekistan remains one of the most insulated regional economies. Nevertheless, there has been a gradual increase in Chinese investment into the country and a commensurate growth in Chinese presence. Uzbek leaders see China as a good partner, and Chinese companies have sought to operate in ways acceptable to Uzbek authorities, a change that might accelerate now that the country has new leadership.

For example, Chinese telecoms firms Huawei and ZTE have both opened manufacturing plants to assemble products which they then sell on the local market.[42] The Uzbek government actively encourages this approach, though most other external investors, concerned about the eventual repatriation of profits, avoid it. Hence, while others shun the market, China is a growing presence there. Although Uzbekistan has been reticent to participate in multilateral initiatives, Chinese engagement has won Tashkent's participation in the SCO. Uzbek leaders are still keener to engage with South Korea than China, but Beijing is also seen an acceptable partner.

With the death of Uzbekistan's long-serving President Islam Karimov, there is clear change happening in Uzbekistan under new President Shavkat Mirziyoyev. Some rebalancing is already taking place, with the new regime focusing its efforts on strengthening its relationships across Central Asia and reassessing its relationships with China, Russia, Iran, and the United States. Renewed Uzbek–Russian engagement has been observed, and a promising, though small, degree of economic liberalization has also begun. Mirziyoyev made a visit to Beijing after Moscow, something that reflects the new leadership's eagerness to maintain a balance of relations between the two powers.

Kyrgyzstan

Of all the Central Asian states, Kyrgyzstan has the highest degree of economic dependence on China. China is building or improving refineries, roads, rail, airports, and mines. Nevertheless, Chinese officials complain regularly about the problems their nationals face in the country. For largely historical, political, and ethnographic reasons, Moscow remains the most significant outside partner—every new Kyrgyz leader makes Moscow their first port of call after election. But Beijing is the most significant player on the ground, and Kyrgyz officials have repeatedly proven acquiescent in the face of Chinese political demands, such as cracking down on Falun Gong protests and banning any Taiwanese nationals or investments in the country.

There is a major asymmetry in economic relations between Kyrgyzstan and China. Kyrgyzstan remains a relatively minor part of the bigger "Silk Road Economic Belt" picture, but the potential investment and financing from it is hugely important to Bishkek. When Bishkek considered joining the Eurasian Economic Union (EEU), many Kyrgyz businessmen were concerned that the heightened tariffs the country would have to impose on imports would negatively affect its critically important import–export business with China. For Beijing, the matter was seen as unimportant, given the small trade flows as a proportion of China's overall global trade. Given the asymmetry in interests, Kyrgyzstan has proven repeatedly willing to bend to Chinese political demands. Because Russian trade and investment cannot replace Chinese, the country has no other options, though Kyrgyz politicians also understand they cannot ignore—indeed must prioritize—the political relationship with Moscow.

Finally, many in Beijing view political instability in Kyrgyzstan, especially during elections, as a negative example. The chaos and instability attending political transitions there are viewed in contrast to the clean transition experienced in Turkmenistan or more recently in Uzbekistan. Occasionally, disorder directly affects Chinese interests. In August 2016, terrorists, including at least one Uighur, attacked the Chinese embassy in Bishkek, killing three (mostly attackers). This incident, while diminishing Beijing's faith in the relationship, will likely lead to a redoubling of bilateral security engagement so that China can feel comfortable that its vital interests are being appropriately guarded.

Tajikistan

The Tajik government is almost completely reliant on aid and remittances and, as with other major investors, will do whatever it needs to guarantee investment. China has undertaken a number of prominent construction projects in Dushanbe and has pursued gold and energy concessions. But much of China's investment into Tajikistan has come in the form of linked loans, and it remains unclear whether and how much Tajikistan will be able to repay. This dependency may make Tajikistan particularly susceptible to Chinese political pressure.

So far, however, there has been little evidence of Chinese assertiveness vis-à-vis Tajikistan. For Beijing, the country is seen primarily as a route to other markets and as a potential security problem. Although Chinese analysts see Tajikistan's security as predominantly a Russian problem, there has been an uptick in attention by China. China has increased its security support for the country, providing barracks, uniforms, and non-lethal equipment, as well as conducting joint training missions to strengthen border forces' capabilities. In addition, Beijing has brought the country into a new High-Level Military Leader Meeting on Quadrilateral Cooperation and Coordination Mechanism in Counter Terrorism by Afghanistan–Pakistan–Tajikistan–China, inaugurated in August 2016.[43]

There is some question about the degree to which Tajik leaders have personally benefitted from Chinese investment, especially in the case of large infrastructure projects, such as the Dushanbe–Khujand road (the only pay road in the region) or Chinese investment in the Talco aluminum factory.[44] The population has a relatively benign view of China, though stories circulate about Chinese workers taking local jobs and women while Tajik men are in working as migrants in Russia or Kazakhstan. In 2011, when the government accepted a Chinese a land loan deal, both the Tajik and Chinese governments blocked coverage of the story that might have fed local concerns about China taking Tajik territory.

Turkmenistan

China's relationship with Turkmenistan revolves largely around energy. Chinese national energy companies are among the few foreign firms that Turkmenistan permits to undertake onshore work in the country. CNPC has developed Turkmen onshore capacity and built infrastructure to support Turkmenistan's exports to China. Because of cancellations and contract disputes affecting export deals with Russia and Iran, Turkmenistan sees China as a crucial economic partner, and Turkmenistan has quickly become one of China's biggest natural gas suppliers.

This does not mean that there are not underlying tensions within the relationship. Restrictions have reportedly been placed on Chinese energy workers after some were alleged to have used local prostitutes. The recent slowdown in domestic Chinese demand for gas has obviated the need for some of the gas pipeline links back to China. This has led to some concerns in Ashgabat about over-dependence on a single customer, and encouraged the leadership to invigorate the long moribund Turkmenistan–Afghanistan–Pakistan–India Pipeline (TAPI) to demonstrate they have alternatives.

It is difficult to discern the degree to which recent issues have affected the overall relationship. Chinese experts express the same concerns about operating in Turkmenistan as most other foreigners there do. And, in fact, while China clearly has a greater level of contact and entry into the country, it is not always clear whether its firms are treated differently than others. As the biggest contributor to the national budget, Beijing ostensibly has a greater leverage. But China is almost solely engaged in energy, while other nations' presence is more diversified. Also, Ashgabat is keen to develop energy relations with other countries. All these factors serve to highlight Turkmenistan's hesitations about being beholden to a single partner.

Implications for the United States and European Union

U.S. influence in the region has reduced dramatically over the last decade. U.S. activity in the region is generally ad hoc and driven by core U.S. interests or a desire by some Central Asian leaders to demonstrate to Russia or China that they have alternative partners. The United States does little to contribute to economic development in the region beyond the energy sector, and has largely abdicated any vision for the region's economic future to China and the various development banks and IFIs. The poor human rights and governance records of many of the governments in the region—something that is not an obstacle for Chinese engagement—further deters closer involvement by Washington.

The United States has launched different efforts to engage the region. The Obama administration first launched the "New Silk Road" project, but that stumbled over a lack of real resources and political commitment. It was too focused on Afghanistan and failed to integrate Iran, China, and Russia into the vision in a realistic way. Failure was exacerbated by sanctions against Iran that continued to place a substantial burden on American companies even after the relaxation of sanctions under the Joint Comprehensive Plan of Action (JCPOA). The "New Silk Road" failed to understand regional dynamics and did not offer long-lasting support for reform efforts.

Today, the United States is pursuing a more limited engagement strategy with the Central Asian governments, focused principally on counter-terrorism cooperation and potentially Afghanistan once again. Outside of another security crisis, there is little that would change the U.S. approach to the region. The calculation seems to be that organic regional development driven by large Chinese and IFI investment could improve regional stability in a more sustained way than episodic U.S. engagement. In other words, many U.S. interests may be served by China's ability to drive regional integration, stability, and economic growth. However, this also means that the United States is increasingly losing its leverage to directly drive the regional agenda, especially compared to China and Russia.

The European Union has suffered from a similar set of problems in the region, though its impetus for engagement was not driven by the conflict in Afghanistan. European interest was instead dictated by member state capitals. The members' varying interests in Central Asia result in occasionally drastic oscillation in strategy. In the wake of the Lisbon treaty and an effort by the EU to strengthen its foreign policy identity, a series of prominent policy documents identified the region as a foreign policy priority. They also laid out a strategy for engagement and regional development, working through institutional structures that support local capacity in a manner that is seen as positive from the ground. Nevertheless, it is not clear that the EU has truly found its way in the region. The level of interest seems to vary depending on which member state has the Presidency, with some members (like Germany or Latvia) focusing attention on the region and others largely oblivious to it.

Central Asian leaders are not unaware of the inconsistencies in EU approach and tend to look at the EU as a secondary player, notwithstanding the fact that it one of the region's largest external trading partners (and Kazakhstan's largest). But the EU has capitalized on the fact that China sees Central Asia as a byway to Europe and on China's belief that European powers understand regional dynamics. European diplomats frequently complain about the difficulties they have engaging with China, but highlight that Central Asia is an area where they find constructive discussion with Chinese counterparts. Be it in terms of undertaking joint projects, or simply learning from each other's experiences, there is a confluence of Chinese and EU interests in Central Asia. In contrast to the United States' more security-oriented history in the region (and sometimes fraught relationship with both China and Russia), the EU engages largely as an aid and investment partner, areas that do not cause as much tension.

This is not to say that there are no openings or success stories for the United States in Central Asia. The State Department has engaged China's Ministry of Foreign Affairs on possible joint projects and efforts. Beijing has approached Washington about connecting on the broader "Belt and Road" initiative, and USAID has undertaken projects in Pakistan along the route of the China Pakistan Economic Corridor (CPEC), despite reticence in Washington about whether the broader "Belt and Road" lacks substance.[45]

The clearest and most positive engagement has been in adjacent Afghanistan, where China and the United States play roles as equal partners in the Beijing instigated Quadrilateral Coordination Group (QCG). QCG is intended to bring Afghan and Pakistani officials together as a prelude to a broader engagement on a peace process in Afghanistan.[46] Beijing and Washington have undertaken joint training programs for Afghan diplomats and other officials. Germany has established a joint training program for mining officials, while the UK is exploring various options for cooperative efforts with China in Afghanistan. This close engagement suggests that, at least in this region, the possibility exists for a relationship that is complementary rather than competitive. Of course, it is possible that this is simply a product of the fact that China is so clearly the more dominant regional actor and the United States has historically played a disinterested role. But there remains a keen desire by Central Asian powers to build strong relations with Washington, in part to balance their relations with Beijing.

Conclusion: Looking Forward

When the earlier chapter was published in this volume ten years ago, it appeared that the United States, Russia, and China were possibly on a collision course in Central Asia or that the three might find a new mechanism for cooperation as they sought to jointly address the security challenges posed in Afghanistan and from the rise of global Islamic terrorism. However, ten years later, the story is quite different.

The U.S.–Central Asia relationship is now a marriage of convenience, activated when specific needs arise. The Central Asian governments have learned that they cannot count on the United States to be a consistent partner in supporting their development. The United States remains heavily engaged in Afghanistan for strategic security reasons, but a lack of broader U.S. interest in Central Asia means that this has not translated into much direct activity in the rest of Central Asia. While the region is unlikely to be an area of competition between the United States and

China, the United States has missed opportunities to engage more attentively and coherently in the region, especially with regimes that are keen to reduce dependence on China and Russia. The U.S. absence will further encourage current autocratic regimes to shun genuine reform.

The China–Russia relationship has flipped in the last decade, with China increasingly becoming the senior partner. To be sure, Russia has not abandoned its core interests in Central Asia, but there is little Russia can do to block China's growing role. The Eurasian Economic Union (EEU) is in many ways a last roll of the dice by Moscow to see if it can secure more than just a historical legacy in the region and build a mechanism for long-term dominant influence. But so far, success seems doubtful, with Kazakhstan expressing concern about declining EEU trade in the wake of collapsing commodities in 2015, and trade figures amongst EEU countries actually going down since the establishment of the entity. In the longer term, the EEU will provide Russia a tool to shape and grow economic exchange with Central Asia, but Moscow lacks China's financial resources and will not be able to compete in regional investment. China, for its part, treats Russia with respect, trying not to embarrass Moscow in the face of its declining empire—but it also will not be deterred by Russia from expanding its regional role or presence.

In the last ten years, China has achieved its primary goals in the region. It has turned a region where security and boundary issues originally drove engagement into a successful laboratory for regional initiative and integration. China has used Central Asia as a launching pad to expand its influence in a huge swathe of territory from Bishkek to Brussels. Not only has China effectively created a security barrier that helps it maintain stability in Xinjiang, but it has also created multiple new channels by which China can achieve broader security, economic, and political goals.

Looking ahead, China is likely to find the next phase of regional engagement more complicated than the last. As it ascends to become the most consequential regional actor, it will increasingly find itself being dragged into regional entanglements and playing roles that previously had belonged to the United States or Russia. Beijing's principle of non-interference will become increasingly untenable as it finds itself having to protect its interests on the ground and arbitrate regional disputes. This is already happening to some degree in Pakistan. Central Asia will remain a testing ground for China's new foreign and security policy approaches, and will offer a glimpse of China's future power projection.

Notes

1 "President Xi Jinping Delivers Important Speech and Proposes to Build a Silk Road Economic Belt with Central Asian Countries," Ministry of Foreign Affairs of the People's Republic of China (hereinafter referred to as FMPRC website), September 7, 2013.
2 Bates Gill and Matthew Oresman, *China's New Journey to the West: China's Emergence in Central Asia and Implications for US Interests* (Washington, DC: Center for Strategic & International Studies, 2003), 25.

3 "Vision and Actions on Jointly Building Silk Road Economic Belt and 21st-Century Maritime Silk Road," National Development and Reform Commission of the People's Republic of China, March 28, 2015.
4 Joshua Eisenman, Eric Heginbotham, and Derek Mitchell, *China and the Developing World—Beijing's Strategy for the Twenty-First Century* (New York: Routledge, 2015), 60.
5 Raffaello Pantucci, "China and Russia's Soft Competition in Central Asia," *Current History* 114 (2015): 272–277.
6 James Zheng Gao, *Historical Dictionary of Modern China (1800–1949)* (Lanham, MD: Scarecrow Press, 2009), 54.
7 "Establishment, Development and Role of the Xinjiang Production and Construction Corps," *China.org.cn*, May 26, 2003.
8 Antonio Giustozzi, "War, Politics and Society in Afghanistan 1978–1992," (PhD dissertation, London School of Economics and Political Science, University of London, 1997).
9 James A. Millward, *Eurasian Crossroads: A History of Xinjiang* (New York: Columbia University Press, 2007), 336.
10 Svante E. Cornell, "The United States and Central Asia: In the Steppes to Stay?" *Cambridge Review of International Affairs* 17 (2004): 12.
11 Tania Branigan, "Han Chinese Launch Revenge Attacks on Uighur Property," *The Guardian*, July 7, 2009.
12 "China-Eurasia Expo, Urumq," British Chamber of Commerce in China, September 2013.
13 "President Xi Jinping," FMPRC website.
14 "Speech by Chinese President Xi Jinping to Indonesian Parliament," ASEAN-China Centre, October 3, 2014.
15 "China and Pakistan," FMPRC website.
16 Mathieu Duchatel et al., "Eurasian integration: Caught Between Russia and China," European Council on Foreign Relations, June 7, 2016. Also see Richard Holmes, "President Xi Jinping's UK Visit: How Britain Can Truly Become China's Best Partner in the West," *City A.M.*, October 20, 2015.
17 "Hualing Group," *Invest in Georgia*, March 4, 2015.
18 Chen Aizhu, "China's CEFC to Take Control of Unit of Kazakh State-Run Oil Firm," *Reuters*, December 15, 2015.
19 "Eximbank Finances Albanian Hydropower Project," *People's Daily*, February 9, 2001.
20 "Spotlight: China, Czech Republic Set Example for Broader Region to Advance Belt and Road Initiative," *Xinhua*, May 5, 2016.
21 Tao Xie, "How China rediscovered Central Asia," *China in Central Asia*, November 16, 2015.
22 Jack Farchy, "China Seeking to Revive the Silk Road," *Financial Times*, May 9, 2016.
23 Selina Williams, Geraldine Amiel, and Justin Scheck, "How a Giant Kazakh Oil Project Went Awry," *Wall Street Journal*, March 31, 2014.
24 Elizabeth Wishnick, *Russia, China, and the United States in Central Asia: Prospects for Great Power Competition and Cooperation in the Shadow of the Georgian Crisis* (Carlisle Barracks, PA: Strategic Studies Institute, 2009), 2.
25 Phillip Orchard, "China and Japan Compete for Southeast Asia's Railways," *Stratfor*, May 4, 2016.
26 Vladimir Odintsov, "China's Strategic Presence in Central Asia," *New Eastern Outlook*, March 24, 2016.
27 Thomas Zimmerman, "The New Silk Roads: China, the U.S., and the Future of Central Asia," New York University Center on International Cooperation, October 2015, 48.
28 "Reversion to the Mean," *Economist*, September 26, 2015.
29 "Aktogay Copper Mine Development in Kazakhstan," *Mining-technology*, December 2015.
30 "Kazakhmys PLC Announces $1.5 Billion Loan Facility to Fund Aktogay Project," *Kazakhmys*, December 16, 2011.
31 Fu Jing, "China Helps Build Belarus Boomtown," *China Daily*, May 15, 2015.
32 Wade Shepard, "Why Is China Building A New City in Georgia?" *Forbes*, August 21, 2016.

33 Oleg Levitin, Jakov Milatovic and Peter Sanfey, "China and South-Eastern Europe: Infra-structure, Trade and Investment Links," European Bank for Reconstruction and Development, March 10, 2016.

34 Hazel Sheffield, "China State Visit: 9 UK Projects the Government Wants to Sell to the Chinese After Hinkley," *Independent*, October 19, 2015.

35 Raffaello Pantucci and Sarah Lain, "Tbilisi Silk Road Forum: Next Steps for Georgia and the Silk Road," *RUSI Publications*, August 2, 2016.

36 Kendrick Kuo and Kyle Springer, "Illegal Uighur Immigration in Southeast Asia," Center for Strategic & International Studies, April 24, 2014.

37 Halimullah Kousary, "The Afghan Peace Talks, QCG and China-Pakistan Role," *The Diplomat*, July 8, 2016.

38 Dmitry Gorenburg, "External Support for Central Asian Military and Security Forces," Stockholm International Peace Research Institute Working Paper, January 2014.

39 Siyao Li, "The New Silk Road: Assessing Prospects for 'Win–Win' Cooperation in Central Asia," *Cornell International Affairs Review* 9 (2016): 5.

40 Casey Michel, "Kazakhstan's Unprecedented Land Protests Only the First Wave of Discontent?" *World Politics Review*, May 19, 2016.

41 Naubet Bisenov, "Kazakh Authorities Resort to Force to Defuse Land Protests," *Intelli News*, May 24, 2016.

42 "The Company that Spooked the World," *Economist*, August 4, 2012.

43 Zhang Tao, "Fang Fenghui Meets With Pakistani Army Chief of Staff," *China Military Online*, May 18, 2015.

44 Farangis Najibullah, "Tajikistan's Transportation Challenge: Ending Dependency On Uzbek Transit Routes," *Eurasia Daily Monitor* 8 (2011).

45 Patrick Mendis and Dániel Balázs, "When the TPP and One Belt, One Road Meet," *East Asia Forum*, April 26, 2016.

46 "The Fifth Meeting of the Quadrilateral Coordination Group (QCG) of Afghanistan, Pakistan, the United States and China," *Pajhwok Afghan News*, May 18, 2016.

5

CHINA'S STRATEGY IN SOUTH ASIA

Jeff M. Smith

Introduction

South Asia is adjoined to China by thousands of miles of shared border, yet separated from the Chinese civilization by the world's most foreboding mountain range. For China, South Asia is both an intimate neighbor and a distant, foreign land. Beyond East Asia, arguably no other region has been more consequential to contemporary Chinese foreign policy than South Asia.[1] During the latter half of the twentieth century, China's engagement with South Asia was framed by its robust strategic partnership with Pakistan and its unspoken rivalry with India, including a shadow competition with Delhi for influence among the smaller states of the region. In the twenty-first century, those trends have endured, evolved, and accelerated. Today South Asia stands at the frontline of a westward expansion of Chinese influence and interests, and at the cross-section of Beijing's counterterrorism strategy, its quest for energy security, its One Belt One Road (OBOR) initiative, its focus on protecting Sea Lines of Communication (SLOCs) and "overseas interests," and its complex relationships with India and Pakistan.

Historical Overview

China–India

Contemporary Sino–Indian relations are profoundly influenced by the war fought over their disputed border in 1962. In many corners of India, the scars from China's month-long invasion have yet to heal, coloring popular perceptions of China with a mix of suspicion, mistrust, and anxiety. After restoring diplomatic relations in 1976, Delhi and Beijing began negotiations on their disputed border in 1981, now the "longest continuing frontier talks between any two countries since the end of the Second World War."[2] In the late 1980s India agreed to de-link progress in bilateral relations from negotiations on the border dispute and the two have since expanded their diplomatic and economic engagement.

Bilateral trade has swelled from $2 billion in 2000 to over $71 billion in 2016. The two countries now conduct some thirty-six annual dialogues and began a program of joint military exercises in 2007. Beijing and Delhi have coordinated strategies on world trade talks, climate change negotiations, and the need to reform global governance institutions, yet convergence on multilateral issues has weakened during the tenures of Xi Jinping and Narendra Modi. Deeper economic and political engagement has diminished neither the legacy of mistrust nor a growing conflict of interests as the two rising powers increasingly see their spheres of interest and influence overlap.

China–Pakistan

China's intimate relationship with Pakistan was long viewed as a byproduct of its longstanding rivalry with India, yet Beijing's ties with the two capitals once looked radically different. The 1950s represented the golden age of China–India relations, while China–Pakistan relations were tainted with acrimony.[3] Both relationships were transformed by the 1962 China–India border war. One year later, Pakistan ceded much of the 5,800-kilometer Shaksgam Valley in Kashmir to Beijing in an agreement Delhi has never recognized. In the early 1970s, Pakistan facilitated a historic rapprochement between the U.S. and China and in the decades to follow Chinese economic and military patronage to Pakistan surged. It's widely believed Chinese nuclear assistance was critical in Pakistan's development of a nuclear weapons capability in the early 1990s.

Today strategic calculations about India still motivate China's relationship with Pakistan but the country has assumed independent significance for multiple Chinese foreign policy objectives: as a conduit to containing Islamist militancy in Xinjiang; as a proxy for defending and promoting Chinese interests in Afghanistan; as a friendly naval outpost in the Indian Ocean; as a source of arms sales and co-production; and as an economic corridor connecting western China to the Indian Ocean.

China and the Rest

Throughout the twentieth century, China repeatedly sought to establish stronger political, military, and economic ties with the smaller powers of South Asia. With few exceptions, those efforts were repeatedly thwarted by India. Yet, three complementary trends beginning in the 1990s opened the door to a major expansion of Chinese influence.

First, India began to take a less invasive, more conciliatory approach to relations with its neighborhood, symbolized by the "Gujral Doctrine."[4] Second, seeking to diminish India's longstanding monopoly of influence, regional capitals began seeking to diversify their economic and security relationships. It's often said China has engaged the smaller nations of South Asia to "contain" India. Yet it's just as true that South Asian capitals have courted China to "balance" against Indian power. Finally, as China galloped into the twenty-first century atop double-digit economic growth, its expanding sphere of power and influence produced a more focused, ambitious, and well-resourced South Asian strategy.

China's Objectives in South Asia

In each South Asian capital, China and Chinese actors have numerous and at times even competing objectives. Nevertheless, we can identify and categorize China's region-wide strategic objectives topically to include: *territorial integrity*; *stability in Tibet*; *maintaining "strategic balance" between China and India*; *counterterrorism*; and *energy security and military power projection*.

Territorial Integrity

China has successfully negotiated a resolution to more than two-thirds of its 23 territorial disputes, including every land border except India and Bhutan.[5] Although China and Bhutan do not maintain formal diplomatic relations, they began negotiations on their disputed, un-demarcated 470-kilometer border in 1974.[6] India has effectively controlled Bhutan's foreign and security policy since a Treaty of Friendship was signed in 1949 and conducted border negotiations on Bhutan's behalf before Thimphu began direct talks with Beijing in 1989.[7]

China claims roughly 750 square kilometers south of the de-facto border, including Jarkarlung and Pasamlung in north-central Bhutan, and the Doklam plateau in the west. The latter is the most strategically sensitive area under dispute, and the source of the most interest and anxiety in India. That's because the Doklam plateau lies adjacent to India's "Chicken's Neck," a narrow, strategically vulnerable land bridge connecting the bulk of India to its isolated northeastern provinces.[8]

In the mid-1990s China offered Bhutan a "package deal" whereby it would renounce its claim to Jarkarlung and Pasamlung in exchange for control of the Doklam plateau. Bhutan demurred and the deal has ostensibly been on offer ever since. In 2012 China again offered to settle the border dispute if Bhutan would establish full diplomatic relations and again the proposal was rejected.

In June 2017, PLA construction crews were spotted extending a road southward in the disputed Doklam area near the India–China–Bhutan tri-border and were confronted by the Bhutanese military. The PLA failed to withdraw, and within 48 hours Indian military forces from nearby Sikkim intervened on Bhutan's behalf. Over one hundred soldiers from each side joined the months-long standoff that followed, which witnessed unusually sharp rhetoric and threats from Chinese diplomats as well as both official and unofficial media outlets.[9] In late August, India and China reached terms on a mutual "disengagement," albeit not a complete withdrawal, officially ending the longest and most volatile standoff between Chinese and Indian border forces in decades.

When India and China assumed their contemporary forms in 1947 and 1949, respectively, they inherited competing claims to an unsettled and un-demarcated border. Cordial negotiations on the dispute began in the 1950s, yet proved short-lived as Beijing confronted an ethnic insurgency in Tibet that intensified in the latter half of the decade.

Beijing accused India of providing moral and material support to Tibetan forces and its position on the border dispute hardened. Negotiations descended into acrimony as the Indian and Chinese militaries grew more adventurous patrolling the unmarked border. The game of brinksmanship devolved into armed clashes in 1959 and eventually a Chinese invasion three years later.

During the war, China assumed control over the largely ungoverned 36,000 square kilometer area of Aksai Chin adjacent to Kashmir—the "Western Sector." In the "Eastern Sector," along India's northeastern border with Tibet, Chinese forces withdrew behind the Indian-claimed "McMahon Line" after considerable advances.

Beijing still claims up to 90,000 square kilometers south of the McMahon Line in India's Arunachal Pradesh, or what China refers to a "South Tibet." In the relatively less-contentious "Middle Sector" smaller patches of territory are claimed by both countries where Tibet meets the Indian province of Uttarakhand.

Begun in 1981, Sino–Indian border talks have produced an elaborate framework to peacefully manage the dispute. Unlike the volatile India–Pakistan Line of Control (LOC) in Kashmir, there has not been a deadly exchange of fire at the China–India Line of Actual Control (LAC) in decades. Yet, while free from violence, volatile stand-offs between Chinese and Indian patrols at the LAC often disrupt bilateral relations at critical junctures. India reports several hundred LAC "transgressions" by Chinese forces annually, most of which occur in the Western Sector along the roughly one dozen stretches where there is no mutual agreement on the location of the LAC.

On multiple occasions between 1960 and 1980 Chinese leaders privately proposed "package deals" or territorial swaps that would enshrine the post-war status quo: China would retain Aksai Chin in the Western Sector and India would retain Arunachal Pradesh in the Eastern Sector. The overtures never received a positive response in Delhi.

After sealing a series of modest border-related agreements between 1993 and 2005, the ongoing negotiations have produced diminishing returns, notwithstanding the "Border Defense Cooperation Agreement" signed in 2013. Most important, rising nationalism appears to be restricting the political space and incentives for territorial concessions in both capitals and the prospects for a "grand bargain" territorial swap appear to be diminishing.

Stability in Tibet

While India sees the border dispute as the principal source of friction in bilateral relations, many in Beijing point to a conflict of interests in Tibet. For decades, Indian leaders have recognized Tibet as an integral part of China; refrained from supporting Tibetan separatists; and even restricted peaceful activities by Tibetan activists at sensitive times. Beijing, however, remains incensed by Delhi's acquiescence to the establishment of a Tibetan Government in Exile (TGIE) in Dharamsala by the Dalai Lama after he fled the Tibetan plateau for India in 1959.

China's leaders harbor extreme animosity toward the Dalai Lama, charging him with promoting unrest and separatism on the plateau despite his official commitment to a "Middle Way" path that foregoes independence.[10] Beijing has repeatedly demanded that Delhi prevent the Dalai Lama from engaging in any "political activities" and Chinese scholars have accused India of undermining Chinese sovereignty and authority by providing the TGIE refuge. China was particularly incensed when the Dalai Lama was granted permission to visit the Chinese-claimed state of Arunachal Pradesh in 2009 and 2017, and when he met with the Indian president in late 2016.

Meanwhile, the question of who will succeed the octogenarian Buddhist leader has emerged as a potentially disruptive issue in Sino–Indian relations. Beijing has claimed the right to name the Dalai Lama's successor, a proposition he has flatly rejected. The Dalai Lama has suggested he may instead break with precedent and choose his own successor—raising the prospect for competing Dalai Lamas—or determine that he is the last in the line of Dalai Lamas.

Beyond India, Tibet remains an important focus of China's relationship with Nepal. Numbering some 20,000, Nepal hosts the second-largest Tibetan exile community after India and has served as the principal transit point for Tibetans entering and exiting the plateau. Nepal closed its borders to Tibetan refugees in 1989 but under a "gentlemen's agreement" with the United Nations allowed Tibetans to transit the country thereafter.[11] By the early 2000s, between 2,000 and 3,000 Tibetans were crossing through Nepal every year, mostly en route to India.

China began taking a greater interest in Nepal's affairs following a series of anti-government protests on the Tibetan plateau in 2008, subsequently followed by a wave of self-immolations by over 100 Buddhist monks in the years to follow. As examined later in this chapter, Chinese diplomatic and economic engagement with Nepal has expanded considerably since then, paralleling a rapid reduction in the flow of Tibetan migrants through Nepal and a crackdown on the Tibetan exile community there.

Maintaining "Strategic Balance" between India and Pakistan

China's approach to India and Pakistan was long guided by a desire to maintain "strategic balance" between the rivals, which Beijing argued contributes to stability on the subcontinent.[12] As Sino–Indian relations improved in the late twentieth century, China's position on the disputed territory of Kashmir, once favorable to Pakistan, grew more consistent with India's.[13] China's leadership now adds India to the itinerary of every South Asia visit, often visiting India first.[14]

During the 1999 Pakistan-instigated Kargil conflict Beijing took a decidedly neutral stance, a significant shift from the 1965 and 1971 Indo–Pakistan wars, when

China offered the latter robust diplomatic support (though not direct military intervention). After Pakistani-based militants launched terror attacks in India in Mumbai in 2008, and in Uri in 2016, Beijing provided little backing to Islamabad.[15]

To be sure, China continues to shield Pakistan-based terrorists from sanctions at the United Nations and still views Pakistan as a regional check on Indian power. Its ongoing political patronage, military support, and activities in disputed Kashmir continue to provoke Indian security concerns.

Yet, evidence suggests Beijing views another Indo–Pakistan conflict as increasingly undesirable, especially since both countries demonstrated a nuclear weapons capability in the 1990s. Today, its growing portfolio of investments in Pakistan, including the $46 billion China–Pakistan Economic Corridor (CPEC), would make an Indo–Pakistan conflict even more costly for Beijing. As Andrew Small argues, China now wants to see relations between the South Asian rivals "function in a stable, predictable fashion."[16]

Counterterrorism

Combating and preventing Islamist terrorism, particularly in Xinjiang, the restive, Muslim-majority province bordering Pakistan and Afghanistan, remains one of China's leading regional priorities. Beijing is particularly concerned about the activities of the East Turkestan Islamic Movement (ETIM), an al Qaeda-linked militant Islamist group dedicated to "liberating Xinjiang from Chinese occupation."[17] The group, which may be no larger than a few dozen militants, operates training camps in the lawless areas of Afghanistan and Pakistan.

Since the 1990s, Beijing has been largely content to outsource both its counterterrorism policy and its Afghanistan policy to Islamabad, relying on Pakistan to contain the ETIM in both countries. Following the 2001 U.S. invasion of Afghanistan, China was torn between anxiety over a large U.S. military presence on its western border, and fear of a more radicalized Taliban returning to power and creating new safe havens for the ETIM. Despite public support for the U.S. war effort in Afghanistan, Beijing largely resisted American efforts to coordinate pressure on Pakistan to withdraw its support for the Taliban.

More recently, however, Beijing has signaled growing impatience with Pakistan's performance as a proxy for its counterterrorism strategy and with Islamabad's efforts (or lack thereof) to resolve the Afghan conflict. In recent years, as discussed on page 000, Beijing has assumed a more prominent role in the Afghan peace process and initiated counterterrorism dialogues with Afghanistan and India.

Energy Security

China's growing appetite for natural resources has transformed it from a largely energy-independent country in the early 1990s to a world-leading consumer and importer of oil and natural gas.[18] Chinese imports of oil grew more than sixfold between 2001 and 2016 from 60 million metric tons (MMT) to 381 MMT.

Similarly, Chinese imports of natural gas nearly quadrupled between 2010 and 2016, from 15 MMT to 70 MMT. Chinese strategists have come to view the country's growing dependence on energy imports as a strategic vulnerability.

The energy that feeds China's economy, including roughly three-quarters of its oil imports, must traverse thousands of miles of open sea, funneled through global chokepoints including the Strait of Malacca. For over a decade the "Malacca Dilemma" created by these long and vulnerable SLOCs has captured the attention of China's strategic planners, and the diversification of China's energy imports is one motivation behind Beijing's OBOR initiative.

Beijing has since pursued a network of alternative overland energy sources to mitigate its dependence on vulnerable SLOCs. In recent years this has produced new, multibillion-dollar gas and oil pipeline deals with Russia, Myanmar, and Kazakhstan. The Malacca Dilemma remains a factor in some of the more consequential changes to China's foreign and defense policies, including its evolving approach to naval power projection, the importance of SLOC protection, and the utility of overseas military bases.

Expanding Trade

At the vanguard of China's expanding influence in South Asia is economic engagement and outreach. Beijing has showered regional capitals with tens of billions of dollars in grants, concessions, and loans, and won contracts for some of the region's highest-profile energy, infrastructure, and power projects. Since 2000, China's bilateral trade with India, Pakistan, and Bangladesh has expanded by factors of 25, 16, and 13, respectively (Table 5.2).

While the region accounted for just 2.6 percent of China's external trade in 2015, for South Asian countries China's economic engagement has been transformative.[19] China has already overtaken India as the top trading partner of Pakistan and Bangladesh. In 2015 it reached parity with India in the Maldives and may soon surpass India in Sri Lanka.[20] China already has a free trade agreement (FTA) with Pakistan and is negotiating FTAs with Sri Lanka, the Maldives, and Bangladesh. FTA talks with India, meanwhile, stalled in the mid-2000s. India, however, remains by far China's most important regional economic relationship, with bilateral trade topping $71 billion in 2016 (Table 5.3).[21]

TABLE 5.1 South Asia in China's Trade Portfolio

2016 Rank Among Chinese Export Markets:	*2016 Rank Among Chinese Import Markets:*
India: 7th	*India*: 27th
Pakistan: 26th	*Pakistan*: 62nd
Bangladesh: 31st	*Bangladesh*: 73rd
Sri Lanka: 53rd	*Sri Lanka*: 100th
Nepal: 116th	*Nepal*: 155th

Source: IMF Direction of Trade Statistics.

TABLE 5.2 South Asia Trade with India and China

2016 Bilateral Trade	China	India
Afghanistan	$440 million	$1.3 billion
Bangladesh	$15.55 billion	$6.4 billion
Bhutan	$5.2 million	$650 million
Maldives	$342 million	$188 million
Nepal	$851 million	$5 billion
Pakistan	$19.6 billion	$2.1 billion
Sri Lanka	$4.66 billion	$4.5 billion

Source: IMF Direction of Trade Statistics 2016.

TABLE 5.3 China's Exports and Imports in South Asia

China Trade 2016	Exports	Imports
Afghanistan	$435 million	$4.5 million
Bangladesh	$14.7 billion	$858 million
Bhutan	$5 million	$13 thousand
India	$59.4 billion	$11.8 billion
Maldives	$342 million	$24 thousand
Nepal	$874 million	$22 million
Pakistan	$17.7 billion	$1.9 billion
Sri Lanka	$4.3 billion	$274 million

India was running trade surpluses with China as late as 2005 but has registered ever-larger deficits in the years since, reaching $47.6 billion in 2016.[22] These deficits have grown despite a trebling and even decline in overall bilateral trade.[23] Indeed, China is running a major region-wide trade surplus, exporting ($98 billion) more than five times as much as it imported ($15 billion) in 2016.[24] Every capital is now running a large and expanding trade deficit with Beijing and, in proportional terms, the trade deficits of the smaller countries are far larger than India's (Table 5.3).[25]

China's Methods in South Asia

Military Deployments

Following their first deployments to the Indian Ocean in 1985, the People's Liberation Army Navy (PLAN) made only infrequent forays to the region, reflecting its modest capabilities and emphasis on coastal defense.[26] The tempo of the PLAN's activity in the Indian Ocean changed dramatically after 2008, the year an international naval task force was organized to combat piracy emanating from war-torn Somalia. Beijing dispatched a PLAN escort fleet to operate an independent anti-piracy mission in December 2008, and by 2016 two dozen PLAN fleets had rotated through the Indian Ocean.[27] The deployments have offered the Chinese navy valuable "blue water" experience and growing familiarity with more than a dozen Indian Ocean ports.[28]

The PLAN's anti-piracy rotations coincided with a conceptual evolution in China's approach to the relative importance of the maritime domain, the value of overseas military deployments and bases, and the necessity of securing China's SLOCs. In 2012, for the first time ever, one of China's semi-annual Defense White Papers emphasized the importance of "safeguarding the security of the international SLOCs."[29]

In the 2015 Defense White Paper the shift was bolder: "The traditional mentality that land outweighs sea must be abandoned and great importance has to be attached to managing the seas and oceans and protecting maritime rights and interests."[30] China, it said, must "strike a balance between rights protection and stability maintenance" while the longstanding focus on "offshore waters defense" was replaced with a new focus on "open seas protection."[31] In 2016 President Xi Jinping unveiled a series of sweeping reforms to the PLA's structure and organization that further elevated the importance of the Chinese navy relative to the long-dominant role of the army.

Perhaps nowhere is this paradigmatic shift more consequential than in the Indian Ocean. A 2014 "Blue Book of the Indian Ocean Region" published by several Chinese think tanks noted: "In the past, China's Indian Ocean strategy was based on 'moderation' and 'maintaining the status quo', but the changing dynamics of international relations necessitates China play a more proactive role in affairs of the region."[32] In 2012 Defense Minister Liang Guanglie signaled a shift in Chinese thinking about the most taboo of subjects: overseas military bases. China, he said, would "consider having logistic supply or short rest [facilities] at appropriate ports of other countries."[33] In January 2015, the official *China Daily* made a similar argument.[34]

Seven months later China announced an agreement for its first "overseas naval logistics support facility" in Djibouti.[35] The facility will ostensibly provide food, water, and fuel for China's anti-piracy task forces and "help the PLA ... play a more active role in ensuring peace and stability at a regional and global level."[36] Critics insist that China's growing military footprint in the Indian Ocean has little to do with combating pirates. After all, from 52 vessels hijacked off the coast of Somalia in 2009, the number had fallen to zero by 2013.[37] Yet, that same year China launched its first-ever nuclear submarine patrol in the Indian Ocean.[38]

Since 2014, Chinese conventional submarines have enjoyed an expanding footprint in the Indian Ocean. In September of that year a *Song*-class diesel electric submarine made the first-ever South Asian port call by a Chinese submarine when it surfaced in Colombo for nearly a week. In November 2014, the Chinese submarine again appeared at Colombo, ostensibly returning from its anti-piracy deployment.[39] In May 2015, a *Yuan*-class PLAN submarine made a port call to Karachi, Pakistan, the first time a Chinese submarine docked at an Indian Ocean port without a support vessel. In January 2016, two Chinese guided-missile frigates and a supply ship docked at Chittagong and conducted drills with the Bangladesh Navy.[40]

Arms Sales

Pakistan and Bangladesh account for the vast majority of China's regional—and indeed global—arms exports. Pakistan is the largest recipient of Chinese arms in the world and the defense trade—which include tanks, combat aircraft, artillery, radar, helicopters, and torpedoes—extends back decades. In recent years, Chinese nuclear and missile assistance to Pakistan has attracted greater scrutiny[41] as the latter has begun developing tactical nuclear weapons and hosts the world's "fastest growing nuclear arsenal."[42]

China and Pakistan have also begun high-profile co-production and co-development projects, including the $500 million JF-17 fighter aircraft. The first JF-17s were inducted in the Pakistani air force in 2010 and Beijing and Islamabad have been seeking export markets since, albeit with little success.[43] In 2015 China announced its largest-ever defense deal, the sale of eight *Yuan*-class submarines to Pakistan at a cost of roughly $5 billion. Four of the eight submarines will be built in Pakistan while China will enjoy the benefit of a friendly facility in the Indian Ocean tailored to support its growing fleet of *Yuan* submarines.[44]

China accounts for over 80 percent of Bangladesh's arms imports over the past decade,[45] including $1.4 billion in sales between 2013 and 2016 alone.[46] Chinese arms exports include anti-ship missiles, tanks, fighter aircraft, frigates, and submarines while Bangladeshi military personnel train in China. The Bangladesh navy operates three Chinese *Jianghui*-class frigates and in 2014 purchased two *Ming III*-class diesel electric submarines for roughly $200 million.[47] In December 2015 Dhaka took delivery of two advanced Chinese *Jingdao*-class corvettes, and has ordered two more.[48] Bangladesh's state-run Khulna Shipyard has begun constructing warships with Chinese firms "supervising the construction and providing the designs and materials."[49]

China—Sri Lanka defense trade dates back to the 1970s when Beijing first provided Colombo with naval patrol craft. Fighter jets, artillery, tanks, and transport aircraft followed in the 1980s and 1990s. While the aggregate value of arms transfers to Sri Lanka are modest, they assumed geopolitical significance after the 2005 election of President Mahinda Rajapaksa, as explored in the "Political Influence" section on pages 000–000.

In 2016, China supplied Afghanistan directly with military aid for the first time during a visit by the head of the PLA,[50] including an initial pledge of $70 million. Kabul received the first shipment of Chinese military supplies in June 2016, including a transport plane, supplies, and ammunition. Chinese Ambassador Yao Jing called it "the beginning of our regular military-to-military exchanges and cooperation."[51]

Nepal is the only other regional recipient of Chinese arms in the twenty-first century. Bearing an eerie resemblance to events in Sri Lanka the same year, in 2005 Nepal's king imposed a state of emergency amid a civil conflict with Nepalese Maoist insurgents. Backed by the U.S. and EU, India suspended arms to the Royal Nepalese Army.[52]

Nepal's monarch, King Gyanendra, appealed to Beijing for military aid, promptly receiving five armored personnel carriers and breaking India's longstanding monopoly on arms exports to Nepal.[53] Later that year, China pledged $1 million in military assistance and sold Nepal $80,000 in small arms and grenades. As in Sri Lanka, the Sino–Nepal relationship was fundamentally transformed in the years to follow, as the following section will show.

Political Influence

Nepal

India has been the dominant force in Kathmandu since it assumed sway over Nepal's foreign and security policies in a 1950 treaty. Since then, Delhi has been virtually the exclusive supplier of commercial and military goods to the landlocked nation.

As mentioned, in 2005 Beijing provided Nepal's monarch five armored personnel carriers and $1 million in military aid and small arms during a blockade of the capital by Maoist forces.[54] Nepal's warring parties reached a Comprehensive Peace Accord one year later that usurped the power of the king, incorporating the Maoists into the military and political process. The group then swept national elections in 2008, electing Prachanda their prime minister.

In Nepal, China's longstanding commitment to political flexibility—a willingness to diplomatically engage all political groups regardless of history, ideology, or prior disposition toward China—proved invaluable. Despite arming King Gyanendra against the Maoists, Beijing quickly formed a working relationship with Prachanda. He reciprocated by breaking protocol and visiting China before India, pledging to safeguard China's "sovereignty and territorial integrity" in a second visit to China in 2009.[55]

As political ties strengthened, by 2013 the number of Tibetans crossing into and through Nepal fell from several thousand per year to 200.[56] During a 2014 visit to Nepal, the Communist Party chief of Tibet insisted there were no "refugees" from Tibet, and anyone crossing the border was doing so illegally.[57] By 2015 the flow of refugees had slowed to a trickle.

An investigation by the *New Yorker* found China rewards Nepalese soldiers by "providing financial incentives to officers who hand over Tibetans attempting to exit China." "Nepalese police," it adds, "have been apprehending Tibetans far inside Nepal, robbing them, and then returning them to Tibet at gunpoint, where they are typically imprisoned and not uncommonly tortured."[58]

In recent years, China–Nepal relations have expanded beyond the Tibet issue, with Beijing leveraging rifts in Indo–Nepal relations to its advantage. In 2015, for example, Nepal's minority Madhesis began protesting against perceived discrimination in a new draft constitution text. Concentrated along the southern border and sharing deep familial links with India, the Madhesis received support from Delhi, which suspended fuel supplies to Nepal in September 2015.

The following month veteran communist KP Sharma Oli was elected prime minister and moved quickly to China to sign an oil trade agreement with Beijing.[59] China provided 1.3 million liters of petrol in relief, breaking India's longstanding monopoly on fuel exports. "Someone had to fill that vacuum that India left. China is now a psychological force in Nepal because of India's support to the blockade,"[60] explained Nepalese Foreign Minister Kamal Thapa.

Beijing increased its annual aid budget to Nepal by over 500 percent to $138 million in 2015. In 2016 Nepal was selected as a board member of the Beijing-based Asian Infrastructure Investment Bank (AIIB) and joined the Chinese- and Russian-led Shanghai Cooperation Organization (SCO) as a dialogue partner.

Throughout 2016 China sought to buttress political support for Oli as he came under fire from domestic opponents[61] and from India. During a trip to Beijing in March, Oli was told China would back his government against "external interference."[62] In July 2016, Oli blamed a "conspiracy" by "foreign elements" when he lost a no-confidence vote and was replaced by former Prime Minister Prachanda.[63]

In contrast to his first term as prime minister, Prachanda chose India for his maiden voyage abroad, signaling a reorientation of relations following criticism Oli had grown too close to Beijing. Two weeks later, Beijing announced it was cancelling a planned trip to Kathmandu by President Xi in October.[64] China's *Global Times* vented:

> Obviously, China feels tricked. When Kathmandu needed Beijing to relieve pressure from New Delhi, it got close to China and signed a series of crucial agreements with Beijing . . . once India's attitude toward Kathmandu relaxed a bit and the former made some promises to the latter, Nepalese politicians immediately put the nation's ties with China on the back burner.[65]

Maldives

As in Nepal and Sri Lanka, China was able to leverage political instability in the Maldives to elevate its influence in Malé in the late 2000s. The two have enjoyed diplomatic relations since 1972. Yet, the country's longtime autocrat, Maumoon Abdul Gayoom, maintained a close defense relationship with India during his decades-long rule, particularly after Indian Special Forces restored him to power after a coup attempt in 1988.

When the Maldives held its first democratic elections in 2008, the winner, opposition candidate Mohammed Nasheed, made no secret of his desire to maintain strong relations with Delhi:

> There is not enough room in the Indian Ocean for other non-traditional friends. We are not receptive to any installation, military or otherwise, in the Indian Ocean, especially from un-traditional friends. The Indian Ocean is the Indian Ocean.[66]

Economic turmoil propelled popular protests against Nasheed in 2011 against the backdrop of a power struggle with allies of former president Gayoom. As the political conflict unfolded, Malé received the highest-ranking Chinese leader to ever visit the country in May 2011, Politburo Standing Committee (PBSC) member Wu Bangguo. In November 2011, China opened its first embassy in the Maldives as anti-Nasheed protests reached a fever-pitch.

Nasheed resigned under duress in February 2012, succeeded by his vice president, Mohamed Waheed. Waheed soon traveled to Xinjiang, where Beijing pledged $500 million in aid and a $150 million loan from China's Ex–Im Bank. In the months to follow Malé welcomed PBSC member Li Changchun and dispatched its defense minister to Beijing, where he was told China was "willing to cement relations between the two countries and their militaries."[67]

Elections in November 2013 brought Gayoom's half-brother, Abdullah Yameen, to power, heralding a further acceleration of China–Maldives ties. Yameen secured a $16 million grant during an August 2014 visit to Beijing and a month later hosted a presidential visit for Xi Jinping in Malé. There, he declared China was one of the Maldives'"closest friends, most trusted allies, and the most dependable development partners." Most important for Beijing, Xi secured a pledge from Yameen to support China's OBOR initiative.[68]

The two applauded the fact that China now accounts for more than a third of the Maldives' tourism industry, the lifeline of its economy. In 2016, one-fourth of all tourists to the Maldives hailed from China, with annual visits from Chinese citizens reaching 324,000, up from 119,000 in 2010.[69] In June 2015, Yameen declared Sino–Maldives relations had reached an "all-time high."

Sri Lanka

When Mahinda Rajapaksa was elected president in 2005 Sri Lanka was embroiled in a brutal, decades-long conflict with the violent separatist Tamil Tigers (LTTE) which claimed some 80,000 lives.[70] Despite a tenuous ceasefire signed in 2002, Rajapaksa planned a major military buildup to crush the LTTE and requested arms from India. With a politically influential Tamil minority of its own, Delhi denied the request.[71] Citing human rights abuses in the war against the Tigers, the U.S. also suspended military aid to Colombo in 2007.[72]

China quickly filled the void. In 2007 Rajapaksa secured $37 million in Chinese ammunition and ordinance. A year later, China "gifted" Sri Lanka six F7 jet fighters[73] and sold Colombo anti-aircraft guns and JY-11 radar.[74] The ceasefire with the LTTE was terminated in 2008 and the following year Rajapaksa launched a scorched-earth offensive that decisively crushed the Tigers, claiming up to 20,000 civilians in the process.

At a parade celebrating the LTTE's defeat, "the majority of the hardware on display was Chinese made."[75] A senior Sri Lankan official later told U.S. officials on Capitol Hill: "We have the United States to thank for pushing us closer to China," referencing the suspension of U.S. military aid.[76]

When Rajapaksa was criticized by the international community for the civilian death toll suffered during his scorched-earth offensive against the Tigers, Chinese patronage proved invaluable when Beijing blocked the UN Security Council from addressing the charges. Sino–Sri Lankan ties expanded dramatically in the years following the conflict: 2012 saw the first-ever visit by a Chinese defense minister to Colombo and the following year the two upgraded their relationship to a "strategic cooperative partnership." In 2014, Colombo enthusiastically endorsed China's OBOR initiative and held its first-ever defense dialogue with Beijing.

In the intensifying Sino–Indian competition for influence among South Asia's smaller powers, Sri Lanka has assumed center stage following a massive infusion of Chinese capital into Sri Lankan infrastructure. Those investments, including in the ports at Colombo and Hambantota, and their implications, are covered in greater detail in the "Infrastructure and Investment" section of this chapter on pages 000–000.

Bangladesh

China has long enjoyed strong political ties with Bangladesh, and in the twenty-first century the two economies and defense establishments have become increasingly engaged. In the years after Bangladesh's 1971 secession from Pakistan amid a bloody civil conflict and the Third Indo–Pakistan War, relations with Beijing were initially quite frosty. However, following a leadership transition in Bangladesh, Beijing and Dhaka normalized ties in 1976 and China began supplying military and economic assistance in the 1980s. By 2000, bilateral trade topped $1 billion and by 2005 China had overtaken India as Bangladesh's top trading partner.[77] The two strengths of the relationship, the defense trade and infrastructure investments, are covered in separate sections of this chapter.

In recent years Bangladesh has subscribed to the principles of "sovereign equality, peaceful co-existence, mutual trust and respect for each other's sovereignty, territorial integrity, and non-interference in each other's internal affairs."[78] In June and December 2015, Beijing welcomed Bangladesh's prime minister and president, elevating relations to a "new dimension." And in October 2016 President Xi Jinping became the first Chinese president to visit Bangladesh in three decades, elevating ties to a "strategic partnership," signing $24 billion in deals, and winning vocal support for the OBOR initiative.

Bhutan

The small Buddhist kingdom of Bhutan has often been characterized as more of an Indian protectorate than an independent state. Nestled on the southern ridge of the Himalayas, Bhutan historically enjoyed strong economic and cultural links with Tibet. However, after a Chinese crackdown in Tibet in 1959 prompted an influx of some 6,000 Tibetan refugees, Bhutan closed its borders with Tibet and reoriented its foreign policy southward toward India.

Delhi effectively assumed control of Bhutan's foreign and national security policies in a 1949 Treaty of Friendship. The two enjoy an open border and India accounts for some 75 percent of Bhutan's imports and 85 percent of its exports while Bhutan receives two-thirds of all Indian foreign aid. Bhutan remains the only Chinese neighbor with which China has yet to establish formal diplomatic relations, having been severed shortly after the Chinese invasion of Tibet in 1950.

Bhutan made a handful of diplomatic gestures toward China in the 1970s, including voicing support for Beijing's "One China" policy. Negotiations over their disputed border remain the principal avenue of bilateral engagement, though Chinese ambassadors to India pay regular "working visits" to Bhutan.[79] In 2007 India and Bhutan signed a revised "Friendship Treaty" which nominally offered Bhutan greater freedom in conducting foreign affairs but reaffirmed the two would "cooperate closely with each other on issues relating to their national interests." Article 4 stated Bhutan was free to import military equipment "*from or through* India."[80]

In 2012 China witnessed arguably its biggest diplomatic breakthrough with Bhutan. That year, former Ambassador to India Zhou Gang conveyed a message to Thimphu: China was prepared to settle the border dispute if Bhutan agreed to establish full diplomatic relations.[81] Months later, Bhutan Prime Minister Jigme Thinley and Chinese Prime Minister Wen Jiabao held the first-ever meeting of Chinese and Bhutanese leaders on the sidelines of a UN conference in Brazil.

In Rio, Thinley told Wen that Bhutan "wishes to forge formal diplomatic ties with China as soon as possible" and settle the border dispute "in a cooperative manner."[82] Shortly after the Brazil meeting, Bhutan imported more than one dozen buses from a Chinese firm.

The diplomatic flirtation provoked a sharp response from Delhi ahead of Bhutanese elections the following year, with Delhi supporting Thinley's more Indophile challenger. Ahead of elections, China applied pressure: a PLA border incursion one week before the first round of voting. China has pursued a policy of "military intimidation followed by diplomatic seduction," according to Bhutanese analyst Talik Jha.[83]

Thinley lost the election to Tshering Togbay, India's preferred candidate, but border negotiations with China have nevertheless continued. At the twenty-third round in August 2015 Bhutan endorsed China's OBOR initiative.[84] Thimphu said it was "willing to continue to deepen exchanges in such fields as tourism, religion, culture and agriculture and further lift the cooperation level with China."[85] Notably, China has fast become Bhutan's largest source of tourists: from fewer than 20 a decade ago, the number of Chinese tourists reached 5,400 in 2014[86] and 9,400 in 2015.[87]

Afghanistan and Pakistan

While China formed an uneasy working relationship with the Taliban when it ruled Afghanistan in the late 1990s, it was largely content to outsource its Afghanistan policy to Pakistan before and after the U.S. invasion in 2001. Since the invasion, Beijing has been a modest contributor of aid and investment and has become increasingly invested in the Afghan peace process. Its principal objective, however, remains ensuring Afghanistan was not used a base of operations for the ETIM terrorist group.

Amid signs of Chinese frustration with the lack of progress on Afghan peace talks and Pakistan's role in the process, in recent years China has begun to engage more directly and robustly with the Afghan government on security issues.

In September 2012, a trip by Public Security Chief Zhou Yongkang marked the first visit to Afghanistan by a PBSC member in decades.[88] The following year Beijing and Kabul signed a terrorist extradition treaty and agreed to intensify cooperation against transnational security threats.[89] In the spring of 2014 a mass knife attack in Kunming in March 2014 attributed to Islamist militants killed 29. In April and May, Xinjiang witnessed the bombing of a marketplace (31 dead, up to 140 wounded) and a train station (3 dead, 79 wounded).

As ballots were being counted for Afghan national elections in July 2014, China appointed former Ambassador to India Sun Yuxi as a special envoy and welcomed the Afghan Army's deputy chief of general staff to Beijing. New Afghan President Ashraf Ghani soon chose China for his first visit abroad, finding Beijing more willing to discuss sensitive security issues than ever before. There, Premier Li Keqiang called on Afghanistan's neighbors to respect its "sovereignty, independence and territorial integrity, not interfere with its internal affairs."[90]

Beijing then hosted Afghan peace talks for the first time, proposing a new "peace and reconciliation forum." It also began more direct outreach to the Taliban through its diplomatic office in Qatar and through "non-publicized" meetings in Doha, Islamabad, and Beijing.[91] Meanwhile, Chinese economic aid to Afghanistan surged from less than $9 million per year between 2001 and 2013 to $80 million in 2014 and $240 million from 2016 through 2019.[92]

In 2015, China continued to take a leading role to bring the Taliban to the negotiating table, but Beijing's activism failed to break the gridlock and the Afghan peace process had again stalled by mid-2016.[93] Nevertheless, that year China proposed forming a new security bloc to include Afghanistan, Pakistan, and Tajikistan and announced it would begin supplying Afghanistan directly with military aid, delivering the first supplies in October 2016.[94]

The shift in China's approach suggests declining confidence in Pakistan's willingness and ability to bring the Taliban to the negotiating table. It also reflects concerns about the safety and security of its growing portfolio of investments (and citizens employed) in Pakistan, and the broader threat instability poses to its OBOR initiative. According to Andrew Small:

> [China] strongly encouraged Pakistan to forge a peace deal between the Afghan government and the Taliban, rather than backing its militant proteges. Chinese interests, from Xinjiang to the new Silk Road schemes, increasingly rely on broad stability in the region, rather than just a defense of narrow security and commercial goals, and it has finally started to bring its influence in Pakistan to bear in trying to achieve them.[95]

Finally, in a further sign of China's evolving approach to counterterrorism, in November 2015 China hosted an unusual meeting with Indian Home Minister Rajnath Singh. According to *Outlook India*, Singh was surprised by the "proactive way China pushed security cooperation with India" and the "change of attitude" shown from China's new security czar.[96]

The report said the two sides "discussed terrorism concerns faced by them from Pakistan and Afghanistan" while Beijing was even willing to discuss the previously taboo topic of its protection of Pakistani-based terrorists from sanctions at the UN Security Council.[97] The meeting was followed in September 2016 by a new India–China High Level Dialogue on counterterrorism.[98]

India

While China and India have found common ground on issues like counterterrorism, rivalrous aspects of the relationship have grown more prominent during the tenures of Prime Minister Narendra Modi and President Xi Jinping.

Mr. Modi prioritized economic outreach to China early in his term, but he also signaled a newfound confidence by inviting the prime minister of the Tibetan Government in Exile to his inauguration; fast-tracking military infrastructure projects along the LAC; rebuking China's claims to Arunachal Pradesh on the campaign trail; and criticizing the "18th-century expansionist mind-set" of some countries from a speech in Japan in September 2014.[99] When President Xi Jinping made his inaugural trip to Delhi a few weeks later, the visit was overshadowed by a three-week-long PLA intrusion across the LAC.

Modi has also added a more overt strategic and defense component to India's "Look East" policy, elevating defense collaboration with Japan, Vietnam, and Australia, among others. In 2015, India invited Japan to become a regular participant in the annual U.S.–India Malabar naval exercises and it has maintained a stake in a Vietnamese oil block in waters claimed by China, raising protests from Beijing.

India under Modi has become an increasingly vocal proponent of "Freedom of Navigation" in the South China Sea. And Delhi's support for a July 2016 UNCLOS Tribunal ruling that invalidated China's Nine-Dash Line claim exceeded that of many European and Asian nations.[100]

Finally, Modi has adopted a "Neighborhood First" policy designed to more vigorously engage India's direct neighbors and ensure India is the regional partner of choice.[101]

Delhi has publicly traded barbs with Beijing over the legitimacy of the PLAN's presence in the Indian Ocean. In December 2012, PLAN Vice Admiral Su Zhiqian declared at a speech in Sri Lanka: "the Chinese navy will actively maintain the peace and stability of the Indian Ocean." In a 2015 lecture, Indian Foreign Secretary Subrahmanyam Jaishankar declared: "Those who are resident in this region have the primary responsibility for peace, stability and prosperity in the Indian Ocean."[102]

An article in the official *China Daily* later argued: "If the Pacific is big enough to accommodate China and the US, so is the Indian Ocean to accommodate India and China."[103]

While legacy disputes over the border and Pakistan still shadow bilateral relations, China's deepening partnerships along India's periphery and the PLAN's growing presence in the Indian Ocean have arguably raised the most alarm in Delhi. The result has been an intensifying competition for influence in regional capitals and rising prospects for friction in the maritime domain.

When a Chinese submarine first surfaced in Colombo in 2014, Prime Minister Modi personally reminded President Mahinda Rajapaksa Sri Lanka "was obliged to inform its neighbors about such port calls under a maritime pact."[104] Yet the same submarine again appeared in Colombo in November 2014 without prior notification to Delhi.

Rajapaksa was upset in national elections just months later and the Sri Lankan station chief of India's intelligence agency, RAW, was expelled shortly after the election. He was involved in organizing and uniting the political opposition, convincing Sirisena to defect and run, and persuading a former prime minister not to contest the election and diminish Sirisena's chances.[105] "The turning point in the relationship," an Indian security official told Reuters, "was the submarines. There was real anger."[106]

If Mahinda Rajapaksa crossed an Indian red line with Chinese submarines in Colombo, the bar for Bhutan was far lower. After Prime Minister Thinley held an impromptu meeting with Chinese Premier Wen Jiabao in 2012, Delhi suspended a key fuel subsidy to Bhutan in the run-up to national elections the following year.

The more vocally Indophile opposition PDP party swept the elections and new Prime Minister Tshering Togbay announced "good relations with India is the cornerstone of our foreign policy."[107] India's national security advisor and foreign secretary traveled to Thimphu shortly afterward to congratulate the new prime minister, advise him on upcoming border talks with China, and apologize for the "unfortunate technical lapse" in India's fuel subsidies.[108]

In June 2014, Prime Minister Modi surprised observers by choosing Bhutan for his first visit abroad,[109] pledging a 50 percent increase in aid and loans to Thimphu and three new hydroelectric plants.[110] Shortly after his departure, Togbay announced China would not be allowed to open an embassy in Bhutan.[111]

To be sure, China too has been more vocal and candid about its desire to serve as an alternative to India for regional capitals. In December 2015, amid a major rift in Indo–Nepal, Chinese Foreign Minister Wang Yi declared: "China has all along believed that countries irrespective of their size are equal. China and Nepal have always treated each other sincerely and as equals. We hope that the same policy and practices will also be adopted by India."[112]

India has also been a frequent target for Chinese nationalist media outlets. The popular *Global Times* has published articles claiming India is "not a first class power,"[113] and criticized the "Indian elites' blind arrogance . . . and the inferiority of its ordinary people."[114] It has warned Mr. Modi's "tougher" foreign policy is "brewing new strategic adjustments."[115] Commentator Shen Dingli claims China "has many ways to hurt India," including sending an aircraft carrier to the Gwadar port in Pakistan. "We can put a navy at [India's] doorstep."[116]

Infrastructure Investment and Construction

In the mid-2000s, Chinese investments in port facilities across the Indian Ocean rim sparked a debate about China's intentions to encircle India with a "String of Pearls." Over time details of China's investments emerged, revealing no explicit military arrangements, and discussion of the "String of Pearls" partially subsided.

Today, however, the region is witnessing a new wave of Chinese infrastructure investments under China's ambitious OBOR initiative. Tens of billions of dollars in Chinese investments have brought desperately needed capital and infrastructure to South Asia and established Beijing as a dominant economic player in many capitals.

On the other hand, some regional actors have viewed China's investment spree with a mix of anxiety and suspicion. Some fear the accumulation of destabilizing levels of Chinese debt; others fear there are grander strategic ambitions behind the ostensibly economic OBOR initiative.

First unveiled at a speech in Kazakhstan in September 2013, OBOR is designed to collate and advance a myriad of overlapping political, economic, military, and energy-related objectives. Beijing endeavors to create a networked web of improved infrastructure and economic linkages across a more integrated Eurasian continent. In the process, it seeks new markets for Chinese exports and capital, new sources of income for its firms, and alternative sources of energy that bypass the Strait of Malacca. With the backing of President Xi Jinping, OBOR is China's most ambitious foreign policy initiative in a generation, leveraging China's $4 trillion in currency reserves to invest "more than $890 billion into more than 900 projects involving 60 countries."[117] Notably, legs of both the continental "Belt" and the maritime "Road" pass through the Indian Ocean and South Asia.

Pakistan

During his 2015 visit to Pakistan, President Xi announced $46 billion in investments in a new China–Pakistan Economic Corridor (CPEC), linking the Chinese-run port of Gwadar in Pakistan's south to China's Xinjiang province. The first project to receive funding from China's New Silk Road Fund was $1.65 billion for a hydropower dam near Rawalpindi, Pakistan.[118]

Chinese foreign direct investment (FDI) in Pakistan[119] has traditionally fallen behind U.S. FDI inflows. After the unveiling of CPEC, that has begun to change. In the 2016–2017 fiscal year, inflows of FDI from China to Pakistan soared to nearly $1.2 billion while inflows from the U.S. sank to $71 million.[120]

CPEC is an amalgamation of 51 separate agreements and MoUs that will come to fruition over the ensuing 10–15 years. Three separate infrastructure corridors of roads, rail, and pipelines are to be paired with major Chinese investments in Pakistan's power sector. Indeed, "the lion's share of China's investment—roughly $35 billion—is expected to go to [21 new] energy projects."[121]

Eyebrows were raised when Chinese state-owned enterprises officially assumed control of the deep-sea port of Gwadar in Pakistan's Baluchistan province. Funded in large part with Chinese capital, the Singapore company originally contracted to run the port sold the managing rights to a Chinese state-backed firm in 2013 on a 43-year lease. By one estimate, "shipping oil to inland China cities via Gwadar is expected to cut shipment times by 85 percent compared with the Malacca strait route."[122]

However, Gwadar has faced trouble realizing its potential. With the goal of eventually processing some 300–400 million tons of cargo.[123] The port's potential remains hampered by security concerns related to a long-running ethnic Baluch insurgency; a lack of infrastructure connecting Gwadar to more developed parts of Pakistan; and a lack of export-ready products in the underdeveloped province of Baluchistan. Nevertheless, China remains committed to building Gwadar into a major "regional hub" and is moving forward with plans to construct a free trade area and $4.5 billion special economic zone adjacent to the port.

In April 2015, Pakistan sought to assuage some of China's security concerns by creating a "special security division comprised of roughly 10,000 troops dedicated to the protection of Chinese engineers, project directors, experts and workers employed on various Chinese funded projects across Pakistan."[124]

India

While China is India's largest trading partner in goods, over the past 15 years it's been only the seventeenth largest foreign investor in the Indian economy. Over that period, Chinese FDI equity inflows[125] amounted to just $1.24 billion, or 0.47 percent of the global total.[126]

In 2014 Xi Jinping pledged $20 billion in Indian investments over the ensuing five years and in the fiscal year to follow Chinese FDI reached roughly $500 million. That's far higher than the previous record of $151 million (2013–14), but well short of the $4 billion annual average suggested by President Xi.

OBOR is unlikely to change this state of affairs. While India has been an eager participant in the Beijing-based Asian Infrastructure Investment Bank (AIIB),[127] it's the only South Asian country to withhold public support for OBOR. Foreign Secretary S. Jaishankar has called OBOR a "national initiative devised with national interest . . . if this is something on which [China] want[s] a larger buy in, then they need to have larger discussions, and those haven't happened."[128]

Indian analyst Samir Saran argues, "A formal nod to [OBOR] will serve as a de-facto legitimization to Pakistan's rights on Pakistan-occupied Kashmir."[129] When Prime Minister Modi visited China in 2015, he told President Xi "very firmly" that CPEC was "not acceptable."[130]

India has, however, remained an active but cautious participant in long-running discussions on a Bangladesh–China–India–Myanmar (BCIM) Corridor.[131] The Corridor envisions a 2,800-kilometer high-speed infrastructure corridor between Kunming, China, and Kolkata India. The fact the Corridor would cross through India's underdeveloped northeastern states, a region Prime Minister Modi has targeted as a priority for development, is particularly attractive for Delhi.

However, progress on BCIM has been slow. In February 2016, Bangladesh, China, and India finished their "strategy papers" on the corridor, though Myanmar had yet to complete its draft.[132] In July 2016 a prominent Chinese scholar accused India of "adopt[ing] opposing, delaying, and hedging measures toward different parts of the initiative."[133]

Nepal

Since 2008 Nepal has received a wave of low-interest Chinese loans and investments in telecommunications infrastructure, hydropower stations, an international airport, and its tourism industry.[134]

The most sensitive and potentially consequential of China's investments relate to the unprecedented cross-Himalayan infrastructure Beijing has begun constructing and planning. China has begun upgrading the cross-border Prithvi highway and in 2016 conducted feasibility studies on a long-rumored extension of the Qinghai Tibet railway connecting Lhasa to the Nepal border.[135] If approved, the project is expected to cost $4 billion and be completed in five years.[136]

In May 2016, for the first time ever, a Chinese freight train departed Lanzhou, Gansu before offloading its goods in Shigatse for road transport on to Kathmandu. The land journey took ten days as compared to the 35-day journey for seaborne goods shipped through Kolkata, India.[137]

Finally, Beijing recently doubled the number of Nepali products getting customs waivers from 4,000 to 8,000 with plans underway to open several new border customs posts along the border.[138]

Sri Lanka

Arguably nowhere have China's infrastructure investments proved more controversial than in Sri Lanka. A month before Sri Lankan President Mahinda Rajapaksa signed a 2007 arms deal with China, he inked a separate contract to lease land to a Chinese consortium at Hambantota, where it planned to build a $1 billion deep-water port.[139] China's Ex–Im bank funded the $361 million and $810 million first and second phases of the port, and a $200 million airport nearby.[140]

Separately, in 2009 a Chinese company was granted an exclusive investment zone adjacent to the country's main port at Colombo and a Chinese-led consortium won a contract to construct and operate a new South Container Terminal there the following year.

In 2011 Rajapaksa unveiled plans for a new $1.4 billion Colombo Port City Project (CPCP) in a partnership with China Harbor Engineering Company (CHEC) that would include a new "mini city" on 230 hectares of reclaimed land. After languishing under government review for two years, Colombo and Beijing finalized the CPCP deal in 2013.

By 2014 China had issued over $5 billion in loans to Sri Lanka, funding and building 70 percent of its infrastructure projects.[141] However, analysts began to wonder if Colombo was accruing unsustainable levels of Chinese debt, and if China would seek to leverage that debt into equity in the ports.[142]

When President Xi Jinping toured Colombo in September 2014, the Hambantota Port was hemorrhaging money. Fewer than 100 vessels berthed at the port in 2013,[143] yet Sri Lanka was paying $30 million per year in interest payments alone.[144] In Colombo President Xi agreed to "ease loan conditions." In return, Rajapaksa quietly granted Chinese firms operating rights to four of the seven container berths at Hambantota on a 35-year lease.[145]

Ahead of 2015 elections, former Rajapaksa ally Maithripala Sirisena defected to the opposition, criticizing Rajapaksa's embrace of Beijing and the billions in Chinese debt he accrued.[146]

In January 2015, he narrowly defeated Rajapaksa and quickly suspended the CPCP over environmental concerns and allegations of corruption during the bidding process. It also objected to a provision in the CPCP contract that granted China 20 hectares of land on a "freehold" basis.[147] CHEC was separately accused of offering millions of dollars in bribes to facilitate Rajapaksa's re-election bid.[148]

However, Sirisena soon found his options with China's port projects were limited. Of the nearly $8 billion in Chinese investments since 2005, less than 5 percent came in the form of grants. The rest were comprised of loans at interest rates above those offered by the World Bank. As a result, Sri Lanka's foreign debt exploded from 36 percent of GDP in 2010 to 94 percent in 2015.[149] Today, more than a third of government revenue goes toward servicing Chinese debt.[150]

In March 2016, ratings agencies downgraded Sri Lanka's sovereign debt rating, and days later Colombo lifted its hold on the CPCP, whose suspension was costing Colombo up to $380,000 per day.[151] A joint venture company with "Chinese majority holding" was granted a 99-year lease but a provision to grant China ownership to 20 hectares of land was removed.[152]

In April 2016, Prime Minister Ranil Wickremesinghe requested an "equity swap"[153] in which Beijing would accept equity in Sri Lankan companies and infrastructure projects to reduce Colombo's debt bill. Sri Lanka's International Trade Minister explained that shrinking the debt would "open up the opportunity for us to take more funds from Chinese Banks."[154]

Meanwhile, at Hambantota, in mid-2015 the Sirisena government approved a feasibility study for an addition to the port by the ostensibly disgraced CHEC, which would control management and operations of the dockyard.[155] "We have $1.5 billion sunk in the project and no revenue. We need to make use of it," a Sri Lankan official told the *South China Morning Post*.[156] In October 2016, Sri Lanka announced it was selling a Chinese company an 80 percent stake in the Hambantota port. "The money from the deal will be used to repay expensive foreign loans," Sri Lanka's finance minister explained.[157]

Bangladesh

China made headlines in 2010 when it announced a $9 billion deal to develop a deep-sea port at Chittagong, Bangladesh, and construct road and rail lines linking Chittagong to China's Yunnan province.

Already Bangladesh's largest port handling 90 percent of its seaborne trade, Dhaka hopes to triple the capacity of Chittagong to 100 million tons with China's help.[158] In September 2015, Bangladesh announced it was granting China a special economic zone outside of Chittagong on 775 acres of land at Anwara.[159]

Yet China has also faced setbacks in its port ambitions in Bangladesh. Throughout 2015 it looked as if CHEC was on the verge of winning a contract to build an $8 billion deep-water port at Sonadia. In early 2016, however, Dhaka unexpectedly awarded Japan a contract to build a port complex at Matarbari, which is just 15 miles from Sonadia.[160]

In late 2015 Dhaka also signaled that it was looking to cancel a deal with China's Harbin Electric International to build a 300MW power plant after "complaints of corruption in the bidding process." The Chinese company faced criticism in the past over the performance of the 80MW Tongi power plant it constructed in 2005, and has been blacklisted by the state-run Eastern Refinery Ltd.[161] Nevertheless, during a visit by President Xi to Bangladesh in 2016, $24 billion in new projects and agreements were reached on power plants, roads, data centers, and various infrastructure projects.

Maldives

China's interest in the Maldives infrastructure dates back to the 1990s when Malé leased China land on the island of Marao to construct a "maritime monitoring hub." Despite little evidence and repeated denials by Malé, Indian security analysts began to suspect China intended to use (or is currently using) Marao as a military and/or submarine base.

However, China's interest and presence in the Maldives was modest before President Mohammed Waheed assumed power in 2012. One of Waheed's first acts in government was to cancel a $300 million, 25-year contract with an Indian-led consortium to upgrade and operate the Malé airport.[162]

By 2014, Chinese investments in the Maldives included a Maldives Ministry of Foreign Affairs building, a national museum, a housing project, and various renewable energy, tourism, and telecommunications projects.[163] That year Yameen said his "government's thinking is changing toward the East."[164]

During a trip to Malé in September 2014, President Xi pledged $100 million in grants and military assistance, including a bridge connecting the capital to the airport island of Hulhule. He also secured loans and awarded a contract to a Chinese company to upgrade the main international airport in Malé, the same airport the Indian consortium was evicted from two years prior.[165]

In July 2015, Yameen moved to amend the Maldives' constitution, overturning a prohibition on land ownership by foreigners. In only the second amendment to the Maldives' 2008 constitution, the text permits foreigners to purchase land if they: a) invest more than $1 billion in the project and b) reclaimed land accounts for at least 70 percent of the completed project area. Critics suggested China was the only country with the financial prowess and land reclamation experience to benefit from such a deal.[166]

Unusually, in a country where the legislative process "includes three main stages and usually takes weeks or months,"[167] the bill cleared a parliamentary committee in one hour and was passed at 1:00 am within 48 hours of being submitted to the parliament.

China has also expressed interest in the atoll of Ihavandhippolhu. The Maldives has outlined an initiative for the atoll, iHavan, which would include "a transshipment port, airport, warehouse, export processing zones, cruise hub, dockyard, and international financial center."[168] The northernmost atoll of the Maldives, it is strategically located along the Seven Degree Channel, the principal east–west sea-trading lane through the Indian Ocean. In August 2014, Xinhua described iHavan as "the link to China's maritime Silk Route."[169]

Regional Perspectives

Views of China's growing influence in South Asia vary across the region, from great optimism and enthusiasm in Pakistan to suspicion and mistrust in India. A 2015 Pew Poll[170] confirms as much, showing 83 percent of Pakistanis with a favorable view of China as compared to just 41 percent of Indians with a favorable view. (Notably, just 24 percent of Chinese surveyed had a positive view of India).

In Pew's 2017 survey, Indian favorability toward China dropped to 26 percent.[171] Unfortunately, polling data across the rest of the region is scarce and unreliable. Bangladesh is the only other country covered in the 2015 Pew poll, with 77 percent viewing China favorably and just 22 percent unfavorably.

It's clear, however, that the elite in several regional capitals have welcomed China's elevated regional profile. This is evident in growing trade and investment links, in official endorsements for China's OBOR initiative in all but India, and in the quickening pace of senior-level diplomatic exchanges.

China has benefitted from consistently downplaying security objectives and interests. As a result, many view Beijing's activities as both non-threatening and a welcome alternative to and hedge against Indian power. Furthermore, China's philosophy of "non-interference" in others' domestic affairs has appealed to many South Asian capitals resentful of Western and Indian criticism of their often unruly democratic practices and transitions.

For the underdeveloped economies of South Asia, China has provided capital and expertise for desperately needed infrastructure. New and improved roads, bridges, and power plants have elevated living standards for millions. The billions of dollars poised to flow from China's OBOR initiative hold the potential to unlock even more of the latent potential trapped in one of the most underdeveloped corners in the world.

However, even those benefitting from China's economic largesse have begun to voice concerns, not least because China's trade with the region is highly imbalanced. In some cases, big-ticket Chinese investments have simply failed to pan out. China's high-profile but stalled $3.5 billion investment in Afghanistan's Anyak copper mine is a case in point.[172]

Elsewhere, Chinese investments have been the target of corruption investigations. In other cases, including in Sri Lanka, Chinese companies have been charged with attempting to influence the elections themselves through bribery.

Finally, the growth in Chinese trade and investments in the region has given rise to a host of expected opposition from displaced domestic industries, accusations that China is "stealing jobs," engaging in unfair trading practices, cyber and intellectual property theft, and exporting poor-quality goods.

Not least in India, Chinese investments in sensitive infrastructure and telecommunications projects have raised an array of security concerns, with a growing portfolio of proposed Chinese investments being rejected on national security grounds. "China's strategists do not draw lines separating economic and security objectives," notes veteran Indian diplomat Shyam Saran. "Each dimension reinforces the other, even though the economic dimension may sometimes mask the security imperative.[173]

Implications for the United States

For Washington, arguably the most consequential impact of China's growing South Asian profile has been the additional momentum it has provided to Indo–U.S. relations. Mutual concerns over China's rise have always represented a substantial, if often unspoken, bond in the contemporary Indo–U.S. partnership. Today, Indian concerns about China are pushing Delhi not just toward more intimate defense cooperation with the United States, but with America's partners in East Asia.

Second, U.S. officials have long seen Afghanistan as a potential avenue of cooperation with Beijing. After years of dismissing U.S. requests to play a more proactive role in the Afghan peace process, China has begun to meaningfully engage Kabul and Islamabad. Today, China appears not only to share America's objectives of containing militancy and promoting stability, it is increasingly willing to proactively engage the parties involved to achieve those objectives.

China's foreign minister has publicly described Afghanistan as a "new highlight" of Sino–U.S. cooperation, and U.S. officials have praised China's more activist role in the Afghan peace process.[174] While it's still too early to identify Afghanistan as a key point of cooperation between Washington and Beijing, their interests at least seem to be coming into greater alignment there.

Finally, China's political inroads into countries like Sri Lanka and Nepal have offered lessons about the efficacy of sanctions and diplomatic isolation in a new, more multipolar international order. In both cases, such strategies, backed by benign intentions in response to violations of human rights or democracy, proved counterproductive. In both cases, they provided China an opening that it swiftly and shrewdly exploited. In both cases, sanctions and isolation proved incapable of dissuading the target country's behavior, or preventing them from obtaining the military or economic assistance they sought. Today, both countries are less prone to economic and diplomatic persuasion and coercion than before.

Conclusion

South Asia holds both great promise and great anxiety for Beijing. It stands at the intersection of a major economic and geostrategic westward push, and Beijing has become increasingly invested in the security and stability of the region as a result.

For the second half of the twentieth century, China's engagement with South Asia was largely limited by, and focused on, its regional rivalry with India. In recent years its interests, influence, and relationships have expanded beyond the confines of that rivalry. Yet the rivalry has endured, and in some cases is intensifying as a result of China's new regional partnerships. One result is the increasing bifurcation of regional politics, with local actors increasingly assuming "pro-India" or "pro-China" labels, and political transitions increasingly viewed through the lens of which power has "won" or "lost," though in governance the distinction is rarely straightforward.

The increasingly zero-sum competition is likely to shape regional politics for the foreseeable future, as the possibility of a transformative diplomatic breakthrough in Sino–Indian relations—like a resolution of the China–India border dispute, a broad understanding on Tibet, or a fundamental change to the China–Pakistan relationship—becomes an exceedingly distant prospect.

Notes

1 The Chinese president's visits to India, Sri Lanka, and the Maldives in 2014, Pakistan in 2015, and Bangladesh in 2016 underscore this point.
2 Francine Frankel and Harry Harding, *The India–China Relationship: What the United States Needs to Know* (Washington, DC: Woodrow Wilson Center Press, 2004), 48.
3 By the mid-1950s Pakistan had assumed the role of an anti-communist, pro-U.S. bastion in the region, hosting American spy planes for missions into the Soviet Union and joining the western security alliances CENTO and SEATO.
4 The Gujral doctrine was named for the Prime Minister who championed the policy, IK Gujral, who served in 1997 and 1998.
5 M. Taylor Fravel, "Regime Insecurity and International Cooperation: Explaining China's Compromises in Territorial Disputes," *International Security* 30 (2005): 46–83.
6 Thierry Mathou, "Bhutan–China Relations: Towards a New Step in Himalayan Politics," in *The Spider and the Piglet: Proceedings from the First International Seminar on Bhutanese Studies*, eds. Karma Ura and Sonam Kinga (Thimphu: Centre for Bhutan Studies, 2004), 388–411.
7 Mathou, "Bhutan–China Relations."
8 The Siliguri corridor is less than 23 kilometers wide at its narrowest point.
9 Jeff M. Smith "High Noon In the Himalayas: Behind the China–India Standoff at Doka La," *War on the Rocks*, July 13, 2017, https://warontherocks.com/2017/07/high-noon-in-the-himalayas-behind-the-china-india-standoff-at-doka-la/.

10 On-again, off-again talks between representatives from Beijing and the Dalai Lama's office have been suspended since 2010.

11 "Tibet's Stateless Nationals: Tibetan Refugees in Nepal," Tibet Justice Center, June 2002.

12 "Pakistan, China Agree on Maintaining Strategic Balance in South Asia," *Daily Times*, February 14, 2015.

13 China previously supported the Pakistani position of holding a referendum in the disputed territory to determine its status. It now says the dispute should be resolved through bilateral negotiations.

14 Chinese leaders visited India first in 2006, 2010, and 2013. It was sixth months after his first visit to India before President Xi arrived in Pakistan, following repeated security-related delays.

15 "China Publicly Names Pakistan for Mumbai Terror Attacks," *Times of India*, June 7, 2016.

16 Andrew Small, "The China Factor," *The Cipher Brief*, October 7, 2015.

17 The ETIM is labeled a terrorist organization by the U.S. State Department.

18 China became a net importer of natural gas and coal in 2007 and 2009, and in 2015 became the world's largest importer of oil.

19 International Monetary Fund (hereinafter referred to as IMF), Direction of Trade Statistics. South Asia represented just 2.6 percent of China's external trade in 2015. That's more than double the 1.2 percent South Asia registered in 2000 but down from 2.7 percent in 2011.

20 IMF, Direction of Trade Statistics.

21 IMF, Direction of Trade Statistics.

22 "India's Trade Deficit With China Mounts to $44.87 billion in 2015," *The Economic Times*, January 13, 2016.

23 India and Nepal are the only countries in South Asia with which bilateral trade was lower in 2015 than it was in 2011. In Nepal's case it was the result of a devastating earthquake and not a secular trend.

24 IMF, Direction of Trade Statistics.

25 In 2015 China exported nearly four times as much to India as it imported; nearly eight times as much to Pakistan; roughly sixteen times as much to Sri Lanka and Bangladesh; and nearly forty times as much to Nepal.

26 PLAN warships made port calls in Pakistan, Sri Lanka, and Bangladesh between November 1985 and January 1986. One year later, the Indian Coast Guard interdicted three Chinese trawlers carrying survey equipment and military charts near India's Andaman and Nicobar Islands. The PLAN's first full transit of the Indian Ocean was in 2000 and its first port call to India in 2005. In 2001 PLAN submarine made an unannounced port call to Myanmar.

27 The PLAN Indian Ocean escort fleets generally consist of two destroyers and a supply ship.

28 Including in Pakistan, Iran, Myanmar, Bangladesh, Sri Lanka, Yemen, Djibouti, Iran, and the Seychelles, among others.

29 Dong Zhaohui, "Safeguarding World Peace and Regional Stability," Ministry of National Defense of the People's Republic of China, April 16, 2013.

30 Anthony H. Cordesman, Steven Colley and Michael Wang, *Chinese Strategy and Military Modernization in 2015: A Comparative Analysis* (Washington, DC: Center for Strategic and International Studies, 2015).

31 Caitlin Campbell, "Highlights From China's New Defense White Paper, 'China's Military Strategy'," U.S.–China Economic and Security Review Commission, June 1, 2015.

32 Robert D. Kaplan, "China's Unfolding Indian Ocean Strategy—Analysis," Center for A New American Strategy, February 11, 2014.

33 Ananth Krishnan, "Maldives for Deeper Ties With China," *The Hindu*, December 12, 2012.

34 Xu Yao, "Overseas Military Bases Not Alliances," *China Daily*, January 14, 2015.

35 Gabe Collins and Andrew Erickson, "Djibouti Likely to Become China's First Indian Ocean Outpost," *China Sign Post*, July 11, 2015.

36 Andrea Ghiselli, "China's First Overseas Base in Djibouti, An Enabler of its Middle East Policy," *China Brief* 16, no. 2 (January 2016): 6–9.

37 David Yanofsky, "Somali Piracy Was Reduced to Zero This Year," *Quartz*, December 27, 2013.

38 In December 2013, a Chinese *Shang*-class SSN crossed the Strait of Malacca, surfacing twice near Sri Lanka and in the Persian Gulf before returning to the Western Pacific three months later.

39 Vijay Sakhuja, "Chinese Submarines in Sri Lanka Unnerve India: Next Stop Pakistan?" *China Brief* 15, no. 11 (May 2015): 15–18.

40 Sanjeev Miglani, "Indian Leader Heading to Bangladesh With China on His Mind," *Reuters*, May 27, 2015.

41 In May 2016 two U.S. congressmen charged China with supplying Pakistan advanced mobile launcher systems for medium-range nuclear-capable ballistic missiles in a potential violation of international law.

42 Hans M. Kristensen and Robert S. Norris, "Pakistan's Nuclear Forces, 2011," *Bulletin of the Atomic Scientists* 67, no. 4 (2011): 91–99.

43 Myanmar was the first to order 16 of the aircraft in 2014 but no details have been disclosed. Nigeria expressed interest in September 2016.

44 Usman Ansari, "Pakistan, China Finalize 8-Sub Construction Plan," *Defense News*, October 11, 2015.

45 "Armstrade Export Values," Stockholm International Peace Research Institute (SIPRI), 2015.

46 Bangladesh's next-largest supplier over that period was Russia, with less than $150 million.

47 They have an expected delivery date before 2019.

48 Paul Pryce, "Bangladesh and Asia's Maritime Balance," Center for International Maritime Security, December 7, 2015.

49 "First Bangladesh Made Warship Launched," *Khulna Shipyard Limited*, November 15, 2012.

50 In 2015 India delivered its first batch of military aid to Afghanistan in the form of four Russian Mi-25 attack helicopters.

51 Ayaz Gul, "China Delivers First Batch of Military Aid to Afghanistan," *Voice of America*, July 3, 2016.

52 Siddhi B. Ranjitkar, "Nepal's China-Card," *Scoop*, January 16, 2006.

53 "Chinese 'Deliver Arms to Nepal'," *BBC News*, November 25, 2005.

54 "Chinese deliver arms."

55 "Prachanda Makes Historic Visit to China," *Lalkar*, November/December 2009.

56 Edward Wong and Bhadra Sharma, "Tibetans Repressed in Nepal, Rights Group Finds," *New York Times*, April 1, 2014.

57 "Nepal Told to Curb 'Anti-China' Activities From Its Soil," *Business Standard*, October 28, 2014.

58 Jon Krakauer, "Why Is Nepal Cracking Down on Tibetan Refugees?" *New Yorker*, December 28, 2011.

59 Nihar R. Nayak, "Nepal's Oil Diplomacy Could Hurt India," Institute for Defense Studies and Analyses, November 11, 2015.

60 "China Has Filled Vacuum Left by India," *The Hindu*, October 18, 2015.

61 Prashant Jha, "Chinese Advice Behind Prachanda's U-Turn on Support to Nepal Gov't?" *Hindustan Times*, May 10, 2016.

62 Press Trust of India, "Nepal Being Developed as a Laboratory, says PM KP Oli as he resigns," *DNA India*, July 25, 2016.

63 Press Trust of India, "Nepal."

64 Yubaraj Ghimire, "Unhappy China Scraps Xi Jinping's Visit to Nepal," *Indian Express*, September 7, 2016.

65 Xu Liang, "Nepal Risks Missing Chance With China," *Global Times*, September 19, 2016.
66 Sergei DeSilva-Ranasinghe, "China–India Rivalry in the Maldives," *The Jakarta Post*, June 17, 2011.
67 Ananth Krishnan, "Maldives for Deeper Ties With China," *The Hindu*, December 12, 2012.
68 Sameer Arshad, "Nasheed Vindicated, But Faces Tricky Run Off," *The Times of India*, September 8, 2013.
69 Republic of Maldives Ministry of Tourism website, www.tourism.gov.mv/statistics/arrival-updates/, accessed on November 20, 2017.
70 The country is comprised of roughly 70 percent Sinhalese Buddhists and 12.5 percent Tamil Hindus.
71 In 2006 India quietly gifted five Mi-17 helicopters to the Sri Lankan air force and substantially aided efforts by the Sri Lankan Navy to target LTTE personnel, supplies, and floating arsenals at sea.
72 Daya Gamage, "US Aid to Sri Lanka Drastically Declined Since 2005, Now Halted: No Strategic Interests in Sri Lanka," *Asian Tribune*, July 24, 2011.
73 Larry Marshall, "Winners and Losers in Sri Lanka's Long War," *Inside Story*, November 13, 2009.
74 Brahma Chellaney, "China Fuels Sri Lankan War," *The Japan Times*, March 4, 2009.
75 Hannah Gardner, "China's Aid Revealed in Sri Lanka's Victory Parade," *The National*, June 9, 2009.
76 S. Prt. No. 111–36 at 1–16 (2009).
77 Ashlyn Anderson and Alyssa Ayres, "Economics of Influence: China and India in South Asia," Council on Foreign Relations, August 7, 2015.
78 "Bangladesh, China Morally Bound to Build a Glorious Future Together: Dhaka Tells Beijing," *Bangladesh News 24*, January 26, 2016.
79 Mathou, "Bhutan–China Relations."
80 "India–Bhutan Friendship Treaty," *Carnegie Endowment for International Peace*, March 2, 2007.
81 Rupak Bhattacharjee, "The Chinese Shadow Over India–Bhutan Relations," *Bhutan News Network*, July 30, 2014.
82 Ananth Krishnan, "China, Bhutan 'Ready' to Establish Diplomatic Ties," *The Hindu*, June 22, 2012.
83 Jha, "China and Its Peripheries."
84 "China and Bhutan Hold 23rd Round of Talks on Boundary Issue," FMPRC website, www.fmprc.gov.cn/mfa_eng/wjbxw/t1292399.shtml, accessed August 27, 2015.
85 "China and Bhutan."
86 Dinah Gardner, "Bhutan Woos Chinese Tourists, But Fears Backlash From India," *South China Morning Post*, July 26, 2015.
87 Bertil Lintiner, "China Turns on Charm Offensive for Himalayan Kingdom of Bhutan," *Yale Global*, September 22, 2016.
88 Andrew Small, "China, the United States, and the question of Afghanistan," testimony before the U.S.–China Economic and Security Review Commission, March 18, 2015.
89 Richard Weitz, "Assessing China's Afghan Peace Play," *China Brief* 14, no. 23 (December 2014): 16–19.
90 Abubakar Siddique, "China Moves Toward Resolving Afghanistan's Peace Problem," *Gandhara*, November 12, 2014.
91 Small, "China, the United States."
92 Zhao Huasheng, "What Is Behind China's Growing Attention to Afghanistan?" *Carnegie Endowment for International Peace*, March 8, 2015.
93 Shannon Tiezzi, "China Joins Afghanistan, Pakistan, and US for Talks on Afghan Peace Process," *The Diplomat*, January 12, 2016.
94 In 2015 India delivered its first batch of military aid to Afghanistan in the form of four Russian Mi-25 attack helicopters.

95 Small, "The China Factor."

96 "China, India Discuss Cross Border Terror From Pak, Afghanistan," *Outlook*, November 20, 2015.

97 "China, India."

98 Ananth Krishnan, "India Holds Key Counter-Terror Dialogue With China Amid Tensions With Pakistan," *India Today*, September 27, 2016.

99 Nitin A. Gokhale, "Modi, Japan and Diplomatic Balancing," *The Diplomat*, September 3, 2014.

100 Subramanyam Jaishankar, "Remarks by Foreign Secretary at Indian Ocean Conference," Indian Ministry of External Affairs, September 1, 2016.

101 Modi invited the heads of every South Asian state to his inauguration. His first two trips abroad were to Bhutan and Nepal, followed in 2014 by a high-profile tour of the island nations of the Indian Ocean. In 2013 Delhi signed new maritime cooperation pacts with Sri Lanka and the Maldives, later adding the Seychelles.

102 Subrahmanyam Jaishankar, "India, the United States and China" (speech for IISS Fullerton Lecture, Singapore, July 20, 2015).

103 Zhou Bo, "China's Subs in Indian Ocean No Worry for India," *China Daily*, July 20, 2015.

104 John Chalmers and Sanjeev Miglani, "Insight: Indian Spy's Role Alleged in Sri Lankan President's Election Defeat," *Reuters*, January 18, 2015.

105 Chalmers and Miglani, "Insight: Indian Spy's Role Alleged in Sri Lankan President's Election Defeat."

106 Chalmers and Miglani, "Insight: Indian Spy's Role Alleged in Sri Lankan President's Election Defeat."

107 Bhattacharjee, "The Chinese Shadow Over India-Bhutan Relations."

108 "NSA, Foreign Secretary to Visit Bhutan on August 8," *Bhutan Observer*, August 6, 2013.

109 Modi was followed to Bhutan by President Pranab Mukherjee months later.

110 "India, Bhutan Not to Act Against Other's Security Interests," *New Indian Express*, November 9, 2014.

111 Brian Benedictus, "Bhutan and the Great Power Tussle," *The Diplomat*, August 2, 2014.

112 Wang Yi, "Nepal Should Not Become 'Boxing Arena' for India, China: Wang Yi," *The Economic Times*, December 25, 2015.

113 Wang Wenwen, "India Wary of US Courtship Efforts," *Global Times Editorial*, September 25, 2016.

114 Hu Zhiyong, "Can Modi's Visit Upgrade Sino–Indian Ties?" *Global Times*, May 11, 2015.

115 Qian Feng, "Beijing Can Heed Modi's Policy Shifts," *Global Times*, September 18, 2014.

116 Ellen Barry, "U.S. Proposes Reviving Naval Coalition to Balance China's Expansion," *New York Times*, March 2, 2016.

117 He Yini, "China to Invest $900b in Belt and Road Initiative," *China Daily*, May 28, 2015.

118 Kyle Churchman, "Beijing's Boldest Plan Yet Faces West," *The National Interest*, January 12, 2016.

119 Between 2005 and 2015 Chinese FDI in Pakistan amounted to $24 billion.

120 The Pakistan Board of Investment, Prime Minister's Office Government of Pakistan. http://boi.gov.pk/ForeignInvestmentinPakistan.aspx accessed November 20, 2017.

121 Daniel S. Markey and James West, "Behind China's Gambit in Pakistan," Council on Foreign Relations, May 12, 2016.

122 Summer Zhen, "Chinese Firm Takes Control of Gwadar Port Free-Trade Zone in Pakistan," *South China Morning Post*, November 11, 2015.

123 Kay Johnson, "Expanded Chinese-Operated Pakistani Port on $46 billion Economic Corridor 'Almost Ready'," *Reuters*, April 13, 2016.

124 Shawn Snow, "Pakistan Deploys Personnel to Protect Chinese Investment," *The Diplomat*, February 21, 2016.

125 Three-quarters of China's FDI into India over that period were directed to the automobile (60 percent) and metallurgical industries (14 percent).

126 "FDI Synopsis on Country China," Government of India Ministry of Commerce & Industry, Department of Industrial Policy & Promotion, September 30, 2015.

127 India is the second-largest shareholder and was elected to the AIIB's first Board of Directors, and is eyeing several infrastructure projects for AIIB funding.

128 Charu Sudan Kasturi, "India Wrinkle on China Silk—Jaishankar Speaks Out on Absence of Consultations," *Telegraph*, July 21, 2015.

129 Samir Saran and Ritika Passi, "Seizing the 'One Belt, One Road' Opportunity," *Observer Research Foundation*, February 3, 2016.

130 "China Defends Projects in PoK, Opposes India's Oil Exploration in South China Sea," *Indian Express*, June 4, 2015.

131 Begun as meeting of think tanks from the four countries in 1999, the "Kunming Initiative" was designed as a forum for promoting trade and growth among the four countries involved. Eventually evolving into the BCIM Forum the project received official endorsement from all four capitals in December 2013. The following June the four held the first "Joint Working Group."

132 Sheikh Shahariar Zaman, "Bangladesh Supports Chinese 'One Belt One Corridor' Initiative," *Dhaka Tribune*, January 26, 2016.

133 Zongyi Liu, "India's Political Goals Hinder Cooperation With China on 'Belt, Road'," *Global Times*, July 3, 2016.

134 Notably, many of China's investments are targeted in Pokhara, where Nepal's Tibetan refugee settlements are concentrated, including plans to build a new airport there.

135 Press Trust of India, "Trans-Himalayan Railways Connecting Tibet, India and Nepal feasible, Says China," Indian *Express*, August 5, 2016.

136 "China–Nepal Rail Link Can Be Extended to India: Chinese Experts," *Central Tibetan Administration*, March 24, 2016.

137 Om Astha Rai, "Coming Soon the Tibet Train," *Nepal Times*, June 23, 2016.

138 "Nepal–China Transit Treaty Is the Most Important Achievement of My Tenure: Mahesh Maskey," *Online Khabar*, June 14, 2016.

139 Gardner, "China's Aid Revealed in Sri Lanka's Victory Parade."

140 Nitin A. Gokhale, "China, India and the Sri Lanka Elections," *The Diplomat*, January 5, 2015.

141 Debasish Roy Chowdhury, "Sri Lanka Looks to China to Buoy Sinking Port," *South China Morning Post*, October 11, 2015.

142 Gokhale, "China, India and the Sri Lanka."

143 Namini Wijedasa, "China Gets Controlling Stake at Hambantota Port," *The Sunday Times*, October 19, 2014.

144 "Hambantota Port Sees Increase in Ship Traffic This Year," *Daily Mirror*, August 26, 2013.

145 Wijedasa, "China Gets Controlling Stake at Hambantota Port."

146 Ankit Panda, "Sri Lanka May Bar Port Visits by Chinese Submarines," *The Diplomat*, March 3, 2015.

147 Gokhale, "China, India and the Sri Lanka."

148 "FCID to Prosecute Chinese Company," *Sunday Observer*, May 1, 2016.

149 Rishi Inyengar, "Sri Lanka Attempts to Repair Relations With China Amid an Escalating Financial Crisis," *Time*, October 19, 2015.

150 Chowdhury, "Sri Lanka Looks to China to Buoy Sinking Port."

151 "Port City Suspension Loss: Whose Baby?" *The Nation*, March 19, 2016.

152 "Sri Lanka Hopes to Sign China FTA in 2017, Economic Plan by June: PM," *Economy Next*, April 11, 2016.

153 Gauri Bhatia, "China, India Tussle for Influence as Sri Lanka Seeks Investment," *CNBC*, April 24, 2016.

154 Ben Blanchard, "Sri Lanka Requests Equity Swap for Some of Its $8 Billion China Debt," *Jakarta Globe*, April 9, 2016.
155 Ankit Panda, "China's Sri Lankan Port Ambitions Persist," *The Diplomat*, July 27, 2015.
156 Chowdhury, "Sri Lanka Looks to China to Buoy Sinking Port."
157 Shiar Aneez, "Sri Lanka to Sell 80 Percent of Southern Hambantota Port to Chinese Firm," *Reuters*, October 28, 2016.
158 Ananth Krishnan, "China Offers to Develop Chittagong Port," *The Hindu*, March 15, 2010.
159 "ECNEC Approves Special Economic Zone for China," *The Independent*, September 16, 2015.
160 Sanjeev Miglani and Ruma Paul, "Exclusive: Bangladesh Favors Japan for Port and Power Plant, in Blow to China," *Reuters*, September 10, 2015.
161 Natalie Obiko Pearson, "Japan Beating China in Race for Indian Ocean Deep-Sea Port," *Bloomberg*, June 23, 2015.
162 Waheed's "Re-Nationalization" of the airport was later ruled unlawful by an arbitration tribunal.
163 Srikanth Kondipalli, "Maritime Silk Road: Increasing Chinese Inroads into the Maldives," Institute of Peace and Conflict Studies, November 13, 2014.
164 Ahmed Naish, "President Yameen Slams Foreign Interference in Independence Day Address," *Maldives Independent*, July 27, 2015.
165 In December 2015 the China Ex–Im Bank loaned the Maldives $373 million to develop a new runway, fuel farm, and cargo complex at INIA airport.
166 Mugdha Variyar, "Chinese 'Land Grab' in Maldives: How India Can Counter Beijing's Expanding Sphere of Influence," *International Business Times*, July 27, 2015.
167 Shubhajit Roy, "New Land Law in Maldives Gives India China Chills," *Indian Express*, July 23, 2015.
168 Devirupa Mitra, "Maldives Offers India Investment Safety Jacket Against China Wave," *Sunday Standard*, March 1, 2015.
169 Chang Yong, "Interview: China–Maldives Relations to Grow in Leaps Through Trade, Investment, Says President," *Xinhua*, August 15, 2014.
170 Bruce Stokes, "How Asia–Pacific Publics See Each Other and Their National Leaders," *Pew Research Center*, September 2, 2015.
171 Global Indicators Database, Pew Research Center, Updated in August 2017 with polling data from Spring 2017. Accessed November 20, 2017. http://www.pewglobal.org/database/indicator/24/
172 Thomas Zimmerman, "The New Silk Roads: China, the U.S., and the Future of Central Asia," Center on International Cooperation, October 2015.
173 Shyam Saran, "What China's One Belt and One Road Strategy Means for India, Asia and the World," *The Wire*, September 10, 2015.
174 Weitz, "Assessing China's Afghan Peace Play."

6

CHINA'S STRATEGY IN AFRICA

Joshua Eisenman and David H. Shinn

Introduction

Over the last decade, Africa has become an integral part of China's larger strategy to secure energy and natural resources, identify profitable investments, exploit emerging markets, gain support for its territorial claims, and validate its political ideology and position as a world leader. To achieve these international and domestic objectives, China's leaders and state-owned firms actively court African political, military, and business elites, whose public support provides external validation for the legitimacy of China's political system. Without a free press or much public debate over foreign policy, China's leaders have a free hand to pursue their goals in Africa using any means at their disposal.

To create economic opportunities and political partnerships, China has taken advantage of openings left by a less engaged Russia and a preoccupied and divided Europe. By 2016, due to its exploitation of domestic shale oil, U.S. trade with Africa was less than half of China's total volume. Meanwhile, China has become Africa's largest trade partner and an important source of aid and investment. As Chinese firms and entrepreneurs expand their operations, however, they increasingly find themselves in competition with rivals from India, Brazil, Turkey, and other emerging economies that have become increasingly active in African markets. Established partners such as Japan and South Korea are also showing renewed interest in Africa.

What follows is an overview of China's objectives and methods across Africa over the last decade. This effort to identify and summarize a Chinese strategy in Africa does not suggest uniformity, nor that it is unswervingly executed at all times by all Chinese ministries and state-run entities, let alone the scores of private Chinese organizations and firms active in Africa. As with all generalizations, we find substantial divergence among individual cases. Still, we believe that there is a method to China's interactions in Africa, which this chapter attempts to elucidate.

Historical Overview

In the 1950s and 1960s, Beijing's primary motivation in Africa was the affirmation of its own communist ideology and support for revolutionary movements. In the 1970s, following the most tumultuous period of Mao Zedong's Cultural Revolution and the deepening of the Sino-Soviet split, an increasingly pragmatic leadership sought to secure China's borders by keeping Soviet resources bogged down in distant conflicts. In the 1980s and 1990s, China's attention to Africa receded as the country turned inward and devoted more attention to relations with the West and overseas Chinese communities in Asia. After the turn of the millennium, however, to support China's growing economy, Beijing began to emphasize more extensive commercial, diplomatic, and political ties with Africa.

The 1955 Asian–African conference at Bandung, Indonesia, marked an important watershed in China's relations with Africa.[1] Premier Zhou Enlai, who led the Chinese delegation, interacted for the first time with delegations from six African countries—Egypt, Ethiopia, Liberia, Libya, and soon to be independent Sudan and Ghana.[2] The Chinese developed a good relationship with the Egyptians and met with representatives of several African liberation movements. Bandung provided a forum for China to condemn colonialism and imperialism in Africa, and to support independence movements in Algeria, Morocco, and Tunisia and Egypt's claim to the Suez Canal.[3]

Building on its success at Bandung, China expanded its engagement with the Afro–Asian world in an effort to mold its thinking and actions in accordance with Chinese ideology. The Soviet Union, which had not been invited to the conference, and its supporters resisted this effort. China sent a delegation to the first Afro–Asian People's Solidarity Organization (AAPSO) Conference in Cairo, which began in late 1957, and took note of Africans' growing role in the movement.[4]

During this period China portrayed itself as the shepherd for a flock of African nations moving toward a "new democratic revolution." At the Moscow Summit of Communist Parties in November 1960, China's state-run press reported that African revolutionaries were "studying Mao's works and using Chinese guerilla methods."[5] Premier Zhou Enlai nurtured the idea that Africa was engulfed in revolutionary zeal and that Soviet revisionists had betrayed the ideals of revolutionary communism. Some African leaders had indeed become steeped in Maoist revolutionary thought and liberation ideology.[6]

Zhou's historic ten-country visit to Africa at the end of 1963 and beginning of 1964 began China's emphasis on the importance of regular, senior, face-to-face contact with African leaders—a practice that continues today.[7] In Africa Zhou unveiled five principles to guide China–Africa relations: opposition to imperialism and colonialism, nonalignment, African–Arab unity, peaceful resolution of disputes, and national sovereignty. These principles are sufficiently vague that they have withstood the test of time, yet China has not always adhered to them. Chinese support in the 1960s for several African revolutionary movements committed to the overthrow of independent governments violated them.[8] Nevertheless, the principles continue to be quoted by Chinese officials and scholars, and were updated and expanded in China's 2006 Africa policy statement and cited in its 2015 second Africa policy paper (Appendix II).[9]

During the Cultural Revolution, the Communist Party of China (CPC) brought African policy to the Chinese people via the state-run press. To reinforce domestic support and publicize its conviction, CPC propaganda promoted what Mao called "righteous struggle" in Africa. This meant supporting Mao-style revolutionary mass movements as an extension of China's own unfinished revolution.[10] By citing Africa as proof of the widespread appeal of Mao Zedong Thought, China aimed to highlight Maoist ideology's broad appeal and establish its position as the vanguard of global proletarian revolutionary orthodoxy.

Beijing aided many African revolutionary forces fighting a guerrilla war by hastening "the development of [African] political opposition groups and guiding them towards conceptions of action closely akin to her own."[11] Speeches, editorials, and publications condemned vestiges of Western colonialism and stressed the role of Maoist ideology and the scope of armed struggles.[12] By asserting that conflicts in Algeria, Cameroon, the Congo, Uganda, and elsewhere were proletarian revolutions, China showcased its influence. Calls for armed struggle and small arms cost little, so Beijing supported revolutionary groups with zealous rhetoric and modest material support.[13]

China's willingness to place geopolitical objectives before ideological consistency grew apace with the Soviet threat. In 1969, roughly 400,000 Soviet troops equipped with battlefield nuclear weapons appeared on China's border. While the Soviets never attacked, the threat prompted Beijing to devise a strategy to cope with the threat. Although Beijing advocated a dual-adversary approach directed against both the U.S. and USSR, in practice the latter was prioritized.[14] China sought to preoccupy Soviet forces in far-off conflicts—particularly in Africa.[15] The CPC supported revolutionary movements that fought against "imperialist forces"—a term synonymous with groups supported by Moscow. This shift from dogmatism to pragmatism was catalyzed by widespread cynicism as the Cultural Revolution's worst days subsided. This less radical approach succeeded in 1971 when 26 African countries supported Beijing's successful effort to displace Taipei on the UN Security Council. In the 1970s China initiated a strategy that prioritized national security interests and was predicated on state-to-state relations, themes that continue today.[16]

In the 1970s the CPC's pragmatists gained power. Although Mao had already been enshrined as "the great leader of the international proletariat and the oppressed nations and the oppressed people," his followers had suffered a crisis of conscience.[17] Maoism had failed to fulfill its promise as a panacea for society's ills. Free from the need to insist all rebel movements were Maoist, and desperately poor, China began promoting African self-reliance. Beijing became willing "to grant ideological autonomy, and when African countries seemed to embark on a policy closely akin to Chinese thinking, Peking refrained from claiming that the Africans were following a Maoist path."[18] China expanded and deepened its state-to-state relations and put most leftist radicals on notice that they could not expect much support.

In the late 1970s and early 1980s, changes in China's domestic landscape diverted attention from Africa. By the time Deng's Xiaoping's reform coalition had wrestled power from the residual Maoists, widespread rural poverty and urban disenchantment required a reorientation of priorities. China's new leadership focused on expanding market forces in the economy. Chinese people were told to get rich, leading many to turn to trade with the West and overseas Chinese communities to make their fortunes. Economic reforms, a receding Soviet threat, and the waning role of revolutionary ideology diverted Chinese attention from Africa. It was not until the nation's need for raw materials and support on diplomatic issues (e.g., repeated Western attempts to condemn China's human rights abuses in the UN in the 1990s) that Beijing turned back to Africa via the Forum on China–Africa Cooperation (FOCAC) framework initiated by President Jiang Zemin in 2000.[19]

China's Africa Strategy

Objectives

China's strategic objectives in Africa were laid out by President Xi Jinping in his December 2015 speech before the FOCAC summit in Johannesburg, titled *Open a New Era of China–Africa Win–Win Cooperation and Common Development*. Xi identified what he called "five major pillars" of the relationship: "political mutual trust," "solidarity and coordination in international affairs," "economic cooperation," "sustained growth of China–Africa friendship from generation to generation," and "mutual assistance in security." The next section explores each of these strategic objectives, followed by a further section that identifies the methods Beijing employs to achieve them.

Political Support

African countries' political support provides external validation for China's domestic political system and foreign policies. The CPC has long prioritized state sovereignty over individual rights, and advocates "non-interference in internal affairs" to protect against foreign interventions in its own domestic politics. Just as Xi has argued that Asian people should control Asian affairs, he has also argued that "Africa belongs to the African people and that African affairs should be decided by the African people."[20] For China, political support from African countries means "promoting mutual understanding and acceptance of and learning from each other's political system and development path," "respecting each other's choice of development path," and support for "issues involving core interests and major concerns."[21] Such pronouncements are a part of China's effort to gain African nations' affirmation of its political system's legitimacy and depict this support as reciprocal.

According to China's second Africa white paper, which was published in December 2015 and is available in Appendix II, "enhancing solidarity and cooperation with African countries has always been the cornerstone of China's independent foreign policy."[22] By identifying its ties to developing countries as a "cornerstone," Beijing juxtaposes its high prioritization of Africa with the continent's relatively low standing among Western nations, particularly the U.S. China continues to cast itself "as the largest developing country" and regularly reiterated that it "will never repeat the past colonial way in its cooperation with Africa."[23]

China promotes its moral authority and leadership of an alliance of developing nations. By identifying itself as the leader of the developing world and framing Western-dominated geopolitics as both anti-Chinese and anti-African, Beijing contrasts itself with the former colonial and "hegemonic" powers. The goal is to enhance solidarity with African nations and the perception of equality even amid stark asymmetries in population, physical size, political and military power, and economic strength.[24]

Solidarity in International Affairs

Increasing China's international influence is another objective in Africa. China wants Africans to support its international aspirations, including countering the global influence of liberalism and universal values, deflecting criticism of Beijing's human rights abuses, and supporting its territorial claims. Chinese rhetoric fuses its interests with those of African nations and calls for collaboration to pursue those "mutual" interests in international institutions. Officials regularly reference decades of "cooperation," "friendship," and "equality" as the basis for longstanding Sino–African solidarity. As Xi said at the 2015 FOCAC summit:

> We Chinese and Africans have forged profound friendship through our common historical experience and in our common struggles. We have always supported each other in trying times. The Tazara Railway and the Convention Center of the African Union built with Chinese assistance are landmarks of China–Africa friendship. What has made China–Africa friendship durable and vigorous is that our two sides have always been guided by the principle of treating each other as equals, promoting win–win progress and common development and enhancing sincere friendship and cooperation. China and Africa will forever remain good friends, good partners and good brothers.[25]

Up until about 2007, Africa remained a key political battleground for Beijing and Taipei's claims to control China.[26] In 2008, with Taipei's support dwindling and the election of the more Beijing-friendly Ma Ying-jeou as Taiwan's president, the two sides undertook an unofficial diplomatic truce that temporarily mothballed their diplomatic rivalry. In 2016, however, the more independence-leaning Tsai Ing-wen was elected president, and Beijing signaled an end to the truce by establishing diplomatic relations with The Gambia, which had recognized Taiwan until 2013, and then with São Tomé and Principe. The political competition is now all but over, with only Burkina Faso and Swaziland still recognizing Taipei. African nations' willingness to abandon Taipei was gratefully acknowledged by Beijing in its 2015 second Africa white paper: "The Chinese government appreciates the fact that African countries abide by the one-China principle, support China's reunification, and refuse to have official relations and contacts with Taiwan."[27]

Beijing has also pressured African countries not to host the Dalai Lama. In 2014, China successfully prevailed upon the South African government to reject the Tibetan spiritual leader's visa application to attend a meeting of Nobel Peace Prize Laureates. While successful, Beijing's ham-fisted political pressure came with some reputational cost: 14 laureates boycotted the meeting, causing it to be cancelled, and South African Nobel Peace Prize winner Desmond Tutu vehemently criticized South African leaders for their decision: "I'm ashamed to call this lickspittle bunch my government," he said.[28]

In 2016, Beijing began seeking African nations' support for China's claims over the South China Sea. That year, several African countries, including Algeria, Gambia, Kenya, Uganda, Sudan, Togo, and Zimbabwe, all expressed support for China's maritime claims.[29] François Ngarambe of the Rwandan Patriotic Front was among Beijing's most zealous supporters. In an interview with the official Xinhua news agency after the UN Secretariat of the Arbitral Tribunal's ruling against China's claims, known as the "Nine Dash Line," Ngarambe denounced the verdict and the United States' involvement: "We support China's position. Related parties should return to the negotiation table to solve their disputes through peaceful means instead of yielding to external forces. External intervention will not bring any good result."[30]

China works to portray Sino–African solidarity as reciprocal, as former Premier Wen Jiabao explained: "As a permanent member of the UN Security Council, China will always stand side-by-side with developing countries in Africa and other parts of the world, and support their legitimate requests and reasonable propositions."[31] In 2015, China reiterated that "it will strengthen coordination and cooperation with [African] countries as well as international and regional organizations."[32]

In 2008, China opposed Western condemnation of election fraud in Zimbabwe. Amid heightened political violence the UN Security Council proposed an arms embargo on Zimbabwe and travel restrictions on President Mugabe and his colleagues, but China opposed the resolution, claiming that it interfered in Zimbabwe's internal affairs.[33] In 2013, China supported the African Union's resolution to the UN Security Council urging a deferral of the International Criminal Court cases against Kenya's president and vice president.[34] China usually opposes any UN Security Council reform proposals that lacks African support.[35]

Economic Cooperation

Since the FOCAC framework's adoption in 2000, China–Africa trade, although relatively small, has grown rapidly. The numbers are extraordinary: China–Africa total trade grew from $40 billion in 2005 to $222 billion in 2014. Between 2014 and 2015, however, China's economic slowdown and sharp drop in African commodity prices caused a dramatic drop in the dollar value of Chinese imports, from $115 to $55 billion, and opened up an Africa-wide trade deficit with China of $53 billion that has created tensions among some Africans (Figure 6.1).

The seeds of this decade-long surge in China–Africa trade—China's need for raw materials and African markets for its export products—were planted in the 1980s and 1990s and grew rapidly during the FOCAC era. During this period, China's exports penetrated African markets and China imported ever increasing supplies of raw materials from Africa. By combining top-quality capital stocks, low labor and capital costs, and government subsidies for energy and infrastructure construction China created powerful economies of scale that provide its export industries a comparative advantage over nearly all African competitors in both capital and labor-intensive production. Massive round-the-clock production kept costs down and allowed razor-thin profit margins to sustain entire export industries. Since 2000, African markets have become awash in low-cost Chinese products (Figure 6.2).[36]

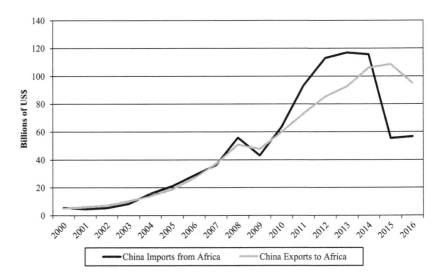

FIGURE 6.1   China–Africa Trade, 2000–2016

Source: Direction of Trade Statistics, IMF.

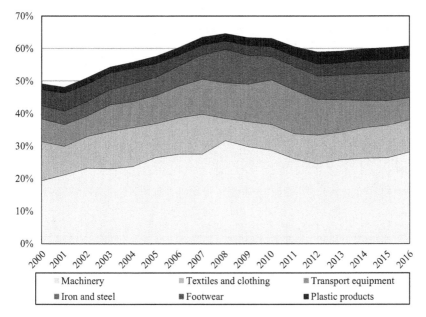

FIGURE 6.2 Percentage of China's Top 6 Exports to Africa FOCAC Era, 2000–2016

Source: Trade Map, International Trade Centre.

Access to African energy and minerals has been another driver of China–Africa trade since the mid-1990s. Natural resources, especially crude oil, are its major African import (Figure 6.3), and a major sector for Chinese invest-ment. China acknowledges these imports and contextualizes them as part of its "win–win" relationship with Africa; that is, financing for large infrastructure projects built by Chinese companies in return for oil and minerals. One 2007 IMF working paper described the trade pattern: "Strong growth of the Chinese and African economies, together with the complementary trade pattern—China imports fuel and other commodities, Africa purchases investment and manu-factured products from China—largely explains their surging trade in recent years."[37]

China first entered the African oil sector in 1997 when the China National Petroleum Corporation (CNPC) purchased 40 percent of Sudan's Greater Nile Petroleum Operating Company. As of 2007 Chinese companies invested an esti-mated $6 billion and built Sudan's oil pipeline infrastructure and a refinery.[38] At its peak production, China obtained 6 percent of its imported oil from Sudan and 65 percent of Sudan's oil exports went to China.[39] China's collaboration with Sudan was its first large-scale investment in African energy and minerals.

In 2013 alone, for example, CNPC purchased $4.2 billion worth of oil and gas assets in Mozambique. The Aluminum Corporation of China acquired $2.1 bil-lion of Chalco Iron Ore in Guinea. China Petrochemical Corporation purchased $1.5 billion of oil and gas assets in Angola. The Jinchuan Group International

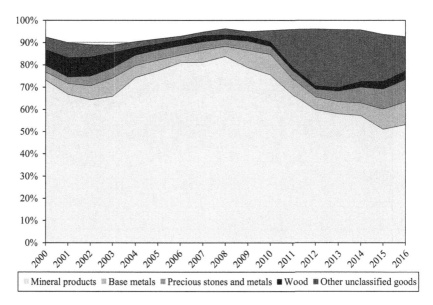

FIGURE 6.3 Percentage of Africa's Top 5 Exports to China FOCAC Era, 2000–2016

Source: Trade Map, International Trade Centre.

Resources purchased for $500 million a 40 percent share of the Metorex Ltd. mining operation in South Africa.

China's oil consumption is increasing and in 2014 surpassed the U.S. as the world's largest net importer.[40] That year, China's total oil imports reached 308 million metric tons or about 57 percent of its total oil consumption. Africa provided 17 percent of China's oil imports in 2000, rising to 28 percent in 2006, and falling thereafter to 22 percent (68 million metric tons) in 2014. Angola has been China's largest African supplier, providing between 12 percent and 17 percent of global imports from 2004 through 2014. Other suppliers include the Republic of the Congo, Equatorial Guinea, Libya, and, in the last several years, South Sudan. Sudan ceased to be a significant supplier after three-quarters of its oil producing areas became part of an independent South Sudan. Since 2010, Africa has also provided about 3 percent of Chinese natural gas imports, primarily from Algeria, Egypt, Equatorial Guinea, and Nigeria.

By value, about three-quarters of Africa's exports to China in 2016 were wood, crude oil and base metals, including iron ore, uranium, aluminum, zinc, phosphates, copper, nickel, cobalt, coltan, diamonds, platinum, tantalum, and gold. About 95 percent of China's imports of iron ore from Africa originate in three countries—South Africa, Sierra Leone, and Mauritania. In 2014, Chinese demand for African oil and metals grew less rapidly than in previous years, even amid a fall in the price of oil and most metals. By the first quarter of 2015, the value of crude oil imports from Africa was 50 percent less than the first quarter of 2014; iron ore imports declined 55 percent while copper imports slid 39 percent.[41] These declines are indicators of the slower pace of Chinese economic growth that President Xi calls "the new normal."

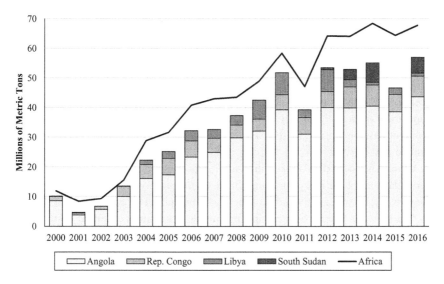

FIGURE 6.4 China's Oil Imports from Africa, 2000–2016

Source: UN Comtrade.

Copper offers an illustrative case of the China–Africa resource relationship. China consumes 45 percent of global copper production and its industrial slowdown is putting downward pressure on copper prices. In 2015, Glencore, the world's largest copper supplier, announced plans to shut down two mines in the Democratic Republic of the Congo (DRC) and Zambia to reduce its copper production by about 20 percent. These countries benefited when copper prices were high, and China imported large quantities, but then experienced the negative effects of an economic downturn.[42] Late in 2016, the price of copper began to rise again and in 2017 Glencore purchased a 31 percent stake in two DRC copper/cobalt mines valued at almost $1 billion.[43]

African countries that export modest quantities of natural resources to China are also suffering from lower commodity prices and China's economic slowdown. Kenya, for instance, has had a large trade deficit with China since at least 2000. In 2015, Kenya imported $6.5 billion from China and exported only $90 million.[44] About 55 percent of all Kenyan exports to China are raw materials (e.g., raw hides and skins, titanium ore, iron ore, and copper). Reduced Chinese demand and falling commodity prices are likely to exacerbate Kenya's trade deficit with China.[45]

Another manifestation of China's economic slowdown is occurring in mergers and acquisitions (M&A). In 2013, China was the largest M&A investor in Africa, accounting for 37 percent of all deals by value. That year, about 80 percent of Chinese acquisitions were in mining and oil. During the first ten months of 2015, however, Chinese acquisitions in Africa were less than $600 million, about 5 percent of their 2013 value.[46]

African timber exports to China increased from 35 percent of total exports in 2000 to 78 percent in 2009, making timber China's third most important commodity import after crude oil and minerals. Rising exports coincided with increased Chinese investment in timber concessions. By 2010, Chinese companies owned about 25 percent of Gabon's timber concessions. They also import large quantities of timber from Mozambique, Zambia, Cameroon, and Equatorial Guinea. Chinese companies are accused of illegally harvesting African forests and although the government has condemned these activities Chinese regulations still permit importing banned raw logs.[47]

China has received the most criticism for importing African endangered species—particularly elephant ivory and rhino horn. China is the world's largest importer of illegal ivory; between 2009 and 2012 nearly 80 percent of illegal rhino horn seizures in Asia were in China. China's surging middle class' unprecedented demand for ivory—figurines, trinkets, bracelets—pushed the price up almost tenfold between 2008 and 2016.[48] Beginning in 2018, China officially banned commercial ivory sales, but it remains to be seen how vigorously the ban is enforced.[49]

Courting Young Africans

Unlike China, Africa has a young and growing population. In 2015, the UN Population Division estimated that 41 percent of Africa's population was under the age of 15, and 19 percent was between 15 and 24. In 2015, Africa made up 1.2 billion of the world's 7.3 billion people; by 2050 the continent's population will more than double, and by 2100 of the 11.2 billion people on earth 4.4 billion will be African.[50]

China wants to influence young Africans' perceptions of its political system and gain their support for its international agenda. From Beijing's perspective, Western governments, academic institutions, and media promote liberal values in Africa that predispose Africans to see China's authoritarian political regime in an unfavorable light. To counter these views, China is hosting and sponsoring tens of thousands of African youth for training both at home and at its top educational institutions.

China uses educational and training programs to identify and cultivate a new generation of African partners who are positively predisposed to working with Chinese and speak their language. According to one long time African resident in Guangzhou, Beijing's strategy is to effect a generational change in African attitudes toward China over the next 10, 15, and 50 years.[51] Mohammed Kimani, a young China-based Kenyan interviewed by Xinhua in 2016, said Africans who go to China "are surprised to discover that Chinese society is very welcoming and friendly. Hundreds of Kenyan youth have been able to lift themselves from poverty after staying in China where they gained business skills."[52]

Still, it remains unclear to what degree China's educational and outreach programs have succeeded in winning younger Africans' hearts and minds. According to Musadabwe Chulu, a Zambian student who received his MA in public affairs from

Peking University in 2016, Africans still face racial discrimination in China: "There is defiantly a racial hierarchy. Americans are on top, followed by Europeans and then Africans."[53] This point was corroborated during meetings with African students at Fudan University in June 2017.

Security

China has a military relationship with all 52 African countries with which it maintains diplomatic relations. In 2015, China issued a military strategy white paper stating that its security interests are now global and increasingly vulnerable to regional conflict, terrorism, piracy, natural disasters, and epidemics (Appendix II). China's armed forces, it said, should safeguard China's expanding overseas interests, which it identified as secure access to energy and resources, strategic sea lines of communication, and defending Chinese personnel and assets abroad.[54] In 2016, China announced the construction of a military installation in Djibouti, which Djibouti's president called a base, but Beijing initially dubbed a naval support facility.[55] In the summer of 2017, the official press admitted that it was, in fact, a base. China's first permanent foreign military outpost underscores the People's Liberation Army Navy's (PLAN) objective to "gradually shift its focus from 'offshore waters defense' to the combination of 'offshore waters defense' with 'open seas protection'."[56]

As the number of Chinese people (the size of the Chinese community is estimated at between one and two million) and firms have increased in Africa, so have the number of security threats they have faced. In some cases, such as in Sudan and Algeria, Chinese nationals were targeted, while in others they were unlucky bystanders. China's most significant security incident occurred in Libya in 2011 following the overthrow of the Mu'ammar al-Qadhafi regime, when it evacuated almost 36,000 Chinese employed by 75 companies working on contracts valued at $20 billion. Libyans looted Chinese work sites and injured dozens of employees.[57]

There have been numerous attacks targeting Chinese interests in Africa. In 2006, China's support for the Nigerian government upset the Movement for the Emancipation of the Niger Delta (MEND), which warned Chinese oil companies to stay out of the Delta. Subsequently, MEND kidnaped more than 20 Chinese nationals. Rebel groups in Sudan's Darfur region objected to Beijing's support for Khartoum and attacked Chinese oilfields and workers, resulting in several deaths. And in 2007, the Zhongyuan Petroleum Exploration Bureau, a Sinopec subsidiary, ignored warnings from the Ogaden National Liberation Front (ONLF) to stay out of Ethiopia's Ogaden region. Nine Chinese employees later died in an ONLF attack on Ethiopian security forces. Then, in 2009, al-Qaeda in the Islamic Maghreb, citing China's crackdown on the Muslim Uighurs in Xinjiang, attacked Chinese highway construction workers in Algeria and killed 24 Algerian security personnel.[58] In 2014, ten Chinese construction workers were kidnapped in northern Cameroon by Boko Haram.[59]

Most security incidents involving Chinese nationals have been random. In 2015, for example, a Chinese embassy worker was among 13 who died when militants bombed the Jazeera Palace Hotel in Mogadishu, and in 2016 a Chinese peacekeeper was killed when militants attacked a UN camp in Gao, Mali; three Chinese nationals were among 18 killed when militants stormed the Radisson Blu Hotel in Bamako.[60] Somali pirates also attacked Chinese ships in the same manner as other nations' vessels. After Chinese ships were attacked and several were seized the PLAN agreed to contribute to anti-piracy operations in the Gulf of Aden. Since 2008, every three months China has rotated two frigates and a supply ship ostensibly to prevent piracy. By 2016 Somali pirate attacks had become rare, yet under the guise of anti-piracy operations the PLAN continues to operate in the region.[61]

Anti-piracy missions have allowed the PLAN to project power far beyond its shores, train its personnel and test naval equipment in a foreign environment, observe foreign navies, and operate submarines in blue water.[62] They have also provided a rationale for establishing naval support facilities in the region and justified the PLAN's expansion into the Indian Ocean and waters around Africa. The Chinese Navy's first port calls to Africa occurred in 2000 in South Africa and Tanzania, followed by a visit to Alexandria, Egypt in 2002, and then no visits until PLAN ships visited African ports in connection with the anti-piracy operation.[63] Since 2010, there have been more than 30 PLA Navy port calls in about a dozen African countries.[64] The PLAN has called in Algeria, Djibouti, Egypt, Kenya, Morocco, Mozambique, Seychelles, South Africa, and Tanzania.[65] Meanwhile, as part of its Maritime Silk Road strategy, China is building commercial ports in countries along the northern and western rim of the Indian Ocean.[66]

Methods

FOCAC

Established in 2000, FOCAC has magnified China's political and economic influence in Africa. It provides a venue for Beijing to regularize and publicize its diplomatic overtures, technical training, debt relief, infrastructure financing, and construction, as well as institutionalize its outreach to African elites and advance conceptions of Sino–African solidarity.

At the Forum's first session in Beijing, 80 African leaders from 44 nations joined President Jiang Zemin's call for a new world order and to redress the inequities of globalization.[22] At the Forum's second ministerial meeting in Ethiopia in 2003, the members agreed on the Addis Ababa Action Plan, which reinforced and legitimized China's expanded presence on the continent. In 2006, China hosted the third ministerial meeting in Beijing and raised the dialogue to a China–Africa summit. Forty-eight African leaders attended the Summit, which concluded with China's pledge to distribute $5 billion in loans to Africa over three years, and create a $5 billion Africa-specific private equity fund—the China–Africa Development Fund (CADF)—to encourage Chinese companies to invest in Africa.[23] Despite an initial infusion of $1 billion from the China Development Bank, however, CADF struggled to raise capital on the private market.[67]

In 2009 at Sharm el-Sheikh, China announced $10 billion in concessional loans, $1 billion for African small and medium-sized businesses, and the cancellation of debt on interest-free loans due to mature that year. It also launched a science and technology partnership, expanded the number of agricultural demonstration centers in Africa to 20, and increased professional training and scholarships.[68] The 2012 FOCAC in Beijing provided a $20 billion credit line for infrastructure, agriculture, and manufacturing projects, scaled up the CADF to $5 billion, and launched the "Initiative on China–Africa Cooperative Partnership for Peace and Security" to deepen security cooperation with the African Union and individual countries.

At the December 2015 FOCAC summit in Johannesburg, Xi announced $60 billion in new financing for ten major initiatives, including $10 billion for an industrial capacity cooperation fund to invest in manufacturing, hi-tech, agriculture, energy, and infrastructure, $5 billion for aid and interest-free loans, and $35 billion for preferential loans and export credits, and it expanded the CADF to $10 billion.[69] China also provided $60 million to support the African Standby Force and the African Capacity for the Immediate Response to Crisis.[70] Simply put, FOCAC has become the primary venue for China-Africa cooperation, and a conduit to channel Beijing's largesse to its African partners.

Party-to-Party Relations and Cadre Training

China's host diplomacy and cadre training harken back to the Mao era, when Beijing exported its communist revolutionary doctrine to African countries. During the 1970s, however, China adopted a non-ideological approach to relationship building, a strategy that endured until the end of the Hu Jintao era in 2012. Since Xi took power, however, China's cadre training has again adopted an ideology-driven approach—although the nature of that ideology has substantially changed from the Mao era. Rather than Maoism, China's diplomacy now features Xi Jinping's vision of the Chinese model of socialist development and national rejuvenation. China now seeks, not only to improve African elites' perceptions of China and "debunk misconceptions," but also to persuade Africans to adopt its illiberal, state-driven development strategy, which it bills as superior to the Western model of political liberalism and free markets.

CPC training is based on sharing its own experiences in governance and management with their African counterparts. "China is actively promoting its new model of China's political and economic development in Africa through political party training programs, which constitute a key component of Chinese foreign policy toward Africa," Yun Sun argues. The CPC maintains that its political outreach and training programs are two-way channels for mutual exchange and learning. China, however, does not appear to have adopted any methods or lessons from its African counterparts. Instead, party-to-party exchanges and cadre training remain the CPC's foremost venue to share its ideology and advance its political agenda with African counterparts. "The goal," Sun explains, "is to educate African political parties on China's experience in economic development and political governance."[71]

Since 2000, China's cadre training among African countries has expanded into a multi-tier approach that includes training programs for senior-level cadre in Beijing and for mid-to-low-level African officials in second or third tier cities.[72] To achieve a generational shift in African perceptions of China, Africa's "younger generation elites receive special attention and resources for training," Sun explained. Between 2011 and 2015, under the auspices of the Sino–Africa Young Political Leaders Forum, the CPC's multilateral African Political Party Leaders program financed training for more than 200 African political leaders under 40.[73] In 2015, the scale and scope of this program was expanded to include hosting and training for 1,000 young African political leaders in China before March 2018.[74]

African delegations often receive lectures at one of China's educational or training institutions; they tour various localities, attend cultural programs, and meet with officials, state-owned enterprises, and private businesses.[75] Topics depend on the African party's expressed interests and CPC objectives, and range from infrastructure financing to Chinese territorial claims. For African political parties in countries with democratic or multiparty systems the CPC's training focuses less on the instruments of authoritarian governance, and more on building governing capacity.

The primary Chinese interlocutor for foreign political party outreach and training is the CPC Central Committee's International Department (ID). Figures 6.5 and 6.6, which are based on reports from the ID's website, depict the changing character of host diplomacy since the leadership change in 2012. While the total number of visits has increased since Xi took power, China has begun to host more African delegations than it sends to Africa. Interviews with ID officials reveal that this change is the result of a countrywide effort to reduce the number and duration of official foreign trips.[76]

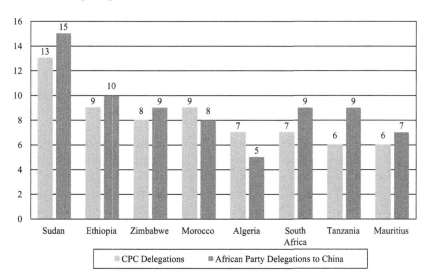

FIGURE 6.5 African Countries with Most Political Exchanges with CPC, 2006–2016

Source: ID-CPC Website.

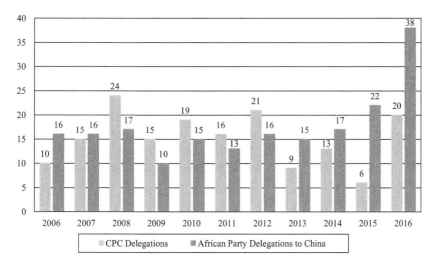

FIGURE 6.6   CPC Exchanges with African Political Parties, 2006–2016

Source: ID-CPC Website.

Tang Xiaoyang believes that Ethiopia has followed the Chinese model of a strong ruling party.[77] Sino–Ethiopian political and ideological affinities date back to the 1970s, when the CPC and the Tigray People's Liberation Front (TPLF), which dominates decision-making in the ruling Ethiopian People's Revolutionary Democratic Front (EPRDF), began their relationship.[78] The similarly non-democratic nature of their domestic politics makes many of the CPC's experiences and lessons relevant for the EPRDF. This shared illiberalism is evident in both parties' efforts to control the media and public opinion.[79] Like the CPC, Aleksandra Gadzala explains, "the TPLF-EPRDF leadership reasons not in economic or developmental terms first and ideological terms second, but vice versa: economic and developmental considerations are to support ideology, not ideology economics."[80]

The EPRDF sent its first senior delegation to Beijing in 1994 and since then the CPC has helped build its party capacity.[81] Senior EPRDF officials were impressed and began attending training programs and importing China's experiences. During one such program at the Central Party School in 2011, for instance, EPRDF cadres received lessons on party organizational structure, ideological work, propaganda, cadre education, and central-local relations.[82] The 2013 EPRDF delegation to China focused on cadre management;[83] the 2015 training program taught the EPRDF how the CPC monitors, guides, and manages public opinion through propaganda, including organizational, technology, legislation, and media relations;[84] and the 2016 delegation focused on youth management.[85] CPC financial support has helped underwrite the EPRDF's new cadre training system modeled after the Central Party School.

South Africa's ANC, which includes the South African Communist Party as part of its coalition, has been another important CPC partner. Unlike Ethiopia, however, there are substantial differences between China's authoritarian political system and

South Africa's democracy. Despite these dissimilarities there is evidence that the CPC's efforts to court the ANC have borne fruit.

In 2008, the ANC and the CPC agreed to enhance cadre training, and since then delegations have been regular visitors to China.[86] Between 2008 and 2012, four groups, including 56 members of the ANC National Executive Committee, visited China for training on the "theories and practice of the ruling parties in China and in South Africa."[87] In August 2015, after returning from an ANC delegation to study CPC organizational structure and local governance in Beijing, the ANC's head of research, Thami Ka Plaatjie, recalled that the ANC guests were treated "like royalty" and explained the purpose of CPC training and its influence on the ANC:

> The advanced study tour was intended to soak the leadership in the latest development models of China, expose them to its political system, [and] party-building models. We left China excited and invigorated, with a view to shaping our organisational thinking going forward.[88]

While in Beijing the ANC inked a five-year party-to-party cooperation agreement and later released a policy paper identifying the CPC as the "guiding lodestar of our own struggle" toward government centralization and a "post-Western," "new world order."[89] The Communist Party of South Africa also received CPC training in 2013 and 2016.[90]

To hedge against the possibility of power transition and expand its information collection activities, the CPC has expanded its outreach to African opposition parties. David Shambaugh explains the objective:

> By maintaining ties with nonruling parties, the ID has been able to keep track of domestic politics in various nations and to establish contacts with a wide range of politicians and experts who subsequently staff governments after they come to power.[91]

Opposition party outreach, however, is not always appropriate and is subordinated if it jeopardizes CPC relations with the ruling party. Ties to opposition political figures in one-party-dominated African states, in particular, could open the CPC to accusations of interference in internal affairs.[92] In Angola, Egypt, Ethiopia, Zambia, and Zimbabwe, among China's most important African partners, the CPC maintains ties only to ruling parties. Still, Liu Naiya, Party Secretary at the Institute of West Asian and African Studies, Chinese Academy of Social Sciences, believes opposition party outreach remains a growth area for the ID in Africa.[93]

The CPC aims to improve African parties' perceptions of China, yet the effectiveness of cadre training and perception management remains unclear. Some, like Shambaugh, argue that CPC has yet to "see any demonstrable improvement in its global image."[94] Others, like Sun, contend that the CPC's efforts to

> help African political parties to absorb, assimilate, and duplicate the Chinese experience constitute a different type of ideological push. It is geographically

expansive, institutionally systematic, and will have a profound psychological and political impact over the choices and preferences of African political parties, thus over African political landscape.[95]

Investment and Financing

China supports stability in African governments, and uses its finance as a hedge against destabilizing regime change. Although modest in relative terms, Chinese direct investment increased rapidly from a low base in the 1990s, yet remains concentrated in a few resource-rich countries, including South Africa, Zambia, Nigeria, Angola, and Zimbabwe.[96] After 2004 the number of Chinese investments in Africa rose steadily, peaking with 532 projects in 2013. Amid the declining profitability of commodity investments and the slowdown in China's economy, however, the number of projects dropped to 311 in 2014 and investment fell 46 percent in the first quarter of 2015 compared to the same quarter in 2014.[97]

China has begun diversifying its investments and helped establish seven African special economic zones (SEZ)—two in Zambia, two in Nigeria, and one each in Egypt, Ethiopia, and Mauritius—that offer incentives including tax breaks and reliable electric power.[98] Optimists argue that the construction of SEZs in Africa's non-resource exporting economies will help reduce trade deficits. Pessimists counter that without significant investment from African firms, the zones will facilitate Chinese firms' displacement of Africa's nascent labor-intensive industries. A study of 97 Ethiopian footwear producers found that Chinese import competition had forced 28 percent of them into bankruptcy and 32 percent lost market share.[99] The networked structure of China's African SEZs further enhances Chinese firms already substantial trade advantages. Consumer goods such as clothes and electronics are often brought into African countries alongside construction materials without paying duties. Meanwhile, labor-intensive African producers outside the zones pay hefty taxes and fees to local authorities for access to basic services and materials.[100]

The 2015 FOCAC Declaration emphasized expanding Chinese financing to support industrialization in Africa.[101] At the end of 2011, about 2,000 Chinese enterprises had invested just over $21 billion in 50 African countries: 30.6 percent in oil and mining, 19.5 percent in banking and finance, 16.4 percent in construction, and 15.3 percent in manufacturing—with the remainder spread among services, technology, wholesale and retail, agriculture, and real estate.[102] By the end of 2014, China's investment stock in Africa exceeded $32 billion (see Figure 6.7).[103] This cumulative figure, however, substantially understates Chinese investment since it omits funds routed through offshore centers such as Hong Kong and the Cayman Islands, and investors that circumvent official reporting requirements.[104]

Since the 2008 financial crisis China has become Africa's most important infrastructure financer and builder, filling a gap left by both private sector and overseas development assistance. Yet, although well publicized, this aspect remains among the least understood components of China's engagement in Africa. Often called "direct investment" or "aid projects," they rarely qualify as either, although many Chinese loans do include a concessional component. Most projects are contracts won

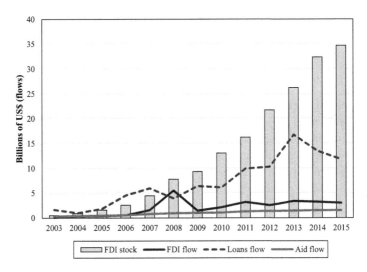

FIGURE 6.7   China's Official Financial Flows to and FDI Stocks in African Countries, 2003–2015

Source: SAIS China–Africa Research Initiative, Johns Hopkins University.

by profit-seeking Chinese construction and telecom companies hired by recipient countries using low-interest, long-term loans provided by Chinese financial institutions, like the Export–Import Bank of China, or the World Bank, African Development Bank (ADB), etc.

China established the Africa Growing Together Fund in 2014 in collaboration with the ADB. China has dedicated $2 billion over ten years to fund both public and private sector projects originating with the ADB; in 2015 seven projects worth $280 million were approved.[105] In 2016, China's Export–Import Bank helped create the $10 billion China–Africa Industrial Cooperation Fund to underwrite investments in manufacturing, agriculture, energy, minerals, technology, and infrastructure.[106] Projects financed by Chinese policy banks tend to use predominantly Chinese materials, employ an agreed-upon percentage of Chinese labor, and are often repaid by shipping oil, minerals or other commodities to China.

There are numerous cautionary tales following the announcement of Chinese financing arrangements. Sometimes funding is less than originally announced, other times project funding or repayment is delayed. The $3 billion loan obtained by Ghana in 2010 from the China Development Bank to finance infrastructure projects is a case in point. Ghanaian oil collateralized the loan, but by 2015, amid falling oil prices, Ghana cancelled half the loan and disbursement of the remaining $1.5 billion has been slow.[107]

The primary African recipients of Chinese infrastructure financing have changed over time. From 2005 to 2008, oil-rich Sudan received the most Chinese-financed infrastructure projects. Between 2009 and 2012, Ghana and Ethiopia moved into the top positions with $6.7 billion and $4.7 billion of financing, respectively. During the same period, Cameroon, Zambia, and Nigeria received infrastructure financing of about $2 billion each. Chinese commitments to non-resource rich countries have also increased, particularly for hydropower, road, and rail projects.[108] The East African Railway, agreed upon in 2014 among China, Kenya, Uganda, South Sudan, and Rwanda, will link Mombasa's port to markets and producers in neighboring states. In West Africa, in 2014 the China Railway Construction Corp. signed a $12 billion contract to build a 1,402-kilometer coastal railway that will link Lagos with Calabar.[109] China's state-run firms have won bids to construct highways in Algeria, Angola, Ethiopia, and Zambia, among other countries. Such infrastructure projects facilitate trade by connecting African natural resource suppliers with Chinese markets, and Chinese goods manufacturers with their African customers.

China provides three types of financial aid to Africa: cash and in-kind grants, interest-free loans, and concessional loans. Grants usually support small or medium-sized projects and fund training programs, technical cooperation, material assistance, and emergency humanitarian aid. Interest-free loans normally fund public facilities and projects to improve people's livelihoods. Grants and interest-free loans have been used to build stadiums, presidential palaces, military barracks, and government buildings. Concessional loans usually fund medium and large infrastructure and manufacturing projects. From 2010 through 2012, almost 56 percent of China's international aid qualified as concessional loans.[110] China's aid flows to Africa have risen steadily since 2003 but still remain a fraction of its loans and investment. In 2015, Chinese aid to Africa totaled about $1.5 billion, compared with nearly $12 billion in loans, and $3 billion in FDI flows. (see Figure 6.7). As this book goes to press there are growing concerns about rising debt levels in numerous African countries including Zambia, Kenya, and Ethiopia.

Since 2000, China has regularly cancelled overdue zero-interest loans that African countries are unable or unwilling to pay.[111] By the end of 2009, China had cancelled $3.6 billion in African debt. In 2014, China announced debt relief for 16 interest free loans totaling $230 million held by Tanzania, Zambia, Cameroon, Equatorial Guinea, Mali, Togo, Benin, Côte d'Ivoire, and Sudan.[112] In 2015, Xi extended debt cancellation to landlocked and small island nations.[113] In 2016, China forgave $40 million of Zimbabwe's debt.[114]

Media and Education

Since 2006, China's state-run media has advanced a multimillion-dollar initiative to enhance China's influence and international image.[115] In Africa, China's primary media outlets—Xinhua, China Central Television (CCTV), and China Radio International (CRI)—enjoy extensive resources that allow them to cover more stories and reach more people than other foreign broadcasters.[116] At a China–Africa Media Cooperation seminar held in Nairobi in 2013, China's Ambassador to Kenya, Liu Guangyuan, explained that these outlets counter the "ongoing conspiracy" whereby a "small number of countries monopolize the international media discourse."[117] The goal, Liu said, is to influence perceptions of China and its engagement in Africa.[118] According to Tichafa Chidzonga at Stellenbosch University: "Media diplomacy is becoming instrumental in reorienting international reporting towards positive perspectives on China's political and social progress in Africa."[119]

China's official media outlets promote a positive image of Africa that taps into the "rising Africa" narrative and emphasizes Chinese solidarity with African actors by countering the overly negative image presented in the Western press.[120] "We hope to strengthen a positive image of Africa," Song Jianing, CCTV Africa's Bureau Chief said in 2013. Douglas Okwatch, a CCTV Africa producer, agreed: "Africa today is so different from what it was ten years ago. There are a lot of opportunities. We try to focus on our strengths."[121]

In 2006, Xinhua relocated its Africa Regional Editorial Office from Paris to Nairobi, where it produces both public news and "internal reference" reports that "provide proprietary information and in-depth analyses for senior government officials, business executives and media leaders."[122] CCTV established its Nairobi newsroom in 2010, and after CPC Propaganda Chief Li Changchun's visit in 2011 the small startup became the largest international broadcasting center in Africa.[123] CCTV deployed dozens of Chinese managers, editors, technicians and reporters to Nairobi and began recruiting African anchors and local staff. By 2012, CCTV's Nairobi Bureau had over 100 employees, including about 70 Africans (primarily Kenyans) and 40 Chinese—many of them young, English-speaking women.[124]

Since 2005, Xinhua has emphasized cooperation and content sharing with dozens of African news outlets.[125] In 2007, the heads of the official news agencies of Senegal, Togo, and Benin visited China, met with Xinhua President Tian Congming, signed "news exchange agreements," and expressed their hopes to "learn from Xinhua experiences and strengthen cooperation with the Chinese state media."[126]

In 2006, CRI began seeking partnerships with national broadcasters in Africa and making its content more accessible to African audiences.[127] In East Africa, CRI established FM radio stations in three cities, broadcasting in English, Chinese, and Swahili. In Kenya, it has a countrywide AM channel and has set up program exchanges with the Kenyan Broadcasting Corp. Meanwhile, in Liberia, CRI began newscasts over the Liberia Broadcasting System,[128] and in 2010, Togo's Radio Lome agreed to broadcast CRI's French language reports.[129]

Africans generally lack knowledge about China due largely to disinterest, minimal contact, and no common language. To fill the void, China conducts both bilateral and multilateral training sessions intended to generate positive reporting about China in the African press and increase the number of media outlets that carry their reports. Journalist training workshops are becoming "one of the key components of China–Africa human resource cooperation and will help enhance the exchange between [the] press of China and Africa," Li Qiangmin, deputy director general of the African Department of China's Foreign Ministry, told participants at a 2006 workshop in Beijing. Xinhua says that during its symposiums "participants gain a thorough and deep understanding of the ongoing changes taking place in China through two weeks of lectures, seminars and tours."[130]

In 2012, Beijing placed its media training programs under FOCAC and hosted the first Forum on China–Africa Media Cooperation.[131] At the opening ceremony, Cai Fuchao, Minister of State Administration of Radio, Film and Television, said the Forum and media exchanges "strengthen mutual understanding and traditional friendship."[132] A second Forum was held in Beijing in 2014, and the next year the China–Africa Media Summit was held in Cape Town before the FOCAC Summit.[133] The third Forum, sponsored by China's Ministry of Foreign Affairs and the State Council Information Office, was held in Beijing in 2016 and included 350 media professionals and officials from 45 African countries.[134] Media cooperation remains "a powerful driving force behind China–Africa Cooperation," Cai told participants.[135]

Like journalist training, educational and vocational training initiatives develop relationships among African and Chinese elites. At the 2006 FOCAC, China increased the number of scholarships for African students to 4,000 by 2009, and increased them to 6,000 by 2015. China also agreed to increase short-term training for African professionals from 10,000 by 2006 to 30,000 by 2015.[136] By 2011, 20,744 Africans were studying in China, 14,428 privately funded and 6,316 on government scholarship:[137] many more than the 2,757 Africans studying in China in 2005, but well below the number studying in the U.S. and France.[138] To close the gap, at the 2015 FOCAC Xi announced the establishment of regional vocational education centers and "capacity-building colleges" to train 200,000 African technicians, educational opportunities for 40,000 students in China, and annual exchanges with 200 African scholars.[139]

The Office of Chinese Language Council International is expanding its worldwide Confucius Institutes Program at African universities, offering startup grants of $100,000 to $150,000 per center.[140] In 2017, there were 46 Confucius Institutes in African universities and 23 Confucius Classrooms in secondary schools in 35 African countries.[141] They offer Chinese-language programs and tutoring services, organize Chinese cultural events, and provide services to help Africans study in China.[142] In 2009, FOCAC announced the 20 plus 20 program whereby 20 Chinese universities established more formal ties with African counterparts.[143]

Chinese universities are also expanding their African studies programs. In 2017, Beijing Foreign Studies University began instruction in at least five more African languages: Comorian, Tswana, Ndebele, Shona, and Tigrinya.[144] In 1998, Peking University opened a Centre for African Studies, the next year Yunnan University established a Centre for Afro–Asian Studies, and Shanghai Normal University established an African Studies Centre in 2000. Zhejiang Normal University, home to China's most robust Africa program, established a Centre for African Education Studies in 2003 and launched its Institute of African Studies in 2007. More research funding is now available to support Chinese researchers' fieldwork in Africa.[145]

To attract African elites to China, Beijing underwrites China–Africa youth gatherings. In 2004, the Communist Youth League of China and All-China Youth Federation hosted the first China–Africa Youth Festival in Guangzhou, including 132 "youth organizations, statesmen and entrepreneurs" from 44 African countries.[146] In 2016, some 600 youths from 36 Asian and African countries attended an event intended to rekindle the Bandung spirit of Afro–Asian solidarity.[147]

China has long emphasized agricultural development and healthcare in Africa. From 2010 through 2012, it trained more than 5,000 African agricultural technicians and established 14 agricultural demonstration centers.[148] The first Chinese medical team arrived in Algeria in 1963, and since then nearly 20,000 Chinese healthcare workers have served in 51 African countries. Between 2010 and 2012 China built 30 hospitals and 30 malaria treatment centers, and in 2015, about 1,200 Chinese physicians were assigned to more than 200 medical stations in 42 African countries.[149] When the Ebola epidemic hit West Africa in 2014, China sent about 1,000 medical staffers and trained some 13,000 medical workers. After the crisis, Beijing pledged $5 million to the UN Ebola Response Multi-Partner Trust Fund and Foreign Minister Wang Yi visited the region to underscore China's commitment to African healthcare.[150]

Not all programs have been effective, however. Initiated in 2005, China's Youth Volunteers Overseas Service Program, whose participants were selected by the China Youth Volunteer Association under the Communist Youth League, had sent only 408 volunteers to 16 African countries by 2009. The program was placed under review in 2010 and subsequently suspended.[151]

Arms Sales and Peacekeeping

China supplies military equipment to African countries and contributes to peacekeeping. During 2007–2010, China's conventional weapons sales were about 22 percent of global deliveries and during 2011–2014 they reached 24 percent.[152] In Sub-Saharan Africa, however, China's small arms transfers were the lion's share: 66 percent from 2006 to 2010.[153] Chinese companies such as North China Industries Corp. (Norinco) and Poly Technologies Inc. sell equipment including armored vehicles, air defense weapons, naval ships, ballistic missiles, fighter aircraft, command and control equipment, battle tanks, long-range artillery, howitzers, and drones.[154] African governments, especially those facing Western sanctions such as Sudan and Zimbabwe, welcome low cost and good quality Chinese weapons, which are increasingly appearing in conflict zones. In 2014, for example, after the outbreak of civil war, Norinco agreed to sell $38 million worth of missiles and small arms to South Sudan. After the first delivery, however, international pressure forced China to cancel the remaining order.[155]

China became active in UN peacekeeping operations in 2000, and by 2017, about 2,100 Chinese were serving in six of the eight UN peacekeeping operations in Africa. Most Chinese peacekeepers are located in Sudan's Darfur Region, South Sudan, the DRC, and Mali.[156] China is the second largest contributor to the UN peacekeeping budget at 10 percent and has more personnel assigned to UN operations in Africa than any other permanent member of the Security Council, but less than countries such as India, Bangladesh, and Ethiopia. China's participation in peacekeeping, although widely praised, serves its interests. Peacekeeping enhances China's image as a contributor to global stability, while testing its troops and equipment under real-world conditions, and allowing the PLA to interact with other militaries.[157] In South Sudan, where the PLA has had a combat battalion since 2015, China evacuated more than 400 personnel from the oil fields.[158]

African Perceptions of China's Contemporary Africa Strategy

Perceptions of China are generally positive in Africa. A 2014 Pew survey conducted through interviews with 7,062 individuals in Tanzania, Kenya, Senegal, Nigeria, Uganda, Ghana, and South Africa found that in all countries (except South Africa) over half of those surveyed hold favorable views of China, perceive China's economic growth as beneficial for their country's economy, and believe that the Chinese government respects personal freedoms.[159] In a subsequent 2015 Pew survey, which looked at favorable/unfavorable views of China in nine countries in Sub-Saharan Africa, China's favorable rating was about 70 percent.[160] Many Africans appear to welcome the benefits of newly constructed roads, schools, communication networks, factories—as well as rising energy and commodity prices driven by Chinese demand.

China has cordial, and in some cases warm, relationships with all 52 African governments that recognize Beijing. Autocratic African governments, like Zimbabwe, Ethiopia, and Sudan, have been particularly attracted to China's political and economic systems. These close relations also extend to the North African countries of Algeria and Morocco. Like many countries, China was forced to adjust its policies in North Africa in the aftermath of the Arab Spring. Relations with Tunisia have since been normalized and ties with Egypt are particularly strong, although Libya remains a challenge. Beijing has cordial relations with the Sahel countries except for Burkina Faso, which recognizes Taipei. China's economic ties are strong throughout the region, including trade with Burkina Faso.

China has good relations with leading countries in West Africa: Nigeria, Ghana, Senegal, Côte d'Ivoire, and Liberia, and in 2016 reestablished diplomatic relations with The Gambia and São Tomé and Principe. The autocratic governments of Central Africa have warm relations with China, largely because Beijing does not hector their leaders over their poor human rights practices and reluctance to democratize. China has close relations with central Africa's most important country, the DRC, with which it has a strong trade relationship and has provided billions in loans.

The six countries in the Horn of Africa present challenges for China because of their internal conflict and problems with neighbors. China has strong economic and political ties with most of them, particularly Ethiopia and Sudan. At the same time, it has struggled to preserve its oil interests in South Sudan, despite its contribution to the UN peacekeeping operation there. China has developed close ties in East Africa with the Kenyan and Tanzanian governments, and has good relations with the four Indian Ocean island governments.

Beijing's economic and political relations with the governments of southern African countries are uniformly strong except for Swaziland, which recognizes Taipei. The CPC has developed especially strong ties with the ruling parties of South

Africa, Zimbabwe, Angola, Namibia, and Mozambique. Angola and South Africa are China's major African trade partners, and a high percentage of China's foreign direct investment has gone to southern Africa.

While China generally has close relations with African governments, elite African perceptions of China are not uniformly positive. The bluntest criticisms of Chinese business practices likened them to European colonialism. "The potential danger, in terms of the relationship that could be constructed between China and the African continent, would indeed be a replication of that colonial relationship," former South African President Thabo Mbeki said in 2006. "It is possible to build an unequal relationship, the kind of relationship that has developed between African countries as colonies. The African continent exports raw material and imports manufactured goods, condemning [it] to underdevelopment."[161]

In 2013, Nigeria's Central Bank governor, Lamido Sanusi, observed that:

> China takes our primary goods and sells us manufactured ones. This was also the essence of colonialism. The British went to Africa and India to secure raw materials and markets. Africa is now willingly opening itself up to a new form of imperialism.[162]

The governor of the Bank of Botswana, Linah Mohohlo, expressed concern that "Africa should be careful not to rely too much on China and its development model as the panacea for its economic ills."[163]

Some African elites, like John Mangudya, the governor of the Reserve Bank of Zimbabwe (RBZ), have refused publicly to criticize the Chinese, even as they are transporting hundreds of millions in hard currency out of the country in "suitcases and depositing cash with a Chinese bank in Johannesburg." In 2015, Mangudya acknowledged that $684 million was illicitly externalized by individuals "under the auspices of free funds for various dubious and unwarranted purposes." That year, in a case bankers called the "just the tip of an iceberg," Chinese diamond mining firm Jinan Mining was investigated for externalizing $546 million. "It's not just the currency; it's also ivory and precious stones. A few of them have been arrested but the fines have not been deterrent," an anonymous RBZ official said. An anonymous source within the ruling ZANU-PF party said the capital flight had "disturbed the political system."[164]

Generally, positive perceptions of China as an African development partner seem to turn negative when large numbers of Chinese enter African communities, usually as traders and entrepreneurs in the local market. Tensions have erupted in urban protests in a number of African countries. Zambia and Zimbabwe, for instance, have seen riots against Chinese merchants and products, and the exclusion of Chinese from business and other communities.[165] In Kampala, Uganda, for instance, local merchants held a two-day strike in 2011 against the "influx of Chinese traders associated with Chinese investments." Issa Sekito of the Kampala City Traders Association explained: "Over the years, we have been complaining to government over the aliens doing petty trade, especially the Chinese—who come in as investors."[166]

Similarly, in 2014, Tanzania's labor unions publicly criticized the government for letting in small Chinese traders.[167]

In January 2015, in Kinshasa, DRC, local protesters attacked and looted about fifty Chinese-owned shops in working-class neighborhoods. Demonstrators shattered windows, broke down doors, and picked shelves clean. "Nothing was touched besides the Chinese stores," said one Congolese who owns dozens of businesses in the area. Thousands of Chinese laborers in the DRC work on Chinese-financed infrastructure projects or run businesses that serve their compatriots. "They sell everything, [and] we're no longer doing any business because of them," complained one local vendor, who said he hoped the looting would be a "lesson" to his Chinese rivals.[168]

If China–Africa trade continues in accordance with existing patterns, China will face increasing criticism at both the grassroots and elite levels. "China inadvertently follows the same pattern of other preceding great powers, spreading the seeds of discontent in a continent with diversified ethnicities and cultures," Eric Kiss and Kate Zhou observe.[169] China's indifference to, or active aid of, autocratic regimes in countries like Zimbabwe, Equatorial Guinea, Guinea, Sudan, and Ethiopia risks partnering with repressive political elites against local people. By selling African governments weapons, censorship technology, and monitoring equipment to maintain social order, Chinese firms are unwittingly tapping into a potential reservoir of unhappiness and distrust.

Implications for the United States

Much of the public discussion on China in Africa has focused on whether China is seeking to, and whether it will, overtake U.S. influence on the continent. Although the United States has diplomatic relations with 54 African countries, the quality of these bilateral relationships varies considerably compared to China. The U.S. prioritizes North Africa, especially Egypt, which Washington considers part of the Middle East. In the aftermath of the Arab Spring and the Libyan revolution, the U.S. struggled to reformulate its policies in North Africa, thus sending mixed signals that strained its relations with Egypt and caused confusion with Libya. Meanwhile, among world regions, Sub-Saharan Africa remains at the bottom of the U.S. foreign policy agenda.

American democracy does not lend itself to long-term strategic thinking. Political power changes every four or eight years in the executive branch, meaning administrations rarely develop lasting foreign policies, and sometimes have trouble thinking beyond the next year. China's Africa policy, by contrast, emphasizes predictability and is based on regularized, high-level personal contacts with African government leaders. Senior officials from the Foreign Ministry, CPC, military, and provincial governments regularly visit Africa and every year China hosts hundreds of African officials. Former President Hu Jintao made six trips to Africa, two as vice president and four as president. Xi Jinping visited Africa on his first overseas trip after assuming the presidency, and then returned to co-chair the 2015 FOCAC summit in South Africa. China's foreign minister has made Africa his first overseas destination every year since 1991.

By contrast, since 1993, U.S. Presidents Bill Clinton and George W. Bush each visited Sub-Saharan Africa twice and President Obama three times. If Cairo is excluded, there have been a number of years since 1991 that the American secretary of state did not visit Africa. The United States receives far fewer African leaders than China, but takes advantage of their presence to arrange high-level meetings at the annual fall United Nations session in New York and World Bank and International Monetary Fund meetings in Washington.

Sometimes China and the United States cooperate in Africa, and other times they compete. While there are disagreements between them, neither country has core security interests in Africa, making the region a natural place to enhance bilateral cooperation. There are numerous areas where China and the United States are already or could cooperate in Africa. Both countries generally seek political stability, economic prosperity, and the minimizing of negative developments such as terrorism, piracy, narcotics trafficking, and international crime. They have collaborated in efforts to encourage stability and reduce conflict in Sudan, South Sudan, and Somalia, and both support UN and African Union peacekeeping efforts and international efforts to combat piracy.

China was instrumental in convincing President Omar al-Bashir of Sudan to accept a hybrid African Union/United Nations peacekeeping force in Darfur, where Chinese peacekeepers subsequently were assigned.[170] Both countries have backed UN initiatives to support the Somali Federal government, neither recognizes the functionally independent region of Somaliland, and both have provided financial assistance to the African Union peacekeeping mission in Somalia to combat extremism.[171] China and the U.S. cooperate with the United Kingdom and Norway to support the Intergovernmental Authority for Development efforts to achieve peace in South Sudan.[172]

There is further potential for U.S.–China security and economic cooperation in Africa. Both countries have unique strengths, for example, in helping jointly to improve African healthcare, agriculture, natural disaster, and crisis relief. Each adds value to malaria prevention programs and can adapt its advanced farming techniques for African conditions. U.S.–China cooperation is most likely when African political and business leaders actively encourage both countries (and perhaps others) to collaborate on specific projects that serve local interests.

The United States has a robust military presence in Africa, although only about 40 Americans are assigned to UN peacekeeping operations on the continent. On the other hand, the United States funds about 29 percent of the UN peacekeeping budget. U.S. military aircraft often over fly or land in African airports, its naval vessels frequently visit African ports, and like China, the United States has been active in anti-piracy operations off Somalia. The Combined Joint Task Force–Horn of Africa base in Djibouti, a major operational center for drone operations in Yemen and Somalia, has more than 4,000 personnel working primarily on counterterrorism, and in 2015–2016 underwent a $1.4 billion upgrade.[173] The U.S. military also has a drone surveillance operation in Niger, Seychelles, and Cameroon and fixed-wing surveillance contract arrangement in Burkina Faso.

Although American and Chinese interests in Africa are often complementary, there are, of course, areas of disagreement. For example, there were disagreements in 2005–2006 over the best approach to end conflict in Sudan's Darfur region. China supported Sudanese President Omar al-Bashir while the U.S. placed sanctions on Sudan. Beijing and Washington also disagreed in 2011 over the future of the al-Qaddafi regime in Libya. Although Beijing did support the UN Security Council resolution that ultimately deposed Qaddafi, there was much consternation in Beijing about that decision. China is also concerned about what it sees as the U.S.' over-reliance on a military response in countries such as Somalia.

More autocratic African leaders sometimes assert (perhaps want to believe) that China will replace the United States in the not distant future as the world's leading power. China is primarily interested in cooperation and is viewed more favorably by autocratic governments because it eschews lecturing them on governance, and in some cases even supplies them the tools of repression. Beijing does not attach political strings (beyond the "One China" policy) to its aid, nor does it interfere to prevent human rights abuses or criticize non-democratic practices.

Washington's political conditionality and the fact that the U.S. has been engaged in controversial African issues have won it friends and foes alike. The U.S. actively encourages African countries to democratize and improve their human rights policies. As a result, many African officials perceive the United States as more arrogant and interventionist, compared to China's more modest, hands off approach. Yet, the United States enjoys an advantage over China in its relations with civil society, non-governmental organizations, think tanks, independent labor unions, opposition political parties, and many university communities. China has minimal contact with most of these groups, perhaps because it has little experience in working with them domestically. Both countries interact well with the African business community, although the Chinese government and business sector has worked harder than their American counterparts to cultivate these relations.

Conclusion

China has become, in the words of Zimbabwe's now deposed strongman Robert Mugabe, "an alternative global power point" in Africa.[174] Beijing has designed a strategy in Africa to ensure access to energy and other natural resources, open new export markets, safeguard its interests in international institutions, and gain external validation for its socialist political ideology. In pursuit of these objectives, Beijing has shown little regard for the financial or humanitarian constraints that give pause to leaders in liberal democratic societies.

Over the last decade, China has expanded its security presence in Africa. The CPC and Xinhua are extending their outreach to African political parties and press outlets, hosting more visitors than ever before and training the next generation of African party cadres and media. Chinese investment and trade have helped many African countries develop their industries and unearth their resources. Yet, China has also faced challenges: its state-run firms lost billions in Libya after the al-Qaddafi regime fell, and despite its contribution to UN peacekeeping in South Sudan, Chinese oil investments have been undermined by civil war. A looming political transition in Zimbabwe could bring similar economic losses.

Although China's trade with Africa is rooted in powerful market dynamics only partially created by Chinese policies, it has generated mixed and often politically charged reactions among many African communities and civil society groups. Criticism that Chinese interests facilitate corruption and poor governance has catalyzed growing criticism of China. Many are frustrated with their governments' inability to manage the China relationship in ways that are more broadly beneficial. China's economic slowdown compounds this problem by contributing to a sharp drop in commodity prices that has expanded African countries' trade deficits with China. Meanwhile, Chinese firms and entrepreneurs in African markets are facing tougher competition from rivals such as India, Brazil, Turkey, and other emerging economies and established partners.

Notes

1 For a detailed description of this period see David H. Shinn and Joshua Eisenman, *China and Africa: A Century of Engagement* (Philadelphia, PA: University of Pennsylvania Press, 2012), 31–38.
2 Shinn and Eisenman, *China and Africa*, 33.
3 Nasser-Eddine, 60–104, has a detailed account of Chinese–Egyptian contacts leading up to diplomatic recognition in 1956; see also Larkin, 16–20. For an account of the Bandung Conference, see Richard Wright, *The Color Curtain: A Report on the Bandung Conference* (Jackson, MS: Banner Books, 1956).
4 Bruce D. Larkin, *China in Africa 1949–1970: The Foreign Policy of the People's Republic of China* (Berkeley, CA: University of California Press, 1971), 20, 32–36.
5 W.A.C. Adie, "Chinese Policy Towards Africa," in *The Soviet Bloc, China and Africa*, eds. Sven Hamrell and Carl Gosta Widstrand (Ussala: The Scandinavian Institute of African Studies, 1964), 53.
6 Patrick Tyler, *A Great Wall* (New York: Public Affairs, 1999), 204.
7 Julia C. Strauss, "The Past in the Present: Historical and Rhetorical Lineages in China's Relations With Africa," *China Quarterly*, 199 (2009): 781–82.
8 CIA, "What the Chinese Communists Are Up to in Black Africa," declassified secret report, March 23, 1971, 7.
9 For a discussion of the principles, see Alaba Ogunsanwo, *China's Policy in Africa 1958–71* (London: Cambridge University Press, 1974), 120.
10 Adie, "Chinese Policy Towards Africa," 44.
11 Larkin, *China in Africa 1949–1970*, 157.
12 Adie, "Chinese Policy Towards Africa," 53.
13 Larkin, *China in Africa 1949–1970*, 156.
14 Samuel S. Kim, "China and the Third World: In Search of a Neorealist World Policy," in *China and the World: Chinese Foreign Policy in the Post-Cold War Era*, ed. Samuel. S. Kim (Boulder, CO: Westview Press, 1984), 184; Harold C. Hinton, *The People's Republic of China, 1949–1979: A Documentary Survey* (Wilmington, DE: Scholarly Resources, 1980), 2414–2423.
15 Richard Lowenthal, "The Sino–Soviet Split and Its Repercussions in Africa," in *The Soviet Bloc, China and Africa*, eds. Sven Hamrell and Carl Gosta Widstrand (Ussala: The Scandinavian Institute of African Studies, 1964), 132.

16 James Lilley and Jeffrey Lilley, *China Hands: Nine Decades of Adventure, Espionage, and Diplomacy in Asia* (New York: Public Affairs, 2004), 155.

17 "Text of the Announcement Issued by Peking Reporting Death of Chairman Mao," *New York Times*, September 10, 1976.

18 Eugene K. Lawson, "China's Policy in Ethiopia and Angola," in *Soviet and Chinese Aid to African Nations*, eds. Warren Weinstein and Thomas H. Henriksen (New York: Praeger, 1980), 172.

19 For a more extensive analysis of China–Africa relations in the 1980s and 1990s see Shinn and Eisenman, *China and Africa*, 43–48, 66–69, 111–114.

20 Niu Honglin, "President Xi Jinping Delivers Speech at FOCAC Summit," *CRI English*, December 5, 2015; Guo Silu and Cen Xinhang, "Yaxin fenghui: Yazhou shi yazhouren de yazhou" 亚新峰会：亚洲是亚洲人的亚洲 [CICA: Asia Is Asia for Asians], *Southern Weekly*, May 22, 2014.

21 "China's Second Africa Policy Year," *Xinhua*, February 4, 2014; Honglin, "President Xi Jinping Delivers Speech at FOCAC Summit."

22 "China's Second Africa Policy Year."

23 "China's Second Africa Policy Year."

24 Yuan Ye, "China, S. Africa Consolidate Ties for Developing World's Benefit," *Xinhua*, June 20, 2006.

25 Honglin, "President Xi Jinping Delivers Speech at FOCAC Summit."

26 For an extensive discussion see Shinn and Eisenman, *China and Africa*, 85–90.

27 "China's Second Africa Policy Year."

28 "Dalai Lama Visa Row Halts Nobel Forum in South Africa," *BBC News*, October 2, 2014.

29 "Kenya Backs China's Approach to South China Sea Disputes," Forum on China–Africa Cooperation (hereinafter referred to as FOCAC), June 12, 2016; "China Praises Togo's Position on South China Sea Issue," *Xinhua*, May 18, 2016; "Zimbabwe: Zim Pledges Support on China Sea Dispute," *All Africa*, June 30, 2016.

30 "Secretary General of Rwandan Patriotic Front: External Intervention Does Not Help to Solve South China Sea Disputes," FOCAC, July 15, 2016.

31 "Speech by Chinese Premier at Opening Ceremony of China–Africa Cooperation Forum," *People's Daily*, December 16, 2003.

32 "China's Second Africa Policy Year."

33 Samuel Ramani, "Zimbabwe: China's 'All-Weather' Friend in Africa," *The Diplomat*, January 11, 2016.

34 Xue Lei, "China as a Permanent Member of the United Nations Security Council," *Friedrich Ebert Stiftung*, April 2014, 13.

35 Lei, "China as a Permanent Member of the United Nations Security Council," 14.

36 Joshua Eisenman, "China–Africa Trade Patterns: Causes, Consequences, and Perceptions," in *Africa and China: How Africans and Their Governments are Shaping Relations With China*, ed. Aleksandra Gadzala (Lanham, MD: Rowman and Littlefield, 2015), 14.

37 Jian-Ye Wang, "What Drives China's Growing Role in Africa?" IMF Working Paper, October 2007, 20.

38 Ali Abdalla, *The Sudanese–Chinese Relations Before and After Oil* (Khartoum: Sudan Currency Printing Press, 2006), 76–80; Shinn and Eisenman, *China and Africa*, 251–252.

39 Zhao Hong, "China–U.S. Oil Rivalry in Africa," *The Copenhagen Journal of Asian Studies* 26 (2008): 100.

40 U.S. Energy Information Administration, "China," May 14, 2015.

41 Kate Douglas, "China's Slowdown: What It Means for African Trade," *How We Made It in Africa*, November 2, 2015.

42 Nastassia Arendse, "China vs Copper: That Sinking Feeling," *Mine Web*, October 6, 2015.

43 Andrew Topf, "Glencore Buys Stakes in Mutanda and Katanga Mines Valued at $960m," *Mining.com*, February 13, 2017.

44 International Monetary Fund (hereinafter referred to as IMF), *Direction of Trade Statistics Yearbook* (Washington, DC: IMF, 2016), 319.
45 Apurva Sanghi and Dylan Johnson, "Deal or No Deal: Strictly Business for China in Kenya?" *Policy Research Working Paper*, World Bank Group, March 2016, 8–9.
46 Valentina Romei, "China and Africa: Trade Relationship Evolves," *Financial Times*, December 3, 2015.
47 Weng Xiaoxue, Louis Putzel, Mercy M. Kandulu, Sigrid-Marianella S. Ekman, Marie-Luce B. Zafinikamia, Samuel Assembe-Mvondo, Paolo O. Cerutti, and Guillaume Lescuyer, "The Africa–China Timber Trade," *Center for International Forestry Research Brief* 28 (March 2014), 1–12.
48 Adam Cruise, "China Pledges to Do More—But Is It Enough to Stop Elephant Poaching?" *National Geographic*, December 8, 2015.
49 Javier C. Hernandez, "In Banning Ivory Trade, China Saw Benefits for Itself Too," *New York Times*, January 2, 2017.
50 "How Will a Population Boom Change Africa?" *BBC News*, September 11, 2015.
51 Benno Muchler and Yiting Sun, "Africa–China: Obstacles Surmounted From Generation to Generation," *The Africa Report*, February 16, 2015.
52 Christine Lagat, "Feature: Young Kenyan Builds Business Acumen in China, Inspires Peers," *Xinhua*, June 27, 2016.
53 Musa Chulu, interview by author July 11, 2016.
54 "Full Text: China's Military Strategy," *Xinhua*, May 26, 2015.
55 Michael Martina, "China Says Starts Construction of Djibouti Military Base," *Reuters*, February 25, 2016.
56 "China's Military Strategy."
57 Shaio Zerba, "China's Libya Evacuation Operation: A New Diplomatic Imperative—Overseas Citizen Protection," *Journal of Contemporary China* 23 (2014): 1093–1094.
58 Shinn and Eisenman, *China and Africa*, 179–181.
59 "Boko Haram Hostages Freed in North, Cameroon Says," *New York Times*, October 11, 2014.
60 "Somalia Blast: Mogadishu Hotel Rocked by Bomb," *BBC News*, July 26, 2015; "Chinese Peacekeeper Among Four Killed in Mali Attacks," *BBC News*, June 1, 2016; Faith Karimi and Erin Burnett, "Mali Hotel Attack: Gunmen Barged in, Shot at 'Anything That Moved'," *CNN News*, November 22, 2015; Jane Perlez and Neil MacFarquhar, "9 Foreigners Killed in Mali Are Identified," *New York Times*, November 22, 2015.
61 "China's Military Strategy"; see Andrew Erickson and Austin Strange, "China's Blue Soft Power: Antipiracy, Engagement, and Image Enhancement," *Naval War College Review* 68 (2015): 71–91 and Susanne Kamerling and Frans-Paul Van Der Putten, "An Overseas Naval Presence Without Overseas Bases: China's Counter-piracy Operation in the Gulf of Aden," *Journal of Current Chinese Affairs* 4 (2011): 119–146.
62 Dinakar Peri, "U.S. Admiral Questions Logic of Chinese Submarines on Anti-Piracy Missions," *The Hindu*, January 9, 2016; "Chinese Submarine on Its Way to Somalia for Anti-piracy Patrols," *Defense Web*, October 1, 2014.
63 Shinn and Eisenman, *China and Africa*, 189–190.
64 Erickson and Strange, "China's Blue Soft Power," 81–82.
65 Erickson and Strange, "China's Blue Soft Power," 81–82.
66 Robert Kaplan, "Center Stage for the Twenty-first Century: Power Plays in the Indian Ocean," *Foreign Affairs* 88 (2009): 22.
67 Deborah Bräutigam, "Mysteries of the China Africa Development Fund," *China Africa Research Initiative Blog*, March 24, 2015.
68 Sven Grimm, "FOCAC—Political Rationale and Functioning," Centre for Chinese Studies of Stellenbosch University, May 2012.
69 "China Promises More Aid to Africa," *Xinhua*, July 27, 2016.
70 "Home Page," FOCAC.
71 Yun Sun, "Political Party Training: China's Ideological Push in Africa?" *Brookings*, July 5, 2016.
72 Ma Hui (International Department, Central Committee of CPC), interview, June 20, 2016.

73 "Zhongfei qingnian lingdaoren luntan zhaokai, Zhonggong tuichu sannian qianren jihua 1000 ming Feizhou qingnian zhengzhijia jiang huoyao fuhua" 中非青年领导人论坛召开，中国推出三年千人计划 1000名非洲青年政治家将获邀赴华 [China Holds the China-Africa Youth Leadership Forum and Launches a Three-Year Plan for Inviting One Thousand Young African Politicians to Visit China], FOCAC, March 30, 2015.

74 "Zhongfei."

75 Interviews with ID official., June 20, 2016.

76 Interviews with Chinese officials in Washington, DC, June 2016 and Beijing, July 2016.

77 Tang Xiaoyang, "Aisaiebiya: fuzhi Zhongguo moshi?" 埃塞俄比亚：复制中国模式？ [Ethiopia: Replicate Chinese Model] *Modern Weekly*, August 29, 2014; Cai Linzhe, "Aisaiebiya xuexi 'Zhongguo moshi'" 埃塞俄比亚学习"中国模式" [Ethiopia Learns from "Chinese Model"], *Phoenix Weekly*, November 12, 2014.

78 Aleksandra Gadzala, "Ethiopia: Toward a Foreign-Funded 'Revolutionary Democracy'," in *Africa and China: How Africans and Their Governments Are Shaping Relations with China*, ed. Aleksandra Gadzala (Rowman & Littlefield Publishers, 2015), 89.

79 Sun, "Political Party Training."

80 Gadzala,, "Ethiopia," 102.

81 "Zhonglianbu juzhang Aiping tan yu Feizhou zhengdangde jiaowang" 中联部局长艾平谈与非洲政党的交往 [Director of ID-CPC Talks about Engagement With African Political Parties], *Guangming Daily*, October 11, 2007.

82 Sun, "Political Party Training."

83 Bai Debin, "Wudegang huijian Aisaiebiya gaoji ganbu yanxiuban yixing" 吴德刚会见埃塞俄比亚高级干部研修班一行 [Wu Degang Meets Delegates of Ethiopian Senior Cadre Seminar], *Gansu Daily*, August 26, 2013.

84 "Aisaiebiya renmin geming minzhu zhenxian zhengdang kaochatuan zaijing kaiban" 埃塞俄比亚人民革命民主阵线政党考察团在京开班 [Ethiopian People's Revolutionary Democratic Front Party Holds Study Groups in Beijing], Research and Training Institute of SAPPRFT, October 9, 2015.

85 Jiang Xuelin, "Aisaiebiya renmin geming minzhu zhenxian ganbu kaochatuan fangwen Guangxi" 埃塞俄比亚人民革命民主阵线干部考察团访问广西 [Officials of Ethiopian People's Revolutionary Democratic Front Visit Guangxi Province], *China News*, February 29, 2016.

86 "Xi Jinping huijian Nanfei feiguoda quanguo zhiwei yanxiuban yixing" 习近平会见南非非国大全国执委研修班一行 [Xi Jinping Meets the Executive Committee of South Africa's African National Congress], ID-CPC, October 11, 2011.

87 Li Shijun, "Zhongfei zhengdang guanxi zhuli Zhongfei zhanlue huoban guanxi" 中非政党关系助力中非战略伙伴关系 [Relations of Political Parties between China and Africa Promotes Sino-African Strategic Partnership], *China News*, October 11, 2012.

88 Thami Ka Plaatjie, "Lessons to Learn from Chinese Experience," *Sunday Independent*, August 2, 2015; Pan Junyu and Zhang Wei, "Nanfei feizhouren guomin dahui gaoji ganbu yanxiuban yixing fangshao, xuexi jiaoliu jiceng dangzuzhi jianshe deng xianjin jingyan" 南非非洲人国民大会高级干部研修班一行访韶，学习交流基层党组织建设的先进经验 [Delegates of South Africa's ANC Senior Cadre Seminar Visit Shaoshan, Study and Exchange Advanced Experience of Establishing Party Organizations at Grassroots], *Shaoguan Daily*, December 9, 2015; "Nanfei feiguoda gaoji ganbu yanxiuban jiang fanghua" 南非非国大高级干部研修班将访华 [Delegates of South Africa's ANC Senior Cadre Seminar Will Visit China], ID-CPC, November 27, 2015.

89 "African National Congress NGC 2015, Discussion Document," African National Congress, 2015; Alex Newman, "South African Regime Embraces Chinese Communism, New World Order," *New American*, August 27, 2015.

90 Jie Bai, "Guojia fuzhuxi Li Yuanchao 10 ri zai Beijing huijian Nanfeigong zongshuji" 国家副主席李源潮10日在北京会见南非共总书记 [Vice President Li Yuanchao Meets General Secretary of South Africa's ANC in Beijing on September 10], *Xinhua*, September 10, 2013; "Nanfei gongchandang ganbu kaochatuan jiang fanghua" 难为共产党干部考察团将访华 [Delegates of South Africa's Communist Party Cadre Seminar Will Visit China], ID-CPC, June 8, 2016.

91 David Shambaugh, "China's 'Quiet Diplomacy': The International Department of the Chinese Communist Party," *China: An International Journal* 5 (2007): 32.

92 Li Chengwen, China's Ambassador to Sudan, interview on July 8, 2007.

93 Liu Naiya, interview, October 23, 2007.

94 Tribune Content Agency, "China's Soft-Power Push," *Foreign Affairs*, July 3, 2015.

95 Sun, "Political Party Training."

96 Miria Pigato and Wenxia Tang, "China and Africa: Expanding Economic Ties in an Evolving Global Context," World Bank paper, March 2015, 10.

97 Janet Eom, Jyhjong Hwang, Ying Xia, and Deborah Brautigam, "Looking Back and Moving Forward: An Analysis of China–Africa Economic Trends and the Outcomes of the 2015 Forum on China Africa Cooperation," *The SAIS China–Africa Research Initiative Policy Brief* 9 (2016): 3.

98 Douglas Zhihua Zeng, "Global Experiences with Special Economic Zones—With a Focus on China and Africa," *The World Bank*, February 2015, 13–14.

99 Tegegne Gebre-Egziabher, "Impacts of Chinese Imports and Coping Strategies of Local Producers: The Case of Small-Scale Footwear Enterprises in Ethiopia," *The Journal of Modern African Studies* 454 (2007): 647–679.

100 Lorenzo Rotunno and Pierre-Louis Vezina, "Chinese Networks and Tariff Evasion," University of Geneva Working Paper, 2010.

101 "Declaration of the Johannesburg Summit of the Forum on China–Africa Cooperation," Presidency of Republic of South Africa, December 5, 2015.

102 China Information Office of the State Council, "China–Africa Economic and Trade Cooperation," August 2013.

103 Eom et al., "Looking Back and Moving Forward," 2.

104 Pigato and Tang, "China and Africa: Expanding Economic Ties in an Evolving Global Context," 9.

105 African Development Bank Group, "Resource Mobilization: Raising Funds and Building Effective Partnerships," November 2015, 14.

106 Miroslav Atanasov, "China Launches Industrial Cooperation Fund to Assist Africa's Development," *CCTV*, February 4, 2016.

107 Thomas Chen, "What Happened to China Development Bank's $ Billion Loan to Ghana," *The SAIS China-Africa Research Initiative Policy Brief* 10 (2016): 1–2.

108 Jeffrey Gutman, Amadou Sy, and Soumya Chattopadhyay, "Financing African Infrastructure: Can the World Deliver?" *Brookings*, March 2015, 27–33. For a good discussion of Chinese-financed hydropower projects, see Deborah Bräutigam, Jyhjong Hwang, and Lu Wang, "Chinese-Financed Hydropower Projects in Sub-Saharan Africa," *The SAIS China-Africa Research Initiative Policy Brief* 8 (2015): 1–8.

109 Koh Gui Qing and Adam Jourdan, "China Railway Construction Wins $12 billion Nigeria deal: Xinhua," *Reuters*, November 20, 2014.

110 China Information Office of the State Council, "China's Foreign Aid," *Xinhua*, July 10, 2014.

111 Eom et al., "Looking Back and Moving Forward," 4.

112 "China's Foreign Aid."

113 Deborah Bräutigam, "Don't Get Excited, China Is Not the New Aid Superpower," *The Guardian*, November 3, 2015.

114 Simon Allison, "Zimbabwe: As Mugabe Fights for His Political Future, Why Is China So Silent?" *All Africa*, July 21, 2016.

115 Iginio Gagliardone, "China and the Shaping of African Information Societies," in *Africa and China: How Africans and Their Governments are Shaping Relations With China*, ed. Aleksandra Gadzala (Lanham, MD: Rowman and Littlefield, 2015), 45–59; Iginio Gagliardone, "China as a persuader: CCTV Africa's First Steps in the African Media Sphere," *Ecquid Novi: African Journalism Studies* 34 (2013): 29; Yu-shan Wu, "The Rise of China's State-Led Media Dynasty in Africa," *South African Institute of International Affairs* (2012): 24, www.saiia. org.za/occasional-papers/31-the-rise-of-china-s-state-led-media-dynasty-in-africa/file.

116 Gagliardone, "China as a Persuader: CCTV Africa's First Steps in the African Media Sphere," 32.

117 "Deepen China–Africa Media Cooperation and Enrich the China–Africa Community of Shared Destinies," PRC's Embassy in Republic of Kenya, November 19, 2013.

118 Gagliardone, "China as a Persuader: CCTV Africa's First Steps in the African Media Sphere," 26; Xin Xin, "Xinhua News Agency in Africa," *Journal of African Media Studies* 1 (2009): 368, 370–1, 373.

119 Tichafa Chidzonga, "China–Africa Media Co-operation: Challenging Western Media Control," Centre for Chinese Studies at Stellenbosch University, August 16, 2016.

120 Gagliardone, "China as a Persuader: CCTV Africa's First Steps in the African Media Sphere," 27.

121 Ibid., 32–33.

122 "Innovations and Successes," *Xinhua*.

123 Gagliardone, "China as a Persuader: CCTV Africa's First Steps in the African Media Sphere," 29–30.

124 Ibid.

125 Shinn and Eisenman, *China and Africa*, 201–203.

126 "Xinhua President Meets Heads of Four African News Agencies," *Xinhua*, June 13, 2007.

127 Gagliardone, "China as a Persuader: CCTV Africa's First Steps in the African Media Sphere," 25.

128 Yu-Shan Wu, "The Rise of China's State-led Media Dynasty in Africa," *South African Institute of International Affairs* (2012): 17.

129 Andy Sennitt, "Ni Hao! Togo, China Sign Broadcast Agreement," *Republic of Togo Official Website*, July 18, 2010.

130 "The 3rd Workshop for African Journalists Held in Beijing," FOCAC, March 13, 2006.

131 "Forum on China–Africa Media Cooperation," *CCTV*, 2012.

132 "Forum on China–Africa Media Cooperation Kicks Off in Beijing," Beijing Government.

133 "The 2nd Forum on China–Africa Media Cooperation," *CCTV*, 2014.

134 Su Yuting, "3rd China–Africa Media Cooperation Forum Opens in Beijing," *CCTV*, June 21, 2016; African Union, "3rd Forum on China–Africa Media Cooperation: Deputy Chairperson, Erastum Mwencha Underscores the Importance of Media in Shaping the Narrative and Promoting the Rich Socio-cultural Diversity and Economic Growth of Africa and China," news release, June 23, 2016.

135 "China–Africa Media Cooperation Gains Momentum—As 3rd Forum Issues Declaration," *Front Page Africa*, July 2016.

136 Kenneth King, *China's Aid & Soft Power in Africa: The Case of Education and Training*, (Suffolk: James Currey, 2013), 69–74.

137 King, *China's Aid & Soft Power in Africa*, 103.

138 Hannane Ferdjani, "African Students in China," Centre for Chinese Studies at Stellenbosch University, September 2012, 10.

139 Ellie Bothwell, "What Chinese Investment Means for African Higher Education," *Times Higher Education*, April 21, 2016.

140 James Paradise, "China and International Harmony: The Role of Confucius Institutes in Bolstering Beijing's Soft Power," *Asian Survey* 49 (2009): 651. Hanban also develops Chinese proficiency tests, selects instruction materials, evaluates teaching quality, and administers international relationships.

141 "Hanban," Confucius Institute.

142 Lai Hongyi "China's Cultural Diplomacy: Going for Soft Power," *Singapore National University, East Asian Institute (EAI) Background Brief* 308 (2006): 9.

143 King, *China's Aid & Soft Power in Africa*, 74–75.

144 "Key Chinese University to add Language Majors amid Boosting Ties," *China Daily*, March 29, 2017.

145 King, *China's Aid & Soft Power in Africa*, 74–75.
146 "Forum on China–Africa Cooperation Addis Ababa Action Plan, 2004–2006," *Xinhua*, October 19, 2006; "China–Africa Youth Festival Opens in Beijing," FOCAC, August 23, 2004.
147 Guo Yan, "China Launches Asian–African Youth Festival to Promote Bandung Spirit," *CRI English*, July 29, 2016.
148 Lu Hui, "Full Text: China's Foreign Aid," *Xinhua*, July 10, 2014.
149 Jiao Feng, "Chinese Doctors in Africa," *China Today*, June 29, 2015.
150 "China, Africa to Join Hands in Post-Ebola Cooperation," *Xinhua*, August 11, 2015.
151 Antonella Ceccagno and Sofia Graziani, "Chinese Volunteering in Africa: Drivers, Issues and Future Prospects," *Annali di Ca' Foscari*, 52 (2016): 307–312.
152 Catherine Theohary, *Conventional Arms Transfers to Developing Nations, 2007–2014* (Washington, DC: Congressional Research Service, 2015), 44.
153 Mark Bromley, Mathieu Duchâtel and Paul Holtom, *China's Exports of Small Arms and Light Weapons* (Stockholm: SIPRI, 2013), 43.
154 Andrew Hull and David Markov, "Chinese Arms Sales to Africa," *IDA Research Notes*, 2012, 25–31.
155 Shai Oster, "China's New Export: Military in a Box," *Bloomberg*, September 29, 2014.
156 In 2016, China had 2,400 personnel in nine operations. See United Nations, *UN Mission's Summary Detailed by Country*, June 30, 2016.
157 Chin-Hao Huang, "From Strategic Adjustment to Normative Learning Understanding China's Peacekeeping Efforts in Africa," *Journal of International Peacekeeping* 17 (2013): 259–263.
158 "China Evacuates Oil Workers From South Sudan Oilfields Over Fighting," *Sudan Tribune*, May 22, 2015.
159 "Global Opposition to U.S. Surveillance and Drones, But Limited Harm to America's Image—Chapter 2: China's Image," *Pew Research Center*, July 14, 2014.
160 Richard Wike, "5 Charts on America's (Very Positive) Image in Africa," *Pew Research Center*, July 23, 2015.
161 Victor Mallet, "The Chinese in Africa: Beijing Offers a New Deal," *Financial Times*, January 23, 2007.
162 Lamido Sanusi, "Africa Must Get Real About Chinese Ties," *Financial Times*, March 11, 2013.
163 Mark Leonard, Wu Xinbo, Bert Hofman, Douglas Rediker, Elizabeth Economy, Michael Levi, Parag Khanna, Sergei Guriev, Lan Bremmer, Hina R. Khar, Evan Ellis, Mahmood Sariolghalam, Linah Mohohlo, Mark Lenard, Angela Stanzel, Agatha Kratz, and Kishore Mahbubani, "Geo-Economics With Chinese Characteristics: How China's Economic Might Is Reshaping World Politics," World Economic Forum, January 2016.
164 Dumisani Ndlela, "Zimbabwe: Panic in Government as Chinese Loot Economy," *All Africa*, April 21, 2016.
165 Barry Sautman, "Racialization as Agency in Zambia–China Relations," in *Africa and China: How Africans and Their Governments are Shaping Relations With China*, ed. Aleksandra Gadzala (Lanham, MD: Rowman and Littlefield, 2015), 127–148.
166 "Uganda Traders Close Shops in Protest," *BBC News*, July 6, 2011.
167 "China in Africa: One Among Many," *Economist*, January 17, 2015.
168 Marthe Bosuandole, "Chinese Become Targets in DR Congo Riots," *Agence France Presse*, January 26, 2015.
169 Eric Kiss and Kate Zhou, "China's New Burden in Africa," in *Dancing With the Dragon: China's Emergence in the Developing World*, eds. Dennis Hickey and Baogang Guo (Lanham, MD: Rowman & Littlefield, 2010), 156.
170 David Shinn, "China and the Conflict in Darfur," *The Brown Journal of World Affairs* 16 (2009): 91–94.
171 "Fact Sheet: U.S. Support for Peacekeeping in Africa," White House, August 6, 2014; African Union, "The People's Republic of China Extends Financial Support to the African Union Mission in Somalia," press release, December 10, 2015.

172 Liesl Louw-Vaudran, "China's Role in South Sudan a Learning Curve," Institute for Security Studies, December 14, 2015.

173 Con Coughlin, "China Deal Threatens Only American Military Base in Africa," *The Telegraph*, July 21, 2015.

174 Patrick Goodenough, "Mugabe Envisages Alternative World Order Headed by China," Cybercast News Services [CNS] (December 3, 2003). Available at www.cnsnews.com/news/article/mugabe-envisages-alternative-world-order-headed-china.

7

CHINA'S STRATEGY IN THE MIDDLE EAST AND THE ARAB WORLD

Sarah Kaiser-Cross and Yufeng Mao

Introduction

In January 2016, President Xi Jinping made his first diplomatic trip of the year, traveling to Saudi Arabia, Iran, and Egypt, a move that signified a new level of importance ascribed to the Middle East. On January 13, six days before Xi's trip, the Chinese government issued its first Arab policy paper (see Appendix II), based on a speech Xi made in June 2014 at the Sixth Ministerial Conference of the China–Arab States Cooperation Forum.[1] In his address, Xi announced that the Middle East was among China's top priorities. Xi detailed China's positions on Palestine and Syria, emphasized its opposition to a nuclear Gulf and "any attempt" to change the political map of the Middle East, and discussed China's stance on regional political issues with unusual candor.[2] Most importantly, both Xi's speech and the policy paper outlined an extensive blueprint for future economic cooperation in the Middle East, underscoring sound business relations as the foundation for China's policy in the region.

The visit, the article, the speech, and the policy paper signaled a historic shift towards a new, bolder Chinese foreign policy in the region. Over the last decade the Middle East and the Arab world have undergone major political transformations and face growing uncertainty. China's increasing economic interests in the region require a more assertive approach and deeper involvement. China has initiated a series of pro-active policies: announcing a Chinese Special Envoy to Syria and new initiatives on the Israeli–Palestinian peace process, exercising its veto on Syria since 2011, playing an active role in the six-party talks that secured a nuclear deal with Iran, and incorporating the Middle East in China's "One Belt and One Road" strategy. China's new assertiveness emanates from its rising international political and military status. Notably, China's strategy is evolving to protect China's expanding interests and to cope with the swift pace of change in the Middle East and the Arab world.[3] Whether

Chinese assertiveness will continue is contingent on domestic developments, regional politics, and China's relationships with the United States and other powers.

Historical Overview

From the founding of the People's Republic of China (PRC) in 1949, until Deng Xiaoping's assent to power in the late 1970s, Beijing's objectives in the Middle East and the Arab world were primarily political. China's priorities included acquiring international recognition by isolating Taiwan diplomatically and gaining international influence at the expense of the United States and the Soviet Union.[4] During this period, China often sacrificed economic interests to achieve political ones.

In the 1950s, China sought to gain wider recognition for the newly established Communist regime. Before the Bandung conference of 1955, China cultivated relations with all governments in the Middle East, including Israel, by highlighting their shared status as third world nations. Israel was the only country in the region to recognize the PRC at the time.[5] Yet, at the Bandung Conference, China terminated contact with Israel, adopted a pro-Arab policy, and began wooing governments including Egypt, Syria, Yemen, Iraq, Morocco, and Sudan. To gain Arab goodwill, China supplied foreign aid and support for Arab nationalists in Palestine, Egypt, and Algeria. As one of the first instances of sacrificing economic interests for political gains in the region, China offered to purchase Egyptian cotton in 1953 though it had no need for imported cotton.[6] Egypt's recognition of the PRC in 1956 initiated a wave of Arab recognition of the PRC in the late 1950s.[7] China's diplomatic strategy was only partially successful, however, as Gulf countries remained U.S. allies, unmoved by Chinese efforts.

Chinese policy took a radical turn after the Sino–Soviet split, when the Soviet Union turned from *Big Brother* to a political competitor in the developing world. After Moscow and Beijing severed their cooperation, China presented itself as a champion for the developing world's struggle against both Soviet and Western imperialism. Consistent with China's own increasingly radical domestic politics, China communicated its foreign policy through militant rhetoric as well as provided material support for revolutionary groups. China became the first non-Arab state to recognize the Palestine Liberation Organization (PLO).[8] Meanwhile, its policy toward Israel grew increasingly hostile, even going so far as to criticize Arab elements negotiating with Israel.[9]

Despite economic difficulties at home, China sought to portray itself as a generous benefactor to the region. Although Chinese donations were small compared to Soviet and U.S. aid packages, China continued to provide aid to Egypt and revolutionary groups in Palestine, Algeria, and Yemen, highlighting China's support for struggling independence movements.[10] In addition, offers made to buy oil from Iraq and Iran in the 1970s aimed to win the goodwill of oil-producers.[11] Prime Minister Zhou Enlai's comments to the Kuwaiti Trade Minister in 1972 underscored China's prioritization of its political goals: "Profit is not the first consideration, but friendship is."[12]

With the continued decline in Sino–Soviet relations in the 1970s and the U.S.–China rapprochement, China allied itself more closely with the U.S. to offset the growing Soviet threat. China readily worked with any anti-Soviet force in the Middle East and moved closer to Western allies such as Lebanon, Iran, and Turkey.[13] In the 1980s, China toned down its militant rhetoric toward Israel, as China and Israel both opposed the Soviet War in Afghanistan, and secretly began exchanging technology.[14] Meanwhile, China's long-term efforts to isolate Taiwan from the Arab world paid dividends when most Middle Eastern countries, including Israel, voted in favor of the 1971 UN resolution to expel Taiwan and give the PRC permanent membership on the Security Council.

Beijing's long-term diplomatic efforts to support Middle Eastern countries paid off after the 1989 Tiananmen Square crackdown. While much of the West condemned Chinese actions and imposed sanctions, President Yang Shangkun received a warm diplomatic welcome from Arab nations including Oman, the UAE, and Kuwait.[15]

China's Present-Day Strategy in the Middle East and the Arab World

Objectives

Four decades after Mao's death, China's objectives in the region have changed dramatically. Today, China's objectives are threefold: securing access to energy in the region, expanding Chinese business further into Middle Eastern markets, and gaining political support.

China recognized the Middle East's vast energy resources and its potential as a growing market as early as the 1990s. By 2016, China had come to depend on Middle Eastern producers for 48 percent of its oil imports (six of China's top ten oil exporters are from the Middle East), 21 percent of its gas imports, and 5 percent of China's overall trade (see Appendix I).[16] Today, China's reliance on Middle Eastern energy and its exports of manufactured goods largely defines its objectives in the region. The Middle East, the Gulf in particular, has become a large market for Chinese goods, services, and contracts. This has led to impressive growth in commercial and diplomatic relations with the region. In recent years, China's political interests have merged with its economic ones. China bases its increasingly necessary political activism on its economic interests, which largely determines which issues China will support. As the security environment in the Middle East devolves, Chinese assets and access to reliable energy imports are placed at risk. Thus, Beijing is becoming more vocal. Beijing seeks to secure Middle Eastern votes in favor of its economic interests and political positions in various international organizations. Beijing is pursuing a more active role in international bodies, using its status in the UN Security Council to voice opinions on regional political issues including Libya, ISIS, Yemen, and Syria. Finally, Beijing hopes its soft power approach will take root, embedding a deep appreciation for Chinese culture in the Middle East in the long run, laying the foundation for strong political and economic relationships and mutual understanding.

Energy

In 2002, China's energy imports exceeded its exports, and by 2014, China had become the world's largest net importer of oil (See Appendix I, 3).[17] Today nearly half of China's oil imports are from the Middle East, highlighting its increased dependence on oil from the Middle East.[18] These dramatic changes underscore China's surging need for energy and its unrelenting quest to secure it.

China has surpassed the U.S. as the largest net importer of oil and gas in the Middle East.[19] The U.S. "Shale Revolution" increased domestic energy production and resulted in reduced imports from Middle Eastern energy producers like Saudi Arabia. As U.S. demand fell, Chinese demand for crude skyrocketed in pace with its surging economic development, spurring Middle Eastern producers to supply energy to China. Greater energy imports also facilitated Beijing's investment in energy infrastructure around the world. To limit its dependence on a single source of energy, China focused on diversifying its energy supplies by funding energy infrastructure projects at home and abroad, including investing in new energy sources in Central Asia, Russia, Africa, and the Americas.

China's $46 billion investment in the China–Pakistan Economic Corridor (CPEC) in Gwadar, Pakistan was an important step in diversifying China's energy sources and trade routes.[20] China is constructing an oil pipeline, as well as refineries and infrastructure, from Gwadar to Xinjiang.[21] (As discussed by Jeff M. Smith in Chapter 5 of this volume, China's investments in Gwadar are threatened by instability in Baluchistan and Xinjiang.) For China's Gulf energy partners, investments that facilitate transporting crude across the continent reduce prices and increase efficiency. Saudi Arabia and Iran recently expressed interest in investing in CPEC, unsurprising given Gwadar's strategic location for two of China's major energy suppliers.[22] Long-term aims in Gwadar include China's fulfillment of its One Belt One Road initiative, connecting China and the Middle East, and expediting the movement of oil from Middle Eastern wells to Beijing.

Oil and natural gas deals between China and Russia may temporarily quench China's thirst for energy and reduce its reliance on Middle Eastern suppliers.[23] However, due to the high reserves in the Middle East and relatively low costs to transport oil from the Middle East to China, it is likely that Middle Eastern oil will constitute the bulk of Chinese imports for the foreseeable future. China's dependence on Middle Eastern oil is so extensive that supply disruptions could adversely affect its economy. Even speculation on potential disruptions has caused negative effects in the past. To prepare for possible disruptions by the Iraq War, China increased its purchase of oil in January 2003 by 77.2 percent, in comparison with the previous year, driving the average price up by 51 percent and contributing to the country's trade deficit that month.[24]

In recent years, China's major oil companies, CNPC, the China National Petroleum and Chemical Corporation (Sinopec), and China National Offshore Oil Corporation (CNOOC), as well as other smaller oil companies, received contracts for upstream exploration and production, oil refining, and infrastructure building in the region. For example, in 2013, Sinopec made its first Egyptian acquisition, purchasing one-third of the Egyptian assets of Apache, an American company.[25] The same year, PetroChina acquired one quarter of interest in Iraq's West Qurna-1 oil field project.[26] Despite such investments in oil production in North Africa, Iraq, and Syria, China continued to import nearly 31 percent of its oil from the Gulf alone in 2016, inextricably tying Chinese interests to the security of the Strait of Hormuz.[27] In March 2017, during Saudi Arabian King Salman's visit to Beijing, state-owned companies Saudi Aramco and Norinco announced plans to build refineries and chemical plants in China to expedite the use of Saudi yields.[28]

Markets

In addition to being an important source of China's energy imports, the Middle East and Arab world provide important export markets for Chinese products and services and a strategic springboard into operations and markets in Africa. Over the past decade, Chinese exports made significant headway in regional markets. China has increased its trade volume with the Middle East by a hundredfold in less than two decades, from under $2.27 billion in 1989, to $58.49 billion in 2005, and $204.2 billion in 2016.[29] The Middle Eastern markets have great potential for growth and the Chinese are pursuing greater market shares.

Over the last decade, the largest markets for Chinese goods and services have been in the Gulf region. Between 2005 and 2015, the trade volume between China and the Gulf region increased over fourfold, from $44.7 billion to $191 billion.[30] Among these countries, Saudi Arabia became the largest destination for China's exports, followed by the UAE, whose imports of Chinese commodities grew from $416 million in 2000 to $11 billion in 2015.[31] Increasing imports of Gulf oil and exports of goods and services rapidly increased the overall trade volumes between China and the region.

Aside from products, China also exports numerous service contracts to the region. According to China's Ministry of Commerce, during the first ten months of 2015, West Asia and North Africa signed service contracts with China worth $3.11 billion, a 133.8 percent increase from the previous year, making the region the "fastest growing region" in entering service contracts with China as part of its "One Belt and One Road" initiative.[32] To cope with the influx of Chinese contracts, business, and currency, Qatar opened the region's first bank capable of clearing Chinese renminbi, allowing a smoother, more cost effective way to move money directly between the Middle East and China.[33] The UAE followed in May 2017, a move expected to facilitate increased trade and access to renminbi liquidity.[34]

Political Interests

China's growing commercial interests with Middle Eastern and Arab states have reinforced its interest in building strong political relations through economic diplomacy. China pursues its goals through encouraging business growth, regional stability, policies of non-interference, and an appreciation for Chinese history.

While economic prosperity remains the nexus of China's political interests in the Middle East, China has become increasingly involved in regional affairs, pursuing the support of Arab nations in international organizations such as the UN and the WTO, particularly in supporting the one-China principle in relation to Taiwan. In Middle Eastern affairs, China has remained largely neutral until recently, highlighting its dedication to the principle of non-interference. During UNCHR meetings, Middle Eastern countries have consistently sided with China on the issue of human rights, helping shield Beijing from criticism for human rights abuses. Barring dramatic changes in regional politics, the Chinese government expects friendly political relations to continue.

China's leaders have taken the long view, dedicating China's resources to building long-term economic projects that require years of cooperation, cultural exchange, and productive political and business relations. Much like the spread of American soft power in decades past, China aims to build support by promoting Chinese history, language, and culture. China's attempt to win the hearts and minds of the Middle East highlights its devotion to a long-term regional presence.

Methods

To achieve its policy objectives in the Middle East, Beijing has pursued a three-pronged strategy. First, China uses diplomacy to help Chinese businesses make inroads in regional markets, focusing on the energy sector. Second, Beijing tries, with increasing difficulty, to pursue a "neutral partner" approach to regional politics in order to maintain an environment friendly to Chinese business interests. Third, Beijing is cultivating goodwill with the intention of safeguarding China's long-term interests.

Economic Diplomacy

China's diplomatic efforts in the Middle East revolve largely around securing its economic interests. As it does domestically, Beijing inextricably links business and politics: politics work to protect business interests while investments strengthen political ties. Chinese diplomats have made advancing business interests, particularly in the Gulf, a priority. With focused effort in the Persian Gulf, Chinese diplomats work to promote trade while simultaneously emphasizing "non-interference in internal affairs" with its bilateral partners. China uses multiple approaches to expand its political influence and help its firms penetrate local markets.

First and foremost, China has signed trade and investment protection agreements with all Arab and Middle Eastern governments. Since the 1980s, China has established a Joint Commission on Commerce and Trade with each of the regional countries, bringing together government officials, diplomats, business representatives, and experts from China and the Middle East to facilitate communication and examine opportunities for trade. Beijing's diplomatic overtures have targeted the Persian Gulf as a focal point, as Beijing pushes for higher levels of cooperation with oil-rich Gulf economies. To improve trade relations further, China and the Gulf Cooperation Council (GCC) bloc seek to establish a free-trade agreement that would enable more fluid trade between the GCC and China.

Dedicated to promoting regional business interests, the Joint Sino–Arab Chamber of Commerce (established in 1988) has opened branches in all twenty-two Arab countries. On September 10, 2015, the Sino–Arab Chamber of Commerce built the first liaison office in Yinchuan, Ningxia Muslim Hui Autonomous Region, a move that signaled new efforts by China to use local Islamic communities to promote business relationships with Muslim countries in the Middle East. Across China, government-sponsored business associations have mushroomed and are engaged in hosting trade exhibitions and organizing economic delegations to visit the region as well as bring visitors to China. As trade flourished, China has also encouraged government-run research institutions and think tanks to address the long-term impacts of investment projects in the Middle East and educate Chinese leaders on regional issues.[35]

Recently, China has promoted its economic interests in the region through pursuing greater cooperation with local partners. During President Xi's visit to Saudi Arabia in January 2016, aimed at fostering relations with its major energy provider, Xi highlighted the interdependence of the two economies, noting, "one in six barrels of crude oil China imports comes from Saudi Arabia, and one in seven Riyal Saudi Arabia earns from its exports comes from China."[36] Xi expressed enthusiasm toward deepening the bilateral relationship in energy, trade, and investment through the signing of fourteen agreements and memorandums of understanding (MoU). The first MoU established greater cooperation on China's One Belt and One Road Initiative, expanding trade and production capacity between the two states.[37] Xi also emphasized China's stated strategy in the region, which was announced during the 2014 China–Arab States Cooperation Forum. China's vision for comprehensive economic cooperation with its Middle Eastern partners is known as "1+2+3." The "1" refers to energy cooperation and is the most important; "2" represents a focus on infrastructure, bilateral trade, and investment volume; and "3" refers to cooperation in nuclear energy, aerospace technology, and renewable energy technology.[38] In March 2017, Saudi Arabia and China strengthened that commitment to cooperation, signing twenty-one deals worth $65 billion in energy, space, and a range of other fields, including oil exploration, petrochemicals, and renewables.[39]

China supports energy cooperation in the Gulf through investments, projects, and technological exchanges. In addition to direct purchases of oil, Beijing works with governments in the Gulf region to expand bilateral cooperation in exploration, boosting refinery capacity, and attracting investment for the region's petrodollars toward China's refinery and petrochemical industries. For instance, China's national oil companies formed joint ventures with Kuwait, Saudi Arabia, and Qatar to build new refinery and petrochemical plants in China to process Middle Eastern varieties of crude oil more quickly.[40] The opening of the Fujian refinery in 2005, a joint venture by Saudi Aramco, Exxon-Mobil, and Sinopec, is the kind of economic cooperation Beijing continues to pursue. Sino–Saudi cooperation expanded greatly when Saudi Arabia granted Chinese national oil company Sinopec permission to produce natural gas in the Kingdom in 2007, the first such agreement allowing a foreign energy company to operate in Saudi Arabia. As energy ties have strengthened, China and its Middle Eastern partners began collaborating on technology transfers and information sharing, highlighted by a MoU signed by China and Saudi Arabia in January 2016 to work jointly on satellite navigation, among other technologies.[41]

In a similar vein, in March 2016, China and Israel announced the initiation of dialogue regarding a free trade agreement (FTA) between the two nations, facilitating the burgeoning bilateral trade, particularly in advanced agricultural and defense technologies.[42] Israeli exports to China totaled $3.3 billion (5.4 percent of its exports), while China exported $8 billion to Israel in 2015 alone.[43] Israel and China's mutually beneficial commercial relationship in the technological sector paved the way for improved diplomatic relations. In a 2014 address alongside Chinese Deputy Prime Minister Yandong, Israeli Prime Minister Netanyahu announced China is "fast becoming perhaps Israel's largest trading partner, period, as we move into the future." In March 2017, China extended an invitation to Netanyahu to bolster diplomatic ties, resulting in ten bilateral agreements which aim to expand Chinese investment in Israeli technology and innovation.[44] China benefits from a strong Israeli economy, which is predicated on a stable political environment.

Despite U.S. and Israeli protests, China has consistently defended its diplomatic ties with Iran, emphasizing that its energy interests and investments necessitate it supporting Iran to secure its $7 billion annual trade and energy contracts. During negotiations to halt the development of Iran's nuclear program, China carefully balanced its relations with Iran, increasing investment in Iran while also supporting the P5+1 sanctions regimes. Chinese support for the sanctions was strategic. China rallied with major world governments to stop Iran's nuclear program, painting itself as a neutral arbitrator. Lifting sanctions resulted in a net increase in Iranian exports and Chinese investment in Iran, facilitating greater and freer trade between Beijing and Tehran. However, China's unwillingness to support Tehran outright resulted in repercussions, as shown in Iran's cancelation in 2014 of a contract with a Chinese oil company to develop the South Azadegan oilfield.[45] China's need for Iranian energy, and Iran's need for China's economic support, however, generally supersedes political tensions. During Vice President Li Yuanchao's visit to Tehran in

October 2016, Yuanchao declared, "China would develop its relations to strategic levels; on banking cooperation, we have been encouraging [the] Chinese financial system to work with Iran regardless of fears of punishment and sanctions." Iran's response mirrors Beijing's economy diplomacy strategy, as Iranians "welcome Chinese investments in our oil and energy sectors, along a belief that scientific and cultural relations would also provide opportunities for strengthening ties."[46]

Finally, Beijing bolsters its strategy of economic diplomacy by declaring its dedication to non-interference on issues like human rights. Contrasting greatly with U.S. diplomacy in the region, Beijing advocates a policy of "non-interference in internal affairs" as a way to win goodwill with government officials and open the door for increased economic opportunity. Beijing's non-interventionist approach to regional politics is effective, and some in the region have explicitly attributed their willingness to do business with China to it.[47] Whereas the U.S. approaches human rights as integral to development and stable long-term partnerships, China views human rights as separate from economic development and diplomacy.[48] By separating human rights concerns from political and economic cooperation, China emphasizes that business relations are the foundation for a robust bilateral partnership. China's silence on the internal policies of Middle Eastern countries has been largely successful and garnered praise from Gulf monarchs tired of U.S. criticism of human rights records.

Neutrality

The second prong of China's strategy is to adopt a neutral partner approach to regional politics and conflicts. China uses vague diplomatic rhetoric and ambiguous policies to pursue its foreign policy goals without committing itself to any side of a conflict, or any actor. China's policies toward the Arab–Israeli conflict, the Iran–Iraq war, the first Gulf War, the war in Iraq, the Arab Spring, and ISIS are examples of this approach. Since the conflict in Libya, however, regional instability forced China to reassess its traditional policy approach of neutrality. For the first time in decades, China took a determined stance and used its veto power to protect its interests, and the regional balance of power, particularly in Syria.

China's policy in the Middle East is intended not to offend any party, but to appear a neutral arbiter and partner, supporting both sides. Thus, Beijing announces positive, yet ambiguous, concepts like "peace" and "stability" without pledging specific actions or outlining how a "peaceful" region should look. During the war between Iraq and Iran, China sold weapons to both countries without siding politically with either. After Saddam's invasion of Kuwait, China condemned the invasion, but refused to vote for a UN-sanctioned war on Iraq. Beijing also opposed the U.S. war in Iraq, though its criticism was mild, and offered to provide aid and debt relief to the new Iraqi government in an effort to protect China's energy investments in the war-torn country.[49]

China's approach to the Israeli–Palestinian conflict best illustrates the evolution of its foreign policy in the region. Chinese rhetoric toward the conflict is more balanced today than it was historically, when Beijing supported Arab nationalist causes against Israel.[50] Beijing established relations with Israel in 1992, after Israel illicitly exported U.S. military equipment to China, opening a backdoor to U.S. weapons technologies despite U.S. sanctions on China.[51] Israel denied these claims. Since 1992, China's attitude toward the Arab–Israeli conflict shifted from strong support for the Arabs to assuming the role of an impartial mediator. Recent budding trade relations are shifting China's approach to one more supportive of Israel.

On the other hand, China has both reduced its rhetoric on the Palestinians' behalf and urged the Palestinians to give up violence. China insists on a two-state solution and land for peace, though does not hesitate to condemn Israeli military actions in the occupied territories. Since 2002, China has appointed four special Middle East peace envoys that have visited the Middle East, meeting with Israelis, Palestinians, Syrians, and Egyptians. These envoys underscore Beijing's balanced stance, desire for peace in the region, and its intention to have a seat at the table. China has not condemned violence against Palestinians in Israel, yet it voted in favor of Palestinian statehood at the UN. In 2013, China separately invited heads of states from both Israel and the Palestinian Territories to Beijing to discuss the peace process. During his meeting with Palestinian President Mahmoud Abbas, Xi offered a proposal, showing China's willingness to play a greater role in achieving a lasting peace.[52] Chairman of the Standing Committee of the National People's Congress of China, Zhang Dejiang, visited Israel in September 2016, signing an MoU for greater cooperation, commenting, "China understands Israel's security concerns yet we hope at the same time that Israel can prove that it is committed to peace."[53] China continues to support a two-state solution as the key to peace.

Perhaps most indicative of China's willingness to engage with all stakeholders, in 2013, China's former Deputy Foreign Minister, Yang Fuchang, and his delegation toured the Hezbollah museum in southern Lebanon, announcing during the trip, "the will of the Lebanese and Chinese people will render the resistance victorious."[54]

Despite China's best attempts to remain neutral, its expanding interests in the region have slowly required deeper involvement. After the Western-led intervention in Libya, the conflict in Syria, and the rise of ISIS, China has taken a more decisive stance against international interventions in the region. For instance, in an uncharacteristic move, China supported Western-led sanctions after the Libyan government's violent clash with protesters in 2011. Later, however, China abstained from a UN vote authorizing a no-fly zone over Libya. After Gaddafi fled, China suffered significant economic losses, including several oil deals. Politically, China was accused of bowing to Western pressure for sanctions and wavering on its noninterference principle. Based on its sour experience in Libya, in October 2011 China used its veto to thwart a UN resolution to intervene militarily in Syria, and since then, together with Russia, has vetoed five additional resolutions on Syria, the most recent in February 2017.[55, 56] Instead, China has encouraged an internal, Syrian-led transition of power, more directed leadership from the UN, and a unified approach to combatting terrorism.

Although China has become more vocal in the UN, its Syria strategy still adheres to its traditional policy approach: support both sides. To support the existing regime, China vetoed a proposal to report Assad's war crimes to the International Criminal Court. China also sent military advisors, an aircraft carrier, and missile launchers to assist Russia's military offensive in Syria and is also supplying training and aid to the regime.[57] To prove its neutrality to its Saudi allies, China sold hundreds of millions of dollars in arms to the Saudi government.[58] China also invited a delegation from the Syrian National Committee for Democratic Change to Beijing to meet with Chinese Vice Foreign Minister on Africa and West Asia, Zhai Jun, and articulate its position.[59] China quietly sent delegations to discuss diplomatic options for resolution of the conflict with regional neighbors. March 2016 marked the appointment of the first ever Chinese Special Envoy to Syria, Xie Xiaoyan, to manage China's response to the Syria crisis.[60]

Ultimately, China's interest lies in promoting stable economic partners in the region and curbing the appeal of extremist and separatist causes. Despite reports that hundreds of Uighurs have joined ISIS, it is unclear whether China will take an active military role in combating the extremist group.[61]

In addition to Syria, Chinese investments in Saudi Arabia and Iran have forced Beijing to balance its relationships with two major regional powers. As it does elsewhere, China underscores its economic interests as a basis for engagement with both states and refuses to choose between partnering with one at the expense of relations with the other. Productive business relations, China argues, outweigh sectarian and political tensions. Rather than playing Saudi Arabia and Iran off one another, China continues to purchase petroleum and invest in both countries. China's interests, therefore, are served by the de-escalation of tensions, and harmed by sectarian and regional power struggles.[62]

China's attempts to remain neutral face challenges, however. President Xi's visit to Saudi Arabia in January 2016 concluded with an announcement of Chinese support for Saudi Arabia and Yemen's ousted President Abdurabuh Mansur Hadi in defeating the Iran-backed Houthi rebels.[63] This support directly challenges Iran's allies and interests, though was likely part of China's balancing act, as President Xi became the first president to visit Iran after sanctions were lifted, canceling his trip to the UAE.[64] China's increasing willingness to involve itself in sticky regional issues between Saudi Arabia and Iran may indicate a broader policy shift toward a more assertive Chinese foreign policy.[65] Still, Beijing's rhetoric emphasizes the importance of "political negotiations," "win–win solutions," and "collective security mechanism" vis-à-vis the United Nations.[66]

In the Middle East, China's economic and political interests require stability, yet it lacks the resources and the military capacity to unilaterally achieve this objective. Therefore, it free rides on the United States' defense of the waterways around the Arabian Gulf to ensure the movement of commodities like oil. In this way, China benefits substantially from U.S. military presence in the region. Conflict with the United States would not only undermine Chinese efforts in the region, but also hinder China's political and economic interests in both the Middle East and globally. China is happy to work with the U.S. in the Middle East, and instead prioritize its "core interests" in East Asia. U.S. President Trump's aggressive posturing against trade with China, however, may lessen China's willingness to integrate itself quietly in the Middle East, particularly if the U.S. challenges China in its own backyard.

Beijing is at a crossroads when it comes to its involvement in the Middle East. Some Chinese analysts are calling for greater involvement to protect Chinese interests.[67] Indeed, China's vetoes over the Syria issue suggest a more assertive approach to secure its economic interests with Russia and Iran, while its position in Yemen seems to support Saudi Arabia. China's strong economic relationships give China the political leverage to exert influence on regional affairs. Enhanced Chinese involvement, however, is risky. Instead of selectively seeking partnerships with politically stable countries, Beijing's quest for neutrality has led it to open dialogue with all players. As China becomes more deeply entrenched in the region, it will need to manage the delicate balancing act of maintaining cordial relations with all players, yet avoid accusations that is has violated its principle of non-interference in pursuit of its own economic and political interests.

Soft Power

In the last two decades, China has increasingly promoted cultural understanding, which Beijing believes generates goodwill, friendship, and increased communication with its Middle Eastern partners. Unlike traditional notions of soft power— exemplified by images of Coca Cola and Hollywood—China pursues the hearts and minds of the Arab world through a more traditional approach, emphasizing its ancient history and commonalities with its partners. In nearly every meeting, forum, and exhibition, China highlights its historic relationship with the Middle East via the Silk Road—blending culture and commerce. Both epitomize historic civilizations that made great contributions, though currently face the challenges of modernization and the encroachment of Western culture.

To all its partners, whether Arab, Iranian, or Israeli, China concentrates on common visions, histories, and traditions. Common historical legacies are what Chinese Deputy Prime Minister Yandong celebrated in her address to Israeli Prime Minister Netanyahu, noting "the Jewish and the Chinese peoples are peoples of great wisdom . . . we respectively created our splendid cultures that stretch thousands of years of history."[68] In 2013, President Xi welcomed a Saudi delegation, "hailing Saudi Arabia as China's good friend, brother and partner" and emphasized the importance of "supporting . . . Saudi Arabia for choosing a development path that suits its own conditions."[69] Despite China's improved relations with both the West and Israel, Beijing emphasizes its steadfast friendship with the Arabs; during the establishment of the Sino–Arab Cooperation Forum in January 2004, China's Foreign Minister Li Zhaoxing declared: "However the international situations change, Chinese people will always be a sincere friend of the Arab people."[70] Such sentiments foster a sense of common values between China and its Middle Eastern partners.

China remains traditional in its pursuit of soft power, proudly teaching about its ancient civilization.[71] To facilitate cultural and educational exchanges, China has established cultural, art, and language centers throughout the Middle East. While tightly controlled by the Chinese government, "Confucius Institutes" in Bahrain, Jordan, Egypt, Iran, Israel, Lebanon, Morocco, and the UAE offer opportunities for Middle Eastern students to study subjects such as Mandarin, Kung Fu, and Chinese history.[72] The serious study of Chinese in the UAE prompted the president of the University of Dubai, Eesa Bastaki, to suggest that Chinese could become a compulsory language for students in the United Arab Emirates.[73] Exchange programs like those at the University of Dubai also foster intercultural cooperation and provide students opportunities to study in China. In 2014, Saudi newspaper *Arab News* reported more than 3,000 Saudi students in Chinese universities, with Arabic taught at more than forty Chinese universities.[74] Estimates from 2012 record over 10,000 Arab students in China, a 70 percent increase from 2010.[75] Israeli–Sino educational exchanges, too, are facilitating technological collaboration between Israel and China and introducing the next generation to Israeli and Chinese culture.[76] While the fruits of China's labor remain to be seen, China is counting on its investment both at home and in the Middle East to instill positive perceptions of China among the next generation.

China's considerable investments in cultural exchanges and media cooperation underpin its long-term strategy: establishing reliable long-term political and economic relationships to advance its interests. The availability of Chinese perspectives and access to Chinese media is key to that strategy. In 2009, China Central Television (CCTV) began airing Chinese programs in the Middle East, complete with subtitles in Arabic and Mandarin.[77] Based in Dubai, CCTV now broadcasts in several languages, including Chinese and Arabic, with correspondents in Iran, Iraq, Syria, and Lebanon.[78] The year 2016 marked the launch of the region's first Chinese TV channel, including news and Chinese cartoons with voice-overs in Arabic.[79] Similarly, *Al Jazeera* broadcasted a popular multiday segment in China focused on the Middle East, called "Eye on China," including a piece on China's Muslims.[80] *Al Jazeera* also began hosting Chinese Arabic speaking news anchors and conducting live interviews of Chinese officials in Arabic.[81] China proudly notes it has ten Chinese ambassadors fluent in Arabic posted in the Middle East, including UAE, Oman, Iraq, and Sudan.[82] Communicating solely in Arabic and Mandarin limits the need for English as a common medium, creating a direct pathway from Riyadh to Beijing.

The success of Chinese public relations efforts, however, varies throughout the region. Fully aware of Arab suspicion toward the secular nature of the Chinese regime, Beijing has been trying to use the fact that China is home to 20 million Muslims to promote an image of itself as a friend of Islam. Since the 1980s, China gave limited freedoms to Chinese Muslims to engage in Islamic religious activities such as educational exchanges and hajj pilgrimages. China routinely invites Arab visitors to China to meet with the head of the Islamic Association of China, visit Muslim regions of the country, as well as local mosques and Muslim families. Chinese leaders have appealed to Middle Eastern populations by openly criticizing the link between Islam and terrorism. The Director of China's State Administration for Religious Affairs, Ye Xiaowen commented,

> As Chinese Muslims advance with the nation, this is our response to the many turbid misunderstandings that tarnish the Muslim image: Islam is a peace-loving religion. Chinese Muslims love peace, oppose turmoil and separatism, advocate tolerance and harmony, and treasure unity and stability.[83]

The mention of separatism, however, underscores Beijing's anxiety over Chinese Muslims' attempts at independence.[84]

Middle Eastern and Arab Perceptions

China's increased attention to the Middle East has enhanced the perception that China may present an alternative to U.S. leadership in the region. As Egyptian author Ahmed Al-Saeed notes, "Arabs no longer look only to the West to learn about economic success. Today they are increasingly eager to learn from China's way to success."[85] Many in the Middle East and Arab world view China's business-first model and its neutral approach to foreign policy as a welcome departure from U.S. policies of democratization efforts. While the U.S. seeks to spread liberal democracy, China has focused on building new industries and infrastructure. A poll conducted by Pew Research Center between 2007 and 2013 found that 45 percent of nations in the Middle East viewed China positively, while 52 percent viewed China unfavorably.[86] Comparably, China fared quite well, as only 20 percent of the Arab world viewed the U.S. favorably. All nations polled, except Egypt, saw China as a partner or a neutral party.[87] In 2014, however, only Tunisia, Palestine, and Lebanon viewed China favorably, with Israel, Egypt, Jordan, and Turkey viewing China unfavorably.[88] Contrastingly, six of the seven countries interviewed strongly agreed (53–68 percent) that China's economy is helping their country.[89] Most importantly, China's strategy of targeting the youth of the Middle East appears to be successful, as Middle Eastern youth overwhelmingly viewed China in a positive light.[90] The most critical reviews stemmed from older populations.[91]

Unlike Africa, few reports of frustration with Chinese companies have emerged from the Middle East. Chinese investments in Middle Eastern nations do not seem to impact traditional governance indicators such as corruption, rule of law, regulation, accountability, and an absence of violence, as numbers in the Middle East remained relatively consistent, though worsened in 2011, starting with the Arab Spring.[92]

One impediment to China's popularity in the Middle East is its treatment of its Uighur Muslim minority in Xinjiang province. To discourage Uighur separatism the Chinese government has criticized both international and domestic terrorism and extremism. In the 1990s, the Chinese Minister of Religious Affairs, Zhou Guo-hai, explained why crackdowns on Uighurs were necessary, noting that the Chinese "deeply fear Islamic extremism" and "deeply distrust the Koran and what it teaches."[93] More recently, China has sought to delink Islam and Uighur separatist violence in Xinjiang. As China's trade with the Middle East increased, Chinese authorities began to reframe their support for Muslims as unrelated to their fierce opposition to extremism and separatism. The China–Arab States Economic and Trade Forum, for instance, provides a venue for Chinese sponsors to highlight local halal food, Uighur culture, and showcase local mosques to its Muslim visitors.[94] In March 2017, the State Administration of Press, Publication, Radio, Film and Television of China (SAPPRFT) sponsored the release of two Chinese films in the UAE that focus on the lives of Uighurs in China,[95] with the hope of showcasing the Chinese government's support of its Muslim minority.

China's treatment of Uighurs is a factor in relations with its Muslim partners because the Muslim public would likely support the plight of fellow Muslims abroad. In the late 1990s, Saudi clerics, and the grand mufti himself, Sheikh Abdulaziz Bin Baz, called for assistance for their Chinese Muslim brothers in his weekly sermon, declaring, "we have a moral obligation to help our Chinese Muslim brothers," reflecting popular opinion to support oppressed Muslim populations globally.[96] After the events of September 11, the Chinese government denounced terrorism and used the global focus on terrorism to target Uighur separatists, worrying their Saudi allies.[97] Qatar-based *Al Jazeera* reported several times on China's mistreatment of its Uighur population since its Hong Kong office opened. The recent association between Uighurs and ISIS and Al Qaeda has damaged positive associations with China's Muslims. Speculation over whether China intentionally inflated the number of Uighurs fighters in ISIS remains unknown.[98] Increasing evidence, however, points to Uighur fighters present in Syria and Afghanistan.[99] In the July 2016 edition of Al Qaeda's "Islamic Spring" series, Ayman al Zawahiri praised efforts by "East Turkistan" fighters, or Uighurs, and lauded a major Uighur leader.[100] Associations with ISIS and Al Qaeda damaged any positive strides made by the Uighur separatist movement, particularly in the eyes of a Middle Eastern public.

The governments of the Middle East, for their part, sidestep controversy with their citizens by accepting Chinese rhetorical support for Chinese Muslims at face value. Public interest in the Uighur narrative was raised during the Xinjiang riots in July 2009, but has remained a peripheral issue in Arab media. During the riots, however, the Saudi press condemned government actions, labeling China an atheist, Communist regime, though it encouraged a "reasoned [governmental] approach," recognizing China's economic importance and thus discouraging any diplomatic posturing. Iranian clerics have spoken more directly against China.[101] In 2009, for instance, Ayatollah Jafar Sobhani opined, "We just thought that only the bullying West violates Muslims' rights . . . but reports from China indicate . . . Muslims are being mercilessly suppressed."[102]

Rather than supporting a Muslim group with a separatist ideology, Middle Eastern governments have chosen to focus on prosperous business relations. China and Middle Eastern regimes share the same fear: domestic uprisings and violence from separatists or extremists. For both countries, regime stability always supersedes religious empathy.

Implications for the United States

China's growing presence in the Middle East raises concerns about U.S. economic, diplomatic, and strategic interests and assets in the region. Beijing's more assertive foreign policy could impact U.S. calculations. Increased Chinese presence in the region poses little short-term risk to the U.S. but may represent a long-term threat to U.S. dominance.

Economically, China has already eclipsed the U.S. as Saudi Arabia's primary economic partner. Chinese trade with Middle East countries has grown exponentially. Saudi Arabia's former Crown Prince Abdullah recognized the shift as early as 2003 and began a "Look East" policy to diversify the Saudi economy away from U.S. imports of oil, and to expand energy and technical partnerships with Chinese companies like Sinopec.[103] As Chinese demand for oil continues to expand, many worry that U.S. energy security is in jeopardy. Contrary to common beliefs, however, the U.S. has imported less than 25 percent of its energy from the Persian Gulf over the last several decades.[104] The U.S. relationship with its Middle East partners does not revolve exclusively or even predominantly around energy trade.

The most important and exclusive goods the U.S. provides its Middle Eastern partners are high quality, military grade weapons. Unlike China, which emphasizes business first, the United States relationships in the Middle East are primarily based on mutually beneficial security arrangements. The U.S. provides protection, arms, intelligence, and critical resources to its partners that no other country can provide. In 2013, Saudi Arabia officially became "the largest defense market for U.S. weapons makers, as the oil sheikdom increased its defense imports 54 percent from 2013 to 2014."[105] U.S. weapons sales and security agreements with Middle Eastern allies are the glue that holds the relationships together. Additionally, U.S. patrols of the Gulf ensure the flow of goods through Hormuz. At present, only the U.S. military has the capacity to provide such public goods on a long-term basis. In turn, Middle Eastern partners provide the intelligence necessary for the U.S. military to conduct operations in the region, including strategically important air and naval bases from which U.S. armed forces can launch attacks, refuel, and house their forces. Critical U.S. military partners include Saudi Arabia, Egypt, Israel, and Bahrain, which hosts the U.S. Navy's 5th Fleet, as well as the UAE, Qatar, and Kuwait.

Weapons sales and defense contracts remain an integral part of U.S. relationships with Middle East governments, though China has begun to enter in the market as well. In 2015, for instance, after the U.S. refused to sell more weapons to Middle Eastern partners, the Chinese military sold drones to Saudi Arabia and the United

Arab Emirates to assist the military campaign in Yemen.[106] China is also expanding its low-grade weapons sales, though Chinese quality pales in comparison to U.S. defense products.[107] The arrival of two Chinese warships in Iran in October 2014 signaled China's new willingness to "strengthen military ties," and potentially establish strategic bases beyond its own waters.[108] In March 2017, the *South China Morning Post* reported that China will construct the first Chinese drone factory in the Middle East, to be based in Saudi Arabia.[109] These relationships are still in their infancy compared to the decades of developed relations with the U.S. defense establishment. Trump's view of a political world defined by spheres of influence, however, could indicate a broader move by the U.S. to cede some of its regional influence in the Middle East to nations ready to shoulder the burden of providing stability, funding, and defense, like Russia and China.

Outside the defense industry, the U.S. exports significant quantities of automobiles, machinery, and medical equipment to the region. U.S. non-oil trade ties with the Middle East remain strong, with trade volumes rising over the last decade. In 2013, U.S. exports to Saudi Arabia, for instance, increased 313 percent from 2003 levels.[110] China's trade in the Middle East poses little economic threat to U.S. exports, because they compete in different sectors. Politically, however, China's expanding presence poses different, diplomatic challenges for the U.S. as it seeks to maintain its influence and promote liberal democracy.

A decade of unpopular U.S. policies in the Middle East—including strong support for Israel and the Saudi regime, the Iraq War, the deposition of the Gaddafi regime in Libya, and the civil war in Syria—has opened the door for China to expand its influence among Middle Eastern countries. Beijing continues to highlight its non-interference, neutrality, and indifference to human rights violations.[111] In January and again in November 2014, Chinese leadership met with GCC leaders and supported "GCC efforts to protect sovereignty and regional stability."[112] Chinese silence on human rights serves a dual purpose: it reinforces Chinese deference to sovereignty and portrays U.S. human rights reproaches as foreign meddling. China is now acting as a foil to the U.S. in the region, offering an alternative, non-judgmental, political partnership. Ultimately, China's policy of non-interference weakens U.S. human rights policies and political liberalization efforts in the region.

China, however, cannot yet compete with the quality of U.S. weapons provided to Middle Eastern regimes or the strategic value of U.S.–Gulf intelligence sharing agreements. Though U.S. policies may be unpopular in some quarters, governments recognize the unique advantages a U.S. security partnership can provide. The U.S. gives regimes access to U.S. weapons, military training, and intelligence sharing. China, therefore, is unlikely to threaten U.S. strategic interests, at least in the short term, and will remain most concerned with safeguarding its short-term interests. For now, China and the U.S. share immediate interests: stabilizing the region, ending the conflict in Syria, and fracturing ISIS strongholds.

In the long term, however, if U.S. human rights policies and offensive military pursuits continue to negatively affect its diplomatic relationships and its image, while China pursues closer political and economic relations with Arab regimes, China may present itself as an alternative to U.S. leadership in the region. If U.S. popularity continues to decline and Chinese goodwill, economic partnerships, and military capabilities trend upward, a shift in the balance of power in the region could emerge. China's economic interests will, in the long run, draw it into a more active political role in the region. Arab goodwill toward China may also result in calls for greater Chinese military involvement in the region, which could make it increasingly difficult for China to maintain neutrality. As Chinese engagement in the region grows, expectations for leadership will likely grow apace.

Conclusion

Since President Xi took power in 2012, China has adopted a more assertive foreign policy in the Middle East and the Arab world. In the past decade or so, China's economic interests in the region increased dramatically, have demanded more active diplomacy, and have expanded Chinese influence. China's foreign policy in the Middle East and the Arab world remains focused on securing energy supplies and markets for Chinese products and services and expanding political support. China has adopted a three-pronged strategy to achieve these goals. First, the state uses diplomacy to advance Chinese economic interests in the region. Second, while Beijing continues to adopt a "neutral partner" policy intended to maintain an environment friendly to Chinese business interests, Beijing is quietly becoming more active and has begun using political leverage to advance its interests. Third, Beijing exploits its soft power resources to cultivate goodwill in the region to serve China's long-term economic and political interests.

Beijing has decided to expand its influence while trying to not antagonize other players in the region. But China's strategy to pursue energy resources and markets is not without challenges. Neutrality is not always achievable. Some Chinese policies and practices in the region have caused tension with the U.S., particularly over issues of human rights and support for the Syrian regime. Regional conflicts may force Beijing to choose sides between the local actors, particularly, Iran and Saudi Arabia, which may have unforeseen negative consequences. Beijing's image is also threatened by the politicization and potential backlash from China's treatment of Uighurs in Xinjiang. Finally, China will need to balance rising expectations, as China's presence may initiate calls for greater involvement in the Middle East.

Notes

1 Bai Yu, "Xi Jinping Attended the Opening Ceremony of the Sixth Ministerial Conference of Sino–Arab Cooperation Forum and Delivered an Important Speech," *Xinhua*, June 5, 2014.
2 Wang Ze and Zeng Wei, "Xi Jinping's Speech at the Opening Ceremony of the Sixth Ministerial Conference of Sino–Arab Cooperation Forum," *Xinhua*, June 5, 2014.
3 This chapter deals with the twenty-two members of the Arab League, as well as Israel and Iran.
4 For works on the history of PRC-Middle East relations, see Yitzhak Shichor, *The Middle East in China's Foreign Policy, 1949–1977* (London: Cambridge University Press, 1979);

Hashim S. H. Behbehani, *China's Foreign Policy in the Arab World, 1955–1975: Three Case Studies*; John Calabrese, *China's Changing Relations with the Middle East* (London: Printer Publishers, 1991); and Lilian Craig Harris, *China Considers the Middle East* (London: I.B. Tauris, 1993).

5 Yufeng Mao, "Islam in Zhou Enlai's Diplomacy at the Bandung Conference, 1955," in *Bandung: Little Histories*, eds., Antonia Finnane and Derek McDougall (Caulfield East, VIC: Monash University Press, 2010), 89–108.

6 Egypt, Syria, Yemen, Iraq, Morocco, and Sudan, despite opposition from the United States, became the first Arab countries to sever diplomatic relations with Taiwan, grant China recognition, and establish diplomatic relations in the second half of the 1950s.

7 Egypt, Syria, Yemen, Iraq, Morocco, and Sudan, despite opposition from the United States, became the first Arab countries to sever diplomatic relations with Taiwan, grant China recognition, and establish diplomatic relations in the second half of the 1950s.

8 Lilian Craig Harris, *China Considers the Middle East* (London: I. B. Tauris, 1993), 118.

9 For example, in 1965, China condemned Tunisian President Bourguiba for advocating peaceful coexistence with Israel. See Harris, 118.

10 Joseph E. Khalili, *Communist China's Interaction With the Arab Nationalists Since the Bandung Conference* (New York: Exhibition Press, 1970); also see Yitzhak Shichor, *The Middle East in China's Foreign Policy, 1949–1977* (New York: Cambridge University Press, 1979), 114, 124; also see Jiang Chun and Guo Yingde, Zhong A Guanxi Shi 中阿关系史 [The History of Sino–Arabian Relationship] (Beijing: Jingji Ribao chubanshe, 2000), 297.

11 According to Abidi, China was buying oil from Iran to offset its sales of oil to Asian countries in the 1970s. Thus, in addition to good diplomacy in Asia, China also showed to Arab oil-producing countries the prospects of commercial deals. China established official diplomatic relations with Kuwait in 1971, and solidified ties with Oman in 1978, the UAE in 1981, Qatar in 1988, and Bahrain in 1989. Outreach to Saudi Arabia came at the end of the Cold War, in 1990. Mohamed Bin Huwaidin, *China's Relations With Arabia and the Gulf, 1949–1999* (London: Routledge Curzon, 2002), 105–106.

12 "Minutes of Talks Between Chou En-lai and Muhammad al-'Adsani, Kuwaiti Minister of Trade, Peking," December 5, 1972; Hashim S. H. Behbehani, *China's Foreign Policy in the Arab World, 1955–1975: Three Case Studies* (Boston: Kegan Paul International, 1981), 320–328.

13 Guang Pan, "China's Success in the Middle East," *The Middle East Quarterly* (December 1997): 35–40.

17 Yitzhak Shichor, "Molehills: Arms Transfers in Sino–Middle Eastern Relations," *Middle East Review of International Affairs* 4, no. 3 (2000): 71–74.

15 Sarah Kaiser-Cross, "The GCC Pivot to Asia: The Security of US Interests in the Arabian Gulf" (Master's Professional Report, University of Texas at Austin, 2015); Mohamed Bin Huwaidin, "China's Foreign Policy Toward the Gulf and Arabian Peninsula Region," in *China's Relations With Arabia and the Gulf 1949–1999* (New York: Routledge, 2002), 244.

16 See Appendices 1, 3, and 5.

17 "China Is Now the World's Largest Net Importer of Petroleum and Other Liquid Fuels," U.S. Energy Information Administration, March 24, 2014.

18 Among the top ten world exporters of oil to China, six are from the region. They are Saudi Arabia, Oman, Iraq, Iran, UAE, and Kuwait. Abbas Varij Kāzemi and Xiangming Chen, "China and the Middle East: More Than Oil," *World Financial Review*, November 26, 2014.

19 Johnson, Keith, "China Tops U.S. as Biggest Oil Importer," *Foreign Policy*, May 10, 2015.

20 "Pakistan hands over 2000 acres to China in Gwadar port city," *The Indian Express*, November 12, 2015; Warjahat Khan, "Gwadar Port Project Reveals China's Regional Power Play," *NBC News*, May 2, 2016.

21 "Pakistan hands over 2000 acres"; "China's Gwadar Port Nears Completion," *Maritime Executive*, April 14, 2014; The expected pipeline completion date is 2017. "China to Build Mega Oil Pipeline From Gwadar to Kashgar," *The Nation*, June 13, 2016.

22 "Iran, Saudi Arabia eager to join CPEC," *The Tribune*, October 1, 2016.

23 "Russia signs 30-Year Gas Deal With China," *BBC News*, May 21, 2014; "Energy Goes East as Russia and China Seal Multibillion Dollar Deals in Beijing," *RT News*, September 3, 2015.

24 Wu Lei, "China's Oil Safety: Challenges and Counter Measures—With Concurrent Comment on the Influence of the Iraq War," *Xiya Feizhou* 西亚非洲 [West Asia and Africa], no. 4 (2003): 17–21.

25 Julie Jiang and Chen Ding, "Update on Overseas Investments by China's National Oil Companies: Achievements and Challenges Since 2011," International Energy Agency, June 2014.

26 Jiang and Ding, "Update on Overseas Investments by China's National Oil Companies."

27 UN Comtrade Database, https://comtrade.un.org/, accessed October 2016.

28 Blanchard, Ben, "China, Saudi Arabia Eye $65 Billion in Deals as King Visits," *Reuters*, March 16, 2017.

29 See Appendix I; also International Monetary Fund (hereinafter referred to as IMF), Direction of Trade Statistics, www.imf.org/external/pubs/cat/longres.aspx?sk=20096, accessed September 2016.

30 IMF, Direction of Trade Statistics, www.imf.org/external/pubs/cat/longres.aspx?sk=20096, accessed September 2016.

31 IMF, Direction of Trade Statistics, www.imf.org/external/pubs/cat/longres.aspx?sk=20096, accessed September 2016.

32 "Shangwubu: xiya beifei cheng 'yidaiyilu' yanxian fuwu waibao zengsu zuikuai diqu" 商务部：西亚北非成"一带一路"沿线外包增速最快地区 [Department of Commerce: West Asia and North Africa Have Become the Fastest Growing Area Alongside "One Belt One Road" in Outsourcing Services], *China Outsourcing*, December 2, 2015.

33 Umut Ergunsu, "Why Is China's Role in the Middle East Growing?" *Huriyet Daily*, February 19, 2016.

34 "Agricultural Bank of China Starts RMB Settlement in UAE" *Xinhua News Agency*, May 11, 2017.

35 For an example, see *Xiya Feizhou* (West Asia and Africa), the bimonthly journal issued by the Chinese Academy of Social Sciences, http://qk.cass.cn/xyfz/qkml/.

36 To date no Arab nation has defended Taiwan's calls for independence. "Full Text of Chinese President's Signed Article on Saudi Newspaper," January 18, 2016, Ministry of Foreign Affairs of the People's Republic of China.

37 "Full Text of Chinese President."

38 Wang Ze and Zeng Wei, "Xi Jinping zai Zhong A hezuo luntan diliujie buzhangji huiyi kaimushishang de jianghua" 习近平在中阿合作论坛第六届部长级会议开幕式上的讲话 [Xi Jinping Delivers a Speech at the Opening Ceremony of the Sixth Ministerial Conference of the Sino–Arab Cooperation Forum), *Xinhua*, June 5, 2014.

39 Ben Blanchard, "China Appoints First Special Envoy for Syria Crisis," *Reuters*, March 29, 2016.

40 Energy Information Administration, "China Country Analysis Brief," May 14, 2015, www.eia.gov/beta/international/analysis.cfm?iso=CHN, accessed January 4, 2016; Jyotsna Ravishankar, "Middle East and China Move Closer," *Arabian Oil and Gas*, February 18, 2013.

41 "Saudi Arabia, China Elevate Bilateral Ties," *Saudi News*, January 19, 2016. China has also praised its cooperation with Israel on technology.

42 Militarily, Israel has become an important source of China's overseas weapons purchases. Since the cancellation of the Phalcon sale in 2000, Israeli arms deals with China continue to raise tensions between Israel and the United States.

43 Shlomo Cesana, "Netanyahu: China Fast Becoming Israel's Largest Trading Partner," *Israel Hayom*, May 20, 2014; Alexander Chipman Koty, "China–Israel Relations: Why the Tech Industry is Key to Bilateral Trade and Investment," *China Briefing*, June 15, 2016.

44 Raphael Ahren, "In Beijing, Netanyahu Looks to 'Marry Israeli's Technology With China's Capacity," *Times of Israel*, March 21, 2017.

45 Haiyun Mao and Jennifer Chang, "China's New Silk Road Strategy," *Middle East Research and Information Project*, May 20, 2014.

46 "Rouhani Calls for More Active Chinese Role in ME," *MEHR News Agency*, October 9, 2016.
47 "China Strengthens Mideast Oil Ties During Saudi's Visit," *The Seattle Times [Lexis–Nexis]*, January 25, 2006, and Zhou Bo, "Noninterference and Assistance Best for Middle East," *China Daily*, May 28, 2016.
48 Kaiser-Cross, "GCC."
49 China gained that reputation by providing Egypt with monetary donations and offering to send volunteers during the Suez crisis, supporting the Algerian independence war, and being one of the first countries to recognize the Algerian Liberation Front as the legitimate government of Algeria. To use Algeria as an example, China provided generous military and financial aid, including $10 million in credits in 1959 to the Algerian National Liberation Front (Harris, *China Considers the Middle East*, 115). According to Yitzhak Shichor, Egypt, Syria, Yemen, and Iraq were the destinations of most of China's aid offers to the Middle East in 1956–76. In Shichor's account, the total aid offer to these countries in the period reached $381.1 million. See Shichor, *The Middle East in China's Foreign Policy*, 209.
50 P.R. Kumaraswamy, "Israel–China Arms Trade: Unfreezing Times," *Middle East Institute*, July 16, 2012.
51 Ma Zhancheng, "Chinese President Makes Four-Point Proposal for Settlement of Palestinian Question," *Xinhua*, May 6, 2013.
52 Michael Zeff, "High-Ranking Chinese Official Signs Memorandum of Understanding During Visit to Israel," *Breaking Israel News*, September 21, 2016.
53 Roschanack Shaery, "Arabs in Yiwu, Confucius in East Beirut," *Middle East Information Project*, Spring 2014.
54 For example, see "China Decides to Forgive Iraq Debts, Reopen Embassy," *People's Daily*, February 6, 2004.
55 James Reinl, "Syria's War and Veto-Wielding UN Powerplays," *Al Jazeera*, September 30, 2015.
56 "Russia and China Veto UN Sanctions Resolution on Syria Sanctions," *Al Jazeera*, February 28, 2017.
57 Rob Virtue, "Putin's Boost in Battle Against ISIS: China Preparing to 'Team Up With Russia in Syria'," *Express News*, November 29, 2015; Samuel Ramani, "China's Syria Agenda," *The Diplomat*, September 22, 2016.
58 Ramani, "China's Syria Agenda."
59 Yun Sun, "Syria: What China Has Learned From Its Libya Experience," *Asia Pacific Bulletin*, February 27, 2012.
60 Ben Blanchard, "China Appoints First Special Envoy for Syria Crisis," *Reuters*, March 29, 2016.
61 "Beijing Policies in Xinjiang Driving Chinese Muslims to Join Ranks of Islamic State, says US Think Tank" *Agence-France Press*, July 21, 2016.
62 For more reading on Saudi–Iran tensions and shifting policies, see Sarah Kaiser-Cross and Ellen Scholl, "Saudi Arabia Begins to Imagine Life without Oil," *Foreign Policy*, May 9, 2016, and Sarah Kaiser-Cross, "What Are the Saudis Up to With Those Executions? Regional Dominance," *Foreign Policy*, January 8, 2016.
63 Ben Blanchard, "China Offers Support for Yemen Government as Xi Visits Saudi Arabia," *Reuters*, January 20, 2016.
64 Gal Luft, "China's New Grand Strategy for the Middle East," *Foreign Policy*, January 26, 2016.
65 For further reading, see Kaiser-Cross and Scholl, "Saudi Arabia Begins to Imagine Life Without Oil," and Kaiser-Cross, "What Are the Saudis Up to With Those Executions?"
66 "Full text of China's Position Paper on the 70th Anniversary of the United Nations," State Council of the People's Republic of China, September 22, 2015.
67 For example, former Chinese ambassador to Iran, Hua Liming, has called in numerous articles for greater Chinese involvement in regional affairs. See Hua Liming's article

entitled, "Yilang he wenti yu zhongguo de waijiao xuanze" 伊朗核问题与中国的外交选择 [The Iranian Nuclear Issue and China's Diplomatic Options], *Guoji wenti yanjiu* 国际问题研究 [*Journal of International Studies*], no. 1 (2007).

68 Cesana, "Netanyahu: China Fast Becoming Israel's Largest Trading Partner," May 20, 2014.

69 Mu Xuequan, "Chinese President Meets Saudi Arabia Crown Prince," *Xinhua*, March 13, 2013.

70 "Li Zhaoxing: Zhonga hezuo luntan de chengli juyou lichengbei yiyi" 李肇星：中阿合作论坛的成立具有里程碑意义 [Li Zhaoxing: The Establishment of Sino–Arab Forum Is a Significant Milestone], *Xinhua*, January 30, 2004.

71 Mimi Kirk, "Chinese Soft Power and Dubai's Confucius Institute," *Middle East Institute*, June 2, 2015.

72 For more information on Hanban, please see http://english.hanban.org; "Hanban (Confucius Institute Headquarters) 2009 Annual Report."

73 University of Dubai, "Confucius Institute Greatly Contributes to China–UAE Cultural Exchange: Scholar," www.ud.ac.ae/news-ciud/440-confucius-institute-greatly-contributes-to-china-uae-cultural-exchange-scholar, accessed September 2016.

74 Abdul Hanan Tago, "Over 40 Universities in China Teach Arabic," *Arab News*, February 23, 2014.

75 Wagdy Sawahel, "Seeking Soft Power, China Expands Activities in Arab Higher Education," *Al-Fanar Media*, February 1, 2016.

76 Cesana, "Netanyahu: China Fast Becoming Israel's Largest Trading Partner."

77 Ben Flannigan, "China Central Television opens regional bureau in Dubai," *The National*, December 24, 2010.

78 Flannigan, "Central Television."

79 V.M. Sathish, "First Chinese TV Channel in Mideast Aims to Be a Bridge," *Emirates 24/7*, June 14, 2016; Renee Ghert-Zand, "Chinese Learn a New Language of the Mideast," *Times of Israel*, April 30, 2015.

80 Ben Simpfendorfer, "The New Public Relations War: 'Al Jazeera in China'," in *The New Silk Road: How a Rising Arab World Is Turning Away From the West and Rediscovering China*, ed. Ben Simpfendorfer (Basingstoke, Hampshire: Palgrave Macmillan, 2009), 117–119.

81 Simpfendorfer, "The New Public Relations War," 116–118.

82 Hanan Tago, "Over 40 Universities in China Teach Arabic."

83 Elizabeth Van Wie Davis, "Uyghur Muslim Ethnic Separatism in Xinjiang, China," Asia–Pacific Center for Security Studies, January 2008.

84 Please see the section "Regional Perspectives" on pages 000–000 for discussions on how China's treatment of the Uighurs creates potential difficulties with its Arab partners.

85 "More Arabs Want to Know China's Way to Success," *China Daily*, November 6, 2014.

86 "Attitudes Toward China," Pew Research Center, July 18, 2013.

87 "Attitudes Toward China."

88 None of the Gulf nations were interviewed in this poll sample, according to the website.

89 "China's Image," *Pew Research Center*, July 14, 2014.

90 "Attitudes Toward China."

91 "Attitudes Toward China."

92 Worldwide Governance Indicators, World Bank, Data from 2002–2015.

93 Nawaf E. Obaid, Amy Myers Jaffe, Edward L. Morse, and Chad Gracia, "The Sino–Saudi Energy Rapprochement: Implications for US National Security," *The Gracia Group*, January 8, 2002, 36.

94 Massoud Hayoun, "Strange Bedfellows: China's Middle Eastern Inroads," *World Affairs*, January/February 2013.

95 "Chinese Films Introduced to the UAE," *Gulf News*, March 30, 2017.

96 Obaid et al., "The Sino–Saudi Energy Rapprochement."

97 Dan Blumenthal, "Providing Arms: China and the Middle East," *Middle East Quarterly* (2005): 11–19.

98 Justine Drennan, "Is China Making Its Own Terrorism Problem Worse?" *Foreign Policy*, February 9, 2015.
99 Metin Gurcan, "How the Islamic State Is Exploiting Asian Unrest to Recruit Fighters," *Al Monitor*, September 9, 2015.
100 Thomas Jocelyn, "Zawahiri Praises Uighur Jihadists in Ninth Episode of 'Islamic Spring' Series," *Long War Journal*, July 7, 2016.
101 Mohamed Turki Al-Sudaira, "China in the Eyes of the Saudi Media, "Gulf Research Center, 14–16.
102 Al-Sudaira, "China in the Eyes of the Saudi Media," 14–16.
103 John Fakiannakis, "Saudi Arabia Continues to Focus on 'Look East' Policy," *Arab News*, February 11, 2009.
104 "Monthly Energy Review March 2015," Energy Information Agency, March 26, 2015.
105 Noel Brinkerhoff, "U.S. Dominates Weapons Export Market as Profits Grow with Sales to the Middle East," *AllGov*, March 17, 2015.
106 Jeremy Binnie, "UAE, Saudi Arabia Operating Chinese UAVs Over Yemen," *IHS Jane's 360*, December 18, 2015; Franz-Stefan Gady, "Will China Sell Armed Drones to US Ally?" *The Diplomat*, May 16, 2015.
107 Zachary Keck, "China Secretly Sold Saudi Arabia DF-21 Missiles With CIA Approval," *The Diplomat*, January 31, 2014.
108 Brian Murphy, "Iran and China Deepen a 'Blue Water' Friendship," *Washington Post*, October 28, 2014.
109 Minnie Chan, "Chinese Drone Factory in Saudi Arabia First in Middle East," *South China Morning Post*, March 26, 2017.
110 "U.S.–Saudi Arabia Trade Facts," Office of the United States Trade Representative, May 6, 2014.
111 Kaiser-Cross, "GCC."
112 Li Xiaokun and Zhang Fan, "Xi Calls for Early Signing of China–Gulf FTA," *China Daily*, January 18, 2014.

8

CHINA'S STRATEGY IN LATIN AMERICA AND THE CARIBBEAN

R. Evan Ellis[1]

Introduction

Since 1997, when Panama awarded a concession to the Hong Kong-based firm Hutchison Whampoa to operate facilities on both the Atlantic and Pacific sides of the Panama Canal, Chinese activities in Latin America and the Caribbean (LAC) have commanded attention.[2] In both the U.S. and the region itself, interest in Chinese engagement is driven by a combination of hopes and fears. Some businessmen and political leaders look to Chinese markets, and the prospect of loans and investments as opportunities, while others focus on the threat posed by Chinese products and services to Latin American manufacturers. While some Latin American leaders, including the late Hugo Chavez in Venezuela,[3] Evo Morales in Bolivia,[4] and Rafael Correa in Ecuador,[5] have welcomed Chinese engagement to help "liberate" the region from its dependence on Western companies and institutions, the majority focus more on less ideological themes.

To date, U.S. policymakers have not sought to limit Chinese engagement with LAC, and some, such as former Assistant Secretary of State Roberta Jacobson, have noted its potential to benefit the region.[6] Yet many have expressed concern regarding a lack of transparency with respect to specific Chinese activities, and a profound distrust persists regarding China's long-term agenda, or how its behavior in the region might change as its national power continues to grow.[7] This chapter examines China's engagement with LAC, with a focus on how it has evolved, Chinese objectives in the region, its methods for pursuing them, and the impact on the region and the United States.

Historical Overview

Since 1978, when the People's Republic of China (PRC) began to open up to the global economy, its relationship with LAC has passed through three important stages.

1. In 2001, China's acceptance into the World Trade Organization marked the take-off of its trade with LAC. Since then the economic relationship has eclipsed the struggle between the Beijing and Taipei for diplomatic recognition, which had previously dominated interactions with the region.
2. In 2009, Chinese companies began to establish a significant physical presence in Latin America, giving China an increasing stake in the internal affairs of the countries where they were operating.
3. In 2015, decelerating economic growth in China and growing awareness of the difficulties associated with China-backed projects combined to push the region's business and political leaders toward a less starry-eyed, more realistic attitude regarding China and its potential contribution to regional development.

Since China's acceptance into the World Trade Organization in 2001, bilateral trade between the PRC and Latin America and the Caribbean has grown by a factor of 17—from $14.5 billion in 2001 to $258.6 billion in 2014, before falling to $231.1 billion in 2015 and to $213.4 billion in 2016.[8] Prior to 2009, however, that engagement was largely limited to importing Chinese products and the exportation of primary products from the region to China. Both required a minimal, and generally temporary, Chinese presence in LAC.

There was, however, a modest number of ethnic Chinese in the region. Since the late nineteenth century, small groups of Chinese immigrants and their descendants had lived there, principally in Peru, Panama, Brazil, and the Caribbean.[9] A small number of Chinese companies operated in the region prior to 2009. Examples include the mining firm Shougang, working in Peru since 1992;[10] the air conditioner maker Gree, operating a factory in Manaus, Brazil, since 2000; and Chinese appliance maker Haier's factory in the same city since 2005.[11] In the oil sector, China National Petroleum Corporation has operated fields in Venezuela since 1997,[12] in Peru since 1999,[13] and in Ecuador since 2005.[14]

Beginning in 2009–10, Chinese investment in LAC took off,[15] and the physical presence of Chinese firms and personnel expanded apace.[16] China's growing economic involvement in LAC was due to several factors, including the expanded capability and experience of its firms as well as the accumulation of physical, financial, and legal infrastructure to support their activities. During this period, China also made substantial advances in its military engagement with the region. Their arms sales to Latin America expanded in terms of the types, sophistication, and quality of equipment sold, as well as the list of countries which bought them. The People's Liberation Army (PLA) also brought members of LAC countries' militaries to China on a regular basis for training and professional military education (PME) and conducted an expanding array of activities in the region.

By mid-2016, the Chinese government was reporting economic growth of only 6.7 percent,[17] nearly half its annual rate during most of the previous two decades.[18] By mid-2017, both Chinese and Western analysts were questioning whether it was feasible to sustain growth at 6.5 percent.[19] This economic "deceleration," in combination with the election of Donald Trump as president of the United States, has moved China's relations with Latin America into a complex new phase.

On one hand, reduced Chinese growth has diminished expectations among political and business leaders regarding China's potential economic contribution to the region. Such reduced growth has contributed to falling demand for commodities, thus pushing prices down and causing distress in those states which have relied primarily on exporting petroleum, mining, and agriculture products. Overall, the decline in commodity prices caused the dollar value of Latin America's exports to China to fall by $25 billion, or 20 percent from 2014 to 2016.[20]

Latin American expectations have been tempered by growing awareness of the substantial number of Chinese projects that have either not been realized, or experienced considerable difficulties, including "dry canals" (principally railroad projects) in Colombia, Honduras, Guatemala, and Mexico. Examples of problematic Chinese projects include the Mexico City–Queretaro railroad;[21] unrealized refinery projects in Costa Rica, Ecuador,[22] and Cuba; and the postponed Nicaragua Canal, backed by Chinese businessman Wang Jing and his firm HKND.[23] Still other Chinese projects have faced serious difficulties. They include the June 2015 bankruptcy of the Baha Mar resort project in the Bahamas;[24] the blocking of the Dragon Mart wholesale-retail complex in Cancun, Mexico; and violent resistance to projects in the petroleum sector in Tarapoa and Orellana, Ecuador and Caquetá Colombia; as well as similar protests and violence against Chinese mining investments, such as Mirador in Ecuador, Shougang, Rio Blanco, and Las Bambas in Peru.[25] While the Chinese side does not necessarily bear responsibility for such difficulties and unrealized expectations, the image of Chinese initiatives which do not go forward, or which are mired in controversy, has become part of the public image of Chinese business in the region.

At the same time, however, the election of Donald Trump as president of the U.S. in November 2016, and the announcement of the new administration that it would withdraw from the Trans-Pacific Partnership, renegotiate the North American Free Trade Administration, and significantly re-define U.S. economic and other relationships in the Western Hemisphere, drove many Latin American leaders to focus even more on China as an additional economic partner.[26]

China's Objectives in Latin America

Economic Objectives

The objectives of Chinese engagement in LAC, as with the rest of the world, are primarily economic, although that does not make them less strategic, or less important for the region or the United States.[27] They have been consistent with its policy pronouncements, and are well summarized in China's November 2008 and

November 2016 White Papers on the LAC (see Appendix __ for the full text of the latter),[28] as well as the "1+3+6" framework (one plan, three axes of engagement, six areas of cooperation) announced by President Xi Jinping during his July 2014 presentation to the first China–CELAC summit in Fortaleza, Brazil.[29] The "1+3+6" framework highlights the focus of China's engagement in LAC; the three axes are trade, finance, and investment, and the six areas of cooperation are energy and resources, infrastructure construction, agriculture, manufacturing, scientific and technological innovation, and information technologies.[30]

Since the beginning of the twenty-first century, China has focused on seven objectives: four economic and three geostrategic. China's primary economic objectives in LAC are: (1) reliable access to commodities, such as petroleum and mining products, at reasonable prices; (2) access to agricultural goods, particularly animal fodder such as soy and fishmeal, to supply China's agricultural sector; (3) access to markets for Chinese goods and services, as PRC-based companies seek to expand their client base and move up the value-added chain; and (4) access to process and product technologies to support the competitiveness of Chinese entities in strategically valued commercial and defense sectors.

China's interest in LAC commodities is a subset of its search for them globally, reflecting the consumption of raw material to supply its infrastructure construction, and both domestic and export-oriented consumer and capital goods manufacturing. China's sustained high demand for commodities also reflects the construction of housing and commercial real estate on a nation-wide scale as the nation's population has migrated in large numbers from the countryside to the cities.[31] Given the oversupply of housing in many Chinese urban areas, and facing extensive over capacity in many industries, it seems likely China will reduce its commodity imports.

Beyond primary products, China also looks to LAC for agricultural goods. Due to extensive land and water degradation China suffers from a lack of usable land to feed its 1.35 billion people. As the Chinese migrate from the countryside to the cities and become more prosperous, they tend to consume more meat, increasing the demands on limited agricultural land to raise the pigs, chickens, and other animals demanded by Chinese consumers. While the Chinese government, in its 5-year agricultural plan, has sought to maintain near self-sufficiency in the production of food for human consumption,[32] it has needed to import significant quantities of animal feeds, such as soybeans from Argentina, Brazil, and Paraguay, as well as fishmeal from Peru.

China also looks to Latin America and the Caribbean as a market for goods and services. As PRC-based companies seek growth by exporting their products, and move into higher value-added products, the 600 million residents of Latin America and the Caribbean, and the region's middle-income, relatively consumption-oriented culture presents an attractive alternative to those seeking to diversify their client base and move up the value-added ladder.

Finally, China looks to LAC (among other regions) to obtain product and process technologies to expand the capabilities of the Chinese firms and help them improve their competitiveness in strategic sectors, particularly in defense and non-defense. Such competitiveness not only benefits the Chinese company, but also advances the Chinese government's goal of a strong state with a modern, diversified industrial and technology base.

Geostrategic Objectives

As a compliment to China's commercial pursuits, Beijing has three geostrategic objectives in the region: (1) promotion of a "multipolar world" in which key institutions and countries are not dominated by the United States; (2) recovery and unification of territory viewed as "historically Chinese," such as Taiwan and Tibet; and (3) avoidance of an international coalition mobilized in opposition to China's "rise."

While the term "multipolar world" appears frequently in the discourse of Chinese politicians and academics, the value of such a world in supporting China's achievement of other strategic goals is often overlooked.[33] As an example, regimes which actively resist U.S.-backed institutions and policy goals in the region, such as the Bolivarian Alliance of the Peoples of the Americas (ALBA), have become a key customer for Chinese military hardware, consumer goods, and construction services, as well as important sources of petroleum and other commodities. They have also served as key nodes in the resistance to U.S. policies and Western institutions which could present obstacles to PRC pursuit of commodities, foodstuffs, markets, and technology in the region. It was significant that China's November 2016 policy white paper toward Latin America, for the first time, spoke of a multipolar world as an objective to promote, rather than simply a feature of the current global order.[34]

Beyond promotion of a multipolar world, China also seeks to consolidate its claims over Taiwan and Tibet. The LAC is home to 12 of the 23 nations in the world that recognize the regime in Taiwan as the legitimate government of all of China: Paraguay, Panama, Nicaragua Honduras, El Salvador, Guatemala, Belize, the Dominican Republic, Haiti, Saint Kitts and Nevis, Saint Lucia, Saint Vincent, and the Grenadines. Since 2008, Taiwan and the PRC have suspended efforts to change the diplomatic position of the other through personal and national gifts, in order to pursue rapprochement and greater integration between their two nations. Nonetheless, with the victory of the Democratic People's Party (DPP) in the January 2016 elections in Taiwan,[35] that agreement has begun to break down. In March 2016, shortly before DPP leader Tsai Ing-wen assumed the presidency, the PRC established diplomatic relations with Gambia. In December 2016, the African nation of Sao Tome and Principe also recognized the PRC.[36]

Even if the PRC does not resume its effort to convince Latin American and Caribbean nations currently recognizing Taiwan to change their position, PRC diplomats continue to work to ensure that official communiqués following interactions between Chinese and Latin American leaders who do recognize the PRC affirm Beijing's position on both Taiwan and Tibet. In addition, the PRC pursues commercial projects with countries recognizing Taiwan, such as the Jaguar thermoelectric plant in Guatemala,[37] and the Patuca III and Aqua Zarca hydroelectric facilities in Honduras,[38] as well as opening PRC trade and investment promotion offices (CCPIT) there.

As the PRC pursues its goals, it tries to avoid the mobilization of the U.S. and other developed Western powers in a coalition to oppose it, since such coordinated opposition could damage China's access to international markets and financial institutions on which it depends.

China's Methods in Latin America

China's preferred style of doing business in the region often leads its companies to develop close relationships with political elites of the partner nations where they operate, occasionally creating problems. Yet to date, the amount of influence actually achieved by Beijing through such relationships in the region is unclear.

To date, Chinese engagement with Latin America and the Caribbean has been principally bilateral in character. Chinese funds such as the China–LAC Industrial Cooperation Investment Fund, the China–LAC Cooperation Fund, and the BRICS bank raise the prospect of China-financed multi-national projects for the benefit of the region, but such projects are yet to occur.

Economic Diplomacy

China uses a mixture of bilateral and multilateral state-led engagements in Latin America and the Caribbean to pursue its strategic objectives in the region. At the multilateral level, the PRC has engaged with the region through the China–CELAC forum, the Organization of American States (OAS),[39] where it has been an observer since May 2004,[40] and the International Monetary Fund, which it joined in February 2009.

Beijing has proposed large multilateral funds to promote its companies' work in the region. These efforts include the $3 billion fund for the Caribbean, announced in June 2013 during President Xi's visit to Trinidad and Tobago;[41] a $35 billion fund, announced in July 2014 at the end of the China–CELAC summit in Brazil;[42] the BRICS bank, to be initially capitalized at $50 billion;[43] a $10 billion China–LAC Industrial Cooperation Investment Fund, financed principally by China Development Bank;[44] and a separate $5 billion China–LAC Cooperation Fund, with the coordinated efforts of China Export–Import Bank and the Inter-American Development Bank.[45] Despite the promise of such multilateral initiatives, however, meaningful multilateral engagement and projects have been limited: the PRC has largely used the China–CELAC forum to discuss the direction of future cooperation and announce bilateral deals with individual member countries.[46] Of China's proposed multilateral funds, the China–LAC Industrial Cooperation Investment Fund and the China–LAC Cooperation Fund made important advances in 2015, but had not, by the end of 2016, disbursed significant resources to support projects.

With respect to bilateral engagement, the PRC employs a posture toward the region which is, on its face, ideologically neutral and non-judgmental toward the domestic policies and conditions of its partners.[47] This approach has been quite effective in building goodwill toward China in the region, particularly among states such as Venezuela, seeking to escape perceived pressures from Western governments, companies, and multilateral institutions regarding their domestic policies.

The concept of Chinese "neutrality," is, however, misunderstood. China takes great interest in the policies of its Latin American and Caribbean partners on issues, including their position on the diplomatic status of Taiwan or Tibet, and the treatment of Chinese companies and citizens[48] and ethnic Chinese living in the region.[49] Yet by contrast to many Western governments, China seldom publicly confronts its partners or demands policy changes that would force them to lose face. Rather, Beijing arguably prefers to use subtle, often economic pressure in a non-public fashion to secure their goals. One prominent example involves protectionist legislation by the Congress of Argentina against Chinese products. Following repeated, low-key expressions of displeasure, the Chinese government suspended imports of soy oil, worth $2 billion per year, prompting both Argentine Foreign Minister Héctor Timerman and President Cristina Fernandez to travel to Beijing to correct the situation. In the weeks following President Fernandez's trip, Argentina announced the award of $10 billion in trains and other infrastructure work to Chinese companies, and China announced to resumption of soy oil imports from Argentina, although no public linkage was ever made between Argentine protectionism, the cut-off of soy oil imports, the infrastructure contracts, and the resumption of soy oil imports.[50]

A key attribute of Chinese engagement with the countries of Latin America and the Caribbean is government-to-government negotiations. Correspondingly, the PRC Ministry of Foreign Affairs meticulously ranks its relationships with the countries in the region (and elsewhere in the world). In Latin America and the Caribbean, those receiving its highest designation, "comprehensive strategic partner," include Brazil, Argentina, Venezuela, Peru, Mexico, and Ecuador. In addition, China has given Chile and Uruguay its second highest designation, "strategic partner." For nations in both categories, the PRC may establish a high-level cooperation forum that meets annually at the ministerial level to monitor and facilitate projects. Prominent examples include the "Cosban" in Brazil,[51] and the "High-level Mixed Commission" in Venezuela.[52]

In addition to diplomatic overtures and ministerial-level coordination, Beijing uses government-negotiated agreements to lay the groundwork for advancing commercial relationships with its partners. These include Memorandums of Understanding (MoU), expressing interest in deepening cooperation in a particular sector or between particular companies. While such MoUs may carry limited legal weight, for Chinese companies they are important as official encouragement to do business in a specific area. Beyond MoUs, framework agreements also include bilateral trade accords, such the agreements signed between China and Chile (2005),

Peru (2009), and Costa Rica (2010), as well as legal and administrative agreements facilitating commerce, such as reciprocal investment protection accords, or the certification of foreign processing facilities to expedite the movement of goods such as foodstuffs through customs.[53] Within the established framework, Chinese companies (both state-owned and private) pursue specific projects with local partners, generally in coordination with Chinese banks and subcontractors, with coordination with and assistance from the Chinese state in a manner that reflects the size of the company involved, its ties to the central government, and the strategic importance of its industry.

With respect to construction projects, China has been most successful in negotiating government-to-government deals with politically sympathetic regimes whose policies have limited their ability to obtain capital from the West, including the ALBA regimes and Argentina prior to the 2015 election of Mauricio Macri.[54] China has also enjoyed considerable successes among the smaller governments of the Caribbean basin, where large Chinese projects can have an enormous impact, and whose small bureaucracies both lack resources for managing major public procurements and are susceptible to personal inducements.

The Chinese have also facilitated winning construction work in the region by setting up loan funds. Examples include the Heavy Investment Fund and Long-Range and Broad Reach Fund in Venezuela, and the twice-renewed Jamaica Development Infrastructure Program fund.

In a small number of cases, mostly involving real estate and road construction in the Caribbean, Chinese companies have invested some of their own capital in projects. In June 2015, the largest such project to date, the $3.5 billion Baha Mar resort in the Bahamas, filed for bankruptcy amidst a bitter public dispute between the Chinese construction firm, China State Construction and Engineering, the real estate developer, Sarkis Izmirilan, and the Bahamian government. Nonetheless, under the terms of the financing, the principal Chinese lender, China Export–Import bank, controlled the disposition of the assets in bankruptcy, ultimately cutting the local partner, Mr. Izmirilan, out of the deal, and facilitating the takeover of the project, at a bargain price, by another Chinese firm, Chow Tai Fook Enterprises.[55]

Although the Chinese have successfully executed a number of road, bridge, power transmission, and other electric infrastructure projects in Latin America, almost none of the large, high-visibility projects to be done in the region by Chinese companies or businessmen have come to fruition. Examples of such "white elephants" include the $50 billion Nicaragua Canal; the $10 billion transcontinental railroad from Bayovar Peru to Açu, Brazil;[56] the Mexico City–Queretaro railroad project; separate transcontinental dry canal projects spanning southern Mexico, Guatemala, Honduras, and Colombia; major refineries including Cienfuegos in Cuba, the Recope refinery in Costa Rica, and the Refinery of the Pacific in Ecuador; and the Dragon Mart retail-wholesale complex in Mexico. With respect to manufacturing, the Chinese companies operating in the region are diverse, with their investments generally smaller than those contemplated in sectors such as mining and petroleum.

Beyond construction projects, the Chinese have also used loans to national oil companies in the region as vehicles to obtain information about and participate in projects in the sector. The most prominent example was a $10 billion loan to the Brazilian state oil firm Petrobras in 2009, setting the stage for the entry of Sinopec into the sector.[57]

Political Outreach

The Communist Party of China (CPC) has tried to insulate itself against the effects of political change on their commercial projects by enhancing political ties with opposition figures and parties in the region, particularly on the left of the political spectrum. For example, the CPC's relationship with the Peruvian Nationalist Party and its hosting of its leader, Ollanta Humala, in China in 2010,[58] proved useful when he was elected president of Peru the following year, and helped to avoid difficulties with Chinese mining investments in the country that had been negotiated by his predecessor, Alan Garcia.

Although the CPC has traditionally maintained relationships with leftist and minority political parties, it has been less effective in maintaining ties with out-of-power conservative parties. The continuing PRC inclination to enhance party-to-party ties was expressed in the 2008 PRC White Paper toward Latin America and the Caribbean,[59] as well as in the hosting of a China–CELAC forum of political parties in Beijing in December 2015.[60] Such efforts reflect Beijing's own political culture, in which relationships the CPC and current or future leading parties help bolster the relationships between governments. For example, the shift in power in Guyana from the Indo-Guyanese People's Progressive Party (PPP) to the predominantly afro-Guyanese "A Partnership for National Unity" (APNU), which united with the newly formed Alliance for Change (AFC) to capture control of the state in the May 2015 national election, caused difficulties for a number of public projects that had been awarded to the Chinese under the previous government.[61] These included including the Amaila Falls hydroelectric project,[62] modernization of the Cheddi Jagan international airport,[63] and timber concessions of the Chinese company Bai Shan Lin.[64]

Along the same lines as "party to party" relationships, the Chinese have historically used "friendship societies" to maintain unofficial relations with key political actors in countries with which they do not have diplomatic relationships. During the struggle for diplomatic recognition between the PRC and Taiwan in Latin America and the Caribbean, these organizations helped to advance diplomatic recognition among elites in the countries involved. With the PRC's achievement of diplomatic recognition in most countries of the region, these societies have evolved into social entities whose members also have sideline businesses promoting travel to, and commercial deals with, China, as well as maintaining good-will toward the PRC among the country's elites.

Beyond initiatives in the economic and political domains, the Chinese have also sought to advance their influence in the region through educational exchanges and

cultural interactions. The PRC explicitly acknowledged its interest in such activities in its 2008 White Paper toward the region.[65] One leading vehicle for doing
so is its cultural promotion organization, Hanban, which maintains more than 53
Confucius Institutes and Confucius classrooms in the region, providing officially
sanctioned education on Chinese language and culture, as well as sponsoring students from Latin America and the Caribbean to study in the PRC.[66]

Mergers and Acquisitions

In 2002, in the 10th five-year plan, the CPC promulgated its "go out" strategy,
which gave its political "blessing" for Chinese firms to pursue foreign engagement. Chinese companies responded to projections of increasing demand by
acquiring mines and oilfields and developing relationships with international agricultural conglomerates. Similarly, Chinese firms in construction, telecommunications, manufacturing, logistics, and banking sought out ties to foreign markets and
technologies.

In petroleum, most major Chinese initiatives involved purchasing an interest
in companies possessing the rights to significant reserves, once the exploratory
work had already been done. Notable examples include Sinopec's acquisition of a
40 percent stake in the Brazilian holdings of Repsol in exchange for the injection
of $7.1 billion into its operations,[67] the $3.1 billion acquisition by Sinochem of a
40 percent interest in the Brazilian holdings of the Norwegian company Statoil,[68]
the March 2010 $3.1 billion CNOOC acquisition of Bridas, with significant assets
in Argentina,[69] and the $2.4 billion purchase of Occidental Petroleum by Sinopec,
announced in December of the same year.[70] In August 2012, Repsol announced
the sale of its operations in Ecuador to Sinopec,[71] greatly increasing the holdings
of Chinese firms in Ecuador. The largest of such acquisitions, to date, has been
CNOOC's 2013 purchase of the Canadian oil company Nexxen for $15.1 billion,
transferring to the firm important petroleum assets in Colombia and elsewhere in
the region.[72] Chinese companies also continued to acquire positions in the region
by buying minority stakes in companies operating there, including Sinochem's purchase of a 10 percent interest in the Brazilian holdings of the French company
Perenco,[73] and Sinopec's $4.8 billion acquisition of a 30 percent stake in Galp
Energy in March 2012.[74] Chinese companies have also begun to move beyond
the acquisition of companies with access to proven reserves, into more risky but
lucrative exploration and development projects. The most prominent example is
the 10 percent stakes acquired by both CNPC and CNOOC in the development
of the Libra oil field in the deep waters off of Brazil, with a possible 8–12 billion
barrels of recoverable oil, making it potentially the largest block that the Brazilian
government has auctioned.[75]

China's activities in the mining sector has paralleled that in petroleum, with its
companies acquiring rights to major mines, developed by others and needing the
injection of a significant amount of capital to take the project forward. As in the
petroleum sector, Chinese firms have also purchased minority positions in some

strategically valuable mining projects, including the September 2011 $1.95 billion acquisition of a 10 percent interest in the firm CBMM, which specializes in rare earth elements.[76] Major examples include the Toromocho, Galleno, Pampa de Pongo, Don Javier, and Rio Blanco mines in Peru, Itaminas in Brazil, Corriente in Ecuador, and Sierra Grande in Argentina. Indeed, in Peru, by the end of 2015, Chinese firms had $19.1 billion in investment commitments, representing a third of all planned mining investments in the country.[77]

In electricity production and transmission, China's largest company, State Grid, has established a significant presence in Brazil, beginning with the 2010 $1 billion acquisition of seven power companies in the country,[78] the 2012 acquisition of the Brazilian assets of the Spanish company ACS,[79] and continuing with acquisitions that include State Grid's multiphase $10.4 billion acquisition of CPFL during the period 2016 to 2017.[80] Other deals include the $1 billion acquisition of the Brazil holdings of Duke Energy by the Chinese firm Three Gorges in 2017.[81]

Chinese firms have also used mergers and acquisitions in their attempts to secure reliable access to agricultural goods and associated technologies from Latin America and the Caribbean. Chinese firms have largely been frustrated in their attempts to acquire land in Latin America and the Caribbean or set up facilities to compete with the logistics infrastructures of established agricultural conglomerates such as ADM, Dreyfus, Bunge, and Cargill.[82] Initiatives to this end, such as a project by the Heilongjiang-based firm Beidahuang to create an agricultural production complex on leased land in Rio Negro Argentina, and planned investments in agro-industrial facilities in Brazil by Sanhe Hopeful and Chongqing Grain, have not gone forward. Nonetheless, Chinese entities such as the wholesale purchaser China National Cereals, Oils and Foodstuffs Corporation (COFCO) have begun to obtain needed agricultural export infrastructures in the region, as well as key technologies through acquisitions. The two most prominent examples are the 2014 purchase of Nidera for $1.2 billion,[83] and the acquisition of H.K. Noble for $1.5 billion the same year.[84] Even with such activities, and with massive imports of animal feedstock such as soybeans from the region, China's inability to meet its growing demand for animal protein, and possibly political pressures from Latin American partners, has driven it to import meat from countries of the region such as Mexico, Brazil, and Argentina.[85]

Clustering Investments

With growing sales volumes and experience with the local partner, the Chinese began to construct final assembly facilities in the region, and in some cases, establish clusters of suppliers to support them. Their objectives for such manufacturing investments include improved client service, and often avoidance of taxes on imported finished goods. Such investments have been concentrated in large countries with access to additional markets through trade accords. Chinese suppliers can use Brazil to access the countries of MERCOSUR, and Mexico to access the U.S. and Canada through NAFTA.

Examples of Chinese manufacturing investments in the region include Jialing and Jincheng, which established motorcycle facilities in Colombia in the 1990s; the Chinese appliance manufacturers Haier and Gree, which established facilities in the Brazilian manufacturing hub of Manaus; Sany Heavy Industries with a factory in Sao Paulo; and Xuzhou Construction Machinery Group (XCMG) in Minas Gerais. Chinese companies in the Latin American auto sector include Shanghai Automotive Industry Corporation (SAIC), Anhui Jianghuai Automobile Corporation (JAC), Foton, and Chery,[86] among others. Nonetheless, such investments have not always done well, particularly major investments in manufacturing facilities in Brazil just prior to that nation's sharp economic downturn in 2014.

Chinese products such as motorcycles, appliances, cars, and heavy machinery first entered Latin American markets through local partners. The partners play a particularly important role in this sector, facilitating the Chinese manufacturer's legal presence in the country and providing a local retail network and knowledge of the local market. Despite the enormous volume of Chinese products sold to Latin America and the Caribbean, there are relatively few Chinese "traders" operating in the region. Most Chinese products are imported into the region through Latin American businessmen or companies. With respect to high-value-added products such as motorcycles, cars, and heavy equipment, however, Chinese companies sell to the region through relationships with local partners who provide sales, distribution, and service networks, although Chinese and local associates may partner on final assembly facilities and distribution hubs in the region.

In the services sector, Chinese companies in the region have demonstrated a range of behaviors depending on their specific industry. In banking, China Development Bank and China Ex–Im bank have played a key role in financing Chinese firms' infrastructure projects in the LAC, while other banks such as ICBC[87] and China Construction Bank[88] have established a branch banking presence in the region.

In telecommunications, the company Huawei, and to a lesser extent ZTE, although relatively small in China, have built a substantial presence in Latin America from the ground up, constructing 3G and 4G networks for governments and private telecommunications companies, as well as selling telephones and data devices. Perhaps because Huawei and ZTE have built their business in the region from the ground up, and because their business depends on client service, the two have been among the best Chinese companies in integrating large local staffs with Chinese managers and technical personnel.

While Chinese companies have made significant advances in operating in the region, such as in winning contracts, working with local partners, and addressing the concerns of local actors impacted by their projects, such challenges are an inherent part of the industries in which Chinese activities are concentrated in the region, including mining, petroleum, and construction. The barriers of language, culture, and operating in pluralistic democracies continue to produce both manageable and insurmountable barriers for Chinese firms in LAC countries.

Military Activity

The client base for the Chinese defense industry has expanded in LAC beyond Venezuela to include Bolivia, Ecuador, Trinidad and Tobago, Peru, and Argentina, among others.[89] Chinese companies have advanced from sales to ideologically sympathetic allies, such as Venezuela, Ecuador, and Bolivia, to more independent countries with more sophisticated militaries, such as Argentina[90] and Peru.[91] Just as Chinese manufacturers are growing and diversifying their capabilities to offer products in strategically important, high value-added sectors such as autos, heavy equipment, and electronics, Chinese defense companies are supplying an ever-broader list of clients with increasingly capable array of military goods.[92]

Defense sales and gifts by Chinese companies in Latin America and the Caribbean have expanded from clothing and small arms, to advanced weapons systems such as fighter aircraft, radars, armored combat vehicles, and military ships. Chinese defense companies like AVIC and Norinco have successfully moved up the value-added chain and diversified their product, offering increasingly sophisticated weapons systems such as the K-8 and subsequently L-15 fighters sold to Venezuela,[93] the VN-1 and VN-16 armored personnel carriers also sold to Venezuela,[94] the Z-9/H-425 helicopters sold to Bolivia,[95] military trucks and buses sold to Bolivia and Peru, and self-propelled artillery vehicles and offshore patrol craft, such as the P-18, sold to Trinidad and Tobago. In July 2015, the Peruvian army took delivery on the first 27 of 40 Type 90B 122mm Chinese rocket launch vehicles.[96] In July 2016, China signed an agreement to provide 31 armored vehicles to Bolivia as part of a broader $30 million defense support agreement with that country,[97] and in August 2016, it provided 10,000 new rifles and three riverine patrol boats to the Ecuadoran army.[98]

Chinese defense companies such as Norinco, AVIC, and PolyTechnologies are increasingly present at military expositions in the region such as the Fidae air show in Chile, the annual LAAD exposition in Brazil, and SitDef in Peru.

The increasing competitiveness of Chinese military goods in the region has principally challenged sales by Russian companies, with the previously noted Chinese sale of Type 90B self-propelled artillery in Peru and the VN-1 and VN-16 armored personnel carriers in Venezuela, occurring at the expense of competing Russian systems.

Despite such progress, Chinese military sales and donations to the region continue to be hindered by issues of quality and aftermarket support. Major issues include cancellation of the contract to supply radars to Ecuador in 2010 because of the inadequacy of the systems supplied to the conditions in which they were deployed,[99] the crash of three of the K-8 fighters sold by the PRC to Venezuela,[100] concerns over the quality of the FC-1 fighter by the Argentine Air Force that contributed to the rejection of the deal,[101] and problems with the first group of Type 90B artillery systems provided to Peru.[102]

Beyond arms sales, extensive military education and professional exchanges exist between the PLA and LAC countries' armies. In China's first public defense strategy white paper, released in May 2015, the PRC recognized the conduct of international security cooperation as a "strategic task" of the nation's armed forces.[103] Correspondingly, of those countries that recognize Beijing, virtually all their militaries send officers to professional military education courses in the Changping district of Beijing, Nanjing, Shijiazhuang, and other sites. These training courses, which include lessons on the operation and maintenance of Chinese military equipment, can range in duration from weeks to a year or more.[104] The PLA also provides technical training for Latin American and Caribbean militaries in the operation and maintenance of the equipment that it sells to the region, as well as in other select topics such as information warfare and space activities, principally in the PRC.[105]

The Chinese People's Liberation Army (PLA) has also been increasingly active in Latin America and the Caribbean itself. In addition to regular visits to the region for professional military exchanges, members of the PLA have received training at Colombia's Tolemaida military base, not far from U.S. forces, and at Brazil's renowned jungle warfare school in Manaus,[106] among other facilities.[107] Over the past decade, the PRC has progressed from participation in *multilateral* humanitarian operations in the region—deploying military police to the MINUSTAH peacekeeping force in Haiti from 2004 through October 2012[108]—to increasingly sophisticated *bilateral* engagements. These include an earthquake response exercise, held with Peru in November 2010[109] and the deployment of the PRC hospital ship *Peace Ark* to the Caribbean in December 2011[110] and its return December 2015, visiting Peru, Mexico, Grenada, and Barbados before the end of 2015.[111] The PLA is also beginning to conduct non-humanitarian activities in the region. In October 2013, for instance, a Chinese naval flotilla with two guided missile frigates engaged in combat exercises in the region, including interactions with the Chilean armed forces[112] and, subsequently, with the navies of Argentina and Brazil.[113] In 2015, the PLA Navy's 20th Task Force made a high-visibility port call in Havana just as the U.S. was conducting sensitive diplomatic negotiations with the country. In space services China's state-owned Great Wall Industries has helped to develop and has launched satellites for governments in Brazil, Venezuela, Bolivia, and Ecuador.[114]

Despite such advances, China has not, as it has done in Djibouti, shown interest in establishing formal military bases in the region. Although it could eventually seek bases in Latin America to defend its interests growing overseas commercial and strategic interests, the U.S. presence in the region may precipitate a more cautious approach.[115]

Regional Implications and Perspectives

China's growing presence and the nature of its engagement with Latin America and the Caribbean has had important economic and political implications for the region. It has fostered divisions among member states about how to engage China, made it more dependent on primary product exports, transformed its infrastructure, and fueled trans-pacific organized crime. Each of these topics is discussed below in turn.

How to Engage China?

An important division has emerged within Latin America and the Caribbean, paralleling the 1960s debate over import substitution industrialization as strategy to engage with the global economy.[116] The contemporary version of this debate focuses on how best to engage with China and other Asian countries in ways that advance the prosperity and development of LAC.[117] One group, whose collective position is represented by the Pacific Alliance (Mexico, Colombia, Peru, and Chile, and candidate members Costa Rica and Panama) and new governments elected in Argentina in 2015 and coming to power in Brazil in 2016, advocates a strategy of free markets and free trade, focusing on achieving transparency and efficiency within a framework of strong institutions. A second group, embodied by the socialist populism of the ALBA regimes, advocates reliance on the state and government-to-government deals with the PRC to advance development. In this framework, the prior government of Brazil represents a third path, insofar as that it used the state and national industries such as Petrobras to negotiate with China, yet also engaged China through market competition with a strong bureaucracy and formally open public procurements.

Much of these differences toward how to engage with China have their roots in the debates on economic development within Latin America itself, with the populist governments of ALBA representing an approach focused on state ownership of key industries and state-led development. This is in contrast to the Pacific Alliance countries, which focus more on the private sector for growth in general. In the prior generation of developmental debates in Latin America, in a less interdependent global economy, however, the orientation of the statist populists against the United States, the region's principal trade and investment partner, led them to advocate endogenous growth. In the current era, the attempt by populists to move away from dependency on the United States has led them to embrace the PRC as an alternative, while using their political control to suppress objections from their own left-of-center coalition regarding the perceived exploitative terms of those interactions.

Advocates of each of the three approaches to engaging China have confronted serious domestic crises, with the populist governments of both Venezuela and Argentina suffering major setbacks in 2015 national elections and Ecuador's president, Rafael Correa, being succeeded by the more pragmatic Lenin Moreno, who came from Correa's Alianza Pais movement. Meanwhile, the centrist socialist Dilma Rousseff was removed from office by impeachment in August 2016 and replaced by the more market-oriented president Michael Temer, although Temer's ability to advance significant new policies has been paralyzed by the nation's unfolding corruption scandal, and his own political future cast in doubt by legal challenges, including the possible invalidation of the election which brought him to power.[118] The future of the Pacific Alliance also remains uncertain, with each member facing its own set of difficult internal political issues.[119] In Colombia, the government has been distracted, while assuming the presidency of the Alliance in June 2016, by challenges flowing from the 2016 peace accord that it signed with the Fuerzas Armadas Revolucionarios de Colombia (FARC).

Increasing Dependence on Primary Product Exports

As in Africa, Chinese exports to LAC in value-added consumer and capital goods has provided stiff competition for the region's manufacturers. Meanwhile, Chinese investment in and imports of raw materials have tilted the economies in favor of low-value-added economic activities.[120] Amid sustained high prices, LAC countries exports came to be dominated by primary product exports. During the 2015–2016 global downturn in commodity prices, however, LAC countries' overcapacity in these sectors compounded already grave problems of poverty, inequality, insecurity, and weak institutions.

Infrastructure Transformation

Increased trade between Latin America and Asia, mostly China, has encouraged the modernization and expansion of the region's Pacific Coast port infrastructure, as well as connections between those ports, the interior of the continent, and its Atlantic coast. Virtually every major and mid-size port on the Pacific Coast of Central and South America is being expanded, including La Union at the intersection of El Salvador, Honduras, and Nicaragua,[121] Buenaventura in Colombia,[122] Manta in Ecuador,[123] and smaller ports such as Paita in Peru.[124]

The Hong Kong-based firm Hutchison Whampoa has won port concessions in Panama (as previously mentioned), the Bahamas, Mexico, Argentina, and Ecuador, which it has administered in the style of other multinational logistics companies. Hutchison's principal advance in the region occurred in the late 1990s and early 2000s, and the company has not established a presence at a major new port since withdrawing from the port of Manta in 2009 amidst a dispute with the Ecuadoran government.[125] Expanding trans-pacific trade is also a key driver of a new third set of locks for the Panama Canal to accommodate the new generation of large merchant ships, as well as the possible construction of an ambitious $50 billion canal across Nicaragua. In the Caribbean, the widening of the Panama Canal is driving new port projects to receive the larger ships, including the expansion of Freeport, the new port complex in Mariel, Cuba,[126] and the possible construction of a new port at Goat Island, Jamaica.[127]

Major new road infrastructure projects driven by trade with Asia, China in particular, include the Manta–Manaus corridor linking Ecuador's Pacific coast to the interior of Brazil, three "bi-oceanic" corridors similarly connecting Peru's coast,[128] and an "inter-oceanic" corridor connecting the north of Chile to the interior of the continent.[129] While only a portion of such projects involves Chinese companies and capital, such as a proposed trans-continental railroad link from Bayovar, Peru, to Acu, Brazil,[130] trade with China is a key driver. In addition to impacting logistics, roads and rails also alter patterns of human interaction. Peru's southern bi-oceanic corridor, for example, has opened up the once isolated interior region of Madre de Dios, bringing greater commerce, but also making the region more accessible for those engaged in illegal logging, mining, and other criminal activities.[131]

Beyond transportation, Chinese companies and loans are also transforming the electrical infrastructure of the region. As noted previously, the Chinese power company State Grid has invested over $4.3 billion in electricity transmission infrastructure and other assets in Brazil since entering the country in 2010, including the $10.4 billion acquisition of CPFL, and plans to invest billions more. In 2015, the firm won a major contract for the construction of a 2,500-kilometer transmission line linking Brazil's enormous new Belo Monte hydroelectric facility (currently under construction) to the national power grid,[132] although the project has been delayed by environmental objections and the unfolding bribery scandal in the country.[133] China is also helping to construct a multitude of wind, solar, hydroelectric, and nuclear energy projects in the region. Major examples include $900 million in planned investments by China Sky Solar in Chile's Atacama Desert,[134] eight hydroelectric facilities in Ecuador,[135] and construction of new nuclear reactors in Argentina's Atucha complex.[136] Such projects are made possible by a combination of inexpensively priced Chinese components and long-term finance from Chinese banks, lowering the price of such electricity generation to levels at which it is competitive with traditional sources.

Illicit Activity

Expanding trade and commercial infrastructures between China and Latin America and the Caribbean has fueled trans-pacific organized crime. Activities of concern include Chinese gangs' extortion of local ethnically Chinese communities,[137] smuggling of Chinese nationals through the region toward the U.S. and Canada, trafficking in contraband goods,[138] the supply of precursor chemicals from Chinese manufacturers for illegal drug production in Latin America,[139] the illicit sale of Chinese arms to criminal and terrorist groups in the region,[140] and the purchase by Chinese companies of illegally obtained minerals and scrap metal from Latin America.[141] Trans-pacific money laundering is another growing problem, due in part to the increased number of activities by Chinese companies doing business in Latin America, and expanding infrastructures for trans-pacific financial movements.[142] Such illicit activities represent a growing challenge for Latin American and Caribbean security forces, which generally lack contacts in China and personnel proficient in Mandarin Chinese (let alone Chinese dialects Cantonese and Hakka) to effectively investigate cases involving actors on both sides of the Pacific.[143] Collaboration against organized crime, such as the PRC's sending of an undercover police officer to Argentina to help dismantle a Chinese organized crime ring operating in that country, may be an indication of things to come.[144]

Implications for the United States

As China's relations with LAC continue to mature and evolve, they impact the U.S. in primarily negative ways. For both American and LAC elites, accustomed to living in a region economically, politically, and culturally dominated by the U.S., China's rapidly expanding presence has been disorienting. China's growing presence undermines the U.S. policy agenda in the region, alters the dynamic of U.S. security relationships, and creates opportunities for the PRC to act against the U.S. through the hemisphere during a major global conflict.

Promoting Illiberal Capitalism

China's strong economic growth over the last four decades, despite its authoritarian political system, sends a message to LAC that the approach advocated by the U.S. is not the only path to prosperity. China's choice to build its multilateral engagement with Latin America and the Caribbean around CELAC, which explicitly exclude the United States—rather than the OAS of which the U.S. is a member—reinforces efforts by those such as Venezuela that would like to advance a regional multilateralism that excludes the United States. Moreover, China's expanding engagement with LAC complicates efforts by the U.S. government to advance its policy agenda in the region in areas such as democracy, human rights, trade, and governance.

China's markets and investments have empowered states pursuing policies contrary to U.S. proscriptions regarding democracy, human rights, and transparency to continue their illiberal course. Since 2005, China has provided over $62 billion in loans to Venezuela;[145] over $17 billion to Ecuador,[146] including $7.5 billion in new credits offered in January 2015;[147] loaned Bolivia at least $7 billion;[148] and extended a $11 billion line of credit to Argentina in the run-up to that nation's October 2015 presidential elections.[149] Yet, while such Chinese engagement has helped to empower such regimes, it has not necessarily been sufficient to sustain them in power, as seen in the loss of elections by in-power anti-U.S. parties in the November 2015 Argentine presidential run-off, and the December 2015 election for the Venezuelan national assembly.

China's appeal as an alternative to the U.S. may also be tempered by some of the difficulties of working with Chinese companies. Examples include concerns over the quality of Chinese manufactured products and infrastructure projects, firms' preference for using Chinese laborers and subcontractors, environmental concerns, and tensions with the local community, as seen with the Las Bambas,[150] Rio Blanco,[151] and Marcona[152] mines in Peru. Alleged malfeasance by Chinese companies, such as the timber company Bai Shan Lin[153] and the telecommunications company Datang[154] in Guyana, have also raised concerns.

Security Concerns

While militaries of the region have maintained relationships with, and purchased arms from, Europe and other Asian countries, China's military engagement is differentiated by its scale and China's implicit position as global rival of the United States. Even absent hostilities between the U.S. and the PRC, China's military engagement with Latin America and the Caribbean complicates the relationship that the U.S. briefly enjoyed after the Cold War as the principal major-power security partner for most countries of the region. When U.S. forces train Latin American partners also working with the PLA, they now must consider the risk that sensitive information about U.S. tactics, techniques, and procedures, as well as U.S. systems and institutions, will flow to the PLA.

If the U.S. suspends or reduces military support due to budgetary constraints or human rights concerns,[155] those partners have the option to seek similar support from the Chinese. Moreover, as Chinese defense companies offer increasingly sophisticated and reliable military goods for sale in the region, the U.S. Foreign Military Sales (FMS) and Foreign Military Financing (FMF) systems are challenged to become more agile to meet the equipment needs of its partners, who increasingly have viable Chinese alternatives.

China's activities in Latin America and the Caribbean, both military and non-military, also expand its options for acting against the U.S. in the context of a major military conflict involving both nations.[156] While such a conflict is neither desirable nor imminent, if the struggle put the continuity of the Chinese communist regime at risk, the PRC would likely consider the use of all of China's global assets (both commercial and military) to aid the war effort. China's disposition to employ both commercial and military assets in a time of national need is illustrated by its use of commercial ships and airlines to evacuate its personnel from Somalia in 1991,[157] and again in 2013, when extracting Chinese nationals from Libya.[158]

During a conflict China could leverage its influence as purchaser of commodities and a source of credit to persuade Latin American and Caribbean nations not to join an international coalition opposing the PRC, or to permit U.S. use of the region's bases, airfields, ports, airspace, or territorial waters to support the war effort. Chinese companies operating in LAC could also help introduce and sustain covert forces in the region to conduct intelligence, sabotage, and other operations. If a LAC nation agreed to receive and resupply Chinese military ships, aircraft, or other assets on its territory, the Chinese companies' experience in the hemisphere (especially with maritime logistics and port operations), coupled with PLA officers' knowledge and personal relationships facilitated by the aforementioned joint military training sessions, could allow the Chinese to establish an operational military capability in the region more rapidly than commonly presumed.

Conclusion

This work has shown that China's engagement with Latin America and the Caribbean is profoundly affecting the political and economic dynamics and structure of the region, as well as its relationship with the U.S. Such impacts have profound implications for the U.S. strategic position in the region, and U.S. national security.

The key findings from this chapter include the following:

1.   While China's objectives in Latin America are principally economic in nature, they are nonetheless strategic and tied to China's position in the global economy, its prosperity, and possibly its survival as a regime.
2.   China's official policy of neutrality in the internal affairs of the region's governments does not mean that it is indifferent to its companies, nationals, or ethnic Chinese residents of the region. As China's national power and associated confidence has grown, it has shown itself increasingly willing to use its influence to protect and advance its interests, although seldom doing so in the way that the U.S. has historically done.
3.   China's companies are becoming increasingly adept at functioning in the region, working with local partners, and engaging with local governments, labor forces, and communities, although there is great variation in the performance of those firms in doing so.
4.   Chinese military engagement with the region is non-trivial and growing, consistent with openly stated Chinese government policy and strategy.
5.   Chinese engagement is profoundly transforming the region, deepening its dependency on primary product exports, expanding and modernizing its port, rail, and road infrastructure, and increasing trans-pacific criminal activities along with growing legitimate commerce.
6.   China's position in Latin America and the Caribbean impacts not only the U.S. pursuit of policy objectives there, but creates new vulnerabilities in the region that must be considered if the U.S. ever becomes engaged in major hostilities with the PRC.

Barring an unforeseen domestic crisis in China, the country will continue to expand and consolidate its position throughout the developing world, particularly in LAC. The decelerating growth of the Chinese economy,[159] coupled with increasing knowledge regarding the difficulties of doing business with Chinese firms, will slow, but not stop, their expansion in Latin America. Falling commodity prices will continue to diminish the perceived benefits in Latin America of developmental strategies focused on exporting primary goods to China. At the same time, falling profitability of domestic bank loans will accelerate the impetus of Chinese companies and banks to seek more profitable investments in Latin America. Although some may seek opportunities to invest in lower-value-added manufacturing, Chinese makers of moderately priced, higher-quality capital and consumer products will increasingly pressure their Latin American and Caribbean competitors. Decelerating Chinese growth and the likelihood of a weaker yuan are thus likely to make Chinese products more competitive in both the region and third country markets like the U.S. and Europe.

In the short-term, however, changes in China's investment posture in the region have been muted by other factors. These include a deep recession, compounded by a political crisis, in Brazil, site of the greatest number of Chinese investments, particularly in manufacturing, petroleum, mining, electricity infrastructure, and telecommunications, as well as the unfolding collapse of Venezuela, where Chinese companies have multiple oil sector investments pending. On the other hand, Chinese negotiations with the Russian company RusAl and the Canadian company Noranda to buy bauxite facilities in Jamaica[160] suggest that the Chinese are cautiously using depressed international commodities prices to acquire commodity sector assets at depressed prices. With respect to loan-backed Chinese construction projects, 2016 was another record year for Chinese loans to the region.[161] Such data, in combination with the construction of two new multibillion-dollar multilateral funds,[162] and the extension of a $7.5 billion line of credit to the government of Bolivia,[163] suggest that, with some adjustments in the partners with whom they are doing the most work, Chinese companies are moving forward even more aggressively than previously.

Such progress notwithstanding, the increasingly challenging nature of China's engagement with the region will be compounded by continuing internal difficulties in its biggest partners in the region, including Brazil and Venezuela. At the same time, the region's expanding engagement with other Asian actors, including India, Japan, and Korea, will expand the competition for the PRC as its government and companies engage with the region.

The new administration of Donald Trump in the U.S. will also present both opportunities and challenges for the PRC in its relationship with the region. As seen during President Xi's November 2016 trip to the region and participation in the APEC leaders' summit in Lima, Peru, the U.S. withdrawal from the Trans-Pacific Partnership (TPP) gives the PRC an opportunity to advance its own multilateral free trade model for the region, the Free Trade Area of the Asia Pacific, from which the U.S. is notably excluded, and which advantages China by containing far fewer restrictions against non-tariff barriers and protections of intellectual property than the TPP. Similarly, the relatively hostile posture that the Trump administration has adopted toward Mexico creates new opportunities for China to expand its trade and investment with that country as part of Mexico's diversification away from the U.S.

For the U.S., the shift in the region toward a more balanced and nuanced understanding of the benefits and pitfalls of engaging with the PRC creates an opportunity for working more effectively as a partner, lending its experience and helping to strengthen the region's institutions to more effectively realize the opportunities arising from engaging with the PRC and other partners across the Pacific in the framework of free trade, transparency, and the rule of law.

The possible collapse of the diplomatic truce between the PRC and Taiwan, as noted previously, may also create new imperatives for the PRC to reach out to states of Central America and the Caribbean with loan-based construction projects and other incentives to change their diplomatic relations. Such changes could even lead the PRC to abandon its caution and openly embrace and fund the Nicaragua Canal.

For the PRC, engagement with Latin America will continue to offer an important market, destination for loans and investment capital, technology partner, and source of agricultural goods and primary products. Yet Latin America also offers the PRC a space in which it can forge a cooperative relationship with the United States and work with the U.S. on shared challenges to the benefit of the region, including cooperation on the rules for global supply chains involving China, intermediate producers in the region and the U.S., as well as cooperation on transpacific organized crime, and possibly even public health issues of shared concern, such as the Zika virus.

For Latin America and the Caribbean, continuing engagement with the PRC, particularly if conducted by strong institutions through a transparent framework, dominated by the rule of law, and in coordination with the U.S. and other international actors, may advance the developmental goals of the region. But to realize such opportunities, the states of Latin America will need a clear strategic concept for how to approach the relationship to achieve those benefits, as well the political courage to maintain the continuity of policy to both persist in that course and adapt as circumstances evolve.

Notes

1 The author is a professor of Latin American Studies at the U.S. Army War College Strategic Studies Institute. The views expressed in this article are strictly his own.
2 Caspar W. Weinberger, "Panama, The Canal and China," *Forbes*, October 4, 1999.
3 Reyes Theis, "Alianza China con Venezuela es comercial y no ideológica," *El Universal*, April 7, 2010.
4 Lorena Canto, "El Izquerdista Evo Morales es el Favorito," *El Nuevo Herald*, October 10, 2014.
5 "Rafael Correa: CELAC–China Relationship Could Improve An 'Unfair World Order'," *Ecuador Times*, January 10, 2015.
6 Roberta S. Jacobson, "China's Latin America Presence Not a Threat: U.S. Official," *Xinhua*, November 13, 2013.
7 See, for example, Teddy Ng, "US Embassy in Nicaragua Voices Fears Over Chinese-Led US$50b Canal Project," *South China Morning Post*, January 7, 2015.
8 International Monetary Fund (hereinafter referred to as IMF), Direction of Trade Statistics, accessed April 23, 2017.
9 See, for example, R. Evan Ellis, *China in Latin America: The Whats and Wherefores* (Boulder, CO: Lynne Rienner, 2009).
10 Amos Irwin and Kevin Gallagher, "Chinese Investment in Peru: A Comparative Analysis," The Working Group on Development and Environment in the Americas at Tufts University, December 2012.
11 R. Evan Ellis, *China on the Ground in Latin America: Challenges for the Chinese and Impacts on the Region* (New York: Palgrave Macmillan, 2014), 90.
12 Wan Zhihong, "Venezuela, China Ink $16b Oil Deal," *China Daily*, September 18, 2009.
13 Karl Royce, "CNPC Units Negotiate Sapet Deal," *Business News Americas*, April 26, 2001.
14 "China Oil Firm Buys EnCana Assets in Ecuador," *China Daily*, September 15, 2005.
15 Taotao Chen and Miguel Pérez Ludeña, "Chinese Foreign Direct Investment in Latin America and the Caribbean," *UN ECLAC*, November 2013.
16 For a detailed analysis, see Ellis, *China on the Ground in Latin America*.
17 Neil Gough, "What China's Economic Growth Figures Mean," *New York Times*, July 14, 2016.

18 "World Economic Outlook: Adjusting to Lower Commodity Prices," IMF, October 2015, 2.
19 Douglas Bulloch, "Why China's 6.5% GDP Growth Target Is A Burden On Their Economy," *Forbes*, March 29, 2017.
20 International Monetary Fund (IMF), Direction of Trade Statistics, accessed April 23, 2017.
21 "Incomoda a China la suspensión del tren México-Querétaro," *Proceso*, February 2, 2015.
22 Chinese loans for or investment in Ecuador's Refinery of the Pacific has been under discussion since prior to 2008, but has not moved forward. Nonetheless, following a December 2015 trip to the PRC, Ecuador's Vice-President Jorge Glas affirmed continuing Chinese interest in funding part of the project. See "Ecuador says ties with China 'at best ever' stage," *Sina*, December 20, 2015.
23 "Nicaragua's $50bn Canal Plan Delayed," *Financial Times*, November 27, 2015.
24 Erin Carlyle, "Baha Mar Resorts To Chapter 11 Bankruptcy, Blames China Construction for Delays," *Forbes*, June 29, 2015.
25 Cecilia Sanchez, "Mexico Halts Chinese Mega-Mall Project After Damage to Environment," *Los Angeles Times*, January 28, 2015. For a detailed discussion of such protests, see Ellis, *China on the Ground in Latin America*, Chapters 7 and 8.
26 R. Evan Ellis, "La Lucha por Venir para la Columna Vertibral de America Latina," *Instituto de Investigaciones Estratégicas de la Armada de México*, March 17, 2017.
27 R. Evan Ellis, "China's Activities in the Americas," Testimony to the Joint Hearing of the Subcommittee on the Western Hemisphere and the Subcommittee on Asia and the Pacific, U.S. House of Representatives Foreign Affairs Committee, September 10, 2015.
28 "Full Text: China's Policy Paper on Latin America and the Caribbean," *China Daily*, November 6, 2008. "Full text of China's Policy Paper on Latin America and the Caribbean," *Xinhua*, November 24, 2016.
29 For a discussion of the consistency of Chinese activities in Latin America with plans announced in such documents, see R. Evan Ellis, "The Strategic Context of China's Advance in Latin America: An Update," *The Asia Centre*, April 2017.
30 "Xi Jinping Attends China-Latin America and the Caribbean Summit and Delivers Keynote Speech, Comprehensively Expounding China's Policies and Propositions Toward Latin America, Announcing Establishment of China-Latin America Comprehensive Cooperative Partnership of Equality, Mutual Benefit and Common Development, and Establishment of China-CELAC Forum," Ministry of Foreign Affairs of the People's Republic of China (hereinafter referred to as FMPRC website), July 18, 2014.
31 For more detail on this process, see Fan Zhang, *China's Urbanization and the World Economy* (Northampton, MA: Edward Elgar Publishing, 2014).
32 Margaret Myers, "China Eyes Latin America to Fill Its Kitchen Cupboard," *Caixin*, August 1, 2014.
33 See, for example, Jane Perlez, "Xi Jinping of China Calls for Cooperation and Partnerships in U.N. Speech," *New York Times*, September 27, 2015.
34 "China's Policy Paper on Latin America and the Caribbean," 2016.
35 Richard C. Bush, "Taiwan Election: Voters Turn Their Backs on Closer Ties With China," *CNN*, January 16, 2016.
36 "China Focus: China, Sao Tome and Principe Resume Diplomatic Ties," FMPRC website, December 29, 2016.
37 "Central America–China Ties to Deepen," *Latin America Monitor*, May 2011.
38 Chris Davis, "Chinese Dam Business in South America on the Rise," *China Daily*, January 20, 2014.
39 "China to Further Cooperation With Organization of American States," *China Daily*, March 1, 2016.
40 "China Opposes Taiwan Observer Status in OAS," *China Daily*, June 7, 2004.
41 Joshua Goodman, "China's Xi Offers Caribbean Nations $3 Billion in Loans," *Bloomberg*, June 3, 2013.

42 "China Offers 35bn Fund to Finance Infrastructure Projects in Latin America," *Merco Press*, July 18, 2014.

43 Unmesh Rajendran, "BRICS Bank: The New Kid on the Block," *The Diplomat*, July 28, 2014.

44 "China Launches Fund for LatAm Industrial Cooperation," *Xinhua*, September 1, 2015.

45 Zhang Enqi, "Introduction of the China-LAC Cooperation Fund," *China–CELAC Forum*, June 2, 2015.

46 Yang Yi, "First China–CELAC Forum Ministerial Meeting Concludes in Beijing," *Xinhua*, January 9, 2015.

47 "China's Initiation of the Five Principles of Peaceful Co-Existence," FMPRC website, accessed October 28, 2015.

48 For a discussion of the Chinese use of economic leverage in the form of soy oil imports to punish Argentina for protectionist measures again Chinese products, see R. Evan Ellis, "Chinese 'Face' and Soft Power in Argentina," *The Manzella Report*, January 1, 2014.

49 In August 2013, for example, during a visit to the PRC by Jamaican Prime Minister Portia Simpson Miller, Chinese Premier Li Keqiang reportedly raised the issue of robberies and other crimes against ethnic Chinese shopkeepers in Jamaica. See "Police implement new security measures for Chinese nationals," *The Gleaner*, August 28, 2013.

50 See, for example, Ellis, "Chinese 'Face'."

51 An Lu, "China, Brazil Launch 20-bln-USD Fund to Support Production Capacity Cooperation," *Xinhua*, June 27, 2015.

52 "Venezuela y China evalúan cooperación hasta el 2025," *El Universal*, June 30, 2015.

53 Lety Du, "China autoriza importación de carne de cerdo de México," *Xinhua*, April 7, 2012.

54 Nonetheless, projects agreed upon between China and Argentina's previous socialist government, including the construction of hydroelectric facilities on Argentina's Santa Cruz river, and the construction of two nuclear reactors, have continued under President Macri.

55 Muhammad Cohen, "Bahamas' Beleaguered Baha Mar Casino Resort To Open With Chinese Characteristics," *Forbes*, March 9, 2017.

56 Mitra Taj and Marco Aquino, "Peru's President Throws Cold Water on Chinese Railway Proposal," *Reuters*, September 13, 2016.

57 Emma Graham-Harrison, "UPDATE 2-China's Sinopec Signs Brazil Deal With Petrobras," *Reuters*, April 15, 2010.

58 "Ollanta Humala se reúne con miembros del Partido Comunista de China," *El Comercio*, April 13, 2010.

59 "China's Policy Paper on Latin America and the Caribbean."

60 "First Meeting of China–CELAC Political Parties' Forum closes in Beijing," International Department of Central Committee of CPC, December 9, 2015.

61 See, for example, R. Evan Ellis, "Chinese Commercial Engagement with Guyana: The Challenges of Physical Presence and Political Change," *China Brief* 13, no. 19 (September 2013): 13–16.

62 Kiana Wilburg, "Govt. Must Be Open to Talks on Amaila Falls Project or else . . . Jagdeo Warns," *Kaieteur News*, November 9, 2015.

63 Abena Rockcliffe, "CJIA Contractor Nails Jagdeo's Lies," *Kaieteur News*, December 4, 2015.

64 "GPL Cuts Power to BaiShanLin Headquarters," *Kaieteur News*, November 29, 2015.

65 "China's Policy Paper on Latin America and the Caribbean."

66 "Worldwide Confucius Institutes," Confucius Institutes Online, http://english.hanban.org/, accessed April 3, 2017.

67 Joao Lima, "Sinopec to Invest $7.1 Billion in Repsol Brazil Unit," *Bloomberg*, October 1, 2010.

68 Fabiana Frayssinet, "Brazil and China, Oiling the Wheels of Business," *Asia Times*, May 25, 2012.

69 Yvonne Lee and Nisha Gopalan, "CNOOC Acquires Argentina Oil Assets," *Wall Street Journal*, March 14, 2010.
70 Wan Xu and Yvonne Lee, "Sinopec Buys Occidental Unit for $2.45 Billion," *Wall Street Journal*, December 12, 2010.
71 Ilan Brat, "Repsol to Sell Ecuador Oil Affiliate to Sinopec," *Market Watch*, August 1, 2012.
72 Arron Daugherty, "China's CNOOC Expects 69MBoe From Colombia unit Nexen in 2014," *Business News Americas*, January 21, 2014. Indeed, the deal gave CNOOC an interest in the venture with Exxon Mobil that discovered commercially significant quantities of petroleum in the waters of Guyana's continental shelf, which became a subject of a major dispute between Guyana and Venezuela in 2015. See R. Evan Ellis, "Venezuela's '9-Dash-Line' in the Caribbean," *Latin America Goes Global*, June 28, 2015.
73 Jeff Fick, "Perenco's Brazil Unit to Sell 10% Stake in Offshore Blocks to Sinochem," *Wall Street Journal*, January 8, 2012.
74 "Sinopec and Galp Close Petrogal Brazil Transaction," *Sinopec*, April 1, 2012.
75 "CNOOC and partners to develop Brazil's Libra field," *Offshore Technology*, October 22, 2013.
76 Andrew Hobbs and Penny Peng, "Chinese Companies Pay $1.95 Billion for CBMM Stake, Xinhua Says," *Bloomberg*, September 1, 2011.
77 "Chinese Companies Make Up One-Third of Peru's Mining Investment Portfolio," *Andina*, December 27, 2015.
78 "State Grid Acquires 7 Brazilian Power Companies," *Global Times*, December 21, 2010.
79 Charlie Zhu and Michele Chen, "UPDATE 2-China's State Grid to Buy Brazil Assets From Spain's ACS," *Reuters*, May 29, 2012.
80 "China State Grid Completes Purchase of Stake in Brazil's CPFL Energia," *Macauhub*, January 25, 2017.
81 "Duke Energy Completes Sale of International Business in Brazil," Duke Energy Company, January 29, 2017.
82 R. Evan Ellis, "Las iniciativas por parte de las firmas agrícolas chinas para establecer su presencia en América Latina y el Caribe," in *Política Exterior China: relaciones regionales y cooperación*, eds. Raquel Isamara León de la Rosa and Juan Carlos Gachúz Maya (Puebla, México: Benemérita Universidad Autónoma de Puebla, 2015), 307–336.
83 Jason Rogers, "Cofco of China Taking Control of Nidera to Boost Food Supply," *Bloomberg*, February 28, 2014.
84 Naveen Thukral and Michael Flaherty, "China's COFCO to Pay $1.5 Billion for Stake in Noble's Agribusiness," *Reuters*, April 2, 2014.
85 "China aumentará la importación de carne argentina," *Noticias Agropecuarios*.
86 Para un excelente estudio de caso, unos de los pocos que existe sobre empresas chinos, vea China-Brasil Business Council, "Chinese Investments in Brazil: A New Phase in the China-Brazil Relationship," May 2011.
87 "Aprueban el ingreso chino al Standard," *Clarín*, November 11, 2012.
88 Cristiane Lucchesi, Dakin Campbell and Giulia Camillo, "Construction Bank Agrees to Buy Majority of Brazil Bank," *Bloomberg*, November 1, 2013.
89 For a detailed discussion of Chinese military activities in the region, see Ellis, "Should U.S. be worried . . ." See also R. Evan Ellis, "China–Latin America Military Engagement: Good Will, Good Business, and Strategic Position," U.S. Army War College Strategic Studies Institute, August 2011.
90 Wendell Minnick, "Argentina, China Could Jointly Develop Fighters," *Defense News*, February 22, 2015.
91 Perú selecciona el sistema táctico de lanzacohetes múltiples Norinco tipo 90B," *Infodefensa*, January 10, 2014; see also "El Ejército de Perú adquiere sistemas de artillería chinos por 38 millones de dólares," *Defensa*, December 27, 2013.
92 For a relatively concise, updated summary of China's most recent military sales to the region, see R. Evan Ellis, "Should U.S. be Worried About Chinese Arms Sales in the Region?" *Latin America Goes Global*, May 11, 2015.

93 "Venezuela adquiere aviones chinos de entrenamiento de combate L15," *Infodefensa*, April 4, 2014; see also "Venezuela habría cerrado la compra del avión de entrenamiento chino L15 'Falcón' y piensa también en Sukhoi," *Defensa*, April 9, 2014.

94 Richard D. Fisher and James Hardy, "Venezuela Signs Up for VN1, Hints at Chinese Amphibious Vehicles Buy," *IHS Jane's 360*, November 23, 2014.

95 Angélica Melgarejo, "Morales entrega 6 helicópteros chinos multipropósito," *La Razón*, September 13, 2014.

96 Cesar Cruz Tantalean, "Peru Receives Chinese Tactical MRLs" *IHS Jane's 360*, July 21, 2015.

97 "Bolivia y China firmarán acuerdo de cooperación militar por $us 30 millones," *Los Tiempos*, August 3, 2016.

98 "China donó a Ecuador 10 mil versiones 'modernas' de fusiles AK47," *El Universo*, August 16, 2016.

99 Victor Vega, "Ecuador Rejects Chinese Radars," *Ecuador Times*, May 5, 2013.

100 "Venezuela Receives More Chinese K-8 Trainers," *DFNS.net*. March 16, 2016.

101 R. Evan Ellis, "Argentina at the Crossroads—Again," *Military Review*, March-April 2017.

102 Angel Paez, "Compraron con fallas lanzador de cohetes chino que costó US$ 38.5 millones," *La Republica*, http://larepublica.pe/politica/1001678-compraron-con-fallas-lanzador-de-cohetes-chino-que-costo-us-385-millones, accessed April 5, 2017.

103 "China's Military Strategy," Ministry of National Defense of the People's Republic of China, May 26, 2015.

104 R. Evan Ellis, "The Strategic Dimension of China's Engagement with Latin America," William J. Perry Center for Hemispheric Defense Studies, October 2013.

105 See, for example, Ellis, "China–Latin America Military Engagement."

106 Eben Blake, "Chinese Military Seeks Jungle Warfare Training From Brazil," *Global Business Times*, August 10, 2015.

107 Ellis, "China's Activities in the Americas."

108 Colum Lynch, "In Surprise Move, China Withdraws Riot Police From Haiti," *Foreign Policy*, March 25, 2010.

109 "Saludan fortalecimiento de cooperación militar entre Fuerzas Armadas de Perú y China," *Andina*, November 23, 2010.

110 "Vicepresidente de Costa Rica destaca misión humanitaria de buque," *Xinhua*, November 25, 2011.

111 Li Qing, "China's Naval Hospital Ship Peace Ark Visits Mexico," *People's Daily*, November 15, 2015.

112 "PLAN's Taskforce Conducts Maritime Joint Exercise With Chilean Navy," Ministry of Defense of the People's Republic of China, October 14, 2013; see also Strike Nahuel, "Armadas de China y Chile Realizaron Ejercicios Navales," *Noticias FFAA Chile*, October 16, 2013.

113 "Ejercitos conjuntos entre armadas China y Brasileña frente Rio de Janeiro," *TodoParaMexico*, October 28, 2013; initially published as "PLAN Taskforce Conducts Joint Maritime Exercise with Brazilian Navy *Jiefangjun Bao* [PLA Daily], October 28, 2013, and captured by U.S. Naval War College newsletter, November 2013, but subsequently removed from *Jiefangjun Bao* website.

114 For a detailed discussion of Chinese space and satellite technology partnerships in Latin America, see Ellis, "The Strategic Dimension of China's Engagement With Latin America," 64–84.

115 Ankit Panda, "After Djibouti Base, China Eyes Additional Overseas Military 'Facilities'," *The Diplomat*, March 9, 2016.

116 James H. Street and Dilmus D. James, "Institutionalism, Structuralism, and Dependency in Latin America," *Journal of Economic Issues* 16 (1982): 673–689.

117 For a more detailed discussion, see R. Evan Ellis, "Latin America's Foreign Policy as the Region Engages in China," *Security and Defense Studies Review* 15 (2014): 41–59.

118 Anthony Boadle and Daniel Flynn, "Brazil Court Postpones Case That Could Unseat Temer," *Reuters*, April 4, 2017.

119 R. Evan Ellis, "O novo ambiente estratégico do Transpacífico: uma perspectiva dos EUA," *Política Externa* 23 (2015): 37–48.

120 Matt Ferchen, Alicia Garcia-Herrero, and Mario Nigrinis, "Evaluating Latin America's Commodity Dependence on China," *BBVA Research*, January 2013; "Alba y neoliberalismo: desvestidos por China," *Nación*, September 22, 2012.

121 "De un proyecto portuario y un corredor logístico," *La Nacion*, August 24, 2012.

122 R. Evan Ellis, "New Developments in China–Colombia Engagement," *Manzella Report*, October 27, 2014.

123 Neptali Palma, "Concesión de puerto de Manta con otra prórroga," *El Universo*, August 26, 2014.

124 "TPE instalará nueva s grúas pórtico y de muelle en Paita," *Gestión*, October 25, 2015.

125 "Ecuador buscará reemplazo a Hutchison para operar puerto de Manta," *El Universo*, March 19, 2009.

126 Marc Frank, "Cuba: Port Upgrades and Free Trade Zones," *America's Quarterly*, 2014.

127 Latonya Linton, "Government, China Harbour Agree on Terms for Goat Island Project," *Jamaica Information Service*, February 26, 2014.

128 Monte Reel, "Traveling From Ocean to Ocean Across South America," *New York Times*, February 19, 2014.

129 "Brazil/Bolivia/Chile inter-oceanic corridor ready for 2011," *Merco Press*, July 6, 2009.

130 Tim Johnson and Vinod Speeharsha, "China's Great Railroad Dream: Traversing South America," *Miami Herald*, November 2, 2015.

131 Dan Collyns and Tom Philips, "Pacific-Atlantic Route Drives Up Fears of Crime and Destruction," *The Guardian*, July 14, 2011.

132 Vanessa Dezem, "China's State Grid Expands in Brazil With Belo Monte Contract," *Bloomberg*, July 17, 2015.

133 Luciano Costa, "China's State Grid Asks Brazil to Speed Up Power Line License: Source," *Reuters*, January 3, 2017.

134 "Chinese Sky Solar to Invest US$ 900 million in Chile for Energy Projects," *Nueva Mineria y Energia*, June 28, 2012.

135 R. Evan Ellis, "Are Big Chinese Energy Investments in Latin America a Concern?" *The Manzella Report*, November 23, 2013.

136 Lyu Chang, "CNNC Inches toward $6b Nuclear Plant Deal in Argentina," *China Daily*, November 6, 2015.

137 See, for example, Gustavo Carabajal, "Mafia china en la Argentina: en los últimos seis años cometió 40 asesinatos," *La Nacion*, December 20, 2015.

138 R. Evan Ellis, "Chinese Organized Crime in Latin America," *Prism* 4 (2012): 67–77.

139 "Capo mexicano capturado coordinaba el tráfico de drogas de Colombia y China," *Noticias 24*, March 12, 2012.

140 "China dice que carguero detenido en Cartagena llevaba material militar 'ordinario'," *El País*, March 4, 2015.

141 See, for example, Natalie Southwick, "Knights Templar Control Mexico Iron Mines Supplying China," *Insight Crime*, December 4, 2013.

142 See, for example, Aaron Daughterty, "Colombians Charged in Massive China-Based Money Laundering Scheme," *Insight Crime*, September 11, 2015.

143 For a more detailed discussion of this challenge, see Ellis, "The Strategic Dimension of China's Engagement With Latin America," 117–134.

144 See Mike LaSusa, "Argentina Targets 'Chinese Mafia' With Operation 'Dragon's Head'," *Insight Crime*, June 14, 2016.

145 "China–Latin America Finance Database," *The Dialogue*, www.thedialogue.org/map_list/, accessed April 5, 2017.

146 "China–Latin America Finance Database."

147 Nathan Gill, "China Rescues Ecuador Budget From Deeper Cuts as Crude Drops," *Bloomberg*, January 13, 2015.

148 "UD pide explicaciones al Gobierno sobre deuda con China," *Erbol Digital*, October 19, 2015. China has also become an important investor in the nation's mining

sector. See "10 empresa chinas ejecutan proyectos en el sector minero," *Erbol Digital,* May 30, 2015.

149 Ken Parks, "Argentina–China Deals Reflect Asian Country's Growing Influence," *Wall Street Journal,* July 20, 2014.

150 Marco Aquino, Mitra Taj and Leslie Adler, "At least One Killed in Protests at MMG's Las Bambas Project in Peru," *Reuters,* September 28, 2015.

151 "Acusan al alcalde de Sapalache de apoyar violencia de Rio Blanco," *El Comercio,* November 23, 2011.

152 Milagros Salazar, "Social Responsibility Missing in Growing Trade Ties," *Inter Press Service,* February 3, 2010.

153 "Deciding Bai Shai Lin's Fate," *Kaieteur News,* July 24, 2016.

154 "Controversial Sale of Govt Shares in GT&T . . . Chinese Company Fails to Pay in Full," *Kaieteur News,* December 9, 2015.

155 See, for example, Joshua Partlow, "U.S. Blocks Some Anti-Drug Funds for Mexico Over Human Rights Concerns," *Washington Post,* October 18, 2015.

156 R. Evan Ellis, "China's Activities in the Americas," Testimony, Testimony to the Joint Hearing of the Subcommittee on the Western Hemisphere and the Subcommittee on Asia and the Pacific, Foreign Affairs Committee, U.S. House of Representatives, September 10, 2015.

157 Christopher D. Young and Ross Rustici, *China's Out of Area Naval Operations: Case Studies, Trajectories, Obstacles and Potential Solutions* (Washington, DC: National Defense University Press, 2010).

158 Xiong Tong, "China Continues to Bring Citizens Evacuated From Libya Back Home," *Xinhua,* March 5, 2011.

159 Mark Magnier, "China Surprises With 7% Growth in Second Quarter," *Wall Street Journal,* July 21, 2015.

160 Alphea Saunders, "Chinese Want a Part of Noranda Too?" *Jamaica Observer,* February 15, 2016.

161 "China–Latin America Finance Database."

162 See, for example, "China to Provide $2 billion for Latin America and the Caribbean Co-Financing Fund," Inter-American Development Bank, March 16, 2013.

163 "Sepa en qué ocupará Bolivia el crédito por US$7.500M otorgado por China," *America Economia,* October 20, 2015.

PART III

Conclusion

9

CHINA'S EVOLVING POWER, POSITION, AND INFLUENCE IN THE DEVELOPING WORLD

Joshua Eisenman and Eric Heginbotham

Stepping Out

When we published *China and the Developing World*, a decade ago, many themes that permeate this volume had only just begun to materialize. Whereas in 2007, China had remerged as an energetic economic and geopolitical force, by 2018, its presence has become a well-accepted fact of life throughout the developing world. Beijing's economic expansion and its diplomatic "charm offensive" have been so successful that many perceive that China may soon displace the U.S. as the leading global power. In his speech at the 2017 Davos meeting in the wake of Donald Trump's election as U.S. president, a confident President Xi Jinping emphasized Chinese leadership for the next stage of globalization:

> China's development is an opportunity for the world; China has not only benefited from economic globalization but also contributed to it. Rapid growth in China has been a sustained, powerful engine for global economic stability and expansion. We will open our arms to the people of other countries and welcome them aboard the express train of China's development. . . . China's development is both domestic and external oriented; while developing itself, China also shares more of its development outcomes with other countries and peoples.[1]

Development with Chinese characteristics has gone global. Beijing has deepened its bilateral relations with partners throughout the developing world and continues to expand its influence in international and regional forums. Chinese leaders have cultivated developing countries as "strategic partners" and have created new regional institutions to facilitate the country's engagement.

Under the "going out" strategy, which was first advanced in 1997 and formally initiated in 1999, Chinese firms have been transformed from novice newcomers to global powerhouses, and have become deeply enmeshed in international trade, banking, and mergers and acquisitions.[2] The growth in China's trade with the developing world has consistently outstripped that with the developed world, and Beijing's policy banks (most notably the China Ex–Im Bank and China Development Bank) have deployed hundreds of billions in capital in an unprecedented global infrastructure financing campaign than dwarfs that of the World Bank. Since 2013, infrastructure financing has been accelerated under President Xi Jinping's One Belt, One Road (OBOR, a.k.a. the Belt and Road) initiative, which was added to the constitution of the Communist Party of China (CPC) at its 19th National Congress in October 2017.

Elements of continuity and evolution in China's political approach to the developing world are summarized in the introduction to this volume and are evident in each chapter. Beyond adherence to the one-China policy, Beijing continues to expand ties with developing countries regardless of their ideology or political system, and, although it increasingly supports friendly regimes in various parts of the world, it generally does not intervene openly in political conflicts. Although they have never renounced the right to use force, Chinese leaders profess a determination to avoid the "power politics" that have ensnared other major powers and instead promote national interests via a proactive and multifaceted engagement rooted conceptually in the traditional Westphalian principles of the equality and sovereignty of all states. Throughout the first decade of the twenty-first century, China's risk-adverse leaders generally adhered to Deng Xiaoping's admonition to "maintain a low profile" and worked to settle or shelve border disputes.

After the 2009 global financial crisis, however, Chinese leaders came to believe that the historic trend towards multipolarity had accelerated and that developing states were becoming ever more important economic, political, and military partners. China's new self-confidence was reflected in Xi Jinping's notion of "major power diplomacy with Chinese characteristics" and his call for more active engagement to shape the international environment in China's favor.[3] China has become an increasingly active participant in international institutions, taking a leading role in United Nations peacekeeping operations and almost doubling its contributions to and vote share in the International Monetary Fund.[4] Beijing has also created and funded numerous Sino-centric regional organizations (e.g., the China–Africa Cooperation Forum and the China–Community of Latin American and Caribbean States Forum) that provide regional venues for Chinese leadership. Other organizations like the Asian Infrastructure Investment Bank (AIIB) enhance the perception that China has emerged as the champion of globalization, though it is unclear whether such institutions complement or challenge existing international institutions.[5]

China's self-confidence is also manifested in its more assertive posture with regard to disputes around its immediate periphery. Beijing has employed numerous coercive measures to advance its territorial claims and isolate and placate other claimants, often reacting to actions taken by others but doing so disproportionately and in ways that alter the status quo in its own favor. Yet while Beijing moves to affirm its territorial claims and regain what it sees as its rightful position as a major world power, it shows little interest in destroying the international order. Instead, China has sought opportunities to influence and adjust international norms and build institutions that better serve its own interests.

In the introduction, we introduced four key questions that each of this book's authors addressed in his or her regional chapter. This concluding chapter pulls together the threads of the regional chapters in an effort to examine these four questions across all six regions: First, how does China define its interests in the developing world, and have those interests evolved or changed over time? Second, what means does it use to achieve those ends? Third, how effective has China been in pursuing its objectives? And fourth, what are the implications for developing countries and U.S. interests in these regions? Below, we address these questions, comparing the patterns and trends evident in 2017 to those we found in our 2007 study and identifying patterns of similarity and difference over time and across regions. We then discuss implications of those findings for the evolving international system and for U.S. policy.

China's Objectives in the Developing World

There are various formulations of China's "core national interests" (核心利益), but all assume three overlapping objectives.[6] First, China's leaders seek to ensure the continued rule of the Communist Party; second, they seek to maintain and defend China's sovereignty and territorial integrity; and third, they want to maintain an international environment conducive to China's continued economic growth.

Despite propaganda efforts to portray Chinese policies as rooted in solidarity with the developing world, the drivers of Chinese policies are primarily domestic, and regime survival remains Beijing's foremost objective, informing all other interests. The priority on regime survival is evident in the content and character of its diplomacy, party-to-party relations, defense of sovereignty norms in international politics, and in its near single-minded emphasis on economic development.[7] As Deng Xiaoping said in 1992: "Development is the hard truth" (发展是硬道理).[8] At Davos in 2017, Xi—in a comment reminiscent of both Deng and U.S. President Abraham Lincoln's Gettysburg Address—said: "Development is of the people, by the people and for the people."[9]

The emphasis on economic growth to enhance domestic stability shapes China's engagement with the developing world. Chinese leaders view economic growth and welfare as central to regime survival, and they view trade as a critical engine of growth. For more than a decade, developing countries have supplied the minerals, metals, timber, and energy demanded by the Chinese industrial, construction, and manufacturing sectors. To secure steady access to those resources, Chinese companies have, since the early 2000s, moved to purchase upstream energy and mineral assets, primarily in developing countries. These countries have also become important outlets for Chinese consumer products, enabling Chinese firms to build brand loyalties in emerging markets.[10]

Improved living standards are integral to Xi's "China Dream," with its goal of achieving a "moderately well off" society (小康社会) by 2021. For many years, officials in Beijing viewed rapid economic growth as essential to absorbing China's growing workforce and avoiding social instability. Since the Third Plenum of the Communist Party's 18th Congress, however, leaders have emphasized balanced growth, environmental protection, and eliminating structural imbalances within the economy. That said, old habits die hard. Local and many central government officials continue to use GDP growth rates as the yardstick of success. Moreover, Xi's "Made in China 2025" is a plan to comprehensively upgrade and strengthen the country's manufacturing capability. Nevertheless, as wage structures continue to shift in China and as environmental concerns mount, some labor-intensive industries (e.g., textiles and leather goods) are shifting production to developing states.

The developing world is also a locus of Beijing's efforts to maintain or defend its "territorial integrity." After a "diplomatic truce" from 2008 to 2016, the competition for diplomatic recognition between Taipei and Beijing appears to have resumed with the election of Tsai Ing-wen in Taiwan. In its quest to contain separatist impulses in Tibet, China periodically sanctions countries and foreign organizations that give the Dalai Lama a platform or afford him anything approaching recognition.[11] Chinese activities to secure its claims to features in the South China Sea have included the use of hard power and coercive measures directly against rival claimants. China has also solicited public support from at least 66 mostly developing countries for recognition of its maritime territorial claims in the South China Sea, and employed a variety of economic and political means to purchase the loyalty of the smallest and weakest states in ASEAN (Laos and Cambodia) to divide the organization and prevent unified opposition from coalescing.[12]

More broadly, China has found common interests with developing states on a range of political-economic issues (e.g., environmental priorities and trade-offs, trade policy, technology standards, and the form and function of international institutions) and has sought to partner with the largest and most influential of them to foster a more "democratic" international order. Interests on these issues often align across regime types. Despite India's long history of vibrant democratic governance, New Delhi's votes in the UN General Assembly on various issues are more closely aligned with those of Beijing than they are with Washington's.[13] In Beijing's case, support for norms related to state sovereignty and non-intervention are motivated by a desire to insulate itself from international condemnation, sanctions, and intervention related to its human rights abuses and harsh policies toward minorities in Tibet and Xinjiang. Although the BRICS and other developing state forums are as riven with division and suspicion as they are united by common interest, China nevertheless sees them as working to democratize international politics and limit the United States' scope for unilateral action.

Characteristics of China's Engagement

As this book's chapters make clear, China's relations with developing countries display three principal characteristics: first, Beijing benefits from and sometimes exploits asymmetry in its relations with developing countries; second, China pursues a "package" approach—bringing economic, political, and other means to bear in a coordinated, albeit imperfect, manner; and third, Beijing advances its interests through a network of interlocking and self-reinforcing bilateral, regional, and global engagements. Each developing country's ability to derive benefits from its relationship with China depends primarily on its capability to develop and implement a coordinated national strategy that carefully considers the combined implications of these three characteristics over the short, medium, and long term. If a developing country ignores these realities or fails to consider their full implications, it is unlikely to achieve its own objectives vis-à-vis China, a much larger, richer, and generally better coordinated state.

Asymmetric Engagement

Asymmetry is the most pervasive and enduring aspect of nearly all of China's bilateral relationships, a fact that then-Foreign Minister Yang Jiechi reminded a security forum of the Association of South East Asian Nations (ASEAN) of in 2010 when he said: "China is a big country and other countries are small countries, and that's just a fact."[14] Indeed, China's nominal GDP ($11.4 trillion in 2016) dwarfs that of every other developing country and is more than double India ($2.3 trillion), Brazil ($1.8 trillion), and South Africa ($280 billion) combined.[15] In 2016, Chinese exports made up more than half of all exports from the developing world.[16]

Although asymmetry is ever-present in China's relationships with nearly all developing countries, Beijing can choose to either highlight and exploit it or downplay it. China's comprehensive "package" approach (discussed immediately below) magnifies the perception of asymmetry, while egalitarian diplomacy and calls for "brotherhood" and "equality" diminish it. Regional forums like FOCAC and the China–Community of Latin American and Caribbean States (CELAC) Relations Forum invariably alternate locations between China and different partner countries in these regions. Symbolically, this places China on par with entire regions, and practically it enhances Beijing's already disproportionate agenda setting power. Beijing never fails to play the impressive and gracious host, with banquets replete with constant references to solidarity, state-sovereignty, and the equality of all nation states.

Comprehensive Engagement

Chinese foreign policy involves "multi-centric, multi-layered and multi-pivotal sub-networks of regional and international cooperation that are interconnected and interwoven," explained former Vice Minister of Foreign Affairs He Yafei.[17] Chinese foreign policy also now emphasizes a broad array of collaborative enterprises including foreign aid, educational and cultural exchanges, media cooperation, military assistance and training, and political cadre education. Beijing looks to combine these elements (discussed individually in the following pages) into a comprehensive package that creates synergies among China's various interests and allows the state to target resources and apply leverage to achieve its objectives. The breadth of Beijing's "comprehensive diplomacy" is well illustrated in its November 2016 white paper on Latin America and the Caribbean, which lists five broad areas of cooperation (i.e., political, economic, social, cultural, and peace and security) subdivided into 37 specific programs (see Appendix II).

China's economic diplomacy, party-to-party relations, military diplomacy, and cultural outreach are often woven into a package that appears irresistible. China's policy banks have become the developing world's go-to lenders. Between these, and its massive state-owned commercial banks, China has 20 of the largest 100 banks in the world (ranked by total assets).[18] China's state-owned and semi-private infrastructure and telecoms firms have become the face of the country's overseas presence, building railroads, dams, airports, highways, and fiber optic networks for dozens of countries.

To be sure, not all of China's overseas engagement is state directed—or even directly state-supported. Chinese small and mid-sized entrepreneurs (which account for a rapidly growing, and often unaccounted for, share of overseas trade and investment) generally operate independently in the developing world.[19] Even large SOEs target deals based primarily on prospective profitability, and they have proven willing to resist political pressure to invest in deals they deem particularly unpromising.[20] Nevertheless, Beijing regularly influences investment decisions in ways that further its political objectives.

While economic tools are perhaps the most persuasive in Beijing's toolkit, China's comprehensive engagement goes beyond economics and aims to build a stable, multifaceted, and mutually beneficial set of bilateral relationships. Chinese leaders have recognized that broader relationships must be "high-quality" and go beyond profits to include a "sense of justice" (义利观).[21] China's relations with developing states now emphasize a wide array of collaborative enterprises, including foreign aid, educational and cultural exchanges, media cooperation, military assistance and training, and political cadre training.

Interlocking Engagement

While all major states conduct diplomatic activities at the bilateral, regional, and global levels, China's engagement consists of a particularly tight latticework of institutionalized relationships, and its focus on creating or interfacing with regional organizations is distinctive in the degree, if not type, of effort involved. By building a dense network of interlocking relationships, Beijing hopes to build a stable, durable, and mutually reinforcing structure that will further its interests.

Regional Engagement

Beginning in the mid-1990s, China enhanced its engagement with regional organizations and groupings around its immediate periphery. In 1995, China initiated the Shanghai Five dialogue with Russia, Kazakhstan, Kyrgyzstan, and Tajikistan to discuss regional confidence-building measures. With the addition of Uzbekistan, the group evolved into the Shanghai Cooperation Organization (SCO) and the scope of its activities expanded to include counter-terrorism and, to a limited extent, economic cooperation. In their chapter on Central Asia, Raffaello Pantucci and Mathew Oresman argue that the SCO serves two key functions for Beijing: enhancing stability in areas adjacent to the Muslim minority population in Xinjiang and mitigating the reemergence of regional competition with Russia. In 2017, the SCO admitted India and Pakistan as full members, despite concerns that the organization could become less cohesive and focused.[22]

The pattern of deepening engagement with regional institutions is replicated across every developing region. Beijing established relations with ASEAN in 1991, and today is involved in 11 ASEAN ministerial-level mechanisms across a wide range of economic, political, cultural, and security areas. It has maintained an ambassador to ASEAN since 2008, and has participated in the China–ASEAN Free Trade Area since 2010.[23] In Latin America, China was admitted as a permanent observer to both the Organization of American States (OAS) and Latin American Parliament in 2004. In 2015, Beijing and Latin American leaders held the inaugural meeting of the China–Community of Latin American and Caribbean Countries (CELAC) Forum, at which Xi Jinping established a target for Chinese investment in Latin America of $250 billion within ten years.[24] Notably, the CELAC forum, unlike the OAS, does not include the United States.[25]

China's regional diplomacy in Africa is orchestrated largely under the Forum on China–Africa Cooperation (FOCAC), which convened its first Ministerial Conference in Beijing in October 2000. In 2006, FOCAC was elevated to a ministerial-level summit, with meetings held every three years. A private equity fund, the China–Africa Development Fund, was created to take equity stakes in promising African companies., yet as of June 2017 many of those investments have fallen short of expectations.[26] The 2015 FOCAC summit, held in South Africa, included leaders from 48 African nations. At the meeting, President Xi announced numerous new economic and social initiatives designed to highlight China's commitment to African development.[27] China and Arab partners established the China–Arab States Cooperation Forum (CASCF) in 2004.[28] As Sarah Kaiser-Cross and Mao Yufeng explain in their chapter on China in the Arab world, the CASCF and China–Gulf Cooperation Council strategic dialogue established in 2010 have created new venues for Beijing to expand relations with the Sunni-dominated Gulf States, which had been limited by China's close relations with Shia Iran.[29]

Bilateral Relations

Although China's creation of regional organizations is among the most distinctive features of Beijing's approach to the developing world, its bilateral relations remain the foundation. Indeed, as R. Evan Ellis argues in his chapter on China in Latin America, multilateral forums boost legitimacy and visibility, but binding deals are primarily pursued bilaterally. Across the developing world, Beijing has deepened its bilateral relationships and maintains "strategic partnerships" with some 67 states.[30]

China's approach towards individual countries is tailored in accordance with its specific interests there. China's relations with nearby states are generally deeper and more complex, with a mix of political and economic interests, and sometimes territorial disputes, at play. Its more distant relationships, by contrast, tend to prioritize economic objectives. China's relations with emerging major developing powers (including the BRICS countries and the developing members of the G-20) cut across regional lines and also tend to be multidimensional—with several overlapping political, economic, and security components.

Within each developing region, Beijing places considerable emphasis on its relations with large and important anchor or "hub" states where circumstances of geography, politics, or economics make relations with China particularly propitious. These relationships tend to receive more attention in Beijing and have been relatively stable over time. In East Asia, they include Indonesia and Thailand; in South Asia, Pakistan and India; in Central Asia, Kazakhstan; in Africa, South Africa, Egypt, and Ethiopia; in the Middle East, Iran; and in Latin America, Brazil and Argentina. This list is not definitive, and has and will continue to evolve over time. For example, some states, like Venezuela under Hugo Chavez, received special attention and financing from Beijing for a limited period of time for political reasons. Small, but strategically located states, like Cambodia and Laos, are more susceptible to Chinese influence, and have served as useful "nail-house" votes in consensus-governed ASEAN, but should not be regarded as strategic partners.

Engaging Global Institutions

Since the 1980s, China has become an increasingly active contributor to international institutions. China's participation reassures other states that it is committed to the international system, provides venues to advance Chinese interests, and helps "lock in" Chinese policymakers in ways that help reduce conservative domestic opposition to reform. China's expanded involvement in global institutions also serves to highlight and promote Beijing's efforts to lead the developing world by reforming and shaping global institutions in ways that ostensibly increase the voice of developing countries. Beijing has pushed for years to change quotas and vote shares in the World Bank, IMF, and Asian Development Bank, although the process has been painfully slow.[31] In the World Bank, it has advocated greater transparency in the selection of the president and an end to Western dominance, and has consistently sought to expand the prominence of the G-20 vis-à-vis the G-7.[32]

China's support for reforming international institutions advances Beijing's broad interest in promoting a more democratic or multipolar international order, but those reform efforts are sometimes limited by narrower national interests. In the UN Security Council, for instance, where China enjoys its privileged status as a permanent member (P-5), some see China providing rhetorical support for expansion of the membership yet working behind the scenes to stymie change.[33] The so-called group of four (G-4), including Germany, Japan, India, and Brazil, argues that the P-5 does not represent the distribution of global wealth or power and that they should be added as permanent members. Since 2005, China has strongly opposed Japanese accession, and only supports India if it dissociates its bid from Japan.[34] Meanwhile, Beijing has voiced support for the "Uniting for Consensus" group of 13 states, which opposes the G-4 in favor of more representation by developing states.

Modes of Engagement

China's interwoven approach to its relations in the developing world makes separate discussions of individual aspects of its engagement difficult. Nevertheless, with the understanding that these elements are not employed in isolation, we attempt to identify and explain the specific economic, political, security, and soft-power means that constitute China's strategy towards the developing world.

Economics

Most of the chapters in this volume identify economic means as the most prominent and efficacious aspect of China's foreign policy. Below, we assess the growth of China's trade with and investment in the developing world and then outline aspects of China's support for it. We address the issue of economic diplomacy in support of political ends in the subsequent section.

Trade

Promoting trade is an important state objective, which enables China to leverage comparative advantages to grow its economy—with attendant benefits for the Chinese people and state capacity. Trade growth is not purely, or even primarily, a function of state-led promotion activities, but Beijing works to tip the balance in favor of its firms and entrepreneurs. Chinese corporations, including SOEs, private, and semi-private firms, often work closely with state policy banks and diplomats, who are empowered to help promote exports. According to one analysis, Chinese commercial service attachés working in China's African embassies outnumber U.S. Foreign Commercial Service officers working in the region by some fifteen to one.[35]

The rapid expansion of Chinese trade has become a key driver of GDP growth. GDP grew by a real compound annual growth rate of 9.1 percent between 1978 and 2015, while trade increased by an average of 12 percent. Trade growth has slowed considerably since 2012, partly due to government policies designed to enhance domestic consumption and, more importantly, the slowing of the Chinese economy.[36] China's trade grew by a 3.52 percent in 2014, *shrank* by 9.85 percent in 2015, and shrank again by 4.02 percent in 2016. These trends are even more pronounced in China's trade with developing countries (Appendix I). Private firms accounted for 38.1 percent of trade in 2016.[37]

For China, developing countries have become increasingly important raw material suppliers and are growing markets for its manufactured products. China's trade with developing countries has come to account for an increasing percentage of the country's overall trade volume. In 1990, developing countries represented only 15 percent of total Chinese trade, but by 2000, that figure had grown to 19 percent, and by 2010, it had reached 31 percent. After peaking around 34 percent in 2012, the percentage has plateaued, as China's economic slowdown has reduced the need for raw materials and the price of oil and metals like copper and iron ore has fallen. If and when commodity prices fully recover, developing countries are likely to once again regain their leading position.

The value of China's trade with the developing world was $29.4 billion in 1990 (measured in constant 2016 USD) and rose to $1.2 trillion in 2016 (about 33 percent of China's total foreign trade)—a real compound annual growth rate (CAGR) of 15.4 percent—compared to a 12.1 percent CAGR for China's total trade over that period. China's trade volume by region were: Southeast Asia, 12.4 percent of total Chinese trade; the Middle East, 5.5 percent; Latin America, 5.7 percent; Africa, 4.1 percent; South Asia, 3.0 percent; and Central Asia, 0.9 percent.[38]

Investment

Developing countries play a central role in China's "going out" foreign investment strategy. As early as 1999, China had amassed about $155 billion in foreign reserves and was looking to gain returns while generating work for its SOEs.[39] That year, at the Fourth Plenum of the 15th National Party Congress, Jiang Zemin launched the so-called going out strategy (走出去战略), encouraging firms to "establish branches overseas" and "explore international markets."[40] Subsequent decisions during the 2000s provided funding mechanisms to facilitate outward investment. China's move outward began slowly—and primarily involved SOEs in the extractive and construction industries—but has diversified and gathered momentum since 2010. China's non-financial FDI flow increased from $3.6 billion (in 2016 USD) in 2003 to some $141.2 billion in 2015—a real CAGR of 36 percent.[41]

According to official figures, as of 2015 about 57 percent of China's total (outward) FDI stocks were in developing states (excluding investment in offshore financial centers), with the largest accumulations in Asia (25 percent of total), Africa (12 percent), and Latin America (5 percent).[42] In some sectors, Chinese firms also have their own sizable war chests and may sometimes prefer to invest their own funds. Much of CNOOC's $15 billion 2012 purchase of Canada's Nexen, for example, came from the firm's own cash reserves.[43] Notably, although Chinese investment in all these regions has increased markedly over the last decade, it is often not the largest investor. For example, Chinese investments in Africa during 2014 accounted for 7 percent of all FDI in the region, far less than France's 21 percent.[44] In 2015, Chinese investment in Africa dropped to just 3 percent of the global total.[45] China accounted for about 9.5 percent of total FDI in Southeast Asia in 2016, while Japan accounted for about 14.5 percent and the United States for about 12 percent.[46] In short, China has gone from having virtually no FDI stake in these regions to being a major player. But it is not the singularly dominant actor it is sometimes portrayed as, but rather one among several important investors. One reason for this is that journalistic accounts often wrongly conflate equity investment with debt finance.

Loans, Financing, and OBOR

For two decades, China has promoted a "going-out" policy among its corporations. Financing for Chinese-built projects in developing countries comes from a variety of sources, the most important being China's policy banks, established in 1994 to finance projects important to Chinese economic growth. The Export–Import Bank of China (China Ex–Im Bank) and the China Development Bank provide large volumes of soft loans to developing countries under the condition that they hire Chinese SOEs to complete projects.[47] The loan portfolio of these two banks and 13 regional funds exceeds the $700 billion outstanding loans from all six western-backed multilateral banks combined (including the World Bank, Asian Development Bank, Inter-American Development Bank, European Investment Bank, European Bank for Reconstruction and Development, and African Development Bank).[48] Once terms are reached with a host country, funds may be transferred directly into the Beijing-based bank accounts of China's state-owned enterprises, which execute the project using Chinese materials and labor.

In September 2013, Beijing provided an overarching framework for this effort, when President Xi Jinping announced the Silk Road Economic Belt initiative, during a speech delivered at Nazarbayev University in Kazakhstan. The next month Xi proposed building a twenty-first century Maritime Silk Road to promote maritime cooperation between China and Southeast Asian nations.[49] Somewhat confusingly, the "belt" portion is continental, while the "road" portion is maritime. The Silk Road Economic Belt (SREB) runs through Central Asia, West Asia, the Middle East, and Europe. The Maritime Silk Road (MSR) connects China to countries in Southeast Asia, Oceania, and parts of North and East Africa—the South China Sea, South Pacific, and Indian Ocean regions. Designed to improve connectivity between China and more than 60 countries, OBOR is overseen by the National Development and Reform Commission, Ministry of Foreign Affairs, and Ministry of Commerce, all under the auspices of the State Council.[50] Projects include virtually all types of transportation infrastructure, including rail, roads, ports, airports, electricity generation, telecommunications, and various other forms of connectivity.[51]

In October 2013, the same month that OBOR was introduced, Xi Jinping announced China's intention to establish the AIIB, which will complement the OBOR initiative. The AIIB began operations in December 2015 with 57 founding member states—37 from Asia and 20 outside of it.[52] Initial capital was $100 billion, about two-thirds of the capital of the Asian Development Bank and about half that of the World Bank.[53] Although the AIIB is headquartered in Beijing, its president reports to an international board, and although China holds the largest voting bloc (26 percent) it remains a minority stakeholder. Beijing has also created the Silk Road Fund, backed by China's sovereign wealth fund but open to private investors.[54] Established in December 2014, the Silk Road Fund is capitalized at roughly $55 billion.[55] The AIIB's slow start and the Silk Road Fund's limited scale means that the preponderance of financing for OBOR projects come from China's policy banks.[56]

While there are many unanswered questions about the initiative, it is clear that OBOR takes China's finance and infrastructure construction efforts to a new, and far riskier, level. Beijing intends to allocate at least $1 trillion to the initiative, and scores of multinational corporations, both Chinese and foreign, are angling take full advantage.[57] The framework has subsumed many projects that were being considered long before OBOR was launched, but the political backing implied by the OBOR imprimatur, written into the Chinese Constitution in October 2017, may lead to more projects being launched with less careful assessment of likely risks and returns. Because these projects involve loans, heavy OBOR funding may exacerbate the debt problems of already poor states and further burden deeply indebted Chinese banks. China now owns more than half of some African nations' foreign debt, and many expect Beijing will have to write off significant portions in the years ahead.

Economic Assistance

China provided substantial economic assistance to developing states during the 1950s, 1960s, and early 1970s, but cut back on those expenditures in the late 1970s, 1980s, and 1990s as it sought to rebuild its own economic position. Over the last decade, however, foreign aid has reemerged as an important part of the Chinese foreign policy toolkit, and Beijing released white papers on the subject in 2011 and 2014 (see Appendix II). The budget for foreign assistance has grown rapidly over the last decade, with an average annual increase of 29.4 percent between 2004 and 2009. Between 2009 and 2012, China's aid disbursements totaled $14.4 billion, or about a third of China's total aid from 1950 to 2008.[58] Unfortunately, the Ministry of Commerce, which coordinates China's assistance programs, does not provide year-on-year tracking, complicating systematic evaluation.

Chinese economic assistance comes in three varieties: grant aid (36 percent of the 2009–2012 total); interest-free loans (8 percent); and concessional loans (56 percent).[59] These funds go to support a wide range of programs: emergency assistance, technical aid and instruction, healthcare and medical facilities, low-cost housing, education, state capacity building, infrastructure development, and environmental protection. In terms of distribution, some 52 percent went to Africa over this period, 31 percent to Asian states, and 8 percent to Latin America and the Caribbean.[60]

China's approach to foreign assistance differs in several respects from the members of the OECD's Development Assistance Committee (DAC), private Western donors like the Gates Foundation, and multilateral institutions like the World Bank. Rather than poverty alleviation, China's assistance, particularly its concessionary loan aid, is primarily focused on infrastructure development tied to Chinese business contracts. It is nearly always distributed on a state-to-state basis. Unlike Western countries and institutions which often place economic or political conditionality on their aid, Chinese aid does not require subsequent audits and comes with "no political strings attached."

The predictable result is that Chinese aid is often easier for corrupt foreign leaders to "capture" and channel towards politically important regions, constituencies, and cronies.[61] While China's foreign aid programs could focus more on grants and be made more transparent to safeguard against abuse by recipient governments, the approach taken by the DAC states and the Bretton Woods Institutions has also faced criticism. Angus Deaton, who won the 2015 Nobel Prize in Economics for work on poverty, argues that the West's approach to aid "undermines what poor people need most: an effective government that works with them for today and tomorrow."[62] Some therefore favor China's "development first" approach, with its focus on state capacity and infrastructure.[63]

Politics

Under Mao Zedong, China supported revolutionary and anti-colonial movements around the developing world. After Deng Xiaoping's accession in 1978, political goals were (with the exception of efforts to isolate Taiwan) generally subordinated in favor of economic ones. Today, Beijing continues to abjure political disputes, practice non-intervention, and actively engage governments of all political types. But the reemergence of political elements reminiscent of the Mao era have crept back into China's agenda. Economic means are increasingly employed to achieve political ends. China has stepped up political outreach and educational activities by government departments and the Communist Party to deepen relations, improve the image of the state and its governing system, and to enhance policy coordination among "major developing states." In his address at the 19th national party congress in 2017, Xi Jinping said China's model of socialism "offers a new option for other countries and nations who want to speed up their development while preserving their independence, and it offers Chinese wisdom and a Chinese approach to solving the problems facing mankind."

Economic Diplomacy

Economic diplomacy has become the most visible and well-articulated aspect of China's external engagement, encompassing many of the elements discussed previously—trade promotion, foreign direct investment, and the financing and execution of infrastructure projects. The most obvious manifestation is what might be called China's "MoU diplomacy." When Chinese leaders conduct summit meetings, they often travel with large business delegations and sign MoUs worth hundreds of millions, if not billions, of dollars. In Islamabad in April 2015, for example, Xi Jinping and Pakistan's President Nawaz Shari signed 51 MoUs worth nearly $28 billion as the first phase of a larger Pakistan–China Economic Corridor Project said to be worth more than $50 billion.[64] During the December 2015 FOCAC meeting, Xi Jinping pledged some $60 billion in funding support, mostly in the form of loans and export credits and $5 billion in assistance to Africa.[65]

In addition to serving China's immediate economic interests, trade delegations also serve as the core of Beijing's "comprehensive diplomacy," and work to highlight Chinese largesse and deepen political relations. In some cases, MoU diplomacy is deployed to cement a political understanding. When Philippine President Rodrigo Duterte visited Beijing in October 2016, having signaled that Manila was prepared to compromise on territorial disputes in the South China Sea, he brought home $24 billion in pledges for investment and credit.[66] A year later, a Chinese delegation visiting Manila recommitted to funding 12 initial projects, including two bridges in Manila, a major dam, an irrigation project, and construction of an industrial park as well as two drug rehabilitation facilities.[67] Two months after Cambodia blocked an ASEAN statement on the South China Sea in July 2016, the Cambodian Chamber of Commerce signed an MOU on trade and investment promotion with a Chinese trade representative, leading a delegation of leaders from 47 Chinese enterprises.[68]

The dollar values discussed at these meetings hold out the promise of profits and economic growth for smaller partner nations. But MoUs are, of course, not legally binding contracts, and many do not reach fruition. Others involve deals for which negotiations have been ongoing (in some cases for years), but which are pushed forward to correspond with a political meeting or leaders' summit.

"Democratizing" International Relations

China has benefitted as much as any country—and more than most—from the current global geopolitical order and free trade regime. Beijing supports and underwrites key international institutions, but as discussed above, it has also sought to modify and "democratize" the international order in ways that give greater representation to itself and developing states.[69]

Chinese official sources depict the international system as evolving towards multipolarity, and developing states as primary drivers of that process. They portray multipolarity as objectively better than U.S. hegemony and bipolarity and its emergence as a natural progression that cannot be resisted or easily manipulated. The Chinese definition of multipolarity appears to differ in important ways from the Western (and especially U.S.) international relations literature. In the Chinese lexicon, it refers more to the autonomy or independence of other states in the system and their ability to influence events at the regional level; that is, freedom from hegemony, rather than the existence of states with the independent capability to challenge the leading state.[70]

China's embrace of emerging multipolarity takes a number of forms. At the bilateral level, Beijing has placed increasing emphasis on developing strategic relations with what it now calls "major developing states." It has, with various subsets of those states, also formed international organizations to pursue common objectives through collective action—and it has linked the operation of those institutions to make them mutually reinforcing. The BRICS grouping, established in 2009, includes what might be regarded as the core major developing states—Brazil, Russia, India, China, and South Africa. The BRICS have pursued primarily political-economic objectives, such as the reform of financial institutions and opposition to farm subsidies by developed nations. It has established a $100 billion currency reserve to lessen dependence on the IMF and nationally held dollar-denominated reserves, as well as a New Development Bank (NDB), also with $100 billion in authorized capital.[71]

Nevertheless, as Niu Haibin has argued: "It is important that China not see the BRICS group only as an economic platform, but that it also values its importance at the political and soft-power level."[72] Following Russia's annexation of the Crimea in 2014, the other members of the G-8 suspended Russian participation in that body. Australia, which hosted the 2015 G-20 meeting, suggested Russia might also be excluded from the G-20. In response, the BRICS foreign ministers issued a joint statement warning against Russian exclusion.[73] According to Niu, this "showed the value of the group in preventing one of its members from becoming geopolitically isolated."[74] The BRICS Joint Working Group on Counter-Terrorism met for the first time in 2016.[75] As China assumed the BRICS' chairmanship in 2017, Foreign Minister Wang Yi indicated that Beijing would look to expand the group's political and security capacity.[76]

China has also promoted the role of the G-20, established in 1999, as a more important alternative to the G-7—naturally enough, given China's membership in the former and exclusion from the latter. It has worked with the BRICS states within the G-20 to coordinate positions and push for reform of global governance, with BRICS leaders meeting informally on the G-20 sidelines.[77] Although China has never joined the G-77 (the group of developing nations within the United Nations that now numbers some 134 countries), Beijing supports the group and has formed the G77+China. Together with most members of that group, China has backed the Sustainable Development Goals (SDG), adopted by the UN in 2015 as the successor to the Millennium Development Goals (MDG). Unlike the MDG, the SDG applies goals to all states, not just developing ones.[78]

Beijing faces several challenges in the push for greater democracy in international affairs. The sharp downturn in China's GDP growth since 2015 and widespread environmental degradation tarnish the nation's image as a model for other developing states. Ultimately, Beijing's success may hinge on its ability to get its own economic house in order, as well as on its ability to manage disputes and conflicts with India and (potentially) Russia. It has, however, created much of the institutional framework to boost the role of "major developing states" in international affairs—and to advance its own national interests in the process.

Non-intervention and the Defense of Sovereignty Norms

China continues to emphasize the norms of state sovereignty and non-interference in its engagement with developing states. Chinese diplomats regularly reference the decades-old mantra of the Five Principles of Peaceful Coexistence, the first of which is mutual respect for territorial integrity and sovereignty. For many other developing states, which warily guard their autonomy, the norms of state sovereignty and non-interference remain equally sacrosanct. But while China stridently promotes its "principle" of non-intervention, the interpretation and application of that principle has evolved over time and is now being reevaluated in light of the threats Chinese people and firms are facing in developing countries.

At the most basic level, non-interference references Beijing's policy of near universal engagement, with the one requirement that states adhere to the one-China policy and recognize Beijing rather than Taipei. When leadership changes occur in partner states, whether by election or force, Beijing has deftly established cordial relations with the successor government. Faced with the problems of governing, new leaders in developing countries are generally willing to overlook China's former support for political rivals. Indeed, Beijing's willingness to work with whomever holds power makes it attractive to new leaders—especially those that capture power by force. At least in the short term, this often rebounds to the advantage of Chinese business, and this approach may encourage Chinese SOEs to see less risk in politically turbulent parts of the world. But it can also backfire. In Libya and South Sudan, billions of dollars in Chinese investments and equipment were destroyed during violent, long-lasting political transitions.

In its international politics, particularly within the UN Security Council, China continues to defend the norm of state sovereignty. Although it is more prone to abstain rather than veto resolutions, it has sometimes used its veto to quash actions that it feels violate the principle of state sovereignty.[79] Beijing's 2011 vote on Libya sanctions was an important exception. Despite significant economic interests and investments in the country, Beijing voted in favor of sanctions and later abstained from a UNSC vote authorizing a no-fly zone when important Arab and African bodies supported tough action. After Gaddafi's fall from power in October 2011, China evacuated some 35,000 nationals and the 75 Chinese enterprises (including 13 SOEs) in Libya abandoned or otherwise lost billions of dollars' worth of construction materials and machinery.[80] A few months later, Beijing, claiming it was misled by the West about the Libya mission's intention, joined with Russia to veto UN intervention in Syria. Beijing and Moscow came together again in 2017 to veto another UNSC resolution that would have imposed sanctions on 21 Syrian people and organizations linked to chemical weapons attacks.[81]

Party Outreach and Cadre Training

Since Xi Jinping's accession to power in 2012, Beijing's engagement with the developing world has assumed more political tones. Outreach by the International Department of the Central Committee of the Communist Party of China (ID-CPC) is a historical and ongoing feature of Chinese foreign policy and supplements the diplomacy conducted by state organs (e.g., the MFA) and leaders. The Party's political outreach generally looks to engage in ways that avoid the appearance of intervention in domestic affairs. In autocracies, the ID-CPC may avoid interaction with the opposition, while in liberal democracies, it maintains ties with both ruling and opposition parties.

As Joshua Eisenman and David H. Shinn explain in their chapter on China's relations in Africa, the CPC has expanded its host diplomacy, cadre training, and outreach to political parties in Africa and throughout the developing world. Political cadre training done by the ID-CPC and media training programs run by the official Xinhua News Agency, are explicitly political and are intended to improve foreign perceptions of China and legitimize the ruling party. In 2014 and 2015, some 2,000 officials of South Africa's African National Congress (ANC) were trained by the CPC, and Beijing is financing the ANC Political School and Policy Institute, modeled on the China Executive Leadership Academy in Shanghai.[82] Ethiopia was perhaps the earliest and most eager student of Chinese cadre training, and has dispatched delegations regularly to China since 1994.[83] During a public talk at Fudan University in Shanghai in May 2017, Arkebe Oqubay, a Minister and Special Advisor to the Prime Minister of Ethiopia, identified party-to-party relations as the first of three Sino–Ethiopian links (along with government-to-government and people-to-people).[84]

Over the last decade, led by Xinhua and CCTV, China's state-run media has advanced an initiative to enhance China's influence and international image.[85] Since 2005, Xinhua has emphasized cooperation, content sharing, and media training programs with dozens of news outlets throughout the developing world.[86] China wants to improve younger generations' perceptions of its political system and gain elite support to counter what Beijing sees as Western efforts to portray Chinese practices in an unfavorable light. In 2017, for instance, Renmin University in Beijing hosted a ten-month development studies and media exchange with 48 students from Africa, South Asia, and Southeast Asia. Training topics include China's political, cultural, media, and economic studies. Counselor Liu Yutong, Chief of the Public Diplomacy Division at the MFA's Information Department, welcomed the journalists with a speech about Chinese stability and growth—and questioned the wisdom of Britain's exit from the EU and the U.S. election of Donald Trump.[87]

Security and Military

China's security role in the developing world is modest but growing. It is actively engaged in military diplomacy and peacekeeping; increasingly identifies the protection of overseas interests as an important military task; is rapidly improving its ability to dispatch and maintain forces overseas; has overcome its aversion to overseas bases; and is developing a defense industry capable of exporting both small and big-ticket military systems to a range of buyers throughout the developing world.

Military Diplomacy and Peacekeeping

Until recently, China paid scant attention to military diplomacy. The PLA Navy's first fleet visit to a foreign port occurred in 1990, and it did not conduct a joint exercise with a foreign military until 2002. The policy origins of China's expanded military and security engagement in the developing world can be found in the 1998 National Defense White Paper, which presented China's comprehensive "new security concept" and contained the first official use of the term "military diplomacy."[88] The new security concept emphasized the need to mitigate security tensions between states and broadened the definition of security to include regime security and security against terrorist and other internal dangers.

Since our first volume in 2007, the PLA has considerably expanded the depth, breadth, and frequency of its "military diplomacy" (军事外交) activities. As of 2008 (the last time China released figures), China had military attaché offices in 109 countries, and 98 countries had established attaché offices in China.[89] Its military diplomacy now encompasses a wide range of peaceful military-related activities that improve military-to-military relations and support China's national interests.[90] These activities include high-level military visits and exchanges, dialogue mechanisms, educational exchanges, disaster relief, port visits, combined training activities, weapons sales, and UN peacekeeping activities.

China has steadily increased the number of combined exercises conducted with foreign militaries, and, as Eric Heginbotham's Southeast Asia chapter highlights, expanded their scope to include more elements of the PLA and more operational categories. In 2015, the PLA participated in 24 joint exercises with foreign militaries.[91] With the 2007 launch of China's first large (14,000-ton) hospital ship (the *Peace Ark*), the PLA Navy (PLAN) can now deliver medical care to coastal areas around the world and has participated in limited disaster relief.

China's self-identification as both a major power and a developing country, and its desire to give its forces real world experience, makes peacekeeping operations a natural fit. China first dispatched personnel to participate in UN peacekeeping in 1990, and has steadily increased its financial and material contribution since that time. China is now consistently among the top contributors of peacekeeping personnel and the largest from among the permanent members of the UN Security Council. For many years, it dispatched only support forces, civilian engineers, and police, but in 2013, it dispatched its first combat forces to Mali and in 2014 sent a battalion of combat troops to a peacekeeping mission in South Sudan.[92] In 2015, China committed 8,000 troops to the UN peacekeeping standby force, roughly 20 percent of the total.[93] As of August 2017, 2,654 Chinese peacekeeping personnel (including 2,466 troops) were serving in UN peacekeeping operations.[94]

Power Projection

With the second largest defense budget in the world—though lagging well behind the United States—China has built considerable combat capabilities in all domains.[95] Chinese defense budgets began rising rapidly in 1996, increasing from roughly $20 billion (in constant 2016 $US) to $143 billion in 2016—an aggregate of more than 600 percent, or a compound annual growth rate of 10 percent per year.[96] Although its priorities during the 1990s and 2000s were oriented to nearby missions, especially Taiwan scenarios, the PLA has since developed a modest but significant power projection capability—larger warships, amphibious lift, at sea replenishment capabilities, improved anti-submarine warfare capabilities, a large force of modern fighters, and, most recently, large cargo aircraft.

PLA forces have increasingly been deployed to protect Chinese overseas interests. In 2004, Hu Jintao directed the PLA to prepare for New Historic Missions (新的历史使命) and popularized the discussion of military missions other than war, including the protection of China's growing national interests abroad.[97] Beijing's 2008 white paper on China's National Defense further identified a "diversified" mission set, including "counter-terrorism, stability maintenance, and emergency rescue and international peacekeeping."[98] The 2013 defense white paper highlighted growing Chinese overseas interests and included a section on "protecting overseas interests," which stipulated that "vessel protection at sea, evacuation of Chinese nationals overseas, and emergency rescue have become important ways and means for the PLA to safeguard national interests."[99]

China's security footprint in the developing world is surprisingly small relative to its economic heft. France, for example, which has a GDP less than quarter of China's, is much more heavily engaged in African security issues. Nevertheless, China's military has become significantly more active over the last decade. Most notable are China's muscular responses to territorial and maritime disputes in Southeast Asia and Northeast Asia; its growing interest in sea-lane protection and participation in the counter-piracy mission in the Gulf of Aden; its evacuation of Chinese nationals and others from conflict zones in Libya (2011) and Yemen (2015); and its construction of a long-run naval facility in Djibouti.[100] In addition to peacekeeping and combined training, various PLA and PLAN units have been dispatched on operational missions. In 2011, the PLA helped evacuate Chinese from Libya, and again from Yemen in 2015. In the Libyan case, the PLA diverted a destroyer from the Gulf of Aden to Libya and also flew 40 sorties using four Il-76 transport aircraft to evacuate more than 1,600 Chinese nationals to Sudan.[101] In March 2016, the PLA established an Overseas Operations Office within its Joint Staff Department Operations Bureau to oversee non-combatant evacuation (NEO) operations, peacekeeping, and other non-war overseas contingencies. China dispatched its first anti-piracy detachment to the Gulf of Aden in 2008 and, as of July 2017, the PLA had dispatched a total of 26 task forces, generally consisting of two warships, helicopters, and a resupply vessel.[102] Taken together, these trends suggest China's global security presence will continue to grow for the foreseeable future.

Although China has long eschewed overseas bases as hegemonic, its position has evolved as Chinese overseas interests have expanded and the PLAN has faced the challenges of operating overseas without dedicated facilities. According to Shen Dingli at Fudan University:

> Setting up overseas military bases is not an idea we have to shun; on the contrary, it is our right. Bases established by other countries appear to be used to protect their overseas rights and interests. As long as the bases are set up in line with international laws and regulations, they are legal ones.[103]

In 2017, the PLAN opened a naval "support facility" in Djibouti adjacent to military outposts operated by the U.S., France, and Japan; it is equipped with maintenance shops for ships and helicopters, weapons stores, and a contingent of up to 10,000 soldiers.[104]

Arms Sales

During the Mao era, China provided weapons either for free or on concessionary terms to revolutionary groups or leftist partner states. Today, however, China limits arms transfers to paying customers. Chinese arms sales peaked during the Iran–Iraq War, exceeding an estimated $4 billion in 1987 in inflation-adjusted 2016 U.S. dollars, then declined afterward to a low of about $450 million in 2005. With improvements to China's military-industrial base, Beijing has reemerged as a sizable arms supplier, with annual sales of between roughly $2 billion–$3.5 billion from 2010 to 2016 (see Figure 9.1).[105]

China now sells corvettes, frigates, and fighter aircraft, and a range of anti-ship and anti-aircraft missiles, in addition to tanks, artillery, and small arms. Weapons sales include maintenance and training packages that facilitate continued security collaboration. Chinese arms sales have been primarily to either nearby low-income states, such as Bangladesh and Pakistan, or oil-rich but technologically weak countries, such as Iran or Nigeria (see Table 9.1). Chinese arms exports to Bangladesh have accounted for 80 percent of that country's arms imports over the last decade. Some buyers, such as Turkey and Venezuela, have used Chinese purchases to signal their dissatisfaction with Washington. China has licensed production or agreed to limited joint weapons development with Pakistan, Thailand, and Indonesia. As Jeff

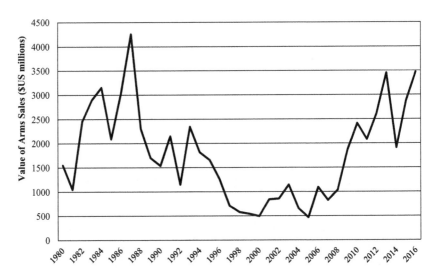

FIGURE 9.1 Value of Chinese Arms Sales, 1980–2016 (In Constant 2016 U.S. Dollars)

Source: SIPRI Arms Transfer Database. All values are expressed in what SIPRI refers to as "trend indicator values" (TIV), designed to capture the value of systems exported in a uniform way, rather than the actual dollar value of agreements. We have adjusted SIPRI's constant 1990 figures to 2016 dollars.

TABLE 9.1 Value of Chinese Arms Sales—Top Recipients, 2007–2016 (Cumulative Sales in Constant 2016 U.S. $ Millions)

Pakistan	9,220
Bangladesh	2,911
Myanmar	1,982
Algeria	1,381
Venezuela	1,021
Tanzania	578
Iran	524
Morocco	480
Indonesia	476
Nigeria	450
Turkmenistan	382
Turkey	349

Source: SIPRI Arms Transfer Database. See source note concerning TIV under Figure 9.1.

M. Smith notes in his chapter, China and Pakistan have jointly developed the JF-17 aircraft and are marketing it to countries in the Middle East and South America.

China's arms sales to Sudan are among its most controversial, though Beijing's role has evolved considerably. In the late 1990s and early 2000s, Beijing supplied Khartoum with arms and helicopter gunships that were used against southern rebels and civilians during the North–South civil war. Prior to the 2008 summer Olympics, however, as world attention focused on the bloodshed in Sudan, China came under increased scrutiny and in 2011 supported a referendum on South Sudan independence. China still refused to sanction the Umar al-Bashir government and hosted its "old friend" in Beijing in 2011 and 2015.[106] After South Sudan became a sovereign country, China's state arms' dealer Norinco began supplying Juba until media reports revealed that its sales were fueling armed conflict, leading to a secession of sales. China also dispatched peacekeepers to South Sudan in 2014 as part of the UN's Mission in Sudan forces, and its forces suffered casualties, including two deaths, there in 2016.

Soft Power with Chinese Characteristics

Beijing's impetus to become a "cultural major power" (文化大国) predates Xi and was discussed in our 2007 volume. A broad conceptual framework was adopted in 2004 under the official formulation "China's peaceful rise," and a subsequent white paper was issued in 2011, as both a guide for Chinese policymakers and an effort to reassure external audiences. Since 2013, Xi Jinping has spoken repeatedly on the need to increase China's "soft power" (软实力) by, among other things, creating a compelling Chinese narrative and strengthening Beijing's capacity to convey its message overseas.[107] "Soft power" is the ability of one nation to shape the preferences of others through its appeal and attraction at the popular, elite, or government levels.[108] Because soft power helps shape others' preferences, it increases the perception of congruence between Chinese interests and those of others.[109]

According to Chinese analysts, the nation's history makes it a "cultural major power" with great natural advantages.[110] In 2004, Beijing launched the Confucius Institute program to cultivate the study of Chinese language and culture abroad. According to the Confucius Institute Headquarters website, in 2017 there were 500 institutes around the world. Although these are clustered in developed countries, with 109 in the United States alone, many developing states also host institutes. Skeptics question whether Beijing-backed Confucius Institutes are being used to influence university research agendas and impinge on academic freedoms.[111]

China promotes other types of "person-to-person" exchanges, including foreign students studying in China. Beijing sponsors tens of thousands of foreign youths for training both in their home countries and at Chinese universities and vocational schools. According to the Ministry of Education, there were 442,773 international students studying in China in 2016, up from about 290,000 in 2011. Of foreign students in 2016, some 49,022 received scholarships from the Chinese government, an increase of 20 percent from 2015.[112] In 2016, more than 264,976 foreign students in China hailed from Asia, but thousands of students are from other developing regions. For at least two consecutive years, the greatest increase was in the number of students from Africa, who numbered some 61,594 in 2016, up 23.7 percent from 2015. China is looking to expand job opportunities for graduates, so it can retain and utilize these young Chinese-speaking foreigners.[113]

Evaluating China's Strategy Towards the Developing World

China's strategy toward the developing world is intended to enhance the perceived legitimacy of the CPC, increase the living standards for the Chinese people, and expand Beijing's power and influence around the world. China has been largely successful in achieving these aims, but it has also not been without failures, and the scale of risk has risen apace with its overseas profile in recent years.

Chinese engagement with the developing world has undoubtedly helped Beijing achieve its economic objectives. China's "going out" strategy has opened developing markets to Chinese-made products and expanded access to the raw materials China needs to meet domestic demand. Its investments and loan financing for infrastructure, catalyzed through the OBOR initiative, have provided sustained opportunities to redeploy China's considerable productive capacity in the construction, telecom, and other sectors. All of this facilitates China's pursuit of its centenary goals, the lifting of living standards for the Chinese people, the power of the Chinese state, and (most importantly for China's leaders) the perceived legitimacy of the Communist Party.

While China's strategy has been remarkably successful to date, its future is uncertain. At home, Chinese leaders understand that economic growth is overly dependent on investment and exports, though they remain ambivalent about rebalancing towards more efficient growth. At the same time, Beijing's policy banks regularly finance projects regarded as too risky by Western counterparts, and the decline in commodities prices has exacerbated that risk.[114] China's existing loans to friendly governments in Zimbabwe, Venezuela, and Sri Lanka already portend tens of billions of dollars in potential losses. China provided tens of billions of dollars in loans and aid to Venezuela between 2007 and early 2016, and, as of mid-2017, the latter still owed China $62 billion.[115] With oil prices stuck under $60 per barrel and Venezuela unable to service its debts fully, Beijing has been forced to accept debt restructuring.

OBOR represents a massive and unprecedented expansion of connected lending to international borrowers that enmeshes the already deeply indebted Chinese banking system in some of the world's most precarious economic and political environments. The lending program's sheer size requires Chinese government and party organs, many with little experience in international operations, to vet scores of projects across a myriad of regulatory, linguistic, and cultural environments. Many poor countries, especially in Africa, are happy to take cheap Chinese loans now and let future leaders and citizens pay them back. China's response has often been to grant loan forgiveness and then provide more loans, creating a serious moral hazard problem. Many governments are banking on China's continued largesse and are thus happy to take whatever they are offered. However, Beijing, which saw its foreign reserves drop by more than 20 percent between 2014 and 2017, cannot write off bad loans *ad infinitum*.

OBOR could also open new opportunities for fraud and corruption. China, which itself ranks an unimpressive 79 on Transparency International's 2016 corruption index, is building hundreds of projects in some of the least accountable countries in the world, such as Turkmenistan (154), Kyrgyzstan (136), Cambodia (156), Myanmar (136), and Pakistan (116). On an OECD 8-point scale of risk by recipient country, the portfolio of states that China's banks extended loans between 2013 and 2015 entailed an average risk rating a full point higher (i.e., riskier) than the World Bank's.[116] Xi himself seemed to recognize the challenges when he called for a "stable, sustainable and risk-controllable financial security system" to supervise the OBOR initiative.[117]

In the political realm, Chinese diplomacy has generally been successful in developing relationships and gaining influence. Beijing has certainly seen failures and setbacks, and has addressed such problems by expanding the depth and breadth of its bilateral political relations with developing states and through existing and newly created multilateral regional organizations. By institutionalizing relations via diplomatic arrangements, party-to-party dialogues, economic agreements, military forums, and person-to-person exchanges, Beijing has created numerous overlapping personal networks that enable the rapid return to normal relations if unexpected crises disrupt the relationship.

China's overseas image is moderately favorable, though it varies widely, depending on location and issue. According to a 2017 Pew survey conducted in 38 countries, an average of 47 percent of respondents hold a favorable image of China, compared to 38 percent holding an unfavorable view. The United States was viewed favorably by 50 percent, down sharply from 2015, when 69 percent viewed it favorably. China is viewed most favorably in Africa (average of 58 percent in six countries surveyed) and Latin America (49 percent average in seven countries), while the perception is less positive in regions closer to China, where security concerns weigh heavily, and in most of the Middle East, where many have reservations about China's treatment of its Muslim Uighur population. A separate 2015 Pew survey found that just 34 percent had a favorable impression of China's respect for human rights.[118]

Influence, defined as the ability to bring about changes in another state's intended behavior in ways that advance one's own aims, is notoriously difficult to measure, as it involves counter-factual analysis. That said, China appears to have successfully influenced other states on issues of marginal importance to the other state, where the costs of taking the desired action are small. Vague official statements supporting China's position on the South China Sea, for example, are costless for African and Middle Eastern states. Similarly, acquiescence to Beijing's single-minded efforts to marginalize Taipei and the Dalai Lama also have minimal political costs for states beyond China's immediate periphery. South Africa, however, suffered a minor indignity when it acceded to China's demands and refused the Dalai Lama a visa, thus prompting the cancelation of a conference of Nobel laureates in Pretoria.[119]

Conversely, there are few clear cases of China's ability to translate its combined economic, political, military, and soft influence into favorable outcomes when the stakes are high for the other state. Yet, China's efforts to minimize opposition to its consolidation of its territorial claims in the South China Sea arguably represent at least a partial success. Beijing has achieved a *fait accompli* in the South China Sea by reclaiming 3,200 acres of land on seven features and thereby turning reefs and rocks into significant military outposts.[120] Such measures have alarmed the states most directly affected, including Vietnam and the Philippines, and fueled wariness in larger regional states like Indonesia and Malaysia. Beijing has responded by offering a blizzard of trade, aid, and arms deals and by leveraging its asymmetric relationship with Cambodia and Laos to thwart joint statements by ASEAN.

China's impact on the economic, governance, and environmental welfare of the partner states in the developing world is mixed. China is, by far, the largest trade partner of developing states in every part of the world, and the loan portfolio of its policy banks and regional funds exceeds that of all Western multilateral banks combined.[121] Chinese activity is stimulating growth and building infrastructure in regions that are chronically short of capital and investment. Even in Southeast Asia, where Japan, the United States, and other Western countries are major actors, most states suffer from infrastructure financing deficits.[122] In sub-Saharan Africa, China's aid and investments are distributed across a wider range of recipient states than is assistance from Western states and international organizations. Some of the difference is explained by Beijing's willingness to engage the least savory African regimes, but it also reflects the more limited (and focused) interests of Western firms, states, and international organizations in Africa.

Needless to say, countries have been affected differently by their engagement with China. During the commodities boom of the 2000s and early 2010s, growth rates rose rapidly among resource-rich countries. At the same time, imports from

China had significant displacement effects on domestic African and Latin American producers of labor intensive manufactured products, like textiles and food processing.[123] The pattern was more mixed in East Asia, where the region's integrated production chains contribute to the specialization among states.[124] Roughly 50 percent of Indonesian exports to China are raw materials, while Taiwan, Korea, and Malaysia export mostly intermediate, capital, or consumer goods.[125]

China's corporations have a poor record of environmental protection at home, and they have contributed to degradation overseas, especially when local governments suffer from poor capacity, weak oversight, or endemic corruption. Some firms have been accused of cutting corners, ignoring safety standards, using secondhand or low-quality materials and equipment, and building environmentally destructive projects. Complaints have come from Laos, Vietnam, and Cambodia regarding environmental damage and droughts from Chinese hydropower projects along the Mekong River; from Indonesia regarding an ill-fated, over-budget coal power plant and a failed high-speed rail project; from Myanmar regarding Chinese firms clear-cutting forests; and from Korea and West Africa about harm done to the marine environment by Chinese trawlers' fishing practices.[126]

Facing growing public resentment at home, the Chinese government has become more attuned to environmental issues. It has passed new environmental regulations and promoted the State Environmental Protection Administration to ministerial status, changing its name to the Ministry of Environmental Protection in 2008.[127] Both the Chinese state and its companies have adopted or signed international compacts designed to protect the environment overseas.[128] Nevertheless, enforcement responsibilities and oversight remain weak at home, and Beijing has even more difficulties policing its corporations—especially small and mid-sized private firms—overseas. China's lack of conditionality, lax oversight, and poor corporate citizenship contribute to, or at least do not discourage, rent seeking and corruption in partner states.[129] The problem is likely to worsen as rising labor costs in China push more "dirty" manufacturing to relocate to cheaper and less well-regulated developing countries.

China's expansion in the developing world may also adversely affect the spread of liberal values. After a remarkable wave of democratization from the mid-1970s to the mid-2000s, the tide appears to have turned. According to the 2017 Freedom House report, those countries experiencing a net decline in freedom have exceeded the number experiencing a net gain every year between 2006 and 2016. In 2016, 67 countries saw declines while just 36 improved.[130] In some countries, like Russia, Venezuela, and Zimbabwe, autocrats have maintained the facade of democracy (e.g., elections and private press outlets) while stripping them of all meaning.[131] Others, like Ethiopia, seem to have borrowed more directly from China's authoritarian state-led development model.

China's attractiveness as an economic model has increased due to its sustained economic growth and as neoliberal economic practices have lost the confidence of policymakers in developing states—particularly in the wake of the global financial crisis of 2008. More recently, however, reduced growth rates and rising debt levels in China have diminished the attractiveness of the "China model." Moreover, with the decline in commodities prices, Chinese investments and debt financing for resource-related infrastructure has saddled some countries with unsustainable debt, again diminishing the popularity of China as both partner and model. Only time will tell whether the billions of dollars Beijing has spent on enhancing and projecting its soft power—the Confucius Institutes, CPC cadre training programs, Xinhua media training, film festivals, think-tank exchanges, student scholarships, etc.—will succeed in improving foreign perceptions of China.

Implications for the United States

Beijing and Washington's relations with the developing world are not primarily zero-sum. To a significant extent, interests are parallel—that is, separate and non-overlapping in either a competitive or cooperative sense. Chinese timber purchases from Africa, for instance, are a link in the global supply chain. They supply Chinese furniture manufactures, which, in turn, sell their finished products to furniture stores from Boston to Beijing to Bangkok. But although Washington and Beijing pursue their economic and political interests vis-à-vis developing states in ways that often neither directly benefit nor harm the other, that dynamic could change if the Sino–U.S. relationship evolves dramatically for the worse.

In some important respects, American and Chinese interests coincide. Both benefit from stability and prosperity in the developing world. Yet they attribute these outcomes to different sources. Washington has long maintained that free and fair elections and an open society are essential for long-term political stability, while Beijing believes that economic security precedes political development.[132] The bloody aftermath of the Arab Spring has dampened Washington's interest in actively supporting democratic change through revolutionary means, though it continues to promote democratic and liberal values. After the election of Donald Trump, it remains to be seen whether Washington will revert to traditional modes of active interventionism or adopt a more isolationist "America first" foreign policy.

In the context of U.S. military operations in the Middle East, the United States benefits from China's efforts to engage, stabilize, and invest in Central Asia. Although Beijing is primarily motivated by a desire to insulate Xinjiang from radicalizing influences based in Central Asian states and provide security for Chinese projects and personnel, its efforts are no less in U.S. interests. American and Chinese interests align in their joint effort to buttress the Afghan government, law enforcement cooperation to combat narcotics smuggling, and anti-piracy patrols off the Somali coast. American companies and investors also benefit from improved global growth and improved economic efficiencies that result from China's policy banks financing tens of billions of dollars' worth of transportation infrastructure around the developing world.

Yet, some Chinese activities in the developing world do threaten peace and stability. China's massive land reclamation projects in the South China Sea have changed the status quo and tested U.S. security assurances to its partners. Its actions have undermined confidence that Beijing's territorial ambitions will remain limited, and that as its military power grows it will not employ coercive means to secure Chinese interests at the expense of other states. The United States and its allies have yet to find an appropriate response to China's island building. Washington is reluctant to become too deeply involved in territorial disputes and instead hopes to lead from behind. Yet regional states lack the capacity, either independently or in combination, to coordinate such efforts without strong U.S. backing. The United States is likely to continue supporting the UN tribunal's 2016 decision that challenges the legality of Chinese claims and to assert freedom of navigation patrols near the Spratly Islands. If Chinese efforts to alter the *status quo* resume, Washington is likely to take additional counter measures, increasing the possibility of military confrontation.

The United States would be well served to deepen its presence and influence in the developing world. By many standards, U.S. engagement with and assistance to the developing world in areas from health care and food aid to institution-building, environmental leadership, military engagement, media, NGOs, and a raft of other areas remain deeper and better considered than China's. Yet many of these efforts gain little attention and are not well understood. Of much greater concern, U.S. efforts could be severely undercut should funding for the U.S. Department of State, the U.S. Agency for International Development, and other parts of the U.S. foreign policy establishment be significantly reduced. The U.S. government is already far less involved in promoting trade and investment than is China. This puts U.S. firms at a disadvantage in competing with Chinese counterparts, and it undermines the larger effort to maintain U.S. relevance and influence in the developing world. Washington should increase funding for the Foreign Commercial Service, U.S. Ex–Im Bank, and other federal programs that improve U.S. corporations' international competitiveness. The United States has the resources to maintain its global leadership position; the question in these uncertainly political times is whether it will choose to do so.

Conclusion

China's interests in the developing world remain primarily economic, but political and security interests have gained increasing prominence, especially since Xi Jinping's accession to Party leadership in late 2012 precipitated a new impetus to "strive for achievements." China's sheer size and its ability to mobilize resources on a grand scale provide it unique leverage. Beijing's strategy has been largely successful in achieving its aims, but its policies have sometimes met with indifferent or uncertain outcomes. China's policy banks have greatly expanded developing states' access to capital, but with few checks to guard against abuses by host country leaders. In ways described above, Beijing has become increasingly adept at hedging against most forms of acute, short-term political risk (i.e., regime change), yet many Chinese investments and loan financing deals entail significant long-term repayment risk. Beijing's non-interference principle would seem to preclude the use of conditionality or military force to enforce contracts. Yet, if a global economic crisis were to precipitate a raft of defaults, or vice versa, the unprecedented size of OBOR lending would likely require policy responses from Beijing that further enmesh it in the politics of foreign countries. In the final analysis, each country's ability to derive long-term benefits from its relationship with China will vary considerably based largely on its leaders' capacity, honesty, and willingness to assert their country's long-run national interests.

Notes

1 Xi Jinping, "President Xi's Speech to Davos in Full," *World Economic Forum*, January 17, 2017.
2 At the National Foreign Investment Conference on December 24, 1997, President Jiang Zemin said: "It's important to combine 'bringing in' and 'going out' ("引进来"和"走出去"), both are indispensable." This appears to be the first time that "going out" was mentioned publicly. Prior to sanctioning at the central government level, however, several provinces (e.g., Guangdong) had already begun to encourage provincial level firms to seek economic opportunities abroad. The first Central government publication calling on "SOEs to 'go out'" was published by the State Council on February 1, 1999 as Document 17, *Circular Encouraging Enterprises to Carry Out Overseas Processing and Assembling of Materials*. www.gov.cn/english/official/2005-07/29/content_18334.htm. "Going out" was publicly touted by President Jiang Zemin at the September 1999 Fortune Global Forum in Shanghai under the theme "China: The Next 50 years," and formally ratified in 2000 at the 3rd session of the 9th National People's Congress.
3 For more on this concept see: Michael Swaine, "Xi Jinping's Address to the Central Conference on Work Relating to Foreign Affairs: Assessing and Advancing Major- Power Diplomacy with Chinese Characteristics," *China Leadership Monitor*, no. 46 (March 19, 2015): 1–19.
4 Mark Weisbrot and Jake Johnston, "Voting Share Reform at the IMF: Will it Make a Difference," Center for Economic and Policy Research paper, April 2016.
5 "China's Xi Jinping Seizes Role as Leader on Globalization," *The Wall Street Journal*, January 17, 2017; "China Now the Unlikely Champion of Free Trade in the Trump Era," *The Globe and Mail*, January 20, 2017.
6 On the Chinese use of the term "core national interests," see Michael D. Swaine, "China's Assertive Behavior, Part One: On 'Core Interests'," *China Leadership Monitor*, no. 34 (Winter 2011): 1–25. See Chinese definition at The State Council Information Office of the People's Republic of China, "China's Peaceful Development" (white paper), September 6, 2011, available from the State Council Information Office of the People's Republic of China website.
7 As Xi Jinping said at Davos in 2017: "China has come this far because the Chinese people have, under the leadership of the Communist Party of China, blazed a development path that suits China's actual conditions." See Xi, "President Xi's Speech to Davos."
8 Deng, Xiaoping. "Speeches in SEZs from January 18 to February 21, 1992." *People's Daily*, December 29, 2000.
9 Xi, "President Xi's Speech to Davos."
10 Yuval Atsmon, Jean-Frederic Kuentz, and Jeongmin Seong, "Building Brands in Emerging Markets," *McKinsey Quarterly*, September 2012.
11 Andreas Fuchs and Nils-Hendrik Klann, "Paying a Visit: The Dalai Lama Effect on International Trade," *Journal of International Economics* 91, no. 1 (September 2013): 164–177; Nick Macfie, "China Slaps New Fees on Mongolian Exporters Amid Dalai Lama Row," *Reuters*, December 1, 2016; Robin Yapp and Sao Paulo, "Dalai Lama Snubbed in Brazil After Chinese Fury at Mexico Talks," *The Telegraph*, September 18, 2011; "Thailand Rejects Chinese Pressure Over Dalai Lama," *United Press International*, February 11, 1993.

12 Wang Wen and Chen Xiaochen, "Who Supports China in the South China Sea and Why," *The Diplomat*, July 27, 2016.

13 George J. Gilboy and Eric Heginbotham, *Chinese and Indian Strategic Behavior: Growing Power and Alarm* (Cambridge: Cambridge University Press, 2012), 72.

14 John Pomfret, "U.S. Takes a Tougher Tone With China," *Washington Post*, July 30, 2010.

15 GDP estimates are from International Monetary Fund (hereinafter referred to as IMF).

16 IMF, Direction of Trade Statistics.

17 He Yafei, "China's Major-Country Diplomacy Progresses on All Fronts," *China.org.cn*, March 23, 2016.

18 "The 100 Largest Banks in the World," *Banks Around the World*, updated May 7, 2017. By a different accounting, Chinese banks held six of the top 23 positions (including all of the top four) in 2016. Will Martin, "These Are the 23 Biggest Global Banks—All with More than \$1 Trillion in Assets," *Business Insider*, April 21, 2017.

19 Eve Cary, "SOEs Declining Role in China's Foreign Investment," *The Diplomat*, July 3, 2013; "China's Overseas Direct Investment Surges 53.3% in First Ten Months," *China Daily*, November 18, 2016.

20 See, for example, Wenjie Chen, David Dollar, and Heiwai Tang, "Why Is China Investing in Africa? Evidence From the Firm Level," The Brookings Institute, August 2015.

21 Xi Jinping used the phrase three times in his 2014 Foreign Affairs Work Conference (FAWC) speech. See "The Central Conference on Work Relating to Foreign Affairs was Held in Beijing," Ministry of Foreign Affairs of the People's Republic of China, November 29, 2014.

22 Kallol Bhattacherjee, "India, Pakistan Become Full Members of SCO," *The Hindu*, June 9, 2017.

23 State Council of the People's Republic of China, "Timeline of China–ASEAN Relations over 25 Years," *English.gov.cn*, September 7, 2016.

24 "China–CELAC Trade to Hit \$500 Billion: Xi," *Xinhua*, January 8, 2015.

25 For more on the significance of this, see the chapter in this volume by R. Evan Ellis.

26 Joshua Eisenman and David H. Shinn, interview with Hao Rui, General Manager Research and Development, China–Africa Development Fund, June 22, 2017.

27 Yun Sun, "The Sixth Forum on China–Africa Cooperation: New Agenda and Approach?" The Brookings Institution, January 2015.

28 Xu Xin, "Backgrounder: China-Arab States Cooperation Forum," *Xinhua*, May 12, 2016.

29 "Press Communique of the First Ministerial Meeting of the Strategic Dialogue Between the People's Republic of China and the Cooperation Council for the Arab States of the Gulf," Ministry of Foreign Affairs of the People's Republic of China, June 4, 2010.

30 He Yafei, "China's Major-Country Diplomacy Progresses on All Fronts," *China.org.cn*, March 23, 2016; Feng Zhongping and Huang Jing, "China's Strategic Partnership Diplomacy: Engaging With a Changing World," European Strategic Partnership Observatory (ESPO) Working Paper, no. 8, June 2014.

31 Xiao Ren, "China as an Institution-Builder: The Case of the AIIB," *Pacific Review* 29, no. 3 (2016): 436.

32 "The Case for Reform at the World Bank," *Financial Times*, August 10, 2016.

33 China has, for example, lobbied African states to demand veto power, making it less likely that the proposals for reform will be accepted. Julian Borger and Bastien Inzaurralde, "Russian Vetoes Are Putting UN Security Council's Legitimacy at Risk, Says US," *The Guardian*, September 23, 2015.

34 "India's Alliance With Japan for UNSC Hampering its Chances," *The New Indian Express*, October 18, 2016.

35 Mwangi S. Kimenyi and Zenia A. Lewis, "New Approaches from Washington to Doing Business With Africa," *This Is Africa Online*.

36 Joong Shik Kang and Wei Liao, "Chinese Imports: What's Behind the Slowdown," IMF Working Paper, May 2016.

37 "China's Trade Surplus Down 9.1% in 2016," *China Daily*, January 13, 2017.

38 IMF, Direction of Trade Statistics (DOTS).

39 Foreign reserves continued to accumulate rapidly through June 2014, when they reached $3.993 trillion, before falling to about 3.051 trillion in November 2016. PRC State Administration of Foreign Exchange website, viewed December 12, 2016.

40 "Genghao di shishi 'zouchuqu' zhanlu" 更好地实施走出去战略 [Better Enforce "Going Out" Strategy], the Central People's Government of the People's Republic of China website, March 15, 2006.

41 National Bureau of Statistics of China, 中国统计年鉴 [China Statistical Yearbook], Beijing, various years. Current dollar figures converted to 2016 constant using GDP deflator.

42 Offshore financial centers include Hong Kong, Singapore, the Cayman Islands, and the Virgin Islands. The developed states of Asia are not included in the figures presented.

43 "China's CNOOC to Buy Nexen for $15.1 Billion," *Financial Post*, July 23, 2012.

44 "The African Investment Report 2015: An FDI Destination on the Rise," *Financial Times* report, 2015.

45 "The African Investment Report 2016: Foreign Investment Broadens Its Base," *Financial Times* report, 2016.

46 Association of Southeast Asian Nations, "Foreign Direct Investment (FDI) Dashboard."

47 The third bank, the Agricultural Development Bank of China, has a domestic focus.

48 James Kynge, Jonathan Wheatley, Lucy Hornby, Christian Shepherd and Andres Schipani, "China Rethinks Developing World Largesse as Deals Sour," *Financial Times*, October 13, 2016.

49 "Chronology of China's Belt and Road Initiative," *Xinhuanet*, March 28, 2015.

50 Rob Koepp, *"One Belt, One Road": An Economic Roadmap* (Beijing: The Economist Corporate Network, March 2016).

51 "推动共建丝绸之路经济带和21世纪海上丝绸之路的愿景与行动" [Vision and Actions on Jointly Building Silk Road Economic Belt and 21st-Century Maritime Silk Road], National Development and Reform Commission of the PRC, March 28, 2015.

52 Jane Perlez, "China Creates a World Bank of Its Own, and the U.S. Balks," *New York Times*, December 4, 2015; Mike Callaghan, "The $100 Billion AIIB Opens for Business: Will China's Multilateral Ambitions Soar or Sour?" *Lowey Institute*, January 19, 2016.

53 "Why China Is Creating a New 'World Bank' for Asia," *The Economist*, November 11, 2014.

54 "China to Establish $40 Billion Silk Road Infrastructure Fund," *Reuters*, November 8, 2014.

55 "Our Bulldozers, Our Rules," *Economist*, July 2, 2016. On May 14, 2017, at the OBOR Forum in Beijing, President Xi increased the Silk Road Fund from $40 billion to $55 billion.

56 James Kynge, "How the Silk Road Plans Will Be financed," *Financial Times*, May 9, 2016. The Export–Import Bank lent $80 billion for projects in 49 countries in 2015, compared to $27.1 billion for the Asian Development Bank (and less than $2 billion for the AIIB).

57 This conclusion is based on interviews with businessmen in Beijing and Shanghai in May and June 2017. Total funding, which will primarily involve debt financing, remains uncertain but has been estimated at between $1 trillion and $4 trillion. "Our Bulldozers, Our Rules." "推动共建丝绸之路经济带和21世纪海上丝绸之路的愿景与行动" [Vision and Actions on Jointly Building Silk Road Economic Belt and 21st-Century Maritime Silk Road], National Development and Reform Commission of the PRC, March 28, 2015.

58 James T. Areddy, "China Touts $14.4 Billion in Foreign Aid, Half of Which Went to Africa," *The Wall Street Journal*, July 10, 2014.

59 Information Office of the State Council of the People's Republic of China, "China's Foreign Aid (2014)," July 2014.

60 Information Office of the State Council of the People's Republic of China, "China's Foreign Aid (2014)," July 2014.

61 Alex Dreher, Andreas Fuchs, Roland Hodler, Bradley C. Parks, Paul A. Raschky, and Michael J. Tierney, "Aid on Demand: African Leaders and the Geography of China's Foreign Assistance," Aid Data, Working Paper 3, October 2016.

62 Angus Deaton, "Why Poor Countries Need Strong Government More than Anything Else," *Market Watch*, October 12, 2015.
63 Ron Matthews, Xiaojuan Ping, and Li Ling, "Learning from China's Foreign Aid Model," *The Diplomat*, August 25, 2016.
64 Mateen Haider and Irfan Haider, "Economic Corridor in Focus as Pakistan, China Sign 51 MoUs," *Dawn*, April 20, 2015.
65 Winslow Robertson and Lina Benabdallah, "China Pledged to Invest $60 billion in Africa. Here's What that Means," *Washington Post*, January 7, 2016.
66 Andreo Calonzo and Cecilia Yap, "China Visit Helps Duterte Reap Funding Deals Worth $24 Billion," *Bloomberg*, October 21, 2016.
67 Ben O. de Vera, "China Commits Financing for 12 PH Infra Projects," *Philippine Daily Inquirer*, October 2, 2017.
68 "ASEAN Deadlocked on South China Sea, Cambodia Blocks Statement," *Reuters*, July 26, 2016; "Cambodia, China Sign Trade Deal," *Xinhua*, September 9, 2016.
69 Michael D. Swaine, "Chinese Views on Global Governance Since 2008–2009: Not Much New," *China Leadership Monitor*, no. 49 (Winter 2016): 1–13.
70 Brantly Womack, "Asymmetry Theory and China's Concept of Multipolarity," *Journal of Contemporary China*, 13(39), May 2004.
71 "BRICS Development Bank to Lend $2.5 Billion Next Year," *Reuters*, October 16, 2016.
72 Niu Haibin, "A Chinese Perspective on the BRICS in 2015," *Global Memo*, February 6, 2015.
73 "G20: BRICS Muscle Up Over Russia," *The Interpreter*, March 31, 2014.
74 Niu, "A Chinese Perspective on the BRICS in 2015."
75 "First Meeting of the BRICS Joint Working Group on Counter Terrorism," Ministry of External Affairs, Government of India, September 14, 2016.
76 "Political, Security Cooperation on BRICS Agenda in 2017: China," *The Hindu*, March 9, 2017.
77 Huifang Tian, "The BRICS and the G20," *China & World Economy*, Vol. 24, Issue 4, 2016. See also, "BRICS Leaders' Informal Meeting on the Margins of the G20 Summit," Ministry of Foreign Affairs of the People's Republic of China, September 4, 2016.
78 "7 Reasons the SDGs will be Better than the MDGs," *The Guardian*, September 26, 2015.
79 Ren Mu, "China's Non-intervention Policy in UNSC Sanctions in the 21st Century: The Cases of Libya, North Korea, and Zimbabwe," *Ritsumeikan International Affairs* 12 (2014): 101–134.
80 "China Counting Financial Losses in Libya," *Global Times*, March 4, 2011.
81 Jane Onyanga-Omara and John Bacon, "Russia, China veto U.N. plan for Syrian sanctions," *USA Today*, February 28, 2017.
82 Stephanie Findlay, "South Africa's Ruling ANC Looks to Learn from Chinese Communist Party," *Time*, November 24, 2014; "Beijing Will Increase Sway Over African Policy-making," *Oxford Analytics Daily Brief*, August 8, 2016.
83 Yun Sun, "Political Party Training: China's Ideological Push Into Africa," Brookings Institution, July 5, 2016.
84 Lecture by Arkebe Oqubay School of Public and International Affairs, Fudan University, China, 26 May 2017.
85 Iginio Gagliardone, "China and the Shaping of African Information Societies," in *Africa and China: How Africans and Their Governments Are Shaping Relations with China*, ed. A. W. Gadzala (Lanham, MD: Rowman and Littlefield, 2015), 45–59; Iginio Gagliardone, "China as a persuader: CCTV Africa's First Steps in the African Media Sphere," *Ecquid Novi: African Journalism Studies* 34, no. 3 (2013): 29; Yu-shan Wu, "The Rise of China's State-led Media Dynasty in Africa," *South African Institute of International Affairs Occasional Paper*, no. 117 (2012): 24.
86 Shinn and Eisenman, *China and Africa*, 201–203; "Forum on China–Africa Media Cooperation," *CCTV*, 2012.
87 Alpha Daffae Senkpeni, "China Launches Studies Exchange Program for African Journalists," *Front Page Africa*, March 2017.

88 "China's National Defense (white paper)," Information Office of the State Council of the People's Republic of China website, July 1998. On the development of the concept prior to 1998 and its definition, see Anil Kumar, "New Security Concept of China: An Analysis," Institute of Peace and Conflict Studies Series on Inside China, 2012.

89 "China's National Defense in 2008," Information Office of the State Council of the People's Republic of China website, January 2009.

90 For various Chinese definitions, see Jin Canrong and Wang Bo "Youguan Zhongguo tese junshi waijiao de lilun sikao"有关中国特色军事外交的理论思考 [On the Theories of China's Military Diplomacy], *Taipingyang xuebao*太平洋学报 [Pacific Journal] 23, no. 5 (May 2015): 17–25.

91 Luo Zheng, "Zhongguo junshi waijiao xian daguo dandang, jinnian canjia 24 chang zhongwai lianyan" 中国军事外交显大国担当 今年参加24场中外联演 [Chinese Military Diplomacy Demonstrates Great Power Role, Participates in 24 Combined Exercises with Foreign Militaries This Year], *PLA Daily*解放军报, December 23, 2015.

92 Courtney J. Fung, "China's Troop Contributions to U.N. Peacekeeping," *USIP Peace Brief*, July 26, 2016.

93 Fung, "China's Troop Contributions to U.N. Peacekeeping."

94 United Nations, "Contributors to United Nations Peacekeeping Operations As of August 31, 2017," accessed November 2017.

95 Eric Heginbotham et al., *The U.S.–China Military Scorecard: Forces, Geography, and the Evolving Balance of Power 1996–2017* (Santa Monica, CA: RAND Corporation, 2015); Roger Cliff, *China's Military Power: Assessing Current and Future Capabilities* (Cambridge University Press, 2015). Although China's "anti-access, area denial" capabilities (a Western appellation) have garnered many of the headlines, China now has very substantial conventional forces. The PLA Air Force and Navy operate about 800 fourth-generation fighter aircraft, the PLA Navy's submarine force includes about 40 modern submarines, and the surface fleet is moving from a primarily frigate force to one built around destroyers.

96 Richard A. Bitzinger, "China's Double-Digit Defense Growth," *Foreign Affairs*, March 19, 2015.

97 Roy D. Kamphausen, "China's Military Operations Other Than War: The Military Legacy of Hu Jintao," paper presented at SIPRI Conference, April 2013; Cheng Jian, Mo Jun and Lan Liqing, "Xinshiji xinjieduan wojun lishi shiming zhongyao lunshu de jiazhi he yiyi" 新世纪新阶段我军历史使命重要论述的价值和意义 [The Great Value and Meaning of Historic Missions of Our Military in the New Century], *Xinhua*, September 27, 2005.

98 "China's National Defense in 2008," Information Office of the State Council of the People's Republic of China website, January 2009.

99 "The Diversified Employment of China's Armed Forces," *Xinhua*, April 16, 2013. Some PLA officers have published articles advocating the military expand its capabilities to rescue Chinese nationals under threat abroad. See Han Xudong, "Guofang daxue jiaoshou: baohu haiwai Zhongguoren jidai wozu zhunjian junshi liliang jieru" 国防大学教授: 保护海外中国人 亟待我组建准军事力量介入 [Chinese National Defense University Professor: We Must Urgently Establish Military Forces for Intervention in Order to Protect Overseas Chinese Citizens], *Global Times* 环球时报, October 25, 2011; Yue Gang, "Zhongguo junli ying hanwei haiwai liyi, juebu rongren paihuai beiju zaiyan" 中国军力增长应捍卫海外利益 绝不容忍排华悲剧再演 [The PLA Must Protect China's Overseas Interests and Never Tolerate Any Anti-Chinese Tragedy Again], *Sina News*, April 18, 2013.

100 Michael D. Swaine and M. Taylor Fravel, "China's Assertive Behavior—Part Two: The Maritime Periphery," *China Leadership Monitor* 35 (2011): 1–29.

101 "The Diversified Employment."

102 Zhou Bo, "Station Looks Beyond Anti-Piracy Mission," *China Daily USA*, March 18, 2016.

103 Shen Dingli, "Don't Shun the Idea of Setting up Overseas Military Bases," *China.org.cn*, January 28, 2010.

104 "China Opens First Overseas Base in Djibouti," *Aljazeera*, August 1, 2017.

105 SIPRI Arms Transfer Database, www.sipri.org/databases/armstransfers, accessed January 15, 2017.

106 "Sudan's Bashir in China for Talks," *Al Jazeera*, June 27, 2011; "China's Xi Calls Indicted Sudan's Bashir 'Old Friend'," *Al Arabiya*, September 1, 2015.

107 Feng Wenyan, ed., "Xi Jinping tan guojia wenhua ruanshili: zengqiang zuo Zhongguoren de guqi he diqi" 习近平谈国家文化软实力：增强做中国人的骨气和底气 [Xi Jinping Discusses National Cultural Soft Power: Strengthening Chinese Character and Integrity], *Xinhua*, June 25, 2015.

108 Joseph Nye coined the term "soft power" to describe the importance of U.S. cultural and political influence. See Joseph S. Nye, Jr., *Bound to Lead: The Changing Nature of American Power* (New York: Basic Books, 1990).

109 See Goh on influence in different types of cases and for the "multiplier" effect. Evelyn Goh, "The Modes of China's Influence: Cases from Southeast Asia," *Asian Survey* 54, no. 5 (September/October 2014): 825–848.

110 Yu Yuanquan "中国文化软实力建设任重道远" [Shouldering the Heavy Responsibility of Building China's Soft Power], 对外大转播 [*International Communications*], 2007 (1); and 陈新光 [Chen Xinguang], "美国软实力衰退于中国软实力提升" [U.S. Soft Power Weakening, Chinese Soft Power Rising], 中国日报 [*China Daily*], June 23, 2015.

111 Hagar Cohen, "Australian Universities the Latest Battleground in Chinese Soft Power Offensive," *Australian Broadcasting Corporation*, October 13, 2016; Ron Grossman, "U. of C. Profs Want China-Funded Institute Evicted from Campus," *Chicago Tribune*, May 4, 2014; Javier Espinoza, "'UK Schools Advance Chinese Propaganda,' Activists Say," *The Telegraph*, March 30, 2015. Not all agree with the negative assessment. See, for example, Hilary Lamb, "Rethink the Influence of Confucius Institutes, Suggests Study," *Times Higher Education*, February 2, 2017.

112 2016年度我国来华留学生情况统计 [2016 Statistics Regarding Foreign Students in China], Ministry of Education of the People's Republic of China, March 1, 2017.

113 Zhang Xin, "China is Attracting a Massive Influx of International Students, but What Are the Policies in Place to Help Them Stick Around?" *Global Times*, April 21, 2016.

114 "China Rethinks Developing World Largesse as Deals Sour," *Financial Times*, October 13, 2016.

115 "China Could Have a Say on Venezuela's Future," *Bloomberg*, July 18, 2017.

116 "China Rethinks Developing World Largesse."

117 "Xi Calls for Advancing Belt and Road Initiative," *Xinhua*, August 18, 2016.

118 Richard Wike, Bruce Stokes and Jacob Poushter, "Global Publics Back U.S. on Fighting ISIS, But Are Critical of Post-9/11 Torture—Part 2: Views of China and the Global Balance of Power," *Pew Research Center*, June 23, 2015.

119 Karin Brulliard, "Controversy Over Dalai Lama Leads to Cancellation of S. Africa Peace Conference," *The Washington Post*, March 25, 2009.

120 "Military and Security Developments Involving the People's Republic of China 2016," Department of Defense, April 2016.

121 James Kynge, Jonathan Wheatley, Lucy Hornby, Christian Shepherd and Andres Schipani, "China Rethinks Developing World Largesse as Deals Sour," *Financial Times*, October 13, 2016.

122 "How China's Belt and Road Is Transforming ASEAN," *South China Morning Post*, January 8, 2017.

123 Matthias Busse, Caren Endrogan and Henning Muhlen, "China's Impact on Africa— the Role of Trade, FDI, and Aid," Ruhr University Institute of Development Research and Development Policy Working Paper, 2014.

124 Ronald U. Mendoza, Keven C. Chua, and Monica M. Melchor, "Revealed Comparative Advantage, International Production Chain and the Evolving ASEAN–China Trade Linkages," *Journal of Asian Development Studies* 4, no. 1 (March 2015): 23–36.

125 Sumedh Deorukhkar and Le Xia, "Gauging the Impact of China's Growth Slowdown on Emerging Asia," *BBVA Research, Asia Economic Watch*, March 2, 2016.

126 Joshua Eisenman and Devin Stewart, "China's New Silk Road Is Getting Muddy," *Foreign Policy*, January 9, 2017.

127 David H. Shinn, "The Environmental Impact of China's Investment in Africa," *Cornell International Law Review* 49, no. 1 (Winter 2016): 25–67.

128 Carla P. Freeman and Yiqian Yu, "China as an Environmental Actor in the Developing World—China's Role in Deforestation and the Timber Trade in Developing Countries," in *Handbook on China and Developing Countries*, ed., Carla P. Freeman (Cheltenham, UK: Edward Elgar Publishing, 2015).

129 Frank Stroker, "Perceptions of Chinese Firms in Africa Tainted by Corruption and Other Abuses," *Corporate Compliance Trends*, February 27, 2015.

130 Arch Puddington and Tyler Roylace, *Freedom in the World 2017: Populists and Autocrats: The Dual Threat to Global Democracy* (Washington, DC: Freedom House, 2017).

131 Javier Correles, "The Authoritarian Resurgence: Autocratic Legalism in Venezuela," *Journal of Democracy* 26, no. 2 (April 2015): 37–51; Lilia Shevtsova, "The Authoritarian Resurgence: Forward to the Past in Russia," *Journal of Democracy* 26, no. 2 (April 2015): 22–37.

132 Some other East Asian states, including Japan, have views on political development and economic aid that are similar to those of China. Maiko Ichihara, *Understanding Japanese Democracy Assistance*, Carnegie Institute paper, March 2013.

APPENDIX I

Data

(1) Trade Statistics: Regional (billions $)

	2000	2001	2002	2003	2004	2005	2006	2007
World								
Imports	225.17	243.57	295.44	412.84	560.81	660.22	791.79	956.26
Exports	249.21	266.71	325.75	438.37	593.65	762.35	969.22	1218.15
% Growth		7.57	21.74	37.03	35.63	23.22	23.79	23.48
Developed World								
Imports	169.54	183.44	218.22	293.16	387.11	433.80	504.87	595.29
Exports	209.14	221.61	268.42	357.79	480.50	610.09	754.18	911.55
% of China's Trade	79.82	79.38	78.34	76.47	75.15	73.38	71.50	69.30
% Growth		6.96	20.14	33.76	33.28	20.32	20.61	19.68
Developing World								
Imports	48.33	51.07	61.85	94.05	134.09	170.48	212.52	273.52
Exports	39.39	44.20	56.54	79.72	112.02	150.54	212.65	304.04
% of China's Trade	18.49	18.67	19.06	20.41	21.32	22.57	24.14	26.56
% Growth		8.62	24.27	46.77	41.63	30.44	32.44	35.84
Regions of Developing World								
Africa								
Imports	5.54	4.65	5.37	8.35	15.63	21.09	28.74	36.21
Exports	5.00	5.97	6.91	10.12	13.72	18.60	26.60	37.15
% of China's Trade	2.22	2.08	1.98	2.17	2.54	2.79	3.14	3.37
% Growth		0.73	15.64	50.35	58.91	35.24	39.43	32.56
Central Asia								
Imports	1.05	1.02	1.44	2.01	2.82	3.49	4.32	6.96
Exports	0.77	0.49	0.94	2.06	3.02	5.23	7.74	12.70
% of China's Trade	0.38	0.30	0.38	0.48	0.51	0.61	0.68	0.90
% Growth		-17.02	58.26	70.34	43.46	49.37	38.28	62.96
Latin America								
Imports	5.36	6.64	8.25	14.71	21.37	26.16	33.60	50.71
Exports	6.90	7.85	9.04	11.20	17.39	22.45	34.42	49.51
% of China's Trade	2.59	2.84	2.78	3.04	3.36	3.42	3.86	4.61
% Growth		18.17	19.27	49.87	49.58	25.41	39.94	47.32
Middle East								
Imports	10.10	9.40	9.77	14.98	22.22	31.78	41.59	49.15
Exports	7.39	7.90	10.83	15.55	19.95	26.71	37.23	55.20
% of China's Trade	3.69	3.39	3.32	3.59	3.65	4.11	4.48	4.80
% Growth		-1.08	19.03	48.22	38.14	38.68	34.77	32.39
South Asia								
Imports	1.89	2.31	2.88	4.89	8.36	10.74	11.62	15.94
Exports	3.80	4.14	5.45	7.19	11.22	15.96	23.40	35.14
% of China's Trade	1.20	1.26	1.34	1.42	1.70	1.88	1.99	2.35
% Growth		13.54	29.09	44.98	62.14	36.35	31.15	45.88
Southeast Asia								
Imports	22.18	23.23	31.19	47.33	62.95	75.02	89.55	108.38
Exports	17.34	18.57	23.57	30.93	42.90	55.48	71.33	94.25
% of China's Trade	8.33	8.19	8.82	9.19	9.17	9.17	9.14	9.32
% Growth		5.77	31.02	42.88	35.28	23.27	23.28	25.96

Source: International Monetary Fund, Direction of Trade Statistics.

2008	2009	2010	2011	2012	2013	2014	2015	2016
1131.92	1003.89	1393.91	1741.43	1817.34	1949.30	1963.11	1601.76	1589.46
1428.87	1202.05	1578.44	1899.28	2050.09	2210.66	2343.22	2280.54	2136.59
17.77	-13.86	34.74	22.49	6.23	7.56	3.52	-9.85	-4.02
673.23	613.19	822.17	990.37	994.28	1094.36	1107.23	948.39	965.96
1025.87	861.83	1110.10	1307.05	1390.88	1485.02	1542.10	1504.95	1403.50
66.35	66.87	65.01	63.10	61.67	62.00	61.52	63.19	63.59
12.76	-13.19	31.00	18.90	3.82	8.14	2.71	-7.40	-3.42
364.54	302.90	444.10	611.49	656.89	672.96	685.73	506.26	490.08
399.61	337.36	463.37	585.84	653.40	719.48	795.88	770.24	726.98
29.84	29.02	30.53	32.89	33.88	33.47	34.41	32.88	32.66
32.30	-16.21	41.73	31.94	9.43	6.27	6.40	-13.84	-4.66
55.87	43.17	63.49	93.14	112.99	116.88	115.65	55.48	56.67
50.71	47.63	59.80	72.90	85.17	92.51	105.94	108.41	94.88
4.16	4.12	4.15	4.56	5.12	5.03	5.15	4.22	4.07
45.29	-14.81	35.79	34.67	19.34	5.67	5.82	-26.04	12.76
8.23	6.85	13.50	21.00	23.96	26.99	20.90	15.04	12.07
22.59	16.67	16.45	18.58	21.31	23.24	24.06	17.56	18.01
1.20	1.07	1.01	1.09	1.17	1.21	1.04	0.84	0.81
56.84	-23.68	27.36	32.12	14.36	10.97	-10.48	-27.50	-7.45
71.02	63.54	90.26	118.23	124.45	125.77	126.21	103.63	101.17
68.87	54.68	88.57	118.38	131.04	131.25	132.37	127.44	112.19
5.46	5.36	6.02	6.50	6.61	6.18	6.00	5.95	5.73
39.60	-15.49	51.26	32.31	7.98	0.59	0.61	-10.64	-7.66
81.95	57.73	89.65	137.17	148.84	159.89	164.95	104.35	87.79
70.10	60.64	75.98	96.50	102.32	116.03	137.94	129.72	116.41
5.94	5.37	5.57	6.42	6.49	6.63	7.03	6.03	5.48
45.71	-22.15	39.93	41.08	7.48	9.86	9.77	-22.72	-12.76
21.55	15.20	22.97	26.15	22.64	21.09	20.25	16.97	14.82
44.25	41.88	57.57	71.25	70.53	75.26	85.86	94.33	97.87
2.57	2.59	2.71	2.68	2.41	2.32	2.46	2.87	3.02
28.82	-13.25	41.10	20.94	-4.35	3.42	10.13	4.89	1.25
117.01	106.32	154.35	192.47	195.73	198.87	208.09	186.40	196.03
114.14	106.39	138.24	169.86	203.92	243.84	271.70	278.90	264.34
9.03	9.64	9.84	9.95	10.33	10.64	11.14	11.99	12.36
14.08	-7.98	37.55	23.84	10.30	10.77	8.38	-3.02	-1.06

(2) Trade Statistics: Top Five Trade Partners per Region (billions $)

	2000	2001	2002	2003	2004	2005	2006	2007
Africa	10.54	10.62	12.28	18.47	29.35	39.69	55.34	73.36
(% of Total)	(2.22)	(2.08)	(1.98)	(2.17)	(2.54)	(2.78)	(3.14)	(3.37)
South Africa	2.05	2.22	2.58	3.87	5.91	7.27	9.86	14.04
Angola	1.88	0.77	1.15	2.35	4.91	6.95	11.83	14.13
Nigeria	0.84	1.15	1.18	1.86	2.18	2.83	3.13	4.34
Egypt	0.91	0.96	0.94	1.09	1.58	2.15	3.19	4.67
Algeria	0.20	0.29	0.43	0.75	1.24	1.77	2.09	3.83
Central Asia	1.82	1.51	2.39	4.07	5.84	8.72	12.06	19.65
(% of Total)	(0.38)	(0.30)	(0.38)	(0.48)	(0.51)	(0.61)	(0.68)	(0.90)
Kazakhstan	1.56	1.29	1.96	3.29	4.49	6.80	8.36	13.87
Turkmenistan	0.02	0.03	0.09	0.08	0.10	0.11	0.18	0.35
Kyrgyz Republic	0.18	0.12	0.20	0.31	0.60	0.97	2.23	3.78
Uzbekistan	0.05	0.06	0.13	0.35	0.58	0.68	0.97	1.13
Tajikistan	0.02	0.01	0.01	0.04	0.07	0.16	0.32	0.52
Latin America	12.27	14.50	17.29	25.91	38.76	48.61	68.02	100.21
(% of Total)	(2.59)	(2.84)	(2.78)	(3.04)	(3.36)	(3.42)	(3.86)	(4.61)
Brazil	2.84	3.71	4.47	7.99	12.33	14.81	20.29	29.72
Mexico	1.82	2.58	3.98	4.94	7.11	7.76	11.43	14.97
Chile	2.12	2.12	2.56	3.53	5.36	7.09	8.80	14.66
Venezuela	0.35	0.59	0.48	0.74	1.33	1.94	4.35	5.84
Columbia	0.19	0.23	0.32	0.46	0.80	1.13	1.76	3.36
Middle East	17.49	17.30	20.60	30.53	42.17	58.48	78.82	104.35
(% of Total)	(3.69)	(3.39)	(3.32)	(3.59)	(3.65)	(4.11)	(4.48)	(4.80)
Saudi Arabia	3.10	4.08	5.11	7.34	10.29	16.11	20.14	25.36
UAE	2.49	2.83	3.90	5.81	8.15	10.78	14.21	20.04
Iran	2.49	3.32	3.74	5.62	7.04	10.09	14.43	20.62
Iraq	0.97	0.47	0.52	0.06	0.47	0.82	1.14	1.45
Turkey	1.20	0.91	1.38	2.60	3.41	4.88	8.07	11.78
South Asia	5.68	6.45	8.33	12.08	19.58	26.70	35.02	51.08
(% of Total)	(1.20)	(1.26)	(1.34)	(1.42)	(1.70)	(1.88)	(1.99)	(2.35)
India	2.91	3.60	4.95	7.60	13.60	18.72	25.07	38.70
Pakistan	1.16	1.30	1.80	2.43	3.06	4.26	5.25	6.89
Bangladesh	0.92	0.97	1.10	1.37	1.97	2.48	3.18	3.46
Sri Lanka	0.46	0.40	0.35	0.52	0.72	0.98	1.14	1.43
Nepal	0.20	0.15	0.11	0.13	0.17	0.20	0.27	0.40
Southeast Asia	39.52	41.80	54.77	78.25	105.86	130.50	160.88	202.63
(% of Total)	(8.33)	(8.19)	(8.82)	(9.19)	(9.17)	(9.17)	(9.14)	(9.32)
Malaysia	8.05	9.43	14.27	20.13	26.25	30.73	37.12	46.44
Vietnam	2.47	2.82	3.26	4.63	6.74	8.19	9.95	15.12
Singapore	10.82	10.94	14.02	19.35	26.70	33.25	40.86	47.20
Thailand	6.62	7.22	8.56	12.66	17.34	21.81	27.73	34.63
Indonesia	7.46	6.74	7.93	10.23	13.47	16.80	19.08	25.00

Source: International Monetary Fund, Direction of Trade Statistics.

2008	2009	2010	2011	2012	2013	2014	2015	2016
106.58	90.80	123.29	166.04	198.16	209.39	221.59	163.89	151.55
(4.16)	(4.11)	(4.15)	(4.56)	(5.12)	(5.03)	(5.15)	(4.22)	(4.07)
17.80	16.04	22.23	45.43	59.95	65.15	60.38	31.23	35.57
25.30	17.05	24.81	27.67	37.50	35.91	37.07	19.71	15.58
7.27	6.38	7.76	10.78	10.57	13.59	18.10	14.89	11.23
6.24	5.86	6.96	8.80	9.55	10.21	11.62	12.87	11.33
4.53	5.13	5.17	6.42	7.74	8.15	8.70	8.38	8.13
30.82	23.52	29.96	39.58	45.26	50.23	44.97	32.60	30.17
(1.20)	(1.07)	(1.01)	(1.09)	(1.17)	(1.21)	(1.04)	(0.84)	(0.81)
17.55	13.98	20.31	24.89	25.65	28.56	22.42	14.27	13.07
0.83	0.95	1.57	5.48	9.72	10.03	10.47	8.64	5.90
9.34	5.28	4.17	4.98	5.16	5.14	5.29	4.34	5.79
1.61	1.91	2.48	2.17	2.88	4.53	4.27	3.50	3.67
1.50	1.40	1.43	2.07	1.86	1.96	2.52	1.85	1.75
139.90	118.23	178.83	236.62	255.50	257.01	258.58	231.07	213.36
(5.46)	(5.36)	(6.02)	(6.50)	(6.61)	(6.18)	(6.00)	(5.95)	(5.73)
48.41	42.44	62.50	84.50	85.48	89.86	86.90	71.81	67.58
17.55	16.15	24.68	33.34	36.69	39.24	43.49	43.90	42.85
17.51	17.50	25.78	31.40	33.22	33.91	34.15	32.00	31.37
9.48	7.13	10.25	18.03	23.77	19.18	16.95	12.15	8.02
4.10	3.37	5.91	8.23	9.39	10.45	15.51	11.13	9.38
152.05	118.37	165.64	233.67	251.16	275.92	302.89	234.06	204.20
(5.94)	(5.37)	(5.57)	(6.42)	(6.49)	(6.63)	(7.03)	(6.03)	(5.48)
41.85	32.57	43.23	64.40	73.40	72.23	69.27	51.83	43.28
28.19	21.22	25.60	35.08	40.39	46.12	54.60	48.35	40.80
27.63	21.15	29.33	45.06	36.54	39.79	51.80	33.85	31.65
2.58	5.11	9.87	14.24	17.56	24.86	28.49	20.58	18.36
12.57	10.07	15.11	18.75	19.11	22.25	23.03	21.58	19.66
65.80	57.08	80.54	97.40	93.17	96.35	106.11	111.30	112.69
(2.57)	(2.59)	(2.71)	(2.68)	(2.41)	(2.32)	(2.46)	(2.87)	(3.02)
51.86	43.41	61.74	73.90	66.57	65.49	70.65	71.65	71.19
7.00	6.78	8.67	10.56	12.42	14.22	16.01	18.96	19.60
4.68	4.58	7.05	8.26	8.45	10.31	12.55	14.71	15.55
1.68	1.64	2.10	3.14	3.17	3.62	4.04	4.57	4.66
0.38	0.41	0.74	1.19	2.00	2.25	2.33	0.85	0.90
231.16	212.71	292.58	362.33	399.65	442.71	479.78	465.30	460.38
(9.03)	(9.64)	(9.84)	(9.95)	(10.33)	(10.64)	(11.14)	(11.99)	(12.36)
53.51	51.86	74.19	89.92	94.77	105.99	102.05	97.41	88.47
19.48	21.04	30.09	40.20	50.45	65.48	83.55	90.17	99.23
52.42	47.83	56.92	63.06	68.75	75.47	79.24	79.17	73.37
41.16	38.17	52.96	64.74	69.68	70.84	72.52	75.51	76.97
31.60	28.28	42.73	60.58	66.32	68.42	63.66	54.19	54.09

(3) China's Oil Imports by Region, 2000–2016

	2000	2001	2002	2003	2004	2005	2006	2007
World								
Metric Tons	70.27	60.26	69.41	91.02	122.81	126.82	145.17	163.16
% Growth		-14.25	15.19	31.14	34.93	3.26	14.48	12.39
Developed World								
Metric Tons (millions)	5.21	4.03	7.52	8.22	14.66	13.53	16.74	15.78
% of Total	7.41	6.70	10.84	9.03	11.94	10.67	11.53	9.67
% Growth		-22.56	86.43	9.32	78.28	-7.73	23.74	-5.73
Developing World								
Metric Tons	60.03	51.10	55.46	76.10	101.75	106.25	123.43	137.02
% of Total	85.44	84.81	79.91	83.61	82.85	83.78	85.02	83.98
% Growth		-14.88	8.53	37.21	33.71	4.42	16.18	11.01
Regions of Developing World								
Africa								
Metric Tons	11.99	8.43	9.37	15.65	28.93	31.72	40.94	43.08
% of Total	17.07	13.98	13.50	17.19	23.56	25.01	28.20	26.40
% Growth		-29.74	11.23	66.97	84.90	9.65	29.06	5.22
Central Asia								
Metric Tons	0.73	0.66	1.02	1.22	1.31	1.31	2.73	6.10
% of Total	1.04	1.09	1.47	1.34	1.07	1.03	1.88	3.74
% Growth		-10.13	54.75	19.19	7.69	0.20	107.86	123.75
Latin America								
Metric Tons	0.23	0.19		0.84	2.91	4.28	9.45	10.25
% of Total	0.32	0.32		0.92	2.37	3.37	6.51	6.28
% Growth		-15.47			247.01	47.06	120.95	8.52
Middle East								
Metric Tons	37.65	33.86	34.39	46.26	55.78	59.85	65.60	72.76
% of Total	53.58	56.19	49.55	50.83	45.42	47.19	45.19	44.60
% Growth		-10.07	1.57	34.52	20.58	7.29	9.61	10.91
South Asia								
Metric Tons			0.03	0.04				
% of Total			0.04	0.04				
% Growth				34.84				
Southeast Asia								
Metric Tons	9.04	7.89	10.49	11.88	12.53	9.08	4.71	4.82
% of Total	12.86	13.09	15.11	13.05	10.20	7.16	3.25	2.95
% Growth		-12.73	33.00	13.20	5.48	-27.47	-48.12	2.24

Source: UN Comtrade.

Note: The sum of regional oil imports is unequal to the total of oil imports from developing world because the Caucuses, developing European countries, and Pacific Islands countries are not included.

2008	2009	2010	2011	2012	2013	2014	2015	2016
178.89	203.79	239.31	253.77	270.98	281.74	308.38	335.49	381.01
9.64	13.92	17.43	6.04	6.78	3.97	9.45	8.79	13.57
12.70	17.52	18.64	24.57	28.97	28.00	37.40	47.57	64.34
7.10	8.60	7.79	9.68	10.69	9.94	12.13	14.18	16.89
-19.52	37.95	6.42	31.76	17.94	-3.36	33.58	27.18	35.25
155.79	173.71	209.09	217.90	242.58	254.60	269.85	289.58	316.67
87.09	85.24	87.37	85.87	89.52	90.37	87.51	86.31	83.11
13.70	11.50	20.36	4.22	11.33	4.96	5.99	7.31	9.35
43.57	49.00	58.47	47.16	64.25	64.15	68.48	64.45	67.82
24.35	24.05	24.43	18.58	23.71	22.77	22.21	19.21	17.80
1.13	12.48	19.33	-19.35	36.25	-0.16	6.75	-5.88	5.23
5.82	6.26	10.34	11.50	11.20	12.59	6.72	6.10	3.23
3.25	3.07	4.32	4.53	4.13	4.47	2.18	1.82	0.85
-4.62	7.57	65.13	11.22	-2.59	12.42	-46.66	-9.26	-47.05
12.68	13.07	20.67	23.12	27.36	27.41	32.89	42.53	51.87
7.09	6.41	8.64	9.11	10.10	9.73	10.67	12.68	13.61
23.72	3.06	58.12	11.88	18.32	0.16	20.01	29.30	21.96
89.62	97.46	112.77	130.03	134.90	146.50	158.33	170.16	182.98
50.10	47.83	47.12	51.24	49.78	52.00	51.34	50.72	48.02
23.16	8.76	15.70	15.31	3.75	8.59	8.08	7.47	7.53
						0.02		
						0.01		
4.01	7.62	5.41	4.27	3.53	2.67	2.16	4.16	10.77
2.24	3.74	2.26	1.68	1.30	0.95	0.70	1.24	2.83
-16.73	89.96	-29.03	-21.13	-17.17	-24.44	-19.22	92.97	158.89

(4) Top Ten Oil Exporters to China, 2000–2016

		2000	2001	2002	2003	2004	2005	2006	2007
(1) **Saudi Arabia**	Metric Tons (millions)	5.73	8.78	11.39	15.08	17.24	22.18	23.87	26.33
	% of Total Imports	8.16	14.57	16.41	16.57	14.04	17.49	16.44	16.14
	% Growth		53.19	29.76	32.39	14.35	28.62	7.63	10.31
(2) **Russian Federation**	Metric Tons	1.48	1.77	3.03	5.25	10.77	12.78	15.97	14.53
	% of Total Imports	2.10	2.93	4.36	5.77	8.77	10.08	11.00	8.90
	% Growth		19.59	71.55	73.43	105.05	18.60	24.95	-9.01
(3) **Angola**	Metric Tons	8.64	3.80	5.71	10.10	16.21	17.46	23.45	25.00
	% of Total Imports	12.29	6.30	8.22	11.10	13.20	13.77	16.15	15.32
	% Growth		-56.01	50.18	77.08	60.43	7.74	34.30	6.59
(4) **Iraq**	Metric Tons	3.18	0.37	0.54		1.31	1.17	1.05	1.41
	% of Total Imports	4.53	0.62	0.77		1.06	0.92	0.72	0.87
	% Growth		-88.31	44.29			-10.42	-10.64	35.02
(5) **Oman**	Metric Tons	15.66	8.14	8.04	9.27	16.35	10.83	13.18	13.68
	% of Total Imports	22.29	13.51	11.59	10.18	13.31	8.54	9.08	8.38
	% Growth		-48.02	-1.17	15.20	76.36	-33.73	21.70	3.75
(6) **Iran**	Metric Tons	7.00	10.85	10.63	12.39	13.24	14.27	16.77	20.54
	% of Total Imports	9.96	18.00	15.32	13.62	10.78	11.25	11.55	12.59
	% Growth		54.95	-2.00	16.59	6.80	7.82	17.51	22.45
(7) **Venezuela**	Metric Tons		0.06		0.44	0.33	1.93	4.20	4.12
	% of Total Imports		0.09		0.49	0.27	1.52	2.89	2.52
	% Growth					-24.68	476.61	117.96	-2.04
(8) **Kuwait**	Metric Tons	0.43	1.46	1.07	0.91	1.25	1.65	2.81	3.63
	% of Total Imports	0.62	2.42	1.54	1.00	1.02	1.30	1.94	2.23
	% Growth		236.81	-26.72	-15.19	38.22	31.24	70.69	29.30
(9) **Brazil**	Metric Tons	0.23			0.12	1.58	1.34	2.22	2.32
	% of Total Imports	0.32			0.14	1.28	1.06	1.53	1.42
	% Growth					1174.87	-14.80	65.49	4.17
(10) **United Arab Emirates**	Metric Tons	0.43	0.65		0.86	1.34	2.57	3.04	3.65
	% of Total Imports	0.61	1.08		0.95	1.09	2.02	2.10	2.24
	% Growth		50.94			55.63	91.07	18.55	19.95

Source: UN Comtrade.

2008	2009	2010	2011	2012	2013	2014	2015	2016
36.37	41.86	44.65	50.28	53.92	53.90	49.67	50.54	51.01
20.33	20.54	18.66	19.81	19.90	19.13	16.11	15.07	16.11
38.11	15.09	6.66	12.61	7.23	-0.02	-7.86	1.77	0.93
11.64	15.30	15.24	19.72	24.33	24.35	33.11	42.43	52.48
6.51	7.51	6.37	7.77	8.98	8.64	10.74	12.65	16.57
-19.88	31.50	-0.41	29.42	23.35	0.08	35.97	28.16	23.69
29.89	32.17	39.38	31.15	40.15	40.01	40.65	38.71	43.74
16.71	15.79	16.46	12.27	14.82	14.20	13.18	11.54	13.81
19.59	7.62	22.40	-20.90	28.90	-0.35	1.59	-4.78	12.99
1.86	7.16	11.24	13.77	15.68	23.51	28.58	32.11	36.21
1.04	3.51	4.70	5.43	5.79	8.35	9.27	9.57	11.43
31.72	285.08	56.89	22.57	13.87	49.92	21.54	12.37	12.77
14.58	11.74	15.87	18.15	19.57	25.47	29.74	32.06	35.06
8.15	5.76	6.63	7.15	7.22	9.04	9.65	9.56	11.07
6.61	-19.50	35.18	14.40	7.79	30.17	16.78	7.80	9.36
21.32	23.15	21.32	27.75	21.93	21.41	27.46	26.62	31.30
11.92	11.36	8.91	10.93	8.09	7.60	8.91	7.93	9.88
3.83	8.56	-7.90	30.15	-20.98	-2.34	28.26	-3.08	17.58
6.46	5.27	7.55	11.52	15.29	15.55	13.79	16.01	20.15
3.61	2.58	3.15	4.54	5.64	5.52	4.47	4.77	6.36
57.06	-18.51	43.30	52.61	32.76	1.71	-11.36	16.13	25.86
5.90	7.08	9.83	9.54	10.49	9.34	10.62	14.43	16.34
3.30	3.47	4.11	3.76	3.87	3.32	3.44	4.30	5.16
62.33	20.00	38.94	-2.94	9.94	-10.93	13.65	35.87	13.24
3.02	4.06	8.05	6.71	6.05	5.26	7.02	13.92	19.16
1.69	1.99	3.36	2.64	2.23	1.87	2.28	4.15	6.05
30.50	34.28	98.32	-16.62	-9.87	-12.94	33.42	98.19	37.64
4.58	3.31	5.29	6.74	8.74	10.28	11.65	12.57	12.18
2.56	1.62	2.21	2.65	3.23	3.65	3.78	3.75	3.85
25.41	-27.78	59.81	27.44	29.82	17.52	13.39	7.87	-3.10

(5) China's Natural Gas Imports by Region, 2010-2016

	2010	2011	2012	2013	2014	2015	2016
World							
Metric Tons (millions)	15.21	26.07	34.06	42.59	50.26	56.80	70.82
% Growth		71.39	30.66	25.04	18.01	13.00	24.68
Developed World							
Metric Tons	4.83	4.65	4.64	4.33	5.56	9.36	18.90
% of Total Imports	31.72	17.83	13.64	10.16	11.05	16.49	26.69
% Growth		-3.67	-0.07	-6.82	28.34	68.57	101.92
Developing World							
Metric Tons	10.38	21.42	29.40	38.09	44.66	47.37	51.92
% of Total Imports	68.23	82.15	86.31	89.43	88.85	83.41	73.31
% Growth		109.35	36.73	29.32	16.43	16.43	9.61
Regions of Developing World							
Africa							
Metric Tons	0.39	1.01	0.81	1.57	2.20	1.86	1.32
% of Total Imports	2.55	3.89	2.37	3.68	4.38	3.28	1.86
% Growth		161.26	-20.30	94.07	40.41	-15.41	-29.03
Central Asia							
Metric Tons	2.60	10.37	15.81	19.95	20.95	21.93	25.31
% of Total Imports	17.07	39.80	46.42	46.84	41.69	38.61	35.74
% Growth		299.56	52.40	26.18	5.02	4.66	15.41
Latin America							
Metric Tons		0.14	0.002		0.07	0.04	0.25
% of Total Imports		0.55	0.00		0.13	0.07	0.35
% Growth			-98.95			-36.09	525.00
Middle East							
Metric Tons	4.46	6.26	8.32	11.21	13.10	12.71	14.59
% of Total Imports	29.34	24.03	24.44	26.31	26.06	22.37	20.60
% Growth		40.38	32.87	34.61	16.92	-3.02	14.79
South Asia							
Metric Tons					0.12		
% of Total Imports					2.08		
% Growth							
Southeast Asia							
Metric Tons	2.93	3.63	4.53	5.44	8.11	9.28	10.46
% of Total Imports	19.25	13.92	13.31	12.77	16.13	16.34	14.77
% Growth		23.89	24.97	19.99	49.06	14.49	12.72

Source: UN Comtrade.

(6) Top Ten Natural Gas Exporters to China as of 2016 (millions)

		2010	2011	2012	2013	2014	2015	2016
(1) Turkmenistan	Metric Tons (millions)	2.59	10.37	15.69	17.71	18.74	20.40	21.63
	% of Total Imports	17.05	39.76	46.06	41.58	37.29	35.92	30.54
	% Growth		299.62	51.35	12.87	5.84	8.85	6.03
(2) Australia	Metric Tons	4.21	3.76	3.83	3.81	3.90	5.78	12.38
	% of Total Imports	27.68	14.43	11.24	8.94	7.75	10.17	17.48
	% Growth		-10.64	1.73	-0.58	2.41	48.23	114.19
(3) Qatar	Metric Tons	1.91	3.26	5.60	7.75	7.31	5.69	6.99
	% of Total Imports	12.54	12.49	16.45	18.20	14.53	10.02	9.87
	% Growth		70.68	72.07	38.36	-5.76	-22.06	22.85
(4) United Arab Emirates	Metric Tons	0.47	0.63	0.82	1.09	3.67	5.16	6.23
	% of Total Imports	3.10	2.43	2.41	2.57	7.31	9.09	8.80
	% Growth		34.53	29.59	33.00	235.93	40.55	20.74
(5) Malaysia	Metric Tons	1.23	1.62	1.93	2.67	3.10	3.43	2.77
	% of Total Imports	8.06	6.20	5.68	6.27	6.16	6.05	3.91
	% Growth		31.96	19.57	38.04	16.03	10.88	-19.24
(6) Myanmar	Metric Tons				0.15	2.20	2.88	2.86
	% of Total Imports				0.36	4.38	5.08	4.04
	% Growth					1323.98	31.07	-0.69
(7) United States of America	Metric Tons	0.04	0.16		0.11	0.79	2.87	2.86
	% of Total Imports	0.27	0.61		0.26	1.58	5.06	4.04
	% Growth		281.46			609.09	262.29	-0.35
(8) Indonesia	Metric Tons	1.70	1.99	2.43	2.46	2.57	2.87	2.91
	% of Total Imports	11.19	7.62	7.14	5.78	5.12	5.05	4.11
	% Growth		16.69	22.55	1.17	4.53	11.52	1.39
(9) Papua New Guinea	Metric Tons					0.29	1.59	1.57
	% of Total Imports					0.57	2.79	2.22
	% Growth						454.37	-1.26
(10) Uzbekistan	Metric Tons			0.11	2.10	1.79	1.13	3.16
	% of Total Imports			0.33	4.92	3.56	2.00	4.46
	% Growth				1791.78	-14.78	-36.55	179.65

Source: UN Comtrade.

APPENDIX II

Relevant Official White Papers Issued under the 18th Central Committee of the Communist Party of China, November 2012–October 2017

1. January 2017: China's Policies on Asia–Pacific Security Cooperation[1]

The State Council Information Office
The People's Republic of China

Contents

Preface

Conclusion

Preface

The Asia–Pacific region covers a vast area with numerous countries and 60 percent of the world's population. Its economic and trade volumes take up nearly 60 percent and half of the world's total, respectively. It has an important strategic position in the world. In recent years, the development of the Asia–Pacific region has increasingly caught people's attention. It has become the most dynamic region with the strongest potential in the world. All parties are attaching greater importance to and investing more in this region. With the profound adjustment of the pattern of international relations, the regional situation of the Asia–Pacific area is also undergoing profound changes.

China is committed to promoting peace and stability in this region. It follows the path of peaceful development and the mutually beneficial strategy of opening up, and pursues friendly cooperation with all countries on the basis of the Five Principles of Peaceful Coexistence. It has participated in regional cooperation in an all-around way and taken active steps in response to both traditional and nontraditional security challenges, contributing to lasting peace and common prosperity in the Asia–Pacific region.

I. China's Policies and Positions on Asia–Pacific Security Cooperation

Currently, the situation in the Asia–Pacific region is stable on the whole, with strong momentum for peace and development. The Asia–Pacific region is a stable part of the global landscape. To promote peace and seek stability and development is the strategic goal and common aspiration of most countries in the region. Political mutual trust among countries has been strengthened, and major countries have frequently interacted and cooperated with one another. To address differences and disputes through negotiation and consultation is the major policy of countries in the region. Regional hot spot issues and disputes are basically under control.

The region has secured steady and relatively fast growth, continuing to lead the world in this respect. Regional integration has gathered pace, with booming sub-regional cooperation. Free trade arrangements in various forms have made steady progress, and a new phase has emerged for dynamic connectivity building. However, the Asia–Pacific region still faces multiple destabilizing and uncertain factors. The nuclear issue on the Korean Peninsula is complex and sensitive; the reconciliation process in Afghanistan remains slow; and disputes over territorial sovereignty and maritime rights and interests continue to unfold. Some countries are increasing their military deployment in the region, a certain country seeks to shake off military constraints, and some countries are undergoing complex political and social transformations. Nontraditional security threats such as terrorism, natural disasters, and transnational crimes have become more prominent. Asia's economy still faces significant downward pressure as a result of its structural problems as well as external economic and financial risks.

As an important member of the Asia–Pacific family, China is fully aware that its peaceful development is closely linked with the future of the region. China has all along taken the advancement of regional prosperity and stability as its own responsibility. China is ready to pursue security through dialogue and cooperation in the spirit of working together for mutually beneficial results, and safeguard peace and stability jointly with other countries in the region.

First, we should promote common development and lay a solid economic foundation for peace and stability in the Asia–Pacific region. To enhance the convergence of economic interests is an important basis for sound state-to-state relations. Common development provides a fundamental safeguard for peace and stability, and holds the key to various security issues. Considerable achievements have been made in economic cooperation. On this basis, we should accelerate the process of economic integration and continue to advance the building of free trade areas and connectivity as well as comprehensive economic and social development. We should implement the United Nations 2030 Agenda for Sustainable Development and narrow the developmental gap in the region, so that all countries and people of all social strata will enjoy the dividends of development, and the interests of countries will be more closely intertwined.

Focusing on common development, China has put forward and actively promoted the Belt and Road Initiative and initiated the establishment of the Asian Infrastructure Investment Bank and the Silk Road Fund. We welcome continued participation by all countries for mutually beneficial outcomes.

Second, we should promote the building of partnerships and strengthen the political foundation for peace and stability in the Asia–Pacific region. Asia–Pacific countries have unique diversities. Countries may become partners when they have the same values and ideals, but they can also be partners if they seek common ground while reserving differences. The key is to remain committed to treating each other as equals and carrying out mutually beneficial cooperation. How major countries in the Asia–Pacific region get along with each other is critical for maintaining regional peace and development. Major countries should treat the strategic intentions of others in an objective and rational manner, reject the Cold War mentality, respect others' legitimate interests and concerns, strengthen positive interactions, and respond to challenges with concerted efforts. Small and medium-sized countries need not and should not take sides among big countries. All countries should make joint efforts to pursue a new path of dialogue instead of confrontation and pursue partnerships rather than alliances, and build an Asia–Pacific partnership featuring mutual trust, inclusiveness, and mutually beneficial cooperation.

China calls for the building of a new model of international relations centered on mutually beneficial cooperation. China is committed to building partnerships in different forms with all countries and regional organizations. China has committed itself to working with the United States to build a new model of major-country relations featuring non-conflict, non-confrontation, mutual respect, and mutually beneficial cooperation. China is committed to deepening its comprehensive strategic partnership of coordination with Russia and establishing a closer partnership with India. It is also pushing for the improvement of its relations with Japan. Chinese leaders have repeatedly elaborated on the concept of a community of shared future on many different occasions. China is working to construct a community of shared future for countries along the Lancang-Mekong River and between China and the Association of Southeast Asian Nations (ASEAN) as well as in Asia and the Asia–Pacific area as a whole.

Third, we should improve the existing regional multilateral mechanisms and strengthen the framework for supporting peace and stability in the Asia–Pacific region. All parties concerned should adhere to multilateralism, oppose unilateralism, further support the development of regional multilateral security mechanisms, push for close coordination between relevant mechanisms, and play a bigger role in enhancing mutual understanding and trust, and expanding exchanges and cooperation in the field of security dialogues.

Committed to pushing forward the building of regional security mechanisms, China initiated with relevant countries the Shanghai Cooperation Organization (SCO), Six-Party Talks, Xiangshan Forum, China–ASEAN Ministerial Dialogue on Law Enforcement and Security Cooperation, and Center for Comprehensive Law Enforcement and Security Cooperation in the Lancang-Mekong Sub-Region. China has actively supported the Conference on Interaction and Confidence-Building Measures in Asia (CICA) in its capacity and institution building, and participated in the ASEAN-led multilateral security dialogues and cooperation mechanisms. Within various regional mechanisms, China has made a large number of cooperation proposals in the field of nontraditional security, which have strongly promoted relevant exchanges and cooperation. China will shoulder greater responsibilities for regional and global security, and provide more public security services to the Asia–Pacific region and the world at large.

Fourth, we should promote the rule-setting and improve the institutional safeguards for peace and stability in the Asia–Pacific region. To live together in peace, countries should follow the spirit of the rule of law, the international norms based on the purposes and principles of the Charter of the United Nations, and the widely recognized rules of fairness and justice. International and regional rules should be discussed, formulated, and observed by all countries concerned, rather than being dictated by any particular country. Rules of individual countries should not automatically become "international rules," still less should individual countries be allowed to violate the lawful rights and interests of others under the pretext of "rule of law."

China has firmly upheld and actively contributed to international law and regional rules and norms. To practice the rule of law in international relations, China, together with India and Myanmar, initiated the Five Principles of Peaceful Coexistence in 1954. China has acceded to almost all intergovernmental international organizations and more than 400 international multilateral treaties so far. China is committed to upholding regional maritime security and order, and enhancing the building of institutions and rules. In 2014 China presided over the adoption of the updated Code for Unplanned Encounters at Sea at the Western Pacific Naval Symposium held in China. China and ASEAN countries will continue to fully and effectively implement the Declaration on the Conduct of Parties in the South China Sea (DOC) and strive for the early conclusion of a Code of Conduct (COC) on the basis of consensus in the framework of the DOC. In addition, China has taken an active part in consultations on setting rules in new areas such as cyberspace and outer space, so as to contribute to the formulation of widely accepted fair and equitable international rules.

Fifth, we should intensify military exchanges and cooperation to offer more guarantees for peace and stability in the Asia–Pacific region. China faces diverse and complex security threats and challenges, as well as the arduous task of safeguarding national unity and territorial integrity. Building strong national defense and armed forces that are commensurate with China's international standing and its security and development interests is a strategic task in China's modernization drive, and provides a strong guarantee for its peaceful development. China's armed forces provide security and strategic support for the country's development and also make positive contributions to the maintenance of world peace and regional stability.

China's armed forces have called for, facilitated, and participated in international security cooperation. China has followed the Five Principles of Peaceful Coexistence, conducted all-around military exchanges with other countries, and developed nonaligned and nonconfrontational military cooperation not targeting any third party. It has worked to promote the establishment of just and effective collective security mechanisms and military confidence-building mechanisms. On the basis of mutual respect, equality and mutual benefit, and mutually beneficial cooperation, China has increased interactions and cooperation with the armed forces of other countries, and intensified cooperation on confidence-building measures in border areas. China has promoted dialogue and cooperation on maritime security, participated in United Nations peacekeeping missions, international counterterrorism cooperation, escort missions and disaster-relief operations, and conducted relevant joint exercises and training with other countries.

Sixth, we should properly resolve differences and disputes, and maintain a sound environment of peace and stability in the Asia–Pacific region. Most of the hot spot and sensitive issues in this region have been left over from history. To handle them, the countries in the region should follow the tradition of mutual respect, seeking common ground while reserving differences, and peaceful coexistence, and work to solve disputes properly and peacefully through direct negotiation and consultation. We should not allow old problems to hamper regional development and cooperation, and undermine mutual trust. For disputes over territories and maritime rights and interests, the sovereign states directly involved should respect historical facts and seek a peaceful solution through negotiation and consultation in accordance with the fundamental principles and legal procedures defined by universally recognized international law and modern maritime law, including the UN Convention on the Law of the Sea (UNC-LOS). Pending a satisfactory solution to disputes, the parties concerned should engage in dialogue to promote cooperation, manage each situation appropriately, and prevent conflicts from escalating, so as to jointly safeguard peace and stability in the region.

China is committed to upholding peace and stability in the South China Sea, and working for peaceful solutions to the disputes over territories and maritime rights and interests with the countries directly involved through friendly negotiation and consultation. This commitment remains unchanged. China has actively pushed for peaceful solutions to hot spot issues such as the nuclear issue on the Korean Peninsula and the Afghanistan issue, and played its due role as a responsible major country.

II. China's Security Vision for the Asia–Pacific Region

Visions guide actions, and to solve new problems new visions are required. Old security concepts based on the Cold War mentality, zero-sum game, and stress on force are outdated given the dynamic development of regional integration. In the new circumstances, all countries should keep up with the times, strengthen solidarity and cooperation with openness and inclusiveness, make security vision innovations, work to improve regional security systems, and explore a new path for Asian security.

1. Concept of Common, Comprehensive, Cooperative, and Sustainable Security

At the Fourth Summit of the Conference on Interaction and Confidence-Building Measures in Asia (CICA) held in May 2014, Chinese President Xi Jinping called for a concept of common, comprehensive, cooperative, and sustainable security, and a path of security featuring wide consultation, joint contribution, and shared benefits in the Asia–Pacific region.

Common security means respecting and ensuring the security of each and every country involved. We cannot just have the security of one or some countries while leaving the rest insecure, still less should we seek "absolute security" of oneself at the expense of the security of others. We should respect and accommodate the legitimate security concerns of all parties. To beef up a military alliance targeted at a third party is not conducive to maintaining common security.

Comprehensive security means upholding security in both traditional and non-traditional fields. We should take into full account the historical background and reality concerning regional security, adopt a multipronged and holistic approach, and enhance regional security governance in a coordinated way. While tackling the immediate security challenges facing the region, we should also make plans for addressing potential security threats.

Cooperative security means promoting the security of both individual countries and the region as a whole through dialogue and cooperation. The countries involved should engage in sincere and in-depth dialogue and communication to increase strategic mutual trust, reduce mutual misgivings, seek common ground while resolving differences, and live in harmony with one another. We should bear in mind the common challenges and actively foster the awareness of meeting security challenges through cooperation. And we should expand the scope of and explore new ways for cooperation, and promote peace and security through cooperation.

Sustainable security means that the countries involved need to focus on both development and security to realize durable security. All the parties should focus on development, actively improve people's lives, and narrow the wealth gap so as to cement the foundation of security. We should advance common development and regional integration, and push for sound interactions and the synchronized progress of regional economic and security cooperation in order to promote sustainable security through sustainable development.

This security concept is in tune with globalization and the historical trend of the times featuring peace, development, and mutually beneficial cooperation. Rooted in regional integration, it has gathered the wisdom and consensus of the countries in the region, reflects the urgent need of all parties to cope with security challenges through cooperation, and opened broad prospects for regional security cooperation.

2. Improving the Regional Security Framework

The key to maintaining the long-term stability of the Asia–Pacific region is to build a security framework which is oriented to the future, accords with regional realities, and meets all parties' needs.

First, the future regional security framework should be multilayered, comprehensive, and diversified. Countries in the Asia–Pacific region differ in their historical traditions, political systems, levels of development, and security concerns. In this region, there are ASEAN-led security cooperation mechanisms and platforms such as the SCO and CICA, as well as military alliances formed in history. Given such a diversity, a consistent security framework in this region is not foreseeable in the near future, and it will be normal to see multiple mechanisms advancing together in the evolution of a regional security framework. All the countries involved should play their respective roles in safeguarding regional peace and stability. China promotes the building of a security framework in the Asia–Pacific region, which does not mean starting all over again, but improving and upgrading the existing mechanisms.

Second, building the future security framework should be adopted as a common cause by all the countries in the region. As multipolarity is becoming a global trend, regional security affairs should be decided by all the countries in the region through equal participation. The development of a regional security framework involves the common interests of all the countries in the region, and requires the active participation and contribution of all parties. The Asia–Pacific area is a region where major powers come into frequent contact and where their interests are concentrated. The major powers should jointly promote a regional security framework, so as to effectively deal with the increasingly complex security challenges in the region. Relevant bilateral military alliances should be made more transparent and avoid confrontation, so as to play a constructive role in the sphere of regional peace and stability.

Third, the future regional security framework should be based on consensus. It will be a long and gradual process to put in place such a framework, which cannot be completed overnight. All parties should continue to strengthen dialogue and cooperation, and steadily advance the development of a regional security framework on the basis of building consensus. At the current stage, the parties should continue to focus on nontraditional security cooperation, and start from the easier tasks before moving on to more difficult ones, so as to build trust and lay a solid foundation for the framework.

Fourth, the development of a regional security framework should be advanced in parallel with the development of a regional economic framework. Security and development are closely linked and mutually complementary. Equal consideration should be given to both a security framework and an economic framework—the main components of the entire regional structure—to ensure their parallel development. On the one hand, the improvement of the security framework will help ensure a peaceful and stable environment for economic development; on the other, faster regional economic integration will provide solid economic and social support for the development of the security framework.

III. China's Relations with Other Major Asia–Pacific Countries

1. China–US Relations

Since 2015 the overall relationship between China and the United States has remained stable and even made new progress. The two countries have maintained close contacts at the leadership and other levels. President Xi Jinping paid a state visit to the US at the invitation of President Barack Obama in September 2015, and met him again during the UN Climate Change Conference in Paris in November of the same year. In late March 2016, the two presidents had a successful meeting during the Nuclear Security Summit in Washington. In September they met again during the G20 Hangzhou Summit, and committed themselves to building a new model of a major-country relationship. Premier Li Keqiang met President Obama when attending high-level meetings of the 71st Session of the UN General Assembly. In June the same year the Eighth Round of the China–US Strategic and Economic Dialogue, the Seventh China–US High-Level Consultation on People-to-People Exchanges, and the Second China–US High-Level Joint Dialogue on Cybercrime and Related Issues were held in Beijing, and achieved fruitful results. In addition, the two countries have made steady progress in practical cooperation in various fields, and maintained close communication and coordination on major regional and global issues like climate change, the Korean and Iranian nuclear issues, Syria, and Afghanistan.

The two countries have maintained communication and coordination in the field of Asia–Pacific affairs through bilateral exchanges and relevant mechanisms at all levels, and agreed to build a bilateral relationship of positive interaction and inclusive cooperation in the region. The two countries have stayed in a state of communication and cooperation on regional and global affairs, including climate change, counterterrorism, marine environmental protection, combating wildlife smuggling, and disaster prevention and reduction within multilateral frameworks such as APEC, East Asia Summit (EAS), and ASEAN Regional Forum (ARF). Moreover, the two sides have smoothly carried out trilateral personnel and agriculture training cooperation projects in Afghanistan and Timor-Leste.

China–US military relations have generally maintained a momentum of steady progress. Since 2015 the two militaries have continued to improve their two mutual-confidence-building mechanisms: the Mutual Notification of Major Military Activities and the Rules of Behavior for the Safety of Air and Maritime Encounters. In 2015, they held their Joint Humanitarian Assistance and Disaster-Relief Field Exercise and Disaster Management Exchanges in China and the US, respectively, and participated in Khaan Quest 2015 multinational peacekeeping military exercise and Exercise Kowari, a China–US–Australia trilateral military exercise. In January 2016, a working meeting of officials from the two ministries of defense was held in Beijing, and in May a video conference was held between the Chinese Chief of the Department of the Joint Chiefs of Staff of the Central Military Commission and the US Chairman of the Joint Chiefs of Staff. From late June to early August 2016, Chinese Navy Fleet 153 participated in RIMPAC 2016, a joint military exercise in Hawaii. In July and August the same year, the US Chief of Naval Operations and Chief of Staff of the Army each made a visit to China.

China is willing to promote the sustainable, sound, and stable advance of bilateral relations, and work with the new US administration to follow the principles of no conflict, no confrontation, mutual respect, and mutually beneficial cooperation, increase cooperation in bilateral, regional, and global affairs, manage and control divergences in a constructive way, and further bilateral relations from a new starting point, so as to bring benefits to the two peoples and other peoples around the world.

2. China–Russia Relations

China and Russia are each other's biggest neighbor and strategic partner of cooperation and priority in diplomacy. Over the years, China–Russia relations have gained healthy, stable, and fast development, and made new achievements through joint efforts. In 2001 the two countries signed the Good-Neighborly Treaty of Friendship and Cooperation, which established the idea of a lasting friendship in legal form. In 2011 the bilateral relationship was upgraded to a comprehensive strategic partnership of coordination based on equality, mutual trust, mutual support, common prosperity, and lasting friendship. In 2014 the China–Russia comprehensive strategic partnership of coordination entered a new stage.

This partnership has presented a more positive momentum of development at a high level. President Xi Jinping and Russian President Vladimir Putin have met frequently. During the latter's visit to China in June 2016 the two sides signed three joint statements: the Joint Statement by the People's Republic of China and the Russian Federation, Joint Statement by the People's Republic of China and the Russian Federation on Strengthening Global Strategic Stability, and Joint Statement by the People's Republic of China and the Russian Federation on Cooperation in Information Cyberspace Development. In September that year the two heads of state met for the third time, during the G20 Hangzhou Summit, and agreed to increase their firm mutual support on issues concerning each other's core interests, energetically promote the idea of a lasting friendship established in the Good-Neighborly Treaty of Friendship and Cooperation, actively promote their development strategies and their efforts to promote the Belt and Road Initiative and Eurasian Economic Union, hold a Year of Media Exchange, and maintain close coordination and cooperation in international and regional affairs, so as to inject strong vigor into bilateral relations.

China and Russia have maintained good cooperation in Asia–Pacific affairs. The two sides continue to strengthen their cooperation within regional multilateral frameworks, safeguard the purposes and principles of the Charter of the United Nations and universally recognized norms governing international relations, uphold the achievements of World War II and international justice, advance the process of a political solution to regional hot spot issues, and contribute more positive energy to regional peace, stability, development, and prosperity.

China–Russia military relations have made further progress. In 2015 the two militaries jointly commemorated the 70th anniversary of the victory of the World Anti-Fascist War, and sent high-ranking officers and teams to each other's commemoration activities and military parades. The two militaries successfully held joint maritime drills twice in a year for the first time. China participated in all events of the international military skill competition hosted by Russia, and the first Chinese Military Culture Week was held in Russia. In 2016 the two militaries maintained positive interaction. The First Joint Computer-Enabled Anti-Missile Defence Exercise was held. China participated in the international military games in Russia and Kazakhstan. In September China and Russia conducted the Maritime Joint Exercise 2016. The two militaries have also maintained close coordination within the defense and security cooperation framework of the SCO.

3. China–India Relations

Since 2015 the China–India strategic and cooperative partnership for peace and prosperity has been further deepened. The two countries have set the goal of forging a closer development partnership, made new progress in exchanges and cooperation in various areas, and stayed in close communication and coordination on regional and international issues.

The two countries have held frequent exchanges of high-level visits, and enhanced political mutual trust. President Xi Jinping met Indian Prime Minister Narendra Modi on the sidelines of the Seventh BRICS Summit in Ufa in July 2015, the 16th SCO Summit in Tashkent in June 2016, the G20 Hangzhou Summit in September 2016, and the Eighth BRICS Summit in October 2016. In November 2015, Premier Li Keqiang met Indian Prime Minister Modi during the leaders' meetings for East Asia cooperation in Malaysia. Indian President Pranab Mukherjee visited China in May 2016, and Prime Minister Narendra Modi visited China in May 2015. Practical cooperation between the two countries has made solid progress in various areas. The two countries have maintained communication and coordination on international affairs and enhanced collaboration in the UN, BRICS, G20, China–India–Russia, and other mechanisms. They have cooperated on climate change, the WTO Doha Round of negotiations, energy and food security, reform of international financial and monetary institutions, and global governance. Such cooperation has helped safeguard the common interests of China, India, and other developing countries.

The relations between the Chinese and Indian militaries remain healthy and stable in general, with increasingly close communication and exchanges, and pragmatic cooperation in greater breadth and depth. Eight rounds of defense and security consultation and six joint military anti-terrorism training exercises have been held so far. Sound cooperation in personnel training, professional exchanges, and other fields is being carried out. The two sides have also conducted border defense cooperation, which plays a positive role in maintaining peace and tranquility in the border areas between China and India. Military leaders of the two sides visited each other in 2015 and 2016, and reached an important consensus on strengthening pragmatic cooperation between the two militaries and working together to maintain peace and stability in the border areas.

4. China–Japan Relations

Since 2015 China–Japan relations have maintained the momentum of improvement which started at the end of 2014. Upon invitation, President Xi Jinping met

Japanese Prime Minister Shinzo Abe on the margins of the APEC Economic Leaders' Meeting and the Asian–African Summit. He attended and gave an important speech at the China–Japan Friendship Exchange Meeting. Premier Li Keqiang met Prime Minister Abe during the China–Japan–ROK Trilateral Summit Meeting in 2015 and during the Asia–Europe Meeting in 2016. During the G20 Hangzhou Summit in September 2016 President Xi Jinping had another meeting with Prime Minister Abe. The two sides resumed contacts at government, parliament, and party levels in an orderly way. Three rounds of high-level political dialogue were held and exchanges and cooperation in various areas were steadily pushed forward. However, complex and sensitive factors still remain in bilateral relations. In response to Japan's negative moves concerning historical and maritime territory issues, China urges Japan to abide by the four political documents and the four-point principled agreement on bilateral relations, properly manage and control disputes and conflicts, and avoid creating obstacles to the improvement of bilateral relations.

Since the end of 2014 defense exchanges between the two countries have gradually resumed and developed. In November 2015, the Chinese and Japanese defense ministers met during the ASEAN Defence Ministers' Meeting. The defense chiefs of the two countries have met several times on other multilateral occasions. In 2016 the defense ministries of the two countries conducted working-level exchanges. Since 2015, defense ministries of the two countries have held two expert panel consultations on the establishment of air and maritime contact mechanisms, with consensus reached on most matters.

China has continued developing friendly and cooperative relations with other countries in the Asia–Pacific region, with enhanced political mutual trust, strengthened economic and trade relations, closer people-to-people and cultural exchanges, and enlarged defense cooperation, so as to jointly promote peace, stability, development, and prosperity in the Asia–Pacific region.

IV. China's Positions and Views on Regional Hotspot Issues

1. Nuclear Issue on the Korean Peninsula

China's position on the Korean Peninsula nuclear issue is consistent and clear-cut. China is committed to the denuclearization of the peninsula, its peace and stability, and settlement of the issue through dialogue and consultation. Over the years, China has made tremendous efforts to facilitate the process of denuclearization of the peninsula, safeguard the overall peace and stability there, and realize an early resumption of the Six-Party Talks. In January and September this year the Democratic People's Republic of Korea (DPRK) conducted two nuclear tests and launched missiles of various types, violating UN Security Council resolutions and running counter to the wishes of the international community. China has made clear its opposition to such actions and supported the relevant Security Council resolutions to prevent the DPRK's further pursuit of nuclear weapons. China will continue to work with the international community and strive for denuclearization and long-term peace and stability of the peninsula and of Northeast Asia as a whole. At the same time, other parties concerned should not give up the efforts to resume talks or their responsibilities to safeguard peace and stability on the peninsula.

2. Anti-Ballistic Missile Issue

The anti-ballistic missile issue concerns global strategic stability and mutual trust among major countries. China always holds the view that the anti-ballistic missile issue should be treated with discretion. Forming Cold War style military alliances and building global and regional anti-ballistic missile systems will be detrimental to strategic stability and mutual trust, as well as to the development of an inclusive global and regional security framework. Countries should respect other countries' security concerns while pursuing their own security interests, and follow the principle of maintaining global strategic stability without compromising the security of any country so as to jointly create a peaceful and stable international security environment featuring equality, mutual trust, and mutually beneficial cooperation.

Despite clear opposition from relevant countries including China, the US and the Republic of Korea (ROK) announced the decision to start and accelerate the deployment of the THAAD anti-ballistic missile system in the ROK. Such an act would seriously damage the regional strategic balance and the strategic security interests of China and other countries in the region, and run counter to the efforts for maintaining peace and stability on the Korean Peninsula. China firmly opposes the US and ROK deployment of the THAAD anti-ballistic missile system in the ROK, and strongly urges the US and the ROK to stop this process.

3. Afghanistan Issue

China supports peace and reconstruction in Afghanistan, and hopes to see an Afghanistan that is united, stable, prosperous, and at peace with its neighboring countries. Since 2015 China has increased assistance to Afghanistan in support of that government's capacity building. In the wake of a 7.8-magnitude earthquake in northern Afghanistan in October 2015 China provided assistance for disaster-relief efforts. China believes that only an inclusive reconciliation process that is "Afghan-led and Afghan-owned" can provide the ultimate solution to the Afghanistan issue. China will continue to play a constructive role in advancing the reconciliation process in Afghanistan.

4. Counterterrorism Cooperation

At present, the counterterrorism situation in the Asia–Pacific region is undergoing complex and profound changes. The region faces severe security and stability challenges posed by violent and extremist ideologies spreading at an ever-faster pace, more active terrorist and extremist forces, rising threats from cyber terrorism, and frequent violent terrorist activities, in particular the infiltration of international terrorist organizations and the inflow of foreign terrorist fighters.

Terrorism is a common scourge of the international community and humanity as a whole. The Chinese government opposes terrorism in all forms and calls on the international community to cooperate in fighting terrorism on the basis of the purposes and principles of the Charter of the United Nations and other universally recognized norms governing international relations. China believes that dialogue among different civilizations should be enhanced and a holistic approach taken to eliminate the breeding grounds of terrorism by addressing both its symptoms and root causes by political, economic, and diplomatic means. At the same time, there should be no double standard in fighting terrorism, which should not be associated with any particular country, ethnicity, or religion.

5. Maritime Cooperation

The overall maritime situation remains stable in the region. It is all parties' common interest and consensus to maintain maritime peace, security, and freedom of navigation and overflight. However, nontraditional maritime security threats are on the rise. The ecological environment in many marine areas has been damaged. Marine natural disasters occur frequently, and leaks of oil or hazardous chemicals happen from time to time. In addition, there are often cases of piracy, smuggling, and drug trafficking. Misunderstandings and lack of mutual trust among some countries about traditional security issues also pose risks to maritime security.

China has called for evenhanded, practical, and mutually beneficial maritime security cooperation. It adheres to the purposes and principles of the Charter of the United Nations, the fundamental principles and legal system defined by universally recognized international laws and modern maritime laws, including the UNCLOS and the Five Principles of Peaceful Coexistence, in dealing with regional maritime issues, and is committed to coping with traditional and nontraditional maritime security threats through cooperation. Maintaining maritime peace and security is the shared responsibility of all countries in the region, and serves the common interests of all parties. China is dedicated to strengthening cooperation and jointly tackling challenges with all relevant parties so as to maintain maritime peace and stability.

China has indisputable sovereignty over the Nansha Islands and their adjacent waters. China has always been committed to resolving disputes peacefully through negotiation and consultation, managing disputes by setting rules and establishing mechanisms, realizing mutually beneficial outcomes through cooperation for mutual benefit, and upholding peace and stability as well as freedom of navigation and overflight in the South China Sea. China and the ASEAN countries stay in close communication and dialogue on the South China Sea issue. When fully and effectively implementing the DOC, the two sides have strengthened pragmatic maritime cooperation, steadily advanced the consultations on COC, and made positive progress. China resolutely opposes certain countries' provocations of regional disputes for their selfish interests. China is forced to make necessary responses to the provocative actions which infringe on China's territorial sovereignty and maritime rights and interests, and undermine peace and stability in the South China Sea. No effort to internationalize and judicialize the South China Sea issue will be of any avail for its resolution; it will only make it harder to resolve the issue, and endanger regional peace and stability.

Issues concerning the Diaoyu Islands and maritime demarcation in the East China Sea exist between China and Japan. The Diaoyu Islands are an integral part of China's territory. China's sovereignty over the Diaoyu Islands has a sufficient historical and legal basis. China and Japan have maintained dialogues on issues related to the East China Sea and held several rounds of high-level consultations. They have had communication and reached consensus on crisis management and control in the air and waters of the East China Sea, maritime law enforcement, oil and gas exploration, scientific research, fisheries, and other issues. China is willing to properly manage the situation and resolve related issues through continued dialogue and consultation. China and the ROK have extensive and in-depth exchanges of views on maritime demarcation, and launched relevant negotiations in December 2015.

V. China's Participation in Major Multilateral Mechanisms in the Asia–Pacific Region

1. China–ASEAN Cooperation

China regards ASEAN as a priority in its neighborhood diplomacy, and firmly supports ASEAN's integration and community building as well as its centrality in regional cooperation. Following the principles of mutual respect, equality, good-neighborliness, and mutually beneficial cooperation, China and ASEAN have further strengthened strategic dialogue, enhanced political mutual trust, and deepened practical cooperation in economy and trade, connectivity, finance, security, maritime affairs, and cultural and people-to-people exchanges, making continuous progress in their relations. During his visit to Southeast Asia in 2013 President Xi Jinping announced that China wants to build a closer China–ASEAN community of shared future.

In 2015 the China–ASEAN Defence Ministers' Informal Meeting was held in China for the first time. The two sides also held the Telecommunication Ministers' Meeting, AEM-MOFCOM Consultations, Transport Ministers' Meeting, and Prosecutors-Generals' Conference. In November of the same year, the two sides signed the Protocol to Amend the Framework Agreement on Comprehensive Economic Cooperation and Certain Agreements Thereunder Between China and ASEAN, which marked the conclusion of the negotiations on an upgraded China–ASEAN Free Trade Area.

The year 2016 sees the 25th anniversary of the China–ASEAN Dialogue and the Year of China–ASEAN Educational Exchanges. On September 7, the 19th China–ASEAN Summit to Commemorate the 25th Anniversary of China–ASEAN Dialogue was held in Vientiane, Laos. Premier Li Keqiang attended and reviewed with ASEAN leaders the progress in bilateral relations, summarized experiences, and outlined the direction for future development. The two sides have also held meetings of their ministers of foreign affairs, economy and trade, quality management, and inspection. A series of commemoration events have been hosted, including the Reception in Commemoration of the 25th Anniversary of China–ASEAN Dialogue Relations, Ninth China–ASEAN Education Cooperation Week, Second China–ASEAN Governors/Mayors Dialogue, International Conference to Celebrate the 25th Anniversary of China–ASEAN Dialogue Relations, and China–ASEAN Week.

2. ASEAN Plus Three (APT) Cooperation

ASEAN Plus Three (APT) cooperation is the main vehicle for East Asia cooperation. China has called upon all parties to increase their input in implementing the Report of the East Asia Vision Group II and ASEAN Plus Three Cooperation Work Plan 2013–2017, actively advanced the Chiang Mai Initiative Multilateralization (CMIM) process, and supported the greater readiness and effectiveness of the CMIM and the capacity building of the ASEAN+3 Macroeconomic Research Office after its upgrading to an international organization, so as to contribute to East Asia's economic and financial stability. China has also pushed forward the negotiations on trade in goods and services, and the model of access to investment markets under the Regional Comprehensive Economic Partnership (RCEP), and encouraged other parties to issue the Joint Statement on RCEP Negotiations.

On September 7, 2016, the 19th ASEAN Plus Three Summit was held in Vientiane, Laos, during which Premier Li Keqiang made six proposals on enhancing APT cooperation: to reinforce financial security cooperation, to expand trade and investment cooperation, to promote agricultural and poverty reduction cooperation, to increase the level of connectivity, to create new models for industrial cooperation, and to expand cultural and people-to-people exchanges.

Since 2015 China has vigorously promoted practical cooperation within the APT framework, and held a series of events, including the Seventh East Asia Business Forum, Training Program on Understanding China, Ninth and Tenth Workshops on Cooperation for Cultural Human Resource Development, East Asia High-Level Investment Forum, Sixth Roundtable Meeting on Food Security, Second East Asia Modern Agricultural Workshop, exchange activities for young scientists, "Return to China" Project Cultural Event Series, Fourth International Workshop on ASEAN Plus Three Connectivity Partnership, Third and Fourth ASEAN Plus Three Village Leaders Exchange Programs, and 14th Asian Arts Festival.

3. China–Japan–ROK Cooperation

As major countries in East Asia, China, Japan, and the ROK are the main drivers of East Asia economic integration. Stronger trilateral cooperation will be conducive not only to the development of the three countries, but also to regional stability and prosperity.

In 2015 China–Japan and ROK–Japan relations improved to some extent, ushering in a new phase of greater practical cooperation among the three countries in various fields. The Sixth China–Japan–ROK Summit was held on November 1 in Seoul, the Republic of Korea, where leaders of the three countries had an in-depth exchange of views on trilateral cooperation and international and regional issues of common interest, reiterated the importance they placed on trilateral cooperation, and agreed to properly handle relevant issues in the spirit of "facing history squarely and working together for the future" and enhancing cooperation in political, economic, trade, fiscal, financial, and cultural fields as well as on sustainable development. The meeting issued the Joint Declaration for Peace and Cooperation in Northeast Asia and other joint statements in agricultural, educational, and economic and trade sectors, which further enriched the trilateral cooperation and charted a course for future cooperation.

Since 2015 a number of meetings, forums, and events among China, Japan, and the ROK have been held, including the Ministerial Meetings on Foreign Affairs, Tourism, Water Resource, Environment, Finance, Economic and Trade, Agriculture, Culture, Health and Disaster Management, Central Bank Governors' Meeting, Meeting of Heads of Personnel Authorities, Trilateral Police Affairs Consultation and Counter-Terrorism Consultation, Director Generals' Meeting on Forestry Cooperation, Meeting of the Committee for Promoting Exchanges and Cooperation Among Universities, Northeast Asia Trilateral Forum, Tabletop Exercise on Disaster Management, Workshop on Marine Sciences and International Forum for Trilateral Cooperation, and several rounds of negotiations for a Free Trade Area.

4. East Asia Summit (EAS)

The East Asia Summit (EAS) is a leaders-led strategic forum. Remarkable progress has been made in EAS cooperation since 2015. Called for by China, the Fifth EAS Foreign Ministers' Meeting decided to extend the deadline of implementing the Plan of Action to Implement the Phnom Penh Declaration on the EAS Development Initiative to 2017.

At the 11th EAS held in Vientiane, Laos, on September 8, 2016, Premier Li Keqiang pointed out that cooperation in economic development and cooperation in political security were the two engines propelling the EAS, which should coordinate and synchronize with each other. On economic development, all parties should render strong support to regional connectivity, step up construction of free trade areas, and strengthen cooperation in social undertakings and people's livelihood. On political security, China advocates the new security concept featuring common, comprehensive, cooperative, and sustainable security, and supports all parties to strengthen cooperation on nontraditional security, discuss the building of a regional security framework, and properly settle hot spot and sensitive issues.

China actively promotes cooperation in various areas of the EAS. Since 2015 China has hosted the Second EAS New Energy Forum, Second EAS Clean Energy Forum, EAS Wildlife Protection Symposium, EAS Track II Seminar on Maritime Cooperation for Security in the Indian and Pacific Oceans, Fifth EAS Workshop on

Regional Security Framework, and the Fourth and Fifth EAS Earthquake Search and Rescue Exercises.

5. ASEAN Regional Forum (ARF)

The ARF has become an influential and inclusive platform for official multilateral security dialogue and cooperation in the Asia–Pacific region. All parties have been making confidence-building measures their core mission, promoting preventive diplomacy based on consensus, and steadily enhancing cooperation in nontraditional security fields.

On July 26, 2016, the 23rd ARF Ministerial Meeting was held in Vientiane, Laos. The Chinese side pointed out that the forum should focus on confidence-building measures throughout the whole process, and explore a preventive diplomacy mode compatible with the regional situation step by step on the basis of consensus. All sides should further strengthen dialogue and cooperation, enhance understanding and mutual trust among regional countries, work together to cope with nontraditional security threats and other challenges, and enable the forum to make greater contributions to regional peace and security.

China has actively led practical cooperation within the framework of the ARF. Since 2015 it has hosted the Workshop on Cyber Security Capacity Building, Third ARF Workshop on Space Security, ARF Seminar on Maritime Risk Management and Cooperation, ARF Workshop on Marine Oil Spill Emergency Response and Management and Disposal Cooperation, ARF Workshop on Strengthening Management of Cross-Border Movement of Criminals, ARF Workshop on Green Shipping, and ARF Workshop on Urban Emergency Rescue.

6. ASEAN Defence Ministers' Meeting Plus (ADMM-Plus)

The ADMM-Plus is the highest-level and largest defense and security dialogue and cooperation mechanism in the Asia–Pacific region. It has played a vital role in enhancing mutual trust and promoting pragmatic cooperation among the defense ministries and armed forces of all parties.

On November 4, 2015, at the Third ADMM-Plus held in Kuala Lumpur, Malaysia, the Chinese side pointed out that all parties should push for the building of an open, inclusive, transparent, and even-handed regional security cooperation framework, keep deepening pragmatic defense cooperation, properly handle disputes, manage and control risks, and jointly safeguard regional peace and stability.

In 2016 the Chinese military participated in the ADMM-Plus peacekeeping and demining joint exercise in India and the maritime security and counterterrorism exercises in Brunei and Singapore. From 2017 to 2020 China and Thailand will co-chair the ADMM-Plus Experts' Working Group on Counterterrorism.

7. Lancang-Mekong Cooperation (LMC)

The establishment of the Lancang-Mekong Cooperation (LMC) framework was an important initiative put forward by Premier Li Keqiang at the 17th China–ASEAN Summit in November 2014. This initiative aims to enhance good-neighborliness and friendship among the six countries along the Lancang-Mekong River through pragmatic cooperation, promote sub-regional economic and social development, and forge a community of shared future for solidarity, mutual assistance, even-handed consultation, shared benefits, and mutually beneficial cooperation in the sub-region. The LMC framework has China, Cambodia, Laos, Myanmar, Thailand, and Vietnam as its members.

The LMC has registered encouraging progress. One leaders' meeting, one foreign ministers' meeting, and three senior officials' meetings have been held by November 2016. In November 2015, the First LMC Foreign Ministers' Meeting was held in Jinghong, in China's Yunnan province, at which the foreign ministers of the six countries announced the start of the LMC process, reached broad consensus on the direction of future cooperation and the structure of the LMC, and put forward proposals for a number of cooperation projects.

On March 23, 2016, the First LMC Leaders' Meeting was held in Sanya, in China's Hainan province, officially launching the LMC framework. Leaders of the six countries reviewed past progress, shared their vision for the future of the LMC, and agreed to coordinate their strategies for development, make overall planning of their cooperation resources, share the benefits of development, and build a community of shared future among the Lancang-Mekong countries. The meeting confirmed the "3+5" mechanism of cooperation: the three cooperation pillars of political and security issues, economic and sustainable development, and cultural and people-to-people exchanges; and the five key priority areas of connectivity, production capacity, cross-border economic cooperation, water resources, and agriculture and poverty reduction. The meeting issued the Sanya Declaration of the First Lancang-Mekong Cooperation Leaders' Meeting and the Joint Statement on Production Capacity Cooperation Among the Lancang-Mekong Countries, and adopted a joint list of early-harvest programs in areas such as connectivity, water resources, public health, and poverty reduction.

8. Shanghai Cooperation Organization (SCO)

Since 2015 the Shanghai Cooperation Organization (SCO) has maintained sound and steady development. Progress has been made in political, security, economic, and cultural cooperation, leading to the firmer international standing and greater influence of the SCO.

President Xi Jinping attended the 15th Meeting of the Council of the Heads of State of the SCO member states on July 9–10, 2015 in Ufa, Russia, where they signed the Ufa Declaration of the Heads of State of SCO Member States and the SCO Member States Agreement on Border Defence Cooperation, and approved important documents including the Shanghai Cooperation Organization's Development Strategy until 2025 and the SCO Member States 2016–2018 Cooperation Program on Combating Terrorism, Separatism, and Extremism.

Premier Li Keqiang chaired the 14th Meeting of the Council of the Heads of Government (Prime Ministers) of the SCO member states held in China on December 14–15, 2015. The leaders at the meeting laid out plans for cooperation in various fields for the next stage, issued the Statement of the Heads of Government (Prime Ministers) of SCO Member States on Regional Economic Cooperation, adopted the resolution on Preparation for Creating the SCO Development Bank and the SCO Development Foundation (Specialized Account), and witnessed the signing of the Program of Interaction Between the Customs Agencies of the SCO member states for 2016–2021 and the Memorandum of Understanding between the Secretariat of the SCO and the Secretariat of the UN Economic and Social Commission for Asia and the Pacific.

On June 23–24, 2016, the 16th Meeting of the Council of the Heads of State of the SCO member states was held in Tashkent, Uzbekistan. President Xi Jinping attended the meeting. The heads of the member states signed the Tashkent Declaration on the 15th Anniversary of the SCO, approved the Action Plan for 2016–2020 on Implementation of the SCO Development Strategy Toward 2025, and adopted the Memorandums of the Obligations on the Entry of the Republic of India and the Islamic Republic of Pakistan to the SCO.

Since 2015 meetings of heads of various departments including Security Council secretaries, foreign ministers, defense ministers, economic and trade ministers, culture ministers, and heads of emergency response agencies have been held. These meetings deepened and expanded cooperation in various fields, and increased the SCO's international influence. China has promoted and participated in SCO cooperation across the board. China's bilateral relations with other SCO member states, observer states, and dialogue partners have continued to grow.

9. Conference on Interaction and Confidence-Building Measures in Asia (CICA)

On April 27–28, 2016, the Fifth Meeting of the Ministers of Foreign Affairs of the CICA member states was held in Beijing. President Xi Jinping attended the opening ceremony and delivered an important speech. The meeting issued the Declaration on Promoting Peace, Security, Stability, and Sustainable Development in Asia Through Dialogue and adopted the 2016–2018 Cooperation Initiative of the CICA Member States for Drug Control and the 2016–2018 CICA Initiative for the Implementation of Confidence-Building Measures for the Development of Small and Medium Enterprises.

China has actively implemented the confidence-building measures of CICA in all fields and made innovative efforts in the cooperation platform of CICA. Since 2015 China has hosted the founding conference of the CICA Youth Council, founding assembly of CICA Business Council, First CICA Non-Governmental

Forum and Third Think Tank Roundtable, which have helped to implement the confidence-building measures in cultural and economic fields, and promoted dialogue and exchange among young people, NGOs, and think tanks.

VI. China's Participation in Regional Non-Traditional Security Cooperation

1. Disaster Relief

Since 2015 the Chinese government has been actively involved in and promoted exchanges and cooperation on disaster relief in the Asia–Pacific region. China hosted the Eighth SCO Meeting of Heads of Emergency Prevention and Relief Agencies and the Third China–Japan–ROK Tabletop Exercise on Disaster Management, co-hosted with Malaysia the Fourth ARF Disaster Relief Exercise, and participated in the Third UN World Conference on Disaster Risk Reduction, Asian Ministerial Conference on Disaster Risk Reduction, International Drill of the Emergency Prevention and Relief Agencies of the SCO Member States, the Ninth APEC Senior Disaster Management Officials' Forum, and International Search and Rescue Advisory Group Asia–Pacific Regional Earthquake Response Exercise.

In January and July 2015 and in May 2016, when Malaysia, Myanmar, and Sri Lanka were hit by devastating floods, China immediately provided relief supplies to the three countries. In the wake of severe earthquakes in Nepal in April 2015 China sent rescue and medical teams and transportation detachments to the country and provided mobile field hospitals in support of disaster-relief efforts.

The Chinese government will continue to work with relevant parties to improve mutual visits of officials, information sharing, personnel training, technological exchanges, simulation exercises, scientific research cooperation, material reserves, and emergency aid, to enhance practical bilateral and multilateral cooperation in disaster relief, and improve disaster mitigation and relief capacity in the Asia–Pacific area.

2. Counterterrorism Cooperation

Since 2015 China has cooperated with a number of neighboring countries in combating terrorism-related human smuggling, and arrested a number of terrorist suspects and human smugglers active in the region. These efforts dealt a heavy blow to the illegal human smuggling networks of the "Eastern Turkistan Islamic Movement" (ETIM) and other terrorist organizations, and effectively countered and prevented the infiltration efforts of the ETIM and other terrorist organizations.

China has held bilateral anti-terrorism consultations with the US, Russia, Canada, the United Kingdom, India, Pakistan, the ROK, and Indonesia, hosted the 13th ARF Inter-Sessional Meeting on Counterterrorism and Transnational Crimes, and promoted cooperation on combating Internet-spread violent and terrorist audios/videos and cross-border terrorist activities. In addition, by taking an active part in the APEC Counterterrorism Working Group, the Global Counterterrorism Forum, and the ASEAN plus China Meeting on Transnational Crime at ministerial level, China has strengthened exchanges in anti-terrorism cooperation.

China, Afghanistan, Pakistan, and Tajikistan have established a coordination mechanism on counterterrorism cooperation among the military forces of the four countries, aimed at conducting coordination on situation analysis, verification of clues, sharing of intelligence, capacity building, joint training and personnel training, and providing mutual assistance.

3. Cooperation in Combating Transnational Crimes

The Chinese government places high importance on combating transnational crimes, and is committed to fully and earnestly implementing the United Nations Convention Against Transnational Organized Crime (UNTOC). China has concluded 123 judicial assistance and extradition treaties with 70 countries, and actively promoted the establishment of bilateral judicial and law-enforcement cooperation mechanisms with the US and Canada. These efforts have provided a solid legal basis and effective platform for China's cooperation with relevant countries in combating transnational crime in all forms.

China is actively involved in international cooperation in combating transnational organized crimes and maintains sound cooperation with the UN and other international and regional organizations. It has facilitated law enforcement and security cooperation along the Mekong River and conducted multiple joint actions with Southeast Asian countries in combating transnational crimes, and effectively fought against human trafficking, telecom fraud, economic crimes, and drug-related crimes that are prevalent in the region. In October 2015 China hosted the China–ASEAN Ministerial Dialogue on Law Enforcement and Security Cooperation with the theme "Security for Prosperity" and the Ministerial Meeting on Law Enforcement and Security Cooperation along the Mekong River. In the Second Safe Mekong Joint Operation by China, Laos, Myanmar, and Thailand, over 10,000 suspects were arrested, more than 9,000 drug-related cases were solved, and a large quantity of narcotics was seized.

China stands ready to enhance judicial and law enforcement cooperation with relevant countries in a joint effort to fight transnational crimes, and calls on all countries to enhance their political will for international cooperation, overcome differences in legal systems, promote cooperation within the framework of the UNTOC, including cooperation on extradition, provide wide judicial assistance, and cooperate in the recovery and disposal of criminal proceeds. China also encourages countries concerned to negotiate and conclude bilateral extradition and judicial assistance treaties for more concrete outcomes in cooperation to combat transnational crimes.

4. Cyber Security

Currently, cyber security is acquiring greater importance. Asia–Pacific countries are placing high importance on cyber security, increasing input and actively conducting dialogue and regional cooperation on this issue. China is a staunch supporter of and an active participant in international efforts to ensure cyber security. It believes that cyberspace should be used to promote economic and social development, maintain international peace and stability, and improve the well-being of mankind. Countries should strengthen dialogue and cooperation on the basis of mutual respect, equality, and mutual benefit, and build a peaceful, secure, open, and cooperative cyberspace and a multilateral, democratic, and transparent international internet regime. It is imperative that a universally accepted international code of conduct is formulated within the UN framework.

Since 2015 China has continued to promote cyber security within the UN framework and has been deeply involved in the process. China and other SCO member states have jointly submitted an updated version of the International Code of Conduct for Information Security to the UN General Assembly. China has contributed to the endeavors to formulate international rules governing cyberspace by taking an active part in and facilitating the efforts of the UN's Group of Governmental Experts on Cyber Security to produce its final report, which affirms that the principles enshrined in the Charter of the United Nations, including sovereign equality, non-interference in others' internal affairs, and non-use of force, also apply to cyberspace. China has also played a constructive role in the UN Internet Governance Forum and the High-Level Meeting on the Overall Review of the Implementation of the Outcomes of the World Summit on the Information Society.

China has continuously strengthened bilateral dialogues and practical cooperation on cyber security with countries in the region. China and Russia have signed the Information Security Cooperation Agreement and held a new round of consultation on cyber security. China–Japan–ROK, China–ROK, and China–EU dialogues on cyber security have been held. China and the US held the High-Level Joint Dialogue on Cybercrime and Related Issues.

China attaches great importance to and takes an active part in regional mechanisms under the ARF, BRICS, and SCO in order to promote balanced and inclusive development of network security cooperation in the region. China is actively involved in the BRICS Expert Working Group on Cyber-Security and the SCO Expert Group on International Information Security, and has worked on the Asian–African Legal Consultative Organization to establish a Working Group on International Legal Issues Concerning Cyber Space. China also hosted the Second World Internet Conference.

5. Cooperation on Maritime Security

The year 2015 was the year of China–ASEAN maritime cooperation. Maritime cooperation is a key part of building the twenty-first century Maritime Silk Road. China and the ASEAN countries conducted a series of exchanges and cooperative events on maritime security, scientific research, and environmental protection. China and Thailand conducted a scientific expedition in the Andaman Sea, and held the Fourth Joint Committee Meeting on Marine Cooperation. China and Malaysia signed the Memorandum of Understanding on the Establishment of the China–Malaysia Joint Oceanographic Research Center. The construction of the China–Indonesia Center for the Oceans and Climate, and the Joint Oceanic Observation Station, proceeded in an orderly way. The Third China–Southeast Asian Countries Marine Research and Environmental Protection Cooperation Forum was also held.

China has actively participated in and advanced dialogues and cooperation on maritime security. Since 2015 China has hosted the Asia–Pacific Heads of Maritime Administrations Conference, the multitask exercise "Cooperation for Law Enforcement 2015" of the North Pacific Coast Guard Agencies Forum, International Training Course for Lighthouse Management Personnel in the Asia–Pacific Area, and the Asia–Pacific Mass Rescue Operation Training Course and Tabletop Exercise. China has continued its cooperation with Australia and Malaysia in the search for Malaysia Airlines Flight MH370, and provided 20 million Australian dollars for follow-up search-and-rescue efforts in this regard.

China has vigorously supported the capacity building and development of the Information Sharing Center (ISC) under the Regional Cooperation Agreement on Combating Piracy and Armed Robbery, and accredited maritime police officers to the ISC. In June 2016, as requested by Vietnam, China dispatched vessels and airplanes to assist in searching for and rescuing Vietnamese airplanes which had crashed, along with their crew members. From December 2008 to January 2016 Chinese fleets sent to the Gulf of Aden and Somali waters as escorts conducted 909 missions, escorting 6,112 Chinese and foreign civilian vessels.

6. Cooperation in Non-Proliferation and Disarmament

China supports and takes an active part in international arms control, disarmament, and nonproliferation efforts, and stands for the complete prohibition and thorough destruction of nuclear weapons. China has earnestly implemented the outcomes of all the review conferences of the Treaty on the Non-Proliferation of Nuclear Weapons (NPT), and played a constructive role in the Ninth NPT review conference and the P5 Conference on Implementing the NPT. China stands ready to work with all parties through unremitting efforts to achieve the three NPT goals of "nuclear nonproliferation and disarmament, and peaceful use of nuclear power."

China holds that establishing a Southeast Asia Nuclear-Weapons-Free Zone is of great significance for promoting regional and global peace and stability. China supports the efforts of ASEAN countries to establish a Southeast Asia Nuclear-Weapons-Free Zone, and stands for the early signing and going into effect of the protocol to the Treaty on the Southeast Asia Nuclear-Weapons-Free Zone. China has solved all the remaining issues concerning the protocol with ASEAN, and looks forward to the signing of the protocol at an early date. China will continue to participate constructively in consultation between ASEAN and the five nuclear countries, and facilitate consultation between ASEAN and the other four nuclear countries to resolve their differences so that the protocol can be signed and come into effect at an early date.

China stands for the complete prohibition and thorough destruction of all weapons of mass destruction, including chemical weapons, opposes the development, stockpiling, and use of chemical weapons by any one, and supports the purposes and goals of the Convention on the Prohibition of the Development, Production, Stockpiling, and Use of Chemical Weapons and on Their Destruction, and the work of the Organization for the Prohibition of Chemical Weapons (OPCW). China is earnest in fulfilling its obligations under the Chemical Weapons Convention in its entirety, and attaches great importance to and supports international exchanges and cooperation under the convention.

In 2015 China held the 13th Regional Meeting of National Authorities of Asian State Parties to the Convention on the Prohibition of the Development, Production, Stockpiling, and Use of Chemical Weapons and on Their Destruction, hosted the Advanced Protection and Assistance Course with the OPCW, and held the Training Course on National Points of Contacts of States in the Asia–Pacific Region together with the UN Security Council 1540 Committee. China also participated in the Asian Senior-Level Talks on Non-Proliferation, ARF Inter-Sessional Workshop on Non-Proliferation, and other related events.

Conclusion

The Chinese people are working hard to realize the Chinese Dream of the great renewal of the Chinese nation. In this process, China will bring greater opportunities and benefits for development and cooperation in the Asia–Pacific region. China's development adds to the momentum for world peace. China will firmly follow the path of peaceful development and the policy of "building friendship and partnership with neighboring countries" to create an amicable, secure, and prosperous neighborhood. China remains committed to the principles of amity, sincerity, mutual benefit, and inclusiveness in conducting neighborhood diplomacy and the goal of maintaining and promoting stability and prosperity in the Asia–Pacific region. China stands ready to work with all countries in the region to pursue mutually beneficial cooperation and steadily advance security dialogues and cooperation in the Asia–Pacific region, and the building of a new model of international relations so as to create a brighter future for this region.

2. December 2016: The Right to Development: China's Philosophy, Practice, and Contribution[2]

The State Council Information Office
The People's Republic of China

Contents

Preamble

    I. The Philosophy of the Right to Development Abreast with the Times
    II. The System Ensuring the People's Right to Development
    III. Effectively Realizing Economic Development
    IV. Enhancing Political Development
    V. Promoting Cultural Progress
    VI. Promoting Social Development
    VII. Accelerating Environment-Friendly Development
    VIII. Promoting Common Development

Conclusion

Preamble

Development is a universal human theme, providing for people's basic needs and giving them hope of better life. The right to development is an inalienable human right, symbolizing dignity and honor. Only through development can we address global challenges; only through development can we protect basic civil rights of the people; only through development can we promote the progress of human society.

China, with a population of over 1.3 billion, is the largest developing country in the world. Development is the top priority of the Communist Party of China (CPC) in governance and national revitalization, and the key to resolving all other problems. Based on its prevailing conditions, China adheres to the Chinese socialist path and to the philosophy that development is of paramount importance. China integrates the principle of universal application of human rights with the country's reality. While striving to enhance the people's well-being through development and materialize their right to development, China endeavors to achieve higher-level development by protecting their right to development. In this regard, China has made notable progress and blazed a path in protecting human rights during the development of human civilization.

Since the 18th CPC National Congress in 2012, the CPC Central Committee with Xi Jinping as its core has highlighted the idea of people-centered development. In the course of realizing the Two Centenary Goals[1] and the Chinese Dream of revitalizing the Chinese nation, it has focused on safeguarding and improving people's well-being, advancing all social programs, and protecting people's rights to equal participation and development. The aim is to share development benefits and achieve common prosperity among all people of the country.

On the 30th anniversary of the publication of the "Declaration on the Right to Development by the United Nations," China, dedicated to advocating, practicing, and promoting the right to development, is willing to join the international community to share its philosophy and experience in this regard and to boost sound development of global human rights.

I. The Philosophy of the Right to Development Abreast with the Times

Equal access to development opportunities and development benefits are the ideals of human society wherein each and every citizen can achieve well-rounded development and enjoy full right to development.

The Chinese people are diligent, wise, innovative, and progressive. In traditional Chinese culture, concepts such as "moderate prosperity" (*xiao-kang*), "great harmony" (*Datong*), "having ample food and clothing" (*fengyi zushi*), and "living and working in peace and contentment" (*anju leye*) fully reflect the Chinese people's aspiration for and pursuit of a better, happier life. In the long course of history, the Chinese people have always striven for better and shared development opportunities, conditions, and benefits. In ancient times, China was for long the world leader in agriculture, and contributed to human progress with extraordinary development achievements. Studies reveal that until the mid-nineteenth century, China's GDP and per capita GDP were the world's highest. Before the sixteenth century, China contributed 173 of the world's top 300 innovations and discoveries.

After the Industrial Revolution started in the eighteenth century, China began losing its leadership. Foreign aggression and expansion by Western colonialists completely destroyed conditions for development in China. Repeated invasions by foreign powers, particularly from the West, from 1840 to 1949, and China's corrupt ruling class and backward social system, reduced China to a semi-colonial and semi-feudal society. There was constant warfare, an unstable society, economic depression, no security of livelihood, and extreme poverty. *The Cambridge History of China: Republican China 1912–1949* describes China's situation in the first half of the twentieth century as follows: "the great majority of Chinese merely sustained and reproduced themselves at the subsistence level . . . the standard of life for many fell short even of that customary level."[2] "As a system, China's economy which was 'pre-modern' even in the mid-twentieth century ceased to be viable only after 1949."[3] In these 110 years, the Chinese people struggled arduously for their right to development and equal access to development opportunity. The Chinese people are fully aware of the value of development and of their right to development.

The founding of the People's Republic of China (PRC) in 1949 ushered in a new era for China's development. The PRC has provided full development opportunities and conditions to the people, and vast scope to realize that right. Through more than 60 years of effort, China's overall national strength has greatly increased;

standards of living have achieved a historical leap from poverty to moderate prosperity; the people's right to development in economy, politics, culture, society, and environment has been effectively protected.

China feeds more than 20 percent of the world's population with less than 10 percent of the world's arable land. Through more than 30 years of reform and opening-up, China has lifted 700 million people out of poverty, accounting for more than 70 percent of the global reduction in poverty. China has established the world's largest social security system, and average life expectancy had grown from 35 years in 1949 to 76.34 years in 2015, ranking high among the developing countries. The level of education has soared: in 1949, more than 80 percent of the national population was illiterate, and the enrollment rate of school-age children was only 20 percent. In 2015, net enrollment rates were as follows: primary school-age children—99.88 percent; nine-year compulsory education—93 percent; high school—87 percent. The enrollment rate for higher education has reached a level approaching that of medium-developed countries. According to the "China National Human Development Report 2016" released by the United Nations, China's Human Development Index (HDI) in 2014 ranked 90th among 188 countries, already in the high human development group.

Over the years, proceeding from reality and following the trend of the times, China has maintained the people's principal position in the country and created its own path by taking the central task of economic development and upholding the Four Cardinal Principles[4] and the policy of reform and opening-up to serve its practice of Chinese socialism, and following the philosophy of innovative, balanced, eco-friendly, open, and shared development, and thus contributed to enriching and improving the concept of right to development.

The rights to subsistence and development are the primary, basic human rights. Poverty is the biggest obstacle to human rights. Without the production and supply of material goods, it is difficult or even impossible to realize any other human right. Development is a means of eliminating poverty. It provides necessary conditions for realizing other human rights, and releases human potential. The right to development is incorporated into other human rights, while the latter create the conditions for people to facilitate development and realize the right to development. Safeguarding the right to development is the precondition for realizing economic, cultural, social, and environmental rights, and obtaining civil and political rights. China appreciates the articulation in the UN's "Declaration on the Right to Development":

> The right to development is an inalienable human right by virtue of which every human person and all peoples are entitled to participate in, contribute to, and enjoy economic, social, cultural and political development, in which all human rights and fundamental freedoms can be fully realized.

The people hold the principal position concerning the right to development. China values the people's supremacy and regards the people as the fundamental driver of development, striving for the people, relying on the people, and sharing among the people. It takes improving popular well-being and well-rounded development as the starting point and ultimate goal, and fully mobilizes people's enthusiasm, initiative, and creativity to participate in, contribute to, and benefit from development. To build a moderately prosperous society in all respects and realize the Chinese Dream of revitalizing the Chinese nation means to provide better education, more secure employments, more satisfying income, more reliable social security, better medical services, more comfortable housing, and a better environment, so that all individuals can develop, contribute to society, and share the opportunity to pursue excellence and realize their dreams.

The right to development is a unity of individual and collective human rights. China values both individual and collective human rights as well as balance and mutual promotion between the two. "The free development of each individual is the condition for the free development of all people." Only through individual development can a collective develop; only in a collective can individuals achieve well-rounded development. The right to development is a human right owned by each individual as well as by the country, the nation, and the entire population. The right to development can be maximized only in the unity of individuals and collective. China values the articulation in UN's "Declaration on the Right to Development": "Equality of opportunity for development is a prerogative both of nations and of individuals who make up nations." They are all entitled to participate in and share the benefits of development on an equal basis.

The realization of the right to development is a historical course. There is no end either to development or to realizing the right to development. The latter is an ongoing process of improvement. China is still in the primary stage of socialism and will long remain so. The inadequacy in meeting the ever-growing material and cultural needs of the people because of backward social production will remain the principal social problem. As a major developing country, China faces challenging problems and heavy tasks in development. In pursuit of more equal participation and development, China needs consistent efforts to fully realize the people's right to development.

The protection of the right to development must be sustainable. Sustainable development is a prerequisite for materializing the right to development, an embodiment of intergenerational equity. Unbalanced, uncoordinated, and unequal development reflects unsustainable development, as does an extensive development model. China is pursuing a sustainable approach to production, utilization, and consumption of natural resources. China now follows a sustainable and resilient socio-economic development path so as to meet the needs of both present and future generations. China has a development mindset of balance and sustainability, regarding the harmonious development between humanity and nature, between economy and society, as a new means of realizing and protecting the right to development.

The right to development must be enjoyed and shared by all peoples. Realizing the right to development is the responsibility of all countries and also the obligation of the international community. It requires governments of all countries to formulate development strategies and policies suited to their own realities, and it requires concerted efforts of the international community as a whole. China calls on all countries to pursue equal, open, all-around and innovative common development, promotes inclusive development, and creates conditions for all peoples to share the right to development. Global economic governance must be based on equality. It must better reflect the new world economic pattern, give an enhanced voice and representation to emerging markets and developing countries, ensure that all countries enjoy equality of rights, opportunities, and rules in international economic cooperation, and ensure the right to development is shared.

II. The System Ensuring the People's Right to Development

China has established an integrated system of legislature, strategy development, planning, and judicial remedy to ensure its people's right to development, and makes continued efforts to improve it. The people's right to development is realized through a framework of institutions, strategies, policies, and measures that are constructive, practical, efficient, and compulsory.

1. The Constitution and Laws

China has established a legal system with Chinese characteristics. With the Constitution at the core, it is based on laws related to the Constitution, the civil laws, the commercial laws, and other major branches of the laws, and consists of laws, administrative regulations, and local regulations, providing a legal basis for the people's right to development.

As the nation's fundamental law, the Constitution establishes and protects the people's right to development in all respects. In the Preamble, equal development is set as the fundamental guiding principle, and the nation's core task is to "promote the coordinated development of the material, political and spiritual civilizations, and to turn China into a socialist country that is prosperous, powerful, democratic and culturally advanced." The Constitution establishes such principles as the people's democracy and equal development, and stipulates that "all power in the People's Republic of China belongs to the people"; "the people administer state affairs and manage economic and cultural undertakings and social affairs through various channels and in various ways in accordance with the provisions of law"; "the state develops a relationship of equality, unity and mutual assistance among all of China's nationalities." Article 33 of the Constitution sets the fundamental principle that "the state respects and preserves human rights." In Chapter II, the Constitution stipulates the Chinese citizens' right to economic, political, cultural, and social development.

China has promulgated and implemented a series of laws and regulations to protect the right to development of all citizens, especially that of the ethnic minorities, women, children, senior citizens, and the disabled. The Law on Regional Ethnic Autonomy stipulates that people of all ethnic minority groups shall

> speed up the economic and cultural development of the ethnic autonomous areas, work toward their unity and prosperity, and strive for the common

prosperity of all ethnic groups and for the transformation of China into a socialist country with a high level of culture and democracy.

The Law on the Protection of Women's Rights and Interests stipulates that

women shall enjoy equal rights with men in all aspects of political, economic, cultural, social and family life. It is a basic state policy to realize equality between men and women. The state shall take necessary measures to gradually improve various systems for the protection of the rights and interests of women and to eliminate all kinds of discrimination against women.

The Law on the Protection of Minors stipulates that "minors shall enjoy the right to life, the right to development, the right to being protected, and the right to participation." The Law on the Protection of the Rights and Interests of the Elderly stipulates that

the state shall protect the lawful rights and interests of the elderly. The elderly shall have the right to obtain material assistance from the state and society, the right to enjoy social services and social preferential treatment, and the right to participate in social development and share the achievements in development.

The Law on the Protection of Disabled Persons stipulates that "disabled persons shall enjoy equal rights with other citizens in political, economic, cultural, social, family life and other aspects."

2. National Development Strategies

The world is a colorful place, with many different development patterns. Summarizing its historical experience and based on its prevailing conditions, China has chosen a socialist path. It strives to build socialism with Chinese characteristics, create a beautiful life for the Chinese people, and realize the people's right to development.

To build socialism with Chinese characteristics, China sets its national development strategies based on the need to protect and realize its people's right to development. In the early 1980s, the CPC proposed the "three-step" development strategy: First, to double the 1981 GNP and ensure the provision of basic material needs by 1990; second, to double the 1991 GNP by the end of the twentieth century and bring people's living standards to a level of "reasonable prosperity"; and third, to quadruple that new GNP to the level of moderately developed countries by the mid-twenty-first century, and bring the Chinese people an affluent life.

At the 15th CPC National Congress in 1997, the third step was made more specific, and a new "three-step" strategy for the first half of the twenty-first century was put forward. First, in the first decade of the twenty-first century, to double GNP compared to the 2000 level, raise levels of prosperity, and form a relatively complete socialist market economy; second, with ten more years' hard work, to further develop the economy and improve various institutions by the centenary of the founding of the CPC; and third, to achieve basic modernization and complete the building of a socialist country that is prosperous, democratic, and culturally advanced by the centenary of the founding of the People's Republic of China in the mid-twenty-first century.

After entering the twenty-first century, the CPC set itself the strategic task of building a "moderately prosperous society in all respects." Since the 18th CPC National Congress in 2012, the Party's Central Committee, with Xi Jinping as its core, has set the "people's wish for a better life" as its goal of governance, and defined the Two Centenary Goals. That is, to enable the people to live prosperous lives and complete the building of a moderately prosperous society in all respects by 2020, the centenary of the CPC (founded in 1921), and to bring China's per capita GDP on par with that of moderately developed countries, and build China into a modern socialist country that is prosperous, strong, democratic, culturally advanced, and harmonious by the centenary of the PRC (founded in 1949) in the mid-twenty-first century.

To achieve the Two Centenary Goals, the CPC strives to promote coordinated progress in economic, political, cultural, social, and ecological areas, and to implement the Four-pronged Comprehensive Strategy, viz., building a moderately prosperous society in all respects, driving reform to a deeper-level, fully implementing the rule of law, and strengthening Party discipline. Based on economic growth, the Party will continue to build the socialist market economy, promote democracy, advanced culture, ecological progress, and a harmonious society, and ensure that the people are better-off, that the nation grows stronger and more prosperous, that the environment is clean and beautiful, and that the people's right to development is protected and promoted in a more solid and effective manner.

3. Overall Development Plans

In accordance with the goal to build a modern socialist country and the associated development strategies, the Chinese government regularly makes national development plans to ensure the people's right to development. In the period between 1953 and 2001, it issued national development plans every five years addressing issues concerning the country's economy, culture, and society. After 2006 the plan has been changed to a program which is less detailed, with fewer numerical targets to guide the macro-economy and social development. To date China has made 13 consecutive five-year plans (including the program starting from 2006) for the nation's economic and social development. These plans have connected the country's overall development goals to the concrete plans to implement them, and are divided into different stages to steadily promote the people's right to development, with mid- and long-term guidelines, goals and directions, basic requirements, and specific measures.

On October 29, 2015, the Fifth Plenary Session of the 18th CPC Central Committee approved the "Suggestions of the CPC Central Committee on Developing the 13th Five-Year Program for National Economic and Social Development." On March 16, 2016, the Fourth Session of the 12th National People's Congress approved by vote the "Outline of the 13th Five-Year Development Program of the People's Republic of China for National Economic and Social Development." Following the new philosophies on development and based on universal participation and benefits, China stresses equal opportunities, with an emphasis on ensuring basic living standards, improving the people's well-being, and realizing a moderately prosperous society for all the people. China has made breakthroughs in equal access to the fruits of development, mainly in increasing the supply of public services, carrying out poverty eradication programs, enhancing the quality of education, granting equal access to educational resources, promoting employment and entrepreneurship, bridging the income gap, establishing a fairer and more sustainable social security system, enhancing public health and fitness, and strengthening the balanced development of the people.

China ensures its people's right to development also by making national human rights action plans. It has issued the "National Human Rights Action Plan" 2009–2010, 2012–2015, and 2016–2020. In these plans, the government puts the people's right to development at the core of human rights, and strives to address the most immediate problems that are of the most concern to the public. While promoting the sound and rapid development of the economy and society, China ensures that all members of the society enjoy the rights to equal participation and equal development.

4. Special Action Plans

The Chinese government formulates special action plans in the fields of economy, culture, society, and environment to ensure people's right to development. It has implemented a wide array of action plans in areas such as poverty alleviation, the internet, innovation and entrepreneurship, science and technology, trade, and regional development. Specifically, these plans have been designed to promote entrepreneurship and innovation among farmers, to send agricultural specialists to rural areas to develop agriculture, to develop rural and agricultural resources in support of rural migrant workers who return to their home villages to start businesses, to improve people's lives by developing high-tech industries in selected counties, to transform the growth model of the western areas through science and technology, and to revitalize the old industrial bases in the Northeast through science and technology. The state has effectively implemented a series of action plans regarding educational development, health improvement, awards for high-caliber professionals, and the cultural industry, such as the action plans to revitalize education in the twenty-first century, to enhance teachers' status in the stage of compulsory education in rural areas, to promote special education, to help girls who have dropped out of school to return to campus, and to support the more developed cities in the eastern areas to train professionals for the western areas. China has implemented a series of action plans regarding employment, social security, food and medical care, disability prevention, and health and fitness, such as the Spring Breeze Action Plan to promote employment, and other plans to realize full coverage of social security, to eliminate malaria, to prevent and control nosocomial infection, to carry out rehabilitation programs for children with impairments and disabilities, to reduce the number of newborns with defects and disabilities, to prevent incidences of disability, and to improve the nutritional status and fitness of the Chinese. The state has issued action plans on pollution prevention and control, energy conservation, and biodiversity, such as action plans to prevent and control water pollution, to reduce high-risk pollutants, to utilize coal in a clean and efficient manner, to upgrade and renovate coal power for energy saving and emissions reduction, to build obstacle-free cities or counties for the disabled, and to protect biodiversity.

China has also made special plans to ensure the right to development of ethnic minorities, women, children, the elderly, and the disabled. The plans include those on the development of ethnic minorities, of women, of children, of the elderly, and of disabled persons, with clear goals and targeted policies for different groups to solve the problems hindering their development, ensuring that they can pursue self-development and enjoy the fruits of reform on an equal basis.

5. The Judicial Remedy Mechanism

China is making enhanced efforts to strengthen judicial protection and remedy to ensure the people's right to development. It has built a judicial remedy mechanism in this regard to prevent and punish infringements of people's right to development.

The government is driving the reform of the judicial relief system to a deeper level to ensure the right to development of disadvantaged groups. The state provides judicial relief to victims of crimes or parties suffering from infringements of civil rights who cannot obtain effective compensation through litigation, and provides help to parties in certain types of cases who are in dire need of relief and are entitled to such relief. Eligible parties mainly receive relief money, and help in the forms of consultation and education. Judicial relief complements legal aid and litigation relief, and is linked with other forms of social relief and aid. The government is conducting research on opening first-aid fast track at hospitals for those injured in criminal cases, providing psychotherapy for victims with severe PTSD cases, and sending social workers to help immobilized victims, so as to further enhance judicial relief.

In 2014 the state issued the "Opinions on Establishing and Improving the National Judicial Relief System (trial)," which was followed by a marked expansion in the scale and increases in the number of judicial relief cases. In 2014 and 2015, the central government and local governments allocated a total of RMB 2.47 billion and RMB 2.95 billion for judicial relief funds, benefiting over 80,000 parties concerned in 2014. In 2013–2015 people's courts at all levels reduced or exempted a total of RMB 625 million for litigation parties, ensuring the right to litigation of the poor.

The government strives to strengthen the effectiveness of legal aid, and ensures the right of impoverished people to judicial relief. In 1994, China began to form a legal aid system, providing free consultation, agency, criminal defense, and other legal services to people in need. In 2003, the State Council issued the Regulations on Legal Aid to define the scale of legal aid, delegating the power to the people's governments of provinces, autonomous regions, and municipalities directly under the central government to supplement the issues to be covered by legal aid, and set the standards for receiving legal aid in light of the local conditions. Currently there are 23 provinces that have expanded the scope of issues covered by legal aid, and 19 provinces have adjusted the standards for receiving legal aid. The Criminal Procedural Law (revised in 2012) included suspects as recipients of legal aid, alongside defendants. Over the past five years, the number of legal aid cases has been growing by 11.4 percent annually, and women, children, the elderly, the disabled, and rural migrant workers have received timely and higher quality legal aid services. In May 2015, at its 12th meeting, the CPC Central Leading Group for Overall and Further Reforms reviewed and approved the "Opinions on Improving the Legal Aid System," with measures to further enlarge the coverage of legal aid for civil and administrative lawsuits, reduce the thresholds for receiving legal aid, and gradually make legal aid available to low-income groups to benefit people in need.

The government strengthens judicial remedy to protect the right to development of disadvantaged groups. China has always attached importance to the judicial protection of the right to development and other basic human rights in criminal cases. The state punishes crimes targeted at women, children, the elderly, the disabled, and rural migrant workers, and strengthens the protection of special groups' rights to healthy physical and psychological development and their economic and social rights. The government strives to prevent or severely punish the abduction and trafficking of women and children, and such crimes have been effectively curbed. The state has issued "Opinions on Punishing Sex Crimes Against Minors" and "Opinions on Handling the Infringements of Minors' Rights and Interests by Guardians," so as to enhance the judicial protection of minors' rights and interests. The state has promulgated "Opinions on Safeguarding the Legitimate Rights and Interests of Disabled Persons in Procuratorial Work," mandating severe punishment for crimes that infringe upon the rights and interests of disabled people in accordance with the law.

The government attaches importance to the role of arbitration, and protects the equal right to development of certain groups. By ending disputes through arbitration and punishing infringements according to law, China endeavors to strengthen procedure-based protection of the people's rights. By the end of 2015, 80 percent of township- and community-level employment and social security centers had set up organizations to mediate labor disputes, up by 14 percent from the 2014 figure. A total of 2,919 administrative divisions at or above county level (about 91 percent of the total) had arbitration offices for labor disputes, up by 208 percent compared with the figure of 946 at the end of the 11th Five-Year Plan period (2006–2010). In 2010–2015, China's mediation and arbitration organizations handled a total of 7.57 million cases, bringing 90 percent to a conclusion.

III. Effectively Realizing Economic Development

China always considers economic development as the central task, laying a solid foundation for safeguarding the right to development. At the same time, economic development is strengthened by safeguarding the people's right to development. Since the reform and opening-up policy was launched in 1978, China has witnessed rapid economic growth, and has become the world's second largest economy. There have been two historic leaps in living standards, from living in poverty to having access to basic material needs, and then to moderate prosperity.

The right to subsistence of the poor is effectively guaranteed. The poverty reduction campaign in China is the most significant sign of China's progress in human rights. Since the end of 1978, China has realized "the most rapid large-scale poverty reduction in human history over the last 25 years."[5] According to the existing rural poverty standards, it has reduced the number of those living in poverty by more than 700 million, which is more than the total population of the United States, Russia, Japan, and Germany, and cut the rate of poverty to 5.7 percent, becoming the first country to complete the United Nations Millennium Development Goals. By the end of 2015, the number of rural people living in poverty had fallen to 55.75 million. In the five autonomous regions of Inner Mongolia, Guangxi, Tibet, Ningxia, and Xinjiang, and in the provinces of Guizhou, Yunnan, and Qinghai, where ethnic minorities are concentrated, the number of rural people living in poverty had fallen to 18.13 million. China's poverty reduction campaign has effectively contributed to granting its disadvantaged people the right to development, laying a solid foundation for the building of a moderately prosperous society in all respects. In November 2015, the CPC Central Committee and the State Council issued "Decision on Winning the Tough Battle Against Poverty," making comprehensive arrangements for poverty eradication work in the following five years. In March 2016, the "Outline of the 13th Five-Year Program for the National Economic and Social Development of the People's Republic of China" was published, in which the Chinese government made strategic plans for the full implementation of the overall goal of poverty eradication. In order to realize the ambitious goal of relieving the rural poor population of poverty by 2020, China is carrying out a basic strategy of targeted poverty alleviation and targeted poverty eradication.

The right to work is fully realized. Economic development creates more jobs. Urban and rural employment continued to increase from 761 million in 2010 to 775 million in 2015. Within these figures, urban employment increased from 347 million to 404 million, representing an average annual increase of more than 11 million. In 2015 urban employment increased by 13.12 million, and the registered urban unemployment rate by the end of the year was 4.05 percent, showing steady progress in this work. From 2008 to 2015, the central government assigned a total of RMB 305.51 billion as subsidies to be used in employment. Since 2009, the Chinese government has implemented a policy of financial discount for small-sum guaranteed loans to women. By June 2016, a total of RMB 279.4 billion in loans had been provided to 5.38 million women, supporting more than 10 million, including women classified as poor, to start their own businesses or find work. The number of women in employment has increased continuously and their positions have improved. In 2014, employed women accounted for 45 percent of the total workforce in China, and female professional and technical personnel accounted for 46.5 percent of the national total.

The government strengthens skill training to promote more equitable sharing of job opportunities through capacity-building. By the end of 2015, the total number of skilled workers in the country had reached 167 million, of whom 45.01 million were highly skilled. The government actively promotes transfer of the rural labor force to employment in local or nearby places, ensuring that 65 percent can find employment within the local county economy. The government vigorously develops the service industry, creating jobs for rural migrant workers, and setting up farmers' markets and food stalls with reduced or zero fees. As a result, more than 80 percent of rural migrant workers have found jobs in small and micro businesses. The government also encourages rural migrant workers to return home and start businesses. By the end of 2015, 4.5 million rural migrant workers had returned home to start businesses, and rural small and micro businesses amounted to 6.99 million. By the end of 2014, China had 15.46 million private enterprises, and nearly 50 million self-employed businesses, representing increases of 83 percent and 44 percent over 2010; these businesses employed 250 million people. Internet entrepreneurship has helped nearly 10 million people find employment, and "internet+" is an important channel for creating jobs. The government takes measures to guide graduates to find employment through multiple channels, encourage entrepreneurship, and offer better employment services to graduates and give more assistance to those experiencing difficulties in finding jobs.

In recent years, the employment rate of new college graduates has been above 70 percent every year, and the overall employment rate at the end of the year has exceeded 90 percent. By aiding enterprises and offering employment support and assistance, the government helps unemployed persons and people having difficulty in securing jobs to find employment, and devotes particular attention to zero-employment families. From 2011 to 2015, more than 5.5 million unemployed urban people found jobs every year, while an annual average of almost 1.8 million people having difficulty in securing jobs found employment. Steady progress has been made in the employment of people with disabilities. During the 12th Five-Year Program period (2011–2015), the government helped 1.52 million urban residents with disabilities to find jobs. In 2015, 21,596,300 disabled people of working age across the country found jobs.

The people's basic living standards have greatly improved. In 1978, the Engel coefficient of urban households was 57.5 percent and that of rural households was 67.7 percent; in 2015, the figures dropped to 29.7 percent and 33.0 percent, respectively. From 1978 to 2015, urban residents saw an increase in their residential area from 6.7 square meters per capita to more than 33 square meters; the corresponding figures for rural residents were 8.1 square meters to more than 37 square meters. A housing security system with government-supported low-rent housing and economically affordable housing as the main forms is in place. In 2015, the national investment in residential buildings reached RMB 8,024.77 billion. Within this program, 7.72 million units of government-subsidized urban housing were completed, and construction on another 7.83 million units already started. The central government provided RMB 36.5 billion to subsidize the renovation of substandard houses for 4.32 million poor rural households around China. From 2011 to 2015, under the government-subsidized urban housing project, China built a total of 40.13 million new units, renovated 21.91 million households in shantytowns, and moved a large number of people with housing difficulties into apartments, realizing "livable" residences. From 2011 to 2015, public finance at all levels subsidized barrier-free reconstruction for 675,000 families with disabled members, improving their quality of life.

Travel conditions have greatly improved. From 1978 to 2015, highways in service rose from 890,000 km to 4.58 million km, and the civil aviation passenger throughput grew from 2.32 million to 915 million. In 2015, the total mileage of expressways open to traffic in China reached 123,500 km, the operating mileage of high-speed railways reached 19,000 km, 94.5 percent of villages had paved road access, and 94.3 percent of villages had access to bus services.

The people's living standards have significantly improved. From 1978 to 2015, the annual GDP increased from RMB 367.9 billion to RMB 68,550.6 billion, and per capita GDP grew from more than US$200 to above US$8,000. In 1978, per capita disposable income of urban households was only RMB 343.4, and per capita net income of rural households was only RMB 133.6. In 2015, per capita disposable income of all residents reached RMB 21,966; the figures were RMB 31,195 for urban residents and RMB 11,422 for rural residents. By the end of 2015, the total number of phone users nationwide reached 1,536.73 million, and 1,305.74 million of them were mobile phone users, with a penetration rate of 95.5 per 100 people. There were 213.37 million households with fixed broadband internet access, and 785.33 million mobile broadband users. The number of internet users was 688 million, and the household penetration rate of fixed broadband reached 50.3 percent. In 2015, Chinese residents made 127.86 million outbound trips, including 121.72 million private trips. Civilian car ownership was 95.08 million, of which 87.93 million were private cars.

IV. Enhancing Political Development

China continues to enrich and improve a political system suited to its own development by advancing Chinese socialist democracy and rule of law in an all-around way, ensuring effective protection of civil and political rights, and raising the levels of participation in and promotion of the political development process and allowing people to partake in the benefits of political development.

The people's congress system is the fundamental institutional guarantee of political development for the people. According to the Constitution, all power in the PRC belongs to the people, and the National People's Congress (NPC) and the local people's congresses at various levels are the organs through which the people exercise state power. The people's congress system guarantees citizens' rights to participate in development and share the resulting benefits in five ways:

1. Generating and supervising state organs involved in the implementation of the right to development. Paragraph 3 of Article 3 of the Constitution states that all administrative, judicial, and procuratorial organs of the state are created by the people's congresses to which they are responsible and under whose supervision they operate.
2. Formulating laws and regulations to foster development. By September 2016, the NPC and its Standing Committee had formulated the Constitution and 252 laws in effect. By July 2016, local people's congresses and their standing committees with legislative power had formulated 9,915 local regulations in effect.
3. Examining and approving development policy initiatives. Article 62 of the Constitution stipulates that the NPC exercises the functions and powers to examine and approve the plan for national economic and social development and the report on its implementation, and to examine and approve the state budget and the report on its implementation, among others.
4. Providing an open mechanism for the expression of public opinion. People express and claim their reasonable development interests by means such as the exercise of their rights to raise opinions, suggestions, and criticism, to file appeals and complaints, and to supervise.
5. Properly defining the relationship between public power and development interests.

In recent years China has introduced three major systems that are of relevance— the power list, negative list, and responsibility list. Since 2013 the State Council has published lists enumerating all matters subject to administrative approval by its departments, and prohibited the addition of any unlisted matters, with 618 matters canceled or delegated to lower authorities. In this way, the State Council endeavors to eliminate opportunities for exploiting public posts for profit, and to enhance the procedures for the exercise of power.

Democratic election is an important element of citizens' political rights. Since the policy of reform and opening up was introduced in 1978, great progress has been made toward establishing people's democracy and an equal right to vote. In 2010, the NPC adopted an amendment to the Electoral Law providing wider equality of voting rights. Among other measures it requires that deputies be elected to the people's congresses based on the same population ratio in urban and rural areas.

Between 2011 and 2012, the election of deputies to county-level people's congresses saw more than 981 million registered voters and a turnout rate of 90.24 percent; the election of deputies to township-level people's congresses recorded more than 723 million registered voters and a turnout rate of 90.55 percent. In these elections, measures were taken based on the conditions in each constituency to ensure the right to vote of the 200 million floating population, and to facilitate their voting. The basic principle was that voters cast their votes in the constituencies where their registered permanent residences are, while they may vote by proxy with a letter of entrustment, and voters who have their voter qualification certificates in the constituencies where their registered permanent residences are may vote in the constituencies where they currently live.

The 2,987 deputies elected in 2013 to the Third Session of the 12th NPC included 401 workers and farmers accounting for 13.42 percent, 699 women accounting for 23.4 percent, and 409 deputies from all the 55 ethnic minority groups of China accounting for 13.69 percent.

Consultative democracy is an important channel for orderly participation in the political process. An extensive, multilayered, institutionalized system of consultative democracy inclusive of multiple parties, people's congresses, governments, people's organizations, grassroots, and nongovernmental organizations has been created to expand orderly participation in the political process and ensure the citizen's right to development.

The Chinese People's Political Consultative Conference (CPPCC) is an essential organ for implementing consultative democracy, involving the participation of nine political parties including the CPC, eight people's organizations, 56 ethnic groups, five major religions, and 34 sectors of society. The CPPCC has more than 3,000 committees and over 600,000 members at all levels. In 2015, the CPPCC organized 41 major consultation events, and 107 inspection and survey tours, forming a political consultation framework employing a range of options such as plenary sessions, standing committees' thematic discussions on administrative affairs and thematic consultative seminars, and biweekly consultative seminars.

In the Third Session of the 12th CPPCC convened in 2015, 87.5 percent or 1,948 of the CPPCC members submitted 5,857 proposals, of which 85.1 percent or 4,984 were taken up for consideration. Since the First Session of the 12th CPPCC held in 2013, the rates of proposal handling and response have reached 99.5 percent or above.

Regional ethnic autonomy is an important channel for ethnic minorities to exercise their political rights. China has created the system of regional ethnic autonomy under the unitary system of government to effectively protect the democratic rights of ethnic minorities. Of the 55 ethnic minority groups in China, 44 have established ethnic autonomous areas. Seventy-one percent of the ethnic minorities exercise regional autonomy, and the land area under ethnic autonomous areas accounts for 64 percent of the national territory. By the end of July 2016 ethnic autonomous areas had formulated and amended 967 autonomous regulations and separate regulations in effect, solidifying the legal foundation for ethnic minorities' exercise of their right to development.

Heads of governments of the five autonomous regions, 30 autonomous prefectures, and 120 autonomous counties are citizens from ethnic groups exercising regional autonomy. Leaderships and functional departments of CPC committees, people's congresses, governments, and CPPCC committees at all levels in ethnic autonomous areas contain ethnic minorities, whose proportions are generally close to or higher than the percentages of ethnic minorities in the local population. By the end of 2015 ethnic minority civil servants numbered 765,000—nearly four times the figure in 1978—and 10.7 percent of the total number of civil servants across the country. Ethnic minorities made up 8.3 percent of civil servants at or above county level.

Grassroots democracy is an effective way for people to safeguard and realize equal right to development. China has established a system of grassroots self-governance implemented by rural villagers' committees and urban neighborhood committees. Approximately 98 percent of the 581,000 villagers' committees across the country practice direct election and have formulated village regulations and rules for villagers' self-governance. The turnout rates of direct elections average 95 percent among 600 million eligible voters. The 100,000 urban neighborhood committees in China utilize the services of 512,000 staff and 5.4 million volunteers. Urban residents' participation in democracy has been remarkably broadened and their self-governance capabilities and levels have been improved through multiple channels, including direct elections, gridded management platforms, volunteer services, hearings, coordination meetings, appraisal meetings, community liaison, communities' online forums, and community public concern stations, all contributing to China's system of grassroots self-governance. The workers' congress system has been widely applied in enterprises and public institutions. Separate systems for publicizing enterprise affairs have been established by 4.64 million or 88.6 percent of enterprises and public institutions with trade unions. There are 2.75 million grassroots trade unions across the country, with 280 million members, including 109 million migrant workers from rural areas.

By June 2016, nongovernmental organizations that had registered at offices of civil affairs numbered 670,000, including 329,000 mass organizations, 5,028 foundations, and 336,000 private nonprofit units. These nongovernmental organizations' services and influence extend to education, science and technology, culture, health, sports, communities, environmental protection, public welfare, charity, rural economy, and other fields of public life.

Public participation provides citizens with ready access to decision-making processes. China has furthered democratic legislation and improved the channels and forms of public participation in legislation. Efforts have also been made to establish a system of commissioning third parties to draft legislation and evaluate the drafts, and improve the mechanisms for soliciting public opinion on drafts of laws and regulations and giving feedback on responses. Some local authorities have adopted regulations on administrative decision-making procedures for major issues, which list public participation as an important legal procedure and define the forms and methods of public participation in administrative decision-making. Open solicitation of public opinion, hearings, seminars, and questionnaires are widely applied for this purpose.

In 2007 the State Council enacted Regulations on Open Government Information, emphasizing open information concerning administrative approval, financial budgets and final accounts, government-subsidized housing for the poor, food and drug safety, land appropriation, and household demolition and resettlement. The Regulations provide for prompt and accurate disclosure of government information to the public and protection of their right to know, and ensure effective scrutiny over government work while enhancing transparency in government information and efficiency in law-enforcement.

Channels of public participation in judicial processes have been steadily broadened. The number of people's assessors has now surpassed 220,000. From 2003 when China piloted the people's supervisor mechanism to April 2016, there were more than 48,000 people's supervisors, who had exercised supervision over 49,000 cases of job-related crimes. By the end of 2015, there had been nearly 800,000 people's mediation committees with more than 3.9 million people's mediators, who had, in the most recent eight years, investigated and resolved more than 67 million cases of disputes.

Public complaint filing has taken on more diversified forms, further broadening the channels for public political participation. The national complaint filing system has opened to the public for online complaint filing, resolution, and result appraisal through computers, mobile phones, and the social media app WeChat's public accounts platform. A total of 1.41 million cases were filed online in 2015, of which 140,000 were aimed at offering suggestions.

V. Promoting Cultural Progress

The Chinese government endeavors to restructure China's cultural system, free and develop cultural productivity, so as to create equal opportunity for all citizens to enjoy benefits of cultural development and to have access to cultural development opportunities, and ensure realization of their right to cultural development.

The building of a public cultural service system has been accelerated. In 2015, the Chinese government issued "Opinions on Accelerating the Building of a Modernized Public Cultural Service System" and "Guidance for National Basic Public Cultural Services (2015–2020)," presenting an all-around plan for accelerating the building of a modernized public cultural service system, promoting standard basic public cultural services and equal access, and protecting the people's basic cultural rights and interests. China has accelerated public digital cultural programs, such as the National Public Culture Digital Platform, and the National Digital Culture Network (www.ndcnc.gov.cn/). By the end of 2015, the National Cultural Information Resources Sharing Project had completed one national center, 33 provincial centers, 2,843 municipal and county centers, 35,719 township and town (sub-district) stations, and 700,000 village (community) stations. China has improved the public cultural infrastructure network and increased the capacity of community-level cultural services. By the end of 2015, China had 2,037 art performance troupes, 3,139 public libraries, 3,315 cultural centers, 2,981 museums, 40 provincial digital libraries, and 479 municipal and prefectural digital libraries. Continuous efforts were made to open public cultural facilities to the public for free, including public art museums at all levels, and basic public cultural services in libraries and cultural centers (stations) at all levels. By promoting projects such as Radio and TV Programs for Each Village and Each Rural Household, Town and Township Comprehensive Cultural Centers, Rural Cinema, Rural Libraries, and Rural Digital Culture, China has greatly enhanced rural cultural service capacity.

Literature, arts, news, publishing, radio, film, television, and sports are thriving. In 2015, China published more than 43 billion copies of newspapers, 2.9 billion copies of periodicals, and 8.7 billion copies of books. The number of books published per capita reached 6.32. A total of 236 million households subscribed to cable TV, including 198 million subscribers to digital cable TV. At the end of the year, the radio coverage rate was 98.2 percent of the total population, and TV coverage was 98.8 percent of the total population. In 2015, China produced 395 TV serials totaling 16,560 episodes, 134,000 minutes of TV animation, 686 feature films, and 202 popular science films, documentaries, animation, and special films. China has adopted value-added tax exemption for revenues from rural cinemas. It has also given support to small and micro cultural businesses, and implemented policies offering construction subsidies, financial support, and differentiated land designation for county cinemas in central and western regions. China has launched an "All People Reading" campaign nationwide. The 2016 "Literary China" series of activities has benefited over 800 million participants, forming a congenial social atmosphere for reading. China has accelerated the development of the sports industry under a policy that has the combined support of government, society, and enterprises. China has launched a nationwide fitness campaign, basically established a corresponding organizational network, and greatly increased the number of sports venues and facilities. In 2015 China allocated RMB 870 million in subsidies to support large sports venues and facilities to open to the public for free or at low cost. In 2014 the sales of the National Sports Lottery reached RMB 174.6 billion, and the funds raised for the public totaled RMB 45.5 billion.

Cultural programs in ethnic minority areas are developing. China has vigorously supported cultural development in ethnic minority areas. Through such programs as the Frontier Cultural Corridor Project and National Cultural Information Resources Sharing Project, China has improved the public cultural service system in ethnic minority areas. By the end of 2015, nine natural and cultural sites scattered in China's ethnic minority areas, including the Potala Palace in Tibet, were added to UNESCO's World Heritage List. Fourteen ethnic minority arts, including Uygur Muqam of Xinjiang, were added to UNESCO's Representative List of the Intangible Cultural Heritage of Humanity, and another four, including the Qiang ethnic group's New Year Festival, were added to the List of Intangible Cultural Heritage in Need of Urgent Safeguarding. Ten experimental zones for cultural protection in ethnic minority areas have been established. A total of 479 ethnic minority heritage items have been included in the four lists of national representative intangible cultural heritage, and 524 trustees from ethnic minority groups have been put on the four lists of national representative trustees of intangible cultural heritage. The book series of explanatory notes on ancient books of ethnic minority groups, titled

Synopsis of the General Catalog of Ancient Books of Ethnic Minority Groups of China, was published in 2014. China has promoted the regulation, standardization, and computerized processing of languages and scripts of ethnic minority groups. Projects have been initiated for the research and formulation of regulations on the transliteration of personal names into standard Chinese from Mongolian, Tibetan, Uygur, Kazakh, Yi, and other ethnic minority languages. China has set up databanks for ethnic minority languages on the brink of extinction, and initiated and implemented the Project for the Protection of Chinese Language Resources. By the end of 2015 a total of 54 ethnic minority groups were using more than 80 spoken languages of their own ethnic groups, and 21 ethnic minority groups were using 28 scripts of their own ethnic groups. Now nearly 200 radio stations nationwide broadcast in 25 ethnic minority languages; 32 publishing houses of various types publish books in ethnic minority languages; 11 film dubbing centers, using 17 ethnic minority languages and 37 ethnic minority dialects, finished the dubbing of movies, amounting to over 3,000 versions from 2012 to 2015. In 2015, China produced many publications in ethnic minority languages, including 69.12 million copies of 9,192 book titles, 196.09 million copies of newspapers, and 12.45 million copies of periodicals.

Cultural development for the elderly, the disabled, and rural migrant workers has received high attention. Relying on public libraries, cultural centers, and other cultural facilities, China has opened a group of demonstration universities for the elderly to meet their multilevel cultural demands. China has also improved the environment for the disabled, encouraging them to participate in cultural and sports activities. By the end of 2015, China had more than 300,000 liaison stations for volunteers helping the disabled, with 8.5 million registered volunteers, providing 100 million interventions on behalf of the disabled. China has issued the "Outline for the National IT Application Development Strategy," enhanced information accessibility of government websites, and encouraged nongovernmental organizations to provide individualized information services to the disabled. The official website of the State Council (www.gov.cn/) has opened a special column for services for the disabled. The China Braille Library and China Digital Library for the visually impaired went online. By the end of 2014, China had set up 1,515 reading rooms for the visually impaired in public libraries at all levels nationwide. By the end of 2015, China had set up 65,918 public e-libraries, mainly to serve the elderly and rural migrant workers.

VI. Promoting Social Development

China pursues shared development and common prosperity for all people as its development goals.

Over the years, China has been committed to developing various social undertakings, establishing and improving various types of social security and social service systems, and continuously improving the provision of social security. It has striven to provide effective social resources and promote equal access to education so that all share the fruits of development.

Protection of the right to health has significantly increased. The infant mortality rate has dropped from 20 percent in 1949, when the PRC was founded, to 0.81 percent in 2015, and the maternal mortality rate has dropped from 1,500 per 100,000 to 20.1 per 100,000. From 1978 to 2015, total national expenditure on health increased from RMB 11.02 billion to RMB 4.10 trillion, of which government expenditure on health increased from RMB 3.54 billion to RMB 1.25 trillion. Per capita health expenditure increased from RMB 11.5 to RMB 2,980.8, the number of medical and health institutions grew from 169,732 to 983,528, and the total number of health workers increased from 7,883,000 to 10,693,900. In 2015, the number of community medical and health service centers reached 361,000, with the coverage of 52.9 percent. The number of beds in social service institutions with accommodation increased from 828,000 in 1991 to 7,329,000 in 2015, of which beds for the elderly increased from 783,000 to 6,727,000, and those for children increased from 7,000 to 100,000. From 1988 to 2015 the government carried out a key state rehabilitation campaign, offering rehabilitation services for 27.98 million people with disabilities. By the end of 2015 there were 7,111 rehabilitation institutions for disabled persons, which employed 192,000 professionals, and 6,352 nursing agencies offering services to persons with learning, mental, and physical disabilities, 2,323 more than the figure in 2010. In October 2016 China published the "Outline of Healthy China 2030" program, advocating that all people make fitness activities part of their life.

A security system covering the whole of society has taken shape. China has established a unified basic old-age insurance system for urban and rural residents throughout the country, and formulated policies to allow workers, and especially rural migrant workers, to participate in basic pension insurance for urban workers and for urban and rural residents. In 2015, 858 million people were covered by the basic pension insurance scheme, and 148 million urban and rural residents were receiving pensions. By the end of 2015 China had established a medical insurance system covering all citizens. The basic medical insurance for urban workers, basic medical insurance for urban residents, and the new rural cooperative medical insurance cover a total of 1,336 million people, keeping the insured rate above 95 percent. The reimbursement rate of hospitalization expenses for workers within the scope of the basic medical insurance exceeded 80 percent, with an increased maximum payment of six times the average annual salary of local workers, and the rate for urban residents within the coverage of the basic medical insurance was around 70 percent, an increase to six times the per capita disposable income of local residents. The reimbursement rates of hospitalization expenses for rural residents within the scope of the new rural cooperative insurance was above 75 percent. From 1994 to 2015, the number of people covered by unemployment insurance increased from 79.68 million to 176.09 million. In 2015, the revenues of the unemployment insurance fund reached RMB 136.46 billion, the expenditure was RMB 73.65 billion, and the average monthly payment to the unemployed was increased to RMB 968.4. The framework of a work-related injury insurance system involving work injury prevention, compensation, and rehabilitation has been established, which has seen the number of insured growing from 18.22 million in 1994 to 214.32 million in 2015. The number of women covered by the maternity insurance program increased from 9.16 million to 177.71 million.

Social assistance efforts continue to increase. In 1997, the Chinese government began to establish a nationwide system of basic living allowances. It promulgated the Regulations on Guaranteeing Basic Living Allowances for Urban Residents in 1999 and the Interim Measures for Social Assistance in 2014, to ensure all citizens have equal access to social assistance. From 1996 to 2015, the number of urban residents covered by the system of basic living allowances increased from 849,000 to 17.01 million, and, from 1999 to 2015, coverage of rural residents grew from 2.66 million to 49.04 million. The government continues to raise the basic living allowances. In 2011, it formally established a dynamic adjustment mechanism for basic living allowances. In 2015, the average basic living allowance line for urban residents was RMB 451 per person per month, and the average monthly subsidy each person received from the government was RMB 317. The average basic living allowance line for rural residents was RMB 265 per person per month, and the average per capita monthly subsidy provided by the government was RMB 147.

China has formulated a series of disaster prevention and relief plans and regulations, gradually strengthening and standardizing disaster relief work. From 2009 to 2015, the central government allocated RMB 69.46 billion as natural disaster relief funds, averaging RMB 9.9 billion for each year. In 2015, China provided medical assistance to 95.24 million people at a cost of RMB 29.85 billion. The government also provides temporary relief to people who suffer sudden, urgent, or temporary difficulties when other social assistance systems cannot cover them at the time, or people who still lack basic necessities after receiving assistance. In 2015, 6.67 million households received temporary relief. The industrial safety and emergency rescue system has been continuously improved. Altogether 32 provincial and 316 municipal emergency rescue centers and 964 emergency rescue bases and teams have been established nationwide, covering coal, non-coal mines, chemicals, and other key industries. In 2015, they took part in 12,438 missions and rescued 44,344 people.

Equal access to education has improved. The gap between urban and rural education has been further narrowed. The Chinese government further promotes the balanced development of compulsory education, carries forward unified reform and development of compulsory education in urban and rural areas of counties, implements such projects as renovation of unsatisfactory compulsory education schools in poor areas, and works to improve conditions for compulsory education schools and teaching venues in rural areas.

The Chinese government strictly follows laws and regulations about compulsory education whereby school-age children should be enrolled in nearby schools without the need to sit exams. It also promotes the school district system and the nine-year compulsory system, under which an elementary school pupil will automatically move on to study in the junior high school in the same school district irrespective of his grades in the elementary school. In 2015, the State Council promulgated the "Notice on Further Improving the Mechanism Guaranteeing Funds for Compulsory Education in Urban and Rural Areas." With this notice, China established a mechanism for the first time that applies common funding standards to both urban and rural areas, with the focus on the latter. The mechanism benefits 140 million students, including more than 13 million children of rural migrant workers, more than 30 million boarding students, about 12 million private school students, and about 5 million small-scale school students and students receiving special education. From the fall semester of 2011, the government started to carry out a nutrition improvement program for rural students receiving compulsory education. The program benefits over 30 million students every year. Efforts have been made to increase the number of rural student enrollments in key universities. Since 2012, the government has implemented special national programs on targeted enrollment in rural and poor areas. In 2015, 75,000 students were enrolled, an increase of 10.5 percent over 2014.

Regional gap in education has further narrowed. The government has increased the college and university enrollment rate of the students from central and western provinces and expanded the scope of the Collaboration Program on Supporting Enrollment in Central and Western Regions. In 2015, the province with the lowest enrollment rate saw the gap with the national average narrowed from 15.3 percentage points in 2010 to less than 5 percentage points. The government has also established the Program on Rejuvenating Higher Education in Central and Western Regions. The central government has provided more funds to strengthen the basic facilities and performance of colleges and universities in these regions.

Educational gap between different groups has further narrowed. Female education has made remarkable progress. In 2013, the number of illiterate females aged 15 and above was 6.7 percent, 17.4 percentage points lower than that in 1995, and the illiterate female population had decreased by more than 70 million compared with 1995. The growth in the number of educated women and the decline in female illiteracy are both greater than those of males.

The government is striving to ensure equal access to compulsory education for children of rural migrant workers. In 2015, compulsory education schools in urban areas of China admitted a total of 13.67 million children of rural migrant workers, with around 80 percent studying at public schools and nearly 6 percent at private schools through a government-funded scheme. In 2016, the State Council promulgated "Opinions on Strengthening Care and Protection of Left-behind Children in Rural Areas" and "Opinions on Strengthening Protection of Children in Difficult Situations" to safeguard the lawful rights and interests of minors. The Chinese government also works hard to offer greater education opportunities to persons with disabilities. There is one independent special education school in every county with a population of more than 300,000 people and a high population of disabled children. The government also supports the establishment of special education resource centers, encourages regular schools to enroll children with special needs, provides convenience for disabled students to take part in college entrance examinations, and promotes integrated education. Almost 90 percent of blind, deaf-mute, and mentally handicapped children have access to compulsory education. It works to improve the system for subsidizing students with financial difficulties, which offers full coverage from preschool education to graduate education. In 2015, the government subsidized more than 84.33 million students throughout China, an increase of 29.36 percent compared with 2009, and spent more than RMB 156.03 billion, 2.25 times the level of 2009.

The quality of education for ethnic minorities has been continuously improved. China has already created an ethnic education system including ethnic minority primary schools, middle schools, vocational colleges, and higher education institutions. Before the PRC was founded in 1949, the illiteracy rate of ethnic minorities in China was above 95 percent, and there was only one higher education institution for ethnic minorities. In the early days of the PRC, there were only 1,300 ethnic minority students in institutions of higher learning across the country, accounting for only 1.4 percent of all students. By 2015 the education level of ethnic minority groups and ethnic minority areas had grown comprehensively. There were 25,955,700 ethnic minority students at that time. There were 32 different types of ethnic minority colleges and universities, and 2,142,900 junior college and college students from ethnic minority groups, accounting for 8.16 percent of the national total. Ethnic minority peoples have expanding access to a broader scope of higher education. Full coverage from undergraduate education to graduate education has been realized for all ethnic minority groups. All of China's 55 ethnic minority groups have graduate students. From 2012 to 2015, under the Program for Training High Caliber Core Personnel for Ethnic Minority Groups, China enrolled and trained 16,000 master's degree candidates and 4,000 doctoral candidates.

VII. Accelerating Environment-Friendly Development

China is committed to the concept of environment-friendly development and strives to expedite the country's ecological progress to deliver a more livable and beautiful environment for the people. It aims to make a good eco-environment a focal point for improving people's living standards, and create sustainable development that benefits all the people.

The basic state policy of environmental protection underpins environment-friendly development. In 1973 China convened its first national work conference on environmental protection, and adopted its first Law on Environmental Protection in 1979. In 1983 China made environmental protection a basic state policy. China became the first country in the world to formulate and implement a national sustainable development strategy when it released China's Agenda 21 in 1994. The year 2000 first saw protection of the eco-environment being incorporated into the national economic and social development program. Since 2013 China has been accelerating ecological progress in an all-around way; the CPC Central Committee and the State Council jointly issued "Opinions on Accelerating Ecological Progress" in 2015. A legal system pivoting on energy conservation and environmental protection has been formed, comprising 32 laws, 48 administrative regulations, and 85 departmental rules of the State Council. Currently, there are 14,257 government agencies involved in environmental protection at all levels.

By the end of 2015 national forestry coverage had reached 208 million ha, representing about 22 percent of China's total land area; the vegetation coverage rate of grasslands had reached 54 percent, and the greenery coverage rate of urban built-up areas was 40.1 percent. Nature reserves have been developing in a unified way. Today China has 2,740 nature reserves, covering a total area of 147.03 million ha.

Environmental governance enhances environment-friendly development. A national integrated decision-making mechanism and regional coordination mechanisms have been established for the protection of the eco-environment, forming an environmental governance system jointly implemented by the government, enterprises, and the public. Research and development in the technology for environmental protection is improving, and there has been continuous reinforcement of environmental monitoring efforts and pollution control capability.

Air pollution control is making steady progress. The proportion of coal consumption in total energy provision is decreasing year by year, while the contribution of hydropower, wind power, nuclear power, natural gas, and other types of clean energy is increasing. Since the beginning of the 11th Five-Year Program (2006–2010), China's energy consumption per RMB 10,000 GDP has decreased by 34 percent, saving 1.57 billion tons of coal equivalent, more than half of the energy saved by the whole world in this period. In 2015 the urban wastewater treatment rate reached 91.9 percent, and the pollution-free disposal rate of urban domestic solid waste was 94.1 percent. Urban park green space per capita reached 13.35 square meters.

Ecological economics fosters environment-friendly development. China has completed a system of working centers for agricultural environmental protection, consisting of two at national level, 33 at provincial level, more than 300 at prefectural level, and more than 1,700 at county level. In the drainage basins of Taihu Lake, Chaohu Lake, Erhai Lake, the Three Gorges reservoir region, and other major drainage basins requiring pollution prevention and control, model areas of diffuse agricultural pollution prevention and control have been established, and 106 national model areas of eco-friendly prevention and control of plant diseases and pests have been set up, covering more than 33 million ha of farmland. More than 100 counties in two batches have been built into national models of ecological farming, prompting the development of over 500 provincial-level model counties. More than 2,000 model sites of ecological farming have been completed.

The agricultural high-tech industry places its emphasis on long-term development. Field water application efficiency in agricultural irrigation has been raised to 0.536. Investments in technological upgrading have been reinforced, and efforts have been made to promote the new industrial development. Between January and September 2016, investments in industrial technological upgrading amounted to RMB 6.6 trillion, an increase of 13.4 percent over the same period of 2015 and accounting for 40 percent of all industrial investments. The tertiary sector has been encouraged and supported to develop faster and generate more green GDP. The expanding internet economy recorded a turnover of RMB 3.88 trillion in the online retail industry in 2015, an increase of 33.3 percent over 2014.

Policy support bolsters environment-friendly development. The state has made active efforts to protect the sustainable development of ecologically fragile areas through integrated planning, targeted treatment, and the ecological compensation mechanism, creating a virtuous cycle for regional eco-environments. Ecological areas of medium fragility make up 55 percent of China's land area, with two thirds concentrated in the western regions. In 2005 the State Council prescribed restrictive development in ecologically fragile areas. The "Outline for the Conservation of Ecologically Fragile Areas in China (2009–2020)" was promulgated in 2008. By 2015 environmental impact assessment had been implemented in all ecologically fragile areas, a 30 percent increase of targeted areas had been brought under the strategy, and models of the ecological industry have been promoted in ecologically fragile areas.

Commitments to international conventions propel environmentally friendly development. China was among the first countries to formulate and implement a national climate change plan, and pledged to achieve its 2020 goals laid out in the "National Plan on Climate Change (2014–2020)" and 2030 goals set out in the "Enhanced Actions on Climate Change: China's Intended Nationally Determined Contributions" released in 2015. Over the years, China has taken effective policy actions to honor its commitments. Moving along the path toward low-carbon development, China enacted the "National Plan for Reducing Ozone-depleting Substances" and achieved ahead of schedule its first-stage hydrochlorofluorocarbons (HCFCs) phaseout goal as part of its commitment to the "Montreal Protocol on Substances that Deplete the Ozone Layer." China's reduction of ozone-depleting substances accounts for approximately half of the total reduction by developing countries. China has eliminated the production, use, and import and export of 17 of the 26 types of persistent organic pollutants listed in the "Stockholm Convention on Persistent Organic Pollutants," and reduced the dioxin emissions of three industries that are major emitters of dioxins by more than 15 percent. Furthermore, the state has established the National Committee for Biodiversity Conservation, enacted the "China Biodiversity Conservation Strategy and Action Plan (2011–2030)," and signed the Minamata Convention on Mercury. China is an active and constructive participant in international talks on climate change, and makes robust efforts to bolster the United Nations Framework Convention on Climate Change. China has made significant efforts in moving the Paris Agreement on greenhouse gas emissions mitigation toward adoption and taking effect, making it one of the fastest major international agreements ever to enter into force and further contributing to the world's sustainable development.

VIII. Promoting Common Development

China upholds the principles of mutual respect, equality of treatment, win–win cooperation, and common development, and promotes the interests of its own people and the common interests of other peoples. China supports the developing countries, especially the least developed countries (LDCs), in reducing poverty and improving people's well-being and the development environment, in order to build a human community of shared future.

Defending the right to development. As an original member state of the United Nations, China participated in drafting the Charter of the United Nations and signed it, facilitated the publication of the "Universal Declaration of Human Rights," upheld the principles prescribed in the "International Covenant on Economic, Social and Cultural Rights" and the "International Covenant on Civil and Political Rights," and facilitated the passing of the resolution on the new concepts of human rights and the resolution on the right to development. China participated in all the previous meetings of the Group of Governmental Experts of the United Nations Commission on Human Rights (UNCHR) for drafting the "Declaration on the Right to Development," and made an important contribution to the formal adoption of the Declaration in 1986. China has always been a co-sponsor of UNCHR resolutions on the right to development, supporting the UNCHR's global debate on realizing the right to development, and consenting to the deliberation of the right to development by the UNCHR as a separate issue. Since the UNCHR was established in 2006, China has been elected as a member four times, and has contributed its wisdom and strength to making the right to development a mainstream issue.

Participating in the formulation of the development agenda. China was the first to voice support for the sustainable development strategy. It has supported and implemented the "United Nations Millennium Declaration," and achieved 13 of the United Nations Millennium Development Goals. While effectively improving the protection of its own people's right to development, China has also promoted the common development of the world. It has helped the international community to pass and implement the 2030 Agenda for Sustainable Development, and issued "China's Position Paper on the Implementation of the 2030 Agenda for Sustainable Development" and "China's National Plan on Implementation of the 2030 Agenda for Sustainable Development." At the G20 Hangzhou Summit, China joined other countries in formulating the "G20 Action Plan on the 2030 Agenda for Sustainable Development" and the "G20 Initiative on Supporting Industrialization in Africa and Least Developed Countries," adding impetus to the overall development of all countries and developing countries in particular. In September 2015 China and UN Women co-organized the Global Summit of Women, and implemented the goals related to the 2030 Agenda for Sustainable Development.

Expanding the path to development. Over the years, based on the principle that all countries are entitled to choose their own social systems and development paths, China has expanded its development mindset and philosophy, and joined other countries in seeking equitable, open, all-around and innovation-driven development. China strives for equitable development for all countries and for developing countries in particular, so that all countries can become participants in and contributors to global development and equitably share the interests of development. China calls on all countries, which share the same development goals yet are at different development levels, to take on common but differentiated responsibilities. China has advocated the developing countries' right to a greater voice in formulating the rules of the global governance system. China keeps the open-door policy while pursuing development. It joins other countries in upholding the multilateral trade regime and promotes the free flow of production factors around the world so that the achievements of development will benefit all parties and people in all countries. China pursues all-around development to achieve balanced development between economy, society, and environment, and to realize harmony between humanity and society, and between humanity and nature. China promotes innovation-driven development, addresses problems arising in development by means of development, and fosters new core competitiveness. China places great value on the leadership of the United Nations, encourages regional economic integration, and improves its competitive development by integrating the strengths and advantages of various parties, so as to fully release its development potential.

Furthering cooperation for development. China adheres to the principle of maintaining integrity and pursuing interests while giving priority to integrity and strives to improve the development capacity of all countries and the international development environment, partnership, and coordination mechanisms for international development cooperation to realize the rights of all people to development. China propels inclusive and mutually beneficial development, while participating in global economic governance. Regarding North–South economic cooperation as the main focus, China continues to expand South–South, tripartite, regional economic cooperation and cooperation with emerging economies and, at the same time, explore more effective means of win–win cooperation. To realize common development the Chinese government endeavors to involve more countries and regions in the Belt and Road Initiative, relying on existing bilateral and multilateral mechanisms such as the Shanghai Cooperation Organization, ASEAN Plus China (10+1) Summit, ASEAN Plus China, Japan, and the ROK (10+3) Summit, East Asia Summit, China–Japan–ROK Cooperation, APEC, Asia–Europe Meeting, Asia Cooperation Dialogue, Conference on Interaction and Confidence-Building Measures in Asia, China–Arab States Cooperation Forum, China–Gulf Cooperation Council Strategic Dialogue, Greater Mekong Subregion Economic Cooperation Program, and Central Asia Regional Economic Cooperation. China has established the Silk Road Fund, initiated the Asian Infrastructure Investment Bank, and set up the Lancang-Mekong River cooperation mechanism, in order to provide financing support for the Belt and Road countries to coordinate programs on infrastructure, resource development, and industrial and financial cooperation.

Increasing development aid. Over the past 60 years China has provided approximately RMB 400 billion in aid to 166 countries and international organizations. It has trained more than 12 million personnel from developing countries, and dispatched over 600,000 people to aid development in other countries. Seven hundred people have given their lives in the course of these programs. Since 2008, China has been the largest export market of the LDCs, and absorbed about 23 percent of their exports. To improve economic growth and standards of living in the developing countries, China will set up a South–South Cooperation Fund, increase its investment in the LDCs, write off certain countries' debts, establish an International Development Knowledge Center, and further the Belt and Road Initiative. In the coming five years China will implement six "One Hundred Programs" targeting developing countries—100 poverty reduction programs, 100 agricultural cooperation programs, 100 trade aid programs, 100 eco-protection and climate change programs, 100 hospitals and clinics, and 100 schools and vocational training centers. One hundred and twenty thousand training opportunities and 150,000 scholarships will be made available to developing countries in China, and 500,000 vocational technical personnel will be trained. China will set up a South–South Cooperation and Development Academy, and give the World Health Organization US$2 million in cash aid.

Providing special treatment. China, as a developing country, is an advocate for a number of trade rights based on the principle of "special and differential treatment," but should not be obliged to provide the same treatment. However, in recent years, China has begun to provide "special and differential treatment" to other developing countries, focusing on protecting the right to development of the LDCs. In 2002, China and the Association of Southeast Asian Nations (ASEAN) signed the Framework Agreement on China–ASEAN Comprehensive Economic Cooperation, offering special and differential treatment with flexibility to new ASEAN member states such as Cambodia, Lao PDR, Myanmar, and Vietnam. In 2006, China joined the Amendment to the First Agreement on Trade Negotiations Among Developing Member Countries of the Economic and Social Commission for Asia and the Pacific. China's General Administration of Customs has issued three documents which have extended the range of countries enjoying its special preferential tariff from African countries to 40 LDCs recognized by the United Nations.

Improving the development environment. China joins other countries in safeguarding international peace, opposes all forms of terrorism, and supports international and regional cooperation in fighting terrorism, in order to create an environment of peace and harmony that promotes development and thereby consolidates peace. In recent years, China has offered solutions to regional flashpoints: involving itself in the Iran nuclear talks; mediating for national reconciliation in South Sudan; proposing a four-step framework for political settlement of the Syrian issue; facilitating the peace talks between the Afghan government and the Taliban; promoting consensus on resuming the six-party talks on the nuclear issue on the Korean Peninsula. To date, China has sent 33,000 military, police, and civilian personnel to join UN peacekeeping missions. Currently there are 2,600-plus Chinese peacekeeping personnel involved in ten UN peacekeeping operations, making China the most active permanent member of the UN Security Council in terms of supplying peacekeeping personnel. In order to support and improve peacekeeping operations, China will join the new UN peacekeeping standby mechanism, take the lead in establishing regular peacekeeping police force units, and organize peacekeeping standby forces. In the coming five years China will train 2,000 peacekeeping personnel for other countries, launch ten demining aid programs, provide US$100 million of non-reimbursable military aid to the African Union, and allocate part of the China–UN Peace and Development Fund to support UN peacekeeping operations.

Conclusion

In the pursuit of development and their right to development, the Chinese people have made strenuous efforts and significant achievements. To promote common development and to build a community with shared future, China has made unremitting efforts and played an important role. It will always be a defender of humanity's right to development, and a force to propel development and progress throughout the world.

There will always be room for improvement in human rights, and the quest to improve people's right to development is always under way. As the world's largest developing country China faces daunting challenges, characterized by pressing problems such as unbalanced, uncoordinated, and unsustainable development. To achieve a higher level of development and better protect the people's right to development, China needs to maintain its efforts. Meeting the people's growing material and cultural needs and giving everyone access to sound development are still the primary tasks of the CPC in its governance of the country.

The Chinese people are working hard to achieve the Two Centenary Goals and the Chinese Dream of the great rejuvenation of the Chinese nation. With the realization of these goals, China will make a historic and unprecedented leap, and the Chinese people's right to development will be further protected.

At the UN Sustainable Development Summit in September 2015, Chinese President Xi Jinping called upon all nations to mark a new starting point with the adoption of 2030 Agenda for Sustainable Development, and unite to chart a path of development that is fair, open, comprehensive, and innovative. China will continue to work with the international community, strengthen cooperation, promote exchanges of experience, and make its due contribution to further increase the level of development of all peoples of the world and build a community with shared future for mankind.

Notes

1 The two goals are to complete the building of a moderately prosperous society in all respects by the centenary of the CPC (founded in 1921) and to build China into a modern socialist country that is prosperous, strong, democratic, culturally advanced, and harmonious by the centenary of the People's Republic of China (founded in 1949).
2 *The Cambridge History of China (Volume 12): Republican China 1912–1949 Part I*, Cambridge University Press, 1983.
3 Ibid. p. 29.
4 The Four Cardinal Principles refer to the principles of adhering to the socialist path, the people's democratic dictatorship, the leadership of the CPC, and Marxism–Leninism and Mao Zedong Thought. The Four Cardinal Principles are the foundation of the state, and the political cornerstone for the survival and development of the Party and the state.
5 "Reducing Poverty on a Global Scale: Learning and Innovating for Development Findings from the Shanghai Global Learning Initiative," a World Bank document on Nov. 14, 2016.

3. November 2016: China's Policy Paper on Latin America and the Caribbean[3]

The State Council Information Office
The People's Republic of China

Contents

Preface

Preface

The world today is undergoing unprecedented historical changes, with multi-polarization and globalization gaining momentum. The rise of emerging markets and developing countries has become an irresistible historical trend. At the same time, the world economy is recovering amidst twists and turns. Global and regional hot-spot issues take place frequently. Traditional and non-traditional security threats are intertwined. Safeguarding world peace and promoting common development remains a daunting task.

China has entered a crucial stage in achieving the great rejuvenation of the Chinese nation. In order to fulfill the "two centenary goals" of building a moderately prosperous society in all respects by 2020 and turning the nation into a modern socialist country that is prosperous, strong, democratic, culturally advanced, and harmonious by the mid-twenty-first century, China has been actively promoting the construction of a socialist market economy, socialist democracy, advanced culture, and a harmonious society, as well as ecological civilization. China adheres to the independent foreign policy of peace and is unswerving in its implementation of the opening-up policy. China stands ready to expand common interests with other countries, promote the construction of a new type of international relations with win–win cooperation at the core, and forge a community of shared future.

The development of China cannot be possible without the development of other developing countries, including countries in Latin America and the Caribbean. Since 2013, the Chinese leadership has set forth a series of major initiatives and measures on strengthening China's relations and cooperation with Latin America and the Caribbean in a wide range of areas, which has provided new development goals and new driving forces for the relations. Building on the previous achievements, the Chinese government hereby releases its second policy paper on Latin America and the Caribbean, to summarize experience, draw a blueprint for the future, provide a comprehensive explanation of the new ideas, proposals, and initiatives in China's Latin America and Caribbean policy for the new era, and promote China's cooperation with Latin America and the Caribbean in various areas.

I. Latin America and the Caribbean: A Land Full of Vitality and Hope

As important members of emerging economies and the developing world, Latin American and Caribbean countries play a major role in safeguarding world peace and development. Since the dawn of the new century, Latin American and Caribbean countries have actively explored development paths suited to their own conditions and attained achievements that have attracted the world's attention.

Faced with changes in the external environment triggered by the global financial crisis, all countries are taking active steps to cope with the challenges and maintain and promote inclusive and sustainable economic and social development. Latin America and the Caribbean as a whole boast huge development potentials and bright prospects, making them a rising force in the global landscape.

II. China's Relations with Latin America and the Caribbean in the New Stage of Comprehensive Cooperation

Though far apart, China and Latin America and the Caribbean have a long history of people's friendship. After the founding of the People's Republic of China in 1949, with the concerted efforts of several generations, the relations between China and Latin America and the Caribbean have gone through a remarkable journey.

In 2008, the Chinese government issued its first policy paper on Latin America and the Caribbean, putting forward the goal of establishing a comprehensive and cooperative partnership featuring equality, mutual benefit, and common development with Latin American and Caribbean countries. In 2014, leaders of the two sides held a meeting in Brasilia and jointly announced the establishment of the comprehensive and cooperative partnership of equality, mutual benefit, and common development. Since then, the relations have entered a new stage of comprehensive cooperation. The two sides have witnessed frequent high-level exchanges and political dialogues, all-round and rapid development in trade, investment, finance, and other areas, and increasingly close cultural and people-to-people exchanges. The two sides have also supported and closely coordinated with each other in international affairs. The establishment of the Forum of China and the Community of Latin American and Caribbean States (China–CELAC Forum) has provided a new platform for cooperation between the two sides, setting the course for simultaneous and complementary development of bilateral and collective cooperation between China and Latin America and the Caribbean.

Based on equality and mutual benefit, the comprehensive and cooperative partnership between China and Latin America and the Caribbean is oriented towards common development. It does not target or exclude any third party. It conforms to the fundamental interests of the two sides and the trends of our times featuring world peace, development, and cooperation, and serves as a shining example of developing countries working together to seek common development, shoulder common responsibilities, and cope with common challenges in the new era.

III. Bringing the Comprehensive and Cooperative Partnership to New Heights

China is committed to building a new relationship with Latin America and the Caribbean with five salient features, namely, sincerity and mutual trust in the political field, win–win cooperation on the economic front, mutual learning in culture, close coordination in international affairs, and mutual reinforcement between China's cooperation with the region as a whole and its bilateral relations with individual countries in the region. We aim to bring the comprehensive and cooperative partnership to a new height by bringing the two sides into a community of shared future in which all countries join hands in development.

- Sticking to the principle of equality and sincere mutual support is the fundamental premise of the development of relations between China and Latin America and the Caribbean. China adheres to the Five Principles of Peaceful Coexistence and maintains that all countries, big or small, strong or weak, rich or poor, are equal members of the international community. China respects the right of Latin American and Caribbean countries to choose their own paths of development and is ready to work with Latin American and Caribbean countries to strengthen exchanges in governance experience, deepen strategic mutual trust, and continue to understand and support each other on issues of core interests and major concerns, such as state sovereignty, territorial integrity, stability, and development.
- The one-China principle is an important political foundation for China to develop its relations with other countries in the world. The Chinese government appreciates that the vast majority of Latin American and Caribbean countries abide by the one-China principle and support China's great cause of reunification. China is ready to establish and develop state-to-state relations with Latin American and Caribbean countries on the basis of the one-China principle.
- Seeking mutually beneficial cooperation and common development is the endogenous driving force for the development of the relations. China is ready to work with Latin American and Caribbean countries to build the new "1 + 3 + 6" framework for pragmatic cooperation (i.e., guided by the China–Latin American and Caribbean Countries Cooperation Plan (2015–2019), utilizing trade, investment, and financial cooperation as driving forces, and identifying energy and resources, infrastructure construction, agriculture, manufacturing, scientific and technological innovation, and information technology as cooperation priorities), actively explore the new "3x3" model for capacity cooperation (which refers to jointly building the three major passages of logistics, electricity, and information in Latin America, enabling healthy interactions among the enterprise, society and government, and expanding the

three financing channels of funds, credit loans, and insurance), and speed up quality improvement and upgrading of the cooperation between China and Latin America and the Caribbean.

- Exchanges and mutual learning, as well as carrying forward the friendship from generation to generation, is the solid foundation of the relations. China stands ready to strengthen exchanges with Latin American and Caribbean governments, legislative bodies, political parties, and entities at the local level and cooperation in the fields of education, science and technology, culture, sports, health, journalism, and tourism. China will actively hold dialogues between civilizations to bring the hearts of our peoples closer, and make contributions to promoting the harmonious coexistence of different civilizations in the world.

- China and Latin American and Caribbean countries share a global responsibility in promoting international cooperation, equity and justice. China is ready to strengthen communication and cooperation with Latin American and Caribbean countries within the international multilateral mechanisms, and jointly safeguard the international order and system with the purposes and principles of the UN Charter as its core. China will advance multipolarization, promote democracy and the rule of law in international relations, and enhance the representation and voice of developing countries. China is ready to deepen South–South cooperation with Latin American and Caribbean countries, consolidate multilateral trading systems, promote global governance reform, and build an open world economic system.

- To promote complementary development of collective and bilateral cooperation is the strategic path for developing China–Latin America and the Caribbean relations. China appreciates and supports the important role played by regional and sub-regional organizations of Latin America and the Caribbean in regional and international affairs. Upholding the principle of equality, seeking mutual benefit and "win–win" results with flexible and pragmatic ways of collaboration, and in a spirit of openness and inclusiveness, China will promote collective cooperation with Latin America and the Caribbean mainly through the platform of China–CELAC Forum, and strengthen dialogue and cooperation with relevant sub-regional organizations and multilateral financial institutions, so as to create a balanced, all-round network of collective cooperation between China and Latin America and the Caribbean.

IV. Further Strengthening Cooperation in All Fields

1. In the Political Field

1. High-Level Exchanges

China wishes to give full play to the guiding role of high-level exchanges, maintain exchanges of visits and meetings at multilateral international events between leaders of China and Latin America and the Caribbean, and strengthen communication on bilateral relations and major issues of common concern.

2. Exchanges of Experience on Governance

The two sides should draw lessons and wisdom from their historical traditions and development practices, and further strengthen exchanges of experience on governance and development, so as to boost common development. Latin American and Caribbean countries are welcome to take an active part in the International Development Knowledge Center established by China.

3. Inter-governmental Dialogue and Consultation Mechanisms

Efforts will be made to give full play to the role of mechanisms such as the high-level coordination and cooperation committee, high-level mixed committee, inter-governmental standing committee, strategic dialogue, mixed committee on economy and trade, and political consultation, and further improve the relevant mechanisms to enhance inter-governmental dialogue and cooperation.

4. Exchanges Between Legislatures

On the basis of respecting each other, deepening understanding and promoting cooperation, the National People's Congress of China wishes to strengthen multi-level, multi-channel friendly exchanges with national parliaments and regional and sub-regional parliamentary organizations in Latin America and the Caribbean through high-level exchanges and exchanges at other levels such as special committees, friendship groups, and offices.

5. Exchanges Between Political Parties

On the basis of independence, full equality, mutual respect, and non-interference in each other's internal affairs, the Communist Party of China wishes to strengthen exchanges and cooperation with political parties and organizations of Latin American and Caribbean countries, so as to further enhance mutual understanding and trust.

6. Local Exchanges

Active support will be given to local governments on both sides to conduct friendly exchanges and cooperation, share experience in local development and governance, and promote cooperation among local governments in relevant international organizations.

2. In the Economic Field

1. Trade

Efforts will be made to tap into trade potentials between the two sides, promote the trade of specialty products, goods with competitive advantages or high added-value, and technology-intensive products, and strengthen trade in services and e-commerce cooperation between China and Latin American and Caribbean countries. Based on the principle of reciprocity and mutual benefit, China will discuss with Latin American and Caribbean countries the establishment of long-term and stable trade relations and various trade facilitation arrangements including the FTA. Trade frictions will be properly handled to promote sound and balanced development and structural diversification of trade between the two sides.

2. Industrial Investment and Capacity Cooperation

China will encourage its enterprises to expand and optimize investment in Latin American and Caribbean countries on the basis of equality and mutual benefit. China wishes to sign more agreements on investment protection, avoidance of double taxation, and tax evasion with Latin American and Caribbean countries, so as to create favorable environment and conditions for investment cooperation between enterprises of both sides.

Upholding the principle of business-led and market-oriented cooperation for mutual economic and social benefits, China will support the efforts of Chinese enterprises to invest and start business in Latin American and Caribbean countries, and align high-quality capacity and advantageous equipment of China with the needs of Latin American and Caribbean countries, in order to help the countries in need to enhance their capacity for independent development.

3. Financial Cooperation

China will support its financial institutions to strengthen business exchanges and cooperation with national, regional, and international financial institutions in Latin American and Caribbean countries and further improve the construction of branch networks in the region. Efforts will be made to enhance dialogue and cooperation between the central banks and financial regulatory authorities of the two sides, expand cross-border local currency settlement, discuss RMB clearing arrangements, and steadily promote monetary cooperation. On the basis of bilateral financial cooperation, and giving full play to the role of China–Latin America Cooperation Fund, concessional loans, special loans for Chinese–Latin American infrastructure, China–Latin American Production Capacity Cooperation Investment Fund, and relevant financing arrangements between China and Caribbean countries, China will actively explore cooperation forms including insurance and financial lease, continuously expand cooperation with regional financial institutions in Latin America and the Caribbean, and support cooperation in key areas and major projects between the two sides.

4. Energy and Resources Cooperation

China wishes to expand and deepen cooperation in the fields of energy and resources with Latin American and Caribbean countries based on the principle of win–win cooperation and sustainable development. Efforts will be made to bring cooperation to upstream business such as exploration and development, so as to consolidate the foundation for cooperation and expand resources potentials; and at the same time, cooperation will be extended to downstream and supporting industries such as smelting, processing, logistics trade, and equipment manufacturing, so as to improve added value of products. China is ready to actively explore with Latin American and Caribbean countries the establishment of mechanisms for long-term supply of energy and resources products and local currency pricing and settlement, to reduce the impact of external economic and financial risks.

5. Infrastructure Cooperation

China will strengthen cooperation on technical consultation, construction and engineering, equipment manufacturing and operation management in the fields of transportation, trade logistics, storage facilities, information and communication technology, energy and power, water conservancy, housing, and urban construction. China will support and encourage competent enterprises and financial institutions to actively participate in the planning and construction of logistics, power, and information passages in Latin American and Caribbean countries, and actively explore new ways of cooperation, such as the Public–Private Partnership (PPP) model, so as to promote the connectivity of infrastructure in Latin America and the Caribbean.

6. Manufacturing Cooperation

China will support its strong enterprises to participate in major resources and energy development projects and infrastructure construction projects in Latin American and Caribbean countries and, using these projects as the basis, to build production lines and maintenance service bases in the region for construction materials, non-ferrous metals, engineering machinery, locomotives and rolling stock, electric power, and communication equipment, with the purpose of reducing costs for resources and energy development and infrastructure construction in Latin American and Caribbean countries. China will encourage its enterprises to go to Latin American and Caribbean countries to carry out cooperation in such fields as automobiles, new energy equipment, motorcycles, and chemical industry, which will cover the whole industrial chain, so that the two sides can complement each other, increase local employment, upgrade the level of industrialization, and promote local economic and social development. Based on business-led and market-oriented principles, discussions will be held on the joint construction of industrial parks, logistics parks, high-tech industrial parks, special economic zones, and other industrial agglomeration areas, so as to help Latin American and Caribbean countries in their industrial upgrading. Exchanges and cooperation between small and medium-sized enterprises of the two sides will be encouraged by building relevant platforms and creating good environment for them.

7. Agricultural Cooperation

Efforts will be made to encourage enterprises on both sides to actively engage in agricultural trade, push for further exchanges and cooperation in agricultural science and technology, personnel training, and other fields, deepen cooperation in livestock and poultry breeding, forestry, fishery, and aquaculture, and jointly promote food security. China will continue to set up and improve agricultural technology demonstration programs, promote the development and demonstration of modern agricultural technologies, and enhance agricultural technology innovation, agricultural production and processing capacity, and international competitiveness on both sides. Bilateral mechanisms for agricultural information exchanges and cooperation will be improved while giving full play to the role of the special fund for China–Latin America agricultural cooperation, and more agricultural cooperation projects are encouraged.

8. Scientific and Technological Innovation

China will actively explore the expansion of its cooperation with Latin American and Caribbean countries in high-tech fields such as information industry, civil aviation, civil nuclear energy, and new energy, to build more joint laboratories, R&D centers, and high-tech parks, support innovative enterprises and research institutions on both sides to carry out exchanges and cooperation, and promote joint research and development. China will encourage dialogue and exchanges between scientific and technological talents on both sides, and support more outstanding young scientists from Latin America and the Caribbean to come to China for short-term scientific research.

9. Space Cooperation

China will actively explore cooperation between the two sides in such fields as communication and remote sensing satellites, satellite data application, aerospace infrastructure, and space education and training, and promote space technology application in disaster prevention and mitigation, agricultural and forestry monitoring, climate change, and other fields. China will pay full attention to the role of space technology as a driving force for the scientific, technological, and industrial development of Latin American and Caribbean countries, and promote sustainable development in science and technology and the economic fields.

10. Maritime Cooperation

China will actively explore cooperation between the two sides in marine science and technology, marine ecological environment protection, marine climate change, marine disaster prevention and mitigation, and other fields, and carry out marine economic development in accordance with local conditions, so as to promote the development of maritime affairs between the two sides.

11. Cooperation on Customs and Quality Inspection

Exchanges and consultations between customs and quality inspection departments from both sides will be strengthened, to promote trade security and facilitation, and ensure product quality and food safety. China will advance the implementation, negotiation, or signing of cooperation documents with Latin American and Caribbean countries regarding customs administrative assistance, animal and plant products, quarantine access, etc. Active steps will be taken to carry out cooperation and exchanges on customs capacity building, trade facilitation, capacity building, goods trade statistics, and standardization.

12. Cooperation Between Trade and Investment Promotion Institutions and Business Associations of the Two Sides

China will deepen its cooperation with trade and investment promotion institutions and business associations in Latin American and Caribbean countries, and facilitate, by making use of relevant mechanisms and platforms for bilateral and collective cooperation, exchanges between enterprises of the two sides, so as to achieve win–win cooperation.

13. Economic and Technical Assistance

Based on full respect for the will of related countries in Latin America and the Caribbean, and in accordance with China's financial capacity and level of economic and social development, China will continue to provide economic and technical assistance to Latin American and Caribbean countries without attaching any political conditions and, in accordance with the needs of related countries, gradually increase the scale of assistance within its capacity. China will innovate the assistance model, giving priority to human resources development, development planning, economic policy consulting and training, infrastructure construction, agriculture and food security, poverty reduction, climate change, and humanitarian assistance.

3. In the Social Aspects

1. Social Governance and Social Development

China is ready to conduct exchanges and cooperation with Latin American and Caribbean countries on strengthening and innovating social governance, to share and learn from each other's experience in governance, jointly promote the modernization of governance system and governance capacity, continuously enhance the level of socialization, rule of law, and refinement of social governance, and ensure social stability and order, as well as long-term national stability.

Efforts will be made to promote further exchanges and cooperation in social development areas such as social welfare and social assistance, strengthen policy sharing, and promote and realize practical cooperation in providing services and assistance to special groups such as the elderly, the disabled, and children, as well as urban and rural disadvantaged groups.

2. Cooperation on Environmental Protection, Climate Change, and Disaster Reduction

China will further develop and consolidate its cooperation with Latin America and the Caribbean under the United Nations Framework Convention on Climate Change (UNFCCC) and other relevant mechanisms, and actively promote consultation, exchanges, and project cooperation to cope with the climate change. China will deepen policy dialogue, information sharing, experience exchange, capacity building, and technical cooperation in the fields of water resources planning and utilization, ecosystem protection, river-lake management, disaster reduction and relief, and Hippophae rhamnoides cultivation. Efforts will be made to promote the establishment of regular multilateral and bilateral meeting mechanisms between relevant departments of the two sides.

3. Poverty Reduction Cooperation

China will promote dialogue and exchanges in fields such as poverty reduction, hunger elimination, and narrowing the gap between the rich and the poor, by sharing information on poverty identification as well as experience concerning targeted poverty alleviation. China will engage in technical cooperation to enhance capacity building for poverty reduction, and promote the formulation of economic and social policies in favor of the poor and disadvantaged on both sides. Efforts will also be made to encourage and support high-level exchanges between relevant departments of the two sides, and hold the China–Latin America Poverty Reduction and Development Forum in a timely manner.

4. Health Cooperation

China will expand exchanges and cooperation in disease control, regional or global epidemic diseases, and response to public health emergencies. The Chinese side will continue to help Latin American and Caribbean countries train medical personnel and improve medical facilities, send medical teams to these countries, and stand ready to provide assistance within its capacity for the prevention and control of sudden outbreak of infectious diseases.

4. In the Cultural and People-to-People Fields

1. Cultural and Sports Exchanges and Cooperation

Regular dialogue will be maintained between the cultural authorities of the two sides, to promote high-level cultural exchanges and implement the plans and the cultural cooperation agreements signed between the two sides. The two sides will support and encourage their high-profile cultural groups and artists to participate or show their works in international art festivals and visual art exhibitions hosted by China or Latin American and Caribbean countries. Efforts will be made to carry out dialogue among civilizations and support "Cultural Exchange Year" activities between China and Latin American and Caribbean countries. Cooperation will be encouraged in the protection of cultural heritage and the fight against theft, illegal excavation, and illegal entry and exit of national borders of cultural properties.

The two sides will strengthen sports exchanges and practical cooperation, encourage their athletes to participate in various sports events held in each other's countries, and build more high-level sports centers. Exchange of experience on advantageous sports of each other will help enhance sports level of both sides.

2. Education and Human Resources Training

China will promote educational exchanges and mobility research projects, as well as cooperation between educational departments and institutions. China will support and encourage the training of talents specialized in the Chinese, English, Spanish, and Portuguese languages, support Latin American and Caribbean countries to promote Chinese language teaching, and continue to advance the construction and development of Confucius Institutes and Confucius Classrooms. China will strengthen human resources development, capacity building, and cooperation in various fields, and increase the government scholarships for students from Latin American and Caribbean countries. Exchanges and cooperation in vocational education will also be carried out in an active manner.

3. Exchanges and Cooperation in Press, Publication, Radio, Film, and Television

China will strengthen dialogue and cooperation in press, publication, radio, film, and television, and encourage the signing of bilateral agreements on radio, film, and television with Latin American and Caribbean Countries. The two sides will encourage the exchanges and co-production of programs and participation in festivals or exhibitions on press, publication, radio, film, or television held in each other's countries, and strengthen personnel exchanges as well as media technology and industrial cooperation. The two sides will support the exchange of resident journalists and carry out joint interviews, exchange of news, and personnel training. Strong and influential internet media from both sides will be encouraged to enhance cooperation in portal development, new media capacity building, and other aspects. The two sides will also encourage the publishing industry on both sides to engage in cooperation and explore the mutual translation of philosophical and cultural classics, so as to translate and publish more classic works.

4. Tourism Cooperation

China will encourage tourism authorities and enterprises on both sides to introduce tourism resources and products to each other and expand tourism cooperation.

China will explore and issue more facilitation policies to promote two-way tourism, and support the negotiation for more direct flights between aviation authorities of the two sides. China will strengthen dialogue and cooperation with consumer protection departments of Latin American and Caribbean countries, with priority given to the protection of consumer rights of international travelers.

5. Academic and Think Tank Exchanges

China will actively support academic research institutions and think tanks on both sides to carry out subject research, academic exchanges, seminars, publications, and other forms of communication and cooperation. Cooperative research between universities of both sides will also be encouraged.

6. Non-governmental Exchanges

China will encourage non-governmental exchanges and support social organizations to carry out various forms of friendly exchanges and public welfare activities. China will promote communication between government departments on youth affairs and youth organizations on both sides, and continue to support the "Future Bridge" Training Program for One Thousand Chinese and Latin American Youth Leaders and the Latin American Youth Cadres Training Program. The two sides will deepen friendly cooperation between women's organizations and promote gender equality and women's empowerment. Non-governmental players of both sides will be encouraged to cooperate in areas such as disaster prevention and reduction, health promotion, and livelihood development at the community level. In time of major natural disasters, domestic humanitarian assistance organizations will be supported in conducting international urgent humanitarian assistance.

7. Consular Cooperation

Efforts will be made to strengthen and expand exchanges and cooperation between the consular departments of the two sides, make good use of the consular consultation mechanism, and earnestly safeguard the safety and legitimate rights and interests of their enterprises and citizens in each other's countries. Support will be given to institutional arrangements to facilitate personnel exchanges between the two sides.

5. International Collaboration

1. International Political Affairs

Efforts will be made to deepen exchanges and cooperation between the two sides in the UN and other international organizations and on other international platforms, maintain communication and coordination on major international and regional issues, promote multipolarization and democracy in international relations, enhance the voice of developing countries in international affairs, and safeguard common interests of both sides as well as other developing countries.

2. Global Economic Governance

China will work to strengthen coordination and cooperation with Latin American and Caribbean countries in international economic and financial organizations and mechanisms such as the Group of 20, APEC, IMF, World Bank, Bank for International Settlements, Financial Stability Board, and Basel Committee on Banking Supervision, advance multilateral trade negotiation processes with the WTO as the core, promote the establishment of a balanced, win–win and inclusive multilateral trading system, and promote economic integration in the Asia–Pacific region. China will call on the international community to continue to promote global economic governance reform, improve and perfect global economic and financial rules, further advance the IMF reforms on quotas and governance, support the World Bank to move forward with shareholding review in accordance with the roadmap and timetable agreed upon by all parties, and increase the representation of emerging markets and developing countries. China will also promote the construction of a global financial security network, to enhance the world's capabilities to respond to systemic shocks, and strengthen monitoring and prevention of global and regional systemic risks.

3. Implementation of the 2030 Agenda for Sustainable Development

China is ready to work with Latin American and Caribbean countries to promote global, win–win cooperation in the implementation of the 2030 Agenda for Sustainable Development adopted by the United Nations Sustainable Development Summit. China will support the international community to improve global partnerships, strengthen the main channel status of North–South cooperation, and urge developed countries to fulfill their commitments on official development assistance, while placing importance on the role of South–South cooperation and trilateral cooperation. China stands ready to provide support and assistance within its capacity to Latin American and Caribbean countries in their efforts to implement the 2030 Agenda for Sustainable Development.

4. Response to Climate Change

China will support the main channel status of the UNFCCC in the international response to climate change. China will adhere to the principles and provisions of the UNFCCC, particularly the principles of equity, common but differentiated responsibilities and respective capabilities, and promote the implementation of the Paris Agreement. China calls on the international community to pay close attention to the special concerns of small island developing states in the Caribbean, promote the establishment of a global climate governance system that is equitable and reasonable for win–win cooperation, and advance the comprehensive, effective, and sustained implementation of the UNFCCC.

5. Cyber Security

Based on the principles of peace, sovereignty, co-governance, and universal benefits, the Chinese government is ready to work with Latin American and Caribbean countries to build a cyber space featuring peace, security, openness, and cooperation, build a multilateral, democratic, and transparent internet governance system, and develop a code of conduct for international cyber space acceptable to all parties and international legal documents against cybercrimes under the UN framework. China opposes any engagement in the destruction of a country's political, economic, or social stability by making use of the internet.

6. On Peace, Security, and Judicial Affairs

1. Military Exchanges and Cooperation

China will actively carry out military exchanges and cooperation with Latin American and Caribbean countries, increase friendly exchanges between defense and military leaders from the two sides, strengthen policy dialogue and set up working meeting mechanisms, conduct exchanges of visits between delegations and vessels, deepen professional exchanges in such fields as military training, personnel training, and UN peacekeeping, expand pragmatic cooperation in humanitarian relief, counterterrorism, and other non-traditional security fields, and enhance cooperation in military trade and military technology.

2. Cooperation in Judicial and Police Affairs

China will speed up the signing process of treaties concerning judicial assistance in criminal matters, and expand cooperation in such areas as fighting crimes, fugitive repatriation, and asset recovery. China will actively carry out police and procuratorial exchanges and cooperation, strengthen and expand cooperation in the areas of extradition, repatriation of criminal suspects, transfer of sentenced persons, and criminal assets attachment, seizure, confiscation, and return, coordinate both sides' positions in international multilateral judicial cooperation, and jointly combat non-traditional security threats such as terrorism and cross-border crimes, including corruption, cybercrimes, drug-related crimes, and economic crimes. Efforts will also be made to negotiate and sign treaties on judicial assistance in civil and commercial matters and conduct judicial exchanges and cooperation between courts of the two sides.

7. Collective Cooperation

Based on the spirit and main objectives of the Beijing Declaration of the First Ministerial Meeting of China–CELAC Forum, the China–Latin American and Caribbean Countries Cooperation Plan (2015–2019), and the Institutional Arrangements and Operating Rules of Chin–CELAC Forum, China is ready to work with Latin American and Caribbean countries to uphold the principles of respect, equality, diversity, mutual benefit, cooperation, openness, inclusiveness, and unconditionality, and actively promote cooperation in various fields under the framework of the Forum. Efforts will be made to give full play to the role of such mechanisms as the ministerial meeting, the dialogue of foreign ministers of China and the "Quartet" of CELAC, and the meeting of national coordinators, hold successfully the sub-forums on political parties, law, youth, think tanks, infrastructure, innovation in science and technology, entrepreneurs, agriculture, non-governmental and local friendship, as well as China–Caribbean Economic and Trade Cooperation Forum, continuously improve the institution building of the China–CELAC Forum, and hold summits to be attended by state leaders of China and CELAC member states when conditions are ripe.

China welcomes the active participation of regional organizations and multilateral institutions of Latin America and the Caribbean in the collective cooperation between the two sides, and will accommodate the needs of the least developed countries, landlocked developing countries, and small island developing countries of the region in the collective cooperation.

8. Trilateral Cooperation

China is ready to carry out trilateral development cooperation in Latin American and Caribbean countries with relevant countries outside the region and international organizations under the premise that such cooperation is proposed, agreed upon, and dominated by countries in the region.

China encourages its enterprises to carry out trilateral cooperation in economic, social, and cultural fields in Latin American and Caribbean countries with relevant parties on the basis of commercial principles.

4. January 2016: China's Arab Policy Paper[4]

The State Council Information Office
The People's Republic of China

Contents

Foreword

    I. Deepen China–Arab Strategic Cooperative Relations of Comprehensive Cooperation and Common Development
    II. China's Arab Policy
    III. Strengthen China–Arab Cooperation in an All-Around Manner
    IV. China–Arab States Cooperation Forum and Its Follow-Up Actions
    V. Relations Between China and Arab Regional Organizations

Foreword

Friendship between China and Arab states dates back to ancient times. Over two thousand years ago, land and maritime Silk Roads already linked the Chinese and Arab nations. In the long stretches of history, peace and cooperation, openness and inclusiveness, and learning from each other, mutual benefit and win–win results have always been the main theme of exchanges between China and Arab countries.

The founding of the People's Republic of China and the independence of Arab countries created a new era for China–Arab friendly exchanges. From 1956 to 1990, China established diplomatic relations with all 22 Arab countries. China firmly supports Arab national liberation movement, firmly supports Arab countries' struggle to uphold sovereignty and territorial integrity, pursue and safeguard national interests, and combat external interference and aggression, and firmly supports Arab countries' cause of developing the national economy and building up the countries. Arab countries have given China strong support in restoring its lawful seat at the United Nations and on issues like the Taiwan question.

After the end of the Cold War, both China and Arab countries have followed the world trend of peace, development, and cooperation, respected each other, treated each other as equals, and committed themselves to deepening the traditional friendship and the bilateral relations. Cooperation in political, trade and economic, scientific and technological, cultural and educational, military, health, sports, news, and other fields has achieved fruitful results, thus enabling the establishment of the friendly and cooperative relationship oriented toward the twenty-first century.

In 2004, China–Arab States Cooperation Forum was set up. Since then, it has developed into a collective cooperation platform covering many fields and with more than ten mechanisms. In 2010, China and Arab countries established the strategic cooperative relations of comprehensive cooperation and common development, and China–Arab collective cooperation entered a new stage of comprehensive development and upgrading. President Xi Jinping delivered an important speech at the opening ceremony of the Sixth Ministerial Conference of China–Arab States

Cooperation Forum, identifying key areas and priority directions of China–Arab collective cooperation, and providing guidance for the development of the China–Arab relations and the Forum.

Since the establishment of diplomatic ties between China and Arab countries 60 years ago, cooperation in all fields has been constantly deepened. China has built comprehensive strategic partnership, strategic partnership, or strategic cooperative partnership with eight Arab countries, and has set up a strategic dialogue mechanism with the Gulf Cooperation Council. Arab countries as a whole have become China's biggest supplier of crude oil and the seventh biggest trading partner. China's proposed initiatives of jointly building the "Silk Road Economic Belt" and the "21st Century Maritime Silk Road," establishing a "1+2+3" cooperation pattern (to take energy cooperation as the core, infrastructure construction and trade and investment facilitation as the two wings, and three high and new tech fields of nuclear energy, space satellite, and new energy as the three breakthroughs), and industrial capacity cooperation, are well received by Arab countries. Both sides have broad consensus on safeguarding state sovereignty and territorial integrity, defending national dignity, seeking political resolution to hotspot issues, and promoting peace and stability in the Middle East. We share similar views on issues such as reform of the United Nations, climate change, and Doha Round trade negotiations, and maintain sound coordination and cooperation. Cultural and educational exchanges are more frequent and people-to-people ties are getting closer with enhanced mutual understanding and friendship between the two peoples.

Over the past 60 years, China–Arab friendly cooperation has made historic leaps in breadth and depth. It has become a model of South–South cooperation and gained the following successful experience: both sides have always respected and treated each other as equals and remained brothers, friends, and partners no matter what happens on the world arena; both sides have insisted on the principle of mutual benefit, win–win, and common development and have pursued common interests and sustainable development no matter what changes or developments take place on either side; and both sides have promoted dialogue, exchanges, and mutual learning among civilizations, and have always respected each other's social system and development path no matter what differences exist in ideology.

The Chinese government has issued the first China's Arab Policy Paper on the basis of reviewing and summarizing the experience in the development of China–Arab relations. It stipulates the guiding principle for developing China–Arab relations, offers the blueprint for China–Arab mutually beneficial cooperation, and reiterates the political will of commitment to peace and stability in the Middle East, in order to promote China–Arab relations to a new and higher level.

I. Deepen China–Arab Strategic Cooperative Relations of Comprehensive Cooperation and Common Development

The world is experiencing profound and complex changes. The trend toward a multipolar world and economic globalization is deepening, and cultural diversity and the information society continue to move forward. Changes in the international configuration and international order are accelerating. All countries in the world are seizing the opportunity to readjust their development strategies, promote reform and innovation, speed up economic transformation, and open up new development horizons. At the same time, the world economy is still in a period of deep transformation, with geopolitical factors becoming more prominent, regional turbulences rising one after another, non-traditional security and global challenges increasing, and the gap between the North and the South widening. It remains an arduous journey to advance mankind's noble cause of peace and development.

China is the largest developing country in the world and is working hard to realize the two centenary goals and the Chinese Dream of national rejuvenation, which is to build a strong, prosperous, democratic, culturally advanced, and harmonious modern socialist country. China will continue to uphold the banner of peace, development, and win–win cooperation, be committed to peaceful development, pursue a win–win strategy of opening up, and promote the formation of a new type of international relations featuring win–win cooperation.

Arab states are situated in the converging area of the Asian and African continents, characterized by religious and cultural diversities, time-honored culture and history, unique resource endowment and great potentials for development. Currently, Arab states are independently exploring the development paths suited to their own national realities. They are committed to pursuing industrialization, enhancing employment, and improving people's livelihood. They are active in promoting peace and stability in the region and are playing important roles in regional and international affairs.

China and Arab states are both developing countries with their combined territory, population, and economic aggregate accounting for 1/6, 1/4, and 1/8 of the world's total respectively. Different in natural endowment and development level, China and Arab countries are all in an important development stage and have a shared mission of rejuvenating the nation. We need to collaborate with each other more closely, and learn from each other along the road of development, strengthen cooperation in seeking common development and promoting regional peace, and echo each other in building a new type of international relations, so as to safeguard state sovereignty, independence, and territorial integrity, and to promote stability, economic development, and well-being of our peoples.

China will continue to carry forward China–Arab traditional friendship, enrich and deepen our all-round, multi-layer, wide-ranging cooperation, promote sustainable and sound development of our strategic cooperative relations featuring all-round cooperation and common development, and safeguard peace, stability, and development of the region and the world at large.

II. China's Arab Policy

Arab states are China's important partners in following the peaceful development path, strengthening unity and cooperation among developing countries, and establishing a new type of international relations with win–win cooperation at its core. China has always approached the China–Arab relations from a strategic height. It is

China's long-held diplomatic principle to consolidate and deepen China–Arab traditional friendship. China will adhere to the right approach to justice and interests and promote peace, stability, and development of Arab states while seeking better development of China, to achieve win–win cooperation, common development, and a better future of the China–Arab strategic and cooperative relations.

China upholds the Five Principles of Peaceful Coexistence, namely, mutual respect for sovereignty and territorial integrity, mutual non-aggression, mutual non-interference in each other's internal affairs, equality and mutual benefit, and peaceful co-existence. China supports the Middle East peace process and the establishment of an independent state of Palestine with full sovereignty, based on the pre-1967 borders, with East Jerusalem as its capital. China supports the Arab League and its member states' efforts to this end. We adhere to political solution to regional hot spot issues, and support the establishment of a nuclear weapon-free and WMD-free zone in the Middle East. We support positive efforts made by Arab states in strengthening unity, curbing the spread of extremist thoughts, and fighting terrorism. China respects choices made by the Arab people, and supports Arab states in exploring their own development paths suited to their national conditions. We hope to enhance the sharing of governance experience with Arab states.

China is willing to have pragmatic cooperation in the principle of mutual benefit and win–win results with Arab states. In particular, in the process of jointly pursuing the Silk Road Economic Belt and the twenty-first century Maritime Silk Road initiative, China is willing to coordinate development strategies with Arab states, put into play each other's advantages and potentials, promote international production capacity cooperation, and enhance cooperation in the fields of infrastructure construction, trade and investment facilitation, nuclear power, space satellite, new energy, agriculture, and finance, so as to achieve common progress and development and benefit our two peoples. China is willing to cooperate with Arab states to promote the new type of cooperation mechanism featuring openness and reciprocity, mutual benefit, and win–win results. According to Arab states' needs, China will continue to provide assistance within our means to Arab states through bilateral and multilateral channels, to help them improve self-development capability and people's livelihood.

China is willing to work with Arab states to contribute to diversified development and mutual learning among world civilizations. We will enhance people-to-people exchanges, strengthen cooperation in such areas as science, education, culture, health, radio, film, and television, deepen understanding and friendship between the two peoples, promote mutual learning and integration between the two cultures, build a communication bridge between the two peoples, and jointly contribute to the progress of human civilization.

China is willing to strengthen consultation and coordination with Arab states, and jointly uphold the purposes and principles of the UN Charter, implement the United Nations 2030 Agenda for sustainable development, safeguard international equity and justice, and make the international order more fair and just. On major international issues, such as the United Nations reform, climate change, food, and energy security, both sides respect each other's core interests and major concerns, support each other's justifiable demand and reasonable propositions, and staunchly safeguard the common interests of developing countries.

III. Strengthen China–Arab Cooperation in an All-Around Manner

1. Political Cooperation

1. High-Level Exchanges

We will keep the momentum of high-level exchanges and dialogues, make full use of meetings between high-level officials to guide the development of China–Arab relations. We will strengthen communication on bilateral relations and important issues of mutual concern, increase exchanges of experience of governance and economic development, consolidate political mutual trust, broaden common interests, and boost practical cooperation.

2. Intergovernmental Consultation and Cooperation Mechanisms

We will further improve the mechanism of China–Arab intergovernmental consultation and cooperation, make the best of bilateral and multilateral mechanisms, such as the strategic dialogue and political consultation, and enhance exchanges and communication, in order to realize common development.

3. Exchanges between Legislatures, Political Parties, and Local Governments

On the basis of mutual respect, deepening understanding, and expanding cooperation, the National People's Congress of China is willing to further expand multi-level and multi-channel exchanges and cooperation with legislatures of Arab states.

In the principle of independence, equality, mutual respect, and non-interference in internal affairs, the Communist Party of China is willing to further enhance exchanges with friendly political parties and organizations in Arab countries, consolidating the political foundation of China–Arab relations.

We will continue to boost exchanges between local governments, strengthen the mechanism of China–Arab City Forum, support the establishment of more sister cities or provinces, and promote exchanges and cooperation on local development and administration.

4. Cooperation on International Affairs

We will strengthen consultation in international affairs, maintain communication and coordination on major international and regional issues, and support each other on issues of core interests or major concern. We will keep closer cooperation and coordination in international organizations and defend the common interests of the two sides and all developing countries.

We will jointly uphold the international order and international system with the purposes and principles of the UN Charter at its core. We are actively involved in building a new type of international relations featuring win–win cooperation and jointly promoting world peace and development. We support the UN in playing a leading role in maintaining peace, promoting common development, and enhancing international cooperation. We support the UN to undergo necessary and reasonable reforms and increase the representation and voice of developing countries, including Arab states, at the UN Security Council.

5. The Taiwan Question

The Taiwan question concerns the core interests of China. The one-China principle is the important basis for China to establish and develop relations with Arab states and regional organizations. Arab states and regional organizations have always been committed to the one-China principle, refrained from having any official relations or official exchanges with Taiwan, and supported China in peaceful development of cross-Straits relations and the great cause of national reunification. China appreciates all these.

2. Investment and Trade Cooperation

1. "The Belt and Road" Initiative

Joint efforts will be made by China and Arab countries to promote the "Belt and Road" initiative under the principle of wide consultation, joint contribution, and shared benefit. China and Arab countries will adopt the "1+2+3" cooperation pattern to upgrade pragmatic cooperation by taking energy cooperation as the core infrastructure construction and trade and investment facilitation as the two wings, and high and new technologies in the fields of nuclear energy, space satellite, and new energy as the "three breakthroughs."

2. Cooperation on Production Capacity

Following the principle of market-oriented business operation in which enterprises serve as the main player and government as the facilitator, we will combine China's advantage of production capacity with demands of Arab states, carry out with Arab states advanced, suitable, effective, employment-oriented, and environment-friendly production capacity cooperation, supporting Arab states in their efforts to realize industrialization.

3. Investment Cooperation

On the basis of equality and mutually beneficial cooperation for win–win results, we encourage and support the expansion and optimization of mutual investment by enterprises from the two sides. We will expand cooperation areas, diversify cooperation methods, broaden investment and financing channels, and strengthen cooperation on two-way investment and financing through equities and debts as well as the use of loans, mezzanine financing, direct investment, and funds. China is ready to continue to provide foreign-aid loan on favorable terms to Arab countries, as well as export credits and overseas investment insurance. We will push for the signing of agreements with Arab countries on avoiding double taxation and tax evasion, thus creating a sound investment environment, providing convenience to investors from both sides and protecting their legitimate rights and interests.

4. Trade

We support the entry of more non-oil products from Arab states into the Chinese market. We will continue to improve the trade structure and push for sustained and steady development of two-way trade. We will strengthen exchanges and consultations between Chinese and Arab trade authorities, complete China–GCC FTA negotiations and sign a free trade agreement at an early date. We will oppose trade protectionism and actively remove non-tariff trade barriers, properly resolve trade disputes and frictions through friendly consultations, and gradually establish bilateral and multilateral mechanisms of early warning for trade disputes and cooperation on trade remedies. We will step up cooperation on inspection and quarantine, speed up the alignment of standards, enhance personnel exchanges and training, and jointly crack down on fake and shoddy goods in exports and exports.

5. Energy Cooperation

We will carry out cooperation on the basis of reciprocity and mutual benefit, promote and support investment cooperation with Arab countries in the field of petroleum and natural gas, in particular, investment cooperation on oil prospecting, extraction, transportation, and refining, and advance the synergizing of oilfield engineering technology service, equipment trade, and industrial standards. We will strengthen cooperation on renewable energy such as solar energy, wind energy, and hydropower. We will jointly build the China–Arab clear energy training center and develop all-round cooperation in related areas.

6. Infrastructure Construction

We encourage and support broader participation by Chinese companies and financial institutions in the cooperation with Arab countries in such areas as railway, highway, ports, aviation, power, communications, Beidou Navigation Satellite, satellite ground stations, and other infrastructure development fields and more extensive cooperation on project operation. According to the priority areas of development and needs of Arab countries, we will be actively engaged in cooperation on major projects in Arab countries to constantly improve Arab countries' infrastructure.

7. Space Cooperation

We will further develop space cooperation with Arab countries, actively explore joint projects in such fields as space technology, satellites and their application, space education, and training, accelerate the applying of the Beidou Navigation Satellite system in Arab countries, and promote exchanges and cooperation on manned spaceflight, so as to enhance the level of cooperation in this field.

8. Civilian Nuclear Cooperation

We will strengthen China–Arab cooperation on the design and construction of nuclear power plants and nuclear technology training. We will be actively engaged in cooperation covering the whole nuclear industrial chain, and promote cooperation between the two sides in basic scientific research, nuclear fuels, research reactors, application of nuclear technologies, nuclear security, disposal of radioactive wastes, emergency responses, and nuclear safety. We will accelerate the joint efforts of building an Arab training center for the peaceful use of nuclear energy, and upgrade the level of cooperation in the nuclear field.

9. Financial Cooperation

We support the establishment of branches in each other's countries by qualified financial institutions from both sides, and multi-sector operation cooperation, as well as strengthened exchanges and cooperation between regulators. We will strengthen monetary cooperation between central banks, discuss the expansion of cross-border currency clearing and currency swap arrangements, and increase financing insurance support. We will strengthen coordination and cooperation in international financial organizations and mechanisms, improve and reform the international financial system, and increase the voice and representation of developing countries. China welcomes the Arab countries to join the Asian Infrastructure Investment Bank and their active role in it.

10. Development of Economic and Trade Cooperation Mechanisms and Platforms

We will give full play to the role of the inter-governmental economic and trade joint commissions, the China–Arab Joint Chamber of Commerce and other bilateral or multilateral mechanisms, make full use of China–Arab States Expo and other platforms, and promote the exchange of visits and communication between governments and enterprises of the two sides.

3. Social Development

1. Health Care

We will strengthen exchanges and cooperation in traditional and modern medicine, pay attention to the prevention and control of communicable and non-communicable diseases, especially to cooperation on information sharing and monitoring of epidemics, and promote exchange of visits by experts from both sides. We will advance cooperation between medical institutions and enhance exchanges on clinical technology. We will continue to send medical teams and continuously improve service.

2. Education and Human Resources Development

We will strengthen cooperation on education and human resources development, expand the scale and innovate the ways of cooperation. We encourage colleges and universities from both sides to carry out joint scientific research in history and culture, scientific and technological application, region and country-specific studies. We will promote the development of China–Jordan University, support China–Arab joint personnel training, expand the scale of exchanges of students, and gradually increase the number of government exchange scholarships, the proportion of graduate students, and the number of disciplines. We will strengthen education of the Chinese language in Arab countries, and support training programs of Chinese language teachers in Arab countries. We will be actively engaged in vocational education exchanges and cooperation, and share best practices.

3. Cooperation on Science and Technology

We will accelerate the development of China–Arab inter-governmental science and technology innovation cooperation mechanism. We will implement the China–Arab partner project of science and technology and continue to improve the science and technology capability of Arab states. Through the China–Arab technology transfer center, we will establish a China–Arab collaboration network of integrated technology transfer. We will implement the "Outstanding Young Scientist Coming to China Project" and encourage the exchanges between young scientific talents of China and Arab states. We will jointly establish a batch of joint national laboratories, joint research centers, and specialized science parks, set up platforms for enterprises to go global and encourage hi-tech Chinese enterprises to innovate, start businesses, and establish R&D centers in Arab States. We will invite Arab technicians to participate in technology training courses for developing countries organized by the Ministry of Science and Technology of China. We will actively promote the application and spread of technological achievements and advanced applied technologies of China and Arab states in each other's countries.

4. Agricultural Cooperation

We will strengthen China–Arab bilateral and multilateral cooperation in such fields as arid zone agriculture, water-saving irrigation, Muslim food, food security, animal husbandry, and veterinary medicine. We encourage agricultural science and technology personnel from the two sides to increase exchanges. We will continue to set up demonstration projects of agricultural technology in Arab countries, scale up agricultural management and technology training, and strengthen project follow-up and evaluation.

5. Cooperation on Addressing Climate Change, Environmental Protection, and Forestry

We will vigorously promote communication and coordination with Arab states within the framework of the United Nations Framework Convention on Climate Change, Convention on Biological Diversity, and United Nations Convention on the Prevention and Control of Desertification. We will be actively engaged in exchanges and cooperation through bilateral and multilateral channels on policy dialogue and information sharing, environmental legislation, water, air, and soil pollution control and treatment, environmental protection awareness, environmental impact assessment, environmental monitoring, environmental protection industries and technologies, bio-diversity protection, prevention and control of desertification, arid zone forestry, forest management, training of environmental staff, and holding seminars. We will work together to enhance our capability of addressing climate change and environmental protection.

4. Culture and People-to-People Exchanges

1. Exchanges Among Civilizations and Religions

We will promote dialogue between civilizations and promote exchanges between different religions. We will build bilateral and multilateral platforms for religious exchanges, advocate religious harmony and tolerance, explore cooperation on eradicating extremism, and jointly contain the breeding and expansion of extremism.

2. Cooperation on Culture, Broadcasting, Film, Television, Press, Publication, and Think Tanks

We encourage regular exchange of visits of cultural officials, friendly partnership between cultural institutions, and experience sharing between the two sides. We encourage mutual establishment of culture centers, and support holding culture years and participating in art festivals hosted by the other side. We will fulfill the plan of "China–Arab exchange of visits by 10,000 artists" and strengthen cultivation of cultural professionals and cooperation of culture industries.

We will enhance China–Arab news media dialogue and cooperation and deepen business exchanges, news articles exchange, and personnel training. We will support joint interviews, joint productions, and joint operation of media institutions. The two sides will boost cooperation on broadcasting, film, and television exchanges, and will continue to hold China–Arab broadcasting and television cooperation forum, conduct translation and authorized broadcasting of television programs, and carry out broadcasting and television technology and industry cooperation. We encourage the two sides to hold film weeks of, send film delegations to, and actively participate in international film festivals hosted by the other side. We will translate and dub some Chinese artistic works into Arabic and vice versa. We encourage Arab States Broadcasting Union to cooperate with China Radio International and the Arabic Channel of China Central Television.

We encourage cooperation of press and publication institutions of the two sides, actively implement the "Memorandum of China–Arab Project of Mutual Translation and Publication of Ancient Books," and encourage and support publishers from the two sides to take part in international book fairs hosted by each other.

We will enhance exchanges of experts and scholars from the two sides and actively explore the establishment of a long-term China–Arab exchange mechanism of think tanks.

3. Exchanges Between Non-governmental Organizations, Youth, and Women

We will continue to enhance non-governmental exchanges, improve the mechanism of China–Arab friendship conference, and provide more support to China–Arab friendship associations. We encourage and support orderly exchanges of various forms between non-governmental organizations and social groups.

We will actively promote China–Arab youth communications, and enhance exchanges between departments of youth affairs and young elites from all walks of life of the two sides.

We will continue to strengthen China–Arab exchanges and cooperation on gender equality and encourage and support high-level dialogues, seminars, cultural exchanges, and capacity-building activities between departments and organizations in charge of women's affairs.

4. Cooperation on Tourism

We encourage tourism departments and businesses to introduce tourism resources and products to each other and carry out tourism cooperation. The Chinese side welcomes Arab states' application for the Approved Destination Status for outbound group tours by Chinese tourists.

5. *Cooperation in the Field of Peace and Security*

1. Regional Security

China calls for a concept of common, comprehensive, cooperative, and sustainable security in the Middle East, and supports Arab and regional countries in their efforts to build an inclusive and shared regional collective cooperation security mechanism, so as to realize long-term peace, prosperity, and development in the Middle East.

2. Military Cooperation

We will deepen China–Arab military cooperation and exchange. We will strengthen exchange of visits of military officials, expand military personnel exchange, deepen cooperation on weapons, equipment, and various specialized technologies, and carry out joint military exercises. We will continue to support the development of national defense and military forces of Arab States to maintain peace and security of the region.

3. Anti-terrorism Cooperation

We resolutely oppose and condemn all forms of terrorism, and oppose coupling terrorism with any specific ethnic group or religion as well as double standards. We support the efforts of Arab States in countering terrorism and support their counterterrorism capacity building. The Chinese side believes that counterterrorism needs comprehensive measures to address both the symptoms and root causes, and counterterrorism operations should comply with the purposes and principles of the Charter of the United Nations and international norms, and respect sovereignty, independence, and territorial integrity of all countries.

China is ready to strengthen anti-terrorism exchanges and cooperation with Arab countries to establish a long-term security cooperation mechanism, strengthen policy dialogue and intelligence information exchange, and carry out technical cooperation and personnel training to jointly address the threat of international and regional terrorism.

4. Consular, Immigration, Judicial, and Police Cooperation

We will earnestly safeguard the safety and legitimate interests of enterprises and citizens of China and Arab states in each other's countries, and actively make institutional arrangements for bilateral personnel exchanges. We will consolidate the results of bilateral cooperation in mutual legal assistance, extradition and repatriation, fugitive repatriation, and asset recovery, and set up cooperation on the signing of treaties on legal assistance, as well as fighting transnational organized crimes and corruption.

5. Non-Traditional Security

We will jointly enhance the capability to cope with non-traditional security threats, support the international community's efforts to combat piracy, continue to send warships to the Gulf of Aden and waters off Somalia to maintain international maritime security, and conduct cyber security cooperation.

IV. China–Arab States Cooperation Forum and Its Follow-Up Actions

The China–Arab States Cooperation Forum was established 11 years ago with dialogue, cooperation, peace, and development as its purposes. The mechanism has been gradually improved, and covered an increasingly wide range of areas. It has become an important platform for collective dialogue and pragmatic cooperation between the two sides based on equality and mutual benefit. China and Arab countries have established a strategic cooperative partnership featuring comprehensive cooperation and common development within the framework of China–Arab States Cooperation Forum, providing a strong support for long-term sustainable development of China–Arab relations.

China will remain committed to the development of China–Arab States Cooperation Forum, and together with the Arab countries, further enrich China–Arab cooperation, make innovative efforts on cooperation models and upgrade the level of cooperation, put into play the leading role of the ministerial meeting, and constantly enrich and improvement cooperation mechanisms in trade, culture, media, non-governmental exchanges, and other fields, so as to promote China–Arab exchanges and cooperation across the board.

V. Relations Between China and Arab Regional Organizations

China attaches great importance to its relations with the Arab League, and respects the efforts by the Arab League in maintaining regional peace and stability and promoting regional development. We support a bigger role of the Arab League in other regional and international affairs. China is willing to continue to strengthen consultation and cooperation with the Arab League in various fields.

China appreciates the active role played by Arab sub-regional organizations such as the Gulf Cooperation Council in maintaining regional peace and promoting development, and stands ready to strengthen friendly exchanges and cooperation with these organizations.

5. May 2015: China's Military Strategy[5]

The State Council Information Office
The People's Republic of China

Contents

Preface

Preface

The world today is undergoing unprecedented changes, and China is at a critical stage of reform and development. In their endeavor to realize the Chinese Dream of great national rejuvenation, the Chinese people aspire to join hands with the rest of the world to maintain peace, pursue development, and share prosperity.

China's destiny is vitally interrelated with that of the world as a whole. A prosperous and stable world would provide China with opportunities, while China's peaceful development also offers an opportunity for the whole world. China will unswervingly follow the path of peaceful development, pursue an independent foreign policy of peace and a national defense policy that is defensive in nature, oppose hegemonism and power politics in all forms, and will never seek hegemony or expansion. China's armed forces will remain a staunch force in maintaining world peace.

Building a strong national defense and powerful armed forces is a strategic task of China's modernization drive and a security guarantee for China's peaceful development. Subordinate to and serving the national strategic goal, China's military strategy is an overarching guidance for blueprinting and directing the building and employment of the country's armed forces. At this new historical starting point, China's armed forces will adapt themselves to new changes in the national security environment, firmly follow the goal of the Communist Party of China (CPC) to build a strong military for the new situation, implement the military strategic guideline of active defense in the new situation, accelerate the modernization of national defense and armed forces, resolutely safeguard China's sovereignty, security, and development interests, and provide a strong guarantee for achieving the national strategic goal of the "two centenaries" and for realizing the Chinese Dream of achieving the great rejuvenation of the Chinese nation.

I. National Security Situation

In today's world, the global trends toward multipolarity and economic globalization are intensifying, and an information society is rapidly coming into being. Countries are increasingly bound together in a community of shared destiny. Peace, development, cooperation, and mutual benefit have become an irresistible tide of the times.

Profound changes are taking place in the international situation, as manifested in the historic changes in the balance of power, global governance structure, Asia–Pacific geostrategic landscape, and international competition in the economic, scientific and technological, and military fields. The forces for world peace are on the rise, so are the factors against war. In the foreseeable future, a world war is unlikely, and the international situation is expected to remain generally peaceful. There are, however, new threats from hegemonism, power politics, and neo-interventionism. International competition for the redistribution of power, rights, and interests is tending to intensify. Terrorist activities are growing increasingly worrisome. Hot-spot issues, such as ethnic, religious, border, and territorial disputes, are complex and volatile. Small-scale wars, conflicts, and crises are recurrent in some regions. Therefore, the world still faces both immediate and potential threats of local wars.

With a generally favorable external environment, China will remain in an important period of strategic opportunities for its development, a period in which much can be achieved. China's comprehensive national strength, core competitiveness, and risk-resistance capacity are notably increasing, and China enjoys growing international standing and influence. Domestically, the Chinese people's standard of living has remarkably improved, and Chinese society remains stable. China, as a large developing country, still faces multiple and complex security threats, as well as increasing external impediments and challenges. Subsistence and development security concerns, as well as traditional and non-traditional security threats are interwoven. Therefore, China has an arduous task to safeguard its national unification, territorial integrity, and development interests.

As the world economic and strategic center of gravity is shifting ever more rapidly to the Asia–Pacific region, the US carries on its "rebalancing" strategy and enhances its military presence and its military alliances in this region. Japan is sparing no effort to dodge the post-war mechanism, overhauling its military and security policies. Such development has caused grave concerns among other countries in the region. On the issues concerning China's territorial sovereignty and maritime rights and interests, some of its offshore neighbors take provocative actions and reinforce their military presence on China's reefs and islands that they have illegally occupied. Some external countries are also busy meddling in South China Sea affairs; a tiny few maintain constant close-in air and sea surveillance and reconnaissance against China. It is thus a longstanding task for China to safeguard its maritime rights and interests. Certain disputes over land territory are still smoldering. The Korean Peninsula and Northeast Asia are shrouded in instability and uncertainty. Regional terrorism, separatism, and extremism are rampant. All these have a negative impact on the security and stability along China's periphery.

The Taiwan issue bears on China's reunification and long-term development, and reunification is an inevitable trend in the course of national rejuvenation. In recent years, cross-Taiwan Straits relations have sustained a sound momentum of peaceful development, but the root cause of instability has not yet been removed, and the "Taiwan independence" separatist forces and their activities are still the biggest threat to the peaceful development of cross-Straits relations. Further, China faces a formidable task to maintain political security and social stability. Separatist forces for "East Turkistan independence" and "Tibet independence" have inflicted serious damage, particularly with escalating violent terrorist activities by "East Turkistan independence" forces. Besides, anti-China forces have never given up their attempt to instigate a "color revolution" in this country. Consequently, China faces more challenges in terms of national security and social stability. With the growth of China's national interests, its national security is more vulnerable to international and regional turmoil, terrorism, piracy, serious natural disasters, and epidemics, and the security of overseas interests concerning energy and resources and, strategic sea lines of communication (SLOCs), as well as institutions, personnel, and assets abroad, has become an imminent issue.

The world revolution in military affairs (RMA) is proceeding to a new stage. Long-range, precise, smart, stealthy, and unmanned weapons and equipment are becoming increasingly sophisticated. Outer space and cyber space have become new commanding heights in strategic competition among all parties. The form of war is accelerating its evolution to informationization. World major powers are actively adjusting their national security strategies and defense policies, and speeding up their military transformation and force restructuring. The aforementioned revolutionary changes in military technologies and the form of war have not only had a significant impact on the international political and military landscapes, but also posed new and severe challenges to China's military security.

II. Missions and Strategic Tasks of China's Armed Forces

China's national strategic goal is to complete the building of a moderately prosperous society in all respects by 2021 when the CPC celebrates its centenary; and the building of a modern socialist country that is prosperous, strong, democratic, culturally advanced, and harmonious by 2049 when the People's Republic of China (PRC) marks its centenary. It is a Chinese Dream of achieving the great rejuvenation of the Chinese nation. The Chinese Dream is to make the country strong. China's armed forces take their dream of making the military strong as part of the Chinese Dream. Without a strong military, a country can be neither safe nor strong. In the new historical period, aiming at the CPC's goal of building a strong military in the new situation, China's armed forces will unswervingly adhere to the principle of the CPC's absolute leadership, uphold combat effectiveness as the sole and fundamental standard, carry on their glorious traditions, and work to build themselves into a people's military that follows the CPC's commands, can fight and win, and boasts a fine style of work.

In the new circumstances, the national security issues facing China encompass far more subjects, extend over a greater range, and cover a longer time span than at any time in the country's history. Internally and externally, the factors at play are more complex than ever before. Therefore, it is necessary to uphold a holistic view of national security, balance internal and external security, homeland and citizen security, traditional and non-traditional security, subsistence and development security, and China's own security and the common security of the world.

To realize China's national strategic goal and implement the holistic view of national security, new requirements have been raised for innovative development of China's military strategy and the accomplishment of military missions and tasks. In response to the new requirement of safeguarding national security and development interests, China's armed forces will work harder to create a favorable strategic posture with more emphasis on the employment of military forces and means, and provide a solid security guarantee for the country's peaceful development. In response to the new requirement arising from the changing security situation, the armed forces will constantly innovate strategic guidance and operational thoughts so as to ensure the capabilities of fighting and winning. In response to the new requirement arising from the worldwide RMA, the armed forces will pay close attention to the challenges in new security domains, and work hard to seize the strategic initiative in military competition. In response to the new requirement coming from the country's growing strategic interests, the armed forces will actively participate in both regional and international security cooperation and effectively secure China's overseas interests. And in response to the new requirement arising from China's all-round and deepening reform, the armed forces will continue to follow the path of civil–military integration (CMI), actively participate in the country's economic and social construction, and firmly maintain social stability, so as to remain a staunch force for upholding the CPC's ruling position and a reliable force for developing socialism with Chinese characteristics.

China's armed forces will effectively perform their missions in the new historical period, resolutely uphold the leadership of the CPC and the socialist system with Chinese characteristics, safeguard China's sovereignty, security, and development interests, safeguard the important period of strategic opportunities for China's development, maintain regional and world peace, and strive to provide a strong guarantee for completing the building of a moderately prosperous society in all respects and achieving the great rejuvenation of the Chinese nation.

China's armed forces mainly shoulder the following strategic tasks:

- To deal with a wide range of emergencies and military threats, and effectively safeguard the sovereignty and security of China's territorial land, air and sea;
- To resolutely safeguard the unification of the motherland;
- To safeguard China's security and interests in new domains;
- To safeguard the security of China's overseas interests;
- To maintain strategic deterrence and carry out nuclear counterattack;
- To participate in regional and international security cooperation and maintain regional and world peace;

- To strengthen efforts in operations against infiltration, separatism, and terrorism so as to maintain China's political security and social stability; and
- To perform such tasks as emergency rescue and disaster relief, rights and interests protection, guard duties, and support for national economic and social development.

III. Strategic Guideline of Active Defense

The strategic concept of active defense is the essence of the CPC's military strategic thought. From the long-term practice of revolutionary wars, the people's armed forces have developed a complete set of strategic concepts of active defense, which boils down to: adherence to the unity of strategic defense and operational and tactical offense; adherence to the principles of defense, self-defense, and post-emptive strike; and adherence to the stance that "we will not attack unless we are attacked, but we will surely counterattack if attacked."

Shortly after the founding of the PRC in 1949, the Central Military Commission (CMC) established the military strategic guideline of active defense, and later, in line with the developments and changes in the national security situation, had made a number of major revisions of it. In 1993 the military strategic guideline of the new era was formulated, which took winning local wars in conditions of modern technology, particularly high technology, as the basic point in making preparation for military struggle (PMS). In 2004, the guideline was further substantiated, and the basic point for PMS was modified to winning local wars under conditions of informationization.

China's socialist nature, fundamental national interests, and the objective requirement of taking the path of peaceful development all demand that China unswervingly adhere to and enrich the strategic concept of active defense. Guided by national security and development strategies, and required by the situation and their tasks in the new historical period, China's armed forces will continue to implement the military strategic guideline of active defense and enhance military strategic guidance as the times so require. They will further broaden strategic vision, update strategic thinking, and make strategic guidance more forward-looking. A holistic approach will be taken to balance war preparation and war prevention, rights protection and stability maintenance, deterrence and warfighting, and operations in wartime and employment of military forces in peacetime. They will lay stress on farsighted planning and management to create a favorable posture, comprehensively manage crises, and resolutely deter and win wars.

To implement the military strategic guideline of active defense in the new situation, China's armed forces will adjust the basic point for PMS. In line with the evolving form of war and national security situation, the basic point for PMS will be placed on winning informationized local wars, highlighting maritime military struggle and maritime PMS. The armed forces will work to effectively control major crises, properly handle possible chain reactions, and firmly safeguard the country's territorial sovereignty, integrity, and security.

To implement the military strategic guideline of active defense in the new situation, China's armed forces will innovate basic operational doctrines. In response to security threats from different directions and in line with their current capabilities, the armed forces will adhere to the principles of flexibility, mobility, and self-dependence so that "you fight your way and I fight my way." Integrated combat forces will be employed to prevail in system-vs-system operations featuring information dominance, precision strikes, and joint operations.

To implement the military strategic guideline of active defense in the new situation, China's armed forces will optimize the military strategic layout. In view of China's geostrategic environment, the security threats it faces, and the strategic tasks they shoulder, the armed forces will make overall planning for strategic deployment and military disposition, in order to clearly divide areas of responsibility for their troops, and enable them to support each other and act as an organic whole. Threats from such new security domains as outer space and cyber space will be dealt with to maintain the common security of the world community. China's armed forces will strengthen international security cooperation in areas crucially related to China's overseas interests, to ensure the security of such interests.

To implement the military strategic guideline of active defense in the new situation, China's armed forces will uphold the following principles:

- To be subordinate to and in the service of the national strategic goal, implement the holistic view of national security, strengthen PMS, prevent crises, deter and win wars;
- To foster a strategic posture favorable to China's peaceful development, adhere to the national defense policy that is defensive in nature, persevere in close coordination of political, military, economic, and diplomatic work, and positively cope with comprehensive security threats the country possibly encounters;
- To strike a balance between rights protection and stability maintenance, and make overall planning for both, safeguard national territorial sovereignty and maritime rights and interests, and maintain security and stability along China's periphery;
- To endeavor to seize the strategic initiative in military struggle, proactively plan for military struggle in all directions and domains, and grasp the opportunities to accelerate military building, reform, and development;
- To employ strategies and tactics featuring flexibility and mobility, give full play to the overall effectiveness of joint operations, concentrate superior forces, and make integrated use of all operational means and methods;
- To make serious preparations to cope with the most complex and difficult scenarios, uphold bottom-line thinking, and do a solid job in all aspects so as to ensure proper responses to such scenarios with ease at any time and in any circumstances;
- To bring into full play the unique political advantages of the people's armed forces, uphold the CPC's absolute leadership over the military, accentuate the cultivation of fighting spirit, enforce strict discipline, improve the

professionalism and strength of the troops, build closer relations between the government and the military as well as between the people and the military, and boost the morale of officers and men;

- To give full play to the overall power of the concept of people's war, persist in employing it as an ace weapon to triumph over the enemy, enrich the contents, ways, and means of the concept of people's war, and press forward with the shift of the focus of war mobilization from human resources to science and technology; and

- To actively expand military and security cooperation, deepen military relations with major powers, neighboring countries, and other developing countries, and promote the establishment of a regional framework for security and cooperation.

IV. Building and Development of China's Armed Forces

In the implementation of the military strategic guideline in the new situation, China's armed forces must closely center around the CPC's goal of building a strong military, respond to the state's core security needs, aim at building an informationized military and winning informationized wars, deepen the reform of national defense and the armed forces in an all-round way, build a modern system of military forces with Chinese characteristics, and constantly enhance their capabilities for addressing various security threats and accomplishing diversified military tasks.

1. Development of the Services and Arms of the People's Liberation Army (PLA) and the People's Armed Police Force (PAPF)

In line with the strategic requirement of mobile operations and multi-dimensional offense and defense, the PLA Army (PLAA) will continue to reorient from theater defense to trans-theater mobility. In the process of building small, multi-functional, and modular units, the PLAA will adapt itself to tasks in different regions, develop the capacity of its combat forces for different purposes, and construct a combat force structure for joint operations. The PLAA will elevate its capabilities for precise, multi-dimensional, trans-theater, multi-functional, and sustainable operations.

In line with the strategic requirement of offshore waters defense and open seas protection, the PLA Navy (PLAN) will gradually shift its focus from "offshore waters defense" to the combination of "offshore waters defense" with "open seas protection," and build a combined, multi-functional, and efficient marine combat force structure. The PLAN will enhance its capabilities for strategic deterrence and counterattack, maritime maneuvers, joint operations at sea, comprehensive defense, and comprehensive support.

In line with the strategic requirement of building air-space capabilities and conducting offensive and defensive operations, the PLA Air Force (PLAAF) will endeavor to shift its focus from territorial air defense to both defense and offense, and build an air-space defense force structure that can meet the requirements of informationized operations. The PLAAF will boost its capabilities for strategic early warning, air strike, air and missile defense, information countermeasures, airborne operations, strategic projection, and comprehensive support.

In line with the strategic requirement of being lean and effective and possessing both nuclear and conventional missiles, the PLA Second Artillery Force (PLA-SAF) will strive to transform itself in the direction of informationization, press forward with independent innovations in weaponry and equipment by reliance on science and technology, enhance the safety, reliability, and effectiveness of missile systems, and improve the force structure featuring a combination of both nuclear and conventional capabilities. The PLASAF will strengthen its capabilities for strategic deterrence and nuclear counterattack, and medium- and long-range precision strikes.

In line with the strategic requirement of performing multiple functions and effectively maintaining social stability, the PAPF will continue to develop its forces for guard and security, contingency response, stability maintenance, counterterrorism operations, emergency rescue and disaster relief, emergency support, and air support, and work to improve a force structure which highlights guard duty, contingency response, counterterrorism, and stability maintenance. The PAPF will enhance its capabilities for performing diversified tasks centering on guard duty and contingency response in informationized conditions.

2. Force Development in Critical Security Domains

The seas and oceans bear on the enduring peace, lasting stability, and sustainable development of China. The traditional mentality that land outweighs sea must be abandoned, and great importance has to be attached to managing the seas and oceans and protecting maritime rights and interests. It is necessary for China to develop a modern maritime military force structure commensurate with its national security and development interests, safeguard its national sovereignty and maritime rights and interests, protect the security of strategic SLOCs and overseas interests, and participate in international maritime cooperation, so as to provide strategic support for building itself into a maritime power.

Outer space has become a commanding height in international strategic competition. Countries concerned are developing their space forces and instruments, and the first signs of weaponization of outer space have appeared. China has all along advocated the peaceful use of outer space, opposed the weaponization of and arms race in outer space, and taken an active part in international space cooperation. China will keep abreast of the dynamics of outer space, deal with security threats and challenges in that domain, and secure its space assets to serve its national economic and social development, and maintain outer space security.

Cyberspace has become a new pillar of economic and social development, and a new domain of national security. As international strategic competition in cyberspace has been turning increasingly fiercer, quite a few countries are developing their cyber military forces. Being one of the major victims of hacker attacks, China is confronted with grave security threats to its cyber infrastructure. As cyberspace weighs more in military security, China will expedite the development of a cyber force, and enhance its capabilities of cyberspace situation awareness, cyber defense, support for the country's endeavors in cyberspace, and participation in international cyber cooperation, so as to stem major cyber crises, ensure national network and information security, and maintain national security and social stability.

The nuclear force is a strategic cornerstone for safeguarding national sovereignty and security. China has always pursued the policy of no first use of nuclear weapons and adhered to a self-defensive nuclear strategy that is defensive in nature. China will unconditionally not use or threaten to use nuclear weapons against non-nuclear-weapon states or in nuclear-weapon-free zones, and will never enter into a nuclear arms race with any other country. China has always kept its nuclear capabilities at the minimum level required for maintaining its national security. China will optimize its nuclear force structure, improve strategic early warning, command and control, missile penetration, rapid reaction, and survivability and protection, and deter other countries from using or threatening to use nuclear weapons against China.

3. Military Force Building Measures

Strengthening ideological and political work. China's armed forces always treat ideological and political building as the first priority, and have endeavored to reinforce and improve their political work in the new situation. They will continue to practice and carry forward the Core Socialist Values, cultivate the Core Values of Contemporary Revolutionary Service Personnel, and carry forward their glorious traditions and fine styles. Moreover, the armed forces will uphold a series of fundamental principles for and institutions of the CPC's absolute leadership over the military, enhance the creativity, cohesion, and combat effectiveness of their CPC organizations at all levels, make great efforts to cultivate a new generation of revolutionary service personnel of noble soul, competence, courage, uprightness, and virtue, and ensure that the armed forces will resolutely follow the commands of the CPC Central Committee and the CMC at all times and under all conditions, and consistently retain the nature and purpose of the people's armed forces.

Pushing ahead with logistics modernization. China's armed forces will deepen logistics reform in relevant policies, institutions, and support forces, and optimize strategic logistics deployment. They will innovate the modes of support, develop new support means, augment war reserves, integrate logistics information systems, improve rules and standards, and meticulously organize supply and support, so as to build a logistics system that can provide support for fighting and winning modern wars, serve the modernization of the armed forces, and transform towards informationization.

Developing advanced weaponry and equipment. Persevering in information dominance, systems building, independent innovation, sustainable development, overall planning, and emphasis on priorities, China's armed forces will speed up to upgrade weaponry and equipment, and work to develop a weaponry and equipment system which can effectively respond to informationized warfare and help fulfill the missions and tasks.

Cultivating new-type military personnel. China's armed forces will continue with the strategic project for personnel training and perfect the system for military human resources. They will deepen the reform of military educational institutions and improve the triad training system for new-type military personnel-institutional education, unit training, and military professional education, so as to pool more talented people and cultivate more personnel who can meet the demands of informationized warfare.

Intensifying efforts in running the armed forces with strict discipline and in accordance with the law. Aiming at strengthening the revolutionization, modernization, and regularization of the armed forces in all respects, China will innovate and develop theories and practice in relation to running the armed forces in accordance with the law and establish a well-knit military law system with Chinese characteristics, so as to elevate the level of rule by law of national defense and armed forces building.

Innovating military theories. Under the guidance of the CPC's innovative theories, China's armed forces will intensify their studies of military operations, probe into the mechanisms of winning modern wars, innovate strategies and tactics featuring mobility and flexibility, and develop theories on military building in the new situation, so as to bring into place a system of advanced military theories commensurate with the requirement of winning future wars.

Improving strategic management. It is necessary to optimize the functions and institutions of the CMC and the general headquarters/departments, improve the leadership and management system of the services and arms, and adhere to demand-based planning and plan-based resource allocation. China's armed forces will set up a system and a working mechanism for overall and coordinated programming and planning. They will also intensify overall supervision and management of strategic resources, strengthen the in-process supervision and risk control of major projects, improve mechanisms for strategic assessment, and set up and improve relevant assessment systems and complementary standards and codes.

4. In-depth Development of Civil–Military Integration (CMI)

Following the guiding principle of integrating military with civilian purposes and combining military efforts with civilian support, China will forge further ahead with CMI by constantly bettering the mechanisms, diversifying the forms, expanding the scope, and elevating the level of the integration, so as to endeavor to bring into place an all-element, multi-domain, and cost-efficient pattern of CMI.

Accelerating CMI in key sectors. With stronger policy support, China will work to establish uniform military and civilian standards for infrastructure, key technological areas, and major industries, explore the ways and means for training military personnel in civilian educational institutions, develop weaponry and equipment by national defense industries, and outsource logistics support to civilian support systems. China encourages joint building and utilization of military and civilian infrastructure, joint exploration of the sea, outer space, and air, and shared use of such resources as surveying and mapping, navigation, meteorology, and frequency spectra. Accordingly, military and civilian resources can be more compatible, complementary, and mutually accessible.

Building a mechanism for operating CMI. At the state level, it is necessary to establish a mechanism for CMI development, featuring unified leadership, military–civilian coordination, abutment of military and civilian needs, and resource sharing. Furthermore, it is necessary to improve the management responsibilities of relevant military and civilian institutions, improve the general standards for both the military and the civilian sectors, make studies on the establishment of a policy system in which the government makes the investment, offers tax incentives and financial support, and expedites legislation promoting military–civilian coordinated development, so as to form a pattern featuring overall military–civilian planning and coordinated development. It is also necessary to push forward with the shared utilization of military capabilities and those of other sectors, and establish a mechanism for joint civil–military response to major crises and emergencies.

Improving the systems and mechanisms of national defense mobilization. China will enhance education in national defense and boost the awareness of the general public in relation to national defense. It will continue to strengthen the building of the reserve force, optimize its structure, and increase its proportion in the PLAN, PLAAF and PLASAF as well as in combat support forces. The ways to organize and employ reserve forces will be more diversified. China will devote more efforts to science and technology in national defense mobilization, be more readily prepared for the requisition of information resources, and build specialized support forces. China aims to build a national defense mobilization system that can meet the requirements of winning informationized wars and responding to both emergencies and wars.

V. Preparation for Military Struggle

Preparation for military struggle (PMS) is a basic military practice and an important guarantee for safeguarding peace, containing crises, and winning wars. To expand and intensify PMS, China's armed forces must meet the requirement of being capable of fighting and winning, focus on solving major problems and difficulties, and do solid work and make relentless efforts in practical preparations, in order to enhance their overall capabilities for deterrence and warfighting.

Enhancing capabilities for system-vs-system operations based on information systems. China's armed forces will quicken their steps to transform the generating mode of combat effectiveness, work to use information systems to integrate a wide range of operational forces, modules, and elements into overall operational capacity, and gradually establish an integrated joint operational system in which all elements are seamlessly linked and various operational platforms perform independently and in coordination. China's armed forces will endeavor to address the pressing problems constraining the capabilities for system-vs-system operations.

They will make further exploration and more efficient utilization of information resources, strengthen the building of the systems of reconnaissance, early-warning, and command and control, develop medium- and long-range precision strike capabilities, and improve the comprehensive support systems. In accordance with the requirement of being authoritative, streamlined, agile, and efficient, they will strive to establish and improve the CMC command organ and theater-level command systems for joint operations.

Pushing ahead with PMS in all directions and domains. Due to its complex geo-strategic environment, China faces various threats and challenges in all its strategic directions and security domains. Therefore, PMS must be carried out in a well-planned, prioritized, comprehensive, and coordinated way, so as to maintain the balance and stability of the overall strategic situation. China's armed forces will make overall planning for PMS in both traditional and new security domains, and get ready to safeguard national sovereignty and security, protect the country's maritime rights and interests, and deal with armed conflicts and emergencies. To adapt to the upgrading of weaponry and equipment as well as changes of operational patterns, China's armed forces will further optimize battlefield disposition and strengthen strategic prepositioning.

Maintaining constant combat readiness. China's armed forces will continue to improve its routine combat readiness, maintain a posture of high alertness, and conscientiously organize border, coastal, and air defense patrols and guard duties. The PLAA will improve its combat readiness system with inter-connected strategic directions, combined arms, and systematized operational support, so as to ensure agile maneuvers and effective response. The PLAN will continue to organize and perform regular combat readiness patrols and maintain a military presence in relevant sea areas. The PLAAF will continue to observe the principles of applicability in peacetime and wartime, all-dimensional response and full territorial reach, and maintain vigilant and efficient combat readiness. The PLASAF will continue to keep an appropriate level of vigilance in peacetime. By observing the principles of combining peacetime and wartime demands, maintaining all time vigilance and being action-ready, it will perfect the integrated, functional, agile, and efficient operational duty system.

Enhancing realistic military training. The PLA will continue to attach strategic importance to combat training in realistic conditions, and strictly temper the troops according to the Outline of Military Training and Evaluation (OMTE). It will constantly innovate operational and training methods, improve military training criteria and regulations, and work to build large-scale comprehensive training bases in an effort to provide real-combat environments for training. The PLA will continue to conduct live-setting training, IT-based simulated training, and face-on-face confrontation training in line with real-combat criteria, and strengthen command post training and joint and combined training. It will intensify training in complex electro-magnetic environments, complex and unfamiliar terrains, and complex weather conditions. It will also set up a training supervision and inspection system, so as to incorporate real-combat requirements into training.

Preparing for military operations other than war (MOOTWs). As a necessary requirement for China's armed forces to fulfill their responsibilities and missions in the new period as well as an important approach to enhancing their operational capabilities, the armed forces will continue to conduct such MOOTWs as emergency rescue and disaster relief, counterterrorism and stability maintenance, rights and interests protection, guard duty, international peacekeeping, and international humanitarian assistance and disaster relief (HADR). They will work to incorporate MOOTW capacity building into military modernization and PMS, and pay special attention to establishing emergency command mechanisms, building emergency forces, training professionals, supporting task-specific equipment, and formulating relevant policies and regulations. Military emergency-response command systems will be tuned into state emergency management mechanisms. China's armed forces will persist in unified organization and command, scientific employment of forces, rapid and efficient actions, and strict observation of related policies and regulations.

VI. Military and Security Cooperation

Pursuing a security concept featuring common, comprehensive, cooperative, and sustainable security, China's armed forces will continue to develop military-to-military relations that are non-aligned, non-confrontational, and not directed against any third party. They will strive to establish fair and effective collective security mechanisms and military confidence-building measures (CBMs), expand military and security cooperation, and create a security environment favorable to China's peaceful development.

Developing all-round military-to-military relations. China's armed forces will further their exchanges and cooperation with the Russian military within the framework of the comprehensive strategic partnership of coordination between China and Russia, and foster a comprehensive, diverse, and sustainable framework to promote military relations in more fields and at more levels. China's armed forces will continue to foster a new model of military relationship with the US armed forces that conforms to the new model of major-country relations between the two countries, strengthen defense dialogues, exchanges and cooperation, and improve the CBM mechanism for the notification of major military activities as well as the rules of behavior for safety of air and maritime encounters, so as to strengthen mutual trust, prevent risks, and manage crises. In the spirit of neighborhood diplomacy of friendship, sincerity, reciprocity, and inclusiveness, China's armed forces will further develop relations with their counterparts in neighboring countries. Also, they will work to raise the level of military relations with European counterparts, continue the traditional friendly military ties with their African, Latin American, and Southern Pacific counterparts. China's armed forces will work to further defense and security cooperation in the Shanghai Cooperation Organization (SCO), and continue to participate in multilateral dialogues and cooperation mechanisms such as the ASEAN Defense Ministers' Meeting Plus (ADMM+), ASEAN Regional Forum (ARF), Shangri-La Dialogue (SLD), Jakarta International Defence Dialogue

(JIDD), and Western Pacific Naval Symposium (WPNS). The Chinese military will continue to host multilateral events like the Xiangshan Forum, striving to establish a new framework for security and cooperation conducive to peace, stability, and prosperity in the Asia–Pacific region.

Pushing ahead with pragmatic military cooperation. On the basis of mutual respect, equality, mutual benefit, and all-win cooperation, China's armed forces will continue to carry out pragmatic cooperation with their counterparts in various countries of the world. In response to the changing situation, China's armed forces will constantly explore new fields, new contents, and new models of cooperation with other militaries, so as to jointly deal with a diverse range of security threats and challenges. Extensive dialogues and exchanges will be conducted with foreign militaries on defense policy, services, and arms building, institutional education, logistics, and other subjects to promote mutual understanding, mutual trust, and mutual learning. The Chinese military will also strengthen cooperation with related countries in personnel training, material assistance, equipment, and technology, so as to strengthen mutual support and enhance respective defensive capabilities. Bilateral and multilateral joint exercises and training, involving various services and arms, will be conducted at multiple levels and in various domains to enhance joint operational capabilities. The Chinese military will work to extend the subjects of such training and exercises from non-traditional to traditional security areas. It will actively participate in international maritime security dialogues and cooperation, and jointly deal with traditional and non-traditional maritime security threats.

Fulfilling international responsibilities and obligations. China's armed forces will continue to participate in UN peacekeeping missions, strictly observe the mandates of the UN Security Council, maintain its commitment to the peaceful settlement of conflicts, promote development and reconstruction, and safeguard regional peace and security. China's armed forces will continue to take an active part in international disaster rescue and humanitarian assistance, dispatch professional rescue teams to disaster-stricken areas for relief and disaster reduction, provide relief materials and medical aid, and strengthen international exchanges in the fields of rescue and disaster reduction. Through the aforementioned operations, the armed forces can also enhance their own capabilities and expertise. Faithfully fulfilling China's international obligations, the country's armed forces will continue to carry out escort missions in the Gulf of Aden and other sea areas as required, enhance exchanges and cooperation with naval task forces of other countries, and jointly secure international SLOCs. China's armed forces will engage in extensive regional and international security affairs, and promote the establishment of the mechanisms of emergency notification, military risk precaution, crisis management, and conflict control. With the growth of national strength, China's armed forces will gradually intensify their participation in such operations as international peacekeeping and humanitarian assistance, and do their utmost to shoulder more international responsibilities and obligations, provide more public security goods, and contribute more to world peace and common development.

6. December 2015: China's Second Africa Policy Paper[6]

The State Council Information Office
The People's Republic of China

Contents

Preface

    I. Establishing and Developing Comprehensive Strategic and Cooperative China–Africa Partnership and Consolidating and Bolstering the Community of Shared Future between China and Africa

    II. Upholding the Values of Friendship, Justice, and Shared Interests and Adhering to the Principles of Sincerity, Practical Results, Affinity, and Good Faith

    III. Promoting the All-Round Development of China–Africa Cooperation

    IV. FOCAC and Its Follow-Up Actions

    V. China's Relations with African Regional Organizations

Preface

The Chinese Government published its first Africa policy paper in 2006. Over the past decade, the policy has been carried out fully and effectively, playing an important guiding role in the all-round development of China–Africa relations. This year marks the 15th anniversary of the establishment of the Forum on China–Africa Cooperation (FOCAC). The Second FOCAC Summit will be held in South Africa in December. As the first China–Africa summit to be hosted on the African continent, it will be a landmark event conducive to strengthening China–Africa unity and spearheading China–Africa cooperation.

Against this backdrop, the Chinese government wishes, with release of its second Africa policy paper, to further clarify China's determination and goodwill to develop friendly and cooperative relations with Africa and expound the new vision, approach, and measures of China's Africa policy under the new circumstances with the aim of guiding the multi-faceted exchanges and cooperation between China and Africa in the years to come.

I. Establishing and Developing Comprehensive Strategic and Cooperative China–Africa Partnership and Consolidating and Bolstering the Community of Shared Future between China and Africa

China and Africa have always belonged to a community of shared future. Over the past five decades and more, they have always been good friends who stand together through thick and thin, good partners who share weal and woe, and good brothers who fully trust each other despite changes in the international landscape. The traditional friendship between China and Africa is deeply rooted in people's minds and has become an invaluable asset for both. China and Africa have long valued sincerity, friendship, and equality, which constitute the underlying rationale for China–Africa relations to grow stronger with time. Based on this tradition, China and Africa will be committed to mutually beneficial cooperation and common development under the new circumstances, adding new substance and injecting inexhaustible impetus to China–Africa relations.

In 2006, the Chinese government proposed a new type of China–Africa strategic partnership featuring political equality and mutual trust, economic win–win cooperation, and cultural exchange. In the past decade, China and Africa jointly formulated and implemented a series of major measures to deepen cooperation, which greatly promoted the rapid development of their friendly and cooperative ties across the board. Political mutual trust between China and Africa has been strengthened. Their coordination and cooperation in international and regional affairs have become closer. Their pragmatic cooperation has borne abundant fruit. China has been Africa's largest trading partner since 2009. In 2014, China's trade volume with Africa rose to four times that of 2006. People-to-people and cultural exchanges have flourished with nearly 3 million visits made between China and Africa every year, garnering greater social and popular support for China–Africa friendship. The scope and depth of China–Africa exchanges and cooperation has been unprecedented. China's contribution to Africa's economic growth has significantly increased.

Tremendous changes have taken place in China and Africa in the past decade, with both shouldering new development tasks. China is striving to achieve the "two centenary goals" and realize the Chinese dream of great national renewal in accordance with the strategy of completing the building of a moderately prosperous society in all respects, comprehensively deepening reform, advancing law-based governance, and applying strict party discipline. Africa is committed to accelerating its industrialization and modernization and forging ahead to fulfill the dreams outlined in Agenda 2063. Both the Chinese dream and the African dream aim to enable people to live a more prosperous and happier life.

The development strategies of China and Africa are highly compatible. Given their respective strengths, China and Africa need each other for cooperation and development. Rare historic opportunities for mutually beneficial cooperation and common development have emerged. China's comparative advantages in development experience, applied technology, funds, and market can help Africa overcome the two major bottlenecks constraining its development—backward infrastructure and inadequate professional and skilled personnel. They can also help Africa translate its natural and human resources advantages and potential into a driving force for development and benefits for people's livelihoods, thereby speeding up industrialization and agricultural modernization, and doing a better job in pursuing economic independence as well as self-reliant and sustainable development and achieving lasting peace and stability.

The international situation has undergone dramatic changes over the past decade. The transition to a multipolar world has gained momentum. The rapid development of emerging markets and developing countries has become an irresistible trend in history, making them a pivotal force for safeguarding world peace and promoting common development. The UN has adopted the 2030 Agenda for Sustainable Development, mandating the realization of inclusive and sustainable development in all countries. Africa has become one of the continents with the fastest economic growth and greatest development potential. It is an important player on the stage of world politics, a new growth pole for the global economy, and a center of human civilization with diverse cultures. China has risen to become the world's second largest economy. It is an active player in the current international system that has helped build it and contributed to it. The current global governance system, however, has yet to fully accommodate the changes. There is a need to increase the representation and voice of developing countries, including China and African nations, in international affairs. China and Africa should make the most of their advantages in political mutual trust and economic complementarity to push for the all-round development of China–Africa cooperation, strengthen South–South cooperation, promote North–South cooperation, and set a good example for the development of a new model of international relations centered on mutually beneficial cooperation.

China–Africa relations have now reached a new historical starting point. Given their shared development tasks, highly compatible strategic interests, and broad prospects for mutually beneficial cooperation, the Chinese and African people will advance side by side with an ever-growing sense of purpose. China is willing to work with African countries to build and develop a China–Africa comprehensive strategic and cooperative partnership featuring political equality and mutual trust, win–win economic cooperation, mutually enriching cultural exchanges, mutual assistance in security, and solidarity and coordination in international affairs. China is devoted, as are African nations, to promoting an all-round development of China–Africa friendly cooperation, working together to pursue development and fulfill dreams, jointly delivering more benefits to Chinese and African people, and making greater contributions to world peace, stability, development, and prosperity.

II. Upholding the Values of Friendship, Justice, and Shared Interests and Adhering to the Principles of Sincerity, Practical Results, Affinity, and Good Faith

Enhancing solidarity and cooperation with African countries has always been the cornerstone of China's independent foreign policy of peace, as well as China's firm and longstanding strategic choice. Under the new circumstances, China will adhere to the principles of its Africa policy—sincerity, practical results, affinity, and good faith, uphold the values of friendship, justice, and shared interests, and push for new leapfrog growth of its friendly and mutually beneficial cooperation with Africa.

"Sincerity" means China insists on the principles of equality, mutual trust, solidarity, and mutual support, and will always be Africa's most trustworthy friend and sincere partner. China respects African countries' independent choice of the way to development as well as their practices and efforts to promote economic and social development and improve people's living standard. It stands ready to exchange governance experience with African countries on the basis of equality and voluntarism, and promote mutual understanding and acceptance of and learning from each other's political system and development path. China has always sincerely supported Africa's development. It never interferes in African countries' internal affairs, never imposes its will on them, and attaches no political strings when providing aid to Africa. On issues involving each other's core interests and major concerns, China will enhance communication and coordination, mutual understanding and mutual support with African countries, and safeguard the common interests of both.

"Practical results" means that China aims to achieve practical and efficient results, seeks cooperation and mutual benefits, upholds the principle of honoring commitments with real actions and results, implements the guidelines and measures for mutually beneficial cooperation with Africa to the letter, and strives to realize the common development of China and Africa while helping Africa achieve independent development. Adhering to the traditional Chinese philosophy of "building a nest to attract the phoenix and teaching people how to fish," China will support African countries' efforts in infrastructure and human resources development to help them overcome these two major bottlenecks that have long been constraining Africa's development, and promote China–Africa industrial alignment and capacity cooperation to facilitate Africa's industrialization and agricultural modernization. China will adhere to the idea of pursuing peace through development and promoting development by maintaining peace, and support Africa's efforts to seek independent and sustainable development, resolve African issues in an African way, and play a more constructive role in regional hotspot issues.

"Affinity" means the hearts of Chinese and African people are connected, and they will live together in harmony, promote inter-cultural dialogue, and enhance exchanges of ideas, policy alignment, and mutual understanding to provide a solid popular and social basis for China–Africa friendship. China will strengthen exchanges and cooperation with Africa in education, science, culture, health, and other social and cultural fields, expand exchanges between Chinese and African people, increase think tank, university, and media exchanges, and support sub-national contacts and cooperation. Chinese and African employees working on each other's soil will be encouraged to get along well with local people, and seek coexistence and common prosperity. The Chinese government encourages Chinese enterprises and citizens in Africa to care more about the well-being of local people and repay local society, create a good environment for the Africans working, studying, and living in China, and constantly extend and consolidate the social basis of China–Africa friendship.

"Good faith" means China cherishes good faith and settlement of problems in an appropriate manner. It views and promotes China–Africa relations from strategic and long-term perspectives, and seeks joint efforts with Africa to create a good environment for friendly and mutually beneficial cooperation. China stands ready to strengthen policy coordination and communication with African countries, adheres to the principles of mutual respect and win–win cooperation, faces squarely and sincerely the new developments and problems confronting their relations through equal and friendly coordination, and ensures that both sides benefit from sincere, friendly, and mutually beneficial cooperation.

Upholding the values of friendship, justice, and shared interests is a hallmark of China's policy toward other developing countries. While valuing friendship and justice as well as shared interests, China places more importance on the former. The core principle is to connect assistance to developing countries, including those in Africa, for their independent and sustainable development with China's own development, achieve win–win cooperation and common development, and promote more balanced, inclusive, and sustainable development of the world at large. China will never repeat the past colonial way in its cooperation with Africa and never pursue development at the cost of Africa's natural and ecological environment or long-term interests.

Providing support and assistance to African countries for their independent and sustainable development conforms to the interests of both African people and the people of the entire world, and is the common responsibility of the international community. While engaging in cooperation with Africa, China always respects and protects the fundamental interests of African countries and their people, upholds fairness, and seeks justice for Africa. It also pursues mutual benefit and win–win results, and sincerely supports and assists Africa in its efforts to realize peace, stability– and development.

The one-China principle is the political precondition and foundation for the establishment and development of China's relations with African countries and regional organizations. The Chinese government appreciates the fact that African countries abide by the one-China principle, support China's reunification, and refuse to have official relations and contacts with Taiwan. China is committed to developing friendly cooperation in an all-round way with all African countries on the basis of the Five Principles of Peaceful Coexistence.

China appreciates the constructive actions of the international community to support and assist Africa in realizing lasting peace and sustainable development. It will strengthen coordination and cooperation with other countries as well as international and regional organizations on the basis of the "Africa-proposed, Africa-agreed, and Africa-led" principle and with an active, open, and inclusive attitude. China will explore tripartite and multilateral cooperation in Africa so as to jointly contribute to peace, stability, and development on the continent.

III. Promoting the All-Round Development of China–Africa Cooperation

1. Enhancing Political Mutual Trust

1. Intensifying High-Level Exchanges

While bringing into play the role of high-level exchanges in providing political guidance, China will maintain the momentum of frequent mutual visits and dialogue between Chinese and African leaders, with a view to facilitating communication on bilateral relations and major issues of common interest, solidifying traditional friendship, and bolstering political mutual trust. China advocates mutual understanding and support on issues involving their respective core interests and major concerns. It calls for safeguarding shared interests, pursuing development together, and deepening cooperation. All these aim to lay a solid political groundwork for the development of bilateral relations between China and individual African countries as well as the overall China–Africa relationship.

2. Boosting Experience Sharing in Governance

China is of the view that countries should respect and support each other's efforts to explore and improve development paths and political systems suited to their national conditions. It is ready to engage in a variety of experience-sharing programs with African countries. Through these programs, they will draw wisdom from each other's civilizations and development practices, increase exchanges of governance experience, and promote common development in accordance with the principles of communication on an equal footing, mutual learning, and shared progress.

3. Improving Intergovernmental Consultation and Cooperation Mechanisms

China will make the most of the coordinating role of bilateral mechanisms such as political consultations between foreign ministries, joint (mixed) committees on trade and economic cooperation and high-level economic and trade cooperation mechanisms, and mixed committees on science and technology. It will further diversify and improve intergovernmental dialogue and consultation mechanisms to promote China–Africa intergovernmental dialogue and cooperation.

4. Promoting Exchanges in Various Sectors Including Those Between Legislative Bodies, Consultative Bodies, Political Parties, the Military, and Local Governments

In keeping with the purpose of deepening understanding and cooperation with mutual respect, China favors increased multi-level, multi-channel, multi-form, and all-dimensional friendly exchanges between the National People's Congress of China and organizations such as the parliaments of African countries and the Pan-African Parliament. These will help further substantiate the China–Africa comprehensive strategic and cooperative partnership.

China stands for expanded and strengthened exchanges between the Chinese People's Political Consultative Conference and relevant institutions such as African national parliaments, the Pan-African Parliament, the Economic, Social and Cultural Council of the African Union (AU), and the economic and social councils of individual African countries.

The Communist Party of China stands ready to expand and deepen diverse forms of exchanges and cooperation with friendly political parties and organizations in African countries based on the principles of independence, equality, mutual respect, and non-interference in each other's internal affairs. It is committed to exploring a new platform for collective communication and dialogue with the aim of enhancing mutual understanding and friendship and deepening exchanges of governance experience. This will also enable them to better understand and recognize each other's governance systems and philosophies, learn from each other, improve governance capacities together, and contribute to the development of state-to-state relations.

Efforts will be made to maintain the momentum of mutual visits between Chinese and African military leaders, and push for strengthened policy dialogue and increased exchanges between young officers.

China supports the establishment of an increasing number of twin province/ state and twin city relationships between China and African countries in a bid to strengthen ties between Chinese and African local governments and facilitate exchanges and cooperation in local development and administration.

2. Deepening Cooperation in International Affairs

China will further enhance exchanges and cooperation with African countries in international institutions such as the UN and on other international occasions. It will maintain communication and coordination with African countries on prominent international and regional issues. It stands for mutual understanding and support on major issues concerning their respective state sovereignty, territorial integrity, national dignity, and development interests, while safeguarding their shared interests as well as those of developing countries.

China will work in concert with Africa to uphold the international order and system underpinned by the purposes and principles of the UN Charter. It is firmly supportive of increasing the representation and voice of developing countries in the international governance system. Supporting comprehensive reform of the UN, China maintains that priority should be given to increasing African countries' representation and voice in the UN Security Council and other UN agencies to address the injustices Africa suffered historically. It is committed, as African nations are, to defending the purposes and principles of the UN Charter, upholding international fairness and justice, and making the world order more just and reasonable.

China calls on the international community to continue to step up the global economic governance reform—in particular, to deliver the promised IMF quota reform as soon as possible—so as to increase the representation and voice of emerging markets and developing countries. It calls for strengthened dialogue between the G20 and Africa and is supportive of Africa's participation in G20 affairs.

China will join hands with Africa to call on members of the international community to realize that they are all in the same boat and should therefore share rights and responsibilities. In this spirit, it calls for efforts to implement the 2030 Agenda for Sustainable Development adopted at the UN Sustainable Development Summit, strengthen all countries' capacities for development, ameliorate the international environment for development, optimize development partnerships, and improve development coordination mechanisms. All these aim to achieve balanced, sustainable, and inclusive growth, jointly create a path of development that is fair, open, comprehensive, and innovative, realize common development, and advance the common interests of mankind. China will continue to uphold and advocate the principles such as equality, mutual trust, win–win results, solidarity, and cooperation while promoting South–South cooperation at a higher level, in a broader scope, and on a larger scale under the new circumstances.

China reaffirms the fundamental role of the United Nations Framework Convention on Climate Change (UNFCCC) in the international response to climate change. It agrees to jointly maintain the solidarity of developing countries, while upholding the principles and provisions of the UNFCCC and its Kyoto Protocol, especially the principles of equity, "common but differentiated responsibilities," and respective capabilities. It is resolved to work for the establishment of an equitable, reasonable, cooperative, and mutually beneficial international climate management system, and promote all-round, effective, and sustained implementation of the UNFCCC. China has taken note of the progress made in the UN Convention to Combat Desertification in Countries Experiencing Serious Drought and/or Desertification, Particularly in Africa. It agrees to jointly safeguard the interests of developing countries and push for the convention's full and effective implementation.

3. Deepening Economic and Trade Cooperation

1. Helping Boost Africa's Industrialization

China will make prioritizing support for Africa's industrialization a key area and a main focus in its cooperation with Africa in the new era. Allowing industrial alignment and capacity cooperation to play a leading role in bringing about overall development will help accelerate the industrialization in Africa, thereby providing a solid foundation for Africa's economic independence as well as self-reliant and sustainable development. In light of their national conditions, development needs, and feasible international rules, China will vigorously support the efforts of African countries to improve their "soft" and "hard" environment for investment and development, to optimize laws and regulations on and government services for attracting and protecting foreign investment, and to remove the two major bottlenecks impeding development, namely, backward infrastructure and inadequate professional and skilled personnel. Efforts will be made to promote industrial alignment and capacity cooperation between China and African countries in an orderly fashion, with the aim to facilitate Africa's industrialization and economic diversification, and increase the level of production, living standards, and employment in African countries. China is supportive of African countries' development of special economic zones, industrial parks, and science and technology parks to attract investment and talents. It will guide, encourage, and support the efforts of Chinese enterprises to jointly build economic and trade cooperation zones in Africa to serve as important platforms for promoting China–Africa industrial capacity cooperation and attracting more Chinese enterprises to invest in Africa, build production and processing bases, and localize their operations in Africa, contribute to the increase of local employment, tax revenue, and foreign-exchange income, and promote the transfer of industries and technologies.

While sticking to the values of friendship, justice, and shared interests, win–win cooperation, the principles of openness and inclusiveness, and market-based operation, China will give priority to building pilot industrial capacity cooperation demonstration zones in African countries with appropriate conditions. China will work together with chosen African countries to bring into full play their governments' role in guidance, coordination, management, and service, increase exchanges of experience in macroeconomic management, and innovate on the cooperation mechanisms in investment protection, finance, taxation, customs, visa, immigration, and exchanges of police officers to help African countries enhance capacity building in law enforcement and improve management and services. They will also work in concert to achieve an early harvest in their industrial capacity cooperation, accumulating development and cooperation experience, providing a demonstration effect, and playing a leading role in bringing along cooperation with other African countries.

2. Helping Boost Africa's Agricultural Modernization

China will prioritize support for Africa's agricultural modernization in its cooperation with Africa in the new era, with increased input and expanded cooperation to help African countries resolve the development problem of this basic industry that has a bearing on their national economy and people's livelihoods as well as economic independence. China is willing to share its experience and technology in agricultural development with African countries, and supports their efforts to improve their agricultural technology and techniques to produce and process agricultural, livestock, and fishery products. This will help them build an agricultural value chain and increase independent grain production capacity to boost food security, enhance the competitiveness of cotton and other specialty industries in the world, generate more income, and improve the livelihood of farmers. China will improve and continue to carry out agricultural technology demonstration projects in Africa, implement the High-Quality and High-Yield Agriculture Demonstration

Project, bolster research and development, promotion, and extensive use of seeds, send senior agricultural expert teams and agricultural vocational training teacher teams, and expand the scale and effect of training in agricultural management and technology. It will build and improve bilateral mechanisms for agricultural cooperation with Africa, give play to the strengths and roles of each side, and strengthen supervision and evaluation of cooperation projects to increase the quality and level of cooperation. China will encourage and promote China–Africa trade in agricultural products. It will encourage and support Chinese enterprises to engage in crop farming, grain storage, stockbreeding, and fishery, and invest in the processing of agricultural products in African countries, helping create more jobs for local people, increase the added value of local products, and generate more foreign-exchange income, and boosting Africa's agricultural modernization. China will also help African countries promote irrigation techniques, effectively use water resources, and improve their capacity to prevent floods and combat droughts.

3. Participating in Africa's Infrastructure Development Across the Board

China will encourage and support Chinese enterprises and financial institutions' expanded involvement in infrastructure development in Africa, give full play to the role of policy-based finance, and innovate on investment and financing cooperation models. While sticking to market-oriented operation, as well as the principles of overall cooperation with emphasis on selected areas and a focus on benefits, China will encourage and support the efforts of domestic enterprises to adopt various models to participate in the construction of railways, highways, telecommunications networks, electric power facilities, regional aviation networks, harbors, water works, and other infrastructure projects as well as water resources development and protection in Africa. They will also be encouraged and supported to participate in investment, operation, and management of these projects. It will encourage bilateral cooperation in the planning and designing, construction, technical standards, supervision, large equipment utilization, and management and operation of the projects.

China stands for pushing forward infrastructure and industrial development in Africa in a coordinated way, with a focus on intensive operation and economies of scale. It will prioritize support for the construction of infrastructure facilities for special economic zones, industrial parks, science and technology parks, etc., to provide favorable conditions for Africa's industrial development and China–Africa industrial capacity cooperation. It will facilitate cross-border and cross-regional connectivity in infrastructure to help accelerate the process of African integration.

4. Strengthening China–Africa Financial Cooperation

China will give full play to financing platforms and tools, which include preferential loans and other means of policy-based finance, the China–Africa Development Fund, special loans for African small and medium-sized enterprises, the

Africa Growing Together Fund, China–Africa industrial cooperation fund, and the BRICS' New Development Bank, and seek innovation in its financial cooperation with Africa. It will support the efforts of Chinese financial institutions to increase exchanges and seek co-financing cooperation with their counterparts in African countries and African regional and global financial and development institutions, and support Chinese and African financial institutions in establishing joint-stock banks based on commercial principles. China will strengthen currency cooperation between the central banks of the two sides, discuss with African countries the arrangements for expanding cross-border local currency settlements and currency swaps, and encourage Chinese and African enterprises to settle their trade and investment in local currencies. It will also support reciprocal establishment of financial institutions, and increase support to financing insurance. China will step up coordination and collaboration with African countries in international financial organizations and mechanisms to improve and reform the current international financial system and increase the representation and voice of developing countries.

5. Promoting the Facilitation of China–Africa Trade and Investment

China will encourage more African commodities to enter the Chinese market and continue to grant zero-tariff treatment to 97 percent of taxable items from the least developed countries that have established diplomatic relations with China, according to the implementation of exchanged notes by both sides. Both Chinese and African enterprises are encouraged to make the most of harbor advantages to build regional logistics and wholesale centers. China will strengthen quality control of the goods exported to Africa and build more sales channels, reinforce cooperation in inspection and quarantine with African countries, and jointly crack down on counterfeit or substandard import and export goods. China will boost customs cooperation with Africa, increase information exchange, mutual recognition of supervision, and mutual assistance with law enforcement, jointly combat commercial fraud, and create a law-abiding and convenient trade environment. China will help African countries enhance capacity building in customs, inspection, and quarantine, provide support to improve trade facilitation, and help boost trade within Africa. China will continue to support the development of the African Free Trade Zone and regional integration, and discuss the establishment of institutionalized trade arrangements with countries and regional organizations in Africa.

While aligning Africa's needs with China's advantages and adhering to the principles of equality, mutual benefit, and win–win cooperation, China is committed to improving the quality and efficiency of China–Africa economic and trade cooperation, helping Africa speed up its industrialization and agricultural modernization, and encouraging and supporting the efforts of Chinese enterprises to expand and optimize their investment in areas such as industry, agriculture, infrastructure, and energy in Africa. It will continue to provide concessional loans and export credit insurance support to qualified projects and moderately increase the concessionality of its concessional loans.

6. Bolstering Resource and Energy Cooperation

On the basis of the principles of win–win cooperation, green development, low-carbon emissions, and sustainable development, China will expand and deepen mutually beneficial cooperation in resources and energies with African countries. It will help African countries strengthen their capabilities in exploration, development, and processing of resources and energies, increase the added value of their primary products, create more local jobs, generate more foreign-exchange income, and turn their resource and energy endowment into achievements in sustainable development and benefits that can be shared by African people. China will innovate on the models of resource and energy cooperation with Africa, and expand whole-industry-chain cooperation in energy and mining sectors. It will support the construction of national or regional power grids in Africa, boost cooperation with Africa in the development of renewable energy and low-carbon, green energy such as wind power, solar power, and hydropower, and promote rational development and utilization of renewable energy sources in Africa in order to serve Africa's industrialization.

7. Expanding Cooperation on the Marine Economy

China will help fully tap into the abundant marine resources and development potential of relevant African countries and support them in strengthening capacity building, planning, designing, construction and exchange of operation experience in marine fishing, offshore aquaculture, seafood processing, maritime transportation, shipbuilding, construction of harbors and harbor industrial parks, and exploration and development of offshore oil and gas reserves, as well as management of the marine environment. It will support the efforts of Chinese and African enterprises to carry out mutually beneficial cooperation in various forms. It will also help African countries develop the marine economy in light of local conditions and explore new areas for Africa's economic growth and China–Africa cooperation, so that African countries' abundant marine resources can better serve their national development and bring more benefits to their people.

4. Strengthening Development Cooperation Between China and Africa

1. Continuing to Increase Development Assistance to Africa

As the largest developing country, China has provided assistance to African countries for a long time and will continue to do so within its capability. China has also received support and assistance from African countries in a timely manner whenever it is stricken by a big natural disaster. It stands ready to continue to provide and gradually increase emergency aid and necessary assistance to African countries in a spirit of sharing weal and woe and standing together through thick and thin with the latter. While providing the assistance in light of its own financial capacity and economic situation and the pressing needs of African countries, China sticks to the principles of no political strings attached, non-interference in others' internal affairs, and no demands imposed on others. China will come up with innovative assistance models and optimize assistance conditions. China's assistance will be primarily used in the areas of human resources development, infrastructure, medical care and health, agriculture, food security, climate change response, desertification prevention and control, and wildlife and environmental protection, and for humanitarian purposes, with the aim to help African countries alleviate poverty, improve people's livelihoods, and build up capacity for independent development.

China will honor its promise to exempt the intergovernmental interest-free loans borrowed by the relevant least developed countries, landlocked developing countries, and small island developing countries in Africa that are not returned when they mature at the end of 2015.

2. Supporting Africa in Strengthening Its Public Health System and Capacity Building

Drawing on the experience in joint fight against Ebola and malaria, China will deepen and expand health cooperation with Africa. It will strengthen communication with Africa on medical and health policies, and support Africa's efforts to strengthen its public health and disease control and prevention system and capacity building. China will actively participate in the preparation for the establishment of an African Center for Disease Control and Prevention, and assist African countries to improve the level of laboratory technology and deliver training to medical personnel, with a focus on assisting in prevention and control of non-contagious chronic diseases, malaria and other insect-borne infectious diseases, cholera, Ebola, AIDS, tuberculosis, and other preventable infectious diseases and newly emerging diseases. By making full use of its own strengths, China will support, on a priority basis, the efforts of African countries to enhance their core capacity in border health quarantine, build infectious diseases monitoring stations, provide medical services to women and children, and improve the departments and services in the existing medical facilities. China will continue to support African countries in health infrastructure development. It will continue to send medical teams to African countries, launch cooperation between counterpart Chinese and African hospitals, and enhance exchanges and cooperation between modern and traditional medicine with a focus on improving local medical services. It will also continue to promote the "Brightness Action" campaign to provide free cataract operation and other short-term free medical services. China stands for increasing paired exchanges and cooperation between Chinese and African medical institutions and drug administration agencies, and supports their cooperation with international and regional organizations such as the World Health Organization and the African Union. It will encourage Chinese pharmaceutical enterprises to invest in Africa in a bid to lower the cost of medicines in Africa and increase the affordability of medical and pharmaceutical products in Africa.

3. Expanding Cooperation in Education and Human Resources Development

China will expand cooperation in education with Africa, supporting educational development in the continent. It will provide more input in light of the social and economic development needs of African countries so as to achieve greater results, and help train more much-needed professionals for African countries, in particular, teachers and medical workers. While enhancing exchanges and cooperation between education administration agencies and institutions on both sides, China will continue to implement the "African Talents Program," gradually increase the number of government scholarships for applicants in African countries, and encourage local governments, institutions of higher learning, enterprises, and social organizations to set up scholarships. It welcomes more African young people to study in China, encouraging and supporting them to play a bigger role in the pragmatic cooperation between China and Africa. China will encourage colleges and universities on both sides to establish partnerships, support exchanges between Chinese and African teachers and students, and magnify the effect of the 20+20 Cooperation Plan for Chinese and African Institutions of Higher Education. Following the principle of integrating learning and knowledge application, China will scale up cooperation in teacher training and vocational education with African countries with the aim to expand the channels for human resources development.

4. Sharing and Popularizing the Experience in Poverty Alleviation

Poverty is the common challenge confronting China and Africa. China will fulfill its promise to the international community to support the implementation of the 2030 Agenda for Sustainable Development. It will actively implement the Program for Strengthening China–Africa Cooperation on Poverty Reduction issued by China and the AU, strengthen China–Africa poverty alleviation cooperation, give play to the role of international poverty alleviation platforms such as the International Poverty Reduction Center in China jointly established by China and the United Nations, and encourage and support governments, academic institutions, enterprises, and non-governmental organizations on both sides to carry out diverse forms of experience exchanges and pragmatic cooperation on poverty alleviation. These will facilitate the sharing of China's successful experience in achieving large-scale poverty reduction by alleviating rural poverty through development. China will strengthen cooperation on demonstration projects to support African countries in enhancing their capability of independent poverty alleviation and development.

5. Stepping Up Science and Technology Cooperation and Knowledge Sharing

China will continue to push forward implementation of the China–Africa Science and Technology Partnership Plan, and encourage strengthened science and technology exchanges and cooperation between China and African countries in the fields of agriculture, water resources, energy, aviation and aerospace, telecommunication, environmental protection, desertification prevention and control, medical care, and marine sector. It will support African countries in building up their capacity in science and technology, and work with them to set up joint laboratories, joint research centers, and science and technology parks in key areas. It will continue to sponsor outstanding young African scientists to conduct short-term research in China, step up training on applied technology and relevant policies, and jointly establish advanced technology application and demonstration bases. China will promote the dissemination of China's science and technology research results and the popularization and application of advanced and applied technology in Africa.

6. Enhancing Cooperation on Climate Change and Environmental Protection

China will boost and consolidate cooperation with Africa under the UNFCCC and other relevant mechanisms, and push for both sides to carry out consultations, exchanges, and cooperation projects in relation to addressing climate change. China will innovate on cooperation areas, deepen pragmatic cooperation, and work in concert with Africa to enhance the capacity for tackling climate change. China stands for closer policy dialogue, and closer bilateral and multilateral coordination and cooperation with Africa in the area of environment. It calls for strengthened cooperation in education and personnel training on ecological protection, environment management, pollution prevention and control, bio-diversity and water resources conservation, and the prevention and control of desertification, as well as in demonstration projects in these areas. It will push forward environment-friendly industrial capacity cooperation and transfer of applied technology. While enhancing exchanges on environmental protection laws and regulations, China will engage in dialogue and cooperation on the conservation of endangered species of wild fauna and flora, step up intelligence sharing and capacity building in law enforcement, and crack down on transnational organized crimes related to endangered wildlife trafficking. While implementing the Convention on Biological Diversity and the Convention on International Trade in Endangered Species of Wild Fauna and Flora and dealing with other related international affairs, China will strengthen communication and coordinate positions with African countries, in a bid to work together to promote the protection and sustainable exploitation of global wild fauna and flora.

5. Deepening and Expanding Cultural and People-To-People Exchanges

1. Expanding Exchanges and Cooperation in Culture and Sports

China will maintain the momentum of high-level contacts, and implement bilateral cultural cooperation agreements and their implementation plans. Encouraging and supporting African countries for Chinese-language teaching, China will continue to set up more Confucius Institutes in African countries, and encourage and support the opening of Chinese cultural centers in Africa and African cultural centers in China. It will support the holding of the "Year of China" events in Africa and the "Year of an African Country" events in China, raise the profile of the "Chinese/African Cultures in Focus" events, and enrich the program of China–Africa mutual visits between cultural personnel and the China–Africa Cultural Cooperation Partnership Program, with the aim to achieve better results in cultural exchanges. China stands for respect of each other's cultural diversity, and will promote China–Africa cultural inclusiveness and common prosperity, thereby enhancing understanding and friendship between Chinese and African people. In addition to promoting exchanges between cultural institutions and personnel, China will strengthen cooperation with Africa in cultural industry and personnel training.

According to the principle of focusing on key areas and doing things within its capability, China will strengthen exchanges and result-oriented sports cooperation with African countries and continue to provide assistance to support the development of sports in African countries.

2. Expanding Tourism Cooperation

China will work with African countries to provide convenience in visa application and other services to facilitate travels by their nationals to their respective countries and regions, support tourism promotion activities in each other's countries and regions, encourage airlines on both sides to open more air routes and operate more flights between China and Africa, and expand personnel exchanges and visits. China welcomes and is willing to give positive consideration to applications of qualified African countries for Approved Destinations Status for outbound Chinese tourist groups, and support Chinese and African enterprises to engage in mutually beneficial cooperation in tourism infrastructure development, thereby improving and optimizing the environment for tourism.

3. Broadening Cooperation on Press, Radio, Film, and Television

China will push forward diverse forms of exchanges and cooperation between Chinese and African media outlets, creating necessary conditions for this purpose and providing guidance and convenience. Dialogue and consultation between relevant government departments will be strengthened for the purpose of deepening media cooperation, enhancing cyberspace management, and sharing experience in handling the relations with media, with a priority given to support capacity building of African media. Support will be provided for the sound development of the China–Africa Press Center, with the aim to increase objective and balanced media coverage on the development of China and Africa and on China–Africa relations so as to promote mutual understanding and recognition between Chinese and African people. China will encourage Chinese and African media organizations to step up cooperation in areas such as journalism studies, personnel training, content exchanges and joint news gathering and production, and new media. China will strengthen technological exchanges and industrial cooperation with Africa on radio, film, and television, and encourage connection and contacts between Chinese and African radio and TV broadcasters. It will continue to promote the digitization of radio and TV broadcasting in Africa, provide related financing, technical support, and personnel training, and encourage Chinese and African enterprises to engage in joint venture cooperation.

4. Encouraging Exchanges Between Academia and Think Tanks

China will encourage Chinese and African universities to carry out joint studies to enhance research strengths of both sides. China will actively implement the China–Africa Joint Research and Exchange Plan and the China–Africa Think Tanks 10+10 Partnership Plan. It will support Chinese and African research institutes and think tanks to engage in multi-forms of exchanges and cooperation, such as joint researches, seminars, and publishing of books. Priority support will be given to joint researches and result sharing in areas that are conducive to promoting China–Africa friendly cooperation, such as governance, development paths, industrial capacity cooperation, and comparison of cultures and laws.

5. Enhancing People-To-People Exchanges

China will continue to enhance people-to-people exchanges to increase mutual understanding between Chinese and African people and push forward cooperation on improving people's livelihoods. It encourages the implementation of the Proposals on China–Africa People-to-People Exchanges and Cooperation, China–Africa People-to-People Friendship Action, and China–Africa People-to-People Friendship and Partnership Program, and supports non-governmental organizations and social groups to engage in diverse forms of friendly exchanges and public benefit activities.

It will promote exchanges between Chinese and African youths and contacts between Chinese and African government departments for youth affairs and youth organizations of political parties, and promote exchanges between outstanding youths from all walks of life in China and Africa. It will encourage and guide Chinese young volunteers to go to African countries to deliver volunteer services, and engage in poverty alleviation, education assistance, and other activities.

China will continue to strengthen exchanges and cooperation with Africa to promote gender equality, deepen exchanges between women's organizations and high-level dialogue on women's issues, maintain good cooperation on multilateral women's affairs, and work with Africa to promote women's causes in China and African countries. It will continue to provide necessary assistance to African countries to benefit women and children, and strengthen cooperation in skills training.

China will engage in exchanges with Africa in such areas as service systems for persons with disabilities and social security policies for them. For this, efforts will be made to step up cooperation in areas including rehabilitation, education, employment, social insurance, and development-oriented poverty reduction.

China will intensify friendly exchanges and cooperation between Chinese and African trade unions.

6. Promoting Peace and Security in Africa

1. Supporting Africa in Realizing Peace and Security

China supports African countries' efforts in independently resolving their continent's issues in their own way. Based on the principles of respecting the wills of African countries, not interfering in African countries' internal affairs, and observing the basic norms governing international relations, China will play a constructive role in maintaining and promoting peace and security in Africa. It will explore means and ways with Chinese characteristics to constructively participate in resolving hot-button issues in Africa and exert a unique impact on and make greater contributions to African peace and security. The Special Representative of the Chinese government on African Affairs will continue to play a contributing part.

China will strengthen dialogue and consultation with African countries and regional organizations on peace and security issues, pursue the principle of securing peace through development and promoting development with peace, and implement the consensus on achieving common, cooperative, comprehensive, and sustainable security. It will support the efforts by African countries, the AU, and sub-regional organizations to build capabilities in safeguarding peace and stability in Africa, and other relevant efforts. It will implement the Initiative on China–Africa Cooperative Partnership for Peace and Security and continue to provide, within its capabilities, support to Africa for its development of collective security mechanisms such as the African Standby Force and the African Capacity for Immediate Response to Crises.

China will uphold justice and safeguard the common interests of Africa and developing countries in multilateral organizations such as the UN. China attaches great importance to and supports the UN's important role in safeguarding peace and stability in Africa, and will continue to support and expand its participation in the UN's efforts in Africa aimed at maintaining and building peace.

2. Deepening Military Cooperation

China will further strengthen military exchanges and cooperation with African countries. It will deepen military-related technological cooperation and carry out joint military training and exercises. China will scale up training of African military personnel according to the needs of the African side, and innovate on the training methods. It will continue to help African countries enhance their capacity building in national defense and peacekeeping to safeguard their own security and regional peace.

3. Supporting Africa in Confronting Non-Traditional Security Threats

China will strengthen cooperation with Africa in intelligence sharing and capacity building, and improve capabilities to confront non-traditional security threats together with African countries. It will support the international community's efforts to crack down on piracy, continue to send naval vessels to participate in the missions for maintaining navigation safety in the Gulf of Aden and in waters off the coast of Somalia, and assist African countries in ensuring navigation safety in the Gulf of Guinea.

China will support the efforts of African countries and regional organizations in improving counterterrorism capabilities and fighting terrorism and help African countries develop their economy and root out the causes of terrorism, with the aim to safeguard regional security and stability and promote long-term peace and sustainable development in Africa. It will strengthen counterterrorism exchanges and cooperation with the AU and priority countries in the region.

7. Strengthening Exchanges and Cooperation in Consular, Immigration, Judicial, and Police Areas

China will support institutional arrangements for the facilitation of personnel exchanges with Africa and guarantee the expansion of friendly and mutually beneficial cooperation and orderly personnel exchanges between the two sides.

China will work with African countries to establish more consular organizations in each other's territory in a planned manner. It will strengthen consular consultation with African countries for both sides to have amicable discussions on urgent problems or issues of common interest in bilateral or multilateral consular relations. China stands for closer exchanges and cooperation between Chinese and African immigration departments to fight illegal immigration, supporting African countries to strengthen capacity building in enforcement of immigration-related laws.

China stands ready to promote exchanges and cooperation between Chinese and African judicial and police departments and the two sides may learn from each other in legal system development and judicial reform. It will support the efforts of Africa to strengthen capacity building in riot control, maintenance of stability, and law enforcement. It stands for concrete and effective measures by both sides to protect the safety, rights, and interests of personnel and organizations from the other side on their own soil.

China will work with African countries to enhance cooperation in judicial assistance and extradition and repatriation of criminal suspects. They will expand cooperation in signing judicial assistance treaties, cracking down on crimes, and pursuing fugitives and recovering criminal proceeds. They will work in concert to crack down on cross-border crimes and ensure the order of and the just and legal rights involved in trade and economic and personnel exchanges. It calls for the two sides to increase communication and cooperation in the areas of jail management, community correction, drug rehabilitation, and transfer of convicted persons.

Part IV. FOCAC and Its Follow-Up Actions

Since its establishment in 2000, FOCAC has become an important platform for collective dialogue between China and Africa and an effective mechanism for their pragmatic cooperation, thanks to the efforts of both sides. In the past 15 years, China and Africa have co-hosted the Beijing Summit and five ministerial conferences, drawn up a series of important programmatic documents on cooperation, and promoted the implementation of measures supporting African development and deepening the friendly and mutually beneficial cooperation between the two sides, reaping fruitful results.

China and Africa have held dialogues through equal-footed dialogue mechanisms such as the Ministerial Conference, the political consultation between Chinese and African foreign ministers on the sidelines of the UN General Assembly sessions, the Senior Officials Meeting, and the consultation between the Secretariat of the Chinese Follow-Up Committee of FOCAC and the African Diplomatic Corps in China, further enhancing mutual understanding and political mutual trust. The forum has served as a platform for all-round pragmatic cooperation, pushing for leapfrog increase in China–Africa trade and mutual investment and promoting mutual benefit and common development. The forum has been a bridge for closer people-to-people exchanges and friendship between China and Africa, promoting bilateral exchanges in all areas, and consolidating and expanding the social and popular support for the friendship between China and African countries. It has helped enhance communication and collaboration between China and African countries in the international arena, facilitating them to work together in safeguarding the overall interests of the two sides and developing countries.

China is willing to work with African countries to enhance the mechanism building of the forum, expand areas and ways of cooperation, enrich mutual cooperation, promote the establishment and improvement of sub-forum mechanisms in the fields of industrialization, agricultural modernization, infrastructure, human resources development, industrial capacity cooperation, finance, science and technology, education, culture, health, poverty reduction, law, locals, youth, women, people-to-people exchanges, think tanks, and media, and deepen cooperation in relevant areas. All these are aimed at enabling China–Africa cooperation to be more pragmatic and effective and achieving more tangible results under the framework of the forum, thereby bringing greater benefits to the Chinese and African people.

Part V. China's Relations with African Regional Organizations

China values and supports the AU's leadership in building a united and strong Africa and promoting African integration and its centrality in safeguarding peace and security in Africa, as well as a bigger role for the organization in regional and international affairs. It appreciates and supports the AU's adoption and implementation of Agenda 2063 and its first ten-year plan. The creation of the Mission of the People's Republic of China to the AU in 2014 has taken China–AU relations to a new stage. China is ready to increase high-level exchanges with the AU, give full play to the China–AU strategic dialogue mechanism, and enhance political dialogue and mutual trust. It will promote cooperation with the AU in areas such as development planning, experience sharing in poverty reduction, health, peace, and security, and international affairs.

China appreciates the positive role of African sub-regional organizations in promoting peace, stability, and development in their respective regions. It stands ready to strengthen friendly exchanges and cooperation with these organizations, and support their capacity-building efforts.

China is eager to establish and improve various dialogue and cooperation mechanisms with the AU and sub-regional organizations in Africa, thereby enhancing China–Africa cooperation at both regional and sub-regional levels in a wide array of fields including political affairs, the economy, trade, and culture.

7. July 2014: China's Foreign Aid[7]

The State Council Information Office
The People's Republic of China

Contents

Preface

Conclusion

Preface

China is the world's largest developing country. In its development, it has endeavored to integrate the interests of the Chinese people with people of other countries, providing assistance to the best of its ability to other developing countries within the framework of South–South cooperation to support and help other developing countries, especially the least developed countries (LDCs), to reduce poverty and improve livelihood. China has proactively promoted international development and cooperation and played a constructive role in this aspect.

When providing foreign assistance, China adheres to the principles of not imposing any political conditions, not interfering in the internal affairs of the recipient countries, and fully respecting their right to independently choosing their own paths and models of development. The basic principles China upholds in providing foreign assistance are mutual respect, equality, keeping promise, mutual benefits, and win–win.

In recent years, China's foreign assistance has kept growing. The following is an introduction of China's foreign assistance from 2010 to 2012.

I. Developing Foreign Assistance Cause Steadily

The scale of China's foreign assistance kept expanding from 2010 to 2012. Besides complete projects and goods and materials, which were the main forms of China's foreign assistance, technical cooperation and human resources development cooperation also saw remarkable increases. Asia and Africa were the major recipient areas of China's foreign assistance. To promote the realization of Millennium Development Goals, China directed most of its assisting funds to low-income developing countries.

1. Financial Resources for Foreign Assistance

From 2010 to 2012, China appropriated in total 89.34 billion yuan (14.41 billion US dollars) for foreign assistance in three types: grant (aid gratis), interest-free loan, and concessional loan.

Grant is mainly offered to help recipient countries build small or medium-sized social welfare projects, and to fund human resources development cooperation, technical cooperation, material assistance, and emergency humanitarian aid. In the three years, China provided 32.32 billion yuan of grants, accounting for 36.2 percent of the total assistance volume.

Interest-free loan is mainly used to help recipient countries construct public facilities and launch projects to improve people's livelihood. In the three years, China offered 7.26 billion yuan of interest-free loans, taking up 8.1 percent of its foreign assistance volume.

Concessional loan is mainly used to help recipient countries undertake manufacturing projects and large and medium-sized infrastructure projects with economic and social benefits, or for the supply of complete plants, machinery, and electronic products. In the three years, the concessional loans China provided to other countries amounted to 49.76 billion yuan, or 55.7 percent of its total assistance volume in the same period.

Foreign assistance budget is put under the unified management of the Ministry of Finance in line with the budget and final accounts system. Concessional loans are raised by the Export–Import Bank of China on the market. As the loan interest is lower than the benchmark interest released by the People's Bank of China, the difference is made up by the state as financial subsidies.

Figure BM2.1 shows the distribution of China's foreign assistance funds according to the income level of recipient countries from 2010 to 2012, according to a white paper on China's foreign aid issued by China's Information Office of the State Council on July 10, 2014 (Xinhua/China's Information Office of the State Council).

2. Distribution of Foreign Assistance

From 2010 to 2012, China provided assistance to 121 countries, including 30 in Asia, 51 in Africa, nine in Oceania, 19 in Latin America and the Caribbean, and 12 in Europe. Besides, China also provided assistance to regional organizations such as the African Union (AU).

Figure BM2.2 shows the income level of the recipient county geographical distribution of China's foreign assistance funds from 2010 to 2012, according to a white paper on China's foreign aid issued by China's Information Office of the State Council on July 10, 2014 (Xinhua/China's Information Office of the State Council).

Figure BM2.3 shows the distribution of China's foreign assistance funds according to projected fields from 2010 to 2012, according to a white paper on China's foreign aid issued by China's Information Office of the State Council on July 10, 2014 (Xinhua/China's Information Office of the State Council).

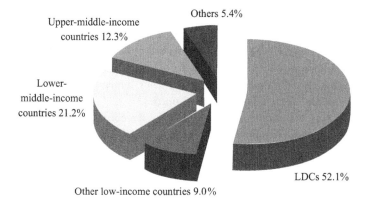

FIGURE BM2.1 Distribution of China's Foreign Assistance Funds According to the Income Level of Recipient Countries, 2010–2012

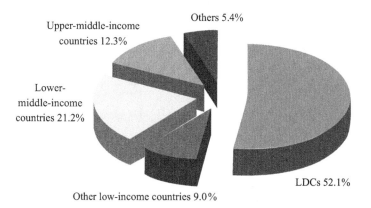

FIGURE BM2.2 Geographical Distribution of China's Foreign Assistance Funds, 2010–2012

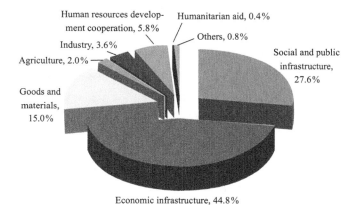

FIGURE BM2.3 Distribution of China's Foreign Assistance Funds According to Projected Fields, 2010–2012

3. Forms of Foreign Assistance

From 2010 to 2012, China provided foreign assistance mainly in the following forms: undertaking complete projects, providing goods and materials, conducting technical cooperation and human resources development cooperation, dispatching medical teams and volunteers, offering emergency humanitarian aid, and reducing or exempting the debts of the recipient countries.

Complete projects. In total, China undertook the construction of 580 such projects in 80 countries, with infrastructure and agriculture as the focus.

Table BM2.1 shows the sectoral distribution of the complete projects from 2010 to 2012, according to a white paper on China's foreign aid issued by China's Information Office of the State Council on July 10, 2014 (Xinhua/China's Information Office of the State Council).

Goods and materials. China provided 96 countries and regions with 424 batches of goods and materials, including mainly office supplies, mechanical equipment, inspection equipment, transport vehicles, articles for daily use, medicine, and medical devices.

Technical cooperation. China completed 170 technical cooperation projects in 61 countries and regions, mainly covering industrial production and management, agricultural planting and breeding, culture and education, sports and physical training, medical and health care, clean energy development, and planning and consultation.

TABLE BM2.1 Sectoral Distribution of the Complete Projects, 2010–2012

Sector	Number of Project
Public Facilities	360
Hospitals	80
Schools	85
Civil construction	80
Well-drilling and water supply	29
Public infrastructure	86
Economic Infrastructure	13*
Transport & communications	72
Broadcasting & telecommunications	62
Power supply	22
Agriculture	49
Agricultural technology demonstration centers	26
Irrigation & water conservancy	21
Agricultural processing	2
Industry	15
Light industry and textiles	7
Building materials & chemical industry	6
Machinery & electronics	2
Total	550

Human resources development cooperation. China held 1,951 training sessions for officials and technical personnel and on-the-job academic education programs in China, training a total of 49,148 people from other developing countries.

Medical teams. China dispatched 55 teams composed of 3,600 medical personnel to 54 countries to provide stationed or touring medical services, treating nearly seven million patients.

Volunteer programs. China sent about 7,000 young volunteers and volunteer Chinese language teachers to over 60 countries.

Emergency humanitarian aid. China extended 1.5 billion yuan worth of materials and cash assistance in emergency humanitarian aid to more than 30 countries.

Debt relief. China relieved nine LDCs and heavily indebted poor countries, namely, Tanzania, Zambia, Cameroon, Equatorial Guinea, Mali, Togo, Benin, Côte d'Ivoire, and Sudan, from 16 mature interest-free loans totaling 1.42 billion yuan.

II. Helping Improve People's Livelihood

One of the important objectives of China's foreign assistance is to support other developing countries to reduce poverty and improve the livelihood of their peoples. China prioritizes supporting other developing countries to develop agriculture, enhance education level, improve medical and health services and build public welfare facilities, and provide emergency humanitarian aid when they suffer severe disasters.

1. Promoting Agricultural Development

Agricultural development is crucial to poverty reduction in developing countries. Through establishing agricultural technology demonstration centers, dispatching agricultural experts to provide consultations and conduct technical cooperation, and training technical and managerial personnel on agriculture in other developing countries, China has taken proactive efforts to help other developing countries raise their agricultural productivity to effectively cope with food crises. From 2010 to 2012, China assisted 49 agricultural projects, dispatched over 1,000 agricultural experts to recipient countries, and provided them with a great quantity of machinery, improved varieties of grain, fertilizers, and other agricultural materials.

Assisting the establishment of agricultural technology demonstration centers. Such centers provide an important platform for China's foreign assistance in agriculture. From 2010 to 2012, China-assisted agricultural demonstration centers were completed in 17 countries, including Benin, Mozambique, Sudan, Liberia, Rwanda, Laos, and East Timor. China passed on advanced and applicable production technologies to local farmers through experiment, demonstration, and training. The demonstration center in Liberia promoted hybrid rice and corn planting in areas of nearly 1,000 hectares, and trained over 1,000 local agricultural researchers and farmers. The demonstration center in Rwanda researched, experimented on, and demonstrated the adaptability of paddy rice and fungi in the context of the local traditional agriculture, and provided technical training to women's associations, paddy rice growers' associations, and other organizations in Rwanda.

Dispatching senior agricultural experts and expert teams. Chinese agricultural experts took an active part in the agricultural planning of the recipient countries. The expert team dispatched to Benin provided expertise to the drafting of the country's Agricultural Law and Agricultural Administration Law. The expert teams sent to Botswana and Guinea-Bissau participated in the formulation of the two countries' agricultural development plans. Chinese experts assisted recipient countries in promoting their agricultural development. The expert team helped Lesotho with its application to the World Health Organization for FMD (foot-and-mouth disease) free membership. The expert team to Mauritania assisted the country in drawing up the plan for building its central laboratory for agricultural comprehensive analysis and testing. Chinese experts actively disseminated easy-to-learn agricultural techniques suited to the conditions of recipient countries. The expert team to Botswana promoted the use of plastic mulch in crop production. The expert team to Mali devised and promoted the use of iron harrows as a means of intensive cultivation in the paddy fields.

Training technical and managerial personnel on agriculture. Taking the characteristics and actual needs of agricultural development in developing countries into consideration, China provided nearly 300 research and training programs of various forms for almost 7,000 agricultural officials and technicians from the recipient countries. These programs covered a wide range of sectors, including management of crop cultivation, forestry, animal husbandry and fishery, national policymaking on rural development and poverty reduction, food security, and agricultural cooperation among developing countries, and issues concerning the agricultural chain, such as technology dissemination and the processing, storage, marketing, and distribution of agricultural products.

2. Improving the Level of Education

From 2010 to 2012, China continuously intensified its efforts of foreign assistance in education by way of constructing and maintaining school buildings, providing teaching facilities, training teachers, offering more government scholarships for foreign students to study in China, and assisting with the development of vocational and technical education, for the purpose of helping other developing countries improve their educational level and support their balanced and equitable development in education.

Improving teaching and learning conditions. China assisted over 80 projects in relation to educational facilities, including the construction and maintenance of primary and secondary schools, universities, and colleges as well as libraries, and has effectively improved the teaching and learning conditions in the recipient countries. China provided large amounts of free educational facilities and materials to the recipient countries, including computers, teaching tools, stationery, and sports equipment, and established university online education networks and distance education systems. In this way, China facilitated the efforts of recipient countries to diversify their means and expand the coverage of education.

Training teachers. In the three years, China trained over 1,000 educational officials, principals, and faculty members from other developing countries by holding over 30 educational training programs, including those for senior administrators of colleges and universities, for higher education management, for vocational education management, for principals and teachers of primary and secondary schools, and for distance education.

Supporting vocational and technical education. Thousands of local people have been trained in the China-assisted Friendship Vocational Training Center in Omdurman. To increase its enrolment, China started the upgrading and expansion project of the center. China took active steps to help the recipient countries develop vocational and technical education. From 2001 to 2012, China dispatched over 400 teachers to Ethiopia to train the local teachers working in agricultural vocational and technical education. A total of 1,800 teachers from agricultural vocational schools and 35,000 agricultural technicians received training.

Increasing government scholarships to foreign students. From 2010 to 2012, the Chinese government assisted 76,845 foreign students to study in China. To promote regional development, China has continuously increased government scholarships to African students and augmented assistance for students from the ASEAN countries and the Pacific island countries to help under-developed countries in these regions develop their human resources.

3. Improving Medical and Health Services

Medical and health care is a major field where China directs its foreign assistance. From 2010 to 2012, China helped recipient countries improve their medical and health services, raise their disease control and prevention ability, and enhance their public health capacity by constructing hospitals, providing medicine and medical equipment, dispatching medical teams, training medical workers, and conducting exchanges and cooperation on disease prevention and treatment with other developing countries.

Constructing medical facilities and providing free medical equipment. China assisted about 80 construction projects of medical facilities, including general hospitals, mobile hospitals, health centers, specialist clinics, and traditional Chinese medicine (TCM) centers, which have effectively alleviated the shortage of medical and health facilities in recipient countries. Moreover, China provided them with about 120 batches of medical equipment and medicine, including color Doppler ultrasound machines, CT scanners, automatic biochemical analyzers, maternal and infant monitors, critical surgical instruments, ICU monitors, and MRI scanners as well as drugs against diseases such as malaria and cholera.

Dispatching medical teams. China dispatched 55 medical teams with 3,600 medical workers to nearly 120 medical centers in recipient countries. They trained tens of thousands of local medical staff, which has relieved to a certain extent the shortage of medical services in recipient countries. The training was carried out through demonstrations, lectures, technical courses, and academic exchanges, covering such topics as the prevention and treatment of malaria, AIDS, schistoso-miasis and other infectious diseases, patient care, and the treatment of diabetes and rheumatism, as well as the TCM of acupuncture application, naprapathy, health care methods, and Chinese medicines. From 2010 to 2012, more than 100 Chinese medical workers were conferred medals by the recipient countries for their out-standing contributions.

Carrying out Brightness Trip activities. Brightness Trip program was actively carried out in both governmental and non-governmental channels to help other developing countries in the treatment of eye diseases. From 2003, China started to send medical teams to provide free surgery for patients with eye diseases in the Democratic People's Republic of Korea, Cambodia, Bangladesh, Vietnam, Pakistan, and other Asian countries. In November 2010, a Chinese Brightness Trip medical team arrived in Africa for the first time and carried out operations for over 1,000 cataract patients in countries including Zimbabwe, Malawi, Mozambique, and Sudan.

Assisting the prevention and control of infectious diseases. From 2010 to 2012, China provided 60 batches of antimalarial medicine, H1N1 influenza vaccine, and cholera vaccine free of charge to other developing countries and held training in the prevention and control of infectious diseases, the expenditure for this purpose accumulating to RMB 200 million. In 2007, China and the Comoros launched a cooperation program of treating malaria with an artemisinin compound, an effective antimalarial drug, which helped the Comorian island of Moheli reduce its incidence of malaria by 90 percent. From 2010 to 2012, while making further progress in Moheli, China started promoting the program on the Comorian island of Anjoyan.

4. Building Public Welfare Facilities

To support other developing countries in improving their people's livelihood and organizing public activities, China actively assisted the construction of urban and rural public welfare facilities, affordable housing, and social activity venues, pro-vided relevant equipment and materials, and conducted technical cooperation on operation and management.

Carrying out well-drilling and water-supply projects. China undertook 29 well-drilling and water-supply projects in other developing countries, and drilled over 600 wells. Despite tough natural conditions and the threat of epidemics and terrorism, senior hydrogeologists and engineering geologists from China helped the recipient countries drill wells and undertake water-supply projects. China helped drill 200 fresh water wells in Kara and Centrale of Togo respectively and 38 wells in Darfur, Sudan and Kator of Juba, South Sudan, all of which were equipped with submersible pumps and generator sets. The China-assisted water-supply project in Zinder, Niger has solved the problem of drinking water for hundreds of thousands of local residents.

Improving people's living conditions. China assisted 80 residential housing and affordable housing projects in other developing countries, totaling about 600,000 square meters in floor space. China's architects and engineers gave full consideration to the living habits and environmental features of the recipient countries in both external and interior design, and exercised strict quality control while making efforts to reduce costs, for the purpose of providing comfortable and endurable houses to local residents.

Assisting the construction of public facilities. China assisted 86 construction projects of public cultural venues, sports venues, office buildings, and conference centers in other developing countries. These projects helped enrich local residents' cultural and recreational life, improve the working conditions of local governments, and create a better cityscape. China assisted the rehabilitation of Sri Lanka's Bandaranaike Memorial International Conference Hall, which was a gift from China in the 1970s and took on new dimensions four decades later. China funded the construction of Gabon's 40,000-seat stadium Stade d'Angondje, which hosted the competition final and closing ceremony of the 28th Africa Cup of Nations in 2012. China assisted the construction of the 20,000-square meter Grand National Theater in Senegal, one of the largest theaters in Africa.

5. Humanitarian Aid

Over the past few years, the world has been frequently hit by severe natural disasters caused by earthquakes, hurricanes, floods, and droughts as well as humanitarian crises caused by wars, and many countries have suffered serious casualties and property losses. China has made quick response to the appeals of the international community by providing relief materials or cash aid and dispatching rescue and medical teams as needed, to help the victim countries with disaster relief and post-disaster reconstruction.

Providing emergency relief materials or cash aid. From 2010 to 2012, the Chinese government provided RMB 1.2 billion worth of emergency relief materials in some 50 batches, including tents, blankets, emergency lights, generators, fuel oil, food, medicine, and water filters, to countries affected by natural disasters or humanitarian crises, such as the earthquake in Haiti, floods in Cambodia, earthquake in Myanmar, floods in Pakistan, hurricane in Cuba, the war in Libya, and the turmoil in Syria. In addition, China provided cash aid totaling RMB 300 million.

Assisting African countries in coping with the food crisis. In 2011 and 2012, the Horn of Africa and the Sahel were stricken by severe droughts and over 30 million people were faced with a serious food shortage. In 2011, the Chinese government provided on three occasions a total of RMB 440 million worth of emergency food aid to the countries of the Horn of Africa, such as Ethiopia, Kenya, Djibouti, and Somalia. In 2012, the Chinese government provided RMB 70 million worth of emergency food aid to Chad, Mali, Niger, and other countries in the Sahel.

Supporting post-disaster reconstruction. In 2010, Pakistan was hit by a severe flood rarely seen in history. The Chinese government promptly carried out rescue work in all aspects and through multiple channels, participated in post-flood reconstruction by helping the victims and rebuilding transportation infrastructure as the country requested. China also provided cash aid to support Pakistan government's compensation packages for victims, and undertook the restoration project of the 340-kilometer national highway network destroyed in the flood-stricken areas, enabling 150 million people to have access to the traffic network. In March 2012, a series of blasts occurred in the north of Brazzaville, the capital of the Republic of Congo. China assisted the construction of settlements for people displaced from their homes and actively supported reconstruction after the explosions.

Helping improve disaster prevention and relief capacity. China helped recipient countries enhance their emergency rescue, disaster prevention, and relief capacity by ways of providing materials and training. Over the three years, China provided over 10 batches of rescue vehicles and equipment, and held 30 training programs on disaster prevention and relief for other developing countries, sharing experience with over 700 officials and technicians.

III. Promoting Economic and Social Development

China has actively helped other developing countries in infrastructure construction, and assisted their efforts in strengthening capacity building and trade development. China has also increased the amount of foreign assistance in environmental protection, helping the recipient countries realize economic and social development.

1. Improving Infrastructure

In light of the economic development of different countries, China arranges grants (aid gratis), interest-free loans, and concessional loans in a well-proportioned manner to help recipient countries with the much-needed infrastructure construction. From 2010 to 2012, China helped build 156 economic infrastructure projects. Exploring its advantages in technology, equipment and materials, and human resources, China effectively cut down investment costs for these projects while ensuring quality.

Supporting development of transport system. During the three-year period, China assisted the construction of over 70 transport projects, including roads, bridges, airports, and ports. For example, China helped build the third section of the Sika Highway that connects Kenya's capital Nairobi to its economic hub Sika, thus making a contribution to the road network that links up Kenya, Ethiopia, and Tanzania. Sri Lanka's Mattala Rajapaksa International Airport, built with Chinese assistance, further improves the country's all-dimensional transport network, and plays a positive role in promoting links and communication between Sri Lanka and its neighboring areas.

Increasing energy supply capacity. China assisted the construction of more than 20 energy projects, including hydropower stations, thermal power plants, power transmission, transformation and distribution grids, and geothermal drilling projects. The Bui Hydropower Station built by China in Ghana boasts the capacity of hydroelectricity generation, farmland irrigation, fisheries development, and local tourism. Its completion has not only powered economic and social development in Ghana, but also benefited other areas in Western Africa. The China-assisted power transmission, transformation, and distribution grids in Dakar, Senegal now provide power to 150,000 local residents, effectively ensuring power supply to the city, which had been troubled by its ageing grid and sudden blackouts until recently.

Promoting the development of information-based societies. China assisted the building of over 60 IT-related projects, including optical cable telecommunication networks, e-government websites, and radio and television frequency modulation transmitters. The telecommunication projects assisted by China in Turkmenistan, Togo, and Eritrea provide high-quality and steady telecommunication systems to these countries, and the number of users has grown exponentially. The optical cable transmission networks assisted by China in Cameroon and Tanzania have effectively promoted the application of fiber cables in African nations.

2. Strengthening Capacity Building

Believing in the ancient Chinese wisdom of "teaching one to fish rather than giving one fish," China shares its experience and technology with other developing countries through human resources and technical cooperation, as well as through volunteer service, to help other developing countries build their own professional teams and enhance their capacity for independent development.

Fast development in human resources cooperation. From 2010 to 2012, China held 1,579 seminars for foreign officials, inviting nearly 40,000 officials from the governments of other developing countries to China. The topics of the seminars covered economics and management, multilateral trade negotiation, politics and diplomacy, public administration, vocational education, and non-governmental organizations. China also held 357 training sessions for about 10,000 technical personnel from other developing countries in the areas of agriculture, health care, telecommunications, industry, environmental protection, disaster relief and prevention, and culture and sports. To help other developing countries improve the ability of their senior management personnel in the public sector, China organized, during the three years, 15 on-the-job academic education programs. Master's degrees in public administration, education, international relations, and international media were granted to 359 officials from 75 developing countries.

Figure BM2.4 shows China's human resources development cooperation from 2010 to 2012, according to a white paper on China's foreign aid issued by China's Information Office of the State Council on July 10, 2014 (Xinhua/China's Information Office of the State Council).

Extensive technical cooperation. During the three-year period, China sent over 2,000 experts to more than 50 countries to conduct technical cooperation, transfer applicable technique, and help improve these countries' technical management capacity in agriculture, handcrafts, radio and television, clean energy, and culture

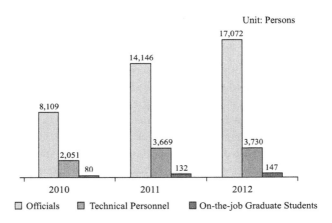

FIGURE BM2.4 China's Human Resources Development Cooperation, 2010–2012

and sports. China also dispatched senior planning and consulting experts to other developing countries to help with the planning of land exploitation, clean energy utilization, river regulation, and economic cooperation. In a technical cooperation program, Chinese experts taught 500 Liberians to weave bamboo and rattan into marketable products. This program has not only created jobs, brought the locals more income, and lifted them out of poverty, but also boosted the bamboo and rattan industry in the country.

The active role of volunteers. China continued to send volunteers to other developing countries to provide services in language teaching, physical education, computer training, traditional Chinese medicine treatment, agricultural technology, art training, industrial technology, social development and international relief for schools, hospitals, government agencies, farms, and research institutes. A Chinese volunteer to Liberia successfully rescued a newborn with gastroschisis, and was awarded the African Star medal. Volunteers to Ethiopia improved the planting method for melons, and local fruit farmers harvested much more than usual that year; the volunteers also taught the locals to build biogas pits so that they could use clean energy more efficiently.

3. Promoting Trade Development

As an active response to the WTO's Aid for Trade initiative, China strengthened its assistance in infrastructure construction and production capacity building for other developing countries. China also stepped up zero tariff treatment to these countries, supported their involvement in the multilateral trading system, and provided training for their economic and trade professionals so as to promote the trade development of these countries.

Improving trade-related infrastructure. During the three-year period, China assisted the construction of 90 large and medium-sized trade-related infrastructure projects, effectively improving transportation for foreign trade in the recipient countries and reinforcing their connectivity with other areas. China also provided commodity inspection equipment, transport vehicles, and other trade-related supplies and equipment to other developing countries. For example, it provided container inspection equipment to Cambodia, Laos, Myanmar, Ethiopia, Egypt, Chad, Cape Verde, Zambia, and Serbia, which has helped these countries improve their commodity inspection capacity and customs clearance ability, as well as effectively combat against smuggling.

Improving trade-related production capacity. China assisted the construction of a number of trade-related production programs, which have helped improve to a certain degree the production capacity of the recipient countries, so that they can better meet the needs of the market and improve the import–export mix. In December 2011, during the eighth ministerial conference of the WTO, China reached agreement with Benin, Mali, Chad, and Burkina Faso—the Cotton-4 countries—on a cooperation program in which China provides cotton seeds, farm machinery, and fertilizers, shares planting technologies, provides training, and supports local companies for technological upgrading and the expansion of industrial chain, so as to promote the development of the four countries' cotton industries and foreign trade.

Promoting export to China. In an effort to effectively boost export to China from other developing countries, in 2005 China decided to offer zero tariff treatment on taxable items in 190 categories to 25 least developed countries in Africa, and further expanded the scope of the treatment in the following years. In November 2011, then Chinese President Hu Jintao announced that China would offer zero tariff treatment to 97 percent of the taxable items from the least developed countries that had established diplomatic relations with China. By the end of 2012, commodities in nearly 5,000 taxable categories exported to China from the least developed countries were enjoying zero tariff treatment. Since 2008, China has been the largest export market of the least developed countries for five consecutive years, buying 23 percent of these countries' exported commodities.

Supporting the least developed countries in joining the multilateral trading system. China is an active participator of the WTO's Aid for Trade initiative. From 2008 to 2010, China made annual donation of 200,000 US dollars to the program, and has increased the sum to 400,000 US dollars since 2011. The donations are used to set up the China Program for Assisting the Least Developed Countries' Accession to the WTO, hold related seminars on accession to the WTO for these countries, and finance their personnel to attend important WTO meetings and do internship at the organization's Secretariat. From 2010 to 2012, China held 18 seminars on promoting trade facilitation and WTO accession, sharing its experience with over 400 government officials from other developing countries.

4. Strengthening Environmental Protection

At the UN conferences on climate change held in Cancun, Durban, and Doha, China shared its experience in energy conservation and emission reduction, and also pledged to increase assistance in the environment sector to the least developed countries, small island countries, and African countries, in a move to help them develop clean energy and improve their capacity in addressing climate change.

Assisting construction projects. China actively cooperates with other developing countries in the areas of clean energy, environmental protection, flood control and draught relief, water resources management, sustainable development of forestry, water, and soil conservation, and meteorological information service. In the three years, China undertook 64 projects in 58 developing countries on the utilization of renewable energy resources, such as solar streetlamps and solar power generators.

Providing materials. From 2010 to 2012, China provided a total of 16 batches of equipment and supplies for environmental protection to 13 developing countries, such as Cambodia, Myanmar, Ethiopia, South Sudan, and the Federated States of Micronesia, and the supplies included wind and solar power generators and lighting equipment, portable solar power supply, biogas equipment, garbage collection trucks, and draining and irrigation equipment. Meanwhile, China proactively promoted South–South cooperation on addressing climate change, and signed the Memorandum of Understanding on Complimentary Supplies for Addressing Climate Change with nine countries: Grenada, Ethiopia, Madagascar, Nigeria, Benin, Maldives, Cameroon, Burundi, and Samoa. Under the framework, China donated more than 500,000 energy-efficient lamps and 10,000 energy-efficient air conditioners to these countries.

Providing assistance in capacity building. During the three years, China carried out technical cooperation with countries like Ethiopia, Burundi, and Sudan, and helped these countries improve their utilization and management of solar power, hydro power, and other clean energy. China also organized 150 training sessions on environmental protection and addressing climate change for over 120 developing countries, providing training to over 4,000 officials and technical personnel in such areas as low-carbon industry development and energy policies, ecological protection, water resources management and water and soil conservation, renewable energy exploitation and utilization, forestry management and desertification prevention and control, and early warning of meteorological disasters.

IV. Foreign Assistance under Regional Cooperation Mechanism

China lays great emphasis on strengthening group consultation with recipient countries through regional cooperation mechanisms and platforms, such as Forum on China–Africa Cooperation (FOCAC) and China–ASEAN Summit, and has, on more than one occasion, announced assistance packages in response to the development needs of various regions.

1. Promoting a New China–Africa Strategic Partnership

Africa is home to the largest number of developing countries. Since the establishment of FOCAC in 2000, China has actively developed its cooperation with

African countries under the framework of the Forum, gradually expanded assistance to the region, and effectively promoted the comprehensive development of its relations with Africa.

Giving priority to agricultural development. China has all along paid great attention to its agricultural cooperation with Africa. From 2010 to 2012, China established 14 agricultural technology demonstration centers, and launched the planning or construction of another eight centers. China also sent a large number of agricultural experts to Africa to carry out technical cooperation, and trained for African countries over 5,000 agricultural technicians. In July 2012, at the Fifth Ministerial Meeting of the FOCAC, the Chinese government promised to provide assistance in building more agricultural technology demonstration centers in Africa, strengthen technical training, demonstration, and popularization, and help African countries improve their ability in food production, processing, storage, and marketing.

Giving support to infrastructure construction and integrated development. Infrastructure has always been the focus of China's assistance to Africa. The Tanzania–Zambia Railway is a landmark project in China's early assistance for cross-border infrastructure construction in Africa. After its completion, China continuously carried out technical cooperation to provide help in the operation and management of the railway. From 2010 to 2012, China built in Africa 86 economic infrastructure projects. In 2012, China announced the establishment of transnational and transregional infrastructure construction cooperation partnership with African countries, rendering support in project planning and feasibility study, and encouraging the participation of capable Chinese enterprises and financial institutions in project construction. China provided active support to Africa in the process to build their own strength through unity and integration, assisted the construction of the African Union Conference Center and Office Complex, and stood up for New Partnership for African Development, helping Africa enhance capacity building.

Promoting medical and health care cooperation. China has long been committed to helping African countries improve their medical and health care conditions. Currently, there are 43 of China's medical teams in 42 African countries. China assisted the construction of 30 hospitals and 30 malaria prevention and control centers, provided 800 million yuan worth of medical equipment and supplies and anti-malaria drugs, and trained over 3,000 medical staff for African countries. China-assisted Tappita Hospital in Liberia, boasting complete and advanced medical equipment, is jointly operated by China, Egypt, and Liberia, which is a meaningful step towards its sustainable operation.

Capacity building. During the three years, China built 150 primary and secondary schools in Africa, and trained a total of 47,000 people of various professions. In 2012, China announced its African Talents Program: to train 30,000 personnel in various sectors for Africa in three years and offer 18,000 government scholarships. In that year alone, China offered 6,717 government scholarships to African countries.

Coping with climate change. China actively helped African countries improve their ability to cope with climate change, and strengthened cooperation with them in meteorological satellite monitoring, new energy development and utilization, desertification prevention and control, and urban environmental protection. A number of the 105 clean energy and water supply projects assisted by China have been under construction or put into operation. In 2012, China started to build for African countries automatic meteorological stations and high-altitude observation radar stations, provide them with forest protection equipment, and carry out personnel training and exchange, in an effort to support Africa to strengthen its capacity in ecological conservation and response to challenges imposed by climate change.

2. Promoting Practical Cooperation with ASEAN

Since China and ASEAN announced the establishment of strategic partnership in 2003, China has conducted active cooperation with ASEAN countries in all fields, focusing on providing economic and technical assistance to low-income ASEAN countries to help the ASEAN narrow internal development gaps.

Supporting multi-level regional cooperation. China has provided funding through multiple channels to support ASEAN in playing its leading role in regional cooperation. From 2010 to 2012, China successively announced assistance measures at China–ASEAN Summits, with particular emphasis on assistance in infrastructure construction. China has assisted the construction of a large number of industrial and agricultural production and infrastructure projects, which have played a boosting role in the economic development of ASEAN countries.

Promoting comprehensive development of agriculture. Since 2010, China has constantly stepped up its efforts in implementing the China–ASEAN Action Plan on Comprehensive Food Productivity Enhancement. It worked with ASEAN countries in setting up 20 experimental stations of improved crop varieties, with the demonstration areas totaling one million hectares. In addition, China built three agricultural technology demonstration centers in ASEAN countries and dispatched 300 agricultural experts and technicians to provide technical guidance. China also worked with neighboring ASEAN countries to set up cross-border monitoring stations for animal and plant disease prevention and control and established a cross-border epidemic joint-prevention and joint-control system.

Boosting capacity building. During the three years, China trained for ASEAN countries over 5,000 officials and technicians in such fields as business conferences and exhibitions, culture and arts, Chinese language, finance and taxation, traditional medicine, control and treatment of infectious diseases, and new energy, as well as agriculture.

3. Supporting the Economic and Social Development of Other Regions

Targeting to common development, China made use of such platforms as Forum for Economic and Trade Cooperation between China and the Portuguese-speaking

Countries (Macau), China–Caribbean Economic and Trade Cooperation Forum, China–Pacific Island Countries Economic Development and Cooperation Forum, China–Arab States Cooperation Forum, and the Shanghai Cooperation Organization to carry out cooperation with developing countries in regions concerned.

Helping Asian and African Portuguese-speaking countries improve livelihood. Since the establishment of the Forum for Economic and Trade Cooperation between China and the Portuguese-speaking Countries (Macau) in 2003, China has conducted assistance cooperation with Portuguese-speaking developing countries, including Angola, Cape Verde, Guinea-Bissau, Mozambique, and East Timor, in fields like culture, education, health, capacity building, and agriculture. From 2010 to 2012, China offered 1.6 billion yuan of concessional loans to the above five countries, and trained over 2,000 personnel for them. In 2011, a training center under the Forum was established in Macau, and it has since hosted over 10 workshops.

Enhancing practical cooperation with the Caribbean countries. China has been actively implementing the assistance measures it announced at the Third China–Caribbean Economic and Trade Cooperation Forum held in 2011. By the end of 2012, under the framework of the Third China–Caribbean Economic and Trade Cooperation Forum, China had provided the Caribbean countries with concessional loans totaling 3 billion yuan mainly for the construction of infrastructure projects. In the meantime, China trained over 500 officials and technical staff for the Caribbean countries, and held training courses for these countries in the establishment of earthquake and tsunami early warning and monitoring system. China also built schools for Antigua and Barbuda and Dominica, dispatched to Dominica medical teams and trained local medical staff, and carried out technical cooperation in agriculture and fishery with Dominica, Grenada, and Cuba.

Supporting sustainable economic development of Pacific island countries. China lays emphasis on developing friendly cooperation with Pacific island countries and supports the Pacific Plan they initiated to boost regional cooperation. Since the first ministerial meeting of China–Pacific Island Countries Economic Development and Cooperation Forum in 2006, China has trained for these countries over 2,500 officials and technicians, and conducted technical cooperation in agriculture and fishery with Fiji, Papua New Guinea, Samoa, Tonga, and the Federated States of Micronesia. China helped Papua New Guinea with malaria prevention and control, dispatched medical teams to Samoa, Vanuatu, the Federated States of Micronesia, Tonga, and Papua New Guinea, and held training courses for health officials, hospital administrators, and pharmaceutical researchers of Pacific island countries.

V. Participation in International Exchanges and Cooperation

With enhanced ability of participating in global affairs, China has within its capacity rendered support to the assistance programs initiated by multilateral development organizations, and has exchanged experience and explored practical cooperation in an increasingly open-minded manner.

1. Supporting Development Assistance Programs of Multilateral Organizations

In recent years, the United Nations and other multilateral organizations have been playing a prominent role in development assistance, particularly in promoting development financing, achieving the Millennium Development Goals, and tackling global development issues. China has rendered support to and took part in the development assistance programs sponsored by the multilateral organizations by ways of voluntary donations, equity financing, etc.

Participating in assistance programs initiated by multilateral organizations. From 2010 to 2012, China contributed in accumulation 1.76 billion yuan to the United Nations Development Programme (UNDP), the United Nations Industrial Development Organization (UNIDO), the United Nations Fund for Population Activities (UNFPA), the United Nations Children's Fund (UNICEF), the United Nations World Food Programme (WFP), the Food and Agriculture Organization of the United Nations (FAO), the United Nations Educational, Scientific, and Cultural Organization (UNESCO), the World Bank, the International Monetary Fund (IMF), the World Health Organization (WHO), and the Global Fund to Fight AIDS, Tuberculosis and Malaria, to support other developing countries in poverty reduction, food security, trade development, crisis prevention and reconstruction, population development, maternal and child health care, disease prevention and control, education, and environmental protection. In the three years, China, through the FAO, dispatched 235 experts to Mongolia, Nigeria, Uganda, and six other countries to provide technical guidance to improve local agricultural production. From 2011 to 2012, China worked closely with the WHO and dispatched 15 experts to Namibia, Nigeria, Ethiopia, and Pakistan to help control the spread of poliomyelitis. In 2012, China set up an educational trust fund under UNESCO to provide teacher training for eight African countries.

Supporting development financing of regional financial institutions. China strengthened cooperation with regional financial institutions such as the Asian Development Bank, the African Development Bank, the Inter-American Development Bank, the West African Development Bank, and the Caribbean Development Bank to channel more capital into the fields of infrastructure, environmental protection, education, and health care in developing countries. By 2012, China had donated a total of 1.3 billion US dollars to these regional financial institutions. Apart from China's investment of 20 million US dollars to establish the Poverty Reduction and Regional Cooperation Fund in the Asian Development Bank in 2005, in 2012 China donated another 20 million US dollars to this Fund to help with the poverty reduction and development of developing countries. By the end of 2012, China had contributed in total 110 million US dollars to the Asian Development Fund of the Asian Development Bank. Furthermore, China supported capacity building of these financial institutions through technical cooperation funds set up in the African Development Bank, the West African Development Bank, and the Caribbean Development Bank.

2. Participating in International Exchanges for Development Cooperation

China actively participated in international exchanges for development cooperation, enhanced dialogue with other countries and international organizations, and shared experience in relation to development cooperation.

Actively participating in research and discussion on global development issues. During the three years, China actively elaborated its principles, positions, and policies at a series of international conferences, including the UN High-Level Meeting on the Millennium Development Goals, UN Conference on Sustainable Development, UN Development Cooperation Forum, UN Conference on the Least Developed Countries, High-Level UN Conference on South–South Cooperation, G20 Summit, WTO's Aid for Trade Global Review, and High-Level Forum on Aid Effectiveness.

Conducting exchanges and dialogue on development cooperation with other countries and organizations. China enhanced dialogue and communication on development assistance with other countries and multilateral organizations to boost mutual trust and mutual learning in an open-minded manner. China held seminars on development assistance and conducted exchanges with the UK, Australia, Switzerland, and the Organization for Economic Cooperation and Development (OECD).

3. Conducting International Cooperation in Foreign Assistance

In order to effectively learn international experience, improve assistance efficiency, and enrich assistance forms, China intensified efforts to promote international cooperation in development assistance, and conducted trilateral cooperation featuring complementary advantage with multilateral and bilateral assistance providers by leveraging each party's strengths on the premise of fully respecting the will of recipient countries.

Jointly holding training programs. China continued to carry out cooperation on training programs targeted at other developing countries with the UNDP, the UNICEF, the FAO, the UNIDO, the United Nations Office for the Coordination of the Humanitarian Affairs (OCHA), the Common Fund for Commodities (CFC), the United Nations Office of the High Representative for the Least Developed Countries, Landlocked Developing Countries and Small Island Developing States (UN-OHRLLS), the World Bank, and the IMF. From 2010 to 2012, together with the above-mentioned organizations, China held about 50 training sessions of themes such as agriculture, trade development, disaster prevention and relief, finance, industrial development, and social and public management.

Sharing experience on development cooperation. China and the World Bank jointly held workshops on international development cooperation featuring capacity development and infrastructure construction, and invited government officials from developing countries to share experience in the field. In October 2011, China and the UNESCO held the China–Africa University President Forum, at which China and Africa held discussions on the prospect of cooperation between Chinese and African universities. China held workshops, for five consecutive years, on South–South cooperation with the International Fund for Agricultural Development to share experience in agricultural development and poverty reduction in rural areas. China and the Asian Development Bank held sessions for five consecutive years on city development in the Asia–Pacific region and development of small and medium enterprises (SMEs).

Piloting trilateral cooperation. China, the UNDP, and Cambodia launched the cooperation project of enlarging cassava export on the basis of the successful training course of cassava planting technique. In March 2012, the UNESCO's Funds-in-Trust for China–Africa Multilateral Education Cooperation funded by China was launched to increase investment in basic education in Africa. At the request of the government of the Cook Islands, in August 2012 China, New Zealand, and Cook Islands reached an agreement on a water supply project in Cook Islands. Once completed, it will provide safe and clean drinking water to local people.

Conclusion

Today, the impact of the global financial crisis still exists, and developing countries, especially the least developed ones, are still confronted with the tough task of poverty reduction and development. The international community should mobilize more development resources to strengthen South–North cooperation, support South–South cooperation, and promote economic and social development of developing countries to eliminate poverty worldwide.

China is endeavoring to build a moderately prosperous society in an all-round way and stays committed to realizing the Chinese Dream of national prosperity and renewal, and happiness of the people. China will follow the trend of the times, which is peace, development, cooperation, and win–win result, keep to the righteous viewpoint on justice and interests, respect and support developing countries' exploration of development paths suited to their own national conditions, actively promote South–South cooperation, and make concrete efforts to help other developing countries promote social and economic development.

China will continue to increase the input in foreign assistance, further optimize assistance structure, highlight key aspects, innovate assistance means, raise the efficiency of capital utilization, effectively help recipient countries improve their people's well-being, and enhance their capability of independent development. China is willing to work with the international community to share opportunities, meet challenges, strive to realize the world's dream of lasting peace and common prosperity, and make greater contribution to the development of mankind.

8. August 2013: China–Africa Economic and Trade Cooperation[8]

The State Council Information Office
The People's Republic of China

Contents

Foreword

   I. Promoting Sustainable Development of Trade
  II. Improving the Level of Investment and Financing Cooperation
 III. Strengthening Cooperation in Agriculture and Food Security
 IV. Supporting African Infrastructure Construction
  V. Stressing African People's Livelihoods and Capacity Building
 VI. Promoting Cooperation under the Multilateral Framework

Conclusion

Appendix I
Appendix II

Foreword

Currently, as the international situation undergoes profound and intricate changes, newly emerging and developing economies have become the major force pushing forward the world's economic development. In tune with the changes in the international environment, China and African countries are, within the framework of the Forum on China–Africa Cooperation (FOCAC), continuing to deepen the new type of China–Africa strategic partnership, vigorously advancing economic and trade cooperation, and actively exploring a common path that reflects both China's and Africa's realities.

China has become Africa's largest trade partner, and Africa is now China's major import source, second largest overseas construction project contract market, and fourth largest investment destination. China–Africa economic and trade development has improved people's livelihoods and diversified economic development in African countries, provided strong support for China's socio-economic development, and contributed to promoting South–South cooperation and balanced world economic development.

Through the common efforts of China and Africa, bilateral economic and trade cooperation now enjoys a consolidated foundation and improved mechanisms, with new common interests and growth points in cooperation constantly emerging. In March 2013, China's President Xi Jinping visited Africa and announced a series of new measures to support Africa's development, providing a powerful impetus for the advancement of China–Africa economic and trade relations.

In 2010, the Chinese government published a white paper on China–Africa economic and trade cooperation. This latest white paper provides a further introduction to the progress of bilateral economic and trade cooperation in recent years.

I. Promoting Sustainable Development of Trade

Against the background of sluggish global economic recovery in recent years, China–Africa trade development has maintained comparatively rapid momentum. In 2009, China became Africa's No. 1 trade partner. In the following two years, the scale of China–Africa trade expanded rapidly. In 2012, the total volume of China–Africa trade reached US$198.49 billion, a year-on-year growth of 19.3 percent. Of this, US$85.319 billion consisted of China's exports to Africa, up 16.7 percent, and US$113.171 billion was contributed by China's imports from Africa, up 21.4 percent. Total China–Africa trade volume, China's export volume to Africa, and China's import volume from Africa all reached new highs.

As the volume of China–Africa trade continues to grow, its proportion to China's and Africa's respective total foreign trade volume has also increased. From 2000 to 2012, the proportion of China–Africa trade volume as a part of China's total foreign trade volume increased from 2.23 percent to 5.13 percent: the proportion consisting of China's imports from Africa up from 2.47 percent to 6.23 percent, and that of China's exports to Africa from 2.02 percent to 4.16 percent. On the African side, the changes are even more remarkable. From 2000 to 2012, the proportion of China–Africa trade volume as a part of Africa's total foreign trade volume increased from 3.82 percent to 16.13 percent: the proportion contributed by Africa's exports to China up from 3.76 percent to 18.07 percent, and that by Africa's imports from China from 3.88 percent to 14.11 percent.

Chinese products exported to Africa are generally of fine quality and well-priced, and fulfill the consumption demands of all social strata in Africa. With the scale of trade expanded, the structure of China–Africa trade has been improved step by step. As the consumption capacity of the African market continues to expand, the amount of technical products that China exports to Africa has increased remarkably. In 2012, the proportion of mechanical and electrical products as a part of China's total commodity exports to Africa reached 45.9 percent. In order to guarantee the quality of products exported to Africa, from December 2010 to March 2011, the Chinese side took special steps to crack down on the potential export to Africa of counterfeit and shoddy products and commodities that violated intellectual property rights. This involved multiple measures, such as prior-to-shipment quality examinations for industrial products that were to be exported to Africa. These measures helped guarantee the quality of Chinese commodities exported to Africa.

Over the past three years, China's import volume from Africa has increased notably, as the trade volume and quantity of bulk commodities, like crude oil and agricultural products, keep rising. Through China–Africa trade, Africa's exporters have obtained access to a stable market, higher pricing, and greater benefits. In the meantime, China has vigorously expanded its imports from Africa by enacting tariff exemptions and setting up exhibition centers for African products. Since January 2012, the 30 least developed African countries that have established diplomatic relations with China have been granted zero-tariff treatment for 60 percent of their exported items. By the end of 2012, 22 of them had seen 910 million yuan worth of tariff exempted, involving US$1.49 billion-worth of goods. In May 2011, an African Products Exhibition Center opened in Yiwu City, Zhejiang Province. By reducing operation expenditures and other supportive policies, the Exhibition Center has attracted over 2,000 salable commodity items from more than 20 African countries.

Sino–African bilateral trade has great potential due to the complementary conditions on both sides, and is significant for the economic development of both China and Africa. China will take multiple measures to promote the healthy development of China–Africa trade. These include implementing the "Special Plan on Trade with Africa," which will expand the scope of zero tariff treatment for African products exported to China and increase China's imports from Africa, and improving the brand building, marketing channels, and quality of China's commodities exported to Africa. In addition, China will help African countries improve their customs and commodity inspection facilities by mobilizing aid for trade, provide support for African countries to promote trade facilitation, and push forward trade development within Africa.

II. Improving the Level of Investment and Financing Cooperation

A poor economic foundation and insufficient construction funds have always been factors limiting the development of African countries. The Chinese government encourages and supports enterprises and financial institutions to increase investment in Africa, striving to improve the quality and level of China–Africa cooperation.

Since 2009, Africa has seen a decrease of foreign direct investment, but an accelerated growth of direct investment from China during this same period. From 2009 to 2012, China's direct investment in Africa increased from US$1.44 billion to US$2.52 billion, with an annual growth rate of 20.5 percent. Over the same period, China's accumulative direct investment in Africa increased from US$9.33 billion to US$21.23 billion, 2.3 times the 2009 figure. The rapid growth of China's direct investment in Africa is indicative of Africa's development potential and investment appeal, and also points to the mutually beneficial nature of China–Africa cooperation.

While increasing aggregate investment, China is also improving the level of its investment in Africa. Currently, over 2,000 Chinese enterprises are investing and developing in more than 50 African countries and regions, and cooperation fields have expanded from agriculture, mining, and building industry to intensive processing of resource products, industrial manufacturing, finance, commercial logistics, and real estate.

In recent years, China has improved its mechanisms for investment in Africa. By the end of 2012, China had signed bilateral investment treaties (BIT) with 32

African countries, and established joint economic commission mechanisms with 45 African countries. The China–Africa Development Fund, established as one of the eight pledges China made at the FOCAC Beijing Summit, had by the end of 2012 agreed to invest US$2.385 billion in 61 projects in 30 African countries, and had already invested US$1.806 billion for 53 projects. According to preliminary statistics, the agreed upon investment projects will bring US$10 billion worth of investment to Africa, increase local exports by about US$2 billion annually, and benefit more than 700,000 people. China's financial institutions have actively expanded financing support for Africa. At the Fourth FOCAC Ministerial Conference in 2009, China announced the establishment of "a special loan for small and medium-sized African businesses." By the end of 2012, the special loan service had promised to offer loans totaling US$1.213 billion, with contract value of US$1.028 billion and loans granted worth US$666 million, providing strong support for the development of agriculture, forestry, animal husbandry, fishing, processing and manufacturing, trade and logistics, and other industries closely associated with people's livelihoods in Africa.

Energy and mineral resource exploitation is the major impetus for the economic booms of many African countries. In this area, Chinese enterprises have helped African countries establish an upstream–downstream-integrated industry chain, transforming resource advantages into economic growth opportunities, and actively participated in local public welfare infrastructure construction. In the Democratic Republic of the Congo, Chinese enterprises have built highways, hospitals, and other public infrastructure while extracting copper-cobalt ores. In the Republic of South Africa, Chinese mineral exploitation and processing enterprises have set up endowment funds to sponsor medical care, poverty reduction, and education in local areas, and built advanced water treatment facilities. Chinese enterprises have sponsored the "Brightness Action" and organized first-rate ophthalmologists to perform cataract extraction surgeries for 623 patients in Zimbabwe and Zambia.

Manufacturing is China's key investment field in Africa. From 2009 to 2012, Chinese enterprises' direct investment volume in Africa's manufacturing sector totaled US$1.33 billion. By the end of 2012, China's investment in Africa's manufacturing industry had reached US$3.43 billion. Mali, Ethiopia, and other resource-poor countries have also attracted a large amount of Chinese investment. Chinese enterprises have invested in sugar refineries in Mali, set up glass, fur, medical capsule, and automobile factories in Ethiopia, and invested in textile and steel pipe manufacturing projects in Uganda. All of these investments have compensated for these countries' unfavorable natural conditions and resources, increased their tax revenues and employment, and extended the value-adding chain of "made in Africa" products.

Chinese enterprises' investments have brought about changes to all dimensions of Africa's social development. For example, those that invest in cash crop cultivation in Zimbabwe have provided interest-free loans to local farmer households, improved production infrastructure, offered technical guidance for the whole production process, organized local employees to visit China, and funded local schools and orphanages. These have promoted the positive interaction and common development of Chinese enterprises and local society.

Service industries that produce zero pollution and consume little energy have become a new highlight of China–Africa cooperation in recent years. Chinese enterprises have invested in finance, trade, science and technology services, power supply, and other fields in Africa. By the end of 2012, China's direct investment in Africa's financial sector had reached US$3.87 billion, accounting for 17.8 percent of its total investment volume in Africa. To some extent, this was able to make up for the lack of sufficient development funds available to local enterprises. In the field of commerce and trade, the construction of the Angola International Trade Center, jointly initiated by Chinese and local enterprises, has been started. When completed, the project will be the largest commercial logistics, convention, and investment service center in southwest Africa. There are now also a large number of small and medium-sized Chinese investors engaged in agricultural and sideline product processing and petty commodity production in Africa. Their products and services are closely linked with African people's livelihoods, playing an active role in meeting local needs, boosting local employment, and promoting China–Africa trade contacts. As the mutual understanding between Chinese and African peoples is deepened and the cooperation between Chinese and African governments enhanced, these small and medium-sized Chinese investors will further incorporate into local society and share the fruits of development with local people.

In recent years, as the economic strength of African countries has increased and China–Africa relations have grown closer, African enterprises have started to invest in China. By the end of 2012, the volume of African countries' direct investment in China totaled US$14.242 billion, increasing by 44 percent over 2009 levels. Of that, the figure for 2012 was US$1.388 billion. Investing countries included Mauritius, Seychelles, South Africa, and Nigeria, and their investments covered petrochemical industries, manufacturing and processing, and wholesale and retail, among other fields. China–Africa investment and financing cooperation has solidified the foundation of Africa's economic development, increased Africa's capacity of independent development, improved Africa's competitiveness in the global economic sphere, and advanced Chinese enterprises' internationalized development. In the future, China will further expand investment and financing cooperation with Africa and fulfill its commitment on the provision of US$20 billion-worth of loans to Africa, which will be used for infrastructure construction, as well as the development of agriculture, manufacturing, and small and medium-sized enterprises. China will give guidance to its enterprises on the establishment of processing and manufacturing bases in Africa, and increase investment in business services, transport, consultation management, and other service industries. China will also encourage its enterprises to carry out multiple-field investment cooperation in Africa, and help African countries improve their external economic development environments.

III. Strengthening Cooperation in Agriculture and Food Security

Agriculture is crucial for stable development and poverty reduction efforts in Africa. It is a pillar industry and a priority field for development in most African countries. China and Africa see favorable conditions and broad prospects for future agricultural cooperation. The Chinese government attaches great importance to its mutually beneficial agricultural cooperation with Africa, and works hard to help African countries turn resource advantages into developmental ones and sustainably develop their agricultural capacities.

In recent years, Sino–African trade in agricultural products has grown quickly. From 2009 to 2012, China's agricultural exports to Africa grew from US$1.58 billion to US$2.49 billion, an increase of 57.6 percent. During the same period, China's agricultural imports from Africa grew from US$1.16 billion to US$2.86 billion, a 146 percent increase. Most imported agricultural products are non-food items, including cotton, hemp, silk, oilseeds, and other such products.

A major reason for the rapid increase in Chinese imports of African agricultural products is the zero-tariff policy that the Chinese government adopted in 2005 for some African products. Agricultural products are a major category benefiting from this policy and, as a result, the export of specialty African agricultural products to China has grown rapidly. One example of the impact of this policy is provided by sesame. China started importing small amounts of sesame from Africa in 2002. After the zero-tariff policy was adopted, sesame imports grew rapidly, from US$97 million in 2005 to US$441 million in 2011, an annual increase of 28.7 percent. This rate of import increase is higher than the average growth rate of all products imported from Africa during the same period.

In recent years, Chinese enterprises have invested in Africa in such fields as breeding improved seeds, planting grain and cash crops, and processing agricultural products. From 2009 to 2012, China's direct investment in African agriculture grew from US$30 million to US$82.47 million, a 175 percent increase. Investment by Chinese enterprises in African agriculture has increased grain supplies in the countries concerned and enhanced the comprehensive agricultural productivity of those countries. In Mozambique, for example, 300 hectares of experimental paddy fields supported by Chinese investment yielded 9–10 tons per hectare for three successive years. With the help of Chinese rice experts, local farmers see their paddy fields yield five tons per hectare, two tons more than previous yields. In Malawi, Mozambique, and Zambia, Chinese enterprises and the China–Africa Development Fund jointly invested in a cotton planting and processing project modeled on having enterprises work with farming households. The project was able to involve tens of thousands of local growers, effectively enhancing local capabilities in cotton processing.

Chinese enterprises have also worked to improve local farmland, water conservancy, and conditions for agricultural production. Currently, the biggest agricultural project in Rwanda is a farmland improvement project supported by investment from the African Development Bank and contracted to Chinese enterprises. When completed, the project will effectively control major rivers and improve the utilization of water resources in Rwanda.

The Chinese government has tried to enhance Africa's self-reliance capacity to develop its agriculture by providing assistance in the construction of demonstration centers of agricultural technology, and sending senior agricultural experts and technicians to teach the locals managerial experience and practical techniques in agricultural production. Since 2006, China has helped set up 15 agricultural demonstration centers in Rwanda, the Republic of Congo, Mozambique, and some other countries, and is planning to establish another seven. At the same time, China has sent technical groups and several hundred technicians to Africa to provide policy consulting, teach practical techniques, and train local staff. With China's aid in a project to breed high-yield and high-quality crop varieties, Chad sees its yields grow by over 25 percent on over 500 hectares planted with improved varieties, and several thousand farmers trained.

In the future, China will advance agricultural cooperation with Africa in all respects while ensuring that this cooperation puts both parties on an equal footing, is mutually beneficial, and advances common development. It will work to establish and improve a mechanism for bilateral agricultural cooperation, and strengthen Sino–African cooperation in the sharing of agricultural technologies, resource varieties, and agricultural information, the processing and trade of agricultural products, agricultural infrastructure construction, and human resource training. China will continue to encourage and support investment by established Chinese enterprises to put money into agriculture or technological cooperation in Africa. It will arrange and launch an appropriate number of agricultural demonstration centers in African countries, depending on their actual needs. China will also work to deepen Sino–African cooperation within the frameworks of the United Nations Food and Agriculture Organization (UNFAO) and the International Fund for Agricultural Development.

IV. Supporting African Infrastructure Construction

Infrastructure construction is a starting point for improving the investment environment and people's livelihoods in Africa, and is of great importance for poverty reduction and development on the continent. The Chinese government encourages enterprises and financial institutions to participate in African infrastructure construction, including transportation, communications, and electric power projects, in a variety of different ways. In 2012, Chinese enterprises completed construction contracts worth US$40.83 billion in Africa, an increase of 45 percent over 2009, accounting for 35.02 percent of China's overseas contract work completed. Africa has been China's second largest overseas contract market for four successive years. Capital, equipment, and technologies from China have effectively helped reduce construction costs for African countries and, as a result, their infrastructure situations have gradually improved.

Chinese enterprises have built numerous city roads, expressways, flyovers, railways, and ports in Africa, effectively improving traffic conditions there and enhancing economic and trade development and personnel exchanges between African countries. In Angola, Chinese enterprises undertook the contract for a project that involved repairing a railway running from east to west through the country.

Chinese communication enterprises have participated in the construction of communication facilities in Africa, such as backbone fiber-optic transmission networks, fixed-line telephone lines, mobile communication, and internet facilities, expanding the coverage of Africa's telecommunication network, raising the network's performance quality, and reducing communication costs. A contract to build a fiber-optic transmission backbone network in Tanzania was also taken on by Chinese enterprises. The network will cover major provinces and cities in Tanzania, link it with six neighboring countries and connect it to seabed optical cables in East and Southern Africa. After the network is completed, there will be three backbone loops, one each in northern, southern, and western Tanzania, and eight international transit links, making communications of East Africa more integrated.

China has also worked closely with African countries in building hydropower stations and power grids, alleviating power crises that have long plagued some African countries. In 2010, Chinese enterprises started to build the Malabo Gas Plant in Equatorial Guinea. After the plant is completed, the country will have a complete power supply system, from power generation to power transmission and power transformation. This will improve the power supply conditions of Malabo City and Bioko Island while promoting agricultural irrigation and ecological tourism in surrounding areas.

The Chinese government and Chinese financial institutions have offered a great number of concessional and commercial loans to Africa for its infrastructure construction. From 2010 to May 2012, China approved concessional loans worth a total of US$11.3 billion for 92 African projects. For example, the Addis Ababa-Adama Expressway of Ethiopia and the Kribi Deep-water Port of Cameroon were both funded by concessional loans from China. Some of China's main commercial banks have also started buyer's credit businesses in Africa, supporting the power grid in Ghana, hydropower stations in Ethiopia, a west–east expressway in Algeria, and other projects.

While undertaking infrastructure projects in Africa, Chinese enterprises have paid attention to localized operation and management styles, and taken an active part in programs benefiting local people. For example, large Chinese communication companies in Africa have raised their localization rate to above 65 percent. They have also cooperated with 1,200 local subcontractors, indirectly providing more than 10,000 job opportunities. In Zambia, Chinese enterprises have repaired roads, hospitals and houses of some mines, and donated sports facilities for communities and money for charity activities, making positive contributions to local development.

Infrastructure construction is a significant part of Africa's further economic and social development. China will deepen cooperation with Africa in transportation, communications, and other infrastructure fields to improve people's livelihoods, steadily push forward Sino–African transnational and trans-regional infrastructure construction partnerships, and enhance exchanges and cooperation in the field of regional integration so as to help Africa improve its capacity for integrated development.

V. Stressing African People's Livelihoods and Capacity Building

Africa has sustained rapid economic growth in recent years, but it still faces severe development problems and the difficult task of accomplishing the UN Millennium Development Goals. While seeking to advance its own development, China tries to offer what assistance it can to Africa without setting any political conditions, and to benefit African people through developmental advances. In recent years, China has implemented measures adopted at the FOCAC ministerial conferences and actively developed cooperation with Africa in areas relating to public amenities, medical and health care, climate change and environmental protection, humanitarian aid, and other fields. China has also strengthened cultural and educational exchanges and scientific and technological cooperation in an effort to improve Africa's ability to develop independently.

Helping build public amenities. China has offered assistance to Africa in digging wells for water supplies, and in building affordable housing, broadcasting and telecommunications facilities, and cultural and educational sites in an effort to improve the productive and living conditions of local people. Since 2009, China has carried out dozens of well-digging projects in the Sudan, Malawi, Zimbabwe, Djibouti, Guinea, and Togo, playing a positive role in easing water problems for local people. It has also provided support for the building of portable dwellings in South Sudan, school houses in Benin, and rural schools in Malawi, and in doing so, improved local living conditions and educational facilities. China's largest aid project in the Central African Republic is the construction of the Boali No.3 Hydropower Station, which, after it is completed, will greatly relieve electricity shortages in Bangui and surrounding areas.

Advancing cooperation in medical and health care. From 2010 to 2012, China helped build 27 hospitals in Ghana, Zimbabwe, and other African countries. China has also sent 43 medical teams to 42 African countries and regions, treating over 5.57 million patients. In recent years, in addition to building hospitals, donating drugs, and organizing medical training programs, China has also launched an initiative, "Brightness Action," to treat cataract patients, provided mobile hospitals, built bilaterally run eye centers, and helped build demonstration and training centers for diagnosis and treatment technologies, effectively advancing Sino–African cooperation in medical and health care.

Working together to address climate change. Environmental protection and climate change are two developmental topics that the world must face, and Africa needs special assistance from the international community in these areas. China pays a great deal of attention to its cooperation with African countries in the field of climate change. Since November 2009, China has carried out more than 100 clean energy projects in African countries, including biogas technology cooperation with Tunisia, Guinea, and the Sudan, hydropower generating facilities in Cameroon, Burundi, and Guinea, and solar and wind power generation in Morocco, Ethiopia, and South Africa. China has also donated energy-efficient lamps, air conditioners, and other materials in response to climate change to Nigeria, Benin, and Madagascar. All of these measures have greatly raised the ability of African countries to respond to climate change.

Offering emergency humanitarian aid. In keeping with humanitarian values, China always offers what materials or cash it is able to give for emergency aid to African countries that suffer from political disorder or have experienced natural disasters. In 2011, China provided 50 million yuan in emergency aid to Tunisia and Egypt to ease the humanitarian crisis caused by refugees stranded in the areas bordering Libya. When the worst famine in 60 years broke out in the Horn of Africa in the same year, China provided the affected countries with emergency aid in the form of grain and cash. In total, this aid was worth more than 400 million yuan, the biggest amount of food aid that the Chinese government has provided since the founding of the People's Republic of China in 1949. In 2012, China granted food aid to affected countries in the Sahel region of Africa.

Supporting cultural and educational exchanges. Cultural and educational exchanges make up an important part of the new type of strategic partnership between China and Africa. By supporting young Africans studying in China, sending young Chinese volunteers to Africa, and developing joint research initiatives, China tries to promote mutual understanding between China and African countries and strengthen the social foundation of their friendship. From 2010 to 2012, China granted 18,743 government scholarships to students from African countries. By the end of 2012, China had sent 408 young volunteers to 16 African countries, including Ethiopia and Zimbabwe. Twenty pairs of leading Chinese and African universities have begun cooperating under the 20+20 Cooperation Plan for Chinese and African Universities. From the launch of China–Africa Joint Research and Exchange Plan in March 2010 to the end of 2012, it had supported 64 projects in the form of workshops, subject research, academic exchanges, and publishing works. The project had also subsidized visits and exchanges for over 600 Chinese and African scholars.

Holding human resource training programs. Human resource training is an important part of capacity building. From 2010 to 2012, China held various training courses for 54 countries and regions in Africa; the courses involved a total of 27,318 officials and technicians, and covered topics relating to economics, foreign affairs, energy, industry, agriculture, forestry, animal husbandry and fishing, medicine and health care, inspection and quarantine, climate change, security, and some other fields. In addition, Chinese medical teams, agricultural experts, and enterprises located in Africa have also trained local people in an effort to enhance local technological capabilities.

Upgrading China–Africa cooperation in science and technology. In 2009, China launched the China–Africa Science and Technology Partnership Plan. This plan aims to promote technology transfer to Africa and research exchanges, as well as the sharing of more scientific and technological achievements. By the end of 2012, China had cooperated with African countries on 115 joint research and technology demonstration projects, including projects relating to cashew pest control technology and resources satellite receiving stations. China also gave 66 African researchers the chance to do post-doctoral research in China and donated 150,000 yuan worth of research equipment to each of the 24 researchers who had returned to their home countries to work upon completing their joint research tasks in China. In December 2011, the Chinese government launched the Science and Technology Action for African People's Livelihood, strengthening its cooperation with Africa through scientific and technological means. It also declared that it would help build a "mobile and modular general clinic" and a "demonstration center for scientific and technological cooperation in gastroenterology" to each African FOCAC member country.

Reducing African debt. From 2010 to 2012, China canceled 16 debts owed by Mali, Equatorial Guinea, Cameroon, Benin, Togo, Côte d'Ivoire, and other countries, greatly reducing the debts of African countries.

VI. Promoting Cooperation under the Multilateral Framework

In recent years, African countries have made intensified efforts to gain strength through unity and they have made substantial progress in terms of economic integration. China firmly supports Africa's self-enhancement through unity, and works hard to strengthen cooperation with the African Union (AU) and African sub-regional organizations in a variety of fields, including infrastructure development, capacity building, and mechanism construction. At the same time, China joins other countries and international multilateral organizations in leveraging one another's advantages to the fullest to help African countries reduce poverty, develop economically, and promote social progress.

China works closely with the AU and African sub-regional organizations not only in traditional areas like infrastructure construction, agriculture, and personnel training, but also in emerging fields like finance, disaster reduction, and intellectual property. The relationship between China and the AU plays an important role in the China–Africa new-type strategic partnership. Early in the 1970s, China started to provide the Organization of African Unity (OAU, now AU) with assistance in a variety of forms, including money, materials, turn-key projects, and training. Since the AU Commission joined the FOCAC in 2011, cooperation between China and the AU has been enhanced. China's largest construction aid project in Africa, the AU Conference Center, was inaugurated in January 2012, at which time the Chinese government decided to provide 600 million yuan in aid to the AU over the next three years.

In recent years, cooperation between China and African regional organizations has been strengthened and become institutionalized. Since 2011, the Chinese government has signed Framework Agreements on Economic and Trade Cooperation with both the East African Community (EAC) and the Economic Community of West African States (ECOWAS), to expand cooperation in promoting trade facilitation, direct investment, cross-border infrastructure construction, and development aid. Evidence of China's efforts in the area of financial cooperation includes China's status as a member state of the African Development Bank (AfDB), the West African Development Bank, and the Eastern and Southern African Trade and Development Bank. China has promised to contribute 615 million US dollars to the African Development Fund (ADF), which is the soft-loan window of the AfDB, and has actively participated in the ADF's Multilateral Debt Relief Initiative to support poverty reduction and regional integration in Africa. The China Development Bank (CDB) has signed an Agreement on Development Financing Cooperation with the Development Bank of Southern Africa, and an agreement to loan 60 million Euros to the West African Development Bank for the development of small and medium-sized enterprises in countries belonging to the West African Economic and Monetary Union (WAEMU). The Export–Import Bank of China and the Agricultural Bank of China have both signed cooperation framework agreements with the AfDB to cooperate on infrastructure project financing and the development of small and medium-sized enterprises. In addition, China has reached relevant agreements with African intellectual property organizations, laying a solid foundation for the advancement of China–Africa economic and trade relations.

China has joined forces with multilateral organizations including the United Nations (UN) and the World Bank (WB) to utilize one another's strengths to the fullest to aid Africa in the fields of agriculture, environmental protection, and training. China was the first country to form a strategic alliance with the UNFAO to foster South–South cooperation. In 2008, China decided to contribute 30 million US dollars to the UNFAO to set up a trust fund. This fund, which is particularly beneficial to Africa, is used to support South–South cooperation between China and African countries under the framework of the UNFAO Special Program for Food Security. By the end of 2012, under said framework, China had sent many agricultural experts and technicians to Ethiopia, Mauritania, and Mali to provide technical assistance in the areas of irrigation and water conservation, crop production, animal husbandry, aquaculture, and agricultural product processing. By doing this, China has played an active role in improving the agricultural production capacities and food security of these countries. In addition, China works cooperatively on climate change and disaster reduction with international organizations, including the United Nations Environment Programme and the secretariat of the International Strategy for Disaster Reduction. In 2012, China promised to contribute US$10 million to the International Monetary Fund (IMF) to provide technical assistance to Africa and improve the macroeconomic management of African countries. Chinese financial institutions established an all-round cooperation framework with the WB in May 2007. The two sides are carrying out feasibility studies on some infrastructure construction projects in African countries. Chinese financial institutions also maintain a good cooperative relationship with the International Finance Corporation (IFC), which is a member of the WB Group, to provide co-financing to telecommunications projects in West Africa and push forward the development of the communications industry in this region.

With an open mind, China has worked to enhance exchanges and mutual learning with other countries to explore practical cooperation in providing assistance to Africa. From 2009 to 2010, in partnership with the UK, China ran three peace-keeping police training classes in China and Ghana for African countries. In 2011, the tripartite agreement on the Liberian Tapeta Hospital cooperative project, signed by China, Egypt, and Liberia, was fulfilled. According to the agreement, the Chinese government was responsible for maintaining medical equipment, and training medical, technical, and managerial personnel for the hospital. The agreement required the Egyptian government to send two to five doctors to the hospital, and made the Liberian side responsible for the hospital's management and operation. This project has trained the backbone staff of the hospital and made outstanding contributions to its operation, winning universal praise.

In the future, China will work more closely with the AU and African sub-regional organizations to support Africa's economic integration and build the capacities of regional organizations. It will do this by promoting transnational and trans-regional infrastructure development and human resources development in Africa, and also by strengthening cooperation with the AfDB and African sub-regional financial institutions. At the same time, China will expand its international cooperative efforts to advance Africa's sustainable development, strengthen cooperation in the fields of agricultural development and climate change, and provide more support to Africa in ecological protection and environmental management.

Conclusion

China–Africa relations have reached a new historic level. Africa, a continent full of hope and thirsty for development, has become one of the world's fastest growing regions, while China, the world's largest developing country, has maintained forward momentum in its development. With increasing common interests and mutual needs, the two sides have great opportunities to accelerate their economic and trade cooperation.

Currently, the Chinese people are working hard to realize the Chinese dream of national revival, while African people are committed to the African dream of gaining strength through unity and achieving development and renewal. With a spirit of mutual respect and win–win cooperation, China will continue to take concrete measures to build a Sino–African community of shared destinies featuring all-round, diversified, and deep cooperation. It will work to advance China–Africa economic and trade cooperation to help both sides make their respective dreams come true. China is also willing to enhance its cooperation with the rest of the world to promote Africa's prosperity and development.

Appendix I

Implementation of the Economic & Trade Measures of the Fourth FOCAC Ministerial Conference

1. The two sides have engaged in enhanced policy dialogue and practical cooperation on climate change. China has, on many occasions, sent senior officials, including the special envoy for climate change negotiations, to African countries to exchange views. During the Cancun Conference, the Durban Conference, the Ministerial Consultation of BASIC countries, and other related negotiations and conferences, China has engaged in dialogue and consultation and also coordinated its position with African countries to uphold the common interests of developing countries. With a view to improving the abilities of African countries to adapt to climate change, China has implemented over 100 clean energy projects in Africa.

2. China has worked to raise the level of its scientific and technological cooperation with Africa. Following the Fourth FOCAC Ministerial Conference, China launched the China–Africa Science and Technology Partnership Plan, which aims to promote technology transfer to Africa and expand the sharing of scientific and technological achievements. The China–Africa Scientific and Technological Cooperation Roundtable was held in Egypt at the end of 2009. China has conducted 115 joint research and demonstration projects with African countries. China has also hosted 66 African post-doctoral students and donated research equipment to 24 returning African researchers who have concluded their joint research projects in China.

3. China has made concrete efforts to fulfill its promise to build up Africa's financial capabilities. By May 2012, China had approved US$11.3 billion in concessional loans for 92 projects, fulfilling its promise six months early. These loans are mainly used for funding infrastructure and social development projects in Africa.

By the end of 2012, the special loan for the development of small and medium-sized businesses in Africa, set up by China Development Bank, had promised to make loans totaling to US$1.213 billion, and US$2 billion had been collected for the second tranche of China–Africa Development Fund. China has canceled debts of interest-free government loans that matured by the end of 2009 owed by all heavily indebted poor countries and least developed countries in Africa that have diplomatic relations with China.

4. China has further opened its markets to African products. All of the 30 least developed countries in Africa that have diplomatic ties with China enjoy zero-tariff treatment for 60 percent of their exports to China, covering 4,762 items. Thanks to this policy, African exports to China have grown rapidly, reaching US$93.2 billion in 2011 and increasing 39 percent year on year. In 2012, African exports to China totaled US$113.17 billion, an increase of 21.4 percent over the previous year.

5. China has scaled up its agricultural cooperation with Africa. By the end of 2012, following the implementation of eight new measures to strengthen cooperation with Africa, China had built seven new agricultural technology demonstration centers for Africa. This increased the number of such centers on the continent to 22. By that time, China had also sent 50 agricultural technology teams to African countries. These teams trained more than 5,000 local technical personnel.

6. China has steadily advanced its health cooperation with Africa. By the end of 2012, China had dispatched 43 medical teams to 42 countries and regions in Africa, where the teams treated more than 5.57 million patients. There are now 1,006 Chinese medical professionals in Africa. China has provided medical equipment, materials, and medicines to 42 countries and regions in Africa, and also to 30 African hospitals and 30 malaria prevention centers.

7. China has further strengthened its human resources development and educational cooperation with Africa. From 2010 to 2012, China ran training sessions with a total capacity of 27,318 trainees for officials and technical personnel from 54 countries and regions in Africa. The training sessions covered the fields of public management, energy, health, social security, and manufacturing.

In the field of education, from 2010 to 2012, China built 28 new schools in Africa, provided equipment to 42 African schools, and funded 18,743 scholarships to students from Africa, 6,717 of which were given in 2012. During the same period, the 20+20 Cooperation Plan for Chinese and African Universities was launched, allowing 20 pairs of Chinese and African universities to conduct cooperative projects. China has also opened 31 Confucius Institutes and five Confucius Classrooms in 26 countries and regions of Africa.

8. China has actively run the China–Africa Joint Research and Exchange Plan. Between its inception in March 2010 and the end of 2012, the program supported Chinese and African scholars working on 64 projects (including 29 research projects, 16 workshops, 16 academic exchanges, and three publication projects) and organized academic exchanges between the two sides involving as many as 600 people. Thanks to the Exchange Plan, the Forum for Chinese and African Think Tanks has become institutionalized. One of the important platforms for exchanges between Chinese and African think tanks, the forum held its second conference in October 2012. The China Development Bank has set up a special fund to support academic exchanges between China and Africa.

Appendix II

Priority Areas of China–Africa Cooperation for the Next Three Years Announced by the Chinese Government at the Fifth FOCAC Ministerial Conference

1. Expanding cooperation in investment and financing to support sustainable development in Africa. To meet this goal, China will provide African countries

with a US$20 billion credit line to be spent on developing infrastructure, agriculture, manufacturing, and small and medium-sized enterprises.

2. Continuing to scale up its assistance to Africa so as to benefit more African people. As part of expanding its aid to Africa, the Chinese government will build more agricultural technology demonstration centers, as necessary, to help African countries increase their production capacities. China will implement the "African Talents Program" to train 30,000 African personnel in various sectors, offer 18,000 government scholarships, and build cultural and vocational skills training facilities in African countries. China and Africa will deepen their cooperation in the health sector, step up high level exchanges in health-related fields, and hold a China–Africa high-level health development workshop when it becomes appropriate to do so. China will send 1,500 medical workers to Africa, while continuing to run the "Brightness Action" campaign in Africa to provide free treatment for cataract patients. It will also help African countries enhance their capacity building in meteorological infrastructure and forest protection and management. The Chinese side will continue to carry out well-drilling and water supply projects in Africa to provide safe drinking water for African people.

3. Supporting the African integration process and helping Africa enhance its capacity for overall development. To support Africa in these areas, China will establish a partnership with Africa that is focused on transnational and trans-regional infrastructure development, support related project planning and feasibility studies, and encourage established Chinese companies and financial institutions to take part in transnational and trans-regional infrastructure development in Africa. China will also help African countries improve their customs and commodity inspection facilities to enhance intra-regional trade facilitation.

4. Strengthening people-to-people friendships to lay a solid foundation of public support for enhancing China–Africa common development. In this area, China proposes to carry out the "China–Africa people-to-people friendship action" to support and promote exchanges and cooperation between non-governmental organizations, women, and youth from the two sides. Also, a China–Africa Press Exchange Center will be set up in China. The two sides will promote exchanges and visits between Chinese and African journalists and press professionals and support correspondent exchanges between their media organizations. China will also continue to implement the China–Africa Joint Research and Exchange Plan by sponsoring 100 programs for research, exchange, and cooperation between academic institutions and scholars of the two sides.

5. Promoting African peace and stability, and creating a secure environment for the development of African countries. To foster security on the African continent, China will launch the "Initiative on China–Africa Cooperative Partnership for Peace and Security," deepen cooperation with the AU and African countries in areas related to peace and security in Africa, provide financial

support for AU peacekeeping missions in Africa and the development for the African Standby Force, and train more AU peacekeepers and officials in peace and security affairs.

Notes

1 State Council website http://english.gov.cn/archive/white_paper/2017/01/11/content_281 475539078636.htm.
2 State Council website http://english.gov.cn/archive/white_paper/2016/12/01/content_ 281475505407672.htm.
3 The State Council of the People's Republic of China website, http://english.gov.cn/ archive/white_paper/2016/11/24/content_281475499069158.htm.
4 *Xinhua*, http://news.xinhuanet.com/english/china/2016-01/13/c_135006619.htm.
5 *China Daily*, www.chinadaily.com.cn/china/2015-05/26/content_20820628.htm.
6 *Xinhua*, http://news.xinhuanet.com/english/2015-12/04/c_134886545.htm.
7 *People.cn*, http://en.people.cn/n/2014/0710/c90883-8753777.html.
8 The State Council of the People's Republic of China website, http://english.gov.cn/ archive/white_paper/2014/08/23/content_281474982986536.htm.

INDEX

Boldface page references indicate tables. *Italic* references indicate figures and boxed text.